The Life
of
Daniel Boone

Daniel Boone *by Alonzo Chappel, c. 1861.* THE FILSON CLUB
HISTORICAL SOCIETY, LOUISVILLE, KENTUCKY.

The Life
of
Daniel Boone

by Lyman C. Draper, LL.D.

Secretary of the
State Historical Society of Wisconsin
1854–1886

Edited by Ted Franklin Belue

STACKPOLE
BOOKS

Published by
STACKPOLE BOOKS
5067 Ritter Road
Mechanicsburg, PA 17055

Printed in the United States of America

10 9 8 7 6 5 4 3 2 1

FIRST EDITION

Library of Congress Cataloging-in-Publication Data

Draper, Lyman Copeland, 1815–1891;
     The life of Daniel Boone/by Lyman C. Draper; edited by Ted
Franklin Belue
        p. cm.
     Includes bibliographical references and index.
     ISBN 0-8117-0979-5
     1. Boone, Daniel. 1734-1820. 2. Pioneers—Kentucky—Biography.
     3. Kentucky—Biography. 4. Frontier and pioneer life—Kentucky.
I. Belue, Ted Franklin. II. Title.

F454.B66D73   1998
976.9'02'092—dc21
[B]

976.9
02
Drap

98-27008
CIP

In memory of Dr. Lyman C. Draper,
who rescued from oblivion
the history of America's first Far West,
and to Dr. Josephine L. Harper,
who opened its door.

And to four great Kentuckians, trailblazers all,
whose life's work continues to inspire:
Daniel Boone, Pathfinder
Bill Monroe, Father of Bluegrass Music
Thomas D. Clark, Historian
David Wright, Artist

Also by Ted Franklin Belue:

The Long Hunt: Death of the Buffalo East of the Mississippi

A Sketch in the life and Character of Daniel Boone

CONTENTS

as a Wagoner.—In Braddock's Defeat.—Escapes.—Sees Some Things of the Upper Ohio Valley, and Learns from John Findlay about Kentucky.

Hunter Life.—Stuart's Mysterious Loss.—His Character.—Remains Subsequently Found.—Neely Returns Alone to the Settlements.—Hunters' Mode of Living.—Daniel and Squire Boone Alone in Kentucky.—Squire Boone Departs for Carolina.—Daniel Boone's Reflections.—His Wanderings.—The Beauty of the Country as Described by Filson and Imlay.—The Blue Licks.—The Buffaloes.—The Ohio.—Big Bone Lick.—Falls of the Ohio.—Boone's Adventure with an Indian.—His Cave on Shawanoe River.—Traditionary Adventure at Dick's River.—His Cautious Habits.—Squire Boone's Return.—Boone's Knob.—The Boone Brothers Ramble Through the Country.—Squire Boone Again Departs for North Carolina and Again Returns to Kentucky.

Explorations of the Taylors.—Of Stone and Others.—McColloch.—Cleveland.—The Long Hunters.—The Boones Explore the Green River Country.—Incidents.—Start for North Carolina.—Neely Gets Lost.—The Boones Robbed by Indians.—Frontier Retaliation.—The Boones Arrive Home.—Sketches of the Long Hunters.

Treaties at Fort Stanwix and Hard Labor.—Projected Ohio Colonies.—Extortions of North Carolina Public Officers.—Regulators.—Daniel Boone's Employments.—Hunts with Joe Robertson.—Meets Isaac Shelby below Holston Settlement.—Settles on Watauga Awhile.—Makes a Trip in 1773 with Benjamin Cutbirth to Kentucky.—Attempts to Remove There and Heads a Large Party.—Repulsed at Walden's Creek, and Abandons the Enterprise.—Indian Depredations on Simon Kenton and Others.—Adventures of Gilbert Christian and Others.—Boone Retires to Clinch.—Western Adventures of 1773.—Green's Bear Fight and Singular Preservation.

1774.—Dunmore's War.—Daniel Boone's Services.—Atrocities and Hostilities on Both Sides.—Squire McConnell Incident.—Spies.—Yellow Creek Massacre.—Boone's Melancholia.—Capt. Russell's Confidence in Boone and the Latter's Subsequent Tour of Kentucky with Michael Stoner.—Ordeal of the Fincastle Surveyors.—

The Clinch Mountain Frontier.—Capt. John Logan, the Celebrated Mingo Chief.

for Kentucky County.—Battle of Cove Springs.—Reinforcements from Virginia and the Yadkin Arrive in Kentucky.

1689 George Boone III (age twenty-three) marries Mary Maugridge (b. 1669), and they live in Bradninch, England.

1702 George and Mary Boone leave the Church of England to become members of the Cullompton Meeting of the Society of Friends (Quakers).

1713 George sends the three eldest Boone children to Abington, north of Philadelphia, in the Quaker colony of Pennsylvania, to investigate possibilities of settling. They are: George IV (age twenty-three), Sarah (age twenty-two), and Squire (age seventeen), who will become Daniel Boone's father.

1717 After enduring a rough eight-week voyage that began in Bristol, England, on October 10, George III and the rest of the family arrive in Philadelphia.

1720 On September 23 in what is now Montgomery County, Pennsylvania, Squire Boone marries Sarah Morgan at the Gwynedd Public Meeting Place of the Quakers.

    In October George III buys a 400-acre tract in Philadelphia County (approximately ten miles east of present-day Reading, in Berks County) and builds a cabin in a portion of Oley Township that on December 7, 1741, is renamed Exeter in honor of George III's birthplace.

1731 After living for about ten years on their 147-acre site, which is within a mile of present-day Chalfont, in Bucks County, Squire and Sarah relocate to a 250-tract in Oley Township and build their cabin near the homestead of George Boone III.

1734   Sarah and Squire Boone's sixth child, Daniel, is born in their cabin on October 22 (according to the Old Style, or Julian, calendar; or November 2, per the New Style, or Gregorian, calendar).

1742   Squire Boone receives first formal rebuke from Friends of Exeter Meeting for his daughter Sarah's (b. January 7, 1724) being "with child" at the time of her marriage to John Wilcoxson.

1747   Daniel receives first "rifle-gun" and begins hunting.

              Daniel's older brother, Israel Boone (b. May 9, 1726), marries out of Quaker faith, prompting Squire's second formal reprimand from Friends.

1748   Squire Boone "disowned" (excommunicated) from Exeter Society of Friends.

1750   On April 10 Squire Boone sells family farm.

              The Boones leave Exeter Township on May 1, beginning their emigration to the Shenandoah Valley.

              Daniel Boone and Henry Miller go on their first long hunt.

1751   The Boones live briefly in a cave on the north fork of the Yadkin River in what is now Davidson County, North Carolina.

              Daniel Boone elects to become a full-time market hunter.

1753   On April 13 Lord Granville grants Squire Boone a 640-acre tract near the confluence of present-day Elisha and Dutchman's creeks.

              On December 29 Squire receives second 640-acre grant on Bear Creek, two miles west of Mocksville, in Davie County.

1755   The French and Indian War begins.

              Boone, a member of Maj. Edward Dobb's North Carolina militia, serves as wagoner in Gen. Edward Braddock's ill-fated march on Fort Duquesne.

              Boone meets trader John Findlay, also serving in Braddock's army.

1756   Boone marries Rebecca Bryan on August 14, and they settle in Rowan County, North Carolina.

              Israel Boone dies of consumption, leaving two daughters and two sons, Jesse (age eight) and Jonathan (age six).

Daniel and Rebecca take in Israel's sons to raise.

1757   Daniel and Rebecca's first child, James, born May 3.

1758   Cherokee Wars erupt.

Boone serves with Gen. John Forbes's Virginia troops.

1759   Boones' second child, Israel, born January 25.

Because of Cherokee raids into the Yadkin Valley, the Boones flee from North Carolina to Culpeper County, Virginia.

Squire Boone sells Daniel a 640-acre tract in Rowan County, North Carolina.

1760   Daniel and Nathaniel Gist (son of famed scout Christopher Gist) hunt the game-rich Holston Valley region of eastern Tennessee.

Susannah, Daniel and Rebecca's third child, born November 2.

1761   Daniel serves in Maj. Hugh Waddell's Cherokee campaigns.

On November 19 the Cherokees sign peace treaty.

1762   The Boones return to Rowan County.

Daniel and Rebecca's fourth child, Jemima, born October 4.

1764   Daniel hunts along Rockcastle Creek.

He sells the farm to relocate on the more remote region of Brushy Mountains on the forks of the Yadkin

1765   Patriarch Squire Boone dies on January 2.

From October through December Daniel and Squire Boone, Jr., with John Stewart, John Field, William Hill, and several others, explore portions of Georgia's Altamaha River region and push southward to Florida.

Daniel buys a lot near Pensacola (but never returns to it).

He returns to his North Carolina home on Christmas Day.

1766   Fifth child and third daughter, Levina, born March 23.

1767   Daniel and Benjamin Cutbirth hunt eastern Tennessee's Watauga country.

Daniel, William Hill, and either Jesse or Squire Boone cross the Blue Ridge and the Clinch to hunt along the west fork of the Big Sandy River.

They build a station camp near present-day Prestonsburg, Kentucky.

1768　　　Sixth child, Rebecca, born May 26.

Regulator movement ignites North Carolina

John Findlay meets Boone for the first time since Braddock's defeat in 1755.

1769　　　Boone appears in court for failure to pay debts.

Findlay pilots Boone and four companions through the Cumberland Gap to Kentucky. Boone's first Kentucky long hunt lasts two years.

Boone captured by Shawnee on December 22.

Seventh child, Daniel Morgan, born December 23, seven months after Boone left to explore Kentucky.

1770　　　Squire Boone and Alexander Neely reach Daniel with supplies.

1771　　　In March Boone returns to his home on the Yadkin with plans to move to Kentucky.

1772　　　The Boones live in Tennessee on a homestead near Sapling Grove.

Boone and companions hunt as far west as French Lick (now Nashville), Tennessee, then enter Kentucky and establish a station camp in a cave at the mouth of Hickman Creek along the Kentucky River.

1773　　　Eighth child, Jesse Bryan, born May 23.

Boone makes his first attempt to settle Kentucky. He leads a party of five families from the Yadkin, beginning on September 26, but more families join along the way. On October 9 Indians attack and kill five, including James Boone, causing the pioneer party to turn back.

Boone settles along the Clinch.

1774　　　Lord Dunmore's War erupys.

Boone defends Clinch settlements.

Boone and Michael Stoner are sent to Kentucky, covering more than 800 miles in sixty-one days, to warn Fincastle surveying crews of impending Indian attacks.

In what is now Mercer County, frontiersman James Harrod establishes Harrod's Town, the first American Kentucky settlement.

The Battle of Point Pleasant is fought on October 10. The Shawnee sue for peace.

1775   Boone acts as Richard Henderson's agent to assemble Cherokee to meet with Henderson and representatives of the Transylvania Company.

On March 13 Boone and a party of about thirty axmen depart from Long Island on the Holston to blaze Wilderness Road leading to Kentucky.

Henderson and Cherokee leaders sign the Treaty of Sycamore Shoals on March 17.

On April 19 shots are fired at Lexington, Massachusetts, beginning the American Revolutionary War.

Despite Shawnee attacks, Boonesborough is established the first week of May.

On June 13 Boone sets off to the Clinch to get his family. In July Rebecca delivers their ninth child, William, who dies several days later. Boone returns with his family on September 8.

1776   On May 23 Indians attack Boonesborough.

The Continental Congress approves the Declaration of Independence.

On July 14, Indians capture Jemima Boone and Fanny and Betsy Callaway; Boone's party rescues the girls on July 16.

1777   Indians attack Boonesborough in April; Boone is shot in the ankle but recovers.

1778   In January Boone heads a party of twenty-six salt boilers to Lower Blue Licks.

Shawnee capture Boone on February 8 and force him to surrender men; Shawnee adopt Boone in March.

Boone escapes and returns to Boonesborough on June 16.

Boone makes foray against the Shawnee, known as the Paint Lick episode.

Boonesborough is besieged from September 7 to 18.

Boone is brought before court-martial on charges of collaboration with the enemy, but he is acquitted and promoted to major of the militia.

After the trial Boone rejoins Rebecca and family in North Carolina.

1779   In September Boone leads a new wave of emigrants from North Carolina to Kentucky.

On December 25 Boone establishes Boone's Station, six miles northwest of Boonesborough.

1780   At Richmond, Virginia, Boone is robbed of $20,000 in depreciated continental script.

His last child, Nathan, is born March 3.

In August Boone joins Gen. George Rogers Clark's 1,100-man army to attack the Shawnee in Ohio country.

The Indians kill Edward Boone in October.

In November Daniel is promoted to lieutenant colonel of Fayette County militia.

1781   On April 7 Boone is appointed coroner of Fayette County.

Shawnee attack Squire Boone's Station in April; Squire is badly wounded.

Boone represents Fayette County in the Virginia legislature.

He is captured in Charlottesville in June by Col. Banastre Tarleton's British rangers but is soon released.

Boone travels to Pennsylvania to visit relatives.

1782   A two-day siege of Bryan's Station begins on August 15.

The Battle of Blue Licks is fought on August 19; Israel Boone is killed in the battle.

In November Boone participates in Gen. George Rogers Clark's retaliatory strike against Indians in Ohio country.

1783   Boone moves either to Marble Creek (where he lives until perhaps 1785), five miles west of Boone's Station, or to Limestone (Maysville) on the Ohio. He sets up a tavern (inn) and surveys.

He is interviewed by author John Filson.

1784   Filson's *The Discovery, Settlement and Present State of Kentucke... To which is added An Appendix, Containing the Adventures of Col. Daniel Boon* is released on October 22, Boone's fiftieth birthday. As of this writing, Filson's work is still in print.

1786   Boone endures numerous lawsuits over land claims.

John Trumbull's first pirated edition of Filson's *Boon* appears; by 1824 Trumbull's version of *Boon* was reproduced in twelve editions in America and Europe, including both French and German translations.

In October Boone participates in Col. Benjamin Logan's Ohio campaign against the Shawnee.

Boone is made trustee of the town of Washington, Kentucky.

1787   In August at Limestone, Boone mediates between the Americans and the Shawnee to negotiate a prisoner exchange.

He is seated in the Virginia assembly in October.

He visits relatives in Pennsylvania.

1788   Boone transports fifteen tons of damaged ginseng to Hagerstown, Maryland.

Late in the year, Boone relocates to Point Pleasant in present-day West Virginia. He builds a cabin on Crooked Creek.

1789   Boone has a trading post at the mouth of the Kanawha. He serves in the Virginia militia.

1791   Boone surveys, hunts, and sells trade goods.

From October through January he serves as a member of the Virginia legislature.

In December Boone is appointed to supply provisions to militia troops in western Virginia.

1792   On February 4 President George Washington accepts Kentucky's petition for statehood. Kentucky is admitted to the Union as the fifteenth state on June 1.

1793   Boone visits Louisville and Paris and hunts along the Kentucky River.

The second edition of Gilbert Imlay's *Topographical Description of the Western Territory of North America*, published in London and Dublin, includes Filson's *Boon*.

1794   Boone testifies at Point Pleasant in court cases over land claims.

Land troubles increase.

1795   Boone moves to present-day Nicholas County, Kentucky, on land
               owned by Daniel Morgan Boone and builds a cabin near Blue Licks
               at Brushy Fork of Hinkston Creek.

               He hunts along Big Sandy.

1796   Boone writes to Gov. Isaac Shelby requesting a government contract
               to clear and widen Wilderness Road; there is no response. Wilder-
               ness Road is officially "opened" as a wagon road into Kentucky on
               October 15.

1797   Daniel Morgan Boone hunts in Spanish Missouri and confers with Lt.
               Gov. Don Zenon Trudeau, who invites the Boones to settle in Missouri.

               While trapping near the mouth of the Great Miami, Daniel Boone is
               interviewed on April 9 by the English traveler Francis Baily; the in-
               terview is published in 1856 in Baily's *Journal of a Tour in Unsettled
               Parts of North America in 1796 and 1797*.

1798   Boone relocates to a cabin on the 400-acre tract one mile from the
               mouth of the Little Sandy River in what is now Greenup County,
               Kentucky.

               He hunts in Tennessee and perhaps North Carolina.

               In November the sheriff of Mason County, Kentucky, issues a warrant
               to arrest Boone after he ignores a court summons to testify in a
               lawsuit over land claims.

               Officials of Mason and Clark counties, Kentucky, put much of
               Boone's land holdings up for sale.

               Boone County, Kentucky, is named in honor of Daniel Boone on
               December 13.

1799   In September Boone, along with Hays, Bryan, and Callaway kin, moves
               to the Femme Osage (now St. Charles County) district of Missouri.

               He receives a grant of 1,000 arpents (850 acres).

               Daniel and Rebecca build a cabin on land owned by son Daniel Mor-
               gan near the present-day town of Matson.

1800   Spanish governor appoints Boone "syndic" (judge and jury) and
               commandant (military leader) of the Femme Osage region; he serves
               in both capacities until the American takeover in 1804 following the
               Louisiana Purchase.

               On October 19 daughter Susannah (Boone) Hays dies.

               Boone and sons Nathan and Daniel Morgan hunt along the Pomme
               de Terre and Niangua rivers, headwaters of the Grand Osage.

1801   Boone and sons Nathan and Daniel Morgan hunt the Bourbeuse River region.

1802   Osage warriors briefly capture Boone during his spring hunt along the Niangua.

On April 6 daughter Levina (Boone) Scholl dies.

1803   Year of the Louisiana Purchase.

Boone is injured in a trapping accident on the Grand River.

That winter he remains hidden for twenty days from an Indian hunting party.

1804   Following the ceding of the Louisiana Purchase, American commissioners strip Boone of his Missouri (Spanish) land holdings.

Daniel and Rebecca move to Nathan Boone's farm.

1805   Boone hunts the Gasconade River region.

He builds a log cabin next to Nathan's stone house as it is being built.

On July 14 daughter Rebecca (Boone) Goe dies.

1807   Meriwether Lewis, governor of Louisiana Territory, appoints Boone justice of the Femme Osage township.

1808   Boone and companions are robbed by Indians while on a hunt.

1809   Boone petitions Congress for reinstatement of his Spanish land titles.

1812   Boone volunteers for War of 1812 duty; he is turned down because of his age (seventy-eight).

Sauk and allied Indian raids increase in Femme Osage Valley and the surrounding district.

1813   On March 18 Rebecca Boone dies and is buried in the Boone family cemetery on a knoll along Tuque Creek on a farm owned by her cousin David Bryan in what is now Marthasville (Warren County), Missouri.

Daniel Bryan, Boone's nephew, publishes a 250-page epic poem, *The Mountain Muse: Comprising the Adventures of Daniel Boone and the Powers of Virtuous and Refined Beauty.*

1814   Boone's handwritten biography and other family papers are lost in the Missouri River when his canoe capsizes.

1815   President James Monroe awards Boone a 1,000-arpent tract of Missouri land, but Boone is forced to sell much of it to pay off old Kentucky claims against him. He sells 300 acres to Jonathan Bryan. He keeps about 180 acres.

     Boone explores and hunts the upper Missouri region.

     The Sink Hole Battle in Missouri is fought.

1816   Boone visits Fort Osage (near present-day Kansas City). In time he explores as far west as Nebraska. Some firsthand reports allege he pushes on to hunt the Yellowstone country, but family members deny such claims.

1817   Boone goes on his last long hunt.

     He is rumored to have returned to Kentucky to settle old debts.

1819   Boone repurchases his 300 acres back from Jonathan Bryan. He resells the tract and the rest of his land holdings for $5,000.

1820   In June artist Chester Harding paints Boone's portrait from life while at the log home of Flanders and Jemima (Boone) Callaway.

     Boone dies on September 26; he is interred next to Rebecca on Tuque Creek.

     In St. Louis, Missouri, on October 11 Chester Harding and engraver James O. Lewis release America's first limited-edition print west of the Mississippi, a full-length fifteen-by-ten-inch engraving, *Col. Daniel Boon.,* rendered from Harding's full-length oil painting of Boone that Harding subsequently destroyed in 1861; the print sells out.

     On December 22 son Jesse dies; he was a member of Missouri's first legislature.

1821   Lord Byron publishes *Don Juan.* The eighth canto of the epic features seven verses dedicated to "The General Boon, back-woodsman of Kentucky."

1823   *The Pioneers,* by James Fenimore Cooper, is published by H. C. Carey & I. Lea. In both name and deed, Cooper's Leatherstocking protagonist, Nathaniel Bumppo, bears a striking resemblance to Daniel Boone. Future works by Cooper offer more of the same fare: *The Last of the Mohicans* (1826); *The Prairie* (1827); *The Pathfinder* (1840); and *The Deerslayer* (1841).

1832   *Sketches of Western Adventure,* by John A. McClung, published in Maysville, Kentucky, wrongfully portrays Boone as a rabid Indian hater.

1833   *Biographical of Daniel Boone, the First Settler of Kentucky,* by Timothy Flint, is published by N. & G. Gilford. Fourteen editions are printed by 1868.

1834   On August 30 daughter Jemima (Boone) Callaway dies.

1839   On July 13 son Daniel Morgan Boone dies.

1845   A delegation of Kentuckians travels to Missouri to retrieve Daniel and Rebecca Boone's remains to inter in Frankfort Cemetery.

        Daniel Boone and the Hunters of Kentucky, by William H. Bogart, is published by J. B. Lippincott.

1847   *The Life of Daniel Boone, the Pioneer of Kentucky,* by John Mason Peck, is published by the University Society Press.

1851   Artist George C. Bingham paints the most famous nineteenth-century Boone depiction, *Daniel Boone Escorting Settlers Through the Cumberland Gap.*

        Lyman C. Draper interviews Nathan Boone and his wife, Olive Van Bibber, in preparation to write his own Boone biography.

1854   Felix Walker's narrative of his toils in 1775 as one of Boone's axmen blazing the Wilderness Trail is published in *DeBow's Review.*

1856   Lyman C. Draper ceases formal work on the manuscript of his proposed work, *The Life of Daniel Boone;* the text covers roughly half of Boone's life and is never completed.

        Nathan Boone dies on October 16.

1859   *The Life of Daniel Boone: The Great Western Hunter and Pioneer,* by Cecil B. Hartley, is published by Lovell, Coreyell, and Company.

1860   Kentucky officials erect fifteen-foot obelisk over the Boones' remains in Frankfort Cemetery; Daniel and Rebecca Boone's graves are opened during construction of the monument.

1861–65 The American Civil War is fought. Union soldiers deface the Boone grave marker in Frankfort, which is restored in 1910.

1874   *Daniel Boone: The Pioneer of Kentucky,* by John S. C. Abbott, is published by Dodd, Mead.

1876   *A History of the Pioneer Families of Missouri,* by William S. Bryan and Robert Rose, is published by Bryan and Brand Press. More than fifty pages of the work are dedicated to Boone's Missouri years.

1891   Lyman C. Draper dies on August 27. He was succeeded in 1887 as corresponding secretary for the State Historical Society of Wisconsin by Reuben Gold Thwaites.

1901   *Boonesborough: Its Founding, Pioneer Struggles, Indian Experiences, Transylvania Days, and Revolutionary Annals,* by George W. Ranck, is published by John P. Morton.

1902   *Daniel Boone,* by Reuben Gold Thwaites, published by D. Appleton Press, ushers in a more modern era of Boone biographies largely based on the Draper Manuscript Collection.

1907   The Edison Company produces a two-reel silent film, *Daniel Boone*; four more silent versions are made in the 1920s.

1910   *Daniel Boone and the Wilderness Road,* by Bruce H. Addington, is published by Macmillan.

1915   The DAR honors Boone Missouri burial site on Tuque Creek with a dedication ceremony and plaque.

1922   *The Boone Family: A Genealogical History of the Descendants of George and Mary Boone,* by Hazel Atterbury Spraker, is published by Tuttle Press. It remains the canon of Boone genealogy and family history.

1926   In a feisty attempt to debunk the growing Boone mythology, Clarence Walworth Alvord published "The Daniel Boone Myth" in the *American Mercury*; Alvord's thesis prompts Louise P. Kellogg's spirited defense, "The Fame of Daniel Boone," in *Register of the Kentucky Historical Society* 32 (July 1934): 185–97.

1932   *Adventures of Col. Daniel Boone,* by Willard Rouse Jillson, is published by Standard Printing Company.

1934   U.S. Treasury issues a bicentennial Boone Memorial half-dollar.

1936   George O'Brien plays the title role in the movie *Daniel Boone,* directed by David Howard; John Carradine stars as the archetypal "white savage renegade" villain Simon Girty.

1939   *Daniel Boone: Master of the Wilderness,* by John Bakeless, is published by William Morrow; reprinted in 1965 by Stackpole Books; reprinted in 1989 by Bison Books.

1947   *The Wilderness Road,* by Robert L. Kincaid, is published in Tennessee by Harrogate Press.

1950   *Virgin Land: The American West as Symbol and Myth,* by Henry Nash Smith, is published by Harvard University Press. It is an analysis of how nineteenth-century Americana shaped the image of Daniel Boone and American culture.

1956   Release of the motion picture *Daniel Boone, Trail Blazer,* starring Bruce Bennett, directed by Ismael Rodriquez and Albert C. Gannaway, and filmed in Mexico.

1964   Fess Parker stars in the NBC television series "Daniel Boone," produced by George Sherman; 165 episodes are produced and air through August 1970.

1966   *Daniel Boone: Backwoodsman,* by John J. and Ima W. Van Noppen, is published by the Appalachian Press.

1968   U.S. Postal Service issues a commemorative Boone postage stamp on September 26.

1973   *Regeneration through Violence: The Mythology of the American Frontier, 1600–1860,* by Richard Slotkin, published by Wesleyan University Press, contains insights concerning the evolution of Boone mythology.

        A novel, *The Court Martial of Daniel Boone,* by Allan W. Eckert, is published by Little, Brown.

1976   *The Long Hunter: A New Life of Daniel Boone,* by Lawrence Elliott, is published by Reader's Digest Press.

1978   *The Life and Adventures of Daniel Boone,* by Michael A. Lofaro, is published by University Press of Kentucky.

1984   *Some Boone Descendants and Kindred of the St. Charles District,* by Lilian Hays Oliver, is published by Dean Publications.

1985   "Daniel Boone: First Hero of the Frontier," by Elizabeth A. Moize, appears in the December 1985 issue of *National Geographic.*

1987   University of Kentucky archaeologist Nancy O'Malley conducts intensive site and documentary investigation of Fort Boonesborough State Park and adjacent environs. The project concludes in spring 1989 and results are published that fall as *Searching for Boonesborough.*

1992   Kentucky celebrates the bicentennial of its statehood.

        Daniel Boone: The Life and Legend of an American Pioneer, by John Mack Faragher, is published by Henry Holt and Company.

        The Columbus of the Woods: Daniel Boone and the Typology of Manifest Destiny, by J. Gray Sweeney, is published by Washington University Gallery of Art.

        Pathfinder Press, Gallatin, Tennessee, reissues a historically correct reproduction of the 1820 Harding-Lewis engraving, *Col. Daniel Boon.*

        Twentieth Century Fox releases a lush remake of *The Last of the Mohicans,* directed by Michael Mann.

1995   Kentuckians reenact the 150th anniversary of the returning of the Boones' remains from Missouri to Frankfort.

1996   *How the West Was Lost: The Transformation of Kentucky from Daniel Boone to Henry Clay,* by Stephen Aron, is published by Johns Hopkins University Press.

        The Long Hunt: Death of the Buffalo East of the Mississippi, by Ted Franklin Belue, published by Stackpole Books, contains much about Boone, Indians, and frontier life.

1997   *A Sketch of the Life and Character of Daniel Boone,* by Peter Houston, edited by Ted Franklin Belue, is published by Stackpole Books. Houston's firsthand account of Boone was originally written in 1842 and housed in the Draper Manuscripts.

1998   *Nathan Boone on the American Frontier,* by R. Douglas Hurt, is published by the University of Missouri Press.

        The Life of Daniel Boone, by Lyman C. Draper, edited by Ted Franklin Belue, is published by Stackpole Books.

ACKNOWLEDGMENTS

Putting all the needed touches on *The Life of Daniel Boone* was a tedious job, and one I could not have done alone. I am glad the book is now out on shelves where it should have been scores of years ago, and I am thankful for all who helped me get it there.

Foremost, the men and women at the State Historical Society of Wisconsin, in Madison, repository of the original Draper Manuscripts, gave permission to transcribe the work and support in getting it published; Harold Miller, the society's archivist, was especially helpful. Of note is the work of archivist emeritus, Dr. Josephine L. Harper, whose *Guide to the Draper Manuscripts* unlocked Draper's literary fortress to the historical world. Reproduction Business Manager Nez Zarragöitia secured photographs.

Kentucky's peerless historian, Dr. Thomas D. Clark, always took time for me. Mining Dr. Clark's incisive letters is finer than panning for gold, and that he stays in touch to offer his help is humbling. Writer and naturalist Allan W. Eckert, of Bellefontaine, Ohio, sent me a watershed in the form of seven diskettes' worth of his meticulous notes, a ream-sized box of old records, and by his white-hot example shows how a writer's writer works. Bill Strode, of Strode Studios, in Prospect, Kentucky, whose roots hearken back to the early days of old "Kaintuck," gave permission to use his photograph of Chester Harding's Boone portrait on the jacket. Neal O. Hammon, of Shelbyville, Kentucky, graciously offered his unpublished essays, maps, and his geographical knowledge of the commonwealth.

At Murray State University in Murray, Kentucky, Dr. Jerry Herndon, professor of English, helped proof my writing. Dr. James W. Hammack, Jr., chair of the Department of History, provided me a workroom, computer, and microfilm reader. Professors Charlotte Beahan, Ken Wolf, and Richard Stieger translated Latin phrases appearing in the work; Dr. Terry Strieter offered one valuable tip. Don Lowry and Hal Rice produced many fine illustrations. The staff of the Harry

Lee Waterfield Library and Forrest C. Pogue Special Collections Library put up with my many requests, which they have done for a long time now.

As in my other works, H. David Wright, of Nashville, Tennessee, a friend, remarkable artist, and modern-day Leatherstocking loaned photographs and art from his collection. Jim and Carolyn Dresslar, of Bargersville, Indiana, generously opened their private collection to me and went the extra mile in procuring good photographs. Dr. Nicholas P. Hermann, archaeologist at University of Tennessee, Knoxville, and Dr. Kim McBride, archaeologist at Department of Anthropology, University of Kentucky, Lexington, provided graphics and data on recent excavations of Logan's Fort in Stanford, Kentucky, as conducted by the Kentucky Archaeological Survey and Logan's Fort Foundation.

Others who helped with illustrations were: Susan Bongiolatti, Washington Gallery of Art, St. Louis, Missouri; Marcus Cope, Benton, Kentucky; Dave Damer, Nashville, Tennessee; Dr. Richard M. Gramly, Buffalo, New York; Lydia Gerbig, Indianapolis, Indiana; Dr. James J. Holmberg and Rebecca Rice, Filson Club, Louisville, Kentucky; Jim Johnson, Golden Age Arms, Ashley, Ohio; Lloyd Jordan, Orlando, Florida; Faye Sotham, State Historical Society of Missouri, Columbia; Chris Steele, Massachusetts Historical Society, Boston.

For compilation of my Boone chronology, which is far from comprehensive, I scrutinized the works of biographers John Bakeless, Lawrence Elliott, Dr. John Mack Faragher, and Dr. Michael A. Lofaro. I also mined the Daniel Boone Papers in the Draper Manuscripts, which has an extensive chronology. Genealogical newsletters from Ken Kamper, historian for the Daniel Boone and Frontier Families Research Association (1770 Little Bay Road, Hermann, MO, 63041), helped me sift fact from fiction in keeping track of Boone's whereabouts. Charles C. Hay III, archivist at Eastern Kentucky University and president of the Madison County Historical Society of Kentucky, mailed me a copy of his useful "Overview of Biographical Sources of Daniel Boone," which appears in volume 1 of *Research Guide to American History* (Meachen Press, 1989).

Other folks that need acknowledging for a variety of reasons are: Dr. Stephen Aron, Department of History, UCLA; E. Carl Barnes, Loudon, Tennessee; Don Bruton, Spruce Pine, North Carolina; Randy Corse, Hagerstown, Maryland; Martin Eden, Oakland, California; William S. Monroe, Rosine, Kentucky; Dr. Timothy C. Nichols, Guntersville, Alabama; Dr. Ralph Stanley, McClure, Virginia; Michael J. Taylor, Cincinnati, Ohio; Richard Taylor, Frankfort, Kentucky; George "Butch" Winter, Union City, Tennessee.

Finally, I would like to thank my wife, Lavina, for putting up with me and the sort of work I do and the sort of life I lead. Her hard efforts, computer expertise, and good cooking keep me and the cats and the house humming.

O n July 6, 1997, an unmanned spacecraft sat on Mars beaming images of the Red Planet's cold, rocky face back to earth and into the homes of millions of transfixed viewers worldwide. The craft's name: *Pathfinder*.

Of course. It was fitting that NASA's new "fist in the wilderness"—a trailblazing orb that had crossed the trackless galaxy—passed forever into history as *Pathfinder*.

Americans are perennially drawn to the "frontier experience" and have long adopted its imagery. For example, the "westering" notion of Mountain Men in the 1800s pushing through South Pass translates easily to the exploration of space—"the Final Frontier."[1] Certainly Col. John Glenn, who in 1962 became the first American to orbit earth, is as brave a pioneer as Jed Smith, who in 1826 became the first American to cross the Mojave.

The origin for the craft's name is obvious: Daniel Boone, America's first Pathfinder. (Though many confuse him with Tennessee's Alligator-Horse and Ring-tailed Roarer David Crockett.) Boone's life, like the frontier saga, is steeped in myth. He was not, as is often believed, the first white man to cross the Blue Ridge into Kentucky. He did not wear a coonskin cap. Nor did he resemble television's depiction of him as "a big man"—the "rippin'est, roarin'est, fightin'est man the frontier ever knew!"[2]

But why all the fuss about this man of humble birth? He was, after all, just a woodsman.

To be sure, Boone was a good man. No Indian hater, he had little blood on his hands and was an adopted Shawnee in a day when some men shot Indians for sport. He was a good husband and father, remaining married for fifty-six years. Rebecca and he raised four girls and five boys of their own and took a few others under their wing as folks were apt to do back in that benevolent but violent day. He was a man whose word was his bond and who paid his debts back to the farthing; indeed, his lack of guile and sense of honor were what caused him to fail at

1

1. Daniel Boone, age eighty-five and four months from his death on September 26, 1820. Rendered from life by Chester Harding. From this original oil portrait Harding made three copies: two busts and a full-length. MASSACHUSETTS HISTORICAL SOCIETY, BOSTON.

land speculation. And though he was a skilled woodsman, he was not, he once admitted, without peer:

> Many heroic exploits and chivalrous adventures are related to me which exist only in the regions of fancy. With me the world has taken great liberties, and yet I have been but a common man. It is true that I have suffered many hardships and miraculously escaped many perils, but others of my companions have experienced the same.[3]

But, his modesty aside, the real Boone was a genuine leader imbued with a sense of wanderlust, whose woodsman's skills and personal traits fitted him for the task. Charismatic, quiet, even-tempered, and rarely willing to utter criticism even of those who opposed him, Boone's genteel ways were the sort that universally garner respect and attract. Whether as scout, militia commander, county representative, or judge, he served where and as he could, earning a solid reputation as a hunter, scout, and a good hand in an Indian fray.

In 1769 John Findley, one of Pennsylvania trader's George Croghan's packhorse men, guided Boone and company from North Carolina's Yadkin Valley to the Holston and through the Cumberland Gap and beyond to the Bluegrass. Once there, Boone directed the proceedings on this, his first Kentucky long hunt, which lasted two years. Financially it was a disaster. But there was another, far greater reward: Boone had seen the New Eden of the West—*Kanta-ke*.

Word of Boone's prowess as a woodsman soared in 1774 when he and Mike Stoner tried to get word from western Virginia to the Fincastle surveyors then mapping out the Bluegrass of the brewing war clouds that burst into Lord Dunmore's War. Boone and Stoner arrived only to find that the surveyors had fled back east—"drove in by Indians," he reported. But their journey was a staggering feat, a grand scout of hundreds of miles through wild, dangerous country.

During the bloody, short-lived episode that year, Boone—promoted to captain of the militia—served as courier and scout along the trans-Allegheny ridge. In a letter sent to Col. William Preston dated August 28, 1774, Capt. John Floyd observed that "Boone has more influence than any man now disengaged; & you know what Boone has done for me by your kind directions, for which reason I love the man."[4]

Well known and tolerably well liked, Boone was neither a hermit nor antisocial. But in roaming the woods he either hunted alone or chose the companionship of just one or two trusted comrades—often one of his own kin—over a band of Long Hunters. This aloofness—a few contemporaries deemed him "taciturn" —also contributed to Boone's mystique.

In 1773 Boone made his first move on Kentucky. He failed and lost a son to the scalping knife. But in his second attempt he and his team of axmen blazed a jagged trail that cut clean from eastern Tennessee's Holston Valley to the junction of Otter Creek and the Kentucky deep in the gentle swells of the

Bluegrass. There in May 1775 he built America's first fort in the Far West: Boonesborough.

Pivotal years they were. In 1776 Boone led a daring rescue to save his daughter and the two Callaway girls from Indians; in 1777 a Shawnee bullet broke his ankle in an attack; in 1778 a war party seized him and his twenty-six salt boilers at the Lower Blue Licks, but Boone escaped in time to warn Kentuckians of an impending Shawnee assault, and that September, Boonesborough withstood a nine-day siege. The next month Boone rose in rank to militia major. In late 1779 he built his second outpost: Boone's Station.

While his exploits were gaining him local notoriety, Boone was losing a fortune in land and suffering personal tragedy. But an event that forever altered his life came in 1783 with the visit of John Filson, a Pennsylvania schoolmaster turned author and land speculator. Filson and Boone met and warmed to each other. As Filson took notes, the pioneer narrated a sketchy account of his life. On October 22, 1784, Boone's fiftieth birthday, Filson released his book, *The Discovery, Settlement and Present State of Kentucke . . . To which is added An Appendix containing The Adventures of Col. Daniel Boon.*

Filson's flamboyant work, followed two years later by plagiarist John Trumbull's feistier version of *Boon,* sold well in the fledgling United States and even

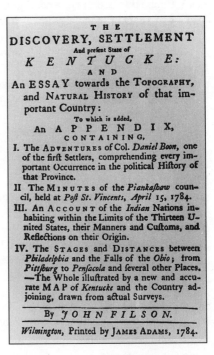

THE
DISCOVERY, SETTLEMENT
And prefent State of
K E N T U C K E:
A N D
An ESSAY towards the TOPOGRAPHY,
and NATURAL HISTORY of that important Country :
To which is added,
An A P P E N D I X,
C O N T A I N I N G,
I. The ADVENTURES of Col. *Daniel Boon,* one of the firft Settlers, comprehending every important Occurrence in the political Hiftory of that Province.
II The MINUTES of the *Piankafhaw* council, held at *Poft St. Vincents, April* 15, 1784.
III. An ACCOUNT of the *Indian* Nations inhabiting within the Limits of the Thirteen United States, their Manners and Cuftoms, and Refleftions on their Origin.
IV. The STAGES and DISTANCES between *Philadelphia* and the Falls of the *Ohio ;* trom *Pittfburg* to *Penfacola* and feveral other Places. —The Whole illuftrated by a new and accurate M A P of *Kentucke* and the Country adjoining, drawn from aftual Surveys.

By *J O H N   F I L S O N.*

Wilmington, Printed by JAMES ADAMS, 1784.

2. John Filson's self-portrait, c.1780s.
THE REUBEN T. DURRETT COLLECTION,
FILSON CLUB HISTORICAL SOCIETY.

3. Title page of Filson's Kentucke.
FILSON CLUB HISTORICAL SOCIETY.

better in England, Germany, Ireland, and France.[5] The humble woodsman's fame grew to global proportions. By the time of his death on September 26, 1820, Boone was a genuine living legend, America's first frontier hero.

Over the next two centuries Boone became all things to all poets, novelists, biographers, historians, folklorists, and moviemakers who set about to remake Boone in their own image: Boone the preeminent Natural Man; Boone the scowling lone-wolf expatriate in his own land; Boone the noble white savage; Boone the knight errant; Boone the Indian killer; Boone as Manifest Destiny's own Jacksonian "tool in the wilderness"; Boone the teetotaling Christian and perfect husband; Boone the "American Moses" and "Columbus of the woods"; Boone the bumpkin, perennial good-old-boy, and ribald oaf who accidentally stumbled into Kentucky, chased Indian women, and relished strong drink.[6] Little wonder many readers conclude that no reliable biography was written until the twentieth century.

But there was one exception, though unfinished and unpublished, tucked away since 1856 in the archives of the State Historical Society of Wisconsin: Lyman C. Draper's manuscript "Life of Daniel Boone."

He was of pioneer stock, this Draper. One who saw him at age fifty-eight noted that he was "a slightly bent, boyish man, an unequal match in bodily strength for most lads of twelve." But though he stood just five foot one and weighed about 100 pounds, he was a giant, a trailblazer.[7]

James Draper, his Puritan forebear, immigrated to Massachusetts in 1647. Jonathan Draper fought the British on Lexington's green in 1775. In 1812 the British thrice captured Jonathan's son, Luke, who spent four months in a Montreal jail before he returned home and to his wife, Harriet Hoisington, near Buffalo, New York. On September 4, 1815, Harriet gave birth to the couple's firstborn child, Lyman.

Solemn and intensely curious, young Lyman spent many a night sitting wide-eyed at the family hearth as his father and grandfather talked of war and Indian raids and recounted tales of the tall Long Knife George Rogers Clark, with his fiery red hair and temper to match. He listened as they told of Samuel Brady, Lewis "Death Wind" Wetzel, the Girtys, Simon Kenton, and Daniel Boone. Armed with their "widder-making" rifles, such border folk, Draper came to believe, opened the first Far West, taming savage beasts, savage wilderness, and savage foes.

Ill suited for farm work, Draper was becoming a man of books by his teens. The frontier beckoned. And via the printed word, he entered his heroes' violent world of flashing musket volleys, keening Shawnee war cries, and aromatic campfires kindled with fat-pine and red cedar and stoked with hickory; he hearkened to thunderous buffalo herds and stood at the blood-drenched killing fields of Braddock's Defeat, the Plains of Abraham, and Blue Licks.

In 1830 Draper took a job as a clerk at Peter Remsen's cotton firm in Mobile, Alabama. Remsen, married to Lydia Chadwick, Draper's cousin, was taken by the lad's passion for history and became his patron. In 1834 Remsen sent Draper to Licking City, Ohio, to begin his education at Granville Literary and Theological Institution. But Draper found the curriculum of classical studies dull, and in its place he wrote, studied politics and history, and interviewed Indians and aging pioneers. He emerged from college in 1837 a born-again Baptist and fervent Democrat.

Though he had earned no degree, Draper emerged with something far greater. Imbued with a deep sense of Christian duty, his newfound "Pioneer Mission"—to rescue the vanishing recollections of frontier folk and to right the errors he read in history books—became a moral quest, a high calling. "For I am a small bit of a fellow," he wrote to an early interviewee. "Yet small as I am, and as 'good for nothing' as I often think myself, I yet feel that I have something to do."[8]

In 1833 seventeen-year-old Draper wrote an essay on Charles Carroll, the last surviving signer of the Declaration of Independence. Published in the *Rochester Gem*, his first literary success stirred in him a grand vision: to be the biographer of America's great, and to save from oblivion the memories of the common folk. To do this, he would write books—books that would sift fact from myth, correct errors, and set the standard for the history of frontier America.

He planned to write twenty titles: comprehensive works on George Rogers Clark, Samuel Brady, the Wetzels; books on William Crawford, Daniel Boone, Simon Kenton, Josiah Harmar, Arthur St. Clair, Anthony Wayne, Ben Lyon, William Whitney, John Sevier, James Robertson, Dunmore's War, Daniel Morgan, Richard Butler; and profiles of outlaws, pioneers, Indians, and heroic exploits.[9]

In 1840 Draper became the editor of the *Mississippi Intelligencer* in Pontotoc, Mississippi, but by 1843 he was living in Buffalo, New York, boarded by his benefactor, Peter Remsen. Seeking interviews, Draper traveled between 1843 and 1852 to Maryland, Pennsylvania, Kentucky, Ohio, Tennessee, Indiana, Illinois, Washington, D.C., Missouri, and Virginia. He collected saddlebags full of notes and kept up a voluminous correspondence.

By 1852 he had begun and shelved several works before settling on "Life of Daniel Boone." That year Peter Remsen died. For Draper it was a personal loss heavy with meaning: it ended his income, made a widow of cousin Lydia, and left her four-year-old adopted daughter, Helen, fatherless.

Twenty-five years younger than sixty-three-year-old Remsen, Lydia was four years older than Draper, and the two had much in common. Remsen had left a trust fund, but Draper felt it his duty to care for Lydia and Helen. But how was he to provide for them and write his books?

In the fall of 1852 he took the Remsens from Philadelphia to Madison, Wisconsin, where he was made corresponding secretary for the state's fledgling Historical Society. The job provided an income and a base of operation, and it gave Draper's efforts greater credibility. But his new duties forced him to lay aside his own work to keep pace with his responsibilities.

In 1854 Draper, age thirty-six, married Lydia Remsen. Besides family and society duties, he penned thousands of letters seeking documents and answers to his queries about frontier life; he plowed archives and transcribed diaries of long-dead soldiers and frontiersmen, stopping only when pain so cramped his hand that he could write no more; and he wrote articles for magazines, encyclopedias, and newspapers. He also served a two-year term as state superintendent of Public Instruction. He was a deacon in the Madison Baptist church from 1856 to 1863 and led in the church's prayer meetings, was its clerk, and for years was its Sunday school superintendent.

His books would have to wait. Besides, he felt he lacked enough data—he must have every detail, he believed. No, he could not write. Not yet.

Meanwhile, Draper kept up his visits back east. Braving accidents, hunger, rain, sleet, snow, hail, and flood, he walked, rode horses, mules, lumber wagons, stagecoaches, steamboats, and trains, traveling more than 60,000 miles, he reckoned, to talk to aging pioneer men and women, Indian elders, and African slaves in an era when few cared about their remembrances.

On October 7, 1865, young Helen Draper died of what was diagnosed as congestive fever. Lyman sank into a melancholia that lasted five years. As he brooded, his health and finances also faltered. Yet the couple survived as the society and its burgeoning library stacks flourished under Draper's capable hands.

4. Lyman C. Draper (1815–1891), at about the age of forty, from a daguerreotype, c. 1855, about the year he shelved forever his unfinished manuscript, "Life of Daniel Boone." THE STATE HISTORICAL SOCIETY OF WISCONSIN, MADISON.

In 1869, when he converted to Spiritualism, the Madison Baptists excommunicated him. But Spiritualism, Draper averred, enhanced the Christian belief in life after death. Many grief-stricken parents of that post–Civil War day made the same conversion in the hopes of contacting lost sons slain in the bloody ordeal.

"It was the possibility of conversing with the spirits of his border heroes," biographer William B. Hesseltine contends, "that ultimately made Draper a convert." As conjurers sat with the Drapers during séances, Lyman summoned the dead to speak to him "useful matter and correct errors." George Rogers Clark and Simon Kenton twice visited out-of-body, he believed; he tested the two table-knocking phantoms and found them not wanting. At times he felt Helen's presence near. Hadean insights from a specter named "Bud" assured him that he could become "a powerful speaking medium." Intrigued, he worked hard to make good the oracle, but he never gained the promised mastery of the arcane. Likewise came the netherworld's decree that he would live to write his books; time would prove that false as well.[10]

What so beset Lyman Draper? Why was this indefatigable worker unable to complete his proposed life's work?

Draper the antiquarian was tireless, inspired, analytical. But procrastination and hypochondria plagued Draper the author. Writing brought strange ills: dark moods, crippling hand cramps, bodily aches, dysentery, blinding migraines, "nervous dyspepsia," liver ailments, and other maladies. Thus assailed, he laid onion poultices on his eyelids, soaked in hot and cold baths, strapped on magnetic battery-charged belts for cure "by electric mode," or sought other faddish snake-oil health remedies.

Once rested, Draper's spirits would rise as he collected material and planned more books that he never wrote, with but two exceptions. To subsidize his work, in 1869 Draper and his collaborator William Croffut released a how-to book on domestic living, *A Helping Hand for Town and Country: An American Home Book of Practical and Scientific Information.* Friends were dismayed: Had he forsaken history? "Others can write of farming," Tennessee historian Dr. J. G. M. Ramsey rebuked him. "You know the border." The publisher's scurrilous dealings ended in a lawsuit, killing forever *Helping Hand* and leaving Draper in debt and embittered, declaring publishers to be the "enemy of writers."[11]

Twelve years later he tried again. In 1881 Cincinnati publisher Peter G. Thompson released Draper's *King's Mountain and its Heroes: History of the Battle of King's Mountain.*

Unabashedly pro-American, *King's Mountain* is a vivid account of the famous battle in which 1,300 homespun Patriots—the "Over-Mountain Men"—whipped His Majesty George III's finest and shot dead one of the Crown's most innovative leaders, Maj. Patrick Ferguson. Draper's version of the epic clash is consummate Draper at his best,—and perhaps too, at his worst. Turgid prose, encyclopedic detail, commas linking sentences that never seem to end, and walls of digressive footnotes mar the book. Still, the mythic saga is there, the story a true one, the analysis and documentation precise, and the work—"a bulky storehouse of information obtained at firsthand," as one reviewer noted—is recognized as "a permanently valuable contribution to American historical literature."[12]

But even with good reviews *King's Mountain* sold poorly. Slated for release in 1880 to mark the battle's centennial, Draper missed his deadline by a year—long after Tennessee's celebration ended. Sales topped 1,000 copies of the edition of 2,600. By September 1882 he admitted, "The book is dead."[13] In 1884 fire swept Thompson's warehouse, torching the remaining copies. Draper was devastated.

After suffering a series of strokes, the bedridden Lydia Draper died in 1888. Seventeen months later Draper wed Catherine T. Hoyt and visited California.

"Still digging away at my historical labors and making good progress," he wrote in 1890, sure that once he began to write, words would pour from his pen. But "It was ever the same story. Ever planning, never doing," observed Reuben Gold Thwaites, who in 1887 succeeded Draper as corresponding secretary at the Historical Society.[14] By now Draper's collection had swelled beyond his control, and though he continually added to it, his sense of organization suffered.

Draper's last days were clouded by accusations from a new generation of frontier descendants charging that he had pilfered papers from their kin. Archivists in Kentucky and Tennessee dubbed him "the man who stole all our documents and carried them off to Wisconsin." But associates rallied to his defense, and the University of Wisconsin conferred upon him an honorary degree of Doctor of Laws.[15]

A stroke took him on August 27, 1891. He died lamenting that he had not written his books and especially regretted that he had not finished "Life of Daniel Boone." He had wasted his life, he said, "just puttering."

But "puttering" hardly describes what he had accomplished, and his efforts were far from wasted. During the celebration of Kentucky's Bicentennial in 1992, Dr. Thomas D. Clark, the commonwealth's distinguished historian laureate, observed that Draper had "saved many valuable manuscripts from destruction, he supplemented the material with his extensive interview notes, he had the patience to travel afar to collect the papers, and he was careful to provide for their permanent housing and management."[16]

"Kentucky and other pioneer states," the venerable Clark concluded, "owe a heavy debt of gratitude to Draper." Yale historian John Mack Faragher agreed, noting in his Boone biography released that year that "Draper's efforts probably preserved those materials from almost certain destruction during the Civil War, and no one has ever proved that he kept anything without permission."[17]

After his death Draper's collection was systematized into its present state of 491 volumes spanning the trans-Allegheny frontier's history. Much of the material is arranged geographically under such headings as Illinois Papers, Kentucky Papers, Virginia Papers, and so on. Other portions are categorized according to intended biographies—Daniel Boone Papers, Simon Kenton Papers, George Rogers Clark Papers. Some sections consist of Draper's ongoing works, such as Draper's "Life of Boone," the Mecklenburg Declaration, Draper's Biographical Sketches, Border Forays, and Draper's Notes.[18]

Time proved Draper's skill to be that of a collector; that he tried as a writer to be encyclopedic shows a lack of historical perspective, a concept he confessed he did not understand. He left as his legacy his work at the State Historical Society of Wisconsin, the progenitor of many such institutions, and his beloved manuscripts,—"so much bricks and stone, ready for the aspiring architects of the future. These will always be of incalculable value to original workers in many branches of Western history," eulogized Reuben Gold Thwaites in 1891 during a memorial service.[19]

Historians, genealogists, and other researchers owe much to Lyman Copeland Draper, this modest, gentle one whose steadfast dedication to his "Pioneer Mission" rescued from oblivion the history of America's first Far West.

Of all his proposed biographies, Draper made the most progress on "Life of Daniel Boone." Perhaps the urge to write the work first stirred within him in 1836, the year he bought a copy of Reverend Timothy Flint's *Biographical Memoir of Daniel Boone, the First Settler of Kentucky* (1833) and to his dismay discovered it rife with tall tales.

Flint's yarns mattered not to an adoring public in search of a hero, and in fact, they probably boosted sales. *Biographical Memoir of Daniel Boone* was, notes modern-day biographer Dr. Michael A. Lofaro, "a runaway best-seller of its day . . . but one that cannot be dismissed out of hand because of Flint's interviews with Boone."[20] By 1868 the work had gone through fourteen editions, but those

5. *Engraving illustration from Timothy Flint's* Biographical Memoir of Daniel Boone *(1833), featuring a mythic exploit and equally mythic coonskin cap, an article that the real Boone "despised."*

who knew the real Boone blasted the book, calling it "little better than a carica-
ture," and Kentucky historian Mann Butler chided Flint for his fabrications. Non-
plussed, the jocular ex-clergyman retorted that his book "was made not for use,
but to sell."[21]

In 1843 Daniel Boone Bryan complained to Draper that Flint had strayed far
from the truth and encouraged him to set the record straight. Should he do so, declared another relative, his work not only would put Flint's "where it belongs, in
the corner," it would become the standard by which other such works would be
measured.[22] Boone books were good sellers too—an important consideration.
So in the 1840s Draper put aside his proposed two-volume George Rogers Clark
epic to begin one on Boone.

Draper wrote to Boone's descendants for answers to his myriad questions
and to assure them of his motives. "I am," he explained, "greatly interested in
Col. Boone. . . . There is a romance about his name that gives the name and history of Daniel Boone a peculiar charm. I anxiously wish to do full justice to his
memory and worth, and present him to the world in his real character."[23]

1851—a busy year for memoir gathering—found Draper in New York, Pennsylvania, steamboating on the Ohio past Kentucky, Ohio, and Illinois to St. Louis,
and journeying westward to Missouri's Green County to call on Nathan Boone,
the aging, last-born son of Daniel and Rebecca—their last surviving child—and
his wife, Olive. Draper arrived that October.

*6. Nathan Boone
(1781–1856), hunter,
scout, surveyor, Mis-
souri dragoon, and a
good woodsman in his
own right at about the
age Draper visited him.
Draper observed that
Nathan resembled the
Harding portrait of his
famous father.* THE STATE
HISTORICAL SOCIETY OF
MISSOURI, COLUMBIA.

Nathan had served in the U.S. Army in the Missouri theater of the War of 1812 and in Osage land to the west. A good woodsman, he was said to bear a striking resemblance to his famed father. As Missouri's fall winds swept the prairie, Draper spent days and candlelit nights in Nathan and Olive's cabin, interrogating them about Daniel Boone's life and times.

They talked long into the brisk nights. Draper's dip pen pumped furiously to keep pace. Often he paused to digress and prod and probe the Boones' memories for dates, events, and exploits, double-checking everything, then checking again.

It was one of Draper's strongest efforts. Besides its trove of firsthand Boone material, the interview includes insights into pioneer life, genealogical data, and notes on Nathan's career.[24] Nearing the end of Draper's three-week stay, Nathan presented him with a magnificent gift—a pack of original Boone family notes wrapped in buckskin.

Draper left the Boone cabin with more than 300 pages of notes. And though he and the Boones continued to correspond, they never again met in person.

Homeward bound, the historian traveled back to New York by stage, his trunk tied to the coach's rear topper. Nearing Fulton, Missouri, the jostle of the stagecoach loosened the ties binding his cargo. The trunk snapped free and bounced away unseen. Miles later Draper discovered the trunk was gone. Frantic, he backtracked the route on foot, handing out notices, inquiring at farms, interrogating passersby, scouring miles of countryside, seeking his lost trunk. Three days later he found it, safe in the hands of an "honest Negro man." Draper returned home triumphant.

His next few years were busy ones. In 1852 he moved to Madison, Wisconsin, and became corresponding secretary of the State Historical Society. Caring for Lydia and her child and his new duties left little time to write.

Finding book writing difficult, instead of writing, he outlined; he visited; he went east to rest and conduct interviews; he wrote thousands of letters; he fretted over publishers; he queried subjects endlessly—no stone would be left unturned.

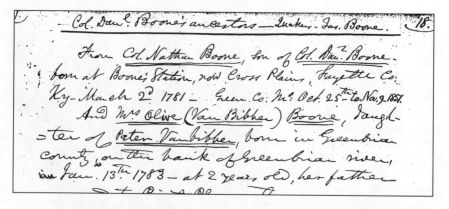

7. *Introductory paragraph of Draper's interview with Nathan and Olive Boone in 1851.* STATE HISTORICAL SOCIETY OF WISCONSIN.

No detail was too small, no sliver of data too fine. He got testimonials from more than sixty Boone kin to assure readers his soon-to-be-released "Life of Daniel Boone" was the real article, surpassing all others.

He did everything but write his book. Time was a pressing enemy. He did not have time enough for his labors, he thought, and so he sought a collaborator.

In 1854 New York writer and artist Benson L. Lossing agreed to help him. Lossing would illustrate the work with woodcuts and edit Draper's thick prose. Inspired, Draper fired off publicity notices to local newspapers. Larger papers picked up the circulars as news of the forthcoming biography on America's first frontier hero began to go nationwide.

NEW LIFE OF DANIEL BOONE

> We copy the subjoined article from the Madison (Wisconsin) *Daily Argus and Democrat*; giving it cheerfully a place in our columns, not only because it pre-announces a book upon a subject very interesting to the people of this State, but because a friend who requests its insertion—a gentleman of the finest literary taste and accomplishments—vouches for the author's personal knowledge, and says he knows the book will be an excellent one.[25]

The book was to be released in the autumn of 1854. According to the unnamed author of this announcement (actually Draper, acting as his own publicist), "More than sixteen years" had been devoted to collecting materials for the work and for "similar volumes on other border heroes of the West." After listing another thirteen titles that would "speedily follow" Boone's biography, the essay ended with ringing approval for the forthcoming book, the *only* authorized and authentic rendering of the famous frontiersman:

> For the work on Boone, the old papers left by the old pioneer have been kindly furnished by his family; which, with the innumerable facts contained in the general collection of MS. papers alluded to, will give the volume a throughly original and authentic character. All the aged direct and collateral descendants of the past sixteen years, have been visited and consulted, and they have freely contributed their facts, family papers and traditions, together with their united approval and commendation of enterprise.

Draper worked feverishly. He wrote a long introduction; he fussed over front matter and illustrations; he inserted into the text entire journals that ran for scores of pages; he completed sixteen hefty chapters spanning Boone's life from birth to his court-martial in 1778; and he wrote an appendix. All parts of the manuscript—more than 800 foolscap pages in all—featured heavily annotated footnotes.

As Draper's work on "Life of Daniel Boone" dragged on, the work itself began to suffer. Somewhere after his first burst of energy, the author's spark seems to dim. The earlier chapters are shorter, more concise, whereas later chapters tend to be longer, lack content headers, and are heavy with extended quotes. Draper the antiquarian was outflanking Draper the writer.

Then, inexplicably, he stopped. In 1856 he shelved the manuscript. He made excuses—"I can write nothing so long as I fear there is a fact, no matter how small, as yet ungarnered."[26] Friends begged him to work on. "Permit me to say in kindness," wrote W. B. Campbell, "that I fear you are a little too fastidious and timid. Why should you hesitate?"[27]

But it was the same story. Draper's twin unexorcised demons, procrastination and hypochondria, had beset him. Not only did he fear going to press lacking facts yet undiscovered, he even feared polishing his notes to put them into workable form, wary that some news brought to him by mail would force him to revamp his material. So he collected, wrote letters, visited back east, did society duties, and attended séances.

Years slipped by. Oddly, in a press release dated March 7, 1884, Draper again announced vague plans for publication of his book—one that he had been working on for more than forty years, time spent "collecting materials for a work on Colonel Daniel Boone."[28] But no book was forthcoming, and this was the last such circular to appear.

Though Draper did not go back to his manuscript, his interest did not dim. In 1888 he queried a Boone relative about some nuance of the woodsman's life. Written in a more tightly cramped scrawl than in his usual flowing script, his letter is a telling one. "You will see by the enclosed," he began in a near apology to his correspondent for his poor penmanship, "that, like other mortals, I have my afflictions—but try to bear them as best I can—and feel more than ever, that my duty is to work while the day lasts, and do what I can to complete my labors."[29]

He kept up his duties "until at last," recalled Reuben Gold Thwaites, who knew him well, "like the patient cat in the familiar fable, he waited too long."[30]

About "Life of Daniel Boone." Not surprisingly, the text has most of the same strengths and weaknesses found in the equally florid and encyclopedic *King's Mountain,* proving that Draper had set out to write for all time the Great Boone Epic. Its digressions from the central hero border on the ponderous, but it is a supremely scholarly, useful work, and often Draper writes with elegance and verve. Even though the author did not finish it, it has many earmarks of a forthcoming book he would have been proud of.

Biographers of Boone and his era, beginning with Reuben Gold Thwaites and on to this day, have mined Draper's manuscript for their own work. Thus, though it remained unpublished for nearly a century and a half, it has stood the test of time as a dense vein of first- and secondhand data on Boone, the Long Hunter teams that invaded the west in the 1760s, Indians and Indian-Anglo relations, frontier Kentuckiana, notable pioneers, and eighteenth-century trans-Appalachian life.

What sort of fellow is Draper's leading man? Underneath his dark linen hunting shirt Boone's heart beats with the pulse of virtue; his eyes see with fore-shadowed vision; his love of nature is unstinting, though he may shoot thirty or so deer a day for the skin-trade. He is wily, heroic, romantic, benevolent, and boasts sterling character and sound judgment—in short, a genteel frontiersman's frontiersman.

Draper was a man of his own Manifest Destiny day. The few times Boone's trusty long-rifle Tick-Licker cracks to kill a "skulking Shawnee," Draper backs his play. And he is a spirited apologist for land speculators, spurious "peace" treaties, and white market hunters and settlers who poached and trespassed on Indian land. Yet unlike many of his more rabid peers of "the-only-good-Injun-is-a-dead-Injun" school of writing, Draper often portrays Native Americans sympathetically as a tragic, much abused race in their last desperate stand against

8. James B. Longacre's line-and-stipple engraving of one of Chester Harding's Boone portraits, from National Portrait Gallery of Distinguished Americans *(1835). Longacre, one of the nation's most distinguished engravers of the nine-teenth century, later became chief engraver to the United States Mint.*

a lashing white tide of Anglo-Americans. Nor does he mince words in condemning shameless acts of barbarism against Indians by frontier blackguards.

Draper's Boone, like John Filson's Boone, is a hard-working, philosophical natural man, a mighty hunter; a Rousseauian white Shawnee and an unchurched Quaker-Deist whom destiny has molded into a providential tool in the wilderness. And like Rev. John M. Peck's teetotaling Boone, who is a paragon of Christian virtue worthy of emulation, Draper's Boone is a good provider and faithful husband.

Here too, as in James Fenimore Cooper's Leatherstocking tales, women are "females," Indians are often "savages," and Draper's "Negroes" are sometimes relegated to playing the role of Sambo. Throughout the work, excerpts from Bible verses abound. Indeed, Draper's prose is heavily influenced by the lyrical English of the King James I (1611) version.

Though other writers may have influenced him, Draper remained his own man. As his footnotes reveal, he did not hesitate to take earlier biographers to task. "Bungling and unreliable," he deemed Alexander Scott Withers' *Chronicles of Border Warfare* (1831). Flint's work, he said, contained "imaginary exploits." Of John McClung's sensational approach to history, Draper chided, "Our beautiful writers are not always our most accurate historians."[31]

But enough. Or, as Dr. Draper might now echo Chaucer's immortal words, "Farwel my book and my devocion."

NOTES

1. For this portion, I owe a debt to Dr. Michael A. Lofaro's astral notions as stated in his well-written introduction to John Bakeless' *Daniel Boone: Master of the Wilderness*, 3rd ed. (University of Nebraska Press: Bison Books, 1989), xi–xix; see also Michael A. Lofaro, "Tracking Daniel Boone: The Changing Frontier in American Life," *The Register of the Kentucky Historical Society* 82 (1984): 321–33.

2. Again, my debt to Lofaro's introduction to the third edition to Bakeless, *Daniel Boone*, xii.

3. "From the New York Statesman: A Visit to Colonel Boon [*sic*]," *Detroit Gazette*, July 4, 1823, found in Draper Manuscripts 6S:338. Draper Manuscripts hereafter cited as DM.

4. John Floyd to William Patterson, August 28, 1774, quoted in Reuben Gold Thwaites and Louise Phelps Kellogg, *Lord Dunmore's War*, (Madison: Wisconsin Historical Society, 1905), 168.

5. For comparison and analysis of John Filson's and John Trumbull's accounts, see Michael A. Lofaro, "The Eighteenth-Century 'Autobiographies' of Daniel Boone," *The Register of the Kentucky Historical Society* 76 (1978): 85–97.

6. For historiography of Boone iconography and typology, see Richard Slotkin, *Regeneration through Violence: The Mythology of the American Frontier, 1600–1800,* 2nd ed. (New York: HarperPerennial, 1996); see also Henry Nash

Smith, *Virgin Land: The American West as Symbol and Myth* (Cambridge, MA: Harvard University Press, 1950). For more recent scholarship, see J. Gray Sweeny, *The Columbus of the Woods: Daniel Boone and the Typology of Manifest Destiny* (St. Louis: Washington University Gallery of Art, 1992). Interesting and relevant material also appears in Arthur K. Moore, *The Frontier Mind* (Lexington: University of Kentucky Press, 1957). For a comparison of the Boone myth with that of frontier icon David Crockett, with whom Boone is often confused, see *Davy Crockett: The Man, the Legend, the legacy, 1786–1986,* ed. Michael A. Lofaro (Knoxville: University of Tennessee Press, 1986).

7. For Draper's life, see Josephine L. Harper, *Guide to the Draper Manuscripts* (Madison, WI: The State Historical Society of Wisconsin, 1983); for the authoritative biography, see William B. Hesseltine, *Pioneer's Mission: The Story of Lyman Copeland Draper* (Madison, WI: The State Historical Society of Wisconsin, 1954); see also Reuben Gold Thwaites, "Lyman Copeland Draper: A Memoir," in *Collections of the State Historical Society of Wisconsin,* ed. Lyman C. Draper, vol. 1, 1903, ix–xxvi; see also Reuben Gold Thwaites, *How George Rogers Clark Won the Northwest,* 6th ed. (Chicago: A. C. McClurg and Company, 1931) 335–59.

8. LCD to William Martin, c. 1842, quoted in Hesseltine, *Pioneer's Mission,* 41.

9. Ibid., 76.

10. Ibid., 229–30.

11. Ibid., 239.

12. Thwaites, *Wisconsin Historical Collection,* xxii.

13. Hesseltine, *Pioneer's Mission,* 282; in 1996 during Tennessee's Bicentennial, the Overmountain Press released a second edition of *King's Mountain and its Heroes.*

14. Thwaites, *Wisconsin Historical Collection,* xxiv; for publications see "Bibliography of Lyman C. Draper," in *Wisconsin Historical Collection,* xxvi–xxix;

15. Quoted in John Mack Faragher, *Daniel Boone: The Life and Legend of an American Pioneer* (New York: Henry Holt, 1992), 343; Hesseltine, *Pioneer's Mission,* 253.

16. Thomas D. Clark, "Draper Collection of Western Americana," *Kentucky Encyclopedia,* ed. John E. Kleber (Lexington: University Press of Kentucky, 1992), 271.

17. Faragher, *Boone,* 343.

18. Harper, *Guide,* xiv.

19. Thwaites, *Wisconsin Historical Collection,* ix.

20. Michael A. Lofaro, *The Life and Adventures of Daniel Boone* (Lexington: University of Kentucky Press, 1976), 137.

21. Quoted by Mann Butler and ancillary data by Judge Hall, n.d., DM 16C:100(3).

22. Quoted in Hesseltine, *Pioneer's Mission,* 114.

23. LCD to Judge Todd, n.d., DM 16C:100.

24. LCD's interview with Nathan and Olive Boone is found in DM 6S, "Draper's Notes"; I am grateful to author Allan W. Eckert for sending me his transcription of Draper's interview with Nathan and Olive Boone.

25. Quoted in DM 1B:47; see also Hesseltine, *Pioneer's Mission,* 132–33, 334, n.18.

26. Thwaites, *Wisconsin Historical Collection,* xviii.

27. Hesseltine, *Pioneer's Mission,* 114.

28. Quoted in DM 13C:11.

29. LCD to Emily Bryan, July 12, 1888, DM 4C:40.

30. Thwaites, *Wisconsin Historical Collection,* xxv.

31. For quotes, see *Life*: chapter iii, n.4; chapter xv, n.4; chapter vii, n.9.

EDITOR'S NOTE: HOW THIS BOOK CAME TO BE AND MY METHODS

What drove me to tackle "Life of Daniel Boone"?

This was a job that needed doing a long time ago. Since 1856 Draper's manuscript has sat on a shelf in the archives of the State Historical Society of Wisconsin. As of 1949 it was available only on microfilm as "Series B. Draper's Life of Boone."

How sad, I often thought as I cranked the microfilm reader to peruse the hundreds of pages etched in Draper's bold cursive script running thirty-five lines or so to a foolscap leaf. Here was this huge manuscript, known only to a few, filled with tales of Boone, frontier lore, Long Hunters, Indians, wild exploits, hunters' skills, genealogical data, descriptions of native flora and fauna, miscellaneous Americana, trans-Appalachian history, and much more. Here was a vast mother lode few would mine. This, I decided one day back in 1990, would not do.

Transcribing the manuscript onto computer disk came first. I began with chapter 8, Draper's treatise on Long Hunters. I spent days in the Forrest C. Pogue Special Collections Library copying from the microfilm in longhand onto a yellow legal pad, and nights at home hunt-and-peck typing into my clunker computer what I had copied that day. My hands gave out; my already bad penmanship got worse. I switched to dictating the text into a hand-held Sony to take home and transcribe from that. In all, it was mighty slow work.

In fall 1991 the Department of History at Murray State University, in Murray, Kentucky, hired me to teach. During the next four or five years I taught full-time and wrote about seventy essays for magazines, anthologies, encyclopedias, and historical journals. Between that I also worked on books and served a seven-week stint as a Hollywood extra in the 1992 release of *The Last of the Mohicans*. After receiving my discharge from the French and Indian War, I stuck what I had copied of "Life of Daniel Boone" into a file and forgot it.

In October 1996 Stackpole Books published my first work, *The Long Hunt: Death of the Buffalo East of the Mississippi,* and in April 1997 my second, Peter Houston's *A Sketch of the Life and Character of Daniel Boone.* Curious, between books I dug out my chapters of "The Life of Daniel Boone" and sent them off to my publisher and made my case. My proposal was accepted.

Eleven more chapters, an appendix, and Draper's whopper Introduction still faced me. To grasp Draper's big blueprint, his vision for the book, it was also essential to decipher of heaps of clippings, notes, plats, testimonials, and letters to Benson J. Lossing, Draper's intended collaborator and illustrator, himself author of several works, including *Pictorial Field Book of the Revolution* (1850).

Aid for the task looming ahead came from Dr. James W. Hammack, Jr., chair of MSU's History Department, who set me up in a room equipped with a microfilm reader and an old computer. After a few false starts—such as getting the wrong microfilm from the supplier; burning out a few of the reader's hard-to-find high-intensity bulbs; witnessing the old computer "freeze up" and having to get it replaced—I was again rolling on Draper, knocking off seven to ten pages of draft daily.

It was on one fateful day in March 1997 when I hammered in the last of Draper's words. Total typed manuscript pages: 1,295. I had forever chained "Life of Daniel Boone" to the printed page via two 3.5" high-density diskettes. Now the real work awaited: editing.

Draper had written and rewritten his draft four or five times. As editor, my first big question was whether to keep his text intact or to cut it. And if to cut, then what? This was, after all, not my book. How much was I to intrude?

"Publish it as it is," was my first thought, "mistakes and all." But I was wary about inflicting such overly punctuated, fustian prose on readers. The text did, I thought, need a touch-up. Nor did I want to pursue my first idea of replicating Benson Lossing's quaint woodcuts to market to folks used to high-resolution television and high-tech motion pictures. Illustrations for the book, I decided, should be crisp black and white photographs, modern and period maps, modern and period art.

Dr. Thomas D. Clark, Kentucky's historian laureate, professor emeritus of University of Kentucky, and author of many books on Kentucky history and the South, offered wise counsel after I sent him a chapter seeking advice on my editorial quandary. "I must say my head was swirling when I got through it. This manuscript presents a fascinating exercise in earlier historical writing, organization, and detail. Reading it is somewhat like looking at a huge and complex framework of an unplanned structure. There are so many details, so many of them dragged in and staked down without much explanation of why they are there."

Whether to leave the text intact, edit it, or rewrite it, that, the venerable Clark said, "presents a real dilemma." "Do you . . . publish it as it is as an example of Draper's attempt at writing history-biography, and take out a proper amount of historical insurance in a somewhat extended introductory essay? Or do you go into the text with a sharp editorial pencil and pare it down to manageable and meaningful proportions? If you took the latter course then you are obligated to engage in deleting so much superfluous materials, the reframing of the context, in giving some sharp degree of coherence to the narrative."

Should I go the latter route, Clark suggested recasting the biography "in a new framework of narration, of presenting Daniel Boone as the central figure, and of giving some element of interpretation to the material."

Clark's thoughts echoed my own. To rewrite "Life of Daniel Boone" would destroy it. I wanted to preserve the integrity of the work.

Using Draper's one published frontier work, *King's Mountain and Its Heroes* (1881), as a stylistic guide, I set my criteria. The author's words and voice would stay his own, including antiquated spellings and usage, but with consistency in spelling and capitalization. (The manuscript was remarkably free of misspellings.) Military titles, abbreviations, and the like have been made consistent with modern usage, except where Draper is quoting someone else.

Where I could not make out a word, I inserted [*wi*] for "word illegible." Where Draper left a blank or skewed a sentence or the microfilm chopped off the text, in its place I used [*wm*], meaning "word (or words) missing." In a few spots where Draper went awry in a sentence and I was not sure what he was going for, I inserted [*?*].

Draper wrote headings only for chapters i, ii, iv, v, vii, viii, ix, xi, and the Appendix. I wrote the rest, including those for his Introduction, keeping them in the proper idiom.

Footnotes no longer appear at page bottoms, as they do in the handwritten text and as Draper did in *King's Mountain,* but instead have been sequentially numbered and moved to the end of each chapter. All of the author's annotations and bibliographic citations, aside from some re-paragraphing, appear as in the original.

Far too many commas caused the text to plod along like an old footsore Clydesdale. Many nineteenth-century authors splattered pages with commas enough to fill a good-sized galaxy, and editors often let them get away with it. Not here. Had Draper subjected his manuscript to a merciless editorial pen the superfluous commas would have been cut. I cut them sharply.

But, I rarely cut commas in textual quotes. Draper had a disturbing way of modifying for inclusion without warning some quotes from narratives and memoirs by correcting spelling and altering punctuation. He also wrote comments in page margins and underlined for emphasis. Not all of his sources were readily available to me, and I was not willing to spend years poring over each first-, second-, and thirdhand source to check syntax. In Draper's Introduction I did restore Dr. Thomas Walker's journal to its original version, as published in J. Stoddard Johnston's *First Explorations of Kentucky* (1898).

I kept my editorial comments lean as much as I could (though many times I could not), trusting the good maxim "to err on the side of brevity," as Civil War historian and author William C. Davis, one of my long-suffering editors, advised. Indeed, as big as the book is, made even more so by its profuse annotations, long introduction, appendix, and front matter, I did not wish to write a companion text of commentary and make the tome any more digressive or imposing or costly. My notes, designated alphabetically, follow Draper's at the end of each chapter, except where I address some matters in his notes, in which case I designate my commentary with my initials "TFB." In notes and commentary herein Draper is cited as "LCD."

    A bit of advice: As you mine the troves herein, go slowly. Pause and ponder the way of this man Draper, his vision, his book, his man Boone. Peruse his footnotes and commentary. No need to rush. What you now hold has been hidden away since 1856. And like the warm tone of a vintage violin, it is meant to be savored.

Nathan Boone Testimonial
NB to LCD, c. 1851, DM 1B:14–15

The facts and papers I have furnished Mr. Lyman C. Draper, now of Madison, Wisconsin, together with many others of an authentic character obtained by him from other aged members of the family, and from surviving companions of my father, the late Col. Daniel Boone, should give to his work on my father the merit it justly deserves, of being the only reliable one extant. From my own personal knowledge of Mr. Draper, and the unusual pains I know he has taken to acquaint himself of the real facts of my father's life, his motives, habits and characteristics, sifting out and discarding not a few erroneous and apocryphal stories, I hope his work, prepared with so much care and faithfulness, and which alone will hand down to posterity any thing like a correct view of my father's public and private career, will meet with a kind reception by all who regard the truth and justice of history generally, and the toils and privations especially of those who, under God, were humbly instrumental in effecting the early settlement of Kentucky and the West. This is alike due to the memory and services of my worthy father, and the untiring zeal and efforts of Mr. Draper for the past fifteen years in the collection of facts, to record his name and actions, in their true light and proper on the pages of our border history.

Wishing for this work that success which I honestly feel that its merits eminently deserve,

I remain, very respectfully,
(signed) Nathan Boone
Green County, Mo.
Sept. 1853

Boone Testimonial #1
DM 1B:2

From our personal acquaintance with Col. Daniel Boone, and our general familiarity with the early history of Kentucky and the West, we cannot but highly appreciate the long and patient efforts of Mr. Lyman C. Draper in collecting materials, from original and reliable sources, for a full and faithful *Life* of that far-famed Kentucky pioneer, and do not hesitate to commend the work to the favorable consideration of all who cherish a love for the deeds of noble daring by which the now mighty west was preserved from the grasp of the Briton and the Savage.
Ezra Farris
Edward Coles
J. M. Peck, Rockspring, Ill. Dec. 1st, 1856
James E. Welch

Boone Testimonial #2
DM 1B:3

We, the undersigned relatives of Col. Daniel Boone, certify that we are satisfied that Lyman C. Draper, has by his long patience and industry, made a large collection of facts and materials, to which we have contributed for a work on the *Life of Col. Daniel Boone* and we commend his work to the public patronage.
Samuel Boone (son of George Boone)
John Scholl (grandson of Edward Boone)
Joseph Scholl (grandson of Daniel Boone)
Edward Boone (son of George Boone)
Daniel Boone
Susan Howell

Boone Testimonial #3
DM 1B:4ff

In view of the facts and documents furnished by us to Mr. Lyman C. Draper, and those he has, with unwearied zeal and faithfulness, collected, during the past sixteen years, from other authentic sources, we unhesitatingly express our belief that his *Life of Col. Daniel Boone* is the only one extant, which we, his descendants and connections, regard as complete and reliable; and, as such, take pleasure in commending it to public favor and confidence.
Higgason Grubbs Boone (grandnephew of Daniel Boone)

Samuel Boone (sons of George Boone)
Joseph Bryan

William T. Bryan (son of Daniel Bryan)
Morgan Bryan

Francis Lamme (daughters of Flanders and Jemima Callaway)
Elizabeth Bryan

John Stuart Pennington (Daniel Boone's nephew; son of John Stuart killed
by Indians in Kentucky in 1769)
Olive Boone (wife of Nathan Boone)
Benjamin H. Boone (son of Nathan and Olive Boone)
Nathan Goe (grandson of Daniel Boone)
S. N. Brown, M.D. (Boone relative)
Sarah Hunter (daughter of Edward Boone)

Is. Boone, M.D. (grandnephew of Daniel Boone)
D. Boone

Daniel Pennington (nephew of Daniel Boone)

Albert G. Boone (son of Jesse Boone, a son of Daniel Boone)
Van Daniel Boone

Daniel Boone (son of Daniel Morgan Boone, a son of Daniel Boone)
Alonzo H. Boone
Edward Boone

Amazon Hays (son of Boone Hays, a grandson of Daniel Boone)
Linvilla Hays
Upton Hays
Samuel Hays

James Boone (oldest son of Nathan and Olive Boone)
Edward Boone Scholl (grandson of Edward Boone, Daniel Boone's brother,
killed in Kentucky October 6, 1780)
Joshua Pennington (son of Hannah, sister of Daniel Boone)

Wilford H. Yor[?] (grandson of Squire Boone, brother of Daniel Boone)
Daniel Boon
Hiram C. Boone

Susan Cockrill (grandniece of Daniel Boone)
Rebecca Boone Grant Lamont (niece of Daniel Boone)
Isaac Van Bibber (grandson of Daniel Boone)
Isaiah Boon (Squire Boone's son, Daniel Boone's brother)

Lafayette Boon (grandsons of Squire)
Granville Boon

Edward Boone Scholl (grandson of Daniel Boone)
Enoch Boone
Levine S. Newman
L. W. Boggs
Panthea Boggs
Nathan B. Goe
James Davison [?]
John Shaw
Robert Hancock

This note appears at DM 1B:32

"I am really astonished at your labor, and the fruits of it, in procuring materials for your future disposition. One thing is certain, that you deserve good credit for your talented and energetic labors thus far: and you have my sincere prayers for your success. In my humble manner, I will think it an honor to assist you with materials so far as I am capable."

Late ex-governor John Reynolds, author of *Pioneer History of Illinois, My Life and Times, and etc.*

*Early Spanish Explorations of North America.—Early English Forays
East of the Appalachians.—"Honorable Major General" Abraham
Wood.—John Lederer's Trek to the Blue Ridge.—Batts and Fallam.—Of
the Enterprising Catholic Missionaries of New France.—La Salle
Discovers the Mississippi.—Knights of the Golden Horse-shoe.—
Colonization, Trade, and More Explorations into America's Interior.—
"Dr. Thomas Walker's Journal, 1750."—Of Christopher Gist's
Expedition into Ohio and Kentucky.—The Treaty of Logstown.—English
Traders and Hunters in the Lands of the Western Waters.—Expeditions
and War.—Capt. Harry Gordon.—Col. James Smith.—Col. George
Morgan.—Western Speculations of the Virginia Dynasty.—Early
Kentucky Forays.—The Fertile Holston Country.—Fort Stanwix Treaty.—
Powell's Valley Settlement.—Joseph Martin's Indian Fight.*

A faithful *résumé* of western discovery and exploration, anterior to Boone's great undertaking with Findlay, and others, seems quite indispensable in paving the way to a correct understanding of the adventurous enterprise of the renowned pioneer of Kentucky.

Who was the earliest discoverer of the Mississippi River, that great historical landmark of the West, history does not inform us. Though Columbus reentered the Gulf of Mexico and explored the bordering portion of the North American coast, evidence is wanting that he ever saw the Great River of the West. On a map accompanying an edition of Ptolemy, painted at Venice in 1513, it is not a little remarkable that the delta of a river corresponding to the Mississippi is traced with more distinctness than upon the maps of the next century. Successive explorers now sailed along the southern shore of Florida till it was thoroughly examined by Garay in 1518;[a] and three years later, a map was drawn up by the arbitrator appointed to decide between the claims of rival discoverers, and on it we find the Mississippi again traced on the part assigned as peculiarly Garay's with the name it subsequently bore for a period, Rio de Espíritu Santo, or River of the Holy Ghost.[1]

Florida, the land of flowers, charmed the attention of the chivalrous spirits of that age. Expedition followed expedition; León,[b] Córdova,[c] and Ayllón,[d] successively found death of the shores on that ill-fated land; and yet the rage for discovery and conquest was not apparently the least damped. In 1528 Pámphilus de

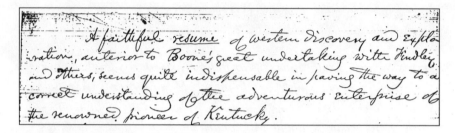

9. *Opening paragraph of "Life of Daniel Boone," from the hand of Lyman C.
Draper.* STATE HISTORICAL SOCIETY OF WISCONSIN.

Narváez undertook to colonize the whole northern coast of the Mexican gulf; but
storms, disease, and famine remorselessly swept off nearly all his devoted followers. A few with Cabeza de Vaca were cast on an island on the coast of the Mississippi, from which, after four years' slavery, De Vaca escaped with four
companions and reached the main land. Viewed as medicine-men by the simple
and credulous natives, they found no difficulty in passing safely from tribe to
tribe, traversing the buffalo plains of New Mexico until they finally reached the
Gulf of California. While De Vaca must have crossed the Mississippi, unless indeed his prison-island was west of the mouth of that river, there is yet nothing in
his narrative to distinguish that stream from other large rivers on his route.

The appearance of De Vaca and his companions among their countrymen in
Mexico relating their marvelous stories and declaring the interior to be "the richest country in the world," naturally enough gave a new impulse to the prevailing
spring for discovery and adventure. Two new expeditions were the result,
planned early in 1539, one of which was led by the Franciscan Friar Mark. Starting from Culican, near the mouth of the Gulf of California, and pushing northwardly through the desert wastes, they reached the Colorado, where in attempting
to enter an Indian town a portion of his party was cut off, when Friar Mark returned with but a slight additional knowledge of the geography of the New
World.[2]

But the other expedition was one of memorable note in the annals of the
West. De Soto and his steel-clad warriors were the first band of European adventurers of whom we have any certain knowledge who pushed their way into the
great Western Valley of North America. Leaving Florida, they at length reached
the Mississippi not very far from the present thriving city of Memphis, on the 1st
of May, 1541; and, crossing the river, wandered in the region of Louisiana,
Arkansas, and as far north as the neighborhood of New Madrid, Missouri, when
they began to retrace their wary steps. In the spring of 1542 the resolute leader of
the intrepid Spaniards, worn down by disappointments and hardships, melancholy
and fever, wasted away and finally died, and with him expired the hopes of his
followers. "Thus perished," in the language of Bancroft,[c] "Ferdinand de Soto, the
Governor of Cuba, the successful associate of Pizarro. His miserable end was the

10. Conquistador musketeer shooting matchlock, or arquebus. Note forked rest, ammunition bandoleer belt strung with wooden pre-loaded charge flasks (called "the Twelve Apostles"), bullet bag, extra "slow-match," and priming flask.

more observed, from the greatness of his former prosperity. His soldiers pronounced his eulogy by grieving for their loss; the priests chanted over his body the first requiems that were ever heard on the waters of the Mississippi. To conceal his death, his body was wrapped in a mantle and in the stillness of midnight was silently sunk in the middle of the stream. The discoverer of the Mississippi slept beneath its waters. He had crossed a large part of the continent in search of gold, and found nothing so remarkable as his burial place."

A second expedition under Friar Mark from the Pacific coast, penetrating up the Colorado, then across the country and over the Rocky Mountain chain, at length reached the upper waters of the Arkansas and Platte in 1542, and finally the Rio Grande, where a "Florida Indian" gave a very clear description of the Mississippi which was substantially confirmed by other Indian accounts. In 1557 a Spanish army of fifteen hundred men under Don Tristán de Luna undertook the conquest of Florida; and though encountering sad disasters by storm on the coast, de Luna sent a detachment into the Coosa country of Alabama which was there joined by Indian allies and pushed forward to wage war with the Natchez, whom they encountered and defeated, when the Mississippi was again reached by Spanish adventurers. Soon after 1580, the Spaniards of New Mexico continually heard of the Mississippi, or Rio Grande del Espíritu Santo, and some seem actually to have reached it. But no vessels had yet entered the Great River of the West for purposes of commerce or exploration. There is, however, a vague rumor of a Portuguese captain, Vincent González, having sailed up a large river between Apalache and Tampico prior to 1630.[3]

For nearly a century after the romantic expeditions of De Soto, Mark, and de
Luna, we have no certain evidence that the footsteps of any adventurous white
man disturbed the stillness of the forests of the mighty Valley of the West. About
the month of March, 1648, some Indian visitors reported to Sir William Berkley,
governor of Virginia, "that within five days journey to the Westward and by
South, there is a high mountaine, and at foot thereof great Rivers, that run into a
great sea; and that there are men that come hither in ships (but not the same that
ours be); they weare apparrell and have red caps on their heads, and ride on
Beasts like our Horses, but have much larger ears."[4] These were probably De
Soto's or De Luna's men or the Spanish adventurers in Mexico. Sir William
Berkley, deeply interested in these relations, determined to make an exploration
with a party of fifty horsemen and as many foot [soldiers], but he was disappointed in its execution.

These Indian reports, in connection with the discussions consequent upon
Berkley's projected exploration, excited in the minds of the enterprising spirits of
the colony an anxious solicitude to acquire some more certain knowledge of the
"high mountaine," and the great rivers and extensive country beyond. Accordingly, on the 27th of August, 1650, Edward Bland, merchant, Capt. Abraham
Wood, Elias Pennant and Sackfort Brewster, gentlemen; together with Robert
Farmer, servant to Mr. Bland, and Henry Newcombe, servant to Captain Wood,
and Pyancha, an Appamattuck war-captain, for a guide, left Fort Henry at the
Falls of Appomattox, now Petersburg, Virginia, taking with them four horses and
provisions, "intending a South Westerne Discovery." They were the same day
joined by Oyeocker, a Nottaway weroance[f] who also accompanied them as a
guide.

Pursuing a south-western course and crossing Nottaway and Meherin rivers,
they evidently struck Roanoke River near an Indian town some six miles below
the junction of the Staunton and Dan rivers, where Clarksville, Virginia, now is.
This stream they named Blandina River and the adjacent country, or rather "continent," they called new Brittaine. The Indians at that period caught many stur-
geon at the falls, which were six miles above the junction, and a little below the
falls were two cliffy islands in a large bay; the upper one, which they named
Charles Island, was "three miles broad and four miles long"; and the other, which
they denominated Berkley Island, was "almost as big"; and "at the lower end of
Charles Island lies a Bay due South from the said Island, so spacious that we
could not see the other side of it." While the length of these islands was very accurately described, their width was far over-estimated; and they naturally produced quite an expansion in the river. There was another island three miles in
length just above these, directly in the mouth of the Staunton, which our explorers
seem not to have observed.[5]

In the evening of the ninth day from their departure they returned to Fort
Henry in safety; and the next year appeared in London a small quarto on "The

11. A Weroance (meaning "Great Lord") of Virginia, c. 1580s, by John White. Note body paint, neck beads, leg tattoos, cane quiver, and bow. BUREAU OF AMERICAN ETHNOLOGY, SMITHSONIAN INSTITUTION.

Discovery of New Brittaine"—"that happy country," as Mr. Bland denominates it in his pamphlet, one hundred and twenty miles south-west of the Falls of Appomattox, where two crops of corn were [harvested] annually and cane grew twenty-five [feet] high and two inches round, which the discoverers imagined to be an indigenous sugar-cane.[6]

This partial success inspired all classes with new hopes and ardent desires respecting South-western discoveries of which this but served as a foretaste. On the 20th of October, 1650, upon Edward Bland's petition, the Assembly of Virginia granted him or any other person permission to "discover and seate to the Southward in any convenient place" and to "have correspondence with the Indians" and "also to receive the benevolence of the well-effected and use all lawful means for effecting thereof" provided they should secure themselves in such settlement with a hundred able-bodied, armed men.[7] In 1652 Col. William Clayborne and Capt. Henry Fleete were authorized to make discoveries in the South and West.[8] The next year Edward Bland, a native of England who had ten years previously been a Spanish merchant and subsequently settled in the colony, died at his residence at Kimages, Charles City County, leaving a widow and only one son, and the same year, Capt. Abraham Wood was authorized to prosecute his discoveries at the South and West, and "diverse gentlemen" were permitted to "discover the Mountains."[9]

Under this authorization, Captain Wood entered renewedly upon his great mission; that he well fulfilled it, the meagre facts handed down to us most honorably attest. Daniel Coxe, in his memorial to King William in 1699 claiming the proprietorship of Carolina or Louisiana, asserts what no one has ever attempted to disprove that Colonel Wood of Virginia, from 1654 to 1664, discovered at different times several branches of the great rivers Ohio and Mississippi; and Coxe further declares that about the year 1678 he himself possessed the journal of a Mr. Needham,[g] who had been employed by Colonel Wood in the prosecution of these adventurous explorations.[10] Another respectable authority informs us that "a large branch of the Ohio called *Wood River,* from Colonel Wood, of Virginia, who discovered it first in 1654 and several times afterwards, of which an authentic account is to be seen in the archives of the Royal Society, besides the accounts we have of that discovery from our historians."[11] Wood's River, or what is now known as the Great Kenhawa or New River, is mentioned in Gist's Journal of 1751 and also so named in Jefferson and Fry's large map of Virginia drawn up in that year; in Dr. Mitchell's map of 1755 and likewise noticed by other early writers and geographers.

Not long after this period we find Abraham Wood distinguished by the title of "Honorable Major General" and granting official commissions to others to engage in Western discoveries—all this, doubtless, in consideration of his own meritorious services in successfully exploring at least the upper portions of the great Western Valley.[12] Of this early intrepid discoverer, whose name must ever remain inseparably connected with the primitive history of the West as the precursor of Marquette and La Salle, little remains to be added. In 1646 a tract of six hundred acres of land adjoining Fort Henry at the Falls of the Appomattox, now Petersburg, Virginia, was granted to him, and there General Wood is spoken of as still residing as late as the commencement of the Indian war in Virginia in 1675, after which we hear no more of him.[13]

John Lederer, a German surgeon, and a man of learning, modesty, ingenuity and enterprise, appeared in Virginia and obtained a commission from the governor Sir William Berkley to explore the south-western parts of that province. Accompanied by three Indians, he set out from the Indian town of Chickahominy, at the Falls of York or Pamunkey River, in March 1669, and proceeded up the stream along the northern shore till they reached the confluence of the North and South Aura, when they crossed the latter into the fork, where, as Lederer informs us, the "great Indian King called Tottopottoma" was slain in battle a few years before "while fighting for the Christians against the Mohocks and Nahyssans, from whence it retains his name to this day." Pursuing the South Aura to its source and thence bearing somewhat northwardly, they crossed the upper part of the Rapidan. When the distant "Apalatean Mountains" were first described, the Indian guides prostrated themselves in adoration and exclaimed, *Okee paeze!—God is nigh*! They soon gained the summit of the Blue Ridge, not very far probably from the confines of Madison, Page, and Rockingham counties; and Lederer named the elevation which he had succeeded in reaching Mount William, in honor of Sir William Berkley. Wandering a few days in the snow, they descended the mountain and returned to the settlements by their outward route.

Dissatisfied with the almost fruitless results of this little expedition, Lederer resolved upon another. Accordingly, in May 1670 he persuaded Major Harris to join him, together from the Falls of the James River passing the Monakin Town, and pursuing a due west course through a mountainous region, they at length reached the Indian settlement of Mohock, located apparently in the fork of the

James and Tye rivers.[14] Here Lederer was ungallantly abandoned by Major Harris and the whole party, except Jackzetavon, a Susquehanna Indian. While Harris and his companions retraced their steps, Lederer and his guide kept steadily on their course up the James River in a south-westerly direction for some distance and finally bore off somewhat to the right of that stream; and, about one hundred miles from Mohock, struck "a stately river," doubtless the Staunton, on the southern bank of which was the Nahyssan town of Sapon. Here they were treated kindly by the savages.

Resuming their journey south-westerly as Lederer thought and about fifty miles by his computation, they arrived at Akenatzy, a small island in a branch of the same river as that at Sapon and upon which was a large Indian town. It is likely that this island town was situated on what is now known as Long Island, in Staunton River and some twenty-five miles above Sapon.[15] While Lederer was at Akenatzy, four Indian ambassadors arrived there curiously painted with representations of singular animals; they were from the Rickahockans beyond the "Apalatean Mountains," and were the only survivors of a party of fifty, the others, during a long and tedious journey of two months, having perished by tempests and in the marshes. This embassy was invited to a night-dance, during which they were suddenly fallen on and all murdered. This piece of treachery so alarmed Lederer and his Indian guide that they stole off without taking formal leave.

After pursuing a south-south-western course, sometimes by a beaten path and sometimes over rocks and hills, they came to the Indian town of Oenock or Shabonaenock, which seems to have probably been on the head waters of Banister River; fourteen miles beyond in the same general direction dwelt the Shackong Indians. Thence onward, west-south-westerly, through thickets and marsh grounds for five days, they arrived at Watary and westerly thirty miles farther to Sara. Sara was undoubtedly the Lower Saura Town, as laid down on ancient and modern maps, on the southern bank of Dan River. "Sara," says Lederer, "is not far distant from the mountains, which here lose their height, and change their course and name; for they run due west, and receive from the Spaniards the name of Saula." The mountains at the Lower Saura Town do bear off westerly along the southern bank up the Irvine or Smith's River.

Leaving Sara, the explorers bent their course south-south-westerly along the western confines of a wet, caney region for three days, when they reached the town of Wisacky, and another day brought them over a river to its southern bank, and a little below, to the great Indian metropolis of Ushery, which proved to be the largest Indian town Lederer had yet seen.[16] At the lower part of the town the river flowed into what he called Lake Ushery, which seemed large to him, though he did not go any farther to explore it, and of its extent he "could neither learn nor guess." The Ushery nation of Indians were those since better known as the Catawbas, and "history knows them chiefly," says Bancroft, "as the hereditary foes of the Iroquois tribes, before whose prowess and numbers they dwindled away."[17] Wisacky was a town of the Usheries.

Lederer traded with the Usheries for some pieces of silver which they had obtained from nations beyond them. Having satisfied his curiosity, and learning that a further journey of two days and a half would bring him to a nation of bearded men whom he supposed to be Spaniards, he concluded it best to direct his footsteps towards Virginia, which he did by taking a more southerly route than his outward one, passing mostly through a dry upland region in which he and his faithful guide were sometimes greatly straitened for water to quench their own and their horses' thirst. At length, on the seventeenth day from Ushery they came to the town of Katearas, "a place of great Indian trade and commerce, and the seat of the haughty Emperor of the Taskiroros." This town was situated on the eastern bank of a small stream, which, from Lederer's rude map and the time consumed in his journey, we should judge was either Eno or the head branches of the Tar River.[18] To save himself from captivity, Lederer yielded up his gun and shot to "his grim Majestie" of the Tuscaroras, "for he was," says our explorer, "the most proud, imperious Barbarian that I met with in all my Marches." Without future misfortune, the good German and Jackzetavon soon passed the Roanoke, Mehemin, and Nottaway rivers and reached "Apanatuck in Virginia" on the evening of the 17th of July, "where," says Lederer, "I was not a little overjoyed to see Christian faces again." During this tedious journey of nearly two months, Lederer and his guide relied mainly on parched maize and such game as happened in their way to supply their necessities, and the wilderness at that season of the year was not wanting in food for their faithful horse.

To his surprise, the honest German explorer found upon his return that Major Harris had been busy not only in exculpating himself from all blame in abandoning Lederer upon the very threshold of his long and interesting exploration, but actually ventured to "report strange things" in his own praise and to Lederer's "disparagement," little supposing the fellow would ever come back to tell a different tale. Ever hopeful, Lederer soon interested a Colonel Catlet to join him in another attempt to penetrate beyond the mountains; and on the 20th of August on the same year, 1670, they left one Robert Talifer's, accompanied by nine mounted whites and five Indian footmen, and that night reached the Falls of the Rappahannock. Continuing their journey up the main fork of that river to its head, they reached the "Apalatean Mountains" on the 26th; and leaving their horses at the foot in charge of some of the Indians, they ascended with much difficulty to the top of one of the highest peaks; there "drank the King's Health in Brandy" and named the elevation *Mount King Charles* in honor of their royal sovereign. Discovering prodigious heights beyond them to a great distance, they despaired of finding a passage for their horses and returned home without accomplishing anything. Lederer speaks of a gap in the mountains, as he learned from the Indians, at a place to the northward called Zynodoa—which we easily recognize for Shenandoah, the name of the principal river in the valley of Virginia.

Returning to the settlements, poor Lederer encountered a storm of opposition from the people who had been made to believe that the public levy of that year all went to meet the expenses of his adventurous travels and discoveries, perhaps supposing that they had been prompted by the self-interest of the governor, Sir William Berkley, who was one of the proprietors of Carolina. Certainly it is that Lederer's personal safety compelled him to take refuge in Maryland, where he had the good fortune to make the acquaintance of Sir William Talbot, who, though at first prejudiced against him, finally entered heartily into his story because satisfied of his persecution and tested his trust-worthiness by comparing his narrative with the Indian relations and translated the account of his discoveries from the Latin in which they were written and had it published in London with a map in 1672.[19] The effect of Lederer's south-western discoveries may in part be inferred from the fact that in less than three years, Joseph and Henry Hatcher and Benjamin Bullington were successfully engaged as Virginia traders to the Saura Indians.[20]

But his bold adventure had also a happy influence in keeping alive the spirit of border exploration. Thus we find that in consequence of "a commission granted by the Hon. Major General Abraham Wood, for ye finding out of the ebbing and flowing of ye water behinde the mountains, in order to the discovery of the South Sea," Thomas Batts, Thomas Woods, Robert Fallam, accompanied by Perecute, a great man of the "Apomatock Indians," and Jack Neson, formerly a servant to Major General Wood, with five horses, set forward from the Appomattox Town in Virginia on Friday, September 1st, 1671. Steering a generally westerly course and crossing some stream flowing into the Roanoke, they reached the "Sapong Town" a little after noon on the fourth day, where they were "very joyfull and kindly entertained, received with firing of Guns, and plenty of provision." Here they engaged a Sapong Indian for their guide to the Tolera Town. The next day, "just as they were to take horse, they heard some Guns goe off the other side of the River," who proved to be seven Appomattox Indians sent to join them in their exploration. And this shows that Sapong was situated on the Southern bank of the river—which was unquestionably the Staunton and the same town that Lederer visited the previous year which he called Sapong. Starting about eleven o'clock, they reached Hanohaskie, twenty-five miles north-west from Sapong, "in an island of the Sapong River."[21] Here they were likewise kindly entertained.

When they departed on the morning of the 6th, Thomas Woods, who was dangerously sick of the "flux," was left at Hanohaskie in charge of the Indians, as also his horse, which had been taken with the staggers. That afternoon the Indian hunters killed a deer. Their route was up the river, and the course indicated agrees correctly with that of the Staunton above the Long Island to the Blue Ridge. During the afternoon of the 8th, they discovered a tree "in the path" marked with a coal *M.A., N.I.;* and towards night they reached out and ascended the mountain, having twice that day crossed the Sapong River. The next day they descended into a "lovely valley about six miles over with curious small risings," beyond which, at the foot of a steep descent, they came to the Tolera Indian Town "in a very rich swamp between a Breach and the main River of Roanoke, circled about with mountains." Here they rested the remainder of that and the two following days, Perecute having "the Ague and Feavor every afternoon." Leaving their horses at the Tolera Town, they renewed their journey on the 12th on foot, pursuing a path which led them over high mountains and deep intervening vallies, passing a number of branches and the main Roanoke River several times, and camped that night beside the Roanoke, "very nigh the head thereof."

On the ensuing day they clambered up a very high mountain whose ascent was so steep and they so weary that they could scarcely keep themselves from sliding down again. Resting awhile on its lofty summit, they viewed the scene beyond them. The vallies tended westwardly. As far as the eye could reach from the north to the south was "a pleasing but dreadful sight, to see Mountains and Hills piled one upon another." After travelling gently descending ground, about three miles beyond the mountain they came to two marked trees—one, as before, with a coal, *M.A., N.I.;* the other having *M.A.* cut into the bark, and "Several other scrablem.ts"; and these trees were "hard by a pretty swift small current tending West, sometimes Northerdly, w.th curious meadows on each side."[22] The "pleasant riseing hills" and the "brave, rich meadows with grass above a man's height" attracted their attention; and as they advanced they discovered many rivers and small streams from the southern mountains all tending northwardly, or to the west-north-west, "to empty themselves in the great River." This day they reached "the great River" itself—which was without doubts New River, the distinctive name of the upper part of the Great Kenhawa. Where they struck the river it ran a north by west course, and the explorers bearing somewhat to the right for half a dozen miles again came to the great river, broader still than before, and here ran west by south and had, they supposed, a western tendency beyond. Wading over the stream, the soil became richer and more stony, "full of brave meadows and old fields."

The next day, September 14th, Batts and his party set forward early following the path, the general direction of which led towards the north-west alternately crossing hills and vallies. "In a clear place on the top of a hill, they saw over against ym. to the south-west a curious prospect of hills, like waves raised by a gentle breeze, riseing one behind another: Mr. Batts supposed he saw houses, but Mr. Fallam rather tooke them to be white cliffs." Such were the trans-Alleghanian views that so frequently arrested the attention and called forth the wonder and admiration of our travellers. Near the middle of the afternoon, having journeyed about twenty-five miles and now both weary and hungry, they took up camp in order to give their hunters a chance to kill some deer. They had not eaten a morsel since they arose that morning, and Perecute continued very ill yet was desirous of going forward. During the day they passed several "brave brooks or small Rivelets."

Nor was the succeeding day much better, for "they lived a dogg's life" of "hunger and ease." "The Indians having done their best, could kill ym. noe meat; the Dear, they said, in such heards, and the ground drye, yt. by the rattling of the leaves, they easily espied. ym." In the afternoon they ventured forward a north-west course "till they came to a current, yt. emptied itself west and by north, as they supposed, into a great River." Fortunately at a time when the gnawings of hunger made anything edible particularly gratifying to their view, they found some "wild goose-barryes" and "exceeding large Haws" and fell to "feeding on these, and ye. hopes of better successe on the morrow." Their hired Tolera Indian guide, while out hunting that day, got lost and seems not to have returned to them again.

"Better successe," as hoped for did not attend them on the 16th. The Indian hunters went early to the woods, and while one soon returned, reporting that he had heard a drum and a gun go off to the northward, the other brought in some "exceeding good grapes" and "killed two turkyes wch. was very welcum, and where wth. they feasted." Refreshed and hopeful, they resumed their journey about ten o'clock, and when they had advanced about ten miles one of the Indians had the additional good fortune to bring down a deer. Presently they had a sight of a curious river "like Thames against Chelcey, but had a fall that made a great noise." Its course there was northwardly, but they supposed its general direction was westwardly, towards "certain pleasant mountains" discernable in that quarter. Their route that day had been something north of west. Upon the high ground near the Falls they took up their camp for the night. Between their camp and the river they found Indian fields "wth. corne stalks in them" and understood after-wards that the Mohetans had lived there not long before.

Sunday, September 17th, was an eventful day. "Early in the morning," says the ancient Journal of the transaction, "they went to seeke some trees to marke, the Indians being impatient of longer stay, by reason it was like to be bad weather, and that it was soe difficult to get provision: They found four trees ex-ceeding fitt for their purpose, yt. had been half barked by the Indians, standing one after another. Then they had this ceremony to proclaime the King in these words: Long live Charles ye. 2d, King of England, Scotland, France, Ireland and Virginia, and all the teretoryes thereunto belonging, defender of ye, faith."

Then, "wth. a pair of marking irons," they commenced the operation of form-ing letters on these peeled trees on the banks of New River. The first tree was marked *C.R.* "for his Sacred Majesty," with a rude representation of a crown sur-mounted with a cross directly over the royal initials. On the second tree was en-graved *W.B.* for the governor Sir William Berkley; and on the third, *A.W.* for the Maj. Gen. Abraham Wood. The fourth tree was marked *T3 R.F.* "for them-selves"; and directly beneath was "*P.* for Perecute, who said he would be an Eng-lishman." On still another tree were marked the initial letters, one under another, of Jack Nesday [Nelson], and four others comprising "ye. rest" of the party.

"After this," continues the narrative, "they left the Indians there, and went themselves down to the River side, but wth. much difficulty, it being a piece of very rich ground, whereon ye. Mohetans had formerly lived, and grown up with weeds and small prickly Locust bushes and thistles. When they came to ye. River side, they found it better and broader than expected, full as broad as ye. Thames over agt. Waping; ye. falls much like the Falls of [the] James River in Virginia, and imagined by the Water Marks it flowed there about three feet. It was then ebbing water; they set up a stick by the water-side, but found it [ebbing] very slowly. The Indians kept such a hallowing for them, that they durst stay no longer to make further tryall least they should leave ym."

They then set their faces homeward. Attaining the summit of the hill, "they took a prospect as far as they could view, and saw westwardly over certain delightfull hills a fogg arise, and a certain glimmering light as from water, and suppose there may be some great Bog." Returning to the Tolera Town, which they reached on Tuesday evening the 19th, they found a Mohetan Indian awaiting their arrival, whose nation, having intelligence of their approach, was afraid they were come to fight them, about which he had been despatched to make inquiry. They satisfied him that these fears were groundless, "and in assurance of friendship, presented him wth. three or four shots of powder." He then informed them that they had been from the mountains half way to the place where his nation then lived and that the next year beyond them was situated "on a plain levell, from whence came abundance of salt." That he could give them no information of the country beyond, inasmuch as Indians who ventured down there never returned; but that "there were a very great company of Indians living upon the Great Water."

Leaving the Tolera Town, where they were kindly entertained, they safely arrived at Hanohaskie the fourth day, where doubtless they sorrowed to find that "Mr. Woods was dead and buried, and his horse likewise dead." Continuing their journey and tarrying one day and two nights at "ye Sapongs" in consequence of "courteous entertainment," and passing the Appomattox Town, "on Sunday morning, being October ye. 1st., they arrived safely at Fort Henry."[23]

It appears quite certain that Batts and party proceeded up the Staunton River, passing over the Blue Ridge into the Virginia Valley, then up the "Roanoke" nearly to its source; crossed the Alleghanies and reached the head waters of Sinking Creek or some stream in that region flowing into New River; and finally struck New River and followed it down, probably to its passage through Peter's Mountain near Parisburg, Giles County, Virginia, where the stream falls over a rocky ledge of some ten or twelve feet in height, forming one of the wildest and most picturesque gorges in the mountains of Virginia. They are called "Peter's Falls."[24] There are no cascades of any magnitude above and none so large below until the Great Falls are reached, a distance of seventy or eighty miles and just below the junction of Gauley and New rivers. The time, route, distance, and circumstances all conspire to this conclusion. And the great salt region to which the Mohetan Indian unquestionably alluded was that which skirted the plains of the Kenhawa, more than a hundred miles below Peter's Falls; and there many years ago "in the latter part of a very dry summer, when the river was lower than it was ever known since it was settled by white people, the top of an old gum was discovered at the edge of low water, and salt water issuing out of it; and it was supposed that the Indians, when in possession of the country, sunk the gum, and perhaps made some attempts at making salt."[25]

12. *The Fox (Mesquakie), c. 1730, fought the French and their Mascouten allies in upper Illinois. Frenchmen captured this warrior and shipped him to Paris, where he died in a dungeon. Note tattoos, quilled hairpiece, trade shirt, bow and quiver full of arrows.* BIBLIOTHEQUE NATIONALE, PARIS.

Thus, on the seventeenth of September 1671, did Thomas Batts and his party formally proclaim King Charles the Second on the banks of New River, an important tributary of the Ohio, precisely a year and nine months before Marquette and Joliet discovered the Upper Mississippi and more than ten years anterior to La Salle's celebrated *Proces Verbal* of taking possession of Louisiana at the mouth of the Mississippi in behalf of the crown of France.

Eminently important as were the services of Wood, Batts, and Fallam in discovering the upper tributaries of the Ohio and thus imperishably connecting their names with the progress of western exploration, we should not fail to award full measure of praise to the early and indefatigable French explorers of the great Mississippi Valley. Though not so early in point of time in reaching the waters of the Mississippi as Wood and Batts, their travels were far more extensive, and the early publication of the narratives of their discoveries have given them a far greater notoriety.

Between the years 1608 and 1629, the enterprising missionaries of New France had explored the country and instructed the natives as far north-west as Lakes Huron and Nipissing. As early as 1639 the adventurous Sieur Nicolet had struck west of the Hurons and found himself among the Winnebagoes of Wisconsin; he explored Green Bay, ascended the Fox River to its portage and embarked on a river flowing west—the Wisconsin; and, adds Father Vimont, "had he sailed three days more on a great river which flows from lake [Green Bay], he would have found the Sea." Here is an evident allusion to the Mississippi, which, the natives representing as the *Great Water,* was misconstrued by Nicolet and Vimont to mean a sea—or, as they expressed it, "the other sea," in contradistinction to the Atlantic.[26] And in 1641, "five years before Eliot of New England had addressed a single word to the Indians within six miles of Boston harbor, the French missionaries planted the cross at Sault Ste. Marie, whence they looked down on the Sioux country and the valley of the Mississippi. The vast unknown West now opened its prairies before them."[27]

Father Claude Allouez, who in 1665 penetrated the wilds on the southern borders of Lake Superior, heard the Indian relations of the Great River called the "Messipi"; and joined three years afterwards by Fathers James Marquette and J. Claude Dablon, these missionaries extended their labors from Lake Superior to Green Bay—"mingling happiness," says Bancroft, "with suffering, and winning enduring glory by their fearless perseverance." Marquette had resolved on attempting the discovery of the Mississippi in the autumn of 1669 but delayed its execution for more than three years, when, joined by the Sieur Joliet, of Quebec, they descended the Wisconsin River with five French and two Indian assistants in two birch-bark canoes and entered the Mississippi, June 17th, 1673, "with a joy," declares Marquette, "that I cannot express." Floating down the great Father of Waters, sometimes landing and enjoying the hospitality of the Indians on its banks, they at length reached the Arkansas, where the Indians at first fiercely attacked the white intruders, but Marquette resolutely presenting the peace-pipe, the Savages desisted because, says the pious narrator, "God touched their hearts." Marquette and Joliet now returning up the Mississippi and ascending the Illinois in due time arrived at Green Bay without loss or injury.[28]

13. French market hunter of the Caribbean, c. 1700, armed with Dutch buccaneer musket.

From the *Jesuit Relations of 1661–'62,* we learn that the missionaries of western New York had heard of the "beautiful river," the Ohio.[29] Hennepin was aware of the existence of "a great river, called Hoio, which passes through the country of the Iroquois," in 1673 or 1674, and we are told that the route from the Lakes by that great river was explored in 1676.[30] Daniel Coxe, in his memorial to King William in 1699, states that he possessed about the year 1676 a journal in English which "seemed to have been written many years before," illustrated by a very large map, describing the country from the mouth of the Mississippi to the Yellow or Muddy River, better known as the Missouri, and containing "the names of divers Nations, and short Hints of the chief Products of each Country; and by Modern Journals of English or French, the most material Parts Thereof are confirmed, the Nations in divers Places there nam'd, continuing still in the same Stations, or very little remote." It is also stated by

Coxe, whose authority appears worthy of credit, that in 1678 a considerable number of persons went from New England for purposes of discovery and proceeded one hundred and fifty leagues beyond the Mississippi as far as New Mexico and then returned home and rendered an account of their journey to the government at Boston, and that four Indians accompanied these New England adventurers. La Salle received most of his information concerning the Mississippi country, which he subsequently more fully explored employing these very Indians for guides and interpreters.[31]

La Salle at length entered upon his laborious western exploration. The year 1679 was consumed in passing Lake Erie and around the Upper Lakes and in bartering with the Indians for furs and peltries. Reaching Lake Peoria on the Illinois River in January 1680, he there erected Fort Crevecoeur. Weakened by the loss of his ship Griffin on the Lakes and the desertion of his men, La Salle returned to Canada for a reinforcement, leaving Chevalier De Tonty in command of the fort and ordering Michael D'Acau and Picard Du Gay, accompanied by Father Louis Hennepin, to explore the Mississippi towards its source.[32] At the close of February 1680 Hennepin's party took their departure in a canoe, descending the Illinois and ascending the Mississippi as high as the Wisconsin, where in April he and his comrades were made prisoners by a band of Sioux Indians and taken first to the Falls of St. Anthony and then up the River St. Francis one hundred and eighty miles to the Sioux villages. After about three months' residence and rambling in this region pretty much at their liberty, they were agreeably surprised by meeting a band of French traders who had penetrated to that remote country by way of Lake Superior, and the poor wandering captives accompanied them on their return to Canada.

Tonty and his companions, in consequence of their sufferings and exposures, abandoned Fort Crevecoeur in September 1680, and retired with much difficulty to the Lakes; and when La Salle, at the close of that year or early in 1681, reached the deserted post on the Illinois, his hopes for a while sank within him, and his bright dreams of great discoveries vanished for a season. Returning to the Miami or St. Joseph's River, he spent the winter among the Indian tribes near the head of Lake Michigan and in June arrived at Mackinac, where great mutual joy was experienced in meeting Tonty and his companions, and all soon set sail for Fort Frontenac on Lake Ontario. La Salle and his party again started upon his western exploration in August 1681, greatly recruited and reinforced, now numbering fifty-four persons and among them were eighteen Savages, Abenakis,[h] and Loups[i] from New England—some of whom may well have been those mentioned by Coxe as having accompanied the New England explorers on their journey to the Mississippi and New Mexico three years before.

In February 1682 they passed out of the Illinois and entered upon the Mississippi; and on the 9th of April ensuing, La Salle erected a column and a cross near the mouth of that stream and formally took possession of the whole country of Louisiana for the French King, and during that year the whole party ascended the Mississippi. La Salle went to France, sought aid from the government, and ob-

14. *"Boeuf de la Nouvelle France," c. 1683. Copied from a drawing by Father Louis Hennepin, who introduced the term* buffalo *to European readers.*

tained after much trouble four vessels and altogether two hundred and eighty persons; and set sail in 1684 for the mouth of the Mississippi but unfortunately struck the coast too far to the westward and finally entered what is now Matagorda Bay, in Texas, and there erected a fort. After a great variety of zig-zag ramblings and untoward adventures in the Texas region in search of the Mississippi, encountering much ill-fortune and greatly reduced by desertion, sickness, and death, La Salle was at length murdered by one of his men March 19th, 1687, probably upon a branch of the Brazos. Of his unhappy followers, those who remained in the fort were mostly killed by the neighboring Indians, while others united their fortunes with savage tribes; a few were taken by the Spaniards, and yet another few, by dint of great perseverance, finally reached the Illinois. And thus perished the adventurous La Salle, like De Soto before him, in the midst of a country he so much contributed to pave the way for ultimate settlement and civilization.[33]

Upon Mitchell's map of 1755[j] is marked "the route of Coll. Welch to the Mississippi in 1698," from Charleston, South Carolina, crossing the Savannah where Augusta was subsequently located, thence through the Creek and Chickasaw nations by way of the Indian towns of Ogeeche, Oconee, Echetee, Chatahoochee, Oakfuskee, and Cousa; and the same authority states that the English made a settlement on the Mississippi during that year, secured a passage from thence to the coast of Carolina, and carried on a trade there for many years.[34] In this same year, 1698, Dr. Coxe despatched two ships to the Mississippi, well manned and provided, under the command of Capt. William Bond, formerly store-keeper of Fort George in New York, to take possession of the country as a portion of the Doctor's Province of Carolina and make a settlement there. One of the ships from some cause turned back, but the other passed up the Mississippi above one hundred miles, taking possession of the country on both sides of the river in King William's name, affixing the arms of Great Britain on boards and trees in several places and making several curious drafts of the coast, river, and bay. Having reached a point about six leagues below the present city of New Orleans, the wind here failing, and seeing a bend in the river, and withal the Indians exhibiting signs of hostility, they turned their course and descended the river, and hence the origin of *the English Turn.*[35]

Early the following year, D'Iberville entered the Mississippi and commenced a French settlement. While his brother Bienville was engaged in exploring the mouths of the Mississippi, on the 16th of the ensuing September he discovered an English corvette[k] of twelve guns ascending the stream, to the commander of which he gave information of the French settlement and occupancy of the country and received for reply that the English had discovered it fifty years before and had the best right to it. The English vessel faced about and departed. This was one of the three ships sent from London by King William to take possession of the Mississippi, two of which proceeded to the Gulf of Mexico, and one of them, as just related, entered the Mississippi, while the other sailed to the Province of Panuco, in New Spain, to concert measures for driving the French from the disputed river,[36] for the Spaniards looked upon the French attempt at settlement as an intrusion upon their territory of Mexico. So anxious was King William that the banks of the Mississippi should be settled by English subjects, he often declared that he would leap over twenty stumbling blocks rather than *not* effect it.[37] Yet the French were suffered to maintain the foothold already gained and extend their settlements and influence in the Mississippi Valley.

In 1710 Col. Alexander Spotswood, a man of great energy of character and unusual political foresight, who had distinguished himself at the battle of Blenheim under the great Marlborough, was appointed lieutenant governor of Virginia. Chalmers pays him the high compliment of having proved himself "the model of provincial governor, whose talents qualified him to rule a kingdom."[38] One of the first objects of his notice was to direct the attention of the British Ministry to the alarming progress of the French in the West, which he proposed to resist by extending their communication between Canada and the Mississippi. By the peace of Athrocyte in 1713, England obtained from France large concessions of territory in America. Louisiana still remained in the possession of France, but whether its extent embraced the whole basin of the Mississippi was a question upon which England had not expressed an opinion, much less yield a quiet acquiescence.

A practical route of the Appalachian Mountains was an important preliminary step, an object which had formerly so much engaged the consideration of Sir William Berkley, but which had latterly been entirely neglected. Those mountains had long been regarded by the great body of the Virginians as an insurmountable barrier to their progress westward, beyond whose rugged and frowning heights in their imagination dwelt only wild beasts and the yet more wild and implacable savages. The French alone were acquainted with the geography and resources of the immense Western Valley, and that knowledge it best accorded with French policy to conceal from the English, who possessed no further acquaintance with that region that what they had derived from the imperfect reports of a few straggling travellers and erratic Indians.

At length, in 1714 Governor Spotswood, with the approbation of the Assembly of his province, led in person an expedition for the discovery of a mountain-passage. Attended by a considerable number of pioneers and gentlemen, and among them a volunteer troop of horses, he marched with his young cavaliers through the shadowy defiles to the head springs of the York and Rappahannock rivers and ascended the summits of the Blue Ridge. Spotswood inscribed his Majesty's name on a rock upon the highest of the mountain peaks, naming it *Mount George,* while the gentlemen present in compliment to their governor bestowed upon the next loftiest peak the name of *Mount Alexander.* The contemporary Virginia historian Jones informs us that the adventurous explorers "passed these mountains." The noble valley of Virginia burst upon their view in all its primeval beauty and grandeur and must have extorted their highest admiration.

In their toilsome mountain march over rocks and stones they had been compelled to take with them a supply of horse-shoes, which were seldom needed in the mellow soil of Lower Virginia. Returning to the settlements with something like the glory and éclat of a great conqueror, Spotswood presented each of his companions with a small golden horse-shoe set with garnets resembling heads of nails, with the inscription on one side *"Sic juvat transcendere montes"* and on the other *"The Tramontane Order."* Thus was instituted the *Tramontane Order,* or *Knights of the Golden Horse-Shoe,* with the motto "Thus he swears to cross the mountains," the object of which was "to encourage gentlemen to venture backward and make discoveries and settlements," and none could wear this golden badge who could not prove he had drank his Majesty's health on Mount George.[39]

This adventure, inconsiderable as it was, suggested to the practical mind of Spotswood an increased scope for Anglo-American colonization. As early as 1716 he proposed the incorporation of a Virginia Indian Company to purchase of the Indians lands on the Ohio, settle them, and from the emoluments of a monopoly of the Indian trade to the northward, southward, and westward of that river, support a chain of forts from Virginia across the mountains to the Ohio settlements; but the law establishing the company was repealed by the Virginia legislature in consequence of the determined opposition of the people as well as opposition in England, and thus the scheme was frustrated, "partly," says Smollet, by the indolence and timidity of the British Ministry, "who were afraid of giving umbrage to the French." In his memorial to the British government, Spotswood foretold with prophetic discernment the latent purpose of aggrandizement which prompted France in extending her settlements in the great Western Valley. Nor is it strange, for that very year two French ships arrived in France from the Mississippi richly laden with the first fruits of the Louisiana colony. The advice of the great and sagacious Spotswood suffered to lead to his supersedure as governor in 1723.[40]

In February 1719 Gov. William Keith of Pennsylvania drew up a report, at the insistence of the British government, relative to the progress and condition of the French in the great valley of West, in which it pretty clearly appears that English traders had already either actually penetrated into the Wabash and Illinois country, or so nearly approached that then remote region as to learn quite minute particulars concerning it. To counteract the designs of the French, who were continually debauching the Indians to their interest, and to protect and encourage English traders in their backwoods commerce with the natives, the establishment of four forts was suggested by Governor Keith—one on Lake Erie near the Miami Indians; another on Lake Ontario near the Iroquois; the third at the fountain head of the Potomac; and the fourth towards the head of the Susquehanna. But these suggestions, neither so comprehensive nor sagacious as Spotswood's and yet proposing something far better than the indolent and timid policy which then characterized the British government, were suffered to pass unheeded.[41]

From 1712 Crozart, a wealthy citizen of France to whom had been granted the monopoly of Louisiana and the absolute ownership of whatever mines he might cause to be opened, commenced his attempts to discover mines and secure a lucrative trade with the Spaniards of New Mexico. He failed in both these objects and in 1717 resigned his privileges to the king again. The celebrated Mississippi Company under John Law was immediately established and, in the following year, a most magnificent scheme adopted. Nothing seemed too extravagant under the magic wand of Law. France had in view the possession of the whole of North America, and Louisiana was considered as the basis of the whole plan. Colonization upon an extensive scale was recommended, transporting five or six hundred families, and none but good peasants at a time provided by government with cattle, provisions, and necessary utensils for a year, which were to be returned or paid for when the colonists should be in a situation to do so.

The Wabash, Illinois, Missouri, Yazoo, and Natchitoches counties were comprehended in the plan and the working of the Missouri Mines proposed. "A large commerce," concludes the memorial of the French government on the subject, "can be carried on between Mexico and Missouri. Missouri has another branch nearly as important; its source is said to be from the same mountain; it is believed that this branch empties itself in the South Sea. The Canadians invited in those parts would soon create establishments for a commerce with Japan and China.

Such would be the importance of such a trade that the truth of these reports is worthy the attention of government."[42] But Law's bank, which was the grand lever of all his stupendous operations, having obtained a circulation of over two hundred millions of dollars and greatly inflated the prices of every thing, suddenly began to totter early in 1720, and this mammoth fabric of false credit soon tumbled into ruins, and with it expired all the vast schemes of Louisiana settlement and enterprise.

About 1724 a band of Pennsylvania Delawares removed to the Upper Ohio for the conveniency of game and in 1728 were followed by that portion of the Shawanoes[1] who had previously resided on the Potomac. Pennsylvania traders soon found their way there, and during their journeying to and from Philadelphia, while carrying on their wilderness traffic, disseminated information concerning the Upper Ohio Valley.[43] And Joshua Gee of London, the friend of Penn and one of the mortgagees of his province, published an ingenious Treatise on Trade in 1729, in which he earnestly urged the planting of British colonies westward as far as the Mississippi and on the rivers falling into it; and ten years later, the same celebrated writer, in connection with Sir William Keith and others comprising a club of American Merchants, gave to the public a tract on Taxing the British Colonies, in which they assert that the British Indian traders were continually obstructed in their attempts to travel and trade westward by the multitude of small forts the French have erected at proper distances between Quebec and the mouth of the Mississippi.[44]

Inability on the part of the French to furnish an adequate supply of Indian goods led some of the western Indians to repair to New York and Albany to trade. This suggested a revival of Spotswood's scheme. Accordingly, in 1730 endeavors were made to obtain a grant from the English crown of those excellent lands on the Ohio and its waters, and those engaged in it proposed to transfer large numbers of Palatines to effect the settlement. But this attempt, like its predecessor, was also frustrated by the same unwise counsels prevailing.[45] About this period, the valley of Virginia began to be settled, which proved another step in the advance of the Anglo-American race towards the great Western Valley. But while the English manifested so much dilatoriness in going forward "to possess the land," that enterprising French officer Bienville in the spring of 1738 explored the Wabash country and the interior region of Ohio and Illinois, and reported the result to his government, together with an account of the Indians inhabiting there.[46]

It is related that some of the Canadians on their way to the Illinois country in 1735, destined to go thence early the ensuing year against the Chickasaws, found "near the *Fine River* or Ohio, the skeletons of seven elephants."[47] In 1739 Longueil, a French officer descending the Ohio from Canada, discovered the mastodontoid remains at the Big Bone Lick in Kentucky, then called the bones of the "unknown animal"; and in 1740, large quantities of them were taken from the Lick to France, where they received the name of "Animal of the Ohio."[48] Thus early was Kentucky visited by white men.

When Spotswood was appointed to the command of the Colonial troops of the Carthagena expedition in 1739, he was gratified with an assurance that his favorite project should be carried into immediate execution; but his death the following year probably retarded the design. It will be pretty safe to conclude that the sending of John Howard and John Peter Salling with a party in 1742 by the government of Virginia to view the western parts of that province was intended as a preliminary step to the effectual accomplishment of that object. Reaching the Ohio, they killed a very large buffalo and constructed a canoe by stretching the hide over a wooden frame-work, and in it they descended that river. They were, however, made prisoners by the French who came from a settlement they had on an island in the Mississippi a little above the Ohio, where they made salt, lead, and etc.[49] The captives were taken to New Orleans as suspicious characters in a fleet of boats and canoes, guarded by an armed schooner. Howard and Salling were at length permitted to return to Virginia, and the government there made out a report to the Board of Trade in which it is stated that the explorers "saw more good land on the Mississippi, and its many large branches, than they judged was in all the English colonies, as far as they are inhabited."[50]

Col. James Patton claimed to have been the first English subject who discovered, at vast expense, Wood's River, as New or Kenhawa River was then called, and the two rivers to the westward of it, probably the Holston and the Clinch prior to 1743, and was the first to apply in that year for a grant of land on those waters.[51] He petitioned the government of Virginia for two hundred thousand acres, offering to pay his "Majesty's rights and all fees accruing" and settle a family on the grant for every thousand acres; but his petition was not granted, as it was feared the Home Government would not approve it lest it should occasion some dispute with France. But Patton's petition was inserted on the Council records with the promise that he should be informed whenever his wishes could be acceded to; and in April 1745 he had notice to attend the Council, who granted to him, Col. James Wood, Col. John Buchanan, Capt. George Robinson, William Parks, John Taylor, and their associates one hundred thousand acres on Wood's River and its waters and "also on two rivers to the westward." On the 10th of October, 1746, this company gave people notice that they would sell to actual settlers at the rate of four pounds, five shillings, current money, for every one hundred acres and appointed Peter Renfroe entry-taker. As soon as the company should comply with the conditions in selling their purchase, they were promised an additional grant of the same amount. At the same time and apparently in the same region, a grant of one hundred thousand acres was made to John Robinson, the president of the Council, and others, and one of fifty thousand to another company.[52]

In April 1748 Dr. Thomas Walker, accompanied by Cols. James Patton, James Wood, John Buchanan, and Capt. Charles Campbell, together with a number of hunters and woodsmen, made an exploring tour down the Holston River. Walker and Campbell were perhaps associated in the land grant just mentioned, or the party may have been examining the country with a view to a new grant, which Dr. Walker and others effected the following year. So far as authentic records show, this was Dr. Walker's first trip to the western waters.[53]

During this year also, Conrad Weiser, long the faithful Indian interpreter in the employ of Pennsylvania, was sent across the Alleghenies to Logstown on the Ohio with presents for the Indians, and perhaps, to sound them with reference to the establishment of a large Anglo-American company, for the erection of trading-houses, and carrying on an extensive Indian trade in that region. Thomas Lee, president of the Virginia Council, and one of the commissioners of that province at the Lancaster treaty four years previously, together with Robert Dinwiddie, then surveyor general for the southern colonies, and eleven prominent citizens of Virginia and Maryland, and John Hanbury, an opulent London merchant, petitioned the king for a grant of land beyond the mountains on which to carry forward the operations of a grand Indian trading association to be styled *the Ohio Company.* The plan was approved, and in March 1749 the king's instructions were sent to the governor of Virginia to grant within that colony, between the Monongahela and the Kenhawa, or on the northern margin of the Ohio, two fifths of which were to be located without delay, at least one hundred families placed on the grant within seven years, and a fort erected and garrisoned sufficient to protect the settlement.[54]

By an order of the Virginia Council of the 12th of June, 1749, leave was granted to a numerous company of adventurers, among whom were Dr. Thomas Walker, Edmund Pendleton, and Nicholas Lewis, denominated *the Loyal Company,* to take up and survey eight hundred thousand acres of land in one or more surveys on the western waters; and four years were allowed the company to survey and purchase rights for the same.[55] While the English were fulfilling Berkley's memorable prophesy—"Westward the course of empire takes its way"— the restless French were far from being idle. Celeron was employed at the head of a party in the summer of 1749, depositing lead plates at the confluence of the several more important rivers with the Ohio, claiming all the Ohio Valley as belonging to the king of France; and at the close of the year a central French power was proposed to be established on the Wabash.[56]

Among the early authentic explorations of Kentucky, that of the party under Dr. Thomas Walker in 1750 holds a conspicuous place in the border history, both on account of the high character of the leader and the early period at which that bold adventure was made.[57] Dr. Walker had doubtless learned that the Ohio could probably be reached by a northerly route from the lower part of the Holston River, and he wished to test its practicability, as well as explore the wild, unknown region between those rivers, with a view, unquestionably, to choice locations for the large grant of the Loyal Company.[58] Having had the pleasure of examining Dr. Walker's original Journal of that adventurous journey, only a few pages of which are missing, we carefully transcribed it and think it of sufficient interest to warrant its insertion entire, with such explanatory notes as may seem necessary.[59]

"Thomas Walker's Journal, 1750"[60]

Having, on the 12th of December last, been employed for a certain consideration to go to the Westward in order to discover a proper place for a Settlement, I left my house on the Sixth day of March, at 10 o'clock, 1749–50, in Company with Ambrose Powell, William Tomlinson, Colby Chew, Henry Lawless & John Hughs. Each man had a Horse and we had two to carry the Baggage. I lodged this night a Col. Joshua Fry's, in Albemarle, which County includes the Chief of the head Branches of James River on the East side of the Blue Ridge.

March 7th. Wee set off about 8, but the day proving wet, we only went to Thomas Joplin's on Rockfish. This is a pretty River, which might at a small expense be made fit for transporting Tobacco; but it has lately been stopped by a Mill Dam near the Mouth to the prejudice of the upper inhabitants who would at their own expense clear and make it navigable, were they permitted.

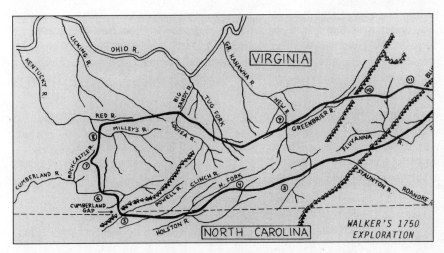

15. The travels of Thomas Walker. 1) Walker's home in Louisa County; 2) Walker's Joplin home on the Rockfish River; 3) Journey delayed by lost horses; 4) Samuel Stalnaker's house; 5) Cumberland Gap; 6) Walker's settlement on the Cumberland River; 7) Western point of exploration; 8) Crossing the Kentucky River; 9) Junction of the New and Greenbrier Rivers; 10) Settlement in Warm Springs Valley; 11) Augusta Court House. MAP BY SAMUEL SISTLER AND ALEXANDER CANADAY MCLEOD, FILSON CLUB HISTORICAL SOCIETY.

March 8th. We left Joplin's early. It began to rain about Noon. I left my People at Thomas Jones's and went to the Reverend Mr. Robert Rose's on Tye River. This is about the Size of Rockfish, as yet open, but how long the Avarice of Millers will permit it to be so, I know not. At present, the Inhabitants enjoy plenty of fine fish, as Shad in their season, Carp, Rocks, Fat-Backs which I suppose to be Tench, Perch, Mullets, etc.

9th. As the weather continues unlikely, I moved only to Baylor Walker's Quarters.

March 10th. The weather is still cloudy, and leaving my People at the Quarter, I rode to Mr. John Harvie's where I dined and returne'd to the Quarter in ye Evening.

11th. The Sabbath.

March 12th. We crossed the Fluvanna & lodged at Thomas Hunt's.

13th. We went early to William Calloway's and supplied ourselves with Rum, Thread, and other necessaries & from thence took the main Waggon Road leading to Wood's or the New River. It is not well clear'd or beaten yet, but will be a very good one with proper management. This night we lodged in Adam Beard's low grounds. Beard is an ignorant, impudent, brutish fellow, and would have taken us up, had it not been for a reason, easily to be suggested.

14th. We went from Beard's to Nicholas Welches, where we bought some corn for our horses, and had some Victuals dress'd for Breakfast, afterwards we crossed the Blue Ridge. The Ascent and Descent is so easie that a Stranger would not know when he crossed the Ridge. It began to rain about Noon and continued till night. We lodged at William Armstrong's. Corn is very scarce in these parts.

March 15th. We went to the great Lick on A Branch of the Staunton & bought Corn of Michael Campbell for our Horses. This Lick has been one of the best places for Game in these parts and would have been of much greater advantage to the Inhabitants than it has been if the Hunters had not killed the Buffaloes for diversion, and the Elks and Deer for their skins. This afternoon we got to the Staunton where the Houses of the Inhabitants had been carryed off with their grain and Fences by the Fresh last Summer, and lodged at James Robinson's, the only place I could hear of where they had Corn to spare, notwithstanding the land is such that an industrious man might make 100 barrels a share in a Seasonable year.

16th March. We kept up the Staunton to William Englishes. He lives on a small Branch, and was not much hurt by the Fresh. He has a mill, which is the furthest back except one lately built by the Sect of People, who call themselves of the Brotherhood of Euphrates, (17th) and are commonly called the Duncards, who are the upper inhabitants of the New River, which is about 400 yards wide at this place.[61] They live on the west side, and we were obliged to swim our Horses over. The Duncards are an odd set of people, who make it a matter of Religion not to Shave their beards, ly on Beds, or eat Flesh, though at first, in the last, they transgress, being constrained to it, as they say, by the want of a sufficiency of Grain and Roots, they having not long been seated here. I doubt the plenty and deliciousness of the Venison & Turkeys has contributed not a little to this. The unmarried have no private Property, but live on a common Stock. They dont baptize either Young or Old, they keep their Sabbath on Saturday, & hold that all men shall be happy hereafter, but first must pass through punishment according to their Sins. They are very hospitable.

March 18th. The Sabbath.

19th. We could not find our Horses and spent the day in Looking for them. In the evening we found their track.

20th. We went very early to the track of our Horses & after following them six or seven miles, we found them all together. We returned to the Duncards about 10 o'clock, and having purchased half a Busshell of meal and as much small Homony we set off and Lodged on a small Run between Peak Creek and Reedy Creek.

March 21st. We got to Reedy's Creek and Camped near James McCall's. I went to his House and Lodged and bought what Bacon I wanted.

22nd. I returned to my People early. We got to a large Spring about five miles below Davises Bottom on Holstons River and Camped.

23rd. We kept down Holstons River about four miles and Camped; and then Mr. Powel and I went to look for Samuel Stalnaker, who I had been inform'd was just moved out to settle. We found his Camp, and returned to our own in the Evening.

24th. We went to Stalnaker's, helped him raise his house and Camped about a quarter of a mile below him. In April, 1748, I met the above mentioned Stalnaker between the Reedy Creek Settlement and Holstons River, on his way to the Cherokee Indians, and expected him to pilate me as far as he knew but his affairs would not permit him to go with me.[62]

March 25th. The Sabbath. Grass is plenty in the low grounds.

26th. We left the Inhabitans, and kept nigh West to a large Spring on a Branch of the North fork of Holston. Thunder, Lightning, and Rain before Day.

27th. It began to Snow in the morning and continued till Noon. The Land is very hilly from West to North. Some Snow lies on the tops of the mountains N. W. from us.

28th. We travelled to the lower end of Giant's Ditch on Reedy Creek.

29th. Our Dogs were very uneasie most of this Night.

30th. We kept down Reedy Creek, and discover'd the tracks of about 20 Indians, that had gone up the Creek between the time we Camped last Night, and set off this Morning. We suppose they made our Dogs so restless last Night. We Camped on Reedy Creek.

March 30th. We caught two young Buffaloes one of which we killed, and having cut and marked the other we turn'd him out.

31st. We kept down Reedy Creek to Holston where we measured an Elm 25 feet round 3 feet from the Ground. we saw young Sheldrakes, we went down the River to the north Fork and up the north Fork about a quarter of a mile to a Ford, then crossed it. In the Fork between Holstons and the North River, are five Indian Houses built with loggs and covered with Bark, and there were abundance of Bones, some whole Pots and Pans, some broken, and many pieces of mats and Cloth. On the West Side of the North River, is four Indian Houses such as before mentioned. we went four miles Below the North River and Camped on the Bank of Holstons, opposite to a large Indian Fort.

April ye 1st. The Sabbath. we saw Perch, Mullets, and Carp in plenty, and caught one of the large Sort of Cat Fish. I marked my Name, the day of the Month, and date of the year on Several Beech Trees.

2nd. we left Holston & travelled through small Hills till about Noon, when one of our Horses being choaked by eating Reeds too gredily, we stopped having travelled 7 miles.

April 3rd. Our horse being recover'd, we travelled to the Rocky Ridge. I went up to the top, to look for a Pass, but found it so Rocky that I concluded not to Attempt it there. This Ridge may be known by Sight, at a distance. To the Eastward are many small Mountains, and a Buffaloe Road between them and the Ridge. The growth is Pine on the Top and the Rocks look white at a distance.[63] we went Seven miles this day.

4th. We kept under the Rocky Ridge crossing several small Branches to the head of Holly Creek. We saw many small Licks and plenty of Deer.

5th. we went down Holly Creek. There is much Holly in the Low Grounds & some Laurel and Ivy. About 3 in the afternoon, the Ridge appeared less stony and we passed it, and Camped on a small Branch about a mile from the top. my Riding Horse choaked himself this Evening and I drenched him with water to wash down the Reeds, and it answered the End.

6th. It proving wet we did not move.

7th. We rode 8 miles over broken Land. It snowed most of the day. In the Evening our dogs caught a large He bear, which before we could come up to shoot him had wounded a dog of mine, so that he could not Travel, and we carried him on Horseback, till he recovered.

8th. The Sabbath. Still Snow.

9th. We travelled to a river, which I suppose to be that which the hunters Call Clinches River from one Clinch a Hunter, who first found it.[64] we marked several

Beeches on the East side. we could not find a ford Shallow eneugh to carry our Baggage over on our horses. Ambrose Powell Forded over on one horse, and we drove the others after him. We then made a Raft and carried over one Load of Baggage, but when the Raft was brought back, it was so heavy that it would not carry anything more dry.

April 10th. We waded and carryed the remainder of our Baggage on our shoulders at two turns of the River, which is about one hundred and thirty yards wide, we went on about five miles and Camped on a small Branch.[65]

April 11th. Having travelled 5 miles to and over an High Mountain, we came to Turkey Creek, which we kept down 4 miles. It lies between two Ridges of Mountains, that to the Eastward being the highest.

12th. We kept down the Creek 2 miles further, where it meets with a large Branch coming from the South West, and thence runs through the East Ridge making a very good Pass; and a large Buffaloe Road goes from that Fork to the Creek over the West Ridge, which we took and found the Ascent and Descent tollerably easie. From this Mountain we rode four miles to Beargrass River. Small Cedar Trees are very plenty on the flat ground nigh the River, and some Bayberry trees on the East side of the River. on the Banks is some Beargrass. We kept up the River two miles. I found some Small pieces of Coal and a great plenty of very good yellow Flint. The water is the most transparent I ever saw. It is about 70 yds. wide.

April 13th. We went four miles to large Creek, which we called Cedar Creek, being a Branch of Beargrass, and from thence Six miles to Cave Gap, the land being Levil. On the North side of the Gap is a large Spring, which falls very fast, and just above the Spring is a small Entrance to a large Cave, which the Spring runs through, and there is a constant Stream of Cool air issuing out. The Spring is sufficient to turn a mill. Just at the foot of the Hill is a Laurel Thicket, and the Spring Water runs through it. On the South side is a plain Indian Road. on the top of the Ridge are Laurel Trees marked with crosses, others Blazed and several Figures on them. As I went down on the Other Side, I soon came to some Laurel in the head of a Branch. A Beech stands on the left hand, on which I cut my name. This Gap may be seen at a considerable distance, and there is no other, that I know of, except one about two miles to the North of it, which does not appear to be So low as the other. The Mountain on the North Side of the Gap is very Steep and Rocky, but on the South side it is not So. We called it Steep Ridge. At the foot of the hill on the North West Side we came to a Branch, that made a great deal of flat Land. We kept down it 2 miles, Several other Branches Coming in to make it a large Creek, and we called it Flat Creek. We camped on the Bank where we found very good Coal. I did not Se any Lime Stone beyond this Ridge. We rode 13 miles this day.

April 14th. We kept down the Creek 5 miles Chiefly along the Indian Road.

15th. Easter Sunday. Being in bad grounds for our Horses we moved 7 miles along the Indian Road, to Clover Creek. Clover and Hop Vines are plenty here.

April 16th. Rai(n). I made a Pair of Indian Shoes, those I brought out being bad.

17th. Still Rain. I went down the Creek a hunting and found that it went into a River about a miles below our Camp. This, which is Flat Creek and Some others join'd, I called Cumberland River.

18th. Still Cloudy. We kept down the Creek to the River along the Indian Road to where it crosses. Indians have lived about this Ford Some years ago. We kept on down the South Side. After riding 5 miles from our Camp, we left the River, it being very crooked. In Rideing 3 miles we came on it again. It is about 60 or 70 yds. wide. We rode 8 (?) miles this day.

19th. We left the River but in four miles we came on it again at the Mouth of Licking Creek, which we went up and down another. In the Fork of Licking Creek is a Lick much used by Buffaloes and many large Roads lead to it. This afternoon Ambrose Powell was bit by a Bear in his Knee. We rode 7 miles this day.

20th. we kept down the Creek 2 miles to the River again. It appears not any wider here than at the mouth of Clover Creek, but much deeper. I thought it proper to Cross the River and began a bark Conoe.

April 21st. We finished the Conoe and tryed her. About noon it began to thunder, lighten, hail and rain prodigiously and continued about 2 hours.

22d. The Sabbath. One of the horses was found unable to walk this morning. I then Propos'd that with 2 of the Company I would proceed, and the other three should continue here till our return, which was agreed to, and Lots were drawn to determine who should go, they all being desirous of it. Ambrose Powell, and Colby Chew were the fortunate Persons.

23rd. Having carried our Baggage over in the Bark Conoe, and Swam our horses, we all crossed the River. Then Ambrose Powell, Colby Chew, and I departed, Leaving the others to provide and salt some Bear, build an house, and plant some Peach Stones and Corn. We travelled about 12 miles and encamped on Crooked Creek. The mountains are very small hereabouts and here is a great deal of flat Land. We got through the Coal today.

April 24th. We kept on Westerly 18 miles, got Clear of the mountains and found the Land poor and the woods very Thick beyond them, and Laurel & Ivy in and near the Branches. Our Horses suffered very much here for want of food. This day we Came on the fresh Track of 7 or 8 Indians, but could not overtake them.

April 25th. We kept on West 5 miles, the Land continuing much Same, the Laurel rather growing worse, and the food scarcer. I got up a tree on a Ridge and saw the Growth of the Land much the same as Far as my Sight could reach. I then concluded to return to the rest of my Company. I kept on my track 1 mile then turn'd Southerly & went to Cumberland River at the mouth of a water Course, that I named Rocky Creek.

26th. The River is 150 yards wide and appears to be navigable from this place almost to the mouth of Clover Creek. Rocky Creek runs within 40 yards of the River Bank then turns off, and runs up the River, Surrounding about 25 acres of Land before it falls into the River. The Banks of the River and Creek are a sufficient Fence almost all the way. On the Lower Side of the mouth of the Creek is an Ash mark'd T.W., a Red Oak A.P., a white Hiccory C.C. besides several Trees blazed Several ways with 3 Chops over each blaze.[66] we went up the North Side of the River 8 miles, and Camped on a Small Branch. A Bear Broke one of my Dogs forelegs.

April 27th. We Crossed Indian Creek[67] and Went down Meadow Creek to the River. There Comes in another [stream] from the Southward as big as this we are on.[68] Below the mouth of this Creek, and above the mouth are the remains of Several Indian Cabbins and amongst them a round Hill made by Art about 20 feet high and 60 over the Top.[69] we went up the River, and Camped on the Bank.

28th. We kept up the River to our Company whom we found all well, but the lame Horse was as bad as we left him, and another had been bit in the Nose by a Snake. I rub'd the wounds with Bear's oil, and gave him a drench of the same and another of the decoction of Rattle Snake root some time after. The People I left had built an House 12 by 8, clear'd and broke up some ground, & planted Corn, and Peach Stones.[70] They also had killed several Bears and cured the meat. This day Colby Chew and his Horse fell down the Bank. I Bled and gave him Volatile drops, & he soon recovered.

April 29th. The Sabbath. The bitten Horse is better. 3 Quarters of A mile below the House is a Pond in the low Ground of the River, a Quarter of a mile in Length and 200 yds. wide much frequented by Fowl.

30th. I blazed a way from our House to the River. On the other side of the River is a large Elm cut down and barked about 20 feet and another standing just by it with the Bark cut around at the root and about 15 feet above. About 200 yards below this is a white Hiccory Barked about 15 feet. The depth of water here, when the lowest that I have seen it, is about 7 or 8 feet, the Bottom of the River Sandy, ye Banks very high, & the Current very Slow.[71] The bitten Horse being much mended, we set off and left the lame one. He is white, branded on the near Buttock with a swivil Stirrup Iron, and is old. We left the River and having Crossed Several Hills and Branches, Camped in a Valley North from the House.

May the 1st. Another Horse being bit, I applyed Bears Oil as before mention'd. We got to Powell's River in the afternoon and went down it along an Indian Road, much frequented, to the mouth of a Creek on the West side of the River, where we camped.[72] The Indian Road goes up the Creek, and I think it is that Which goes through Cave Gap.[73]

2d. We kept down the River. At the mouth of a Creek that comes in on the East side is a Lick, and I believe there was a hundred Buffaloes at it. About 2 o'Clock we had a Shower of rain. we Camped on the River, which is very crooked.

May 3rd. We crossed a narrow Neck of Land, came on the River again and kept Down it to an Indian Camp, that had been built this Spring, and in it we took up our Quarters. It began to rain about Noon and continued until Night.

4th. We crossed a narrow Neck of Land and came on the River again, which we kept down till it turn'd to the Westward, we then left it, and went up a Creek, which we Called Colby's Creek. The River is about 50 yards over where we left it.

5th. We got to Tomlinson's River, which is about the size of Powell's River, and I cut my name on a Beech, that Stands on the North Side of the River.[74] Here is plenty of Coal in the South Bank opposite to our Camp.

6th. The Sabbath. I saw Goslings, which shows that wild Geese stay here all the year. Ambrose Powell had the misfortune to sprain his well knee.

7th. We went down Tomlinson's River the Land being very broken and our way embarrassed by trees, that had been blown down about 2 years ago.

May 8th. We went up a Creek on the North Side of the River.

9th. We got to Lawlesses River which is much like the others.[75] The Mountains here are very Steep and on Some of them there is Laurel and Ivy. The tops of the Mountains are very Rocky and some part of the Rocks seem to be composed of Shells, Nuts and many other Substances petrified and cemented together with a kind of Flint. We left the River and after travelling some Miles we got among the Trees that had been Blown down about 2 years, and were obliged to go down a Creek to the River again, the Small Branches and Mountains being impassable.

10th. We Staid on the River, and dressed an Elk skin to make Indian Shoes— most of ours being quite worn out.

11th. We left the River, found the Mountains very bad, and got to a Rock by the side of a Creek Sufficient to shelter 200 men from Rain. Finding it so convenient, we concluded to stay and put our Elk skin in order for shoes and make them.

May 12th. Under the Rock is a Soft Kind of Stone almost like Allum in taste; below it A Layer of Coal about 12 Inches thick and white Clay under that. I called the Run Allum Creek. I have observed several mornings past, that the Trees begin to drop just before day & continue dripping till almost Sun rise, as if it rain'd slowly. we had some rain this day.

13th. The Sabbath.

14th. When our Elk's Skin was prepared we had lost every Awl that we brought out, and I made one with the Shank of an old Fishing hook, the other People made two of Horse Shoe Nailes, and with these we made our Shoes or Moccosons. We wrote several of our Names with Coal under the Rock, & I wrote our names, the time of our comeing and leaving this place on paper and stuck it to the Rock with Morter, and then set off. We Crossed Hughes's River and Lay on a large Branch of it. There is no dew this morning but a shower of Rain about 6 o'Clock. The River is about 50 yards wide.[76]

May 15th. Laurel and Ivy encrease upon us as we go up the Branch. About noon it began to rain & we took up our Quarters in a Valley between very Steep Hills.

16th. We crossed Several Ridges and Branches. About two in the afternoon, I was taken with a Violent Pain in my Hip.

17th. Laurel and Ivy are very plenty and the Hill still very steep. The Woods have been burnt some years past, and are now very thick, the Timber being almost all kill'd. We Camped on a Branch of Naked Creek. The pain in my Hip is something asswaged.

18th. We went up Naked Creek to the head and had a plain Buffaloe Road most of the way. From thence we proceeded down Wolf Creek and on it we camped.

19th. We kept down ye Creek to Hunting Creek, which we crossed and left. It rained most of the afternoon.

May 20th. The Sabbath. It began to Rain about Noon and continued till next day.

21st. It left off raining about 8. we crossed several Ridges and small Branches & Camped on a Branch of Hunting Creek. in the Evening it rained very hard.

22d. We went down the Branch to Hunting Creek & kept it to Milley's River.[77]

23rd. We attempted to go down the River but could not. We then Crossed Hunting Creek and attempted to go up the River but could not. it being very deep we began a Bark Conoe. The River is about 90 or 100 yards wide. I Blazed several Trees in the Fork and marked T. W. on a Sycomore Tree 40 feet around. It had a large Hole on the N: W: side about 20 feet from the Ground and is divided into 3 Branches just by the hole, and it stands about 80 yards above the mouth of Hunting Creek.

May 24th. We finished the Conoe and crossed the River about noon, and I marked a Sycomore 30 feet round and several Beeches on the North side of the River opposite to the mouth of the Creek. Game is very scarce hereabouts.

25th. It began to rain before the day and continued till about noon. We travelled about 4 miles on a Ridge and Camped on a small Branch.

26th. We kept down the Branch almost to the River, and up a Creek, and then along a Ridge till our Dogs roused a large Buck Elk, which we followed down to a Creek. He killed Ambrose Powell's Dog in the Chase, and we named the Run Tumbler's Creek, the Dog being of that Name.

27th. The Sabbath.

28th. Cloudy. We could not get our Horses till almost Night, when we went down the Branch. We lay on to the main Creek, and turn'd up it.

May 29th. We proceeded up the Creek 7 miles, and then took a North Branch & went up it 5 miles and then encamped on it.

30th. We went to the head of the Branch we lay on 12 miles. A shower of Rain fell this day. The Woods are burnt fresh about here and are the only fresh burnt Woods we have seen these Six Weeks.

31st. We crossed 2 Mountains and camped just by a Wolf's Den. They were very impudent and after they had been twice shot at, they kept howling about the Camp. It rained till Noon this day.

June ye 1st. We found the Wolf's Den and caught 4 of the young ones. It rained this morning. we went up a Creek crossed a mountain and went through a Gap, and then, camped on the head of A Branch.

2d. We went down the Branch to a River 70 yards wide, which I called Fredericks River.[78] we kept up it a half mile to a Ford, where we crossed and proceeded up on the North Side 3 miles. It rained most of the afternoon. Elks are very Plenty on this River.

June 3rd. Whit-Sunday. It rained most of the day.

4th. I blazed several trees four ways on the outside of the low Grounds by a Buffaloe Road, and marked my Name on Several Beech Trees. Also I marked some by the River side just below a mossing place with an Island in it. We left the River about 10 o'Clock & got to Falling Creek, and went up it till 5 in the Afternoon, when a very black Cloud appearing, we turn'd out our Horses, got tent Poles up, and were just stretching a Tent, when it began to rain and hail, and was succeeded by a violent Wind which Blew down our Tent & a great many Trees about it, several large ones within 30 yds. of the Tent. we all left the place in confusion and ran different ways for shelter. After the Storm was over, we met at the Tent, and found all safe.

5th. There was a violent Shower of Rain before day. This morning we went up the Creek about 3 miles, and then were obliged to leave it, the Timber being so blown down that we could not get through. After we left the Creek, we kept on a Ridge 4 miles, then turned down to the head of a Branch, and it began to rain and continued raining very hard till Night.

June 6th. We went down the Branch till it became a large Creek. It runs very Swift, falling more than any other Branches we have been on of late. I called it Rapid Creek. After we had gone 8 miles we could not ford, and we Camped in the low Ground. There is great sign of Indians on this Creek.

7th. The Creek being fordable, we Crossed it & kept down 12 miles to a River about 100 yards over, which We called Louisa River.[79] The Creek is about 30 yards wide, & part of ye River breaks into ye Creek—making an Island on which we Camped.

8th. The River is so deep we Cannot ford it and as it is falling we conclude to stay & hunt. In the afternoon Mr. Powell and my Self was a hunting about a mile & a half from the Camp, and heard a gun just below us on the other side of the River, and as none of our People could cross, I was in hopes of getting some direction from the Person, but could not find him.

June 9th. We crossed the River & went down it to the mouth of a Creek & up the Creek to the head and over a Ridge into a steep Valley and Camped.[80]

10th. Trinity Sunday. Being in very bad ground for our Horses, we concluded to move. we were very much hindered by the Trees, that were blown down on Monday last. we Camped on a Small Branch.

11th. It rained violently the Latter part of the night & till 9 o'Clock. The Branch is impassable at present. We lost a Tomohawk and a Cann by the Flood.[81]

12th. The Water being so low we went down the Branch to a large Creek, & up the Creek.[82] Many of the trees in the Branches are Wash'd up by the Roots and others barked by the old trees, that went down ye Stream. The Roots in the Bottom of the Runs are Barked by the Stones.

June 13th. We are much hindered by the Gust & a shower of Rain about Noon. Game is very scarce here, and the mountains very bad, the tops of the Ridges being so covered with Ivy and the sides so steep and stony, that we were obliged to cut our way through with our Tomohawks.[83]

14th. The Woods are still bad and Game scarce. It rained today about Noon & we Camped on the top of A Ridge.

15th–16th. We got on a large Creek where Turkey are plenty and some Elks.[84] we went a hunting & killed 3 Turkeys. Hunted & killed 3 Bears & some Turkeys.

17th. The Sabbath. We killed a large Buck Elk.

18th. having prepared a good stock of Meat, we left the Creek crossing several Branches and Ridges. the Woods still continuing bad the weather hot & our Horses so far spent, that we are all obliged to walk.

June 19th. We got to Laurel Creek[85] early this morning, and met so impudent a Bull Buffaloe that we were obliged to shoot him, or he would have been amongst us. we then went up the Creek six miles, thence up a North Branch of it to the Head, and attempted to cross a mountain, but it proved so high and difficult, that we were obliged to Camp on the side of it. This Ridge is nigh the eastern edge of the Coal Land.

20th. We got to the top of the Mountain and Could discover a flat to the South & South East.[86] we went down from the Ridge to a Branch and down the Branch to Laurel Creek not far from where we left it yesterday & Camped. my riding Horse was bit by a Snake this day, and having no Bear's Oil I rub'd the place with a piece of fat meat, which had the desired effect.

21st. We found the Level Nigh the Creek so full of Laurel that we were obliged to go up a Small Branch, and from the head of that to the Creek again, and found it good travelling a Small distance from the Creek. we Camped on the Creek. Deer are very Scarce on the Coal Land, I having seen but 4, since the 30th of April.

June 22nd. We kept up to the head of the Creek, and Land being Leveller than we have lately seen, and here are some large Savanna's. Many of the Branches are full of Laurel and Ivy. Deer and Bears are plenty.

23rd. Land continues level with Laurel and Ivy & we got to a large Creek with very high & steep Banks full of Rocks, which I call'd Clifty Creek, the Rocks are 100 feet perpendicular in some Places.[87]

24th. The Sabbath.

25th. We Crossed Clifty Creek. Here is a little Coal and the Land still flat.

26th. We crossed a Creek we called Dismal Creek, the Banks being the worst and the Laurel the thickest I have seen.[88] The Land is Mountainous on the East Side of Dismal Creek, and the Laurels end in a few miles. We camped on a Small Branch.

June 27th. The Land is very high & we crossed several Ridges and camped on a small Branch. it rained about Noon and continued till the next day.

28th. It continued raining till Noon, and we set off as soon as it ceased and went down the Branch we lay on to the New River, just below the mouth of Green Bryer. Powell, Tomlinson and my self striped, and went into the New River to try if we could wade over at any place. After some time having found a place we return'd to the others and took such things as would take damage by Water on our shoulders, and waded over Leading our Horses. The bottom is very uneven, the Rocks very slippery and the Current very Strong most of the way. We camped in the Low Ground opposite to the mouth of Green Bryer.

29th. We kept up Green Bryer. It being a wet day we went only 2 miles, and Camped on the North Side.

June 30th. We went 7 miles up the River, which is very crooked.

July ye 1st. The Sabbath. Our Salt being almost spent, We travelled 10 miles sometimes on the River, and at other times some distance from it.

2nd. We kept up the River the chief part of this day and we travelled about 10 miles.

3rd. we went up the River 10 miles to day.

4th. We went up the River 10 miles through very bad Woods.

5th. The way growing worse, we travelled 9 mile only.

6th. We left the River. The low grounds on it are of very little Value, but on the Branches are very good, and there is a great deal of it, and the high land is very good in many places. We got on a large Creek called Anthony's Creek, which affords a great deal of Very good Land, and it is chiefly bought. we kept up the creek 4 miles and Camped. This Creek took its Name from an Indian, called John Anthony, that frequently hunts in these Woods. There are some inhabitants on the Branches of Green Bryer, but we missed their Plantations.

July 7th. We kept up the Creek, and about Noon 5 men overtook us and inform'd us we were only 8 miles from the inhabitants on a Branch of James River called Jackson's River. We exchanged Some Tallow for Meal & parted. We camped on a Creek nigh the top of the Alleghany Ridge, which we named Ragged Creek.

8th. Having Shaved, Shirted,[89] & made new Shoes we left our useless Raggs at ye Camp & got to Walker Johnston's about Noon. We moved over to Robert Armstrong's in the Afternoon & staid there all Night. The People here are very hospitable and would be better able to support Travellers was it not for the great number of Indian Warriers, that frequently take what they want from them, much to Their prejudice.

July 9th. We went to the hot Springs and found Six Invalides there. The Spring Water is very Clear & warmer than new Milk, and there is a spring of cold Water within 20 feet of the Warm one. I left one of my Company this day.

10th. Having a Path We rode 20 miles & lodged at Captain Jemyson's below the Panther Gap. Two of my Company went to a Smith to get their Horses Shod.

11th. Our way mending. We travelled 30 miles to Augusta Court House, where I found Mr. Andrew Johnston, the first of my acquaintance I had seen, since the 26 day of March.

12th. Mr. Johnston lent me a fresh Horse and sent my Horses to Mr. David Stewards who was so kind as to give them Pastureage. About 8 o'Clock I set off leaving all my Company. It began to rain about 2 in the Afternoon & I lodged at Captain David Lewis's about 34 miles from Augusta Court House.

13th. I got home about Noon.
We killed in the Journey 13 Buffaloes, 8 Elks, 53 Bears, 20 Deer, 4 Wild Geese, about 150 Turkeys, besides small Game. We might have killed three times as much meat, if we had wanted it.

Such are the plain, authentic details, now for the first time published, of Dr. Walker's primitive exploration of Kentucky. While it was peculiarly an adventure of toil and hardship, difficulty and danger, requiring no small amount of foresight, nerve, and perseverance in its accomplishment, still, but little additional knowledge of the great Ohio Valley was really gained. The rich and level region of Kentucky, unsurpassed in natural beauty, of which the Elkhorn country is the center, was not seen by Dr. Walker and his adventurous companions; yet unquestionably their rough and hardy tour, fruitless as it evidently proved to Dr. Walker at the time, had its influence in keeping alive the spirit of western exploration. It furnished, moreover, some rude data for geographers and map-makers. The map prefixed to Washington's Journal, published in 1754, and for which it is quite evident Dr. Walker contributed some of the information, gives the names and localities of Cumberland, Powell's, Hughes', Milley's, Frederick's, and Louisa rivers, and Hunting Creek, but the positions of all, except Louisa or Sandy, are so greatly displaced and erroneously delineated as to afford little or no clue towards their identification. But taking the Cumberland River at the crossing of the old Warrior's Path not far from Cumberland Gap as a starting point, and passing over the coal-basin of the Forks of Kentucky and thence to the Sandy, corroborated by the statements of Walker and Tomlinson, and from Sandy across the mountainous country to the mouth of the Greenbriar, we are not left in doubt as to the general route pursued.

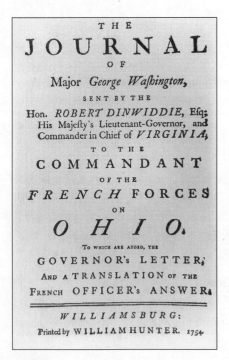

16. Title page of Washington's Journal.

Lewis Evans,[m] in his map and *Analysis,* which shortly after appeared, acknowledged his indebtedness to Dr. Walker for information about the rivers and water-courses of New Virginia. Dr. Mitchell's ancient map of the West in 1755 furnishes us the names and localities of the principal rivers that Dr. Walker discovered and named, placing Powell's River next above the Cumberland flowing into the Ohio; then Lawless and Hughes' rivers uniting and descending to the Ohio; then Milley's and Frederick's rivers uniting to form the Kentucky; and designating the Louisa as the main and western fork of Coal River. It is plain that at that early day, Dr. Walker had but a confused idea of the locality of the several streams he met with and named on his journey and probably was never after fully able to identify them all. Let the names and memories of Thomas Walker, Ambrose Powell, Colby Chew, Henry Lawless, and William Tomlinson ever be held in grateful remembrance for their early daring and hardihood in exploring one of the wildest and most forbidding portions of the Great West.[90]

Christopher Gist, a native of Maryland and a man of unusual border enterprise, was at this time settled near the head of the Yadkin. His services were sought by the grand Ohio Land Company[n] to explore the western country and ascertain the locality of the best tracts of land. He was instructed, September 11th, 1750, to proceed as far as the Falls of Ohio and keep a journal, noting the qualities of the soil, passes in the mountains, courses and sizes of the rivers, number of the cataracts, strength and commerce of the Indians, and report the result fully to the company. On the last day of the ensuing October he set off from Old Town on the Potomac and at length reached the Ohio; thence crossing the country to the Muskingum Town on the Muskingum or Elk's-Eye Creek, where he "read prayers" on Christmas-day to a few graceless traders and a squad of wondering Indians and "talked of salvation, faith and good works." The Lower Shawanoe Town, just below the mouth of the Scioto on either bank of the Ohio, and the large Indian town of Piqua, on the Great Miami, were also visited. He distributed presents and received in return renewed pledges of friendship on the part of the Indians and a promise to meet at Logstown the following summer to conclude a general treaty with Virginia.

Winter had now worn away. On the first day of March, Gist started from the Twightwi or Piqua Town, accompanied by George Croghan,[o] Andrew Montour,[p] and an Indian party as far as Mad River, where they parted company, Gist bearing off to the Little Miami alone on horseback, down which stream he pursued his course some distance and along whose banks he saw herds of forty or fifty buffaloes grazing together in the natural meadows. He at length reached the Lower Shawanoe Town, where he had left his boy-companion, probably a Negro, and his horses; and on his way there, he killed a bear and a buffalo cow. After tarrying three days at the Lower Shawanoe Town and learning that a party of about sixty French Indians was encamped at the Falls, he still resolved on examining the country on the southern shore of the Ohio and, for this purpose crossed the Ohio with his only companion and passed westwardly, apparently as far as the Licking River, when hearing the report of guns in the woods and discovering the tracks and traps of Indian hunters, he determined to abandon his intention of visiting the Falls according to instructions. He yielded more rapidly to this course as he had learned when at the Indian towns of the captivity of several English traders by the French and their Indian emissaries, and he feared that he might be blamed should he be too venturesome in such dangerous times. He once had thought of leaving his boy and horses and going privately on foot to view the Falls; but the boy, being a poor hunter, was afraid he would starve if left long alone, and moreover, Gist thought there was great danger of losing the horses should some of the straggling French Indians hear their bells or discover their tracks.

So facing partly about, they bore off southwardly, crossing a ridge of mountains, from the top of which they saw a fine, level country to the south-west as far
as the eye could behold on a very clear day. This "rich, level land, covered with
small walnut, sugar trees, and red-buds," they soon entered, and passing about
thirty miles through it, they reached the Kentucky—called by Gist the Little Cuttawa. They doubtless saw the charming Elkhorn region. Passing up the Kentucky, they soon found plenty of coal and a far less desirable country. Gist was
compelled by sickness to stop, but taking "a sweat after the Indian manner," he
recovered after tarrying but a single day. In the upper Kentucky region, they
came to a large Indian camp on a small creek capacious enough to contain seventy or eighty warriors; their leader's name as indicated by a rude painting on a
tree was *The Crane.*

They now pursued the *Warrior's Road* a short distance and at length entered
a country of most forbidding rocky mountains and laurel thickets so bad that in
one place they had to cut a passage through better than two miles. In climbing up
the cliffs and rocks one day, two of their horses fell down and were much hurt,
and a paroquet[q] which the Indians north of the Ohio had presented to Gist was so
much injured by the fall that it died; and Gist adds feelingly in his Journal,
"though it was but a trifle, I was much concerned at losing him, as he was perfectly tame, and had been very brisk all the way, and I had still corn enough left
to feed him." In climbing up the rocks, Gist himself also got a fall, which hurt
him considerably. Thus they toiled on their weary way, sometimes themselves
destitute of meat and their horses of grass, at others killing bears and buffaloes
and finding fresh feed in plenty. Meeting such stern experience at almost every
step, they at length reached the Blue Stone and Kenhawa, and crossing the Alleghenies and Blue Ridge, they found themselves once more at Gist's old residence on the Yadkin, May 18th, 1751; but to their great surprise the family was
gone, and soon happening to meet an old man, learned that they had been frightened away the preceding winter by the Indians having killed five persons near
there and had repaired to Roanoke, thirty-five miles nearer the inhabitants. The
next day Gist reached his family.[91]

But the Indians, thwarted probably by the adverse interests of the traders, did
not meet at Logstown as they had promised. In November 1751 Gist made a second exploration in the service of the Ohio Company, passing down on the south
side of the Ohio as far as the Kenhawa and spent the ensuing winter in that quarter.[92] And in the latter part of 1751 Col. John Lewis and his son Andrew Lewis
were engaged in making extensive land locations on the Greenbrier River in behalf of the Greenbrier Land Company, who on the 29th of October in that year
had obtained the passage of an order in the Virginia Council granting them leave
to take up one hundred thousand acres of land on that river.[93]

During the year 1752 two important events transpired which had their bearing upon the ultimate development of the great Western Valley: The treaty of
Logstown, June 13th, by which the western Indians assented to the proposed settlement of the Ohio Company. And secondly, the continued hostile disposition

manifested by the French and their Indian emissaries in seizing English traders, carrying them into captivity, and plundering them of all their goods; and finally, on the 21st of June, two Frenchmen and two hundred and forty French Indians, principally Chippiways[r] and Ottawas,[s] leaving a reserve of thirty Frenchmen, suddenly appeared before the Twightwee town[t] of Piqua because of their attachment to the English; and, in the absence of most of the Twightwee warriors hunting, surprising them in their corn-fields and then attacking their fort, and in the end capturing six of the whites, one of whom being wounded, they stabbed him to death, tore off his scalp, cut out and ate his heart; they killed, besides, one Mingo,[u] one Shawanoe, and twelve Twightwees, among whom was the old Piankeshaw[v] king commonly called Old Briton, from his great friendship for the English, and a Shawanoe chief, both of whose bodies they boiled and ate. Two of the English traders were secreted and escaped, and plunder to the value of three thousand pounds was carried off by the successful assailants, who paid dearly for their booty and prisoners in the loss of thirty-six of their warriors.[94] Such were some of the inhuman and unjustifiable acts of the French, which at length roused the spirit of the English government and her American colonies, and wrested from France that power and dominion which she had so perniciously exercised in North America, and thus paved the way for the ultimate occupancy of the valley of the West by the adventurous Anglo-American race.

At this period nearly all the Indian traders in the Ohio region were Irish-Pennsylvanians chiefly from Lancaster and Cumberland counties. Among the more prominent of them were George Croghan, Alexander Lowry, Robert Callender, Alexander Maginty, and John Findlay,[w] all of whom had a number of men in their employ. As Maginty was returning from a trading-tour to the Cuttawas or Catawbas in Carolina and was encamped "on the southern bank of *Kantucqui* or *Cantucky* River, about twenty-five miles from the Blue Lick Town," in company with Jabez and Jacob Evans, David Hendricks, William Powell, Thomas Hyde, and James Lowry, a party of seventy Caughnawaga[x] Indians from the St. Lawrence River, accompanied by a Low Dutchman named Philip on a war-excursion against the Catawbas, happening to meet this party of white traders on the 26th of January, 1753, attacked and made them prisoners, seizing their goods, skins, furs, horses, and the clothing on their backs, to the value of seven hundred pounds Pennsylvania money.

In justification of their conduct, the Caughnawaga declared that some of the Indians with whom they were at war were in company with the traders; and the latter, discovering that the Caughnawagas were resolved on killing or taking their Indian foes, made resistance in behalf of their Catawba friends and wounded one of the Caughnawagas with a musket ball in the arm; whereupon the Caughnawagas determined on capturing whites as well as Indians and accordingly brought them all off as prisoners. Two days after, Lowry effected his escape and at length safely

reached Pennsylvania. Maginty particularly was beaten and abused in a most cruel
and unfeeling manner by his captors, and all were conveyed first to "the French
fort on the Miamis or Twightee River" and thence to Detroit, where Mons. Celeron
was commandant, who purchased Jacob Evans and Thomas Hyde of the Indians,
while Powell was also retained in that quarter. The other three were sent down the
Lakes to Montreal, where they were taken before the Governor-General of
Canada, who refused to have anything to do with them as they were the Indians'
prisoners. Jacob Evans, Hyde, and Powell subsequently arrived at Montreal, the
two former of whom were imprisoned and finally sent back to France.

Maginty and his three companions detained in the Indian villages near Montreal managed at length to send a letter to the mayor of Albany, giving a brief
statement of their helpless situation, which eventuated in their liberation by the
payment of over seventy-two pounds; and even this was unsatisfactory to the
Caughnawagas, for Ononraquite, their chief at the Falls of St. Louis, near Montreal, sent a message to Col. Myndet Schuyler at Albany complaining that the
ransom received for each prisoner was not sufficient to buy a little Negro slave,
and unless increased, his warriors would not think it worth their while to spare
the lives of captives. In October of the same year, Maginty arrived in Philadelphia in destitute circumstances, when the Assembly voted him six pounds to procure clothing and defray his expenses to his residence in Cumberland County.[95]

In connection with the account of the captivity of Maginty and his companions in
the gazettes of the day is the additional intelligence that "three of John Findlay's
men were killed by the Little Pick Town, and no account of himself."[96] This unquestionably refers to the affair mentioned by Filson, on probably the vague authority of Boone, that "about the year 1767, one John Findlay, and some others,
trading with the Indians, fortunately travelled over the fertile region now called
Kentucke. * * * ᵞ Sometime after, disputes arising between the Indians and
traders, he was obliged to decamp, and returned to his place of residence." The
Little Pick Town here spoken of was probably the same as Es-kip-pa-ki-thi-ki on
Lulbegrud Creek of Red River of Kentucky; and though the accounts are confused and indefinite, we presume that the traders both of Maginty and Findlay's
parties were attacked by the same Indians, at the same time, and at that place,
which is on the waters of the Kentucky and about twenty-five miles south of the
Upper Blue Licks where the Warriors' Road crossed the Licking. Filson plainly
conveys the idea that it was somewhere from the "fertile region of Kentucke" that
Findlay had to decamp.

Next in order of the early western adventurers was James McBride, who,
with a party from Virginia, passed down the Ohio in canoes in 1754; and landing
at the mouth of the Kentucky River, McBride marked on a tree the initials of his
name and the year, which were still visible at the first settlement of Kentucky.
"These men," relates Filson, "reconnoitered the country, and returned home with

the pleasing news of their discovery of the best tract of land in North America, and probably in the world."[97]

During the ensuing nine years of border warfare, many hapless captives were carried into the Indian country north-west of the Ohio, where they spent successive years in wandering with their whimsical Indian masters from village to village and through the boundless forests in quest of game and, at length, returned to their friends and homes to relate their sufferings and adventures, interspersed with hopeful views of a beautiful country in the great West that might yet be opened to settlement and civilization. Among these numerous captives, whose subsequent prominence gave unusual weight and influence to their statements, were Col. James Smith,[z] taken in Pennsylvania in 1755 when a youth of eighteen years, and Col. Arthur Campbell,[aa] captured on the frontiers of Virginia in the summer of 1756 when a mere stripling in his fifteenth year. The former remained in captivity five years and the latter four. Probably none of these many white captives ever saw Kentucky; the region from which they were taken would preclude that idea, and it was not then necessary for the Indians to resort there simply for supplies of game.

It is related that in 1760 Dr. Thomas Walker made a second attempt to reach the beautiful plains of Kentucky but that he penetrated no farther than Dick's River and, of course, failed in the object he had in view. No details of this

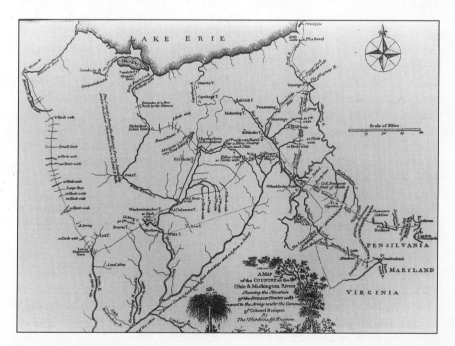

17. Thomas Hutchins's map of the Ohio country, c. 1760, which appeared in Col. James Smith's memoirs of his Indian captivity.

adventure are extant, nor any authority for its performance, save that of vague tradition.[98]   During this year also, Daniel Boone found his way into the Watauga Valley and there cut in the bark of a tree on the bank of Boone's Creek the evidence that he killed a bear there at that early period.[99]

The expeditions of Braddock,[bb] Forbes,[cc] and Bouquet[dd] into the Ohio Valley, of Montgomery[ee] and Grant[ff] into the Cherokee country, and of Byrd[gg] into the vallies of New River and Holston opened to the view of the hardy borderers who mainly composed these pioneer armies fresh and vigorous regions full of enchantment to the lover of nature, replete with hope to the hunter, and big with promise to the humble cultivation of the soil.   Soon after peace with the Cherokees in the autumn of 1761, Daniel Boone passed down the Holston vallies, while Elisha Walden, Henry Skaggs, William Blevins, Charles Cox, and fifteen others, all bold and intrepid hunters, penetrated the vallies of East Tennessee and Southwestern Virginia and spent eighteen months in hunting.

In 1761 one Swift, two Frenchmen, and a few others had a furnace near the Red Bird Fort of the Kentucky for smelting silver ore, which they obtained at a cave three miles distant.[100]   And on Goose Creek, which unites with the Red Bird Fork, was many years ago discovered a well a hundred feet deep, at the bottom of which was found a piece of an iron pot, some coal, and ashes.[101]   In the early settlement of Kentucky, many fruitless efforts were made to find the locality of Swift's silver mine.[hh]   And in the year 1761 the well-known and enterprising Moravian missionary Christian Frederick Post, having visited the Delaware Indians on the Muskingum and obtained their consent to settle among and instruct them in the doctrines of the Christian religion, erected a cabin on the eastern bank of that stream and returned to Bethlehem, in Pennsylvania.   Accompanied by the then youthful John Heckewelder, he returned to his field of labor the following spring and remained till the ensuing autumn, when sickness and Indian alarms induced Post and Heckewelder to return to the settlements.[102]

Notwithstanding the King's Proclamation of October 1763, forbidding the granting of lands or making settlements on the western waters, grants were made, the country explored, and settlements gradually extended.   There was during this year an exploration of a portion of Kentucky hitherto unchronicled which deserves a passing notice.   William Jordan, a captive from Virginia, was at Fort Duquesne when the French evacuated that garrison in 1758 and was taken by a party of Frenchmen to Kaskaskia, in which region he remained till 1763, when he agreed with a fellow prisoner named McCall to make the best of their way on foot to the frontiers of Virginia.   They started, relying upon their guns for means of support, and crossing the Ohio below the mouth of the Green River, they directed their course south of that stream, through what has since become well-known as the Green River Country.   In this region they found wild game in abundance and so tame that it seemed as though they could never have been hunted by white men or Indians.

Jordan and McCall passed over the Kentucky River where it appeared to break through the mountains and then pursued their course through the mountain ranges and defiles, until they at length reached the Cow Pasture settlement in western Virginia. There he married a sister of John Jackson, who was a brother-in-law of the pioneer McAfees[ii] of Kentucky, and both Jordan and Jackson early emigrated to that country. About 1783–4 Jordan settled on Cartwright's Creek, in what is now Marion County, and there lived to an advanced age, where all who knew him regarded him as a worthy and trustful man. His narrative is singularly corroborated by the fact that about thirty-five years ago, Major Long, then acting as deputy marshall of Kentucky under Robert Wickliffe,[jj] was engaged on official business up the Kentucky River a few miles above the village of Irvine, where, on the bank of the river about the point where Jordan said he crossed it, he was shown a beech tree on which was anciently but plainly inscribed—"*McCall 1763.*" What became of McCall is not certainly known.[103]

The company of hunters under the leadership of Elisha Walden passed through Cumberland Gap in the fall of 1763 and hunted for a season on the Cumberland River; and in the fall of 1764, the Blevins connection are also said to have made their fall hunt on Rockcastle River and to have continued their hunts in that quarter for several years afterwards.[104]

Among the papers of Gen. Charles Lee, who had served in America during the conquest of Canada, is found a scheme for establishing two new colonies, one on the Ohio below the Wabash and the other on the Illinois, which appears to have been projected soon after the peace of 1763. A company was to be formed and grants were to be obtained from the king. It was a part of the plan to procure settlers from New England and among the Protestants in Germany and Switzerland. In describing the advantages which he thinks could not fail to flow from these settlements, he discovers an accurate knowledge of the resources of the country and of the facilities of navigation furnished by the great lakes and rivers of the West. In a political view they would be important, protecting the old colonies from the incursions of the western Indians, preventing their intercourse with the Spaniards at the South, and opening a new channel of commerce through the Mississippi and the Gulf of Mexico. The proposal was rejected by the ministers, who had adopted the policy of allowing no settlements in the territory beyond the Allegheny Mountains. Experience proved, however, that this was a short-sighted policy at variance with the interests of the government and hostile to the prosperity of the colonies.[105]

Col. George Croghan, deputy Indian agent under Sir William Johnson, left Pittsburgh in May 1765 on a pacification to the Indian tribes in Illinois and to pave the way for taking possession of that country by the English; but in June, a little below the mouth of the Wabash, he was taken prisoner by the Indians, some of his party killed, and he carried to Vincennes and the Wea town,[kk] and thence, being released, returned home by way of Detroit. In the latter part of August ensuing, Capt. Charles Stirling, with one hundred men of the 42d regiment, left Pittsburgh in bateaux,[ll] descended the Ohio, and on the 10th of October of that year received the formal cession of Fort Chartres by *proces verbal* from Louis St. Ange.[106]

Thenceforward, explorers and explorations increase rapidly in the West, threading the water-courses and penetrating the almost trackless wilds in every direction. Capt. Harry Gordon, chief engineer in the western department of North America, was sent from Fort Pitt in June 1766 to the Illinois country, where he arrived in August. Descending the Ohio, his party killed several buffaloes from a point a hundred miles below Fort Pitt to the Muskingum; and he mentions in his published Journal "Kentucke River," describes the Falls of Ohio, and notes the latitude of the more prominent points on the route. Extracts from his Journal appear in the appendix to Pownall's *Topographical Description of North America.*

James Smith, better known by his subsequent title of colonel, started from Pennsylvania the last of June of the same year for Holston River, and thence travelled westward in company with Joshua Horton, Uriah Stone, William Baker, another James Smith, and a mulatto youth named Jamie to view the country between the Ohio and the Cherokee or Tennessee rivers. They explored the region south of the Kentucky River, where no sign of white men was any where to be seen; and in May 1767 they reached and gave name to Stone's River, a southern tributary of Cumberland, and explored the country along the Cumberland and Tennessee rivers, from Stone's River to the Ohio. At the mouth of the Tennessee, Smith's companions concluded to visit and examine the Illinois country before returning home, but Smith himself wished to return without delay, as he had already over-staid his time; and placing his horse in charge of his fellow-travellers, as it was difficult to take him through the mountains direct to the border settlements, and receiving from them the chief part of their remaining ammunition, he took his departure, accompanied by the mulatto Jamie.

After three months of varied fortune, they reached the frontiers of Carolina in October, and soon after, Smith arrived home on Conococheague, where his wife and friends had supposed him a victim to Indian barbarity, as they had heard that he had been killed and his horse taken into one of the Cherokee towns. Of Smith's companions who went to Illinois, we only know that Stone returned the same year to the Cumberland in company with a French hunter and trapped successfully on Stone's River; and having nearly laded their boat with furs, the Frenchmen, in Stone's absence, stole off with the boat and lading, and Stone returned to the Holston settlements.[107]

During the year 1766 also, Col. George Morgan[mm] passed down the Ohio, visited Big Bone Lick, and proceeded on to Fort Chartres in the Illinois country, where he was one of a Philadelphia firm extensively engaged in the Indian trade;[108] and Benjamin Cutbirth, John Stuart, John Baker, and James Ward set out from the Yadkin settlements across the wilderness of Tennessee to the Lower Mississippi, where they spent two or three years, as shall be more particularly noticed hereafter.

Early in 1767 a new scheme of western settlement was set on foot which seems to have had its origin in the celebrated Patrick Henry—to whom Byron has paid the high and lasting compliment:

"Henry the forest-born Demosthenes,

Whose thunder shook the Philip of the seas."

The young Virginia orator, whose sagacity was equal to his powers of popular eloquence, together with Dr. Thomas Walker, Capt. William Fleming, and probably others, formed the design of planting a colony on the Mississippi near its junction with the Ohio. Captain Fleming was selected by the others to go out at once and reconnoiter the country. "Pardon me," writes Mr. Henry to him, "if I recommend to you a diary. Even the trees, herbs, grass, stones, hills, and etc., I think ou't to be described. The reason I wish you to be so particular is, that a succinct account of your journal may be printed, in order to invite our countrymen to become settlers. The task is arduous. To view that vast forest, describe the face of the country, and such of the rivers, creeks, and etc. as present themselves to view, is a work of much trouble, hazard and fatigue, and will, in my judgement, entitle you to the favorable notice of every gentleman engaged in the Scheme."[109] The contemplated reconnaissance was from some cause not made, and the projected colony was abandoned.

To George Washington was reserved the honor of making the first land surveys in Kentucky, commenced as early as 1767 under the Proclamation of 1763; one was located on both sides of Big Sandy, including the present town of Louisa and the other on Little Sandy, eleven miles from its mouth. Both surveys were made for John Fry, probably as heir of Col. Joshua Fry, who commanded the Virginia regiment in 1754 and upon whose death Washington succeeded to the command, and all those lands are still held under Fry's title. Upon the beginning corner of the Big Sandy survey, Washington cut the initials of his name, and nearly every corner was found well marked, so that this survey, like every thing else attempted by that great man, was accurately made and easily identified more than twenty-five years afterward when the country began to settle.[110] From the time of these primitive Kentucky surveys to the commencement of the Revolutionary War, Washington continued to take a lively interest in the growing importance of the West,[nn] visiting it occasionally in person, and in all probability, but for that event, he would have become a leading settler there and strangely changed the character of all our American history.[111]

Two more hardy hunters than Samuel Harrod and Michael Stoner[oo] never trod the rich vallies of the West. Harrod was the elder brother of James[pp] and William Harrod, so conspicuous in early Kentucky history, and was born in 1735 on the Shenandoah River but taken when very young by his parents to the Big Cove in Pennsylvania. Reared on the frontiers and educated how to use the rifle and thread the mazes of the forest, he had played well his part in the drama of the French war; but with that single interlude, he grew up with gun in hand nothing but a hunter. Stoner, of German descent, was several years younger than Harrod, born on the Schuylkill near Philadelphia in 1748; and losing his parents when four or five years old, he was early placed an apprentice to a saddler in Lancaster, with whom he remained till he was about sixteen years old, when from some cause he left and wended his way to New River in western Virginia. He subsequently went to the Fort Pitt region, where he fell in with Samuel Harrod, when both proceeded together to the Illinois country; and thence, in 1767, they went to the mouth of Stone's River on the Cumberland to indulge in their favorite sports of the chase. Here they were met by Isaac Lindsay and four others from South Carolina, who had crossed the Alleghenies, passed into Powell's Valley, through Cumberland Gap and thence to Rockcastle River, which Lindsay so named from a romantic appearing rock through the fissures of which the waters dripped and froze in columns below. Lindsay and party pursued Rockcastle to the Cumberland and down that stream to Stone's River.[112]

It was about this period that Dr. John Connolly ascended the Cumberland or Shawanoe River nearly four hundred miles to examine the country; and Joseph Nicholson, a well-known Indian interpreter, about the same time hunted on that stream. So highly delighted was Dr. Connolly with the soil and climate that he wished for nothing better than to induce one hundred families to go and settle there, that he might be among them and form the germ of a new government — which he proposed to have bounded by the Ohio northward and westward by the ridge that divides the waters of the Tennessee or Cherokee River southward and westward and a line to be run from the Falls of the Ohio, or above, so as to cross the Shawanoe River above the fork of it.[113] But he seems never to have seriously attempted the accomplishment of his fancied scheme.

Pretermitting Boone's fruitless effort to find the rich and level region of Kentucky in the autumn of 1767, and wintering near the Big Sandy, to be more appropriately noticed hereafter, we shall refer to the meagre events of 1768 so far as they stand connected with western exploration and discovery. During this year, James Knox and Henry Skaggs hunted in Powell's Valley with the famous Indian hunter Dick and in October passed through Cumberland Gap as far northwardly as Rockcastle River, the forbidding defiles of which discouraged their further progress in that direction, they fell short of the rich lands of Lincoln. They pitched their camp on what was once called Station Camp Creek but now known as Robertson's Creek, an upper branch of Laurel River and not far from a noted fountain called the Raccoon Spring. There they enjoyed their Christmas festival on thirty-six marrow-bones, the rich marrow[qq] of which proved to be a most delicious dainty when properly roasted in the camp-fire, as all the early hunters knew full well by happy experience. Soon after Christmas they returned to Virginia.[114]

What was the practical effect of the Fort Stanwix treaty, concluded in November 1768, and the cession there made by the Iroquois Confederacy to the Indiana Company, for losses which they as traders had sustained by the Indian out-burst of 1763, of a large tract between the Monongahela and Kenhawa rivers, and the yet larger cession to the king of all the claim which the mighty Romans of the New World held, by right of conquest, to the country between the Ohio, Great Kenhawa, and the Cherokee or Tennessee rivers, we are not left altogether to conjecture. The extinguishment of the Indian title, so far as the Six Nations had any to so extensive a region of country which had so long attracted the attention of border hunters and explorers, and which the proclamation of 1763 had hitherto prohibited them from settling or encroaching on, must have excited new hopes in the minds of the class of adventurers as virtually opening the way for the speedy extension of the Anglo-American settlements. That Dr. Thomas Walker, who had taken so early and so constant an interest in western exploration and whose home was at the eastern base of the Blue Ridge, was the Virginia commissioner at that treaty doubtless had its effect in quickly spreading the result of that memorable Indian congress of three thousand sons and daughters of the forest through the quiet settlements of Augusta and other portions of the Virginia Valley. The new impetus which now seemed to be given to the exploration of the Ohio Valley may well be attributed to this extinguishment of the claim of the Six Nations to one of the fairest regions of the West.

Near the close of 1768 Gilbert Christian, John Sawyers, John and William Anderson, who had formerly, when connected with Col. William Bird's regiment, penetrated the valley of the Holston and were much pleased with its inviting appearance, set out from Augusta County, Virginia, to make a more thorough examination of the country. Accompanying them were Robert Christian, James McNair, and Nathan Page, the latter of whom joined them on the route. Continuing down the Holston River to Clinch Mountain, they crossed the North Fork of Holston in February 1769, at the present ford above the mouth of that fork, and pursued as low down the main Holston as Big Creek in the present county of Hawkins, in Tennessee. Here they found themselves in the hunting grounds of a large party of Indians, as they judged by the plentifulness of the "sign," when they thought it prudent to return. Re-crossing the North Fork of the Holston, they shortly reached Reedy Creek, on the bank of which, about a mile above its junction with the main Holston, they erected a cabin where they sojourned the remainder of the winter and part of the ensuing spring, each planting corn and making an improvement on that stream—which, however, most of them subsequently lost by an older title held by Edmund Pendleton, probably one of the surveys of the Loyal Company, of which he was a member.

Returning that spring to Augusta, they found, from a point twenty miles east of the ford of the North Fork of the Holston, a cabin erected on every spot where the range was good and where, only a few weeks before, not a solitary settler nor the remotest evidence of civilization was any where to be seen. On their outward journey they found no settlers on the waters of the Holston save three families at the head springs of that river. Thus East Tennessee began to be permanently settled early in 1769, and ten of these hardy adventurers who located on Watauga came from the region of North Carolina where Raleigh has since been established, at the head of whom was James Robertson,[rr] who became one of the most meritorious of the noble band of western pioneers.[115]

Another effect of the Fort Stanwix treaty may be seen in the petition to the king, in December 1768, of George, Augustine, and Samuel Washington, five of the Lees, and twenty-eight other prominent citizens chiefly of Virginia, styling themselves the *Mississippi Company,* for a grant of two and a half million acres west of the Alleghenies between the thirty-eighth and forty-second degrees of north latitude, westward to the dividing line, the Tennessee River, according to the boundary prescribed by the Fort Stanwix treaty; to be exempt from all quit-rents and taxes for at least twelve years, pledging on their part to seat within that period not less than two hundred families on the grant, if not interrupted by the savages or some foreign enemy; and declaring that several of the petitioners were determined themselves to be among the first settlers. Arthur Lee, the agent of the company, presented the petition to the king in Council in the succeeding March, which was read, referred first to a committee, and then to the Board of Trade, where it was soon consigned to an undeserving oblivion.[116] But even such a spasmodic movement on the part of the leading Virginians, with the illustrious Washington at their head and "several" of their number expressing their firm determination to share in person the privations and hardships incident to a new colony, is strongly indicative of the feelings of the more enterprising class of people of that period to settle the rich trans-Allegheny Valley and cause it to blossom as the rose.

But while these notable sons of the Old Dominion were planning their scheme on so magnificent a scale, Dr. Thomas Walker, the veteran explorer of the West and the leading spirit of the old Loyal Company, who had just returned home from Fort Stanwix, where he had served as the Virginia commissioner, was busy in devising how he could best turn to account the new aspect of affairs in the West. The lovely region called Powell's Valley, which he had first visited in 1750, had probably fallen to his share of the old Loyal Company's grant. That valley extends about ninety miles in length and from eight to eighteen wide, skirted on either side by Powell's and Cumberland mountains, with Powell's River meandering centrally through its entire length, and lying partly in Virginia and partly in Tennessee, remarkable for its excellent springs and flowing watercourses, the unusual richness of its soil, and the great size and towering height of its sugar maple, ash, cucumber, elm, buckeye, linn, white and black walnut, oak, poplar, beech, and other forest trees. It was a region well calculated to attract the admiration of all lovers of nature in its wildest and richest aspects, where the hunter could fully gratify his passion for the chase and the farmer could well count on reaping a generous reward for subduing the wilderness and cultivating the soil.

Dr. Walker was anxious to effect the settlement of a valley at once so extensive and lovely, and he deemed it an auspicious moment to commence the enterprise and push forward the borders of civilization fully a hundred miles in advance of their then existing limits. Among his neighbors to whom he made known his wishes was Joseph Martin, a man of uncommon hardihood, who had spent many years as a hunter and was inured to all the privations of a frontier life, and who now entered with spirit into Dr. Walker's plans for the speedy settlement of the Valley. With twenty chosen companions, Martin started from Albemarle— for the new land of promise early in March 1769. The terms upon which he engaged in this toilsome undertaking and the outlines of the manner in which he effected it are best related in the simple narrative written by Martin himself shortly after reaching the Valley and addressed to a friend, probably Capt. William Simms, of Albemarle—a copy of which has fortunately been preserved:

Powell's Valley, May 9th, 1769

Worthy Friend,

Having a few leisure hours, I embrace the opportunity of writing to you. Perhaps it may not be disagreeable to you to hear of our former travels, as well as our present station. The day I parted with you and my other friends, with sorrowful hearts and weeping eyes, I set forward on my tedious journey. The weather proving tolerably good, I got to Staunton in four days; completed my business there; got to Capt. Ingles' on New River, the 14th of the month, being March, where I laid in a sufficient stock of provisions for our journey, viz: seed corn, ammunition, and etc. I then sent the boys on under the care of my brother, and waited for Doct. Walker and my companion Capt. Hord[?], who came up the 16th at night. Next morning we started. Nothing material happened till we got to Holston River, where we were informed, that the day we left New River the Kirtleys, Capt. Rucker and several others, came there, and gave a man five pounds to pilot them a road six days journey nearer than the road we were then going, which confused us very much; for the case stood thus: If they got there first, we were to have twenty one thousand acres where we chose, and they were not to interfere with us.

We immediately hired a pilot, took two of our best horses, about one quart of flour, and pushed on as hard as interest and desire could lead us, leaving the boys to follow after. The third day, to our great mortification, we found we were lost, and after three days' travel more, over mountains, creeks, laurel, canebrakes, and etc., our dogs being spent with hunger, gave out, and ourselves and horses were very little better. We were under the disagreeable necessity of resting part of two days. The second day I found the hunters' track about five miles from our camp. I hastened back as fast as possible to tell the welcome news to my companions. The next day, being the 24th, we set out full of hope once more. With much difficulty I prevented my companions from discharging our pilot with heavy blows. The 26th we got to our long desired place.

April 1st, the boys got to our camp, which was on Saturday. Monday being the 3d, we then began to work, and from then till now, there has been little else but eating and confusion. As to our health, I need not mention it. You may be assured of that yourself, after I tell you, that we have eaten and destroyed twenty three deer, fifteen bears, two buffaloes, and a great number of turkeys. The 15th of April the Kirtleys got to the Valley, very well pleased with the land, till we gave them a letter from Doct. Walker, that informed them if we got to the Valley first, we were to have twenty-one thousand acres of land, and they were not to interfere with us. They endeavored to prevail on us for a part of our land, which we would not consent to. They then pushed home without making any further search for land.

The place we are now settled, is on the waters of Beargrass, called by the hunter's Powell's River, about a mile from the foot of a large ledge of mountains called Cumberland, much resembling our Blue Ridge, only considerably larger and much steeper, running the same course, by the account, three hundred miles; and from Powell's Mountain we are about seven miles. Powell's Mountain runs near the same course of the South West Mountain in Albemarle. From where we crossed it, for nearly six miles, is broken land. There commences our rich Valley, which is in length, by the hunters' account, equal to that of the mountains above mentioned. We have marked off in length about ten miles; in width, some places a mile, some places more, some less; all very rich, and lies very well, with vast quantities of black walnuts and wild cherries. Great signs of old Indian towns. It lies out of all danger from water, being near five miles from Powell's River. Very good springs, bold creeks big enough to support large stocks for many years. I think it considerably warmer here than with you—vast numbers of ticks and gnats. We had abundance of snow fell the 20th of April, though very little lay, and we had frost the 4th. of May. April the 24th, came several gentlemen from Bedford, three from Maryland to get land to settle one hundred families.

This primitive settlement in Powell's Valley was made twenty miles east of Cumberland Gap, at the crossing of Martin's Creek of what was subsequently the great thoroughfare to Kentucky, and known afterwards by the name of Martin's Station and sometimes as Martin's cabins. But little preparation, beyond a rude brush fence, was requisite for planting corn and other vegetables in an old Indian field; and having, towards the close of summer, finished working their crop or, in Southern parlance, "laid by their corn," they concluded to explore Kentucky, of which they had heard something—doubtless in part from Dr. Walker and probably also from Boone, Findlay, and their companions, who must have visited them in May, and not very long after Martin had penned the preceding letter.

Having passed through Cumberland Gap they encamped. Next morning a large party of Indians, who had been on a hunting expedition, came up. The Cherokees, as these probably were, had been admonished by the British Indian agents not to kill any intruders upon their hunting grounds, but they might very properly rob them if they chose to do so, and they seldom hesitated in their choice when an opportunity presented itself; they had the power and were to profit by the operation. The whites on this occasion were saluted on the part of these dusky warriors and greasy hunters, with a liberal use of the word *"brod-der,"* a hearty shaking of hands, and almost any amount of extravagant pantomime expressions of friendship, to which Indians so invariably resort whenever they meditate mischief and wish to throw their intended victim off his guard. They were very loquacious, though unfortunately they possessed not even a smattering of English, nor did any of Martin's party know a word of Indian language. The Indians, however, were not long in discovering the superiority of the guns of the white strangers nor slow in endeavoring to evince their admiration of them and, naturally enough, proposed an even exchange, which of course was rejected. Too well suspecting their object, Martin cautioned his men not to suffer the Indians to take or examine any of their guns; but the Indians, notwithstanding, by a signal, suddenly seized the guns of the party and obtained them all. So quickly was it done that there was scarcely a chance for resistance.

The Indian who snatched Martin's gun, who was a powerful fellow, cast his worthless weapon away and walked off proudly with his prize. Instantly picking up the old fire-lock and stepping rapidly to where the Indians were, among whom was the one who had just played off his swap-game so successfully upon him, Martin indignantly hurled the old thing at the Indian's feet, seized hold of his own, to which the Indian firmly clung, when a violent struggle ensued; Martin at length threw the fellow upon the ground and succeeded in wrenching the gun from his reluctant grasp. The other Indians who, having quickly hopped out of the way, witnessed the exciting scene now raised a great laugh at the expense of their discomfited huge companion. But the fellow himself, who did not seem to relish it quite so well, became very much enraged, talked in a high and menacing tone, accompanied with violent gestures, all which Martin well understood as intended for bold and unmistakable threats of an Indian's revenge. Then robbing the camp, the Indians departed mutteringly.

It so happened that Joseph Martin's younger brother, Brice Martin, had gone out at the moment of this grabbing adventure to drive up the horses, which had been hoppled out for the night; his friends called to him to be on his guard, and thus he saved his gun. Nor is it certain whether the Indians also took the horses, but probably they did so. Martin and his party, with but two guns remaining and despoiled of every thing, abandoned further thought of exploration, retraced their steps to their old camp on Martin's Creek, which, to their grief, they found also plundered of every article that could be carried off. They now broke up and returned home; nor did Martin attempt to re-possess his favorite Valley settlement till several years thereafter.[117]

Such is an outline of the more important efforts in western discovery, exploration, and settlement made in successive order prior to the commencement of Daniel Boone's memorable trip in 1769. Though so much had from time to time been attempted, little or nothing of it had ever reached Boone's ears so far as Kentucky was concerned, beyond what he had vaguely learned from the enterprising John Findlay. The mighty power of the press was then little in vogue to spread a knowledge of these hardy adventures among the comparatively unlettered occupants of the rude cabins scattered sparsely along the frontiers of the North American Colonies.

DRAPER'S NOTES: INTRODUCTION

1. Shipwrecks of Alvar Nuñez Cabeza de Vaca, translated by Buckingham Smith and printed for private distribution at Washington in 1851 for George W. Riggs, Jr.; Shea's *History of the Discovery of the Mississippi River.*

2. De Vaca's Narrative; Shea's *Discovery of the Mississippi.*

3. Shea's *Discovery of the Mississippi* and the authorities there cited—a work of great merit and research.

4. *A Perfect Description of Virginia, and etc.* London, 1649. There is a copy of this work in the Franklin Library, Philadelphia; and re-print in the 2nd volume of Force's *Historical Tracts.*

5. Byrd's Westover MS., 105. Colonel Byrd, who visited these islands in 1733, calls the lower one Sapponi Island, the middle one Occaneeche Island, and the upper one Totero. The Sapponi and Occaneeche Indians formerly lived near the head of what is now known as the Rocky River, a western tributary of the Pedee, and called on ancient maps Sapona River. The Totero Indians resided on one of the upper branches of the Yadkin, apparently what is now known as Arrarat River. These seem to have been all clans of the same nation—probably the Catawba, and were driven from their ancient homes by the Iroquois about the commencement of the seventeenth century and then appear to have taken possession of these islands. Afterwards they went into Virginia, apparently for security against their northern enemies, and Colonel Spotswood took them under his care at Christanna. Dissatisfied at the execution of one of their Saponies for a murder he committed when drunk, they soon after removed in body to the Catawbas; south then went the daughter of the Totero King, the last of her tribe, and fearing she should not be treated according to her rank, poisoned herself with the root of the trumpet plant. Her father had died two years before of pleurisy. In Totero Island was a cave in which this valiant old chief with only two of his men defended himself against a host of northern Indians and at last obliged them to retire. He had made himself terrible to all other Indians by his exploits and had escaped so many dangers that he was esteemed invulnerable.—See Westover Papers, 89, 106.

6. *Discovery of New Brittaine,* London, 1651, from a copy of which, in the British Museum, the transcript had been made which has served as our guide in this notice of the first Anglo-American western exploration.

7. Bland's *Discovery of New Brittaine.*

8. Hening's *Statutes of Virginia,* i:377.

9. Bland Papers, i:147; Hening, i:277, 377, 381; Charles Campbell's *History of Virginia,* 70.

10. Coxe's *Carolina,* the successive editions of which appeared in 1722, 1736, 1737, and 1741, with a large map; the last edition, p. 120, is here cited; Adair, 308, *State of the British and French Colonies,* London, 1755: 107, 118.

11. *The Contest in America,* London, 1757: 176, 177; which is attributed to Dr. John Mitchell, a very accurate writer referred to by Dr. Franklin in his Ohio settlement and who, in 1755, prepared a large map of America at the request of the Lords Commissioners of Trade and Plantations, who furnished him many of the materials from their records.

12. Batt's MS. Narrative of 1671, London Documents, Albany.

13. Hening, i:326; ii:328. For these references, credit is due to that worthy antiquary Charles Campbell, Esq., of Petersburg, Virginia.

14. Probably the Maj. William Harris who represented Henrico County in the Virginia House of Burgesses at the period of 1658.—Howison's *Virginia,* 1:309, notes.

15. Captain Batts visited both these towns the following year, and his MS. Journal aids materially in determining their locality. Like all travelers in a wilderness country, Lederer, on some occasions at least, considerably over-estimated his distances and seems generally to have made slow progress, as some time was necessary each day to kill game and graze the horse, and his ignorance of the country prevented his taking advantage of the best and most discreet routes.

16. About thirty years after Lederer was at Sara, the Saura Indians, in consequence of the incessant inroads of the Senecas, were obliged to abandon their "beautiful dwelling" place—their "Elysian fields," in the language of Colonel Byrd, who visited the locality of the Lower Saura Town in 1733, and retire southwardly to the Pedee. The Saponies, too, about the same period, were driven from their ancient seats, first probably from the Sapon or Staunton, and then from the Sapona or Rocky River of the Pedee, and compelled to take refuge in Virginia, as they were no longer able to resist the attacks both of the Northern Indians, who were their implacable enemies, and several of the southern tribes. The Toteroes, likewise, were forced from their homes on one of the upper tributaries of the Yadkin. Such was the prowess—such the conquests, of the mighty Iroquois, the Romans of the New World.

17. Byrd's Westover MS., 85, 86. Wisacky was very likely located on the north-west fork of what is now known as Sugar Creek in Mecklenburg County, North Carolina, and perhaps at the spot where Charlotte now stands, where the old Indian and trader's path crossed the streams, pronounced by the Catawbas

Sugaw or *Soogaw*, which was probably an abbreviation of Lederer's Wisacky—as, *'Sacky-Soogaw*. From the Upper Saura Town to this point was something like ninety miles, which must have kept Lederer busy to have accomplished in these days. Between the Yadkin and Catawba were extensive prairies, and doubtless then mostly covered with a rank growth of cane, and hence shaded and wet. Colonel Byrd informs us that in 1728 there were half a dozen Catawba towns situated along the banks of the Catawba within a distance of twenty miles; and it is to be presumed that the one Lederer called Ushery was located [on] just some large island in the river, which caused an expansion of the stream, which might very naturally have deceived him into the erroneous notion of a lake. There is precisely such an island in the Catawba, a few miles above the modern Catawba settlement and about a mile below the point where the ancient Trading Path crossed the river—as may be seen by consulting Morizon's old map of the Carolinas, in Jeffrey's *American Atlas,* 1768.

18. On Eno River, or a Creek [*wi*] the Tuscaroras once lived.—Colonel Byrd in 1735, Westover Papers, 104.

19. The writer of this work is indebted to the kindness of President Sparks for the use of his copy of this rare tract. There is also a copy in the valuable library of Harvard College. A vague reference to Lederer's explorations may be found in Oldmixion, edition 1744, i:382. Other historians seem not to have noticed his adventurous efforts.

20. Byrd's Westover MS., 114. About thirty miles below the Lower Saura Town is a small stream flowing into the Dan, called Hatcher's Creek, near which Colonel Byrd in 1733 found the initials of the well-known traders cut in the bank of a large beech tree —"*J.H., H.H., B.B.* lay here the 24th of May, 1673."

21. Hanohaskie could have been none other than the place called by Lederer Akenatzy, located on the Long Island of Staunton River, in the north-west corner of Halifax County, Virginia. This, we should suppose, was only a variation in the orthography for the Indian tribe called by Colonel Byrd "Occaneeche," a clan of the same nation as the Saponies; and both were driven together from the Sapona or Staunton River by the Iroquois to the Rocky River of Pedee and thence to the Saponi and Occaneeche islands in the Roanoke. Subsequently the remnant of the Occaneeches joined the Saponies, and all lived awhile at Germanna, in Virginia, and then joined the Catawbas. The name is variously written. Beside the instances already given, "We Occoneachey" and "A Konichi" on Fry and Jefferson's map of 1751; "Aconeechy" on Mitchell's map of 1755; "Ockoneachey" on Mouzon's map in Jeffrey's *Atlas of 1768;* and "the Okenachee path" is alluded to in the Journal of Batt's expedition. On the maps of Fry and Jefferson, and Mitchell, a town bearing the name of this tribe is laid down on the eastern bank of the Eno River, occupying apparently the present locality of Hillsborough, North Carolina. It was probably only a temporary residence.

22. These interesting memorials of former travellers on the western slopes of the Alleghenies, as well as the same initials at the head of the Staunton at the eastern base of the Blue Ridge, were probably made by General Wood's explorers

between 1654 and 1664; all on the natural route and Indian trails from the Falls of the Appomattox, where Wood resided, across to the Staunton; then up that stream scaling the Blue Ridge, and following the upper part of that river known as the Roanoke to its source, and thence across the Alleghenies. This may be considered another evidence that General Wood and those in his employ did actually discover the Kenhawa or New River, which so long bore the name of Wood's River.

23. *MS. Journal and Relation of a New Discovery Made behind the Apulein Mountains to the West of Virginia,* among the London Documents, Albany, copied from the original unpublished narrative in the British Archives.

The earliest printed account of Batts' exploration is to be found in Beverly's *History of Virginia,* the first edition of which appeared in 1705; and that, though meagre, is in the main a very fair outline. The "infinite quantity of elks and buffaloes, so gentle and undisturbed," mentioned by Beverly, had the good fortune to keep beyond the reach of Batts and his Indian hunters, as no mention is made of them in the Journal. The date of this expedition is variously assigned by historians to 1667, 1670, and 1674; and in some instances, Batts' name is metamorphosed into Bolt, and sometimes into Bolton.

Beverly supposed that Batts did not "cross the great ridge of the mountains," but kept under [*wi*], as the marshes on the Oukfuskie River, which empties into the great gulf between Cape Florida and the mouth of the Mississippi, corresponds to Batts' description. What is here called Oukfuskie was doubtless the Tallapoosa, a large eastern tributary of the Alabama, on the right bank of which was situated the town of Oc-fus-kie. Howison's comment is far more truthful; that it would appear "the explorers crossed the Blue Ridge; passed through the beautiful valley of Virginia; scaled the Allegheny Mountains and penetrated nearly to the salt licks contiguous to the Great Kenhawa, or the Ohio River."

24. MS. letter of Hon. B. R. Floyd, of Virginia.

25. *Sketches of a Journey from Huntsville, Alabama, to Virginia, in 1823,* p. 46.

26. Shea's *Discovery of the Mississippi.*

27. O'Callaghan, *Jesuit Relations;* Shea's *Mississippi.*

28. There are not a few references to early western exploration of a character too vague and uncertain to warrant their introduction into the text of our work, which are nevertheless worthy of a passing allusion.

From the inscription on a stone found in Onondaga County, New York, over thirty years ago, it would appear that some party visited that region in the year 1520; and this antique memorial is supposed by Schoolcraft to have reference to Juan Ponce de León, or some stragglers of his party, in his exploration of Florida—for Florida then extended northwardly at least to the Great Lakes.— *Notes on the Iroquois.*

In Brighton, Lorain County, Ohio, was found in 1838 a stone upon which the name and date of "Louis Vagard, La France, 1533," were plainly engraved, and bearing every mark of antiquity, the date occurring in three different places on the stone and once on another stone found near by. Howe's *Ohio,* 313.

It is stated on the authority of DeWitt Clinton, that in 1669 a band of twenty-three Spaniards passed up the Mississippi and Ohio and destroyed a French missionary settlement in the Onondaga country. *Clinton's Memoir on the Antiquities of Western New York;* cited by Stone, Barber and Howe, and in Clark's *History of Onondaga.*

Some curious instances of great antiquity in what seem to have been traces of axe-cuts in trees have been brought to light. In 1829 a large tree was felled in Ashtabula County, Ohio, in which, about three feet from the ground and near the heart, was discovered what had the appearance of axe-cuts; and counting the annular rings, the year 1479 was indicated as the period when they were made— thirteen years before Columbus discovered America. It was probably the work of the Mound-builders, who are said to have had the art of hardening their copper axes so as to cut like steel.—Howe's *Ohio,* 40, 41.

An oak tree was cut in Canfield, Trumbull County, Ohio, which had some ancient axe-marks, which, when the circles of growth were counted, pointed to 1660 as the year when they were made. Other axe-marks were found on a white wood log in Newburg, Cuyahoga County, Ohio, of about the same age.—Charles Wittlesay's Discourse before the Ohio Historical Society in 1840.

29. Shea's *Mississippi.*

30. Perkins' "Early French Travellers in the West," in *North American Review,* January 1839; also in his *Life and Writings.*

31. Coxe's *Carolina:* 117, 120. In Mitchell's *Contest in America,* p. 90 and 239, it is stated that the English discovered the countries of the Great Lakes, Ohio, and Mississippi, in 1568, 1654, and 1672; and at these two latter dates were the first that found their way to the Mississippi and were soon after cut off on the Isle of Massacre nigh its mouth, whence its ominous name. The assertion that the inland country of North America was discovered by the English as early as 1568 must be founded in error; that of 1654 refers to Captain Wood; that of 1672 must either refer to Batts' exploration of 1671, or the conquest of the Shawanoes and Andastes[?] in [*wi*] 1672 by the Iroquois, who placed the conquered country under the protection of the English. The discovery of 1678 must have been that of the New England party. Isle of Massacre, or Dauphin's Island, in Mobile Bay [*wi*] when visited by Iberville in 1699 presented "a heap of human bones."

32. Spark's *La Salle;* Peck's edition of *Annals of the West,* note 39; in Tonty's Memoir, in French's *Historical Collections of Louisiana,* i:45, this name D'Acau is written "the Sieur Deau"; it is usually written Ducan.

33. Spark's *Life of La Salle* and Perkins' *French Discoveries in the West.*

34. Mitchell's *Contest in America,* 90.

35. Coxe's *Carolina: State of the British and French Colonies in America,* London, 1755: 117; Du Pratz's *Louisiana,* London edition, 1774: 156, 157; *The Present State of Louisiana,* London, 1744, p. 3, says the English passed up the Mississippi before La Salle as high as the English Turn, from whence it derived its name; but the writer probably erroneously used La Salle's name for Iberville's.

36. Charlevoix's *History Nouvelle France,* quarto ed., ii:259–261; *University History* xl:278; Holme's *Annals,* i:468. Martin, the historian of Louisiana, and

Bancroft after him, mention the name of Captain Barr as the English commander whom Bienville met and assert that his vessel was the one sent out by Dr. Coxe. The memorial of Dr. Coxe's was written in 1699 and presented to the king, from whom it passed into the hands of Secretary Vernon, the Ministry, and the Attorney General, and [was] regularly acted on by them all before the close of the year, and all this, of necessity, required considerable time. In that memorial, Coxe speaks of having despatched his two vessels the previous year and having heard the result of the expedition; and this could not well have been so, had it been his vessel that Bienville spoke with in the Mississippi, on the 16th of September, in the year 1699. Charlevoix speaks of the vessel as a corvette, which is a sloop of war—a national craft; and one of the three vessels that sailed from London went to Panuco to concert measures for expelling the French from the Mississippi, which a vessel on a private enterprise, like that of Dr. Coxe's, would never have thought of. Not a word is said by Coxe in his memorial, nor by his son in his work on Carolina, about Captain Barr meeting Bienville; and the younger Coxe expressly states that his father's vessel was *the first* that ever entered the Mississippi from the Gulf of Mexico, which could not have been true had it been Coxe's vessel with which Bienville had the interview.

Keating, Monette, and some others intimate that it was Captain Wood whom Barr and his companions declared had discovered the Mississippi fifty years before; and notwithstanding [the fact that] Keating says, without citing any authority, that it was not the Colonel Wood of Virginia, we doubt not [that] if any Captain Wood was mentioned on the occasion, it was Capt. Abraham Wood, of Virginia. Whether, however, he really discovered any thing more than the upper waters of the Ohio is very questionable, though Jeffrys, in his *History of the French Dominicans,* says Wood spent about ten years "in searching the course of the Mississippi."

37. Coxe's *Carolina,* preface.

38. *History of the Revolt,* i:318; ii:78.

39. Robert Beverly's *History of Virginia,* preface, 2nd edition, 1722, who seems to have been one of Spotswood's party; Hugh Jones' *Present State of Virginia,* 1724; Oldmixon; Wynne. Burk.[?]; Charles Campbell's *History of Virginia,* 107, 112; this learned Virginia historian is a lineal descendant of Spotswood; Holmes; Bancroft; Grahame. The statement in the outline in Howe, which is repeated in Howison, that Spotswood received from his royal sovereign the honor of knighthood with the golden horse-shoe as a reward for his successful discoveries, is unsupported by older authorities.

The late Judge Francis J. Brooke of Virginia stated that his paternal grandfather was one of the Spotswood's party that "crossed the Blue Ridge," and that he had seen the golden brooch, and yet, as Charles Campbell states, it was small enough to be worn on a watch chain. It was about the size of a Spanish silver shilling or eighth of a dollar.

It is understood that a manuscript journal of the Tramontane Expedition is extant in Virginia which is promised to be made public. A very clever historical novel, written by the late Dr. William A Caruthers, entitled *"The Knights of the*

Horse-Shoe," published at Wetumpka, Alabama, 1845, derived its name and subject from Spotswood's adventures.

40. *State of the British and French Colonies,* 1755, 109; Wynne, i:517–518; Smollet, ii:125; Burk, ii:332; Holmes, i:516; ii:39, note; Bancroft, iii:344–345; Grahame, Boston ed., ii:42–43; Howison; Charles Campbell's *History* and MS. Correspondence.

Of Spotswood we may add that he was borne of Scottish parents at Tangier, Africa, on board a man of war, his father being a commander in the British navy, and his earliest years were passed amid the scenes of the camp and the bivouac. At the great battle of Blenheim in 1704, he received a dangerous wound in the breast. In 1710 he was appointed to the government of Virginia, and for thirteen years he proved himself, in the truthful language of Bancroft, "the best in the line of Virginia governors." Retiring to his plantation in Spotsylvania County, named in his honor, he devoted himself several years to agricultural pursuits and the manufacture of iron. After serving as deputy post master general for the Colonies, he was in 1739 appointed commander-in-chief of the Colonial troops in the expedition destined against Carthagena, but died, when on the eve of embarking, at Annapolis, Maryland, June 7th, 1740: "His ashes flew, no marble tells whither."

41. *Collection of Keith's Tracts and Papers,* London, 1740.

42. Bancroft, iii:344; *Pennsylvania Colonial Records,* iii:223–492; Kercheval's *History of the Valley,* 58.

43. Mitchell's *Contest,* 237, says the English had settled on the Ohio as early as 1724, referring, of course, to traders.

44. Anderson's *History of Commerce;* Dillion's *Indiana,* i:62; Pamphlet of Keith, Gee, and others, reprinted by Almon, 1767, p. 7.

45. *State of British and French Colonies,* 109.

46. French's *Historical Collections of Louisiana*, ii:51–52.

47. Bossu's *Travels,* i:179; French's *Louisiana,* ii:83.

48. Rafinesque's *Annals of Kentucky;* Eager's *History of Orange County,* New York, 77.

49. The French settlement here alluded to was probably Fort Chartres, abreast of an island in the Mississippi, near which, on the opposite shore, a plentiful supply of both salt and lead was obtained.

50. Abstract of the official report in Du Pratz, London edition, 1774, note 62, and preface, p. x; Wynne, ii:405, 406; Expediency of securing our American Colonies, and etc., Edinburgh, 1763, 25, 47; Kercheval, 67. Very little reliance can be placed on the statement of the late Hugh Paul Taylor, in his newspaper series of *Notes on West America,* from which Withers derived his account which had been followed by Howe, Ruffner, Butler, De Hass, and others. Taylor wrote from vague traditions, and not having sifted his authorities, has necessarily fallen into numerous blunders in this and various other matters connected with the early story of Western Virginia.

Of John Howard, little is known. Kercheval, in his *History of the Valley,* pp. 6, 67, 73, speaks of him as one of the first explorers and settlers of the South Branch of Potomac, about 1735; that when captured by the French on the Mississippi, his son was with him, and both were sent to France, but nothing criminal appearing against them, they were discharged. They then went to England, and thence probably returned to the South Branch. For a sketch of Salling, see the Appendix.

51. Stephen Holston, who discovered the river which perpetuates his name, was most likely in Colonel Patton's employ. He was probably from Pennsylvania, as the names of both Stephen and Holston were among the earliest of the Swedish settlers there—Day's *Pennsylvania,* 485, 486, 499, 559. Many Pennsylvanians, particularly Germans, were among the primitive settlers of the Virginia Valley. "Some years before 1758," says Haywood, "one Stephen Holston, a resident of that part of Virginia which afterwards bore the name of Botetourt, in his travelling excursions to the south and west, came to the head waters of a considerable river. Allured by its inviting appearance, and by the fertility of the lands on its banks, and by the variegated scenery which it presented, as also by the quantity of game which he saw, he proceeded some distance down the river. When he returned and related to his countrymen what discoveries he had made, they called the river by his name." He erected a cabin and located himself at the head spring of the Middle Fork of the Holston, twenty miles in advance of the nearest settlement. He probably died early. His cabin was yet standing in 1774 and occupied by one Davis, who informed the late Maj. John Redd of Henry County, Virginia, that it was built and inhabited many years before by Holston, from whom the river derived its name.—MS. Statement of Major Redd.

52. MS. letters of Col. James Patton, in the Preston Papers.

53. Dr. Morse states in his *Geography* that it was between 1740 and 1750 the exploration just named was made; Guthrie's *Geography* says it was between 1745 and 1750; and Winterbotham in his *Travels* gives the date "as early as 1748," which is corroborated by Dr. Walker's MS. Journal of his trip of 1750. These early grants must have settled rapidly, for in 1752 the Virginia Legislature opened "An Act to encourage the settlers on the Mississippi," exempting them from taxes for ten years, to which act the king gave his assent, and the next year a further indulgence of five years was added.

54. Spark's *Washington,* ii; appendix *Sketch of the Ohio Company;* Bancroft, iv:42; Perkins' *Annals.*

55. Leigh's *Virginia Code,* ii:347.

56. In the preceding year, some of the western Indians had stolen from Joueaire one of these leaden plates, evidently before it was deposited, containing assumptions of territorial claims by the French, which the Cayugas took to Governor Clinton of New York for explanation; which, in fact, Governor Clinton communicated to the British government December 14th, 1748.—Lee MS.

London Documents, Albany, vols., xxix and xxx; French's *Historical Collections of Louisiana,* ii:49.

57. The date of this exploration has been variously stated. Mann Butler, an authority of the late Hon. John Brown of Kentucky, who had treasured it in [his] memory from conversations with Dr. Walker something like half a century before, gave it as having occurred in 1747. Winterbotham plainly mistakes the Holston trip of 1748 for the one to Kentucky two years later. Mr. H. Taylor thought Dr. Walker informed him that his Kentucky exploration was in 1752; and Marshall, in both editions of his *History,* says it was "about 1758." But it was really in 1750. The late Gov. Isaac Shelby of Kentucky commanded the escort of guards to the commissioners who ran the western extension of the boundary line between Virginia and North Carolina. Dr. Walker was one of the Virginia commissioners. After passing Cumberland Gap in November 1779, the doctor spoke of his having passed that route in 1750; and when they had advanced to Yellow Creek, a mile or two from the gap, he observed to Shelby, "Upon that tree," pointing to a beech across the road to the left hand, "Ambrose Powell marked his name and the year." "I could not realize the idea," said Shelby, "of any white man's having travelled that path nearly thirty years before; but on examining the tree, I found '*A. Powell –1750,*' cut in large, legible characters, and apparently that old": compare Holme's *Annals,* ii: notes 3 and 4, with Bradford's *Notes on Kentucky,* which originally appeared in the *Kentucky Gazette* in 1826 and [was] republished in Stipp's *Miscellany,* Xenia, Ohio, 1827, p. 9.

In 1822 and 1823 the late Professor [Constantine Samuel] Rafinesque visited the aged Shelby and doubtless learned the same facts from him, as he gives the correct year, 1750, in his *Annals of Kentucky,* prefixed to Marshall's work, in 1824. Judge Hall informs us in *Sketches of the West,* i:239, that he has seen a manuscript affidavit of Dr. Walker, that he visited the waters of the Cumberland and gave its present name to that river in April 1750. In a MS. letter of Dr. Walker to Col. William Preston, dated March 23, 1778, when speaking of the claims of the Loyal Company, he says, "I was exploring the country west of the settlements in 1750." On the map prefixed to Washington's Journal of his mission to the Ohio in 1753–'54 is marked on the Cumberland River, "Walker's Settlement, 1750," which was copied upon the maps of Mitchell, Ottens[?], Sayer and Bennett, and several others of that period. And finally, the inedited MS. Journal of that trip, kept by Dr. Walker himself, preserved by the Hon. W. C. Rives of Virginia, whose accomplished lady is a granddaughter of Dr. Walker, completely corroborates and establishes this date.

58. The French maps of De Lisle as early as 1720, and that of Bellin in Charlevoix's *New France* in 1744; Popple's map of North America, 1733; Coxe's *Carolina* with its map, the last edition of which was published in 1744, and the same year appeared the last edition of Oldmixon with Moll's map; and the report of Howard and Salling's trip and adventures in 1742 most probably were known to Dr. Walker and furnished him some vague conception of the Kentucky country. Dr. Walker, moreover, must have been personally acquainted with Salling, as they lived comparatively near each other, and Salling's residence was directly on the

way from Dr. Walker's in Albemarle to the Holston country. The first edition of Lewis Evans' map of the Middle Colonies appeared in 1749, on which, it is believed, was laid down the adjacent Indian countries.

59. TFB: *Here, DM 1:126–48, Draper presents his transcribed and annotated version of Dr. Thomas Walker's journal.*

60. TFB: *In the 1850s, when Draper edited—and at times rewrote—his transcription of Walker's journal for inclusion in this introduction, pages from March 6 to 15 and April 10 to 20, 1749, were missing from the diary. In December 1895 Dr. William C. Rives, a Walker descendant living in New York, discovered the lost pages and sent them to Col. J. Stoddard Johnston, then vice president of the Filson Club in Louisville, Kentucky, who in 1898 published the entire journal for the first time. As Draper sought to include the full journal in his manuscript, I transcribed the entire Walker text verbatim, supplementing it with Draper's notes to keep intact both Draper's vision for his book and the integrity of Walker's original narrative. For Colonel Johnston's well-annotated transcriptions of the complete journals of Dr. Thomas Walker and Christopher Gist, with copious information relative to routes, flora, fauna, topography, and geography encountered during both of these important western expeditions, see J. Stoddard Johnston,* First Explorations of Kentucky *(Louisville, KY: John P. Morton and Company, 1898); for a more recent look at Walker, see Alexander Canaday McLeod, "A Man for All Regions: Dr. Thomas Walker of Castle Hill,"* Filson Club History Quarterly *71 (1997): 169–201.*

61. For an account of the Society of Euphrata, a somewhat distinct sect from the Dunkers who first emigrated from Germany to Pennsylvania in 1719, see Hazard's *Register,* vol. xv, or Day's *Pennsylvania,* 413. Colonel Buchanan, in his MS. Journal, speaks of meeting in October 1745 two of these Ephrata brethren somewhere near the head of Roanoke River.

62. On the 18th of June, 1755, Adam Stalnaker, Mrs. Stalnaker, and three other persons were killed by the Indians on Holston, and Samuel Haydon and Samuel Stalnaker made prisoners, but the latter soon effected his escape. He is subsequently spoken of as Captain Stalnaker and his residence became a prominent frontier station.—MS. Preston Papers.

63. This was Clinch Mountain, in Hawkins County, East Tennessee. A vein of grey and variegated marble extends along the north side of the mountain for fifty miles.

64. This shows a great error in Haywood's *History of Tennessee,* p. 32, where it is stated that in 1761 a party of Virginia hunters passed into Powell's Valley. "They named Clinch River and Clinch Mountain," says Haywood, "from the following circumstance. An Irishman was one of the company; in crossing the river, he fell from the raft into it and cried out *clinch me! clinch me!—*meaning *lay hold of me.* The rest of the company, unused to the phrase, amused themselves at the expense of the poor Irishman, and called the river Clinch." In Popple's map of 1733, Bellin's in Charlevoix, of 1744, and Dr. Amville's, improved by Bolton, in 1752, it is called Pelasippi River; and on the map prefixed to Washington's Journal, 1754, it is given as [*wi*].

65. TFB: *Here Draper speculates on the second sheave of missing pages from the Walker journal, spanning from April 11, 1749, to the last part of the April 19 entry:*

Here the record, for nearly nine days, is unfortunately missing, during which period Dr. Walker and party travelled [in] nearly a western direction over Powell's Mountain to Powell's River, which, with the beautiful valley bearing that appellation, were doubtless named on that occasion for Ambrose Powell. (Haywood informs us that the same party of hunters who, he says, gave name to the Clinch River and mountain in 1761, seeing the name of Ambrose Powell inscribed on a tree near the mouth of Walden's Creek on Powell's River, gave his name to the river, mountain, and valley, which they have ever since retained.) Pursuing their course down Powell's Valley, they came to the remarkable depression in the rocky chain of mountains on their right; and ascending to the summit of the gap, where flowed a fine, cool spring, Dr. Walker and his companions, having a little rum remaining, drank to health of the famous duke of Cumberland, who was then conspicuous for having four years before suppressed the Scotch rebellion which had broken out in favor of "Prince Charlie," the Pretender, and bestowed the duke's name upon the mountain and gap, and also upon the river a little distance to the northward, which they soon reached. (The bestowal of this name at that time upon the mountain, gap, and river all in the honor of the duke of Cumberland is proved by Walker's affidavit referred to by Judge Hall; the statement of Dr. Walker to Isaac Shelby and John Brown; and the declaration of William Tomlinson, one of Walker's party, to the late Daniel Bryan and the late Col. Cave Johnson of Kentucky, who communicated this fact to the author. The printed authorities of Winterbotham and Marshall also fully corroborate this statement. The incident of drinking [to] the duke's health is given on the authority of the late worthy pioneer Col. William Martin of Tennessee.)

(Before the conferring of these new names, Cumberland Mountain, according to Lewis Evans, was known as the Ouasioto and the river as the Shawanoe River. The earliest map extant upon which the name of Cumberland is given to that stream is that prefixed to Washington's Journal, published in 1754. On Mitchell's, Ottens'[?], and other maps, in and after 1755 it is inevitably designated by the name of Cumberland River.)

A mile or two from Cumberland Gap, on a beech tree on the bank of Yellow Creek, Ambrose Powell, as already mentioned, cut his name and the year 1750, and others of the party there carved their initials. ("I saw," says Daniel Bryan, "the initials of the names of Dr. Walker, Ambrose Powell, and party, and a date, cut in the bark of a beech tree on the bank of Yellow Creek, as I passed the tree in the year 1777; but I do not remember the date.") Through Cumberland Gap passed the *Warrior's Path,* leading from the Shawanoe towns in the Ohio country to the Cherokee settlements, which our explorers followed by Yellow Creek to the Old Ford of Cumberland. As Dr. Walker alludes to Clover Creek in his Journal, as will presently be seen, and as the general course of the upper part of the Cumberland River is correctly laid down on the map prefixed to the *Journal of Washington's Tour,* published in 1754, and the name bestowed upon this and other streams by Dr. Walker for the first time given, as well as *"Walker's Settlement"* noted, rendering it pretty certain that the doctor furnished some of the materials used in the construction of the portion of the map; it is therefore highly probable that Dr. Walker and his companions pursued up the river as far at least as the mouth of the Clover Fork, something over thirty miles above the Old Ford, and returned again, and it may be that Dr. Walker gave the name of Clover Creek to what is now known as Yellow Creek. Dr. Walker's Journal, which we shall now resume, re-commences at a point some ten or twelve miles north-west of the Ford and a short distance south of the Cumberland River; and it evidently begins by an allusion to some lick.

TFB: *Here Draper resumes the Narrative with Walker's April 19, 1749, entry.*

66. The extent of this reconnoitering trip of Walker's was probably the southern bank of Laurel River, in Whitley County, Kentucky. Dr. Walker informed the late Hon. John Brown that he went as far as Laurel River, as the MS. notes of Mann Butler's conversations with Mr. Brown show. The point where Walker left the Cumberland was at the Swan Pond, about six miles below Barboursville, Kentucky, and the stream on which he and his companions camped, twelve miles from the river, was unquestionably near the head of one of the forks of Indian Creek, which unites with the Cumberland something like two miles below the Swan Pond. What Dr. Walker denominates Rocky Creek, which he followed southwardly to the Cumberland, is now known as Young's Creek, the mouth of which is about five miles in a direct course from Williamsburg, the county town of Whitley County, or ten or twelve miles following the meanderings of the river. We are indebted to the courtesies of Richard Herndon, Esq., of Barboursville, Kentucky, for a drawing of the peninsula at the mouth of Young's Creek and some facts with reference to that locality. The creek runs within thirty or forty feet of the river and then takes a turn and forms the peninsula, while Walker says it went within forty yards of the river before turning—very likely the river bank has been considerably encroached on since that day—over a hundred years ago. The area embraced in the peninsula is supposed to contain from fifteen to twenty acres, eleven of which are under cultivation, the rest swampy woodland. At an early day, it was covered with a dense cane-brake, which doubtless led to a slight over-estimate on the part of Dr. Walker as to the number of acres. The river here, as Dr. Walker states, is fully a hundred and fifty yards wide. Young's Creek has a sandy bottom for some eight hundred yards above its mouth and above is remarkably rocky.

67. Now Watt's Creek.

68. Big Poplar Creek.

69. This round hill, writes Mr. Richard Herndon, still stands, and though it has been in cultivation a great many years, it is still about fifteen feet high. It is situated about a mile above the mouth of Meadow Creek, in the eastern part of Whitley County—and singularly enough, the stream still bears the name Dr. Walker bestowed upon it.

70. This was Walker's Settlement, noted on the map prefixed to the pamphlet edition of Washington's *Journal of His Tour to the Ohio,* first published at Williamsburg, Virginia, in 1754 and re-printed in London the same year, and also laid down on several maps which appeared in 1755 and after. That this interesting locality has at length been identified should be a matter of gratification to all true lovers of the early history of western exploration. Here the first cabin was erected and the first corn and peach stones planted in Kentucky. This memorable spot is a little over five miles below Barboursville on the northern bank of the Cumberland in Knox County, Kentucky, and three fourths of a mile above the Swan Pond. The pond is some two or three hundred yards from the river, and its size is very correctly given by Dr. Walker.

71. We can state upon the authority of Richard Herndon, Esq., of Barboursville that the Cumberland opposite to and above the Swan Pond "has a sandy bottom and high banks."

72. Going a little to the east of north from the Swan Pond, they must have struck Goose Creek, which forms the Red Bird Fork from the South Fork of Kentucky; they probably followed it some distance below the junction of Red Bird and Goose creeks, where it is fifty yards wide.

73. What Dr. Walker here calls Cave Gap has reference to Cumberland Ford, where the Cumberland seems to have forced its way through Pine Mountain, leaving cliffs on either side consisting of almost interminable heaps of limestone rising to the height of thirteen hundred feet. In the vicinity of these cliffs is a cave of considerable size.

74. Doubtless the Middle Fork of the Kentucky.

75. Probably the North Fork of the Kentucky. For some distance above their mouths, all the three forks of [the] Kentucky may be said to be fifty yards wide, the North Fork perhaps something more. The narrow coal-field of Eastern Kentucky, extending from the Ohio to the Cumberland River, crosses the three forks of the Kentucky River, which is an interesting landmark in tracing Dr. Walker's route.

76. What is here called Hughes River must have been, we think, Quicksand Creek, a large eastern tributary of the North Fork of the Kentucky. It could not have been so wide as fifty yards, though the preceding rains had most likely expanded it beyond its usual size, and it was most probably in the route for our travellers to cross it. Streams, in a wilderness region, are fuller than when the country becomes cleared up, when the sun and air absorb much of the moisture.

77. Licking was probably the stream Dr. Walker here calls Milley's River; it was, most likely, then swollen by the recent rains.

78. This was doubtless Paint Lick Creek, a small stream emptying into the West Fork of Sandy River from the west in what is now Johnson County, Kentucky. The late Samuel Plummer of Kentucky, who for sixty years was much engaged in the eastern portion of that state as a surveyor and who died about 1851, at the advanced age of about ninety-seven years, states in a MS. Narrative before us that about 1794 he was at the forks of Paint and Jenny creeks and there found

the name[s] of Walker and others cut on a beech tree at a salt spring in the forks of the two streams, and some four miles above the junction of Paint Lick Creek with Sandy. There was a date also coupled with the names, which Mr. Plummer thought was designed for 1754, the year of his birth, but probably he mistook the figure *4* for a cypher—as nearly forty years had elapsed since the names and date were inscribed on the tree. Near by was another tree, on which was rudely engraved a buffalo, with an Indian represented as pulling at its tail while another Indian was tomahawking the animal; also the picture of a crane with a gun going south, indicating that the party were under the leadership of the Crane, or belonged to the Crane totem, and there was also cut a moon and a half-moon, showing that the party had been out a month and a half and were still going southward and had killed a buffalo at the salt spring, which has long been known as Plummer's Lick. These trees were long since cut down for wood used in the manufacture of salt. This early discovery of Dr. Walker's name at this point furnishes us an interesting landmark in tracing his route.—MS. letters of S. Plummer and Estes Mars.

This was undoubtedly the West Fork of Sandy. On Evans' ancient map of 1755 and Pownall's of 1776, the upper part of Sandy is called *Frederick's* River.

79. This Louisa River of Dr. Walker's was unquestionably the main or East Fork of Sandy, sometimes called Tug Fork, and so Dr. Walker himself informed the late Hon. John Brown of Kentucky. On the map prefixed to Washington's Journal of 1754, the lower part of Sandy is laid down as *Louisa or Totteroy Creek,* and in Evans' and Mitchell's maps of 1755 it is called *Totteroy or Big Sandy Creek;* but the two main forks are not distinctly indicated on these early maps. From the vague knowledge of the several rivers in the middle and eastern part of Kentucky and the bordering region of Virginia, as variously given by the early explorers of the country, this name of Louisa was sometimes applied to one of the Forks of Coal River, oftener to the Kentucky River, and finally to the east branch of the West Fork of Sandy; and even to this day the West Fork itself is not infrequently spoken of by the people of that region as the *Louisa* or *Levisa* Fork of Sandy, and the thriving town of Louisa is located at the junction of the East and West forks.

In Peck's edition of Perkins' *Annals of the West,* it is said that Dr. Walker bestowed the name of Louisa in compliment to the duchess of Cumberland, the lady of the celebrated duke of Cumberland. But this is a mistake, for the "Bloody Duke" was never married and consequently had no duchess. The name was unquestionably given from Louisa County, Virginia, in which Dr. Walker resided, but the part in which he lived was ultimately attached to Albemarle; and Louisa County received its name in 1742 from one of the royal princesses of England.

80. Pigeon Creek, perhaps.

81. This branch was probably the stream (Island Creek) emptying into Guyandotte on the west, not far below Logan Court-House, Virginia. In connection with the loss of the tomahawk, we may mention the singular coincidence that in August 1845 a youth by the name of Stopher found a fine tomahawk, leather shot

pouch, the remains of a powder-horn, and an Indian pipe sticking under a rocky bank of Salt River at the mouth of a small drain on the west side about two or three hundred yards below the mouth of the Harrodsburg branch, in Mercer County, Kentucky: On one side of the tomahawk is the name of *Thomas Walker,* in fine plain letters. This must have been the tomahawk lost in the swollen branch east of Big Sandy, where it was probably found at a subsequent period by some of the Western Indians, who in after years, in their attacks on Harrodsburg, left this interesting memorial in the neighborhood, and which is still preserved. — MS. letters of the late Gen. Robert B. McAfee; also his sketch of Boone in *Cist's Miscellany,* ii:3.

82. Probably Guyandotte, near Logan Court-House, Virginia.

83. William Tomlinson, one of the party, related to Daniel Bryan that crossing some of the head branches of the Kentucky River over a poor and hilly country, they concluded there was no good country in the West, and then directed their course eastwardly, passing over the worst mountains and laurel thickets in the world, having to cut the laurel with their tomahawks in order to pass through. — Bryan's MS. Statement.

84. TFB: *Draper's note illegible.*

85. TFB: *Draper's note illegible.*

86. Probably Cherry Pond Mountain, between the heads of Guyandotte and Coal rivers.

87. Most likely the head of Big Coal.

88. Perhaps Piney Creek of Kenhawa.

89. TFB: *Draper mistakenly transcribed* shirted *as* shifted. *This is an antiquated term meaning that the men bathed and changed into clean clothes.*

90. Of this noble band of adventurers, it would be gratifying if sketches of all could be given. A full notice of Dr. Walker may be found in the Appendix. Of Ambrose Powell, whose memory alone is perpetuated by the mountain valley and river bearing his name, nothing beyond what is stated in Dr. Walker's journal is known. Colby Chew was an ensign in the French and Indian War, and stationed at Patterson's Fort, on the waters of the South Branch of the Potomac, in which region in April 1758 some mischief was done, as was supposed, by two Indians, when Ensign Chew was sent in pursuit at the head of a party of men, who at length overtaking them at their camp beyond the North Mountain, fired upon them, killing one and mortally wounding the other. Both turned out to be well-known white men dressed and painted in Indian style, who had thus disguised themselves the more successfully to plunder and injure their neighbors. Ensign Chew was much commended for his spirit and enterprise. He probably served on Forbes' campaign and doubtless performed other services during that war. Allusion is made to him by Col. Thomas Lewis of Virginia in a letter among the Preston Papers as having been engaged in surveying lands on the Kentucky River prior to the year 1779—sometime, probably, from 1773 to 1775. Nothing more is known concerning him.

Henry Lawless was killed by the Indians on Jackson's River in West Virginia on the 14th of May, 1757. William Tomlinson lived in Orange County, Virginia, where he raised a family of nine children, and several of his sons served in the Revolutionary War and during the Indian troubles in Kentucky. Visiting Kentucky in the spring of 1779, Mr. Tomlinson removed his family there in the ensuing autumn and settled at Bryan's Station, where, at the memorable attack in August 1782, the old gentleman was the first person at whom the Indians fired. After the Indian War, he settled about three miles from Lexington, Kentucky, where he died at an advanced age, about the year 1802, having been many years a worthy member of the Baptist denomination.

The name of Dr. Walker's other companion, we infer, was Hughes, as that name was bestowed upon one of the rivers which they passed; and perhaps his first name was Frederick, as that name was given to another stream. This name, however, might have been bestowed in honor of Frederick the Great of Prussia, who was then held in high esteem by the English. There was a man named Hughes, an early explorer of Kentucky and Tennessee in 1771, mentioned in the work of Judge Haywood.

91. This narrative of Gist's tour is taken from his journal, furnished to Col. George Mercer, the agent of the Ohio Company, and presented to Gov. Thomas Pownall, who has inserted it entire in the appendix to his *Topographical Description of North America, with Evans' Map and Analysis Improved, Quarto, London, 1776.*

Gist was present at the treaty of Logstown, June 13th, 1752, attending to the interests of the Ohio Company, and was shortly after appointed their surveyor. The Indians agreeing at that treaty not to molest any settlements that might be made on the south-east side of the Ohio, Gist built a cabin and commenced a settlement at a place since called Mount Braddock on Gist's Run, Fayette County, Pennsylvania, and induced eleven other families to settle around him on lands which it was supposed would come within the limits of the company's grant. The next year he was the chosen companion of Washington on his perilous mission to the French garrisons at Le Boeuf and Venango; and during the ensuing French and Indian War, he held the rank of captain and acted as agent for Indian Affairs for the colony of Virginia, for the tribes in the English interest. In this service he met with great embarrassments and perplexities. He was a man of great integrity, perseverance, and fortitude, possessing more than common intelligence, and proving himself eminently useful to Washington on repeated occasions during his movements on the frontiers. He died at his residence in Fayette County, Pennsylvania, about the commencement of the Revolutionary War, leaving an only son, Thomas Gist.

92. In Pownall's *Topographical Description,* extracts are given from the journal of Gist's second tour down the Ohio, but the date there mentioned is 1761— probably a typographical error, as Sparks, who made an examination of the manuscript papers of the Ohio Company, gives that of 1751.

93. Stuart's *Indian Wars of West Virginia;* Leigh's *Revised Code,* ii:347.

94. *Maryland Gazette,* November 9th and December 7th, 1752; *French Policy Defeated,* London, 1755, p. 37; *Colonial Records of Pennsylvania,* v:599, 600; Bancroft, iv:94–95.

95. *Pennsylvania Colonial Records,* v:626–628, 643, 663, 664; *Maryland Gazette,* May 17, 1753, August 22, 1754; *French Policy Defeated,* 38; Rupp's *History of Dauphin, Cumberland, and etc.,* 67. Lewis Evans acknowledged his indebtedness to Col. Alexander Lowry and Alexander Maginty for information used in the preparation of his early map of the West. Lowry was a native of Scotland and early settled in Lancaster County, Pennsylvania, and was long engaged in the Indian trade; was a pilot for Colonel Bouquet's Indian campaigns of 1764, [and] he frequently represented his county in the Legislature; was a militia colonel during the Revolution, taking part in the battle of Brandywine; was subsequently a county judge in Donegal and died in that county in January 1805 at an advanced age. Rough in his intercourse with his fellow men, he was kind-hearted and patriotic.

96. *Maryland Gazette,* May 17, 1753.

97. James McBride was a brother to Capt. William McBride, an early and meritorious settler of Kentucky who was slain at the battle of the Blue Licks and whose son of the same name, who served under Harmar, St. Clair, and Wayne, died in Woodford County, Kentucky, in the summer of 1844 at about the age of seventy-six years.

98. Rafinesque's *Ancient Annals of Kentucky,* prefixed to Marshall's *History* of that state, published in 1824. Though Rafinesque may be set-down generally as visionary and unreliable, yet in this instance full credit may be awarded him, as it appeared from his *Life and Travels,* published in 1836, that in the years 1822 and 1823 he thrice visited the venerable Gov. Isaac Shelby, from whom he evidently learned the date of Walker's first trip of 1750 and *for the first time* gave the date of that event correctly in print; and doubtless from the same source derived these meagre facts of Walker's second trip to Kentucky. It will be borne in mind that Shelby was one of Walker's party in 1779–'80 in running the Virginia and North Carolina western extension boundary line. Though the year 1760 was one of war with the Cherokees, who that summer beleaguered and took Fort Loudon, and Dr. Walker was then commissary to the Virginia troops, yet as the Virginia forces under Colonel Byrd had advanced towards the head of the Holston and were inactive, it is not improbable that Dr. Walker may have taken the occasion to strike off northwestwardly with a party in search of a better country than he had found on his former trip of exploration. The Indian tribes north-west of the Ohio were then at peace, and hence he had nothing to fear from that quarter.

99. Ramsey's *History of Tennessee,* 67; MS. letter of Dr. Ramsey; conversations of the author with various individuals of East Tennessee in 1843 and 1844. TFB: *Whether this or any other hunk of tree bark carved "D. Boon." is the real thing is doubtful, especially since Boone always spelled his name with an "e" and such a "relic" could so easily be faked. Most such "artifacts" are indeed*

spurious, and some intentionally so. Alleged "D. Boon." guns, knives, powder-horns, and other items continue to surface and fetch high prices. See Joe Nickell, *"D. Boone Riddles," in* Ambrose Bierce Is Missing and Other Historical Mysteries *(Lexington: University of Kentucky Press, 1992): 72–93.*

100. Haywood's *Civil History of Tennessee,* 33, 34.

101. Haywood's *Aboriginal History of Tennessee,* 57.

102. Rondthaler's *Life of Heckewelder.*

103. MS. statement of Hon. Robert Wickliffe, Sr., of Kentucky, who knew Jordan well but received the most of this narrative from William Stone, who had it direct from Jordan. Mr. Wickliffe attests to the truthfulness of both Jordan and Stone.

104. Haywood's *History of Tennessee,* 35. This Blevins' hunt may well be questioned, as Haywood says in the same connection that Daniel Boone met them on their hunting tour, informing them that he was engaged in behalf of Henderson and Company to explore the country. Boone certainly made no such exploration.

105. Spark's "Life of General Lee," *American Biography,* xviii:19, 20.

106. MS. New York Paris Documents, xvii: no. 43; *Pennsylvania Gazette,* September 26, 1765.

107. Smith's Narrative; Haywood's *Tennessee,* 77; Pamphlet, *Sketch of Tennessee,* 1810, p. 41.

108. Morse's *Geography,* London quarto ed., 1794, 150; Boston ed., 1805, i [*wi*]; MS. letter of Baynton, Wharton, and Morgan to John Irvin, their agent at Fort Pitt, September 21, 1766.

109. Letter of Patrick Henry, Jr., Louisa, June 10, 1767, to Capt. William Fleming, Augusta County, Virginia, in the *MS. Fleming Papers.*

110. Collins' *Kentucky,* 399; Chief Justice Robertson's Kentucky Address, 1843, p. 9; MS. letter of Hon. Richard Apperson, Mt. Sterling, Kentucky.

111. Spark's *Washington,* ii:346–387; "English Discoveries in the Ohio Valley," by James H. Perkins, in the *North American Review,* July, 1839; also in Perkins' *Annals of the West,* 1st edition, 110; 2nd edition, revised by the Reverend Dr. Peck, 131.

112. MS. notes of conversations with the late venerable William Harrod of Bracken County, Kentucky, son of Capt. William Harrod; MS. letter of G. W. Stoner, son of Michael Stoner, June 24, 1845; Haywood's *Tennessee,* 75. It many be added that Stoner soon found his way back to the frontiers of Virginia, and Lindsay also, in due time, returned to the border settlements and in after years became an early and prominent settler in the Cumberland country. Harrod remained in the West, devoting himself to hunting and trapping, taking buffalo meat to New Orleans to supply the garrison there, and thus continued to employ himself till the spring of 1780, when he was treacherously killed at the mouth of the Tennessee by an Indian hired to commit the deed by a French trader at Kaskaskia, whose inimical conduct towards the American cause led to his imprisonment and the confiscation of his goods. This had been executed by Capt. William Harrod of Clark's regiment, which eventuated in the trader's wrecking his vengeance on the captain's brother, the old hunter of the West.

113. Washington's Diary of 1770; Spark's *Washington,* ii:532, 533. As Baynton, Wharton, and Morgan were driving a large trade between Fort Pitt and the Illinois country in 1766–'67, it is presumable, as Connolly also visited Illinois, that he went at that period in some of the boats in their employ.

114. MS. statement of the venerable Hon. Robert Wickliffe, who knew Knox well; MS. notes of Mann Butler's conversations in 1833 with the late Hon. John Brown of Frankfort; statement of Mrs. Mary L. Smith, daughter of Gen. Benjamin Logan, whose widow became the wife of Colonel Knox; sketches of the late Col. Nathaniel Hart of Woodford County, Kentucky.

115. Haywood, 36, 37; MS. letters of Col. George Christian of Tennessee and Col. Isaac C. Anderson of Virginia, sons of Gilbert Christian and John Anderson, two of this party of explorers whose careers as prominent leaders in the early settlement of East Tennessee will be more appropriately noticed in the forthcoming *Life of Gen. John Sevier,* by the author of this volume.

TFB: *As with of his proposed works, Draper never got around to writing* Life of Gen. John Sevier.

116. *Plain Facts,* Philadelphia, 1781, 69; Butler's *Kentucky,* 1st edition, 381; 2nd edition, 475; Perkins' *Annals,* 1st edition, 108; 2nd edition, 130.

117. MS. statement of the late Col. William Martin of Tennessee, eldest son of Joseph Martin, who had also preserved a copy of the early Powell's Valley letter; MS. narrative of the late Maj. John Redd of Henry County, Virginia, who was one of Martin's party in re-possessing his Powell's Valley settlement. This Joseph Martin was a distinguished border pioneer who subsequently rose to the rank of a general and of whom full and interesting materials have been collected for a memoir and will in due time be embodied in a volume.

It may here be added that Martin and his party failed eventually in securing their twenty-one thousand acre grant, and doubtless because of the inability of the Loyal Company to maintain their title. Among the Virginia archives are the manuscript records of the Virginia commissioners of the Washington District, who in 1781 granted preemptions to Joseph and Brice Martin and Mordecai Hoard for having made settlements, respectively, on Martin's Creek, Beaver Dam Springs, and Indian Creek in Powell's Valley in the year 1769.

EDITOR'S NOTES: INTRODUCTION

a. Francisco de Garay, governor of Jamaica, who in 1518 outfitted four ships commanded by Alonso de Pineda to explore and map the entire contours of the Gulf of Mexico.

b. In 1493 Juan Ponce de León sailed on Columbus' second voyage. He was afterward governor of Puerto Rico and in 1513 became the first European to visit Florida. While exploring Florida's Gulf side in 1521, he was mortally wounded in a skirmish with Calusas warriors and died days later in Cuba.

c. Francisco Fernandez de Córdova explored the Yucatán and Florida in 1517.

d. In 1523 the Spanish Crown granted Lucas Vasquez de Ayllón a license to establish a permanent New World colony. After claiming the coasts of Florida, Georgia, and South Carolina for Charles V, in 1526 he founded the town of San Miguel de Gualdape. Located on Sapelo Sound on the coast of present-day Georgia, this was the first Spanish settlement in what became the United States.

e. George Bancroft (1800–91), transcendental Democrat, New England progressive historian, and author of *History of the United States.*

f. *Weroance* is an antiquated term meaning an Indian chief of Virginia or Maryland.

g. In May 1673 Maj. Gen. Abraham Wood sent James Needham and Gabriel Arthur to the Cherokee town of Chota (once located in what is now Monroe County, Tennessee) to establish trade with the Indians. An Occaneechi warrior killed Needham that September.

h. Eastern Abenaki (meaning "dawn land people") Indians were Algonquian speakers whose territory at the time of Anglo contact spanned much of present-day Maine. The Western Abenaki inhabited what is now New Hampshire.

i. *Loups* originally was the French term for the Mahicans, Algonquians of the Hudson Valley who by 1736 were known as the Stockbridge. The few Mahicans that remain now live on a small reservation in Wisconsin.

j. Dr. John Mitchell was an English cartographer employed by Lord Halifax in 1750 to map the North American colonies.

k. A corvette was a sailing warship smaller than a frigate but larger than a sloop and armed with one tier of guns.

l. Shawanoes, one of many antiquated variant spellings of Shawnee (meaning "person of the south"), were Algonquian-speaking Woodland Indians of the Ohio Valley and staunch defenders of their Middle Ground homeland. Other spellings include Shawnese, Shawanos, Shanwans, Shawanah, and Chaouanons.

m. Lewis Evans was another cartographer loyal to the Crown of George II and a contemporary of Dr. John Mitchell. Dr. Benjamin Franklin of Philadelphia in 1755 first published Evans' map of Kentucky.

n. Formed in 1748 by prominent English Virginians, the Ohio Company sought to explore the trans-Allegheny region, trade with Indians, and acquire land. In 1792 the firm forfeited its 200,000 Kentucky acres with that commonwealth's formation.

o. Irishman George Croghan came to America in 1741 and by 1744 became a licensed Indian trader in Pennsylvania. By the mid-1740s he was leading strings of packhorses and teams of traders into the lower Ohio Valley. In 1752 one of his men, John Findlay, established a trading post in Kentucky at Es-kip-pa-ki-thi-ki (in present-day Clark County) and in 1769 helped lead Daniel Boone to the Bluegrass region. Croghan exerted a strong English influence among the Indians, played a pivotal role as a mediator, and proved hostile to Americans during the Revolution. He died in the 1780s.

p. Andrew Henry Montour, called "the half Indian," was an important man of mixed-blood parentage who assisted fur-trade and business entrepreneurs Conrad Weiser and George Croghan, and sided with the British during the French and Indian War (1755–63). He lived near Fort Pitt and died just prior to the Revolutionary War. A contemporary of Montour's left this striking portrait of him, ample testimony that this multilingual man's life, habits, and even dress were a blend of native and Anglo cultures:

> Andrew's cast of countenance is decidedly European, and had his face not been encircled with a broad band of paint, applied with bear's fat, I would certainly have taken him for one. He wore a brown broadcloth coat, a scarlet damasken lapel waistcoat, breeches, over which his shirt hung, a black cordovan neckerchief decked with silver bangles, shoes and stockings, and a hat. His ears were hung with pendants of brass and other wires plaited together, like the handle of a basket. He was very cordial; but on addressing him in French, he, to my surprise, replied in English.

For a biographical sketch of Andrew Montour, see Charles A. Hanna, *The Wilderness Trail,* 2 vols., 2nd ed. (Lewisburg, PA: Wennawoods Publishing, 1995), 1:223–46.

q. The now extinct Carolina parakeet, whose range once extended as far west as the Great Plains.

r. "Chippiways," or Ojibwa, a large tribe of Algonquian speakers that numbered about 20,000 in the seventeenth century and whose homeland core was the Great Lakes.

s. Ottawa were Algonquians living on Manitoulin Island and in the region of northern Michigan, where they remain today. During the French and Indian War, the Ottawa (of whom Pontiac was the most famous war leader) were allied to the French.

t. Twightwees, or Miami, were Ohio Algonquins whose onomatopoeic tribal name resembled the sandhill crane's strident call.

u. Mingo, or Black Minqua, were an independent Iroquois group living in Pennsylvania and Ohio. The group was composed of several tribes that by the early 1800s became known as the Seneca of Sandusky and later relocated to Oklahoma.

v. The Piankeshaw were one of the six Ohio-Illinois tribes that composed the Miami of the Wabash and Upper Maumee. Also spelled Piankashaw or Peanghichia.

w. John Findlay, a licensed Indian trader and one of George Croghan's men, is an obscure frontier figure. After helping Boone enter Kentucky in 1769, the next year he fled to North Carolina, fearing Shawnee attack, and took up his old ways as a trader. By 1772 he vanished from history. Researchers spell his name variously as Finley, Finlay, Findley, and Findlay. Draper usually spelled it "Findley" but decided it should appear as "Findlay" in the published text.

x. The Caughnawaga were a Mohawk division that by the 1670s resided at Sault Saint Louis (Lachine Rapids) on the St. Lawrence.

y. Here and in other places, Draper used several asterisks to denote ellipses in the original text.

z. James Smith escaped from Indian capture in Montreal in 1759 and returned to his Pennsylvania home. After a brief career as a backwoods guerrilla fighter who dressed and trained his band of rangers Indian-style, he explored the Cumberland basin in 1766, fought in Lord Dunmore's War in 1774, and died in Kentucky in 1812. An articulate, mild-mannered soldier and woodsman who found much to appreciate about Indian life, Smith wrote a lucid memoir of his exploits, as well as a number of Christian tracts and anti-Shaker polemics. Draper elaborates on Smith's activities later in his Introduction.

aa. For more on Col. Arthur Campbell, see appendix v.

bb. On July 9, 1755, Maj. Gen. Edward Braddock, protégé of the Duke of Cumberland, the notorious "Butcher of Culloden," blindly led a force of 1,500 British regulars and American militiamen into a devastating defeat at the hands of 220 Frenchmen and 637 Indians near the forks of the Allegheny and Monongahela. Braddock was killed and only 538 of his men escaped injury.

cc. Brig. Gen. John Forbes came in Braddock's bloody wake and on November 25, 1758, seized control of Fort Duquesne's ruins from the French and renamed the site Pittsburgh.

dd. Col. Henry Bouquet, a Swiss mercenary, was one of George II's North American backwoods military leaders during the Seven Years' War. By his orders to give Indians as "gifts" blankets infected with smallpox, he became one of the first men in the annals of American history to use germ warfare. Bouquet also suggested that to save manpower, the Crown could "make use of the Spanish method to hunt Indians with English Dogs." His former strategy worked with devastatingly predictable results; there is no record that the British ever tried his latter suggestion.

ee. In the summer of 1760 Lt. Col. Archibald Montgomery and Maj. James Grant commanded an invading force of more than 1,300 New York Royal Highlanders and Scots, 300 rangers, 50 Catawba allies, and a dozen guides deep into the Lower Cherokee towns of northwestern South Carolina and northeastern Georgia, torching the towns of Estatoe, Toxaway, Qualatchee, and Conasatche. Montgomery's men killed 60 to 80 Indians and captured 40.

ff. After his and Montgomery's initial success at defeating the French-allied Lower Cherokee, in 1761 the imperious Maj. James Grant invaded the Middle Cherokee towns of southwestern North Carolina and southeastern Tennessee, burning fifteen villages and hundreds of acres of beans, corn, and squash. The Indians signed articles with Great Britain that October.

gg. Col. William Byrd III, a Virginian, served in the French and Indian War with Forbes during his 1758 campaign and in the North Carolina theater in 1760–61.

hh. Rumors of Jonathan Swift's silver mines are more than two centuries old. According to the legend, a certain Jonathan Swift claimed that he and some Frenchmen mined a rich silver vein in eastern Kentucky in the 1760s, but upon returning to the land fifteen years later, he was unable to find the site. Subsequent treasure hunters have not found it either, and most researchers believe the story false. No evidence exists of a Jonathan Swift—whose name recalls the author of *Gulliver's Travels,* one of Daniel Boone's favorite works—living in Kentucky as early as 1760. The germ of the tale is believed to be based upon a misinterpretation of an eighteenth-century Masonic parable.

ii. The McAfee brothers—Robert, James Jr., and George—along with their brothers-in-law James McCoun, Jr., and Samuel Adams, came to Kentucky in 1773, accompanying Capt. Thomas Bullitt's company of about forty men. On that trip, the McAfees briefly left Bullitt's party and hired Hancock Taylor to go with them to survey land near what are now Frankfort and Harrodsburg. They returned to Virginia that summer and in 1779 moved their families to Kentucky.

jj. For Robert Wickliffe, Appendix, see note gg.

kk. The Wea were one of the six divisions of the Miami whose villages were erected along that river. Also known as Ouiatanon, Oiatenon, Oua, and many other variations.

ll. For contemporary descriptions of bateaux and their construction, chapter 6, see note g.

mm. Concerning Pennsylvania trader and Indian agent George Morgan, chapter 13, see note b.

nn. George Washington speculated heavily in the lands encompassing the headwaters of the Ohio, Kenhawa, and Greenbrier, claiming by 1767 to own more than 32,000 prime acres of Indian country. Little wonder then that he had such a strong interest in the Far West and in driving native people from their homes in territory he claimed as his own.

oo. For Michael Stoner, see chapter 10, note d.

pp. For more on James Harrod, see chapter 13, note o.

qq. Besides buffalo tongue, Long Hunters, voyageurs, coureurs de bois, and most other frontiersmen relished buffalo marrow (usually from the shank bones) to the point of gluttony. Hunters roasted the shank bones an end at a time on coals before cracking them open with a belt ax to devour the steamed fat marrow. Hunters ate deer marrow (and tongues) too, but they preferred buffalo marrow.

rr. For more on frontiersman James Robertson, see chapter 16, note r.

CHAPTER 1

Daniel Boone's Ancestry.—Birth.—Childhood.—Boyish Anecdotes.

In May 1769, a little over eighty years ago—Daniel Boone, an obscure individual on the western confines of Carolina, started with an intrepid band of kindred spirits "to wander through the wilderness of America, in quest of the country of Kentucke." This, in his own expressive language, was the object he had in view,[a] and here commenced his great mission of western exploration and adventure. To Boone this passion was uncontrollable—but there was a Providence in it and if he did not see and feel it then, he fully realized and acknowledged it thereafter.[b]

From time immemorial, Kentucky—"the dark and bloody ground"—had been the scene of ruthless contention between different Indian claimants for the sovereignty of the soil. "It was truly a spell-bound land: and the spell continued until it was dissolved in blood."[1] "Yet it was beautiful enough to have stilled human passions."[2]

That fair land—the land of promise—then reposed in the quiet of its primeval beauty and grandeur. Its mellow, virgin soil was canopied with a lordly forest, here and there bestudded with patches of verdant cane and carpeted with a luxuriant growth of wild clover and pea-vine. The buffalo,[c] elk, bear, deer, and other wild game everywhere roamed in fearless security. It was the hunter's paradise. More than forty years thereafter in his hoary old age, Boone declared that "those fertile plains were unequaled on our earth, and laid the fairest claim to the description of the garden of God."[3] Through these rich plains passed the war-trail of the stealthy Indian; the century-beaten path of the buffalo led unerringly to the numerous licks and salt springs of the country. But in all this charming region, the habitation of a white man was no where visible; no ruthless axe had yet invaded this land of forests and green meads.

During the subsequent half dozen years, Kentucky was fully explored and permanent settlement commenced. Seventeen years more rolled away—years of toil, suffering, and border warfare—when in 1792 Kentucky became a member of the American Republic; and now in 1854 she numbers over a million of peaceful,

18. Hunters, speculators, and settlers saw Kentucky as the "New Eden." This idyllic scene of Dismal Creek's 190-foot-high cliffs in Grayson and Edmondson counties is from David Dale Owen's Report of the Geological Survey in Kentucky (1856). LITHOGRAPH BY ROBYN & CO., LOUISVILLE.

happy people.[d] In all this there is something wonderful. Our admiration only equals our astonishment. As a consequence, our curiosity is excited and eagerly do we inquire Who, under Providence, was this "humble instrument" ordained "to settle one of the fairest portions of the New World?"[4] Daniel Boone was no ordinary man, and this volume will aim to delineate, fully and faithfully, the origin and career of that celebrated pioneer of Kentucky.

Several persons bearing the name of Boone were among the earliest settlers of the British American colonies, nearly all of whom were from England and probably from the same original stock. Henry Boone—or DeBone, as it was originally written and hence indicative of its French origin—was one of about two hundred persons, chiefly English Catholics of considerable fortune and rank, who, with their inferior adherents, sailed from Cowes in the Isle of Wight the 22nd of November, 1633, in a large ship called The Ark and the Dove, accompanied by a pinnace, under the leadership of Leonard Calvert as governor; and after stopping at Barbados, St. Christopher's, and Old Point Comfort, sailed up the Potomac, and anchoring at the Indian town of Yoacomoco, and finally ascended the St. Mary's River near the close of March 1634, commenced the settlement of Maryland. Anywhere "religious liberty obtained a home, its only home in the wide world, at the humble village which bore the name of St. Mary's."[5]

The Boones of Maryland became extensive and early began to migrate—some to the eastern shore of that colony, while others found their way into New Jersey and Pennsylvania.[6] It is recorded in a newspaper of that day that Robert Boone, an honest and industrious planter, died of old age February 9th, 1759, at his plantation on the north side of the Severn near Annapolis, Maryland, on the very place where he was born in 1680, from which he never went thirty miles in his life. He left a widow to whom he was fifty-seven years united in marriage.[7]

Long anterior to the commencement of Penn's settlement of Pennsylvania, a little Swedish colony had found a quiet home along the banks of the Delaware. Among these early Swedish adventurers was Anders Bonde, whose name was subsequently Anglicized into Andros or Andrew Boon. He was a native of Sweden and settled on the Delaware in what is now Delaware County, Pennsylvania, as early as 1639 or 1640. All these Swedish pioneers professed the Lutheran faith and were noted for their piety and simple manners. When Andrew Boon had been fifty-four years in the country, he united with his Swedish neighbors in a letter of thanks to their friends in Sweden for having sent them a Christian minister and asked for two more, together with twelve Bibles, three sermon-books, some psalm-books, tracts, catechisms, and primers. They spoke of the richness and productiveness of the soil, their happy and contented condition, and added with pious simplicity: "Our wives and daughters employ themselves in spinning wool and flax, and many of them in weaving, so that we have great reason to thank the Almighty for his manifold mercies and benefits. God grant that we may also have good shepherds to feed us with his holy word and sacraments. We live also in peace and friendship with one another, and the Indians have not molested us for many years."[8] As early as 1685, reference is made to the "lands of Andros Boon and company," in now Delaware County, Pennsylvania,[9] and the names of Swan and Caure Boon occur among the ancient land records of Philadelphia County in 1707 and 1708, while those of Hance and Andrew Boon appear a few years later.[10] The name of Ralph Boon appears in the records of Bucks County as having entered in 1701 the mark of his cattle to record.[11] But between these Swedish Boons and the English Boone family who early settled in Pennsylvania and from whom the Kentucky pioneer descended, there could have been no ties of consanguinity.[12]

Thomas Boone, probably a native of England, was appointed royal governor of New Jersey in 1760 and was the following year transferred to the government of South Carolina, where he for some years served with much acceptance. "He had," says Dr. Hewit, "a good talent for business, and both knowledge and ability equal to the important trust"; and the colony prospered to an astonishing degree during his administration. In 1769, having returned to England, he was appointed one of his majesty's commissioners of customs and was still living at the outbreak of the Revolutionary War.[13]

In 1670 a little band of adventurers set sail from England and planted the first germ of the colony of South Carolina—proclaimed in advance "the beauty and envy of North America." The most of these colonists were members of the established church—the majority of whom, according to Archdale, were "pretended Churchmen"—"loose principled men," who seem to have had the chief control of public affairs. Among this class, as is inferable from the ancient historians Archdale and Oldmixan, was John Boon. Distinguished among the prominent citizens of the colony, he was in 1682 appointed by the Lord's Proprietaries one of a commission of three to decide all causes of complaint which had resulted in a rupture between the colonists and Westoe Indians; and the next year, Mr. Boon was a member of the Parliament of that colony and one of the commissioners for stating and passing public accounts.

About the year 1700 Joseph Boone was known as an enterprising merchant and planter of Colleton County, South Carolina. He was deputed in 1705 by the dissenters of that colony to proceed to England and lay before the House of Lords a petition for redress of religious grievances and disqualifications. Among the few "very handsome buildings" in Charleston mentioned by Oldmixon in 1708 was "Mr. Boone's"; and the same author speaks of "Boone's Island," a little below Charleston, which was at that time "well planted and inhabited." As early as 1704 there was a Nicholas Boone who kept a shop in Boston for the sale of the *Boston News-Letter;* and nine years later, a "Mr. Boon," perhaps the same person, is mentioned as residing in Boston.[14]

With these fragmentary notices of the early Boone emigration to the New World embracing such data as have come to our knowledge, we shall now proceed to speak more directly of the ancestry of Daniel Boone, "backwoodsman of Kentucky."

His earliest ancestor of whom there is any record was George Boone, a native of England, who had a son of the same name born in or near the city of Exeter, Devonshire, in the beautiful peninsula in the southwest of England between the British and English channels.[15] This second George Boone, who was a blacksmith by trade, was married to a Miss Sarah Uppey; he died at the age of sixty and she at eighty, and it is recorded of her that she "never had an aching bone or decayed tooth." Their son, George Boone, was born at the village of Stoak near the city of Exeter in 1666 and learned the trade of a weaver. He was united in marriage to Mary Maugridge, three years his junior, a native of Bradninch, eight miles from Exeter city, and daughter of John Maugridge and Mary, his wife, whose maiden name was Milton. They had nine children, all born in Bradninch, namely, George, Sarah, Squire, Mary, John, Joseph, Benjamin, James, and Samuel, all of whom, except John, were married and left numerous descendants.[16]

Squire Boone, the father of Col. Daniel Boone, the second son and third child of George and Mary Boone, "was born on the fourth day of the week, between eleven and twelve in the forenoon, on the 25th of November, 1696." Like his immediate progenitor, he seems to have learned the weaver's trade; and it will be seen in the sequel that his son Daniel honestly inherited his propensity for distant exploration and frequent change of residence. "A few years before" 1717—as the ancient *Boone Genealogy* has it—George, Sarah, and Squire Boone went to Pennsylvania at the insistence of their parents with a view to examine the country and learn by personal inspection the prospects and inducements for the permanent settlement of the family in that flourishing province. This exploratory visit, judging from the ages of the two brothers and their sister who made it, was somewhere about 1712 to 1714—when, on authority of Daniel Bryan, "Squire Boone was grown, but of small size."[17] Old George Boone and his good spouse, Mary, had embraced the faith of the Friends, or Quakers, and naturally enough turned their attention to Sir William Penn's inviting colony in the wilderness of America, where they would be forever exempt from the dread of such religious intolerance as they had unhappily witnessed in their disjointed times—for but a few years previously, the poor Quakers, simply for conscience' sake, "filled the prisons of the kingdom"; and about thirteen hundred of them, most of whom had been imprisoned several years, were liberated on a single occasion. The hope of bettering their own and children's condition in the New World, where a fee-simple in the soil was cheaply obtained, no doubt had also appropriated influence.

With a favorable report, George Boone the younger in due time returned to England, leaving Squire and Sarah in Pennsylvania. Preparations were now made

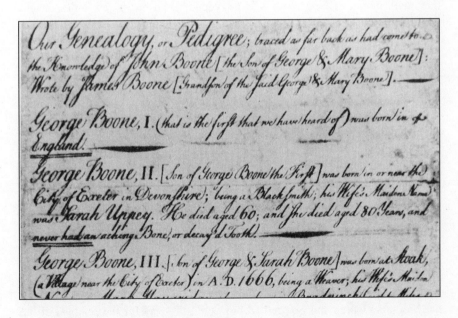

19. James Boone's chronology. STATE HISTORICAL SOCIETY OF WISCONSIN.

for the long-planned removal of George and Mary Boone with their children to the distant shores of America. With the broad Atlantic before them—hardships, risks, and dangers to be encountered—the dim, uncertain, shadowy future in the distance—the bitter parting of kindred, friends, and their loved native valley of the river Exe—all conspired to render such a removal at that day a herculean undertaking. But the old patriarch George Boone never for a moment hesitated or faltered in his purpose; and we may well suppose his good helpmate Mary warmly approved his dutiful intention upon which his heart was so firmly set; and peradventure, something whispered in their minds like the divine command to the patriarch Abraham, "Get thee out of thy country and from thy kindred, and go unto the land which I shall show thee."[e] Like faithful Abraham, they promptly obeyed, "and went out not knowing whither they went"; but the blessing of heaven went with them and their posterity.

The 17th of August, 1717, was the memorable day when George Boone and his family bid adieu to friends and home and left Bradninch, going about eighty miles by land to Bristol, where they took shipping and safely landed at Philadelphia on the 29th of the following September, according to the Old Style of reckoning time, or the 10th of October, according to the New.[f] They at first took up their abode in Abington, now Montgomery County, twelve or fourteen miles north of Philadelphia, celebrated at that day as the residence of Robert Fletcher, a noted public character and prominent member of the Society of Friends. This settlement was composed almost entirely of Quakers.

Remaining here but a brief period, George Boone and family removed to the small hamlet of North Wales in Gwynedd Township, a few miles distant from Abington in a northwesterly direction. On the 31st of the 10th month— October— 1717, George Boone, Sr., produced to the Gwynedd Meeting "a certificate of his good life and conversation from the Monthly Meeting at Collumpton, Devonshire, England, which was read and well-received."[18] This township of Gwynedd, as its name indicates, was originally settled by Welsh emigrants, two only of whom were Quakers, the rest churchmen.[19] But a short period after the first settlement in 1698, all these churchmen united with the Friends and in 1700 erected a log meeting-house, which in 1712 gave place to a stone edifice.

As a pleasing instance of the simplicity alike of the times and people, it may be mentioned that when Sir William Penn about the year 1700 visited his friend Thomas Evans in Gwynedd, the dwelling of the latter was constructed of barked and hewn logs—a refinement far surpassing the common lot of those around him. At the close of the day, when Penn had ascended the steps on the outside to retire to his bed-chamber, Hugh Evans, a lad of twelve years, curious to see so distinguished a guest, went up afterwards to peep through the apertures between the logs and saw the pious founder of Pennsylvania on his bended knees giving audible "thanks to God for such a peaceful and excellent shelter in the wilderness."[20]

At this period we find Sarah Boone married—the same heroic girl who with her brothers George and Squire had pioneered the way for the removal of the family to America. Her husband's name was probably Jacob Stoner, a German of much energy of character who settled himself and young wife in Oley Township, then in Philadelphia County, but now within the limits of Berks.[21] The settlement of his daughter there induced George Boone to visit Oley, and he was so well pleased with the country that he took out a warrant in 1718 for four hundred acres of land and probably removed his family there near the close of the following year, as the ancient *Boone Genealogy* states that he resided in North Wales "about two years."[22] He may not, however, have removed there quite so early. In the subsequent divisions of Oley, the township of Exeter was formed—so named from commemoration of Exeter, England, from near which George Boone came; and it was in that part of Oley which now forms Exeter that he settled, and there he lived to a good old age, surveying with calm delight the increase and prosperity of his worthy descendants around him.[23]

Among his worthy neighbors was Arthur Lee, a native of England and also a member of the peaceful Society of Friends. Some of their nearest neighbors were Indians, who delighted to have such upright, benevolent men in their country. Some of these friendly Indians, having received intelligence that a hostile tribe was about making incursions into the settlements of the whites, came by night, painted and equipped for war, and surrounded Lee's dwelling. This warlike attitude of the Indians alarmed some of the inmates of the house, especially the younger portion of them, who to escape for life made efforts to get out of the house but were prevented by the Indians, who assured them that their object was to protect, not injure them. Learning from Mr. Lee that the report touching the hostile Indians was unfounded, they manifested their joy by firing their guns in the air with a hearty shout of exultation and returned to their homes instead of proceeding against their red brethren as had been their intention. Neither Lee nor Boone were ever molested by the Indians.[24]

The cabin which George Boone erected when he first settled in the country was still pointed out within the last half century, which his son James occupied, preferring himself to remain in his log cabin as long as he lived. The house erected in 1733 is yet in use, and the date may be seen on the corner next to the garden; its present worthy occupant is John Boone, a grandson of James and a great-grandson of George Boone, the old patriarch of the family.[25] George Boone's faithful companion, Mary, died on the 2nd of February, 1740 [or 1741], aged 72 years, and he breathed his last July 27th, 1744, at the age of 78 years, and both were interred in the Friends' burial ground in Exeter. When he died, he left eight children, fifty-two grandchildren, and ten great-grandchildren—in all, seventy, "being as many persons," quaintly adds the *Boone Genealogy,* "as the house of Jacob which came into Egypt."[g]

Among the early Welsh settlers in Gwynedd, who were called ancient Britons, was the Morgan family, from whom descended the celebrated Gen. Daniel Morgan[h] of the Revolution. To Sarah, daughter of John Morgan, a Welsh Quaker, Squire Boone paid his addresses and succeeded in gaining the promise of her hand in marriage.[26] Both were raised in the Quaker faith and thus the proposed union was within the pale of the Society of Friends. The allowing of marriage belongs to the Monthly Meetings. Those who contemplate this relation appear together and propose their intention to the Meeting and, if not attended by their parents or guardians, produce a written certificate properly attested giving their consent. The Meeting then appoints a committee to inquire whether they be clear of other matrimonial engagements; and if, at a subsequent meeting to which the parties also come and declare the continuance of their intention, no objections be reported, they have the Meeting's consent to solemnize their intended marriage. The final ceremony takes place in a public meeting for worship towards the close of which the parties stand up and solemnly take each other for husband and wife. A certificate of the proceedings is then publicly read and signed by the parties and afterwards by the relations and others as witnesses and all entered upon the church record.[27]

Such was the simple ceremony, performed at the Gwynedd Meeting House, which conjugally united Squire Boone and Sarah Morgan. On the 6th day of May, 1720, they declared in Gwynedd Meeting their intention of marriage, to which their parents' consent was given, and at the same time, the old patriarch George Boone, Sr., "openly acknowledged in this Meeting his forwardness in giving his consent to John Webb to keep company with his daughter Mary in order to marry—contrary to the established order amongst us." Whereupon John Webb and Mary Boone formally declared their intention and were married on the 13th of July ensuing. Ten days later, on the 23rd of July, Squire Boone, father and brother of the groom, and John Webb were witnesses.[28] But little has been handed down to us relative to the personal appearance of the newly married couple. According to the manuscript statement of Daniel Bryan, who remembered them both very well, "Squire Boone was a man of rather small stature, fair complexion, red hair and grey eyes; while his wife was a woman something over the common size, strong and active, with black hair and eyes, and raised in the Quaker order." We may pretty safely conclude that Squire Boone descended from Teutonic or Anglo-Saxon ancestry and his wife from the Welsh or ancient Britons, who are traced to Celtic origin and probably through the Cimbri of Jutland.[29] From such an union could only be anticipated a brave, honest, hardy, hospitable, and enterprising progeny—jealous of their liberties and remarkable for their sincerity and fidelity.

Near the close of the year 1730, Squire Boone obtained from Ralph Asheton, one of the members of the Pennsylvania Council, a grant for 250 acres of land situated in Oley, now Exeter or Owatin Creek, about a mile above its confluence with the Monackasy [Monocacy], and about three and a half miles from the junction of the latter stream with the Schuylkill. It is a level tract of red shale land well adapted to grazing purposes, located about eight miles southeast of the present city of Reading and a mile and a half from Exeter Meeting-house.[30] Here Squire Boone removed with his wife and four children, probably early in 1731, and settled down on land of his own in the immediate neighborhood of his parents, the Webbs, and Stovers. We may pretty safely conclude that the period of between ten and eleven years that he resided in Gwynedd after his marriage was devoted in part to weaving and in part to farming—most likely on tenanted land. By industry and economy, a sufficiency of means had been gradually accumulated to purchase a home in Oley, where lands were yet held at moderate prices.

With the help of relatives and friendly Quaker neighbors, a log cabin was speedily erected, a patch of ground cleared and fenced, and the newcomers heartily welcomed to the settlement and snugly domiciled in their new home on Owatin. An allusion to the primitive mode of living in the neighboring county of Bucks at the period under consideration is equally applicable to the Oley region and will appropriately exhibit the unaffected simplicity which Squire Boone and family practiced in common with others. The women were always industrious, generally clothing their families by their own handicraft in spinning and weaving the necessary linen and woolen apparel. Bread, milk, and pie usually composed the frugal morning repast; good pork or bacon and a wheat-flour pudding or dumplings with butter and molasses served for dinner; while mush or hominy with milk, butter, and honey formed the simple evening meal. Chocolate was only occasionally procured and sweetened with maple sugar; and almost every table was bountifully spread with venison and wild turkies in their season. Only a few of the wealthiest farmers had wagons and carts [which] were chiefly in use for going to market.[31]

Amid these simple border customs and unpretending people, Daniel Boone was ushered into being.[32] The fourth son and sixth child of Squire and Sarah Boone, he was born in Oley, afterwards Exeter Township, then Philadelphia, now Berks County, Pennsylvania, the 22nd of October, Old Style, or the 2nd of November, New Style, 1734.[33] He was probably named after Daniel Boone, a distinguished Dutch painter whose pieces are valuable, who died in London in 1698 and who may have been known or distantly related to the family.

Upon Scull's large map of Pennsylvania, published in 1770, "Boone's Mill" is laid down at the crossing of the great public road from Philadelphia to Tulpehocken, over Monackasy Creek in Exeter; and just east of the creek on the north of the road is indicated the locality of the Exeter Quaker meeting-house. This was the Boone settlement in the lovely and picturesque valley of the Schuylkill in which young Boone was born and reared, and with this border region all his youthful associations were connected.

From his infancy, Daniel Boone seems to have possessed in an unusual degree those amiable traits of character that won for him the love and esteem of all his acquaintances. His uncle, John Webb, residing in the same region, who had three little sons and a daughter, was fond of taking his little nephew while yet very young home with him and keeping and petting him for weeks together.[34]

While Daniel was still a very small boy, the small-pox was brought into the neighborhood. To prevent the exposure of her children to this much dreaded and loathsome disease, Mrs. Boone kept them pretty closely confined at home. This

20. *This stone farmhouse, photographed in the late 1800s in Reading, Pennsylvania, stands where the log cabin marking Daniel Boone's birthplace once stood.* STATE HISTORICAL SOCIETY OF WISCONSIN.

severe restraint becoming intolerably irksome to little Daniel and his next older sister, Elizabeth, they talked the matter over in some quiet corner and arrived at the conclusion that their only hope of speedy relief was to take the disease, and once over it, they would again be free to go where and associate with whom they pleased. So after retiring to bed of an evening, they slyly got up and stole off undiscovered to a neighbor's, where they laid down beside a person having the offensive disorder; and returning home with a sort of secret triumph, they quietly crept into their beds as though nothing had happened. Discovering in due time the premonitory symptoms, and suspecting full well to what they would lead, the good Mrs. Boone, looking her little son full in the face, said calmly, "Now Daniel, I want thee to tell thy mother the whole truth." This he did, with childlike simplicity and without the least reserve. "Thee naughty little gorrel,"[i] said his mother chidingly, "why did thee not tell me before, so that I could have had thee better prepared?" But Daniel, as did the other children, got through the disease very easily and secured the freedom for which even in tender years he so much longed and which he so dearly enjoyed.

The sight of Indians must have been among his earliest recollections. They often visited the Oley and Exeter settlements and were kindly entertained by these hospitable Quaker people. It is recorded in the Provincial Records of Pennsylvania that in the summer of 1736 the famous old Delaware chief Sassanoon, or Allummoppees,[j] with several other chiefs, young men, women, and children, numbering twenty-five altogether, arrived at George Boone's on their way to

Philadelphia and there learned the recent death of Patrick Gordon, the lieutenant governor of the province. The Moravian historian Loskiel relates that in February 1742 the celebrated Count Zinzendorf[k] appointed a synod at Oley, where he met many of his Moravian brethren. Three Indian converts assembled with them. Their place of meeting was a barn, there then being no church in Oley. "The appearance of three Indian visitors," says Loskiel, "whose hearts were filled with the grace of Jesus Christ and the love of God, made a deep impression upon all present," and "these three firstlings of the North American Indians were then publicly baptized. These zealous converts could not keep silence but made known to all the white people who came into their tent what great favor had been bestowed upon them. They preached a whole night to a party of Delaware Indians who were in the neighborhood, and by the providence of God were just at that time led to return to Oley; and when one ceased, another began, and their animated testimony of Jesus filled their hearers with admiration."[35]

These and similar bands of red men visiting the neighborhood must have afforded the inquisitive mind of young Boone curious and interesting subjects of study and contemplation, and thus have laid the foundation of that thorough knowledge of the Indian character which he so often in after life brought into requisition alike for his own and the public weal.

In October 1744 Squire Boone took out a warrant for twenty-five acres of land in Oley, adjoining land of Conrad Reiff—thirteen years afterwards Reiff still resided there.[36] While Mr. Boone kept five or six looms employed at home, the cultivation of his farm was not neglected.

During the grazing season, he annually sent his stock several miles distant to a fine range—probably in the neighborhood of his twenty-five acre tract in Oley, which was 5 or 6 miles north of the homestead. Mrs. Boone always accompanied these pastoral migrations to give her personal attention to the dairy—for which, from her habits of industry and neatness, she was well calculated. She regularly took her son Daniel with her as herdsman. In the midst of the range, a rustic cabin was erected for the temporary home of Mrs. Boone and her son; and near by, over-spread with shady trees, was some cool, gushing spring or gurgling rill over which the dairy-house was conveniently located. From the age of ten to sixteen years, young Boone was constantly employed from spring till late in the fall watching the herd while daily roaming through the woods, bringing them up at the close of the day for milking and for nightly herding in the cow-pens.

For the first two or three years of his pastoral life, he constantly carried with him a staff made of a small sapling grubbed up by the roots, properly shaved down, leaving a rooty knob at the end—this he called his herdsman's club. While attending the cattle, he would many a time creep stealthily upon and kill birds and other small game by dexterously throwing his club, in which he became very expert. Occupied in this manner for successive months and years, he studied with the zest of a Wilson or an Audubon the peculiar habits of birds and wild animals— *Experience* and *Observation* were his only teachers, and they formed in young Boone a scholar apt and ardent. There was, withal, a charm and quietness about this nomadic life, reminding one of the patriarchal ages and implanting in Daniel Boone's youthful mind a fervid love of nature in all its varied phases.

Attaining the age of twelve or thirteen years, his father, yielding to the entreaties of young Daniel, purchased him a short rifle-gun,[1] with which he soon became a good marksman and successful hunter. His love for the chase now became a passion with him, and though the walls and rafters of the little cabin in the range were well garnished with fresh food and jerked meat, it was too frequently obtained at the expense of neglecting the cattle by suffering them to stray away and lie out for the night.[37] This early occupation of herdsman—spending so many of his youthful days in the range and wilderness, where game was plenty and attractive, was what—Boone himself used to relate—gave him such an enthusiastic fondness for the wild woods and hunter's life. Thus grew up our young Nimrod, extending his winter rambles, we may well suppose, to the Flying and Oley hills and Neversink mountain range to the north and west of Monackasy Valley, packing home wild meat for family use and peltry to exchange for powder, lead, flints, and Barlow knives[m]—for these comprised the young hunter's simple outfit.[38]

Daniel Boone never went to school a day in his life, as he himself often related to his children. When he was about fourteen years of age, his brother Samuel, nearly seven years his senior, married a very amiable and intelligent young lady named Sarah Day, who taught her young brother-in-law Daniel to read and spell a little and, in a rude manner, to form letters. He could at first do little more than write his own name in an uncouth and mechanical way. To these humble beginnings, he added something as he grew up, by his own practical application. His acquirements were limited to reading, writing, and the rudiments of arithmetic. He could read understandingly and write intelligently. His compositions bear the marks of strong common sense yet, as might be expected, exhibiting defects in orthography, grammar, and style by no means infrequent.[n]

Reared as he was under the peaceful influence of the Quaker faith, he would nevertheless fearlessly maintain his rights as he understood them. On one occasion, a mischievous youth of the neighborhood, by some unmitigated misrepresentation, managed to embroil young Boone and an intimate friend of about the same age in a fierce combat at fisticuffs, in which Boone had one of his front teeth so loosened that it never again became firm in the socket; and a year or two before his death it was pulled out by one of his daughters with her thumb and finger. Subsequently learning their mistake, the young pugilists renewed their friendship, caught the cowardly meddler, and gave him such a pommeling as his baseness deserved.

Another early pugnacious affair of Boone's smacked somewhat, perhaps some might think, of a war of gallantry in the young hunter towards the gentler sex. His father joined some neighbors in the purchase of a seine and each successive spring would catch large quantities of shad in the Schuylkill, not far distant, which enabled them to spread their tables bountifully with these delicious fish in their fresh state, as well as to salt down a yearly supply. On one of these fishing seasons, when Mrs. Boone had assisted in cleaning what shad she wished, she sent word to a poor neighbor woman that she might have the remainder. Mrs. Boone returned home, leaving Daniel from weariness and perhaps broken of rest the preceding night by fishing, to lie down on a dry flat rock on a mild spring day, placing his hat over his face with a view to take a nap. After a while, the woman's two daughters, coming for the shad and seeing a pail of entrails from the fish Mrs. Boone had cleaned, seized the vessel and dashed the contents full in young Boone's face. If it was sport for them, it was anything but a grateful shower-bath to him; and jumping up and rubbing the filth from his eyes and face with no very amiable feelings, and thinking if they were fond of such rough joking they could not reasonably complain if they should be paid off in kind, with principal and interest, he fell to and gave them both a sound beating, sending them home with swollen faces and bloody noses. Their mother ran to Mrs. Boone with a sorry complaint. The latter, though of a quiet turn, was sometimes quite spirited when the occasion required it and now retorted tartly, "If thee has not brought up thy daughters to better behavior, it is high time they were taught good manners. And if Daniel has given them a lesson, I hope for my part that it will in the end do them no harm; and I have only to add that I bid thee good day."[39]

Boone, like most youths, had his crony. Henry Miller was raised on the outskirts of civilization, fearless of self-denials and hardships. Under an exterior somewhat rough was concealed a heart faithful in its friendships and generous in its impulses. The most that could be said to his disparagement was that he was full of fun and frolic. Boone, like Henry Miller, was not a little given to pleasantry and mischief, and each found a congenial spirit in the other.

Squire Boone, in addition to his farming and weaving operations, carried on the smithing business for repairing guns, as well as executing the customary work in that line of a farming community. As this was Miller's trade, he was employed to work in the shop, and Daniel Boone was placed awhile under his instruction in these useful arts—and especially to acquire a mechanical knowledge of what pertained to the [*wi*] gun and rifle. Though Miller was perhaps some two or three years Boone's senior, he was not more ready than the latter to engage in any boyish prank. If some fault-finding or meddlesome neighbor affronted either, one of his wagon wheels would very likely be seen the next morning gracing the roof of his barn or dancing high in some neighboring tree-tops.

George Wilcoxen, a young man entirely unacquainted with the practical use of a gun, expressed a desire to go out a deer hunting. For this purpose, he borrowed Squire Boone's long musket and requested Mr. Boone to load it for him one night that he might lay it away for early morning use. During the evening, Miller and young Boone learning of this sporting design, quietly took away the musket from its position, drew the ball and put in load enough for a half a dozen ordinary charges, and carefully replaced it.° On the morrow at peep of day, young Wilcoxen shouldered his gun and started out to try his luck, ruminating, as he entered the forest, the various gunning instructions with which his friends had favored him. Deer were plenty in the neighborhood, and after he had started, Miller and Boone began to have their misgivings lest the overloaded musket should burst and kill or seriously injure Wilcoxen.

About sunrise they heard a loud report like a small cannon some distance off and soon after, much to their relief, discovered Wilcoxen approaching. Instantly running forward and meeting him, and seeing his face all covered with blood, they exclaimed, "Wilcoxen, how come so much blood on you!" He laconically related his misfortune by saying that "the darned gun" had kicked him over—a result probably as much attributed to his awkward manner of holding the gun as the overcharge of powder. Entering the house with his nose and face badly bruised and a deep gash in his forehead, old Squire Boone wanted anxiously to know what the matter was. When informed, he stoutly protested against the fault being chargeable to the load; that he knew it was a very light load and could, without the least apprehension of danger, have rested the breech of the gun against his nose and discharged it.

Miller and young Boone following Wilcoxen into the house and, finding his injuries were not of a serious character, inquired if he had shot at a deer, and with what success. Yes—he had a pretty fair shot at a short distance; described the glade in which he had fired; but, from the mingled effects of pain and fear, could not tell what had become of the deer; he thought, however, it was a pretty dear shot. Miller and Boone went to the spot indicated and there found the deer dead. This George Wilcoxen was a relative of John Wilcoxen, who about this period married Boone's eldest sister, Sarah; and soon getting over this mishap, learned to do his own loading and thus dispensed with the roguish help of his mischievous young friends.

While Boone and Miller were once partaking of a frugal meal away from home, the former espied a wad of silk in his food and laid it beside his plate, scarcely seeming to notice it; while Miller with great difficulty restrained himself from laughter, as much from Boone's ludicrous gravity on the occasion as anything else. This threatened out-break had barely subsided when Boone discovered a dark looking substance in his dish; and picking out which with his fingers, it proved to be a large worm. Holding it up and eyeing it with mock seriousness, he exclaimed, "You are the chap that produced the silk!" Miller's pent-up merriment now burst forth without restraint.

A distant frolic was on hand. Boone knew full well it would be a waste of time to ask permission of his staid old Quaker parents to attend, so he and Miller, like *Minute-Men* as they were, hastily adjusted their linsey-woolsy[p] hunting-shirts,[q] selected Squire Boone's best nag, mounted him double, and started off after night unseen. Returning at a late hour and passing up Squire Boone's lane, the frolicsome youths attempted to make their horse leap over an old cow reposing quietly in the path; but the cow, suddenly springing up alarmed, threw the horse, who unfortunately broke his neck in the fall. Taking the bridle and saddle, they made off home and, putting them in their proper place, crept slyly into bed and kept their own secret. The old man and family wondered again and again how the poor horse could possibly have managed to break his own neck.[40]

Such comprise the authentic incidents of Boone's boyhood days. They serve to give us something of a satisfactory view of the lights and shadows of border life and explain to us the influences and causes which impelled Boone to his peculiar career of frontier exploration and adventure.

DRAPER'S NOTES: CHAPTER 1

1. Morehead's Boonesborough address, p. 12.
2. Howison's *Virginia,* ii: 234.
3. Boone's MS. memorial to the Legislature of Kentucky, 1812.
4. Boone's Memorial.
5. Oldmixon's *British Empire,* i:324; Chalmer's *Annals,* 207; Chalmer's *Revolt,* i:62; Holme's *Annals,* i:222; Grahame's i:306; Bancroft, i:246.
6. MS. letter of William F. Boone, Esq., of Philadelphia.
7. *Maryland Gazette,* February 15th, 1759.
8. Day's *Pennsylvania Historical Collection,* 305–559.
9. Pennsylvania Colonial Records, i:74.
10. MS. Records of Philadelphia County.
11. MS. letter of John F. Watson, Esq., of Germantown, Pennsylvania.
12. In the burial ground attached to the ancient Swedes church in Southwark District, Philadelphia, there is a head-stone to a grave with the following curious inscription:

> In memory of Margaret Boon, who died ye 17th of June, 1738, aged 57 years. She lived a widow three and twenty year, Five children bore, and by one husband dear, Two of ye same in ye ground lyeth near.

13. Gordon and Howe's *Histories of New Jersey;* Dodley's *Annual Register,* 1761 and 1769; Hewit's *South Carolina;* Grahame's *Colonial History,* Philadelphia edition, ii:420.
14. Massachusetts Historical Collection, second series, viii: 242; third series, vii:66, note.
15. MS. *Boone Genealogy,* written by James Boone, Jr., as dictated by his uncle John Boone, son of George and Mary Boone, who came with his parents to America in 1717, in his sixteenth year, and died in October 1785, in his 84th year, having survived all his brothers and sisters. This curious document is a beautiful specimen of chirography and is deemed worthy of a place in the Appendix, with a preliminary explanation of its authenticity and history. The fullest confidence may be placed in its statements.
16. Their births and deaths occurred as follows: George, born July 13, 1690; for several years a school-teacher; in 1733 appointed a justice of the peace and repeatedly reappointed for many years; and died in Exeter Township, Berks

County, Pennsylvania, November 20, 1753. Sarah, born February 18, 1691–2, was married, it is believed, to Jacob Stover and early removed to the valley of Virginia. The date of Squire's birth appears in the text; he died in the Forks of [the] Yadkin, in North Carolina, on January 2, 1765. Mary, born September 23, 1699, married to John Webb, and died in Berks County January 16, 1744. John, born January 3, 1701–2, O.S., and died unmarried in Exeter, Berks County, October 10, 1785—the last of the Boone emigration of 1717. Joseph, born April 5, 1704; died in Exeter January 30, 1776. Benjamin, born July 16, 1706; died in Exeter October 14, 1762. James, born July 7, 1709, O.S., represented Berks County in the Colonial Assembly in 1758, and died in Exeter September 1, 1785; whose son James, born in 1744, wrote the *Boone Genealogy*. Samuel, the youngest of the children of George and Mary Boone, died in Exeter August 6, 1745, at the age of about thirty-four years. William Boone, a grandson of George and Mary, became a prominent citizen of Berks County; in 1752 and the two following years he was the coroner and in 1755 the sheriff of that county, as the Colonial Records of Pennsylvania show.

17. That one or all of these eldest three of George Boone's children first came to Pennsylvania to look at the country is a tradition yet distinctly retained by his great grandchildren, the late venerable Judge Moses Boone, and the aged surviving Isaiah Boone, Col. Nathan Boone, and Mrs. Rebecca B. Lemond—and this wholly independent of the *Boone Genealogy*. They each corroborate the other. There is also a tradition among them that George, Sarah, and Squire Boone came over with William Penn perhaps on his last visit to Pennsylvania; and Mrs. Lemond thinks that George was Penn's clerk. But this could not have been so, for Penn's last visit to his colony was in 1699, when George, Sarah, and Squire Boone were respectively but nine, seven, and three years of age. Penn remained but two years in the country, and then made his final return to Maryland. His son William Penn, Jr., was in the colony in 1704; but even this date was unquestionably several years anterior to the coming over of George and Squire Boone with their sister. As Thomas Penn and his brother John, then proprietors, came over to Pennsylvania respectively in 1732 and 1734, it is very probable that Squire Boone may have been with one or both at Pennsbury Manor, four or five miles above Bristol on the bank of the Delaware. Joshua Boone, of Oley, an aged grandson of James and a great-grandson of George Boone, says that his ancestor came to Pennsylvania "in the days of William Penn," which is true, as George Boone's emigration was in 1717 and Penn did not die till the following year. This probably explains the tradition of the western branch of the family, that George, Sarah, and Squire Boone came over to examine the country, not literally with William Penn, but . . .

TFB: *The rest of this line concluding Draper's footnote is illegible. For modern-day Boone genealogies, see Hazel Atterbury Spraker,* The Boone Family, *2nd ed. (Baltimore: Genealogical Publishing Company, 1774) and Lilian Hays Oliver,* Some Boone Descendants and Kindred of the St. Charles District *(Rancho Cordova, CA: Dean Publications, 1984).*

18. MS. statement of John F. Watson, Esq., collected at the instance of one of the authors, from the manuscript records of the Gwynedd Monthly Meeting.

19. Gwynedd means "North Wales."

20. Watson's *Olden Time,* p. 60.

21. The *Boone Genealogy* mentions the fact of her marriage and settlement in Oley but does not give the name of her husband, Mr. Thomas E. Lee, a worthy member of the Society of Friends of Amity, Berks County, [*wi*] learned from his aged mother, who was related to the Stover family and who died in February 1853 at the age of nearly ninety-three, that one of old George Boone's daughters was married to a Stover. The late Judge Moses Boone and his surviving brother, Isaiah, learned from their father, Squire Boone, the well-known brother of Col. Daniel Boone, that his name was Stover—and probably Jacob Stover, an enterprising German who in 1731 left Pennsylvania and went to the valley of Virginia, and there obtained a grant for 5,000 acres of land on the south fork of the Shenandoah River, in what was formerly Shenandoah, now Page County, as may be seen by reference to Kercheval's *History of the Valley of Virginia,* p. 65, and Leigh's *Revised Code of Virginia,* ii:346. There was a Peter Stover, who, at a later period, settled Strasburg or Stover's Town, in Shenandoah County, and near the early grant of Jacob Stover. The late venerable Mrs. Rachel Denton, of Barren County, Kentucky, who went to Kentucky with her father, William Scholl, in 1779 from Shenandoah County, Virginia, stated that her father was related to the Boone family and joined Daniel and Edward Boone at the close of that year in erecting and settling Boone's Station. Scholl, of German origin, doubtless descended from the Stover family. It is certain that previous of the name of Stover were early settlers in Berks; there was a Jacob Stover in Union Township in that county about 1740; and also a Jacob Stover in Oley in 1757; see Rupp's *History of Berks,* 238–252.

22. Rupp's *History of Berks,* p. 231.

23. "Oley is a lovely valley, shaped like a horse-shoe, with a brook running down from the toe past the heels. The very name Oley is poetic, which my aged half-sister, Susanna Boone, always said was the Indian designation for horse-shoe, but what the Indians knew of horse-shoes, or how they shod their horses, she never told me." MS. letter of James W. Biddle, Esq., of Pittsburgh.

24. Rupp's *History of Berks County,* p. 231.

25. Statement of Joshua Boone of Oley to Joseph Foulks of Gwynedd, kindly communicated by letter for this work.

26. The records of the Gwynedd Meeting gave the name of Edward Morgan as the father of the young lady who became the wife of Squire Boone [*an entire line is illegible here*] rich evidence should generally be deemed conclusive. There is, however, some [*wi*] of its correctness in this instance. A family narrative, prepared many years since by the present venerable Tabitha Adamson, now in her ninety-fourth year, communicated by Dr. William Carson of Pennsylvania, states: "John Jarmen emigrated to America, in the year 1682; one of his daughters married John Morgan, who emigrated from Wales near the same time. John Morgan had six daughters: Sarah married Squire Boone, the father of Daniel Boone, the

pioneer of Kentucky; Margaret married Samuel Thomas; Elizabeth and Alice married two brothers, David and Jenkins Evans; another daughter married Morris, and Mary married [*wm*] Wright—all Quakers or Quaker families." John Morgan had two sons, Daniel and Edward, the former of whom and his wife were celebrated Quaker preachers. Mrs. Adamson is a granddaughter of John Wright and Mary Morgan and has often heard her parents speak of their Aunt Sarah Boone and of her early removal with "her boys" to North Carolina; MS. statements of Daniel Bryan and Mrs. Rebecca B. Lemond; conversations with Col. Nathan Boone; Mrs. Adamson's narrative.

27. *Encyclopedia of Religious Knowledge,* p. 996.

28. MS. records of Gwynedd Monthly Meeting; correspondence of John F. Watson and Joseph Foulks.

29. The word Welsh signifies foreigners or wanderers and was given to this people by other nations, probably because they came from some distant country. The Welsh call themselves Cymry, in the plural, and a Welshman Cymro, and their country Cymru. A hundred years before Christ, the Cimbri, large in stature, hovered like a cloud over Gaul and Italy. Nothing at first could resist their impetuous career; they bore down all before them, putting to rout no less than five respectable Roman armies and generals. The illustrious Caius Marcus at length took the field and turned back these hitherto resistless hordes.

30. MS. letters of Thomas E. Lee of Berks County, Pennsylvania; MS. Land Office Records, Harrisburg, Pennsylvania.

31. Watson's *Olden Time,* p. 42.

32. The particular birth-spot of noted individuals is a matter of much interest. Of that of Daniel Boone, we can only give the following extract of a letter from James Lee, a worthy Friend of Exeter, in Berks County, who owns and now occupies over one hundred and fifty acres of Squire Boone's old homestead, which the latter sold to William Maugridge: "The house in which I now reside is not the one in which Daniel Bone was born, but that the western end thereof stands upon the same spot, there is, with me, not a shadow of doubt. The circumstance which has led me to this conclusion so fully, is this: Nearly twenty years ago, and shortly after I came to the place, I invited an ancient Friend, and relative of mine (Rachel Lee, whose maiden name was Chivington, who, if now living, would be at least one hundred years of age, and perhaps several years older), to make us a visit at our new home. She said she would be so much pleased [*wi*] did so, for that in her younger days she had used to be there spinning for William Maugridge's family, and she would like to see whether the place looked like it did at that time. She said they lived in an old log house which stood over the spring. Now this could not have been long after Squire Boone, as he, Maugridge, lived there but fifteen or sixteen years, and consequently must have been the same house. My house is of stone, and has been built at two different periods of time; the western end, which is of the latest date, stands over the spring, and probably the eastern end was built whilst the log structure was standing. There is an ancient arch standing

by the spring, under the western end of my house, which, from appearance, must have been built to support a chimney, which of course could have been none other than that of the house in question; for no house could or would have been built and demolished in the intermediate time. There were logs and timber in a stable which I had taken down some years ago, and which evidently had been in use as part of a house formerly, and which may have been a part of Squire Boone's dwelling, but this is a mere supposition."

33. This is the date in the Old Style recorded by Col. Daniel Boone himself in his Family Record, lately obtained on a visit to his son, Col. Nathan Boone, of Missouri. The same data has recently been derived from the ancient records of the Exeter Monthly Meeting and kindly communicated by John F. Watson, Esq., from Germantown and Thomas Pearson of [*wi*], Pennsylvania.

Different writers have assigned different dates for the birth of Daniel Boone, varying from 1730 to 1746. Mrs. Lemond often heard her mother, Elizabeth Boone, who was much older than her brother Daniel and [was] born December 5th, 1732, according to the Quaker records, on February 5th, 1733, according to the Family Register, say that she was two years his senior; and hence Mrs. Lemond placed Colonel Boone's birth in February 1735—which date was, in good faith, furnished by the author of this work to the Rev. Dr. J. M. Peck for his *Life of Boone,* in Sparks' Biography. "My Uncle Daniel," says the aged Isaiah Boone, "was about ten years older than my father, Squire Boone, who was born October 5, 1744, and both were natives of Pennsylvania." This would point out 1734 as Daniel Boone's birth year. Daniel Bryan, too, assigned Boone's birth to 1734, as Bryan's mother, Mary Boone, next younger than her brother Daniel, was born on the 3rd of November, probably Old Style, according to the Quaker Records, or the 10th of November, 1736, according to the Bryan Family Register. All these respective dates, and particularly those of the birth of these sisters, as preserved in their families—the one immediately proceeding and the other succeeding him in the order of their births—tend strongly to corroborate the correctness of the birth-date which Colonel Boone has given of himself in his Family Register and which is preserved also in the records of the Exeter Monthly Meeting. This hitherto doubtful question may now be considered as settled beyond all doubt or cavil.

In its correction, it is worthy of remark that soon after the re-interment of the remains of Daniel Boone and wife at Frankfort in 1845, a newspaper sketch of the Boone family appeared in the *Kentucky Yeoman,* written by the late Gen. R. B. McAfee, from verbal statements derived from Col. William L. Boone, a nephew of Daniel Boone, since deceased, in which Daniel Boone's birth is said to have occurred July 14th, 1732. This date and other matters in that sketch were brought together in such a manner in Cist's *Cincinnati Miscellany,* vol. ii:141, as to convey the idea that they were a part of the *Boone Genealogy,* previously adverted to in this work; and Mr. Perkins so understanding it, gave this date of Boone's birth in the first edition of his *Annals of the West* as really "taken from

the family Record" and cited Cist's *Miscellany* as authority. Thus do errors orig-
inate, grow apace, and finally become incorporated into the standard histories of
the country.

But the birthplace of Colonel Boone has been as variously stated as the
date of his nativity. His Family Record—here approximately five words not legible—of the Gwynedd and Exeter meetings are silent upon the subject. Some authorities have asserted that Bridgsworth[?], in Shropshire, and others that
Somerset County, England, was the place of his birth; others, that he came into
being during the transit of his parents across the Atlantic; while yet others variously state that he was a native of Virginia, Maryland, and of Bucks and Berks
counties, Pennsylvania. The migratory character of the family will best explain
these contradictory statements. Flint was the first to assign Bucks County, Pennsylvania, as Boone's place of nativity, and others since he wrote have followed his
example. The only other original authority pointing out the same county is the
Bryan MS., which gives no further particulars except to add that his, Bryan's,
mother, a sister of Boone next younger than himself, was born in Bucks County,
near Reading, soon after the settlement of the family there. Mrs. Lemond thinks
that her Uncle Daniel, as well as her mother, was born somewhere from fifteen to
thirty miles from Philadelphia—probably referring to North Wales, in Gwynedd
Township, some twenty miles distant. Boone himself stated to the present ex-
Gov. Edward Coles that he was born in Pennsylvania, and Governor Coles thinks
he said near Carlisle, but it might have been near Reading. Col. Nathan Boone
has heard his father, Col. Daniel Boone, repeatedly say he was born in Berks
County, fifty miles from Philadelphia—probably the distance as then reckoned
from Squire Boone's place in Exeter to Philadelphia, and it must now measure
forty-seven or forty-eight miles. One of the earliest sketches of Boone extant, in
a volume entitled *Biographia Americana,* by B. F. French of Philadelphia, published in New York in 1825, gives Berks County as his birthplace. Squire
Boone's purchase of land in Oley, in what is now Berks County, in 1730, almost
four years before the birth of his son Daniel—the repeated declarations of the
latter that he was born in Berks—the strong conviction of his only surviving son,
and the united traditions and belief of the aged members of the Boone connection
in Pennsylvania to the same effect—all go pretty conclusive[ly] to establish
the fact that Daniel Boone was born in what is now Exeter, Berks County,
Pennsylvania.

The only other locality which can at this day lay any plausible claim to the
honor of having given birth to the great Kentucky pioneer, is that asserted by
Flint— near Bristol, Bucks County, on the right bank of the Delaware, "about
twenty miles from Philadelphia." Daniel Bryan, from tradition, [said] that it was
somewhere in Bucks County that Squire Boone's eldest six children, including
Daniel, were born; but his vague idea had evident reference to Gwynedd, in now
Montgomery County. Flint cites no authority whatever—Bryan was plainly in
error; and it need only be added that Squire Boone never owned a foot of land in
Bucks County, as both the records of that county and the old colonial land records
at Harrisburg conclusively shows.

34. John Webb, an Englishman, married Mary Boone and early settled in Exeter, where his wife died January 16th, 1774, in her seventy-fifth year, and he died the ensuing 18th of October in his eightieth year. The names of the children were George, Joseph, Sarah, and Benjamin.

35. Loskiel's *History of the Moravian Indian Missions,* part ii:19–21.

36. *MS. Land Office Records,* Harrisburg, Pennsylvania.

37. Buffalo, bear and elk meat, beef, and venison, cut into small pieces and laid on a scaffold over a slow fire till roasted and thoroughly dried, was well known in the frontier parlance as jerk.

TFB: *Spencer Records, a frontier contemporary of Daniel Boone, wrote in his memoirs (DM 23CC:1–108) how he made buffalo jerk (DM23CC:39–40):*

> We skinned the bull, and cut off all the meat in broad thin pieces, which we laid on the hide, and sprinkled salt thereon, letting it lay till we made a long fire, and placed poles on the forks. Small sticks were then laid on them, and the meat laid on the sticks over the fire, where it remained until half-cooked; it was then turned over and left to lay till morning.... In the morning we put the meat in bags and carried it home.

38. Flying and Oley hills so called from the innumerable flights of turkies on them. Pownall's *Topography,* Des., 27.

39. Prior to 1736 yearly accounts were sent to the governor and Council of Pennsylvania of "tumultuous meeting, riotous behavior, quarrels, contentions, and even outrages amongst the young people and others who assemble as to a merry-making or a publick diversion, at the time of fishing by racks," or dams, in the Schuylkill. These fish-racks impeding the navigation of the river and causing conduct "so unseemly" led to their abatement. *Colonial Records of Pennsylvania,* vol. iv.

40. The two anecdotes of Boone and Miller just related were derived from the present venerable Isaiah Boone, a nephew of the old pioneer, who learned them from his father. The late Judge Moses Boone, another son of the second Squire Boone, corroborated in a general way the early crony-ship of Henry Miller and Daniel Boone. The other youthful events of Boone are given on the respectable authority of the venerable Col. Nathan Boone and lady, to whom Col. Daniel Boone himself communicated them in various familiar conversations when a member of their family.

EDITOR'S NOTES: CHAPTER 1

a. To aver that Boone wrote his *Narrative* "in his own expressive language" or to imply that his biographer and amanuensis John Filson copied his words verbatim is a bit much; that Draper uncritically accepts the whole of Filson's bombast and extensively quotes from it is telling. Boone, although literate, was far from lettered enough to wax as eloquently about great cities of antiquity like Persepolis and Palmyra as he does in Filson's *Kentucke.* But Boone delighted in having his "autobiography" read to him. "All true. Every word true!" he would say. "Not a lie in it!"

b. Boone often reflected in his later years that a benevolent providential hand guided his steps. But, to be sure, he came to Kentucky in the 1760s seeking game and land. As Filson and Draper romanticized the man beyond proportion, one wonders how much Providence Boone really felt during his first Kentucky long hunt and if the Shawnee who caught him and his men poaching on their hunting grounds and confiscated their skins and wares sensed Providence too.

c. East of the Mississippi, buffalo herds were small compared with the truly vast herds that foraged the Great Plains of the trans-Mississippian region. Eyewitness accounts of buffalo herds in Kentucky, the Illinois country, and the Cumberland basin number them between 100 and 600 head. After white settlement, herd size radically diminished because of habitat loss and slaughter. In 1820 an observer spotted what may have been Kentucky's last buffalo herd near the Green River. For a definitive look at buffalo in the East, lifestyles of native and market hunters, and the opening of America's first Far West, see Ted Franklin Belue, *The Long Hunt: Death of the Buffalo East of the Mississippi* (Mechanicsburg, PA: Stackpole Books, 1996).

d. At the time of the 1990 census, Kentucky's population numbered 3,685,296.

e. Draper's paraphrase of Genesis 12:1, King James Version: "Now the Lord had said unto Abram, Get thee out of thy country, and from thy kindred, and from thy father's house, unto a land that I will show thee."

f. On January 1, 45 B.C.E., Julius Caesar inaugurated his Julian calendar for the Roman Empire. Because the Julian calendar was slightly longer than the solar year, in 1582 Pope Gregory XIII initiated the more accurate Gregorian calendar. In 1751 Great Britain and her colonies adopted the Gregorian, or New Style (N.S.), calendar. Adding eleven days to dates from the Julian, or Old Style (O.S.), calendar converts the date to New Style. Boone, born in 1734, insisted upon observing his birthday on the Old Style date of October 20 rather than on November 2, the New Style conversion.

g. A paraphrase of Genesis 46:26, King James Version: "All the souls that came with Jacob unto Egypt, which came out of his loins, besides Jacob's sons' wives, all the souls were three-score and six."

h. For Daniel Morgan, see chapter 2, note f.

i. The *Oxford English Dictionary* defines *gorrel* as a "youth, lad or boy" and notes that after 1650 the term was not in common English usage.

j. In 1715 Sassoonana, also known as Allumapees, succeeded his father Tamanend to become an influential Delaware chieftain of the Turtle Clan; he was a friend of the English until his death in the fall of 1747.

k. Nicholas Lewis Zinzendorf was a Moravian minister to the Delaware who traveled the wilds of Pennsylvania in the mid-1700s.

l. "Rifle-gun" is eighteenth-century terminology for *rifle,* thus making a distinction between long arms fitted with rifled barrels and smoothbore firearms, such as muskets, fusils (lightweight smoothbores; alternate spellings include fusee, fuzil, fuzee), fowling pieces (called "fowlers"), and Indian trade-guns. Long arms built with a rifle's more streamlined esthetics but equipped with unrifled barrels were called "smooth-rifles."

m. Records dated 1745 from Sheffield, England, list John Barlow as a registered cutler. By 1764 Barlow's pen and "clasp" (folding) knives, some types having two to four blades, sold well at home and in the colonies. Revolutionary War ads urged American recruits to sign up and bring their guns and Barlow knives.

n. Boone's sister-in-law Sarah Day taught him as a youth the basics of reading and writing, and he became an avid reader, delving into the Bible and history books. Although one kinsman observed that he "had no relish for fiction," Boone enjoyed a good tale and often took along a copy of *Gulliver's Travels* on his jaunts. Applying quill to paper, he expressed himself well, and although his spelling was poor, Boone, said one relative, "could write a good farmer's hand."

o. To "draw the ball," a shooter fits a screwlike device called a "worm" onto the jag-end tip of a ramrod, rams it down the barrel into the soft lead bullet, and while pushing down, turns the rod until the worm screws into the ball deep enough to extract it. Doubling loading is the standard charge to "proof," or test, a black powder gun. Using "half a dozen charges," as Draper notes, is enough black powder to charge a small cannon. This sort of prank could have had a fatal end.

p. Linsey-woolsey is a coarse woven cloth made by blending spun wool fibers for the warp, the threads strung in the loom lengthwise, with the linen weft, the threads that cross the warp. The term is rarely seen in eighteenth-century texts.

q. Hunting shirts were an identifying badge of Anglo and native woodsmen of Boone's day. In 1824 Rev. Joseph Doddridge observed in *Notes on the Settlement and Indian Wars of the Western Parts of Virginia and Pennsylvania:* "The hunting shirt . . . was a kind of loose frock, reaching halfway down the thighs, with large sleeves, open before and so wide as to lap over a foot or more when belted." Such garments were plain or fancy, sewn of linen, buckskin, or single-print calico in red, blue, white, or another color, and sometimes embroidered with silk thread. They could be made as pullovers or open fronted and were belted with a finger-woven sash tied in back or a leather belt buckled in front.

CHAPTER 2

1742–1755.—The Boones Belligerent.—Prosperity of Squire Boone.—
Settlement of the Yadkin Country.—Squire Boone and Family Remove
There.—Daniel Boone's Early Occupations.—Indian Difficulties.—
French and Indian War.—Boone Engages in the Service as a Wagoner.—
In Braddock's Defeat.—Escapes.—Sees Some Things of the Upper Ohio
Valley, and Learns from John Findlay about Kentucky.

It is curious to observe several notices among the Exeter Meeting Quaker Records, going to show that the Boones were sometimes rather too belligerent and self-willed, calling for the occasional dealing of the Meeting. Sarah, the eldest daughter of Squire Boone, having married in 1742 out of the order, was promptly disowned. Israel Boone, the eldest son, marrying out of the Society in 1747, was also disowned; and his father countenancing this disloyal act and unwilling to retract his error had testimony of disownment issued against him on the 26th of the 3rd month, 1748.[1]

Prosperity attended the steady industry and frugal managements of Squire Boone in his triple occupations of farming, smithing, and weaving; thus was he enabled in March 1749 to take out a warrant for two hundred and fifty acres of land in Exeter, adjoining lands of George, Joseph, and Benjamin Boone.[2] His family had now increased to eleven children, several of whom were married.[3] The choice lands of the settlement were all located, and as more homesteads were needed, it became a matter of much concern and inquiry to what new, fertile, and salubrious country they could migrate where the right to the soil could be cheaply purchased.

Between the years 1735 and 1750 a few resolute adventurers sought a sequestered home in the beautiful but distant frontier west of the Yadkin River in North Carolina, some of whom seem to have wended their way thither from Pennsylvania. From about 1750 family after family, group after group succeeded in rapid progression, led on by reports sent back by the enterprising pioneers of the fertility and beauty of those solitudes, where conscience was free, labor voluntary, and a comfortable living easily obtained.

[wm] sources as these, the fame of the Yadkin country reached the Boone settlement in Exeter.[4]

The dawning of the spring of 1750 was fraught with unusual interest to Squire Boone and his now numerous family. Their removal to the far off Yadkin

Valley was carefully considered and finally resolved on, and Mr. Boone disposed of his lands, surplus stock, and such household articles as were too bulky for a land carriage of fully five hundred miles and made every necessary preparation for the long and tedious journey.[5] With at least one or two teams and a small drove of cattle, they started in the month of April—the women and younger children usually riding, while the men trudged along behind driving the cattle. As Daniel Boone was now in his sixteenth year and had long been accustomed to the duties of herdsman, he took his place in the caravan with his gun on his shoulder, ready to bring down any chance game that might happen in his way. Thus bidding adieu to Pennsylvania and passing through Maryland, they crossed the Potomac and entered the valley of Virginia. Carrying provisions with them, they would pitch their camp each night beside some cool spring or limpid stream, the females preparing the simple meals, and reposing nightly in their covered wagons and before their cheerful campfires. Such was then, as now, the frontier mode of moving, practiced alike for its convenience and frugality.

Tradition says that the Boone family tarried "about two years" on Linnville Creek, six miles north of Harrisburg, Rockingham County, in the Virginia Valley and on the direct route to the Yadkin country.[6] Little Shenandoah River was bordered with the lands of an excellent quality. Its name was derived from one Linnville, an early resident upon its banks—the same probably who a few years later was treacherously slain by Indians in the mountain region above the head of the Yadkin.

Admitting, however, that the Boone connection did sojourn awhile in the Linnville settlement, they must have resumed their journey for their original destination not later than the fall of 1751 or spring of 1752, for we find that Squire Boone's daughter Elizabeth, early in the autumn of the latter year, was united in marriage in the Yadkin Valley to William Grant, a native of Maryland who had been some years residing in that region.[7]

In the Forks of North and South Yadkin, clean and rapid mountain streams, was a lovely and fertile region. Here, upon Dutchman's Creek, a tributary of North Yadkin and at a place called the Buffalo Lick, which was probably at the confluence of Buffalo Creek with Dutchman's, in a rich and undulating country, Squire Boone made choice of a spot for his new home. Between the Yadkin and Catawba, large prairies spread out into a broad expanse with their luxuriant growth of grass, where have since sprung up many a thrifty forest. These native meadows, with the tall and vigorous canebrakes[a] overspreading the bottoms and skirting the streams, furnished food and shelter for wild game and sustenance the whole year for the stock of new settlers. Game was everywhere plentiful, and the Yadkin afforded an ample supply of shad and other delicious kinds of fish in their season. The country was sufficiently elevated above the flat region which stretches for sixty miles back from the sea-coast to render it, with its pure water and serene air, one of the healthiest portions of North America. The oppressive heat of summer was genially tempered by the extensive mountain range on the west, and the nights were delightfully cool and refreshing. Autumn, with its mellow hue and ripened wild fruits, presented a rich variety of vegetation; and the mistletoe, that beautiful twining evergreen, was common in all that frontier region. Such was the Yadkin Valley—emphatically the poor man's home—a land of plenty and happiness.[8]

When all that fair region lay open to the choice of the new settlers, the comparative plenty of cane generally decided the preference of one spot over another. With this paramount consideration in view, Squire Boone's location was made at Buffalo Lick. The soil yielded so generous a return for the little labor bestowed on it that the necessaries of life were secured with scarcely an effort. Daniel Boone worked occasionally during the cropping season for his father, but he had no heart to perform the drudgery of farming. Let but a shower come up to prevent for a while out-door labor, he would take his rifle and glide into the nearest forest; and though the rain should cease in an hour, the excitement of the chase would beguile him on till reminded by the approach of night to retrace his wandering footsteps.

At this period, there were so many buffalo in the wild upper country, particularly of South Carolina, that three or four men with their dogs could kill from ten to twenty in a day; but they soon receded before the advancing settlements or fell prey to the deadly rifle.[b] Deer were so numerous that a common hunter could easily kill four or five a day and, in the autumnal season, as many bears as would make from two to three thousand weight of bear-bacon. Wild turkies filled every thicket, and the water-courses teemed with the beaver, otter, and musk-rat; while wolves, panthers and wild-cats over-ran the country.[9] Nothing could have better suited young Boone's tastes and predilections than such a profusion of game while it lasted. He had hitherto hunted only for recreation; now he began to spend his autumns and winters in the woods because he could unite profit with the pleasure derived from the roving and exciting characteristics of a hunter's life—a life he learned to love too well. Furs and peltries bore a good price and formed not only the frontier currency of that day, but the chief article of remittance to the trading marts on the Atlantic. Every skin passed currently at its standard value. During the summer season, Boone was more or less engaged for his father in teaming produce, pelts, and furs to Salisbury, some twenty odd miles from the Boone settlement.[10]

The nearest Indian towns were those of the Catawbas,[c] some sixty miles distant; the Cherokee villages were yet more remote. The Indians often visited the new settlements on the Yadkin, temporarily pitched their camps at some convenient spot, and drove something of a barter-trade with their white neighbors. They lived on terms of peace and good will with the new settlers. Occasionally some mischief was committed, but it was invariably done, so far as can now be judged, by the Northern Indians[d] in their warlike forays against the Catawbas and other Southern tribes. On the return of the adventurous Christopher Gist from his exploration of the Ohio Valley and the Kentucky country in 1750–'51, he makes this record in his journal:

Saturday: May 18th, 1751.—Set out S 20 M to my own House on the Yadkin River, when I came there I found all my family gone, for the Indians had killed five People in the Winter near that Place, which frightened my Wife and family away to Roanoke about 35 M nearer in among the Inhabitants, which I was informed of by an old Man I met near the place. Sunday, 19th.—Set out for Roanoke, and as we had now a Path, We got there the same Night, where I found all my Family well.[11]

A signal instance at this early period of the devotion of the Catawbas to their white brethren, which ever after manifested itself on all suitable occasions, deserves our special notice. In July 1753 a party of Northern Indians in the French interest made their appearance in Rowan County, into which the Yadkin country had just been organized, committing various depredations upon the scattered inhabitants. A band of faithful Catawbas sallied forth and encountered a detached party of the enemy, killed several of them, and put the rest to flight. The victorious Catawbas obtained the scalps of the slain; and among the spoils were silver crucifixes, beads, looking glasses, tomahawks and other implements of war, all of which were of French manufacture.[12]

About this period Daniel Boone's great skill in hunting and shooting at a mark had become proverbial. Whites and Indians readily conceded it, except a distinguished Catawba of the name of Saucy Jack, who was envious of young

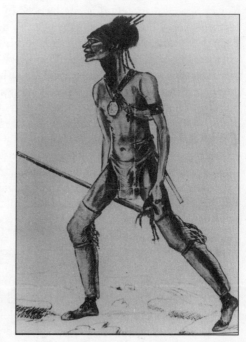

21. Northern war chief (Ottawa) carrying scalp after a foray, c. 1750s. This painted warrior has decorated his roached hair with trade silver and porcupine quill ornaments, wears a breechcloth, moccasins, side-seam leggings, powderhorn, and peace medallion. He is armed with a tomahawk and trade gun. DRAWN BY GEORGE TOWNSHEND, COURTAULD INSTITUTE OF ART, LONDON.

Boone's preeminence with the rifle, and even he at length was constrained to make the reluctant acknowledgment. But he resolved to have no superior alive and, perhaps in his cups, dropped a few careless words unwittingly betraying his intention to seek the first opportunity to sacrifice his successful rival. This quickly reached the ears of old Squire Boone, whose son Daniel then happened to be absent on a hunting excursion, and Quaker as he was, the old gentleman's ire was so much roused that he seized a hatchet and set out in search of Saucy Jack, resolutely exclaiming, "Well, if it has come to this, I'll kill first!" Warning was immediately conveyed to Jack of his danger, who, thinking discretion the better part of valor, fled the country and remained absent until old Squire Boone's anger became appeased and the affair comparatively forgotten. But Saucy Jack never more ventured to promulge such foolish threats; he had very likely the fear of Daniel Boone's unerring rifle constantly before his eyes. The amicable relations which had hitherto existed with the Catawbas influenced the people studiously to avoid every cause of rupture, and so the matter was suffered to die away.[13] This anecdote serves strongly to illustrate the idea we have all along endeavored to inculcate, that Boone's ruling passion was early developed, and that he became learned, if not in the lore of books, at least in that kind of knowledge which excited the envy of the friendly and the terror of the hostile Indians.

The frowns of war at length fell heavily upon the border settlements. The long and bloody Seven Years' conflict commenced in 1754, and in the sequel, the proud *Fleur de Lis* of France yielded the palm to the triumphant Cross of St. George. Though kings and courts had no small pride and interest at stake in this war of personal ambition, yet the people of the Colonies generally had little or nothing to gain, and those especially along the frontier had to bear the crushing miseries of the contest. An all-wise Providence, however, seemed to have designed it for the training of a race of men fitted in after years to meet and conquer the combined power of Britain, her savage allies, and mercenary hirelings. Daniel Boone passed through this school of trial; and though not a conspicuous actor, he nevertheless acquired in its progress that knowledge of men and things which had a marked influence in effecting the subsequent exploration and settlement of the West.

French encroachment upon the Upper Ohio, the erection of forts on Venango and French Creek and preparations for building others, the murder of several persons by the French Indians upon the western confines of Virginia, the capture of a number of English traders in the Ohio country with a declaration that all English subjects should be made prisoners who attempted to trade upon those waters, were alarming facts revealed by the mission of Maj. George Washington to the notice of Governor Dinwiddie of Virginia. Immediately after Washington's return, in January 1754, Governor Dinwiddie dispatched a letter to President Rowan of North Carolina soliciting men to join the troops embodying in Virginia and Maryland to repel these French aggressors.

No time was lost by the government of North Carolina in appropriating means for repairing Forts Johnson and Granville in that province and for raising, subsisting, and paying a body of troops to march to the assistance of Virginia. One thousand pounds were voted for the purchase of arms for the use of the inhabitants of the frontier counties of Anson and Rowan, who were deemed too poor to support unaided the expenses attending the defense of the back settlements against the Indians.[14] About three hundred troops were raised and placed under the command of Col. James Innis of New Hanover County, who marched to Virginia but arrived there too late to join Colonel Washington until after the affair at Fort Necessity.[e] The most of these men were soon recalled, as President Rowan had received intelligence that the French were posting themselves near the back-parts of that province. Capt. Hugh Waddell, by his energy and bravery, proved himself the most useful of the officers of the North Carolina troops and remained in service on the borders of Virginia as late as September 1754, after several North Carolina companies had been disbanded and returned home.[15] It is highly probable that Daniel Boone was with Captain Waddell on this campaign; if not, we may well suppose he shared in the defense of the frontiers of Rowan.

Braddock's fatal campaign of 1755 now properly claims our attention. Boone accompanied the one hundred North Carolina troops under Captain Waddell on that expedition, not as a soldier, but a wagoner, conveying the baggage of the company. Among the large numbers of wagons employed was Boone's cousin, "Daniel Morgan,[f] famed in village groups as a wrestler; skillful in the use of the musket; who emigrated as a day-laborer from New Jersey to Virginia and husbanded his wages so that he had been able to become the owner of a team; all unconscious of his future greatness." It was no mere frolicsome pastime to the drivers; their most unwearied care and patience were requisite in conducting the heavily laden baggage-wagons over hills and mountains, through streams, ravines, and quagmires.

After days and weeks of ceaseless toil in clearing a passage for the army—"stopping," says Bancroft, "to level every molehill, and erect bridges over every creek"—they at length on the memorable 9th of July passed the Monongahela. It was now nearly two o'clock in the afternoon when all were in motion; the advance of three hundred and fifty men under Lieutenant-Colonel Gage, closely attended by a working party of two hundred and fifty more under Sir John St. Clair, followed by Braddock with the artillery, baggage, and remaining regulars, while the slighted provincial companies of Virginia, Maryland, and Carolina sullenly brought up the rear, where their supercilious general had ignobly placed them, strangely supposing them to possess "little courage or good will."

Within seven miles of Fort Duquesne, "with colors flying, drums beating, and fifes playing the *Grenadier's March*," presenting an imposing appearance, "brilliant in their dazzling uniforms, their burnished arms gleaming in the bright summer's sun, but sick at heart and enfeebled by toil and unwholesome diet," the army of twelve hundred chosen men advanced cautiously along a path but twelve feet wide. Leaving a steep conical hill upon their right, they marched to the extremity of the open space, where the path disappeared between the thickly wooded banks of a small brook running into the Monongahela. The guides and light-horse at length entered the timber skirting the little stream and commenced descending towards it, while a number of ax-men were vigorously at work felling trees and clearing the underwood for the approach of the army, the grenadiers acting as a covering party.[16] They little dreamed of the fatal ambuscade into which they were unconsciously entering, or of the disappointment, as sudden as appalling, that so soon awaited all their fondest hopes and brightest prospects.

Intelligence of the advance of an English army represented to consist of three thousand men was early brought to the French by the alacrity and fidelity of their scouts. Vaudreuil, the governor of New France, had given up Fort Duquesne as lost. Contreceur, the commandant of the garrison, could have cherished no solid hopes of success with only a handful of soldiers and a single cannon mounted as if merely to make a show of resistance, the better to secure for himself and garrison the honors of war. There were some brave men among his subordinate officers, and an ambuscade was suggested. Their Indian allies twice in council declined so hazardous an enterprise. "I am determined to go out and meet the enemy," exclaimed De Beaujeu; "and will you suffer your father to go alone? I am sure we shall conquer"; and partaking of his spirit, they rushed forth upon the war-path eager for blood and carnage.

De Beaujeu's heterogeneous band numbered less than two hundred and thirty French and Canadians and six hundred and thirty-seven savages, led on by the renowned Pontiac of the Ottawas,[g] Athanase of the Hurons of Lorette,[h] Gi-ya-so-do, or Big Cross, of the Senecas of Allegheny, Black Hoof and probably Cornstalk of the Shawanoes, and the Delawares,[i] Wyandots,[j] and other tribes by their favorite braves.[17] Securely posted in ambush in two ravines heading near each other, with the trail between and extending either way into the valley below fronting the path, the Indians impatiently awaited the approach of the English and at length poured on them a quick and heavy fire. The British advance was soon driven back, losing their two six-pounders and mingling with the vanguard, which had been ordered forward by the general as a reinforcement and was attempting to form in the face of the rising ground upon the right, a scene of indescribable confusion ensued. All huddled promiscuously together, and fully exposed to the shots of the enemy, Braddock and his officers vainly exerted themselves to form the men, now perfectly infatuated with fear by the scenes of death and carnage around them mingled with the terrific yells of the savages.

The French and Indians were almost of a man invisible, hidden behind trees, logs, bushes, tall wild grass, and in the deep ravines, save a skulking savage would momentarily rush from his covert to bring down some exposed officer or tear a scalp from some fallen foe, while the half-bewildered soldiery fired their platoons aimlessly into the air or tree-tops. "In the midst of the strange scene," says Bancroft, "nothing was so sublime as the persevering gallantry of the officers. They used the utmost art to encourage the men to move upon the enemy; they told them [to break] off into small parties of which they took the lead; they

22. *"Sauvage de la Nation des Shawanoes" by Joseph Wabun, 1796. This painted warrior has roached hair and slit ears garnished with trade silver brooches. Blue beads encircle his neck. Shirt and breechcloth are blue and blanket is white. Leggings are scarlet stroud decorated with tufts of dyed deer hair in metal cones. Ear brooches, arm bands, and nose ring are silver.* BIBLIOTHEQUE NATIONALE.

bravely formed the front; they advanced sometimes at the head of small bodies, sometimes separately, to recover the cannon, or to get possession of the hill; but were sacrificed by the soldiers who declined to follow them, and even fired upon them from the rear."[18]

From every quarter the enemy poured in a deadly fire, and many a gallant officer fell, a sacrifice to his almost superhuman efforts to rally the dismayed regulars and urge them to the charge. Braddock himself exerted every nerve and braved every danger, until at last, after having five horses disabled under him, a ball passed through his arm and entered his right side, and he fell mortally wounded. He "was borne from the field," says Lord Mahon, "by some soldiers whom his aid-de-camp had bribed to that service by a guinea and a bottle of rum to each," although the fallen chieftain "was very solicitous to be left on the field."[19]

Two cannon flanked the baggage, which was now warmly attacked; the Indians were kept at bay for a short time, but they soon obtained possession of the booty, as well as many of the wounded of Braddock's army, who quickly fell victims to the merciless tomahawk. A great many horses and some drivers were killed; among the survivors was Daniel Boone, who cut his team loose and fortunately escaped by flight. This success in securing the baggage partially arrested the attention of the Indians, enabling most of the fugitives to re-cross the river with only fifty of the enemy in pursuit, and these soon returned to share the scalps and plunder. Twelve poor captives were taken and hurried off to Fort Duquesne with their bodies and faces painted black—an unmistakable indication of the sad fate that inevitably awaited them; and that evening they were burnt by the savages on the banks of the Allegheny in sight of the fort and unopposed by Contreceur. One at a time was tied naked to a stake with his hands fastened above his head, then tortured with red-hot irons and lighted pine splinters stuck in his body; and the shrieks of the victim drowned in the horrid yells of his tormentors as they gaily danced around him, gradually became fainter and fainter, until death at length kindly relieved the sufferer. Another and another perished in the same awful manner, until all were sacrificed to this diabolical custom.[20]

During three brief hours on that disastrous day, twenty-six British and Provincial officers were killed and thirty-seven wounded, and seven hundred and fourteen privates slain or disabled, while three officers only and thirty men of the French and Indians fell, and as many more were wounded. The leaders of the contending parties, as was again the case four years later on the plains of Abraham, lost their lives in the desperate strife to gain laurels and territory for their respective royal masters—Braddock surviving only four days, and the brave De Beaujeu falling early in the contest. The French, says Mante, found themselves "surprised in a victory."

Amid the almost universal havoc, the preservation of Washington was indeed providential. Braddock was stricken down; his secretary, young Shirley, was shot dead; and both his English aides wounded early in the action, leaving Washington alone to distribute the orders, who finally, when all was lost, rallied a few faithful

Provincials and successfully covered the retreat. "I expected every moment," said Dr. Craik, whose eye was on Washington, "to see him fall." "Nothing but the superintending care of Providence could have saved him." An Indian chief—I suppose a Shawanoe—singled him out with his rifle and bade others of his warriors to do the same. Two horses were killed under him; four balls penetrated his coat. "Some potent Manitou guards his life," exclaimed the savage. "Death," wrote Washington, "was leveling my companions on every side of me; but, by the all-powerful dispensations of Providence, I have been protected." "To the public," said Davies, a learned divine in the following month, "I point out that heroic youth, Colonel Washington, whom I cannot but hope Providence has preserved in so signal a manner for some important service to his country." "Who is Mr. Washington?" asked Lord Halifax a few months later. "I know nothing of him," he added, "but that they say he behaved in Braddock's action as bravely as if he really loved the whistling of bullets."[21]

To some of the causes which led to this unhappy defeat, casual reference has been already made. Braddock was utterly unsuited for this important command. Though possessing brutal courage, he was haughty, self-sufficient, and overbearing, rejecting counsel of his Provincial and Indian allies, and adhering with stubborn bigotry to a rigid system of tactics adapted only to the open plains of civilized Europe.[22] He coolly told Franklin that Fort Duquesne could hardly detain him above three or four days, and then he should push on to Niagara and, having taken that, to Frontenac. "The Indians are dexterous in laying out and executing ambuscades," replied Franklin cautiously. "The savages," retorted Braddock, "may be formidable to your raw American militia; upon the King's regulars and disciplined troop it is impossible they should make any impression." Despising his foe, in spite of the warnings of the duke of Cumberland, his patron and friend, and scorning to provide against the dangerous ambush of the American savages, was the most capital of all his errors.

His surviving officers declared in a representation to Governor Shirley that Braddock was blamable for neglecting to cultivate friendship of the body of Indians who had proffered their services under Col. George Croghan; had they and the Provincials been employed as scouts and spies to precede the army, they would have seasonably discovered and thwarted the enemy's ambuscade. But instead of these precautions, the whole army was led by only three or four guides. None felt more keenly than Boone these egregious blunders; and to his dying day he would with profound sorrow censure Braddock's conduct generally and reprehend especially his fatal neglect to employ strong flank-guards and a sufficient number of Provincial scouts thoroughly acquainted with the wilderness and all the wiles and strategies of savage warfare.[23]

Colonel Dunbar, with the rear division of the army posted forty miles from the scene of action and having above a thousand troops under his command, instead of marching against the enemy and striving to regain some of the lost ground, or fortifying and sending for reinforcements, was seized with the prevailing infatuation, and to accelerate his flight, ordered all the stores and ammunition and part of the provisions to be destroyed and was actually obliged to send for thirty horse loads of the latter to Fort Cumberland, where he shortly after arrived with the shattered remains of the English army. The French and Indians, now unchecked, spread desolation along the frontiers of Pennsylvania and Virginia. Happily, at the south the Catawbas remained faithful, and the Cherokees renewed their ancient pledges of friendship and peace.[24]

Daniel Morgan, too, escaped the disasters of Braddock's defeat—except, perhaps, received there a shot aimed by an Indian, which entered the back of his neck and passed through his left cheek, knocking out all the rear teeth on that side. It is something remarkable that Boone and Morgan, of kindred blood, natives of the same region of country from which both had early emigrated to a distant frontier, were so singularly brought together in the same perilous service and were both so Providentially preserved for future usefulness of no ordinary character to their native country.

Rejoiced to get off with a whole scalp and his favorite horses, Boone in due time returned to his frontier home on the Yadkin. The experience he acquired in Indian warfare was not lost upon him. He gained too on Braddock's campaign some glimpses of the inviting loveliness of the fertile glades of the upper Ohio Valley. Possessing a naturally inquisitive turn of mind, he had perhaps heard something of the noble utterance of the far-seeing Franklin, who had grasped in advance of his age the comprehensive idea of colonizing the mighty valley of the West and had spoken eloquently in the Colonial Congress at Albany in June 1754 of that "great country back of the Appalachian mountains." He directed attention to the extreme richness of its land; the healthy temperature of the air; the mildness of the climate; and the vast convenience of inland navigation by the lakes and great rivers. "In less than a century," said he with the gift of prophecy, "it must undoubtedly become a populous and powerful dominion." And through Thomas Pownall, who had been present at Albany during the deliberations of the congress, he advised the immediate organization of two new colonies in the West, with powers of self-direction and government like those of Connecticut and Rhode Island: the one on Lake Erie, the other in the valley of the Ohio, with its capital on the banks of the Scion.[k] At this very juncture, too, the king instructed the governor-in-chief of Virginia to grant lands west of the Blue Ridge and Alleghenies, not exceeding a thousand acres to any one person, to all such adventurers as should be desirous of settling them, from which it was thought great additional security would be derived against the growing encroachments of the French.[25]

It was on Braddock's expedition that Boone first met with John Findlay, an Irish lover of adventure who had long been engaged in the wandering life of an Indian trader. Under what circumstances these congenial spirits were brought together tradition does not inform us. Findlay was probably one of the party who,

23. Cumberland Gap, gateway to Kentucky, America's first Far West. COPPER ENGRAVING BY H. FENN, D. APPLETON & CO., NEW YORK, 1872.

under George Croghan, had tendered their services to Braddock and were received in so cold and indifferent a manner. In Boone, an eager listener was found to the simple narrative of Findlay's rambles and discoveries in the Ohio Valley, and more especially in the Kentucky country and the Eldorado of the West. He described to Boone how he could, from North Carolina, find that unequaled land, by passing in a northwestwardly direction and penetrating the Cumberland or Ouasioto Mountain at the great gap, thence pursuing the ancient *"Warrior's Path"*[1] towards the Ohio.

This new stock of border information furnished Boone a fruitful topic for study precisely suited to his peculiar taste and temperament. He scarcely dared to express openly what he secretly cherished—the hope that he might, at no distant day, be permitted to feast his eyes upon that goodly land, the description of which so completely filled his *beau ideal* of a hunter's paradise.

DRAPER'S NOTES: CHAPTER 2

1. MS. letters of John F. Watson and Thomas Pearson. It may be added that some of the Boone connection were members of the established church, according to the authority of J. W. Biddle, Esq., who derived the fact from his aged half-sister, the late Miss Susannah Boone, who died in 1847 at the age of nearly seventy-six years.

2. See MS. Land Office Records, Harrisburg, Pennsylvania.

3. See Appendix for a sketch of Daniel Boone's brothers and sisters.

4. TFB: *In the microfilmed copy of the manuscript, there are an unknown number of words missing between DM 3B:35{1} and 36. The sentence was transcribed as it appears in the original text.*

5. One hundred and fifty eight and three fourths acres embracing the dwelling were sold to William Maugridge, and the remainder of the original tract to Joseph Boone, Sr., both under date April 11th, 1758—the former is now owned by James Lee, the latter by Jacob De Turck[?].—MS. letters of Thomas E. Lee of Berks County, Pennsylvania, 1852–'54.

6. General McAfee's sketch in the *Kentucky Yeoman,* on authority of the late Col. William L. Boone; MS. letter of Joshua Pennington, an aged surviving nephew of Daniel Boone's; on Fry and Jefferson's map of Virginia, drawn in 1751, is laid down the great road from the Yadkin River, "passing through the Blue Ridge in the same gap with the Staunton River, thence up" the valley of Virginia.

7. MS. statement of Mrs. Lemond, only surviving child of William and Elizabeth Grant.

8. It may be interesting to note the opinion of the celebrated Col. William Byrd the Elder of the Yadkin country, several years before its settlement, as derived from Indian traders who passed through that region on their way from Virginia with their merchandise for the Catawba towns. "The soil," says Colonel Byrd, "is exceedingly rich on both sides, the Yadkin abounding in rank grass and prodigiously large trees; and for plenty of fish, fowl and venison, is inferior to no part of the northern continent. There the traders commonly lie still for some days, to recruit their horses' flesh, as well as to recover their own spirits." Colonel Byrd's *History of the Dividing Line,* written in 1728, p. 85.

9. Ramsey's *South Carolina,* ii:598.

10. In 1753, thirty thousand deer-skins were exported from North Carolina.— Wynne, ii:299.

11. TFB: *Quoted in J. Stoddard Johnson,* First Explorations of Kentucky *(Louisville, KY: John P. Morgan, 1898), 162. This work contains the journals of Dr. Thomas Walker and Christopher Gist.*

12. *Maryland Gazette,* December 6, 1753.

13. MS. notes and statements of Isaiah Boone, who derived the facts from his father, Squire Boone.

14. Martin's *North Carolina,* ii:68.

15. *Maryland Gazette,* October 10, 1754.

16. Warburton's *Conquest of Canada,* ii:21.

17. Parkman states that Pontiac and Athanase took part in Braddock's defeat. Gov. Black Snake and Captain Decker, two venerable Seneca chiefs, assured one of the writers of this work that Gi-ya-so-do, or Guyasutha, as more commonly written, whom they both well knew, was in the action, but that neither Farmer's

Brother nor Cornplanter, as has been asserted, was there; and Captain Decker added that the French were also aided by the Shawanoes, Delawares, and Wyandots. The present venerable Col. John Johnston, long the faithful Indian agent of our government in Ohio, mentions the fact that the Wyandots obtained as a part of the spoils of victory a number of horses and then first introduced their use among their people.

18. The following fragment of an ancient backwoods ballad commemorative of Braddock's defeat and often sung in a plaintive strain at many a frontier cabin fire-side has been preserved in the memory of the venerable pioneer Mrs. Lydia Shepherd Cruger, near Wheeling:

> Sir Peter Halket whose courage was great, Fought like a soldier and would not retreat;
>
> He flew through the field, like Cato again, Saying "fight on, brave boys!"—alas, he was slain!
>
> Poor Britons—poor Britons—poor Britons remember,
>
> Although we fought hard, we were forced to surrender.
>
> The Major his son did ride up and down, Courageously fighting for old England's Crown,
>
> Until that he saw all attempts were in vain,
>
> From sighs and from tears he could scarcely refrain,
>
> Poor Britons, and etc.

19. MS. *Journal of Braddock's Expedition,* in the Royal Artillery Library, Woolwrich, quoted in Warburton's Conquest of Canada, ii:24.

20. Smith's Indian Narrative.

21. Bancroft, iv:190.

22. Warburton, ii:18.

23. "Want of intelligence and reconnoitering parties was the sole cause of defeat." General Kane's *Military History of Great Britain.*

24. The chief authorities consulted in the preparation of this narrative of Braddock's campaign have been Sparks, Bancroft, Parkman, Warburton, the gazettes of that day, together with a curious manuscript journal of the campaign preserved in the King's Library in the British Museum and recently published in Craig's *History of Pittsburgh.* Mante's *History of the French War, to 1772;* and the *Review of Military Operations in North America, Dublin Edition, 1757,* by William Livingston, afterwards governor of New Jersey, shed considerable light upon this expedition. The facts of Boone's connection within is derived from his son Col. Nathan Boone and his lady.

25. Bancroft, iv: 127, 167.

EDITOR'S NOTES: CHAPTER 2

a. For an explanation of cane and canebrakes, see chapter 6, note n.

b. In 1702 Piedmont traveler John Lawson reported seeing small droves of buffalo east of the Blue Ridge. In 1722 artist-naturalist Mark Catesby saw buffalo in South Carolina and painted a watercolor of one, which now hangs in Windsor Castle. East of the Appalachians, the beasts were killed out by the early 1700s.

c. The Catawba are a Siouan people who lived along the borders of North and South Carolina's Piedmont, building their towns along the Wateree and Catawba rivers, Twelve Mile and Sugar creeks, and at the forks of the Wateree and Santee at Pine Tree Hill. Although some Catawba traveled west of the Mississippi during the era of Indian removal, most chose to live in their native land, and so the nation endures today.

d. "Northern Indians" may be Draper's reference to the Shawnee, inveterate foes of the Catawba, who in 1763 killed their most beloved chief, Hagler. Catawba warriors avenged Hagler's death by killing his Shawnee assassins.

e. On May 28, 1754, near Great Meadows in now Fayette County, Pennsylvania, twenty-two-year-old Maj. George Washington and forty English troops and native guides attacked a thirty-three-man French reconnoitering party, killing ten, including the commander, Ens. Coulon de Jumonville, and capturing twenty-two. The one escapee fled to Fort Duquesne. Washington erected at the site a small square enclosure of dirt and log ramparts he dubbed Fort Necessity. On July 3 a detachment of French and Indians pursued Washington's half-starved forces to the tiny, roofless fort. On July 4, after enduring a nine-hour cross fire, Washington surrendered. As he and his men retreated and his Indian allies left in disgust, the French fired Fort Necessity.

f. Daniel Morgan (1736?–1802) was a Continental Army officer, frontiersman, and Revolutionary War hero. Genealogists disagree on these key points of Morgan's life: whether he was Daniel Boone's cousin or uncle or even related to him at all; whether he was born in 1735 or 1736; and whether he was born in Hunterdon County, New Jersey, or Bucks County, Pennsylvania.

g. For Pontiac, see chapter 16, note l.

h. At the time of French contact, the Hurons' land was Lake Simcoe, Ontario. In 1649 the Iroquois attacked the Hurons' homeland in an attempt to gain control of the fur trade and scattered the people. One hundred years later a remnant band of Hurons settled at the French Canadian town of Lorette near Quebec.

i. For more on the Leni-Lenape or Delaware, who were Algonquian speakers kin to the Shawnee, see chapter 3, note i.

j. For more on the Wyandots, see chapter 8, note k.

k. "Scion" refers to Ohio's Scioto River, which flows just south of the Upper Sandusky and empties into the Ohio near Portsmouth.

l. The "Warrior's Path," or *Athiamiowee,* meaning "path of the armed ones," was a major native war road bisecting Kentucky north and south. Shawnee and Cherokee warriors traveled it to war upon each other's towns. *Athiamiowee* went north through the Cumberland Gap, crossed the Cumberland, and went on past Station Camp Creek to beyond the Red River near the Shawnee town of Es-kip-pa-ki-thi-ki. It ended in present-day Mason County at the Ohio.

CHAPTER 3

The Bryan Family.—Daniel Boone's Courtship and Marriage.—Personal Appearance of the Newly Married Couple.—Commence House-keeping.—Fort Dobbs Erected.—Adventures of Col. William Byrd.—Incidents of the War.—Daniel Boone Returns to Virginia, Occupation There.—Indian Troubles.—Return to the Yadkin.—Hunts in East Tennessee.—Interesting Memorial.

The Bryan family deserves special notice, alike from their intimate association with the Boones and early connection with the Kentucky story. Morgan Bryan, a native of Ireland, emigrated to America and seems to have settled in the region of York County, Pennsylvania. Marrying Martha Strode, they raised eight strong and healthy children, whose names in their order were— Joseph, Eleanor, Morgan, Samuel, John, James, William, and Thomas. In the year 1731 Joist Hite and Robert McCoy of Pennsylvania obtained a grant for one hundred and forty thousand acres of land in the valley of Virginia, on condition of settling on it their own and a hundred other families, which was shortly after effected by the requisite emigration from Pennsylvania.[1] Among these families appears to have been Morgan Bryan's, who, together with Hite, settled on Opeckon Creek, a few miles from Winchester. Not many years after, the Bryan family removed up the Virginia Valley a hundred and seventy-five miles to the Big Lick near the head of Roanoke, in then Augusta, now Roanoke County, evidently bent on occupying the out-skirts of civilization. That was then a wild frontier greatly infested with wolves, upon which a bounty of five shillings each, Virginia currency, was offered, and during the single year 1744, thrice of the Bryan connection received the premium on the scalps of fourteen wolves.[2]

Still desirous of keeping in advance of others, the Bryans migrated to the Yadkin Valley probably as early as 1746; several of the children were then married and had large families. The Bryan settlement in the forks of the Yadkin was certainly made several years before Squire Boone located in the same region. When the Bryans first settled there, they selected the choicest lands and engaged largely in hunting. The nearest white settlement from which they obtained corn for food and planting was sixty miles distant; and as a consequence, their little supply of corn was carefully husbanded until the crop was raised, relying mainly for sustenance upon milk, game, and the wild fruits of the country. Their horses and cattle kept in good order feeding the whole year exclusively upon the range;

when the range gave out near home, it would be sought farther off, until at length the Bryans would have to drive their stock sixty or seventy miles, and even west of the spurs of the Allegheny, and go occasionally to look after and salt them.[3]

The heart's affections glow as warmly in a cabin as a palace—in the woods as "in cities cag'd"; and if there is less of blandishment, there is more of true love and unadorned simplicity. Little Cupid occasionally found his way into the wild region of the Yadkin and taught that "unsighing people of the woods" how to unite two kindred hearts and trudge along life's journey happily together. The advent of the Boones into the Yadkin Valley was the signal of extending the acquaintance and enlarging the social relations of the Bryans, hitherto pent-up and limited by the circumstances with which they were surrounded. William Bryan, next to the youngest of the seven brothers, was now grown to manhood and meeting with, wooed, and won the fair Mary Boone and in the fall of 1753 was united with her in marriage. At this wedding of his sister, Daniel Boone first saw the young and pensive face of the sweet Rebecca Bryan. She was a daughter of Joseph Bryan and then scarcely fifteen years of age. If Boone's eyes were ever "shined,"[a] as Flint declares, *that* was the time and the occasion; and of one thing we are quite certain, that his heart at all events was "shined" by the love of a noble girl, who was all unconscious of warming into being new feelings and affections of which young Boone had never before been the happy possessor.

They met a second time. It was the next season, during the early general warmth of summer when cherries were ripe and a number of young people were gathered together, sitting socially upon a ridge of green turf beneath the shady trees enjoying the delicious fruit. Boone sat beside Rebecca, musing doubtless in his own mind whether she would make him a worthy help-mate, when, with apparent thoughtlessness, he took his knife and made several sad incisions in one corner of her white cambric apron—an article rarely to be met with in the backwoods of that day. Her mild disposition forbade the thought of hastily checking her seemingly absent-minded lover, as most others would have done under similar circumstances. Boone gained his point. He only resorted to this singular expedient, as he used afterwards pleasantly to relate, *to try her temper;* if it had been fiery, he was certain she would fly into a passion. This was Boone's mode of studying character; and in this instance, the experience of sixty years proved the correctness of his judgment.

What thoughts now almost entirely absorbed young Boone's mind it is needless to conjecture. He had gone to the wars and returned home in safety; and doubtless the fair Rebecca, like Desdemona,[b] loved him all the better for the dangers through which he had passed. If he had hitherto pondered much about the practicality of making important discoveries in the distant enchanting land of Kentucky, he now began to think, for his own comfort and happiness, how he could best secure the conquest of a prize he had discovered considerably nearer home. The autumn and winter after his return from the gory fields of Monongahela quickly wore away; and in the spring of 1756, Boone led to the Hymeneal altar the object of his affections. In the beautiful language of Scripture, he "took

Rebecca, and she became his wife, and he loved her."[c] As old Squire Boone for several years held the office of justice of the peace in Rowan County, he probably officiated on the joyous occasion. And to add to the interest and hilarity of the season, two other young couples were, [*wi*] time and place, made happy in the marriage union.

Behold that young man exhibiting such unusual firmness and energy of character, five feet eight inches in height, with broad chest and shoulders, his form gradually tapering downwards to his extremities; his hair moderately black; blue eyes arched with yellowish eye-brows; his lips thin with a mouth peculiarly wide; a countenance fair and ruddy with a nose a little bordering on the Roman order. Such was Daniel Boone, now past twenty-one, presenting altogether a noble manly, prepossessing appearance.[d] Flint, in his bit of sentimental romance, represents Boone as encountering the fair Rebecca in one of his nocturnal rambles and mistaking her bright eyes for those of a deer, almost eventually fatally; and closes by describing her as a "flaxen-haired" beauty. In all this there is not the least semblance of truth. Rebecca Bryan, whose brow had been fanned by the breezes of seventeen summers, was like Rebecca of old, "very fair to look upon,"[e] with jet black hair and eyes, complexion rather dark, and something over the common size of her sex, her whole demeanor expressive of her child-like artlessness, pleasing in her address, and unaffectedly kind in all her deportment. Never was there a more gentle, affectionate, forbearing creature than this same fair youthful bride of the Yadkin. Such were the couple who had now solemnly vowed, for better or for worse, to love and cherish each other till inexorable death should dissever the union.

Boone and his young wife now commenced home-keeping in a small way, occupying for a while a cabin in his father's yard, and then settling on a small stream called Sugar-Tree, an upper tributary of Dutchman's Creek, a few miles northwardly of Squire Boone's in the Bryan settlement. All this region is within the limits of the present day county of Davie, which is esteemed one of the most prolific of the grain-growing districts of North Carolina. The lands along Sugar-Tree Creek are level and mostly of a rich, black, gravelly character; and here Boone erected a cabin and cleared a small farm, where he continued for ten years to reside, except forced at intervals to abandon it by Indian alarms and invasions.[4] His time in the cropping season was employed at home, to raise and secure a sufficiency of provisions for family use; and when not occasionally engaged in wagoning, the rest of the year, especially the fall and winter, was spent in hunting to obtain a plentiful supply of fresh and jerked meat, and with the furs and skins to procure in exchange such articles beyond their own production as the simple wants of himself and family required. "The first inhabitants," says the historian Ramsey of South Carolina, speaking of the frontiers, "being easily supplied with all the necessaries of life, esteemed the country, especially when at peace with the Indians, as an asylum from the toils, cares and diseases incident to man. This happy and contented state of mind contributed, with the salubrious nature of the climate, to procure for them an exemption from disease."

24. *"Col. Daniel Boon." James O. Lewis' line-and-stipple engraving of Chester Harding's original full-length portrait. Harding destroyed the oil portrait in 1861, and this engraving—released as a limited edition in St. Louis two weeks after Boone's death—is the only full-length image from life and the first print published to authentically depict the dress of the American woodsman.* ORIGINAL ENGRAVING HOUSED AT MISSOURI STATE HISTORICAL SOCIETY; REPRODUCTION BY PATHFINDER PRESS.

While the southern frontiers were not yet actually suffering the horrors of war, the dread notes of preparation were mutteringly heard in the distance. During the year 1756, the province ordered the erection of a fortification between Third and Fourth creeks of the Yadkin in Rowan County, which received the name of Fort Dobbs in honor of the governor. It was an oblong square fifty-three feet long by forty-three wide; the opposite angles were twenty-two by twenty-four feet high, having three stories, each of which was so well provided with loop-holes that above one hundred muskets could be discharged at a time. This fortress was made sufficiently commodious and located centrally that in times of imminent danger the inhabitants of the Yadkin country might resort there for safety.

At a treaty held by Governor Glen with the Cherokees the previous summer, assembled under a spreading tree in the western highlands of South Carolina, the privilege was freely granted to erect forts in their country for their protection against the designs of the French. Fort Prince George was accordingly built and garrisoned high up the Savannah River and within gun shot of the Indian town of Ke-o-wee.

Col. William Byrd and Col. Peter Randolph visited the Cherokees in 1756 as commissioners from Virginia in order to cement more strongly the bonds of friendship and alliance and engage them more heartily in the British cause. In the midst of negotiations promising the most successful results, a few fugitive Cherokees returned to the nation who had been north to assist the Virginians against the common enemy, and several of whose companions had been treacherously waylaid and murdered by a party of savage monsters in human shape, on the confines of that province, on the pretense of their having pilfered some poultry. The horrid act, however, was instigated alone by the hope of gain on the part of the base perpetrators by endeavoring to palm off the scalps of the slain as having been taken from hostile Indians, for which a considerable reward had been offered. The few Cherokees who fortunately escaped brought the melancholy tidings to their people, producing at once the utmost rage and excitement. "Death to the Virginia ambassadors" was wildly shouted from every quarter.

Amid the exciting scene, the renowned At-ta-kul-la-Kul-la, or the little Carpenter, for nearly thirty years the steady friend of the English, hastened to the commissioners, apprised them of their danger and urged them to conceal or barricade themselves as well as they could and not to appear abroad on any account. A council was called. "Whatever else we may do," exclaimed At-ta-kul-la-Kul-la, "let us never violate our faith or the laws of hospitality by imbuing our hands in the blood of those who are now in our power. They came to us in the confidence of friendship, with belts of wampum,[f] to cement a perpetual alliance with us. Let us conduct them safely back to their own settlements; and then, if we fail to obtain satisfaction, we can take up the hatchet."

It was proposed that Colonel Byrd should be sacrificed in revenge for the loss of their countrymen. In the council was a distinguished young war-chief named Si-lou-ee, or the Young Warrior of Es-ta-to-e, who on some former occasion had contracted an acquaintance and friendship with Colonel Byrd. Every

25. *"The Three Cherokees, Came Over from the Head of the River Savanna to London, 1762. 1: Their interpreter that was poisoned. 2: Outacite or Mankiller. 3. Austenaco, or King. 4: Uschesees ye Great Hunter, or Scalpper." Lt. Henry Timberlake took this Cherokee delegation to London, where Sir Joshua Reynolds and Francis Parsons painted and engraved their portraits.* BUREAU OF AMERICAN ETHNOLOGY, SMITHSONIAN INSTITUTION.

night this faithful Indian came to him in his tent and told him not to be afraid, that they should not kill him. After many days' deliberation, however, the determination was contrary to Si-lou-ee's expectation, that Byrd should be put to death, and some warriors were dispatched as executioners. Si-lou-ee attended them, and when they entered the tent, he suddenly threw himself between them and their intended victim and exclaimed to the warriors, "This man is my friend: Before you get at him, you must kill me!" On this they desisted and returned, and the council respected the principle so much as to recede from their determination. It was a noble act on the part of the young chieftain and a magnanimous exercise of forbearance on the part of the Cherokee council. The treaty was now resumed and amicably concluded, permission granted for the erection of a fort on the Tennessee River, and a pledge given to send more warriors to the aid of their Virginia brothers.[5]

In the course of the year, Maj. Andrew Lewis was sent by Virginia to build the fort according to the stipulation. Capt. Paul Demere was left to garrison it with a small body of two hundred men, three fifths of whom were provincials, having a train of twelve pieces of artillery.[6] Major Lewis, before returning to Virginia, advised Governor Dobbs of North Carolina that the French by correspondence and emissaries contrived to influence the Cherokees, who began to show evident signs of displeasure at seeing so many well-armed white people in the heart of their nation. On the receipt of this information, Capt. Hugh Waddell was dispatched with a small party to reinforce Captain Demere. The original fort appears to have been located on the northern bank of the Tennessee, just below the mouth of Four Mile Creek and nearly opposite to Chotee; and this seems to have been abandoned, and Fort Loudon erected on the southern bank of the Tennessee, a few miles lower down and about one mile above the junction of the Tellico.[7]

The year 1757 passed away, and there was yet no real danger in the Yadkin country. The war had thus far resulted disastrously to the English cause—driven from the Ohio Valley; compelled to surrender Fort Necessity; overwhelmingly defeated at Monongahela; Fort William Henry on Lake George carried and its garrison inhumanely massacred;[g] frontier forts in New York, Pennsylvania, and Virginia taken, their inmates butchered, burned, or hopelessly captivated; well-digested campaigns miscarried; the whole northern frontier, by swarming bands of French and Indians, rendered almost one continued scene of unexplained terror and desolation. Gen. William Johnson had gained a victory over Dieskau,[h] and Col. John Armstrong made a successful expedition against Kittanning;[i] all else wore an aspect sad and gloomy.

But in 1758 the salutary effect of Pitt's new administration began to be powerfully felt, as well in Great Britain as the Colonies; new life and energy were infused into every department. Expeditions wisely planned were vigorously executed. Louisbourg,[j] Frontenac,[k] and Duquesne[l] successively fell into the hands of the victorious English and their only check was that of Abercrombie at Ticonderoga.[m] These unfortunate results paved the way for the capture of Niagara and Quebec the following year and the ultimate conquest of all Canada and, with it, the final downfall of French power and dominion in North America.

A body of Cherokees early in 1758 joined Colonel Washington at Winchester with a view to participating in General Forbes' projected campaign against Duquesne. The Raven Warrior made an unsuccessful scout and, returning, produced two white men's scalps which he pretended he had taken from the enemy. In this, however, he was detected by the other warriors as having endeavored to palm off scalps which he had brought from his own nation; and so highly were they offended at his baseness that they threatened his life. A consciousness of his guilt and a dread of being called to a severe account by his own countrymen were the reasons which many of them assigned for his abrupt and unsatisfactory departure. Others of the Cherokees who had been tempted to take part in the expedition, with the prospect of rich presents from the king's stores, came forward so early that they grew weary, discontented, and troublesome, and finally most of them went off in a fit of ill-humor.[8]

On their way home during the month of May, they are said to have killed the cattle, destroyed the plantations, and carried off the horses of the frontier inhabitants of Virginia; and the people, after suffering a great deal of very ill treat-ment from them, at last betook themselves to their arms, and in two or three skir-mishes which ensued, twelve or fourteen of the Cherokees were killed, several wounded, and the rest put to flight. They still continued their robberies, though not so openly as at first, being awed by the number of militia in actual service.

In palliation of the conduct of the Cherokees, it has been said that the horses on the frontiers ran wild in the woods, and it was customary for both whites and Indians to appropriate them indiscriminately to their own use; and even if justly belonging to the border settlers, the Indians probably possessed no very nice sense of the rights of property. Be this as it may, returning home highly provoked and besmeared with blood, they met a party of Cherokee warriors under the con-duct of Col. William Byrd marching to the assistance of General Forbes. When made acquainted with the usage their brethren had received, they were extremely irritated and were only appeased and with difficulty persuaded to continue on the rout when informed that the Indians alone were the aggressors. Their frequent de-sertions during the season, inducted by bad treatment, led to apprehensions of some premeditated blow against the frontiers, especially if General Forbes' expe-dition should happen to miscarry.[9]

George Turner, a person well suited for the purpose, was dispatched to the Cherokee nation by the Earl of Loudon, commander-in-chief in North America, to solicit as large a number of their warriors as possible to join the troops on the Vir-ginia frontiers. At-ta-kul-la-Kul-la, O-con-nos-to-ta, and several influential chiefs engaged warmly in the enterprise. But on the appointed day of rendezvous at Cho-tee the 21st of June, they refused to go till fall, as their conjurers had pre-dicted that much sickness and death would be the consequence should they go be-fore that time; and At-ta-kul-la-Kul-la particularly pledged himself that in the autumn he would, if desired, join General Forbes at the head of three hundred warriors.[10] A body of them accordingly went to Forbes' assistance in the fall, but so coldly were they treated by that commander that even At-ta-kul-la-Kul-la, so long the devoted friend of the English, left the army late in November and re-turned in disgust to his people.[11] Shortly anterior to his arrival, the Cherokees had been still further provoked by an unwarranted attack on a number of their hunters by Captain Wade and a party of Virginians.[12]

Driven from Fort Duquesne, the French retired down the Ohio, and some of their most active emissaries, well-supplied with spirituous liquors, arms, and am-munition, hastened among the already disaffected Cherokees at a time when their half-smothered rage needed but the slightest fanning to burst forth in uncontrol-lable fury. While At-ta-kul-la-Kul-la and ninety-odd headmen and warriors of their nation were visiting the governor and Council of South Carolina at Charleston in April 1759, with many professions of peace, their more irascible fellows at home were incited to take up the hatchet and embroil their nation in open hostilities with their white neighbors. Their vengeance first fell upon some unsuspecting soldiers engaged in hunting near Fort Loudon when, at the close of April, they invaded the country along the Yadkin and Catawba rivers, killing

Thomas Adams, John Snap, Daniel Halsey, Joseph Rentford, and Thomas Ellis in the upper branch of the Yadkin; John Hanna and his family, supposed to be seven in number, near Fort Hobbs below South Yadkin; John Mull on the Catawba, together with several others. The friendly Catawba Indians were greatly exasperated when they heard of these murders and instantly sent thirty of their best warriors under Capt. Matthew Tool in pursuit of the enemy. Meanwhile, all the frontier inhabitants were very much alarmed, many of whom desisted from planting, while others fell to fortifying themselves or fled to Fort Dobbs for protection.[13]

The borders of South Carolina also felt the stroke of the merciless Indian tomahawk. A few facts attested by an eye-witness will give some faint idea of the sufferings of the frontier settlers. A young man was shot through the body and through the thigh, one of his arms was broken, and he [was] scalped. A tomahawk was driven into his head, and the muscles of his neck were so far divided that his chin lodged on his breast, and several arrows were shot into his body. In this condition, after he had extracted the arrows, he walked twenty miles before he could get any assistance. Another was found wounded in the woods, where he had lain nine days without bread or water, incapable of helping or even of moving himself. An attempt was made to move him, but he instantly expired. When settlements were attacked by the Indians, some would escape, conceal or lose themselves in the woods, in which condition they have been known to wander two or three weeks living on snakes and such articles of food as the woods afforded. Several who were scalped and otherwise badly mangled had the good fortune to recover, though they received no aid from regular physicians or surgeons.[n] Women and children were oftener the subjects of these barbarities than men, while the latter, by resistance, for the most part obtained the superior boon of being killed outright.[14]

Until this outbreak in 1759, the western borders of the Carolinas had thriven rapidly. They had received large accessions from the frontiers of the more northerly provinces, where five years [of] almost constant massacres had disheartened the people and caused many of them to retire to a region where all the blessings of peace were fully enjoyed. Among those who were thus induced to settle in the backwoods of South Carolina were the families of the Calhouns and Pickens from the valley of Virginia. The tide now turned; while some forted, not a few fled to the old settlements along the Atlantic remote from dread and danger.

While the Bryans and probably some of the Boone connection took refuge in Fort Dobbs, Samuel Boone and family removed to the old settlements in South Carolina, and old Squire Boone and wife, his son Daniel Boone, and son-in-law William Grant, with their families, retired to Virginia and Maryland. When Squire Boone and family removed in 1750 from Pennsylvania to North Carolina, he left his youngest son, Squire, then a lad of six years, with his cousin Samuel

Boone, a gunsmith, to learn the trade at a suitable age. This Samuel Boone, with several others of the Boone relatives, soon after removed to Maryland and settled in or near Georgetown, now in the District of Columbia, which town was laid out by an act of the Maryland Assembly passed May 15th, 1751, and, according to tradition in the Boone family, was named in memory of old George Boone.[15] Here Squire Boone and his son-in-law Grant repaired and remained three years among their connections.[16]

Daniel Boone conveyed his wife and their two little sons in a two horse wagon to Culpepper County, in Eastern Virginia, and there took up his temporary abode in the settlement of the Fields, Greens, and Slaughters, who employed him with his team to transport tobacco to Fredericksburg, the nearest market town. One of his employers sent a Negro with a neck piece of bull beef for Boone's provision during one of his trips to Fredericksburg. Discovering at a glance that the meat was as firm and clammy as though it had really been a part of one of the ancient animals old Noah had driven into the ark and survived the flood, he directed the Negro to lay it down, who, with all imaginable innocence, quietly placed it upon the nearest stump. Sternly eying the bull beef for a moment with no enviable feelings, Boone seized a billet of wood and commenced beating it all around the ground at a terrible rate, without seeming in the least to notice how busy it kept poor Sambo dodging from one place to another to prevent his shins coming in contact with the nimble handspike. Perfectly dumb-founded at this curious exhibition, the Negro asked "Massa Daniel," when he got through with his violent beating process, what it all meant. "Oh, nothing particularly," replied Boone with becoming gravity. "I thought it looked plaguy tough, and I was only trying to see if I could possibly make it tender; but it's all to no purpose." The Negro reported the scene to his old master, who, taking the hint, saw that Boone ever after fared as well as himself.[17]

After the bloody onslaught of the Cherokees on the Yadkin borders in April, a calm ensued; the most of the nation, by repeated letters and friendly strings of wampum, disavowed the act. Governor Lyttleton of South Carolina, however, insisted, on their surrendering, on executing the offending chiefs and strictly interdicted further supplies of ammunition and merchandise on the part of the traders. The Indians brooded over these new wrongs, as they deemed them, and scarcely knew what to do. But Lyttleton, charging that some concert of action was on foot between the Creeks and Cherokees, dispatched a haughty message to the latter that if they desired peace to send deputies to him and they should come and return in safety; yet at the same time, he embodied fifteen hundred men to march against them. The British traders had fled from the nation and taken refuge at Fort Prince George; and the frontier people had betaken themselves to forts of their own construction in each of which some thirty or forty men with their families huddled together.

Just at this juncture, a deputation of over thirty chiefs arrived from the Cherokees, headed by At-ta-kul-la-Kul-la and O-con-nos-to-ta, or the Great War-

*26. William Henry Lyttleton,
governor of South Carolina,
1765–1760.*

rior. Lyttleton reproached them with double-dealing and treated them with no measured contempt and, towards the close of October, marched for the frontiers, promising protection to the Indian delegation; but at Congaree, the governor treacherously seized the Cherokee deputies and upon his arrival at Fort Prince George crowded them all into an insignificant hut. Finally, in December, Lyttleton demanded of At-ta-kul-la-Kul-la twenty-four of his people to be put to death or otherwise disposed of as he should think fit, in retaliation for at least that number of whites killed by the Cherokees. "I have ever been the firm friend of the English," answered the old chief. "I will ever continue so; but for giving up the men, we have no authority over one another." O-con-nos-to-ta and one or two others of the imprisoned deputies were liberated by substituting others in their places, when a patched-up treaty was signed by half a dozen chiefs, in partial duress, professedly sanctioning the retention of the envoys as hostages till twenty-four Cherokees should be delivered up to suffer punishment for the misdeeds of some of their wayward people. This treaty was blazoned forth throughout the colonies as a piece of consummate diplomacy, and Lyttleton, dismissing his troops, returned with an air of uncommon triumph to Charleston.

No sooner had the army withdrawn from their borders than the insincerity of the Cherokees generally began to manifest itself in such a manner that hopes of peace were no longer indulged. Nine of the traders who had, upon the heels of

Lyttleton's short-lived treaty, hurried back to the Indian settlements with fresh supplies of goods to drive a profitable trade were suddenly cut off; some were made prisoners, while a fortunate few chanced to make good their escape. War parties infested all the roads and trails, beleaguered Fort Loudon, and masked the frontiers with savage repine and bloodshed.

With the design to surprise Fort Prince George, about eighty Cherokee warriors suddenly appeared before that fort on the 18th or 19th of January, 1760, headed by Si-lou-ee, or the Young Warrior of Es-ta-to-e, the Round O, Tiftoe, and other war leaders, pretending to have brought two of the Indian murderers demanded by Lyttleton's treaty, and wished to exchange them for two of the hostages and desired admission into the fort altogether that they might see their friends and make the selection. A few only were admitted at a time; their Indian murderers they soon pretended had escaped, and thus whatever intentions they might have had of surprising the fort and releasing the hostages were happily frustrated. They, however, killed a straggling soldier and wounded another and went to John Elliott's trading establishment a mile and a half from the fort, chased and killed him, together with ten other traders and their retainers, made two captives, seized their goods, and strutted in their blankets. For several weeks, they continued to hover around the fort insolent and watchful, making reiterated demands for the hostages, which were of course unheeded.[18]

While Patrick Calhoun with about one hundred and fifty persons, forty of whom were fighting men, were on the first of February removing with their most valuable effects from the Long Cane settlement on the frontiers of South Carolina, they were unexpectedly attacked as they were emerging from a bog fifty miles above Augusta, Georgia, by about one hundred mounted Cherokees; and in half an hour about forty men, women, and children were killed and taken, others dispersed, and several wagons with their loads captured by the enemy. Twenty dead bodies of the mangled slain were afterwards found upon the spot, and many of the children were subsequently discovered wandering in the woods without food or shelter. One man alone brought no less than nine of them to Augusta, whom he had picked up in two different parties, some of them terribly cut with tomahawks and left for dead, others scalped, and all yet alive. On the second of the same month, two Indian spies were captured near Fort Ninety-Six° in South Carolina; and the next day about forty Cherokees fired for two hours incessantly upon that fortress but were repulsed with several of their numbers slain. "We fatten our dogs with their carcasses," wrote one of the defenders to Lyttleton, "and display their scalps, neatly ornamented, on the tops of our bastions."[19] The same day, one Davis, removing to Augusta with twenty-three women and children in charge, was waylaid near Steven's Creek, about twenty miles above Augusta; and after defending himself and party as long as he could and slaying single-handed two of his assailants, he was at length forced to fly when most of the helpless women and children were mangled and killed.[20] Turner's Fort, thirty miles east of Ninety-Six, commanded by Capt. Andrew Brown, was fiercely attacked for four hours, but the Indians were beaten off with the loss of seven of their warriors.

O-con-nos-to-ta appeared before Fort Prince George on the 16th of February and called for Lieutenant Coytmore, the commandant of the garrison, who went out with a small party in hailing distance. The Great Warrior professed peace, saying that he wished to go and see the governor on business of great importance and desired a white man to accompany him. As this was all satisfactory, O-con-nos-to-ta proposed to catch a horse for the white man to ride, and then swung a bridle, which he held carelessly in his hands, thrice over his head. This proved to be a signal for a concealed party of warriors, who instantly discharged twenty-five or thirty guns, mortally wounding Coytmore, and two others slightly. Fearing the hostages might attempt their deliverance, orders were quickly given for binding and ironing them; but in attempting to do this, the Indians rose on the soldiers, tomahawked and stabbed one till he was killed on the spot and badly tomahawked another; when all the hostages were immediately put to death. The remainder of that day and the following night, O-con-nos-to-ta and his party kept up their attack on the fort; and ignorant of the fate of their unhappy fellows in the garrison, they called out repeatedly in their native language, *Fight strong and you shall be assisted!* Their puny efforts against a strong fort well supplied with food, fuel, and ammunition were unavailing.

Near the middle of March, thirty Rowan County rangers who were out on a scout came suddenly upon a party of forty Cherokee warriors busily engaged in skinning a bullock near a deserted house and not far from the Catawba River. After exchanging a few shots, the Indians betook themselves to the house, where a firing was briskly kept up on both sides for several hours, the whites being securely placed behind a fodder-stack and some small out-cabins, which enabled them fully to command both the door and chimney of the house and prevent any retreat on the part of the enemy.

At length one John Perkins, having formerly lost some of his family by the savages, was much exasperated and proposed to set the house on fire. This was quickly seconded by another brave fellow, and these two intrepid men successfully effected their enterprise, and though exposed to the fire of all the Indians, they escaped unhurt. Seeing their impending danger, one of the Indians observed to his comrades that it was better for one to die rather than all should perish. Then, strictly charging them to be ready to issue through the door the moment he should have extracted the fire of the assailants, to which they readily agreed, he darted out-side, skipping hither and thither from one place to another in order to draw as much of their fire as possible. He fell and expired—and though an untutored savage, he was a real hero. Before those of the whites whose guns were empty could re-load, the Indians rushed out of the house and several escaped, but seven of them fell as they ran by the fatal rifles of the rangers. One was said to have remained in the house and perished in the flames; and John Perkins' dog followed one of the wounded fugitives into the river and held him fast till he drowned. None of the rangers were killed. Several dead bodies of the Indians who died of their wounds were afterward found in the woods by different scouting parties, so that altogether, nineteen Indian scalps were obtained, for which quite a bounty was then paid. On one of the slain Indians was found six scalps of white people, freshly taken.[21]

When this brilliant little engagement happened, Colonel Waddell was stationed at Fort Dobbs, where the Bryans and some of the Boones had taken refuge. The few of the Cherokee party who survived this affair on the Catawba, joining with others, attacked Fort Dobbs but were repulsed with loss; and it was believed that of the original forty Indians who entered Rowan County, scarcely one was left alive to relate to his people the successive disasters of this singular border foray. About this time, on the other hand, John Long and Robert Gillespie, on their return from a visit to Colonel Waddell at Fort Dobbs, were both shot and scalped seven miles from the fort, and [Long having been] pierced with eight bullets and Gillespie seven.[22] A woman and four children were likewise butchered in the most barbarous manner. Other events of an equally exciting or tragic a character were not wanting to give a sad variety to the scene then enacting along the Carolina borders.

In April General Amherst detached six hundred Highlanders and as many Royal Americans under Colonel Montgomery, afterwards Lord Eglinton, and Major Grant, to give the Cherokees a sudden chastisement and then rejoin the main army at the north in time to take part in the Canada campaign. Seven hundred Carolina rangers, a few of whom were from North Carolina under Colonel Waddell, attended by a small party of Catawba warriors under their old King Heigler, joined the regulars at Ninety-Six near the close of May, and all marched forward to make a bold stroke at the restless savages in their sequestered homes in the fair vallies of Ke-o-wee and Tennessee. All the towns and villages in the Lower Settlements were laid waste with fire and sword; about seventy Cherokees were killed; forty persons, chiefly women and children, taken; large magazines of corn together with their growing crops destroyed; and the survivors obliged to subsist many months upon horse-flesh and wild roots.[23] At Sugar Town were found the remains of a white prisoner whom the savages had that very morning put to the torture.

Between eight and nine o'clock in the morning of the twenty-seventh of June, Si-lou-ee and other war-leaders at the head of six hundred and thirty warriors suddenly emerged from their ambush in a swampy thicket on the southern bank of the Chow-howee or Little Tennessee, within six miles of Et-cho-wee and just in advance of a narrow defile called Crow's Creek, where the path along the river bank was hemmed in by a lofty mountain. Captain Morrison of the Provincial rangers was shot dead while penetrating the thicket in front, when Captain Williams of the Royal Americans, going to his support, was also slain, the Indians mistaking him for Colonel Montgomery. Lt. Patrick Calhoun of the rangers succeeded Captain Morrison and well sustained the high reputation of the company.[24] The Indians resorted to their usual practice of yelling hideously to intimidate the whites; but the sturdy Highlanders and expert Provincials, far from being deterred, raised three loud huzzas, accompanied with three waves of their hats and Scotch bonnets, and drove the enemy from their looking places, hotly pursuing them over hills and mountains, through streams and vallies. These operations lasted between four and five hours. During the remainder of the day the troops were thrice fired upon by the skulking foe and in the night reached Et-cho-wee and encamped in a hollow square, having lost twenty killed and about sixty wounded. The Cherokees had many rifles among them and were hence enabled to do much execution; fifty of their warriors were supposed to have fallen that day.

Thus far this expedition had been conducted with that energy and celerity so essential to success against the wily Indian. Remaining but a single day at Et-cho-wee and there several times fired upon in camp, Montgomery resolved to retreat and abandon his original design of relieving Fort Loudon. As a number of his horses had been killed and others wounded, he deemed it impossible to go forward with his provisions and baggage and at the same time provide for the removal of his wounded; so at midnight succeeding the 28th, the army, deceiving the Indians by kindling fires in the huts and cabins, silently withdrew. Encountering a few parties of warriors during their return, they either killed them or easily put them to flight. Hastening to Charleston, Montgomery thence sailed for the north, notwithstanding the entreaties of the South Carolina Assembly for him to remain. "I cannot help the people's fears," wrote the haughty Scotch colonel. His hurried departure gave the Cherokees not only occasion to boast of their prowess in having completely driven him and his army from their country and the province, but left them entirely free to desolate the frontier and press the siege of Fort Loudon.[25]

Sad indeed was the condition of that devoted garrison. On the twentieth of March the Overhill Cherokees made an attack on the fort and kept up an incessant firing for four days and nights. The faithful At-ta-kul-la-Kul-la retired with his family into the woods to avoid being a painful spectator of a scene he could not prevent; and O-con-nos-to-ta was absent at the time on a hunt down the Tennessee. No great damage seems to have been done on that occasion; but the garrison, to prepare for the worst, were each put upon the short allowance of a single pint of corn a day. Seeing no Indians, Lt. Maunce Anderson, with a pack-horse man named Thomas Smith, ventured on out the fifty or seventy yards from the fort upon the hill-side, when both were killed and scalped. The last scanty supply of corn was obtained at the rate of sixteen pounds per bushel by almost stripping themselves, women as well as men, to effect the purchase; but no relief came, the Indians were vigilant, and the last month the garrison was without any kind of bread. Many of the soldiers had contracted marriage after the Indian manner with squaws, whose attachment to their distressed husbands and friends in the fort was truly remarkable. They conveyed by stealth hogs and Indian beans, notwithstanding Wil-lan-i-waw, the head chief of Toqua, anxious to hasten the surrender of the garrison by starvation, threatened death to all who should assist the whites; but these devoted Indian women, laughing at his threats, boldly told him they would succor their husbands every day and were sure that should he kill them, their relations would make his death atone for theirs. Wil-lan-i-waw, too sensible of this, did not venture to inflict punishment, so that the pent-up garrison subsisted a long time on the provisions obtained in this manner. Discovering at length that the whites in their straitened circumstances made use of the flesh of lean dogs and horses, the Indians took care that no more of these animals were suffered to go within their reach. Upon much precarious supplies, the soldiers became quite debilitated.

Night and day the enemy kept up so close an investment that none dared to stir out for even wood or water; and so well were the trails guarded that it was almost impossible for any one to escape from the fort. Several ineffectual attempts were made to bring about a peace, but the Cherokee chieftains considered the garrison as starving and told them they must soon be entirely at their mercy. Parties of the soldiers began to desert on nights and throw themselves upon the compassion of the Indians, and the men in general threatened to abandon the fort and betake themselves to the woods rather than remain longer only to perish by the slow and painful process of starvation. At length, on the 6th of August, having had no intelligence from the settlements for over two months, when their situation had become miserable beyond description and the garrison seemingly forsaken of God and man, they resolved to deputize Capt. John Stuart to go to Cho-tee and procure the best possible terms from the enemy.[26]

It was agreed the following day that the fort should be surrendered to the Indians with the cannon, ammunition, and spare arms without fraud; that the garrison should be permitted to march with their arms, a sufficiency of ammunition, and such baggage as they might desire to Fort Prince George or Virginia, escorted by a party of Indians; that the lame and sick might remain in the Indian towns with kind usage till able to go to Fort Prince George; and furthermore, that the Cherokees should provide the men with as many horses as they could conveniently, for which they should be paid. These articles were signed on the part of the garrison by Capt. Paul Demere and on that of the Cherokees by O-con-nos-to-ta and Cun-ni-ca-to-gue, head chief of Cho-tee and the nominal king of the nation. The 8th of August was spent in making preparations for the march; and Captain Demere dispatched a messenger to Virginia with a copy of the reasons of the garrison for their capitulation, the articles of surrender, together with a letter stating that had they not yielded as they did, they would inevitably have been obliged to abandon the fort that day, whatever might have been the consequences; that the Indians appeared desirous of peace and expected the immediate release of the prisoners at Fort Prince George upon the arrival of the Fort Loudon troops; and finally, that Captain Demere and his unfortunate fellow captives flattered themselves that the Indians meant them no harm. Vain hopes! Delusive prospects!

On the 9th the fort was formally delivered to the Indians, and the garrison marched that day about ten miles, encamping at night on a plain two miles from Tillico town; and there, what few Indians accompanied them gradually left until all were gone. They passed the night in quietness. But early in the morning of the 10th, when some of the soldiers were in the act of resuming their march and others were packing up, a large body of Indians were discovered crawling towards them in the tall grass but sixty yards distant, and the alarm was quickly given.

Volleys of small arms and showers of arrows were instantly poured upon the whites, accompanied with horrid yells and screams, which produced such confusion that little or no resistance was made, though Captain Stuart called to the men to stand to their arms. Seeing the utter impossibility of defending themselves, surrounded as they were by seven hundred warriors, they called out to one another not to fire but surrender themselves to the mercy of the enemy. Captain Demere received two wounds at the first fire and [was] directly scalped, when the Indians forced him to dance about some time for their diversion, after which they chopped off one hand or arm, then the other, and finally his legs. The most shocking barbarities were also practiced on the bodies of others.[27]

Beside Captain Demere, Lt. James Adamson, Ens. John Boggers, and Ens. Wintle, together with twenty-five privates, and some accounts add three women, were thus perfidiously slain.[28] It was also stated in one of the newspapers of the time that of a party of ten soldiers who plunged into the river, seven were drowned in attempting to cross; and two of the three survivors, after reaching the Indian town of Hi-was-see, died from the effects of overeating in their half-famished condition. But for the powerful exertions and unwearied efforts of a noble-minded chief known as Ou-ta-ci-te, or the Judds' Friend, perhaps none would have escaped the massacre. "He went around the field," asserts one of the gazettes of that day, "calling upon the Indians to desist, and making such representations to them as stopped the further progress and effects of their barbarous and brutal rage." Over two hundred were saved—an enduring evidence of Ou-ta-ci-te's generous promptings of humanity at a time when all others seemed completely under the influence of the demon of blood.[29]

But the good genius of Ou-ta-ci-te did not always prevail. Stripping the prisoners, their exulting captors carried them to their respective towns, frequently slapping their faces with the bloody scalps of their murdered companions. Reaching the Indian towns, one Luke Croft was gradually tortured to death in an awful manner, after which they cut his body in pieces, placing his head and right hand upon a stake as a spectacle to the prisoners, while they gathered up and burned the other fragments. One Mouncey and their prisoner very narrowly escaped the same fate. While Croft was suffering the most excruciating agonies, the other captives were severely beaten with sticks. The Indians of Sit-ti-co tied one of the female prisoners to a stake, shot her full of arrows, in which miserable condition she died.[30] Such were some of the sickening inhumanities connected with savage warfare.

Captain Stuart was made prisoner by the Round O's brother, pinioned, and conveyed back to Fort Loudon, where his old friend, At-ta-kul-la-Kul-la hastened as soon as he heard he was there, ransomed him at the expense of his rifle, clothes, and all that he could command, and shared with him what little provisions his table afforded. Ten bags of powder with a proportionate quantity of balls were by accident found buried in the fort to prevent their falling into the hands of the Indians. This unlucky discovery would have cost Captain Stuart his life had not the interpreter exercised so much presence of mind as to assure the Indians that the concealment was entirely without the captain's knowledge. With this new supply of ammunition, O-con-nos-to-ta formed the design of attacking Fort Prince George, and a council was called at Cho-tee. Captain Stuart was summoned in attendance and reminded of his obligations to the Indians for having spared his life; and as they resolved to take six cannon and two cohorns[p] on their intended expedition, they told him he must go with them to manage the artillery and write such letters to the commandant of Fort Prince George as they should dictate. And should that officer refuse to surrender, they declare their determination to burn the prisoners one after another in front of the fort and see what effect that would have upon its obstinate commander.

Alarmed at these developments, Captain Stuart privately made known to At-ta-kul-la-Kul-la how uneasy he was at the thought of being compelled to bear arms against his countrymen and how peculiarly he needed his assistance at this trying period to deliver him from these perilous circumstances. The humane old chief, taking Stuart by the hand, assured him he was his friend; that he had already given him one proof of his regard and intended to give another so soon as his brother should return to aid him in correcting the measure. No time was to be lost. So At-ta-kul-la-Kul-la gave out that he was going a hunting for a few days and should take his prisoner with him to eat venison, of which he declared he was exceedingly fond. Accompanied by his wife, brother, a few Indian attendants, and three of the captives, the old chief and Stuart started on the 30th of August, killing game by the way to supply their wants, and on the tenth day fell in on the Holston River with three hundred Virginians under Maj. Andrew Lewis, an advanced party of Colonel Byrd's army. In four days more they reached Colonel Byrd's camp, where the faithful old chief was loaded with presents and thence returned to his nation—ever ready to succor the unfortunate and ever anxious for the peace and true happiness of his people.[31]

Early in the year Col. William Byrd had been ordered with a large detachment of his old Virginia regiment, together with some new levies, consisting altogether of twelve hundred men, to advance to the frontiers of South-western Virginia to act against the Cherokees as occasion might require. He advanced as far as Reed Creek, near the head of the Kenhawa and about two hundred miles from Fort Loudon; but from bad weather, high waters, and scanty supplies, he was greatly retarded in his march, and when the Cherokee hunting grounds near the head of Holston were reached, the weakness of his force and lateness of the season prevented any effective operations. Relieving a number of the Fort Loudon prisoners who escaped from their captivity or were brought in by At-ta-kul-la-Kul-la and others, holding the hostile Cherokees in partial check, and encouraging the friendly portion of the nation to continue their efforts in favor of peace were the chief objects gained by the expedition; and at length the new levies were disbanded, and the old regiment retired to Augusta County for winter quarters.[32]

After Captain Stuart's departure, the designs of the Cherokees against Fort Prince George were abandoned. Sincere desires for peace now began to take the place of former animosities. They had been defeated by Montgomery, lost many of their warriors, and suffered greatly from the destruction of their settlements and means of subsistence. The small pox raged among them, their crops proved scanty, and many of them now began to feel keenly the privation of both food and clothing. At-ta-kul-la-Kul-la [was] untiring in his efforts to bring about a lasting reconciliation; O-con-nos-to-ta hoped that all differences would be made up and the bloody tomahawk buried deep under the tree of peace. "Never," exclaimed Ou-ta-ci-te, "shall there be any more war as long as I and the old warriors live." "I have been through all the towns," the same old chief declared, "and gave my talk of peace, which they fully approved. What is it like to war with the English? We can find none but them only to supply our wants."[33]

Such was the peaceful tendency of things in September; but in the succeeding month, all these fair prospects were, in an evil hour, entirely blasted. Louis Lantinac, formerly a trader among the Cherokees, then a cadet in an English company but now an officer in the French service, made his appearance at Cho-tee with some presents of brandy, ammunition, knives, and hatchets, accompanied by a few fellow emissaries, all zealous and indefatigable in spiriting on the Indians to mischief. Lantinac declaimed bitterly against the English as having nothing less in view than the extermination of the whole Cherokee nation and, at a grand council, striking his bloody hatchet into a log, cried out, *"Who is the man that will take this up for the king of France?"* Si-lou-ee, or the Young Warrior of Es-ta-to-e, leaping forward and laying instantly hold of it, exclaimed "I am not yet weary of war and will give the English more of it. The spirits of our slain brothers still call on us to avenge them; he that will not take up this hatchet and follow me is no better than a woman." Many a fierce look and brandished tomahawk and many a hearty shout of the well-known guttural *ugh!* answered the successful appeal to an Indian's notion of manliness and bravery, and again did the war torrent rush down upon the frontiers.[34]

When Daniel Boone returned to the Yadkin country is not precisely known. He probably was not well pleased with the dull monotony of quiet rural life in Eastern Virginia, where game was scarce and tobacco plenty—his love for the one being only equaled by his hatred for the other. Lyttleton's short-lived treaty may have hastened his return; if so, it is quite probable that he served with the Rowan rangers in the brilliant little affair previously mentioned as having occurred in April of this year on the Catawba and perhaps aided in the defense of Fort Dobbs or even served with Colonel Waddell on Montgomery's campaign. During the autumn Colonel Waddell's command was augmented to four hundred North Carolina troops for the protection of the frontiers of that province, with Fort Dobbs for their headquarters. Certain it is that Boone, in his old age, used to speak familiarly of that fortress, and the probability is that he forted there with his family during this and the ensuing season.

Sometime in the course of this year, he ventured over the mountains, either on a scout or hunt, perhaps both, and penetrated as far as what is now known as Boone's Creek, a small southern tributary of the Watauga River in Washington County, East Tennessee, and about a hundred miles from the Cherokee towns of the Little Tennessee. Here he left a singular memorial of that early adventure across the Alleghenies, perfectly in character with the man. On a tree still standing near that creek is the following ancient inscription, in tolerably plain letters, covering altogether a space of about 14 by 19 inches:

> D. Boon.
> Cilled a Bar on tree
> in the
> year
> 1760

Tradition points out, close by this tree, his camp[q]—a natural one made of rocks and in the center of what is known to have been fine hunting grounds.[35]

DRAPER'S NOTES: CHAPTER 3

1. Leigh's *Revised Code of Virginia,* ii:346; Kercheval's *History of the Valley,* 64.

2. MS. Preston Papers.

3. Daniel Bryan, in his MS. narrative, related that when a boy he was sent by his father, William Bryan, to look after and salt the stock and would frequently be absent several weeks together.

4. The bungling and unreliable work of [Alexander Scott] Withers states that in the year 1756, settlements were made on New River and Holston in Southwest Virginia, and among the daring adventurers who effected them was Daniel Boone; that the lands were taken up and held as *corn rights*—each settler acquiring a title to a hundred acres of adjoining land for every acre planted in corn. So far as Boone was concerned, this statement is wholly erroneous.

5. Burnaby's *Travels;* Jefferson's *Notes;* Martin's *History of North Carolina.*

6. Captain Demere commanded New York's independent companies on Braddock's campaign, and thus he and his men had seen some service.

7. "I saw the remains of Fort Loudon more than fifty years ago; the walls were of brick, much fallen and mouldered."—MS. statement of the late Col. William Martin of Tennessee, July 7, 1842.

8. Sparks' *Washington,* i:93; ii:284.

9. *Virginia Gazette,* May 26, 1758; Hewitt's *Historical Account* in Carroll's *Collection,* i:443.

10. Statement of the Cherokee chiefs at Fort Loudon, June 22, and Turner's letter, August 4, 1758, in MS. *Byrd Papers.*

11. Sparks' *Washington,* ii:322.

12. MS. letter of Governor Fauquier, November 14, 1758, in the Preston Papers.

13. *Maryland Gazette,* May 24, June 21, and July 5, 1759.

14. Ramsey's *South Carolina,* i: notes 209, 210.

15. This, however, is doubtful. It is claimed also to have derived its name from Col. George Beall and is said to have been the founder of the place. Proceedings of the June Meeting, 1858, of the Pennsylvania Historical Society; Squire, son of Samuel Boone, was born while his parents were in South Carolina, in [*wi*], 1760, [*rest of line illegible*].

16. William Grant's family record aids in determining these three years' sojourn in Maryland: His daughter Sarah was born in the Forks of the Yadkin in January 1759; his son William in Maryland January 1761; and his son Samuel in the Forks of the Yadkin in November 1762.

17. Mrs. Lemond, daughter of William Grant, is our authority for stating that her parents and grandparents went to Georgetown. That Daniel Boone retired to Virginia is stated on the authority of Isaiah Boone, who had the fact, as well as the bull-beef anecdote, from his father, Squire Boone, Jr. Colonel Boone himself informed the Hon. Edward Coles, since governor of Illinois, that he once resided awhile in the region of Fredericksburg.

18. *South Carolina Gazette,* February 9th, 1760.

19. *South Carolina Gazette,* February 13th, 1760; Bancroft, iv:350.

20. *South Carolina Gazette,* February 13th; and *Maryland Gazette,* March 20th, 1760.

21. *Maryland Gazette,* May 8th, 1760; Haywood's *Aboriginal History of Tennessee,* 239, 240.

22. *Maryland Gazette,* May 8th, 1760.

23. *Timberlake on the Cherokees,* 41.

24. Patrick Calhoun, when but six years of age, was brought by his parents from Ireland, his native country, to Pennsylvania in 1733; thence he emigrated to Augusta County in the valley of Virginia, the ancient records of which county show him, together with George Ezekiel and William Calhoun, to have been residing there as early as 1746. The melancholy defeat of himself and neighbors fleeing from the Long Cane settlement on the South Carolina frontiers, where he had located in 1756, has been already mentioned. He was an ardent friend of his adopted country during the Revolution and often served in the South Carolina legislature. A cool, steady, plain-spoken, matter of fact man himself, he wished legislative business done in a straight-forward, intelligible manner. It has been related of him that, annoyed beyond endurance by the frequent classical quotations with which the conceited young collegians affected to illustrate their fancy speeches, he one day rose in his place and rebuked one of this class in this wise: "Mr. Speaker: the gentleman is very fond of interlarding his speeches with the *Lettin* tongue, which I suppose few of the members of this assembly understand anymore than myself. I give this warning, therefore, if he don't quit spouting his

Lettin, I'll spout my Irish, and then let me see whether he'll be able to understand that or not." He was little annoyed during the remainder of the session, which was much shortened by the reformation he effected. He died in 1796. Such was the father of our late lamented statesman John C. Calhoun.

25. *Maryland Gazette,* August 7, 1760; Bancroft, iv:351 et. seq; Mante, Hewit, Wynne, Ramsey, and Martin have also been consulted.

26. *Pennsylvania Gazette,* September 4, 1760; Mante, 294–295; Timberlake, 65–66; Martin's *North Carolina,* ii:130.

27. *South Carolina Gazette,* October 18; and *Maryland Gazette,* October 16 and November 6, 1760.

28. It is said in Haywood's *History of Tennessee* that between two and three hundred men, women, and children perished in this massacre and only nine escaped; and à writer in the *Nashville* [wi] in September 1847, in giving a fancy sketch of the siege of Fort Loudon, has somewhat amplified Haywood's exaggerations.

29. *Maryland Gazette,* November 6 and 27, 1760.

30. *South Carolina Gazette,* October 18, 1760; *Pennsylvania Gazette,* February 19, 1766.

30. *Maryland Gazette,* Sept 25; October 13, 16; and November 6, 27, 1760; Hewit, in Carroll's *History Collections,* i:463–464.

31. *South Carolina Gazette,* October 18, 1760; *Maryland Gazette,* April 3, November 6 and 20, December 24, 1760, and February 12, 1761; Timberlake's Memoirs, 6.

32. *Maryland Gazette,* November 27, 1760.

33. *Maryland Gazette,* January 8, 1761; *Pennsylvania Gazette,* February 19, 1761; Hewit, in Carroll, i:466.

34. Ramsey's *History of Tennessee,* 67; MS. letters of Dr. Ramsey; notes of conversations with various individuals of East Tennessee in 1843 and 1844. I am indebted to Dr. J. G. M. Ramsey, the historian of Tennessee, for a full-sized copy of this interesting relic.

EDITOR'S NOTES: CHAPTER 3

a. The tall tale of Daniel Boone "shining" Rebecca Bryan while on a fire hunt was told not only by Timothy Flint. As the legend goes, one dark night, as Boone fire hunts with rifle in one hand and torch held high in the other to spot ("shine") the reflective eyes of white-tailed deer, he spies two orbs glinting at him. He aims, but the eyes vanish. Later he learns to his horror that the eyes he beheld were those of his lady love. That Boone seldom fire-hunted and that no one on either side of the family believed this apocryphal tale mattered little to early biographers.

b. The tragic heroine of Shakespeare's *Othello,* who admired her husband for his great courage.

c. A biblical allusion, Draper quoting from Genesis 24:67, King James Version, regarding Rebekah, daughter of Bethuel, the nephew of Abraham, father of the Hebrews. Rebekah married Isaac and was the mother of Jacob and Esau.

d. Boone was a stout, robust man who stood five feet, eight inches and in his prime weighed 175 pounds.

e. "Rebecca of old" is a second biblical allusion to Rebekah of the Old Testament, this time excerpted from Genesis 24:16, King James Version: "And the damsel was very fair to look upon, a virgin, neither had any man known her: and she went down to the well, and filled her pitcher and came up."

f. For an expanded exegesis on wampum, concerning its uses and significance, see chapter 4, note g.

g. The story of the massacre at Fort William Henry following Lt. Col. George Monro's capitulation to the Marquis de Montcalm is well known. In 1823 the tragedy was recast to achieve new fame in James Fenimore Cooper's *The Last of the Mohicans;* since then, the epic has been retold in word and film (and in the 1990s, with a lively degree of revisionism), but the facts are often forgotten. Monro had to defend Fort William Henry (at Lake George) with 2,372 ailing and half-starved men, only 1,100 of whom were fit to fight and protect the women, children, and slaves. Montcalm's force of 7,626 men included 1,600 Indians. Though Monro's pleas for reinforcements were not met, he held out for four days before signing terms of surrender. As the defenseless English survivors streamed from the fort, Abenaki and Ottawa warriors, incited by French propaganda and rum, attacked, slaughtering the terrified throng. It is impossible to know how many casualties there were. Hundreds were killed and hundreds taken hostage to live as adopted white Indians, to be ransomed, or to die.

h. In Canadian theater of the Seven Years' War, Jean-Arnold Dieskau, Baron de Dieskau, was army commander of seventy-eight companies of troops, second in command, and protégé of Quebec governor Vaudreuil. On September 8, 1755, during the battle of Lake George, Sir William Johnson's forces wounded and captured Dieskau, whom Vaudreuil replaced with Louis-Joseph de Montcalm, Marquis de Montcalm, who in 1759 was killed in the epic clash against Maj. Gen. James Wolfe (who was also slain in the battle) on the Plains of Abraham.

i. About 1724 the Turtle and Turkey clans of the Delaware moved from the forks of the Susquehanna to present-day Jefferson County, Pennsylvania, to a site on the Allegheny River ten miles below the mouth of the Mahoning. There they built Kittanning (meaning "place at the great river"), their first town built along what would become the new route of their western trek. Kittanning became a large and important Delaware village, but bloody conflicts arose between the Delaware and encroaching white settlers. On September 8, 1756, Col. John Armstrong and his Scottish-Irish troops attacked and destroyed Kittanning, but the Delaware soon rebuilt it. Today a city by the same name occupies the site.

j. Louisbourg was the French naval fortress erected at Cape Breton, Nova Scotia, after the Treaty of Utrecht (1713). Built of thick stone walls thirty-five feet high and armed with 250 cannon, it was called the "Gibraltar of the New World." The English seized Louisbourg during King George's War (War of Austrian Succession, 1744–48), but it was returned to French control on October 18, 1748, by terms of the Treaty of Aix-la-Chapelle. In 1758, during the Seven Years' War, English troops led by Cols. Jeffrey Amherst and James Wolfe again captured Louisbourg and its 5,000 defenders.

k. In 1673 Count Frontenac, governor of New France, built Fort Frontenac at the juncture of the St. Lawrence and Lake Ontario. Col. John Bradstreet's English forces captured it on August 25, 1758. Losing Frontenac and Louisbourg strategically cut New France in half, dooming forever French New World rule.

l. In June 1754 at the forks of the Ohio, French troops seized the half-completed English Fort Trent and rebuilt it, calling it Fort Duquesne. Washington failed to retake it in 1754; Braddock failed in 1755. In November 1758, fearing the approach of a large envoy of British troops led by Gen. John Forbes, the French lit the fort's powder magazine and blew it up. Gen. John Stanwix succeeded Forbes on March 15, 1759, and that September began erecting Fort Pitt on the demolished site.

m. Just south of the headwaters of the Hudson, bordering Lake Champlain, the French built Fort Carillon, which the English knew as Fort Ticonderoga. Maj. Gen. James Abercrombie's forces attacked Ticonderoga in July 1758 and were repulsed, mainly because of Abercrombie's inept leadership. The French abandoned Ticonderoga and Fort Frederic in July and August 1759.

n. Scalping was painful but not always fatal. Edward Robinson, who in 1811, at age sixty-six, left Kentucky to trap beaver in the Rocky Mountains, had been scalped years before; he afterward always wore a large handkerchief tied around his head to cover the old wound. To scalp, an attacker would down a victim, grasp the top hank of hair, and at its base cut to the bone a silver-dollar-size incision. Placing a foot on the victim's back for leverage, the attacker yanked the scalp free. Scalps were stretched on small wood hoops and the skin side painted. Scalps were decorated, hung from lodges and cabin garrets, and glorified as war trophies. Scalping goes back to antiquity, and its practice was not restricted by race. In fact, some of the most ruthless scalp hunters, such as Lewis "Death Wind" Wetzel in the East and John "Liver-Eating" Johnston in the West, were white Indian haters who today might be seen as psychopathic.

For a man, woman, or child living through a scalping, the treatment—"pegging the head"—was almost as bad as being scalped. A "doctor" of sorts seated the victim before him and, with a sharp leather awl, bored scores of holes into the bare skull to allow the pink cranial fluid to ooze through to form a scab. After a generous swabbing of poultices, the head was wrapped and the wound slowly healed, as long as it did not get infected.

There were times, though, when the entire scalp was skinned off. According to an observer during the French and Indian War: "Scalping is the cutting of the Skin round the Head, & by drawing quite to the eyes." Such a horrendous wound must have been beyond remedy.

o. Fort Ninety Six, South Carolina, was established in 1772 along a major trade route leading from Charleston to the Cherokee towns.

p. A cohorn, or coehorn, was a small military mortar or field howitzer made with handles for easy carrying for short distances.

q. Most such cryptically marked "D. Boon." and "Dan'l Boon." tree bark, abandoned camps and caves, knives, guns, tomahawks, derelict "salt-boiling" kettles, and other relics usually have a shaky provenance and prove to be fake.

CHAPTER 4

1760–1764.—French Emissaries Instigating Indians.—Grant's Expedition.—Daniel Boone Serves on Byrd's Expedition.—Peace with the Cherokees.—Squire Boone, Sr., Returns from Carolina.—Renewed Indian Outbreak.—Regulators.—Boone Aids in Breaking Up Brigands.— He Extends His Hunts.—Mount Ararat, or Pilot Mountain.

During the winter of 1760–'61, the governors of Virginia, North and South Carolina concerted with General Amherst the plan of the ensuing southern campaign. It was arranged that Lt. Col. James Grant should be detached from the main army with his Highlanders and a few other regulars and, uniting with the troops of South Carolina, should attack the Lower and Middle Cherokee Towns, while the provincials of Virginia and North Carolina under Colonel Byrd should make a simultaneous movement against their Upper Towns.[1] Preparations were accordingly made on such a scale as to encourage a reasonable expectation of the final subjugation of those restless Indians. Though nearly powerless in men and means, the French still dwelt upon the real or imaginary wrongs of the Cherokees and urged them on to war. In May Lantinac brought to Cho-tee nine horse-loads of presents, chiefly powder and lead, a little salt, some brandy, and a few shirts.[2] The scarcity of provisions among the Indians caused much of the ammunition to be necessarily expended in hunting.

At-ta-kul-la-Kul-la met Colonel Grant at Fort Prince George, entreating him to delay that time might be given for the leading men of his nation to come in and conclude a permanent peace; and while pleading for his favor, the old chief was not slow in condemning the conduct of many of his people. Though his sincerity was never doubted, his request was little heeded, as the Cherokees generally had given no evidence of a real desire to effect an adjustment of differences; and under such circumstances, a nominal peace forced upon them by the presence of a powerful army about to overrun their country in case of non-compliance should, like Littleton's, prove only a delusive expedient, morally certain to be repudiated the moment the threatened danger should pass away.

But with a well-appointed army of twenty-six hundred men, one half of whom were regulars, followed by a train of about seven hundred pack-horses and over four hundred head of cattle, Colonel Grant took up his line of march on the 7th of June. His advance corps was a body of ninety Indians, mostly Catawbas under their old King Heigler,[3a] together with some Chickasaws and a few adventurous Iroquois, and about thirty white volunteers dressed and painted in Indian style,[b] all under the command of Capt. Quintine Kennedy.[4]

Passing the dangerous defiles of War-Woman's Creek on the eighth by a rocky path only wide enough for a single pack-horse, winding around between an overhanging mountain of granite and a yawning precipice washed by the rushing stream at its base, they discovered on the following day a rude representation, painted in vermilion on a blazed forest tree, of nine Cherokee warriors equipped with guns and tomahawks, running with a white man as a captive. About half after eight o'clock on the morning of the 10th of June, when the army was passing along the Little Tennessee within about two miles of Et-cho-wee, Captain Kennedy and his Indian corps first encountered the Cherokees upon a high hill upon the right of the army, at the foot of which, with the river close upon their left, the line was obliged to pass for a considerable distance. A smart fire was opened upon them from the opposite shore. Continuing the march, strong parties were sent up the hill to dislodge the enemy, which, after some dispute, was effected, while the main line faced to the left and gave the Indians over the river their whole fire, which quickly dispersed them in that quarter. When hard pressed and driven back in one direction, the Indians soon rallied and re-appeared in another, and thus kept up a galling fire in their desultory mode of warfare.

27. Indian-influenced Anglo guerrilla, c. 1760, tattooed and wearing leggings, shirt, moccasins, breechcloth, and French shortcoat, and armed with modified English Short Land Pattern "Brown Bess" musket. Frontiersmen from this unique, overlooked caste served on campaigns with Col. James Grant as scouts and interpreters. ILLUSTRATION BY LYDIA GERBIG.

After three hours' exposure to this irregular fire, the advance of the long, extended line of troops began to emerge from the narrow defile of two miles in length into an open savanna. Meanwhile, the yells of the Indians denoted too unerringly a concentrated attack upon the rear, which was encumbered with the cattle and pack-horses, when a strong relief party was sent back, the Indians beaten off, the baggage saved, and the dead sunk in the river to save them from savage mutilation. Happily for the whites, the Indians were but scantily supplied with ammunition; after eleven o'clock their fire slackened, and occasional shots were made till two in the afternoon, after which they entirely disappeared. Their force was said to have been not less than one thousand, embracing all the warriors of the Lower, Middle, and Valley Towns, led on by the Standing Turkey and Silou-ee, the latter of whom was wounded in the action. The loss of the whites was one officer and ten privates killed, four officers and forty-eight privates wounded, while that of the Cherokees was never ascertained except that it was large, including many of their headmen and prominent warriors. It was not till midnight that the army with their wounded reached the place of encampment at Et-cho-wee. Among the brave Carolinians who fought that day was Francis Marion,[c] then a humble lieutenant, who in after years attained so deservedly eminent a character among his grateful countrymen.

Now commenced the work of devastation. At one of the towns Silver-Hills, a noted Mohawk, mounted the Round House and, with a loud voice, three times summoned all the Cherokees from their towns and mountains to come and hear the news he had to tell them from the north; but not appearing, he concluded by informing them that since they would not come and hear him, he must burn and destroy their settlements. For thirty days the English army was busily employed in burning and ravaging the towns and hamlets and laying waste the growing crops of the enemy. "Heaven has blessed us," wrote one of the participators in this work of devastation, "with the greatest success, we have finished our business as completely as the most sanguine of us could have wished. All their towns, fifteen in number, beside many little villages and scattered houses, have been burnt; upward of fourteen hundred acres of corn, according to a moderate computation, entirely destroyed; and near five thousand Cherokees, men, women and children, driven to the mountains to starve—their only sustenance for sometime being horse-flesh."[5]

The fugitive Cherokees from the Lower Settlements, whose towns had been destroyed the previous season by Colonel Montgomery, had opened many new fields in the vales and upon the hill-sides along the water-courses of the Little Tennessee and planted them in maize; all these shared the common fate of the others. In but a single town was any old corn found, about twenty bushels at Tessantee. The most pitiful destitution was everywhere observable— the corn mortars unused; no meat but scanty scraps of horse beef; and for sometime past the Indians seem to have subsisted on the boiled stalks of young corn. Even these poor shifts for a pinching support were now utterly swept away. Their only resort was to fall back upon their more fortunate brethren of the Upper Towns who had escaped the general desolation.

In July the English army returned to Fort Prince George, but not without having purchased their success with incredible toil and suffering. They had undergone constant fatigue and unceasing watchings, encountering alternately scorching heat with much wet weather and swollen streams, having nothing better than bowers of boughs to shelter them from storms and night-damps; upwards of twenty days on short allowance, with their legs and feet more or less bruised and cut with rocks and torn with thorns and briars.[6]

Under the influence of At-ta-kul-la-Kul-la and O-con-nos-to-ta, the Upper Settlements of the Cherokees were anxious for reconciliation with the English before the late action and had furnished no warriors to oppose Colonel Grant, and these two chieftains, accompanied by Wil-lan-i-waw and Old Caesar of Hiwassee, were within twenty miles of Colonel Grant on their way to meet him and make peace when they heard of the battle and then returned home determined to remain quiet and let the people of the Middle and Valley Settlements take the consequences of their folly. Now weary of the war, their country laid waste, not a few of their warriors slain in battle, and many of their old people and children dead and dying from actual starvation, their young men and women, once strong and vigorous, greatly reduced and debilitated by long continued privations, the whole nation was constrained to make sincere overtures for peace. Si-lou-ee, who was now absent on a hunt to secure meat for his subsistence, still muttered and chafed with the threat of death by the nation hanging over him if he should commit the least mischief.[7]

The Cherokees were completely humbled. At-ta-kul-la-Kul-la again appeared at Fort Prince George as the representative of the whole nation pleading for peace. Colonel Grant made it *sine qua non* that the Cherokees should deliver up four of their countrymen to be put to death in front of his camp or produce four green Cherokee scalps in the space of twelve nights. The old chieftain was too humane to yield to this barbarous demand, when Grant sent him forward to Charleston to see whether Governor Bull would mitigate its rigor, who readily granted a liberal treaty in which a pacification was provided for between the Cherokees and their ancient enemies, the Chickasaws and Catawbas.[8] "As we all live in one land," said At-ta-kul-la-Kul-la, "let us henceforth love one another as one people."

While the southern army was actively employed, little was accomplished by the northern division under Colonel Byrd. Early in the year, General Amherst gave orders for uniting the detachments of the Virginia regiment and recruiting men for its completion. Byrd, in turn, gave early notice to General Amherst of a great deficiency of arms in both Virginia and North Carolina and earnestly desired five hundred regulars, as he had a larger march to make than Colonel Grant, posts to erect along the course, while those along Grant's line were already made and garrisoned, and the whole route was equally exposed with Grant's dangers and vicissitudes. The regulars were denied him, and he was urged to go forward without delay. Tardiness in furnishing recruits, supplies, and means of transportation greatly annoyed Colonel Byrd and retarded his movements; and in June, to avoid further delay, he was compelled to use his personal credit to obtain provisions and teams and proceed with five hundred men of his regiment, leaving the remaining two hundred under Lt. Col. Adam Stephen to follow as soon as means of subsistence should be provided. Proceeding to his old camp on the Kenhawa, and thence to Capt. Samuel Stalmaker's old place on the Middle Fork of Holston, he was still detained by want of supplies and means of conveyance and prevented from making a simultaneous movement with Colonel Grant against the Cherokee towns, according to the original plan.[9] While Grant had thirteen hundred regulars and as many more Colonial troops, Byrd's Virginia force at no time exceeded eight hundred men, including a few militia.

In August Colonel Byrd wrote to General Amherst, fully explaining his situation. He was still two hundred miles from the nation and had a road to make and open the whole way; he was building a block-house and throwing up an entrenchment around it for the security of the troops and provisions. Only sixty militia had joined him, who were certainly not sufficient to garrison the necessary posts for three hundred and thirty miles in advance of the settlement. The enemy having retired from Colonel Grant to the Upper Towns would increase the difficulties of approaching them successfully; and from the Upper Settlements, large bodies of Cherokees were detached to hunt between the French Broad and Holston rivers and watch the motions of the Virginian army. If Colonel Grant with his formidable force could only burn fifteen towns and over-run the country below the mountains not more than sixty miles from his advanced post, how could it be expected that he, with his pitiful number of Virginians, could proceed through a wilderness two hundred miles from his outermost post to attack thirty-two towns in the remotest part of the nation defended by their united force? Colonel Grant had the whole winter before him to provide everything for his well-appointed army, while he was not even thought worthy of the contractor's notice till the middle of June and had double Grant's distance to march. At-ta-kul-la-Kul-la, with forty-three Indians from all parts of the nation, had visited him in July to solicit peace; but his hands were tied, and he presumed he appeared in a very despicable light to the Indians, as he really did to himself, for he was neither enabled to chastise them or empowered to negotiate a peace. Since Colonel Grant had retreated, it appeared impossible to do anything more offensively as well from deficiency of numbers as want of carriages for transportation, and without a prospect of doing any service for his country or credit to himself, Colonel Byrd proposed, after completing the fortification of his camp, to resign his command to Lieutenant Colonel Stephen.

Shortly after, Colonel Waddell joined the Virginia forces with five hundred North Carolinians. Though they had early been ordered to embody for this service, they only rendezvoused at Salisbury late in the summer, and then had to tarry there sometime for want of arms. Daniel Boone was among these troops and, ever after, spoke freely of Byrd's dilatoriness and want of enterprise, for the old pioneer, even at that early period, had a poor opinion of a body of men destined against a wily Indian foe wasting their time and energies in cutting roads and erecting forts. A sudden and unexpected blow without giving them time to learn the strength of the force employed against them, or to lay their artful ambuscades, almost universally succeeded, while tardiness in road-making or fort-building, as in the case of Braddock and Forbes, and afterwards of St. Clair,[d] was almost morally certain to be followed by defeat, failure, or misfortune.

Colonel Byrd retiring from the command, Colonel Stephen marched without molestation to the Long Island of Holston, about one hundred and forty miles from the enemy settlements, and set about the construction of a fort on the northern bank of that river and nearly opposite to the upper end of the Long Island, in compliance with Governor Fauquier's instructions.[10] "It was situated," says Haywood,e "on a beautiful level and was built upon a large plan, with proper bastions; the walls thick enough to stop the force of a small cannon shot, and the gates spiked with large nails, so the woods was all covered." Fort Robinson was the name assigned to this fortress. When nearly completed, about the middle of November, Cun-ni-ca-to-gue, head chief of Cho-tee and nominal king of the Cherokees, arrived accompanied by about four hundred of his people deputed by the nation to sue for peace.[11] A treaty was finally concluded on the 19th of that month, satisfactory alike to both the whites and Indians. Trade was to be restored, prisoners delivered up, and friendly offices interchanged. Ens. Henry Timberlake repaired with three companions at the request of the Indians to the Cherokee towns, that the nations might be convinced of the good intentions and sincerity of the English towards them and also to collect what captives yet remained in the settlements.[12] A portion of the Virginia regiment continued all winter in garrison at Fort Robinson under the command of Capt. John McNeil, an experienced officer who survived the disasters of Braddock's defeat.

And the Cherokees pledged anew to their white brothers the friendship, "which," says Bancroft beautifully, "was to last as long as the light of morning should break above their villages, or the bright fountains gush from their hillsides. Then they returned to dwell once more in their ancient homes. Around them nature, with the tranquility of exhaustless power, renewed her beauty; the forests blossomed as before; the thickets were alive with melody; the rivers bounded exultingly in their course; the glades sparkled with the strawberry and the wild flowers; but for the men of that region the inspiring confidence of independence in the mountain fastnesses was gone. They knew they had come into the presence of a race more powerful than their own; and the course of their destiny was irrevocably changed."

The return of Colonel Waddell's regiment to North Carolina gave Boone an opportunity to indulge himself in one of his old fashioned hunts far away from settlers and settlements and exempt once more from the fear of the mortal redskins.[13] So at the head of a party of Yadkin hunters, he roamed through some of the lovely vales of East Tennessee and Southwestern Virginia, gratified beyond expression with the great plentifulness of the game and highly delighted with the

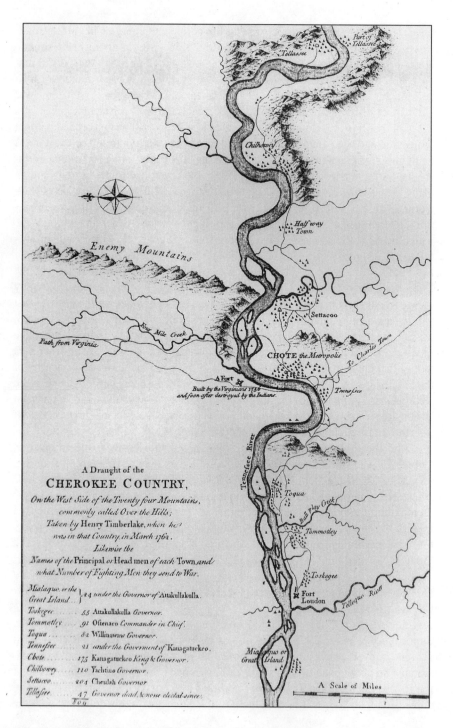

28. "A Draught of the Cherokee Country," by Lt. Henry Timberlake, March 1762.

charming valley of the Holston. Another party of hunters, composed of Elisha Walden, Henry Skaggs, William Blevins, Charles Cox, and fifteen others, about the same time visited Cartier's Valley in East Tennessee and finally passed into Powell's Valley, where they hunted eighteen months.[14]

With the opening of 1762, abandoned cabins and deserted plantations were again occupied by the border settlers, who had long been habituated to flee for safety and join their fellow fugitives in some pent-up fort, where they would pass an irksome, ungainful life of squalidness and ease. During the successive years of 1759, '60, and '61, the Yadkin settlers resorted to their forts whenever alarms were given of Indian invasions; the danger once over, they would venture back distrustfully to their homes, only to fly again upon the earliest intimation of the massacre of some unsuspecting neighbor.[15] At the dawn of peace, joy sparkled on the countenances of every cabin occupant along the wide-extended frontiers.

Boone shared largely in the common joy and felt peculiarly happy to find himself and little family once more comfortably domiciled in their quiet home on Sugar Tree Creek, under their own vine and fig tree,[f] with none to molest or make them afraid. There the soil yielded an abundant return for a slight cultivation, the sugar-maples furnished their luxurious sweets, the range for small herds, like Boone's, was yet inviting; and as deer, though getting scarce, were yet to be found in the forests and mountain regions remote from the settlements, we may be quite sure that such a hunter as Boone always kept a bountiful supply in the family larder.

During this year, his parents and their son-in-law William Grant and family returned from Maryland, bringing with them Squire Boone Jr., who had from boyhood been living with his cousin Samuel Boone and learning the gun-smith trade, from whom was purchased between one and two years of the remaining period of his apprenticeship.[16] All this long journey from Maryland to the Boone settlement on the Forks of Yadkin was performed by Mrs. Boone on horseback, the whole party camping each night in the open air before a cheerful, blazing fire kindled beside some fallen giant of the forest.

The year 1763 brought with it no unusual event to Daniel Boone. During the year, the British authorities were much engaged in providing governments for the new territories acquired by conquest from France; and as some of the North-Western Indians had commenced hostilities under the influence of that master-spirit Pontiac, a treaty with the Southern tribes was deemed advisable. Accordingly, a treaty was held with the Creeks, Cherokees, Chickasaws, Choctaws, and Catabaws at Augusta, Georgia, in November, at which were present the governors of Virginia, North and South Carolina, and Georgia, and Capt. John Stuart, the newly appointed superintendent of Indian Affairs for the Southern colonies. A

29. *"Hysac, or the Woman's Man," Creek Indian, after a pencil drawing by artist John Trumbull, July 1790. Typical period Southeastern Indian dress featured European-style coat, turban, silver gorgets and nose ring, and ostrich feather.* BUREAU OF AMERICAN ETHNOLOGY, SMITHSONIAN INSTITUTION.

large amount of presents were given to the Indians, good talks and white belts[g] freely interchanged, and the Creeks and Cherokees granted a tract of country on the frontiers of Georgia, with the proceeds of sales of which to discharge their indebtedness to the traders.[17]

Displeased with the terms of this grant as taking umbrage at something else not now known, a large party of Creeks made a sudden irruption into the Long Cane Settlement in the back part of South Carolina on the 24th of December and killed fourteen persons of both sexes, greatly mutilating their bodies. Other persons were at the same time missing. The frontier people of that province fled to forts, of which there were two stockaded at the Long Canes; in one were thirty-seven men and one hundred and three women and children. Many persons also fled for shelter to the forts at Ninety-Six and Hard Labour. Eleven days after the massacre at the Long Canes, a party of twenty men went from Capt. Patrick Calhoun's fort in that settlement, who were fired upon and one of their number wounded in the shoulder, upon which, as their guns, wet with snow, were unfit for use, the whites retreated.[18] This little out-burst on the part of the Creeks was soon quieted; nor do we learn that its brief alarming influence extended so far north as the Yadkin settlements.

Unalloyed good is not the lot of man. When the long and sanguinary French and Indian War ended, its consequences began to develop themselves. It had stained the principles of many of the inhabitants as to endanger the peace and happiness of society. When settlements were broken up by savage inroads, industry was at an end. The prospects of reaping were so faint that few had the resolution to sow. Those who took up their abode in forts had nothing to do. Idleness is the parent of every vice. When they sallied out, they found much property left behind by others who had abandoned their homes. To make use of such derelict articles did not appear to them in the odious colour of theft. Cattle were killed—horses stolen—household furniture and plantation tools taken into possession in violation of private rights. The wrong-doers lived easily at the expense of the absentees and acquired such vicious habits that when the war was over, they despised labor and became pests to society. To steal was easier than to work. The former was carried on extensively and the latter rarely attempted. Among all kinds of theft, none was so easy in execution, none so difficult in detection and at the same time so injurious in its consequences as horse-stealing. On the labors of that useful animal the cultivation of the soil depended for raising the provisions necessary for their support. A horse when grazing is as easily caught by a thief as by his owner and will as readily carry the one as the other to a distance where he might be sold or exchanged, to the serious injury of a helpless family. Practices of this kind became common and were carried on by system and in concert with associates living remote from each other. The industrious part of the community were oppressed and the support of the families endangered.[19]

These difficulties were increased from an inefficient system of government. This was particularly true of the back parts of South Carolina, where were only justices of the peace to enforce the laws, who, instead of exerting their authority to suppress horse-stealing and other crimes, were themselves often the greatest villains and liberal sharers in the profits of this nefarious business. Before such officers it was difficult to procure the commitment of criminals; crimes the most glaring were winked at, witnesses suffered to absent themselves, evasions and subterfuges of every kind resorted to, and the guiltiest of wretches permitted to go free. The inhabitants groaned under these frustrations of justice. Despairing of redress in a legal channel, they took the law into their own hands. In the year 1764 Thomas Woodward, Joseph Kirkland, Barnaby Pope, and others of the best and most orderly inhabitants held a consultation on what was best to be done. They drew up an instrument of writing [to] which they and their associates generally subscribed. In it they bound themselves to make a common cause in immediately pursuing and arresting all horse-thieves and other criminals. Such when caught were tried in a summary way by the neighbors and if found guilty were sentenced to receive a number of stripes on their bare backs, more or less in proportion to their misdeeds. They were then advised to leave the neighborhood and informed that if they returned, their punishment would be doubled. This mode of proceeding was called Regulation and its authors and friends Regulators.

The horse-thieves, their associates, and other criminals, who from causes already mentioned were numerous, made a counter common cause in supporting themselves against these Regulators. Most of the inhabitants favored one or the other of these parties. The one justified their proceedings on the score of necessity and substantial, though irregular, justice; the other alleged the rights of British subjects to a legal trial by a court and jury. Though the former meant well, yet justice is of so delicate a nature that form as well as substance must be regarded. It is therefore probable that in some cases the proceedings of the Regulators may have so far partaken of the infirmities of human nature as to furnish real grounds of complaint against them. Their adversaries made such high colored representations of their conduct that the civil authority interposed.

One Scouil or Scofix was empowered by the governor of South Carolina to put a stop to the measure of the Regulators, but his conduct, character, and standing in society rendered him in the general estimation, and especially in the opinion of the Regulators, very unfit for the office. He erected something like a royal standard and called some of the Regulators to answer for their transgressions, some of whom were sent under a guard to Charleston for imprisonment. Warm blood ensued on both sides; and the Scouilites on the one hand and the Regulators on the other arranged themselves under their representative leaders and formed camps in opposition to each other. A civil war was on the point of commencing; both parties were armed and prepared for the last extremity, and each was only waiting to return the fire of the other, yet neither daring to meet the consequences of beginning hostilities. A flag was at length sent from one to the other—a parley followed; and an agreement was entered into to break up their camps, go home, and respectively petition the governor for a redress of grievances. And thus, five years after the organization of the Regulators, courts were established; and in less than two years more thirty-two horse-thieves alone were tried, convicted, and punished, and the cause of justice at length completely vindicated.[20]

North Carolina was not entirely exempt from the rapine of these desperadoes. Forting upon her frontiers had produced similar effects upon the naturally vicious and indolent. Scorning to work, and ashamed to beg, several of the more hardened of this class banded together in the mountain region in the rear of the Yadkin settlements, where, in a quiet nook, they had formed a rude fort for the receptacle of their ill-gotten plunder and for their protection in case their secluded retreat should happen to be discovered. Others, perhaps more timid, remained at their homes in the settlements, secreting their robber-friends by day and aiding them by night in their villainous pursuits. One Owens and wife and a man named Harmon were of the party, consisting of fully a dozen altogether, who had their head-quarters among the mountains in the wilderness. Two of this desperate band managed to kidnap a daughter of one of the Yadkin settlers, probably designing to doom her to the basest of purposes. The whole country was roused, and the people formed themselves into different bands to go in pursuit, strongly suspecting that the girl had been taken by the outlaw-gang who had long prowled among and depredated upon that suffering community.

Daniel Boone, in common with his neighbors, was shocked by an event at once so bold and aggravating. He placed himself at the head of one of these pursuing parties composed of the unhappy captive's father and five or six sympathizing friends; and while pressing forward far into the wilderness, the lost girl suddenly came running to them; she thought they were the robber-band until fortunately recognizing the well-known features of her father in the party. The meeting under the circumstances between the parent and daughter was peculiarly affecting; all seemed equally to partake in the joy—for the lost one was found again. She soon related her simple story: how the two bandits had abducted her, hurrying her through the woods by night and day, almost exhausting her delicate form as well by anxiety of mind as exposure, fatigue, and the laceration of her limbs by rocks and brambles. When at length thinking themselves secure from pursuit and perhaps well-nigh their forest-fort, the robbers employed their first leisure in getting embroiled in a dispute, most likely involving their respective claims to the captive-maiden; words soon led to blows, and during a severe encounter the young lady had the good fortune to escape from her desperate captors. Boone and his party, with the rescued girl for their guide, soon reached the spot where she left the rival bandits in fearful contention and found one of the combatants weltering in his gore and senseless. The other had fled. The wounded brigand was conveyed to Salisbury Jail; but whether he died of his wounds or his life paid the forfeit of his crimes, tradition is silent. We have in this instance another illustration of the maxim that when rogues fall out, the honest and oppressed obtain their rights.

About a year after this affair, a quantity of stolen goods were found concealed under the fodder-stack of one Cornelius Howard, a resident of the Yadkin country who had hitherto borne a good character. The evidences of his guilt so multiplied against him that he confessed his connection with the clan without reserve and piloted a large party, prominent among whom were Daniel and George Boone, to the secret fort in the mountain region many miles remote from the frontier settlements. The brigands' mountain fortress was at length discovered beneath an over-hanging rocky cliff, with a large natural chimney and a considerable area in front well-stockaded. It was the most secluded and fitly chosen place for its object, Boone used to say, that could well be imagined. There was no beaten path leading to or from it—so careful were its wily occupants to avoid every sign that might chance to lead to their detection. Led on by Howard, Boone and his party suddenly surrounded the encampment and captured several of the freebooters, among whom were Owens and his wife. Harmon and a few others of the most active of the band managed to effect their escape, and others of the party were probably absent. Stores had been robbed, horses and cattle stolen, farming utensils and almost every conceivable article taken by this daring and well-appointed band. The prisoners once secured, search was instituted for their hoarded plunder. Goods were found in tree-gums with a layer of straw and ashes on top, intended to convey the idea of leach-tubs.[h] A large quantity of silks, dry goods, log chains, farming implements, and household articles were recovered.[21]

Mrs. Owens was found within the rock-house on a bed, either sick or more probably feigning herself ill, and expressed a strong desire to see Cornelius Howard. He had scarcely appeared in sight, when she quickly drew a pistol and would have shot him on the spot, had not the deadly weapon been snatched from her hand by some of the by-standers. Failing in this, she gave him a pretty fair specimen of law invective, branding him as a second Judas in the turpitude of his conduct. The culprits were bound and taken to Salisbury Jail to await the rigors of the law and satisfy the demands of justice. Mrs. Owens' sobriquet of Judas Howard became familiarly known throughout that region; and several years thereafter that unfortunate man was stealthily shot from his horse at the crossing of a stream—thus suffering the terrible penalty of having betrayed the outlaws of the Yadkin. But the clan was entirely broken.[22]

It is safe to conclude that hunting, in Boone's estimation, was of the first importance, while farming was only secondary consideration. As newcomers rapidly settled in the country and opened extensive clearings, game gradually became more scarce, both from the habit of many wild animals to retire before the advancing settlements and from the increased number killed to meet the additional demands of new settlers. So Boone had necessarily to extend his hunts to more distant and less frequented regions.[23] These long, rambling excursions gave him an opportunity of thoroughly exploring every portion of the rugged mountain region of western Carolina, where were many picturesque scenes and not a few of singular wildness and grandeur.

The celebrated Mount Ararat, or Pilot Mountain, some forty miles north of Boone's residence, was and still is considered a great natural curiosity. The name is said to be a translation of an Indian appellation signifying Pilot and so called by aborigines, as the mountain served as a peculiar guide to their hunting and war-parties in their forest wanderings through an extent of surrounding country for sixty or seventy miles. It rises, an isolated pile, in the midst of an extensive plain, exhibiting a striking symmetry of pyramidal structure to the height of eighteen hundred feet, its sides all covered with trees and vegetation. From its summit, covering nearly the area of an acre, rises perpendicularly a vast, stupendous rock to the height of over two hundred feet, presenting the appearance of an ancient castle with its lofty battlements. Up this pinnacle there is but a single passage, which is on the north side through cavities and fissures of rock, narrow, steep, and difficult. The summit once reached, the prospect from the beautiful level is truly grand and enchanting, embracing within its range the wide-stretching forest, the distant Blue Ridge and its mountain heights on the northwest, the towering Suara Mountains at the eastward, and the silvery Yadkin meandering down from its hilly sources through a rich and lovely valley.[24]

Other wonders of equal grandeur were not wanting to gratify the curiosity and elevate the feelings of so true a lover of nature as Daniel Boone. Mount Mitchell, or the Black Mountain, a peak of the Blue Ridge in what is now Yancey County, has an elevation of over six thousand, four hundred feet, which considerably exceeds any summit in the United States east of the Rocky Mountains.[i] Roan Mountain is over six thousand feet high, with an extensive plain upon its top;

Grandfather Mountain exceeds five thousand, five hundred feet in elevation; and Table Mountain, four hundred feet.[25] These towering peaks, with their dizzy heights, with many a bounding mountain stream issuing from their nooks and gorges, with their cataracts and waterfalls, cliffs and promontories, are well calculated to impress the beholder with a reverential sense of the stupendous works of the Almighty Architect.

DRAPER'S NOTES: CHAPTER 4

1. MS. letters of General Amherst, Governor Fauquier, and Colonel Byrd, in the *Byrd Papers.*

2. *Pennsylvania Gazette,* July 9, 1761.

3. In 1762 a party of seven Shawanoes waylaid some Catawbas near the Waxaws in South Carolina and killed old King Heigler, the most noted chief his nation ever had. It was singular that six years afterwards, in May 1768, a party of Shawanoes were discovered asleep near the Catawba town by a band of Catawba warriors, who fired on them, killed three on the spot, captured three others, while the seventh escaped wounded but was subsequently found dead in the woods; and among the captives was old King Heigler's murderer, who, with his fellow prisoners, was tortured to death in the usual barbarous manner of the Indians. One of the victims was very young and pleaded hard for his life, begging that his tender age might be taken into consideration, assuring them that he had engaged in the expedition against his own wishes at his brother's insistence and had never killed or hurt a human being. The stern Catawbas were inexorable.

4. Early in 1758, among the reinforcements from Great Britain arrived at New York, was the regiment of Highlanders. The Iroquois Indians, in alliance with the English, were furnished with arms and encouraged to join the army. The Highlanders "were," says Hewit, "in many respects well qualified for the service. It is impossible to describe how much the savages were delighted with the dress, manners, and music of this regiment. Their sprightly manner of dancing, their dexterity in the use of arms, and natural vivacity and intrepidity the savages greatly admired and expressed a strong inclination for attending the Scotch warriors to the field. To prevent them from joining the enemy it was not only necessary to employ those warriors, but it was thought they might be rendered useful for scouring the dark thickets before the regular army. Lieutenant Kennedy, to encourage them, entered into their humor, and, in order to lead them, dressed and painted himself like an Indian. They gave him a squaw, and the nation to which she belonged having made him a king, no small service was expected from the new alliance." Kennedy, it is believed, served on Forbes' campaign and the next year, under General Amherst, was dispatched with a flag of truce to the St. Francois Indians on the St. Lawrence, who detained him in captivity. When released, he was sent south with a few Iroquois to aid Grant in his expedition against the Cherokees.

5. Tasse, Noockasse, Noyeewee, Canuga, Whatoga, Eyoree, Cowhee, Usanah, Cowitchee, Burning Town, and Allejoy, on the Et-cho-wee branch of the

Tennessee. On the Stickoey branch, and called the Back Settlement, or Out-Side Towns: Stickoey, Kittoa, Tuckoritchie, and Tessantee. Et-cho-wee was destroyed the previous year by Colonel Montgomery.

6. *Pennsylvania Gazette,* August 6; *Maryland Gazette,* August 13, 1761; Hewit's *Historical Account;* Ramsey, Martin, and Bancroft.

7. In the summer of 1770 Si-lou-ee conveyed a message from the Cherokee nation to Governor Botetourt of Virginia, complaining of the encroachment of the frontier people of that province; and on the 2nd of September following, he passed through Salisbury, North Carolina, on his return home, sick of fever, and proceeded about ten miles farther, where he was found lying in the woods by a planter, who kindly carried him to his house and had him properly cared for; but he died the next day, September 5th, greatly regretted by his people.

8. James Grant was a native of Scotland and early embraced the profession of arms. He came to America in 1758 as major of Montgomery's regiment of High-landers and that year was defeated in an injudicious advance upon Fort Duquesne and taken prisoner. Near the close of 1759 he was exchanged and the next year served with Colonel Montgomery against the Cherokees. Promoted to the rank of lieutenant colonel, he led the successful expedition against the Cherokees in 1761, which has been narrated. In October 1763, upon the organization of East Florida as a British province, he was appointed its first captain general and governor-in-chief, which office he continued to hold till the summer of 1773. He was promoted in 1772 to the colonelcy of the 55th regiment of foot and in 1774 was assigned to the lieutenant governorship of Fort George, near Inverness, Scot-land. While governor of East Florida, he expressed to the British government his joy, in common with the people of his province, on the repeal of the Stamp Act; yet in February 1775, as a member of the House of Commons, he aided in mea-sures of Colonial oppression and declared that the Americans would not fight and would never dare face an English army.

In 1776 he was sent to America to assist in suppressing the rebellion, with the rank of major general for that special service, and took part in the battle of Long Island and, in January 1777, in the battle of Assumpink Creek, New Jersey. In August 1777 he was appointed a major general in the regular service and par-ticipated that year in the battles of Brandywine and Germantown. He was with the British advance in Monmouth battle in June 1778 and, in December of that year, with a large land and sea force, after some severe fighting, captured from the French the island of St. Lucia, in the West Indies. He was made in November 1782 a lieutenant general and in 1796 a full general in the British service. Soon after the Revolutionary War, he was appointed governor of Stirling Castle, Scot-land, and continued to fill these high military positions till his death, which oc-curred at his seat at Ballendalloch, Scotland, April 13th, 1806, in his eighty-sixth year. His bravery was not a little dimmed by his overweening arrogance and superciliousness.

9. On the 18th of June, 1755, a party of Indians killed five persons and took Captain Stalmaker and one Samuel Hydon prisoners on Holston; Stalmaker fortu-nately escaped.—MS. Preston Papers.

10. Lieutenant Colonel Stephen and Maj. Andrew Lewis were brevetted colonels to prevent their being subject to the command of a junior officer. MS. letter of Governor Fauquier, July 1st, 1761, in the *Byrd Papers.*

11. Or, Kan-a-ga-tuck-o, according to Timberlake's orthography.

12. In September 1760 At-ta-kul-la-Kul-la delivered up Captain Stuart and his companions, as already mentioned, and in November following brought in ten other prisoners to Colonel Byrd and reported forty or more on their way. Others were that fall and early winter delivered up at Fort Prince George. Between the 10th of February and 27th of April, 1761, seventy men and forty-three women and children were redeemed at that garrison, then commanded by Capt. Lachlan McIntosh. In the spring of 1761 Wil-lan-i-waw took in a number more to Virginia, so that in October of that year, but about forty white captives remained in the nation, only about thirteen of whom were Fort Loudon soldiers.

13. Hugh Waddell was the Washington of North Carolina. He served with the troops of that province on the Virginia frontiers in 1754 and shared in Braddock's disastrous campaign, soon after which, returning home, he was deported by Governor Dobbs to treat with the Cherokees and Catawbas and strengthen their friendship at that critical period. In 1756 he was ordered to reinforce Captain Demere at Fort Loudon, probably for a short period while the Cherokees were inimical. He was engaged in 1759–'60 in defending the frontiers of North Carolina, repelling attacks on Fort Dobbs, and serving on Montgomery's campaign; and in 1761 serving with Colonels Byrd and Stephen till peace was concluded. In 1765 he first discovered the approach of the stamp-ship to that province, laden with the hated stamps of tyranny, and gave notice to the people who gathered in the night and prevented their distribution. "Colonel Waddell," says Seawell Jones, "delighted in war, for it was his profession; and he commanded the sympathies of the people of Brunswick. He could march them to battle against the Stamp Act; he might do so against the governor." He became one of the popular leaders in the Regulators, when he held the rank of general. He died at Fort Johnson, North Carolina, April 9th, 1773, in the 39th year of his age, of a dropsy and mortification of his lungs. "Every virtue," said the *Cape Fear Mercury,* "that can endear a man in private life or render him valuable in society, were General Waddell's. In his military character, he was calm, humane and brave; in his friendships, steady and sincere; in the public service of his country, faithful and unwearied; in his domestic affections, warm and tender; in his disposition, benevolent and social. His loss, therefore, is lamented by all. He endured a long and painful disease and with a mind conscious of its own worth, he closed the last scene with cheerfulness and resignation."

14. The authority of the account here given of Byrd's campaign, and Boone's connection with it, are: *Pennsylvania Gazette,* June 4, September 17 and 24; MS. correspondence of General Amherst, Governor Fauquier, and Colonel Byrd in the *Byrd Papers;* Timberlake's *Narrative;* MS. notes of conversations with Col. Nathan Boone and lady; and Haywood's *History of Tennessee.* It should be observed that Judge Haywood, writing from traditionary statements, has fallen into an error in assigning 1758 as the date of Byrd's campaign and the erection of

Fort Robinson. Byrd was that year engaged in Forbes' expedition against Fort Duquesne.

15. "I was born February 10, 1758. When I was yet a baby, my father forted from the Indians, and forted as many as three different times, during the last of which, I can recollect some things that happened in the fort." MS. narrative of the late Daniel Bryan of Kentucky.

16. This Samuel Boone was the son of Samuel and grandson of old George Boone. During the Revolutionary War, he filled large contracts with Congress for guns and lost all he possessed by the operation; and in the fall of 1783 emigrated to Kentucky. He spent most of the year 1787 among the Chickasaw Indians, working at his trade. He settled in Shelby County, Kentucky, and there died about 1809 at a good old age. He was the father-in-law of the venerable Judge Moses Boone of Indiana and grandfather of the present Col. William P. Boone, a prominent attorney of law of Louisville, Kentucky.

17. McCall's *History of Georgia*, i:301; Martin's *North Carolina*, ii:179.

18. *Pennsylvania Gazette*, February 2 and 23, 1764.

19. Ramsay's *South Carolina*, i:210–11.

20. Ramsay's *South Carolina*, i:211–14.

21. The venerable Samuel Boone states that his father, George Boone, recovered a number of cattle stolen from the range by this daring band.

22. MS. notes of conversations with Col. Nathan Boone and lady.

23. It is stated by Haywood that in the fall of 1764, the Blevins connection made their fall hunt on Rock Castle, near the Crab Orchard in Kentucky, and continued to hunt in that region for several years afterwards; and that Boone came among them to obtain information of the geography of the country for Henderson and company who had employed him for that purpose. Dr. Peck partially adopted Haywood's assertion. There is no evidence, not even tradition, to sustain this statement, and it must be regarded as erroneous. Boone's connection with Henderson and the Company's purchase and settlement of Transylvania will be fully noticed in its proper place.

24. Morse's *Geography;* Wiley's *North Carolina Reader.*

25. DeBow's *Review,* August 1851; Wiley's *North Carolina Reader.*

EDITOR'S NOTES: CHAPTER 4

a. King Heigler or Hagler, in the Catawba tongue Nopkehe was much revered among the Catawbas and was a trusted diplomat, friend, and ally to the English. During the era of Anglo conquest and colonialism, which often came in the form of rum and brandy, he blamed "ardent spirits" as "the Very Cause" of violence among his young men.

In 1764, after the Cherokee Wars, the English herded the tribe, including the courageous Catawba warriors who had fought alongside the king's finest, onto a 144,000 acre-reservation in northwest South Carolina. But by 1842 the U.S. government had stripped the Catawba of the claim and, in a sad attempt to make what remained of the tribe agriculturists, granted them a tract of 630 acres on the west side of the Catawba River in their ancient homeland. Today the Catawba maintain the small reservation near Rockhill, South Carolina.

b. White market hunters, such as Long Hunters or white backwoods scouts, called "spies," often dressed in full or partial native garb, partly for convenience, partly from necessity, and partly because of the daunting look of bravado it gave them. Such dress was practical, comfortable, and marked one as a true woodsman. James Smith, Samuel Brady, and many others adopted the "white Indian" look and dressed their militia units in the native fashion and schooled them in native tactics. Daniel Boone wore his Indian-influenced dress as a badge of distinction when he served in 1780 as Kentucky's Fayette County representative and sat in the Virginia Assembly at Richmond among the likes of Thomas Jefferson. "I recollect very well when I saw Col. Boone," John Redd told Draper. "He was dressed in real backwoods stile, he had on a common jeans suit, with buckskin leggings neatly beaded. His leggings were manufactured by the Indians." See John Redd to LCD, c. 1848, DM 10NN:101. For more on such men and such dress, see chapter 7 in Ted Franklin Belue, *The Long Hunt;* also, "Indian-Influenced Woodsmen of the Cane," in *The Book of Buckskinning VII,* ed. William H. Scurlock (Texarkana, TX: Scurlock Publishing, 1995), 42–77.

c. South Carolinian Francis "the Swamp Fox" Marion (1732–95) earned his fame in the Revolution's southern theater. He was a lean man (he ate sparingly to stay fit for combat) and a teetotaler (unusual in those rum-swilling days). The mythic exploits of this one of Huguenot descent place him among America's war heroes. His British foe, Col. Banastre "Bloody Ban" Tarleton, once complained that the "devil himself could not catch" the wily Swamp Fox. High praise indeed.

d. It was Maj. Gen. Arthur St. Clair—not George A. Custer—who handed Indians their greatest victory against the United States. In 1787 Congress appointed him governor of the Old Northwest Territory, the lands above the Ohio. Ongoing conflicts and encroachment pitted a confederation of British-allied Algonquins in that Middle Ground region against American interests. In fall 1791 St. Clair marched his army from Fort Washington on the Ohio to the Great Miam, where he built Fort Hamilton. He then proceeded to the south of Greenville Creek to erect Fort Jefferson, then bivouacked his troops on the upper Wabash at St. Mary's Creek. On November 4 Blue Jacket (Shawnee) and Little Turtle (Miami) led more than 1,000 Indians in a rout of St. Clair's army of 1,400. He left behind 632 dead soldiers, 200 dead camp followers, and hundreds of wounded. Twenty-two Indians were killed.

News of the fiasco enraged President George Washington: "To suffer that army to be cut to pieces, hacked, butchered, tomahawked by a surprise—the very thing I guarded him against!! Oh God, Oh God, he is worse than a murderer! How can he answer to his country? The blood of the slain is upon him—the curse of widows and orphans—the curse of Heaven!" Arthur St. Clair died a penniless, broken man in 1818.

e. John Haywood, early Tennessee historian and author of *Natural and Aboriginal History of Tennessee* (1823).

f. Draper's paraphrase of I Kings 4:25, King James Version: "And Judah and Israel dwelt safely, everyone under his own vine and fig tree, from Dan even to Beer-she'ba, all the days of Solomon."

g. "White belts" refers to a belt of white wampum. Indians esteemed wampum as sacred and used it in at least two important ways: to seal treaties and, by presenting wampum strings during council talks, to give emphasis to speeches. Wampum making was arduous. Indians drilled white wampum from a conch's inner spiral; purple wampum, of varying shades of light red to dark purple (erroneously called "black wampum"), was punched and drilled from the thick shell of the quahog clam.

Purple and red "beads," or "grains," were worth three times the value of white wampum. Grain size varied. Grains from the William Penn belts are one-fourth inch wide by three-eighths to a half-inch long. For wampum strings, artisans strung grains on narrow deerskin strips three feet long and tied off the ends. Woven wampum belts might signify war or peace or be used to create alliances, prevent disputes, or identify a messenger. One belt described by Pennsylvania trader Conrad Weiser in 1748 was "25 grains wide and 265 grains long, in all containing almost 7,000 grains." A belt given in 1776 by Indian agent George Morgan (1742–1810) to Delaware chief Guyashusta at Fort Pitt was about seven inches wide, over six feet in length, and made of 2,500 beads.

English and Dutch traders, realizing how fluid a commodity wampum was, flooded native markets with European manufactured porcelain wampum and made great profits, which helped bring about the demise of the manufacture and use of the real article.

h. A leach tub was a hopper used to leach saltpeter (potassium nitrate) from guano-heavy cave dirt or night soil dug from beneath outhouses. A V-shaped vat was built of saplings and lined with straw and twigs for filtration. Once the dirt was heaped in the tub, the maker poured water on the mix to leach from it the "mother liquor"; the leachate is a key ingredient of black powder, which consists of ten parts sulfur, fifteen parts charcoal, and seventy-five parts saltpeter. Settlers also used leach tubs to leach lye from wood ashes to make soap.

i. Draper's eloquence of the beauty of this portion of the Blue Ridge is not without merit. Mount Mitchell is the highest mountain in North Carolina and eastern North America. Fittingly, Twentieth-Century Fox used the lush region described herein for its woodland backdrop in the 1992 motion picture *The Last of the Mohicans*.

CHAPTER 5

1764 –1768.—Daniel Boone's Hunting.—His Father's Death.—Tate
Incident.—Explores Florida.—Boone's and Cutbirth's Hunts.—Cutbirth
and Others' Adventures in the West.—Indians Attack the Linnville
Party.—Boone's Removal to the Upper Yadkin.—Tryon's Boundary
Line.—Fire-hunting.—Boone and Hill Attempt to Find Kentucky.—
Incident of the Cherokees.—Boone Hunting on Watauga. Surprised and
Captured by the Cherokees.

As early as 1764–'65, on his shorter trips, Boone began to take his oldest son, James, then seven or eight years of age, with him both for company and early to initiate him into the fascinating mysteries of the hunter's life. Spending several days in the woods together, they would sometimes be caught by a cold, snowy spell of weather, when Boone would have much difficulty in keeping little James warm during an inclement night by hugging the little fellow closely to his bosom in the open hunting camp. Though a blazing fire was always kept up during the night when the weather was such to require it, yet it was often the case that while one side of a person would be uncomfortably warm, the other would be shivering or benumbed with cold. James Boone, as he grew up, continued to accompany his father on his hunts, and not unfrequently on such occasions in the fall of the year, they would be absent two or three months and return home laden with many of the richest spoils of the chase.[1]

On the 2nd of January, 1765, Squire Boone, the father of Daniel, died at his residence at the Buffalo Lick in his sixty-ninth year, leaving behind him an unblemished reputation and numerous respectable descendants.[a] He had served several years as a justice of the peace and was esteemed a useful and honored member of society.[2]

Near Boone's, in the Sugar Creek Settlement, lived a noted old hunter named Tate, who spent much of his time in the woods. Boone once, returning from a hunting tour, went to his father-in-law's, Joseph Bryan's, to thrash out rye for his own use and, learning the wants of Tate's family in consequence of his protracted absence, obtained permission of Mr. Bryan also to thrash out some grain for them. Such acts of charity were so common among the pioneers as scarcely to excite notice; and though they were not blazoned abroad by the adulatious newspaper puffs, they were nevertheless observed by that Good Being who assures us that while he loves a cheerful and ungrudging giver,[b] we should never let our right hand know what our left hand doeth.[c] On his way home with his own grain, Boone left at Tate's what he had designed for that needy family. Returning from the wilderness, Tate expressed displeasure at Boone's generosity; and this coming to Boone's ears and soon after meeting Tate, he gave him a severe flogging and said he would do it again should he ever throw out anymore jealous intentions; that he would be grateful to any person who, under similar circumstances, would befriend his family as he had attempted to befriend Tate's; but he could not brook the idea of real kindness being misconstrued in a manner so provokingly unkind. In his old age, Boone would sometimes allude to this instance of man's ingratitude.[3]

Upon the acquisition of the Floridas,[d] Col. James Grant was in October 1763, appointed to the government of East Florida.[e] Early in the following year, he issued a proclamation inviting settlers to that province by the offer of free grants of one hundred acres of land to every Protestant emigrant, one third to be settled in three years and the whole in ten years; otherwise, at the expiration of that period, the unsettled portion [was] to revert to the Crown. For two or three years this liberal offer attracted considerable attention both in this country and Europe. Denys Rolle, a member of the British Parliament, obtained a large grant on the St. John's River [and] settled upon it two hundred English planters, of whom fifty were miserable females picked up in the purlieus of London. He hoped to reform them, but death soon removed a portion; and after a few years, all but fifteen of the remaining original emigrants had absconded, chiefly to Georgia.[f] Another colony of fifteen hundred Greeks, Corsicans, and Minorcans was brought out by a Dr. Turnbull, who induced them to leave their native land by liberal promises which he never fulfilled;[g] and once in Florida, he treated them for many years with more severity than so many slaves.

Near the close of the summer of 1765, Maj. John Field, William Hill, one Slaughter, and two others arrived from Culpeper County, Virginia, and shared Daniel Boone's hospitality at his humble home on Sugar Tree Creek. They were old acquaintances and on their way to explore Florida. Field had, during the preceding year, made a trip to that province soon after the promulgation of Governor Grant's proclamation, when sickness, want of time, or some other hindrance prevented anything like a general examination; and who more likely to join him in such an enterprise than his old friend Boone, an ardent admirer of nature and a real lover of adventure? Long had Boone been meditating a removal to some region superior to the Yadkin Valley; and the great problem to be solved was where could that more desirable region be found? Perhaps Florida, the land of flowers, oranges, and magnolias, and famed as possessing the fabulous fountain of rejuvenescense was the long sought-for El Dorado; he was willing at all events to go and see for himself. And his younger brother Squire Boone, not then quite twenty-one and but recently married, would gladly relinquish the company of his young wife awhile with the fond hope of finding a paradise home on some of the pellucid streams of Florida.[4] John Stuart, too, a young man chiefly raised on the

Yadkin, who had about two years before married [to] the youngest sister of the Boones, volunteered to share in the enterprise.

Daniel Boone gave his good spouse a hearty smack and ejaculated a sincere "God bless you!"—at the same time faithfully promising her if it should please Providence that he would eat his Christmas dinner with her and the children. All mounted on horseback, each equipped with a gun, ammunition, and a few articles of clothing, the eight adventurers departed. Major Field, the leader of the party, was a man of uncommon enterprise. He had served as a captain of Forbes' campaign and also on the frontiers of Virginia, as well as a major of volunteers on Bouquet's expedition of 1764; and several years after this Florida exploration, he lost his life in the memorable battle of Point Pleasant.[h]

William Hill was a great quiz and consequently the life and spirit of the whole company. Whenever they chanced to stop for a meal of victuals or a night's entertainment, he would be sure to make himself quite at home and commence playing off his favorite antics and witticisms, and particularly if there were any young women in the family. He had a way peculiarly his own of snapping paper wads, bits of sticks, or kernels of corn at the girls, constantly annoying them with his various exhibitions of roguery. Sometimes he encountered his equal among the frank and fearless girls of the Carolina and Georgia borders. At one place, while sitting at breakfast, with the horses saddled and fastened at the door, one of the young girls upon whom he had been playing his pranks slipped out and unloosed his horse. Apprised of it, Hill ran out and caught the animal; and while he was absent, the mischievous girls snatched up his knife, thrust the blade for a few minutes into the fire, and then carefully replaced it beside the plate. Hill presently returning and resuming his seat, attempted with his knife to cut some butter, which as quickly slid from the heated blade, when the girl roguishly remarked, "Mr. Hill, somehow your knife seems ashamed of the butter." Suspecting the trick, he quietly laid the knife down and as unconcernedly drew out his jack-knife, observing that he knew that was never ashamed of anything. On another occasion, eating out of a very dirty noggin, he sarcastically remarked to his hostess that hers was a very fortunate noggin as it had evidently escaped many a hard scouring.

At length they entered Florida and explored sufficiently in the eastern, middle, and western portions of the province to satisfy the Boones, at least, that their fancied land of beauty and loveliness was not to be found there. They encountered great difficulties in getting their horses and baggage through the wet, miry regions, wading, swimming, and rafting streams and dragging their weary limbs over an almost impassable section of country until man and beast were well-nigh exhausted. Stuart, probably searching for game, got lost and almost starved before he found his companions. A part of their route was almost entirely destitute of game, and they had nearly perished with hunger, when they came to an encampment of Seminole Indians. By a happy stroke of policy, Squire Boone presented an Indian girl with a small shaving glass, the only article he retained among his baggage that might be dispensed with. As she gazed upon it, there she

30. Seminole chikee, built of log stilt frame, elevated floor, and thatched pal-
metto frond roof. Note corn pounding block. Such open-air construction was
well suited to Florida's tropical climes and trade winds, but some Seminoles
opted for semipermanent pine-log cabin homes. BUREAU OF AMERICAN ETHNOL-
OGY, SMITHSONIAN INSTITUTION.

saw mirrored her own face; all this was unaccountably mysterious to the simple
Indian maiden. Eagerly did she first look upon one side and then the other to discover, if she could, the object of her delighted vision; and though she could not
comprehend the singular representation of her own well-known features, form,
dress, and trinketry, yet she was highly gratified with it. With extravagant delight
she hastened to her mother with the precious gift, and in a few minutes the starving travelers were furnished with venison and honey in abundance and treated
with the most liberal hospitality that an itinerant camp of Indians could offer.[i]
    Our explorers visited the region of St. Augustine and proceeded several days
up the St. John's River, some distance above Rolle's Settlement; [they] examined
Middle Florida and also the region back of Pensacola, which was then in the
province of West Florida. The palmetto with its [*wi*] leaves and magnolia with its
magnificent white flowers skirted the streams, interspersed with many a majestic
oak and, here and there, extensive groves of the fragrant orange. Along the
water-courses the soil was rich, but a few hundred yards back, the surface became
more elevated and so sandy as to appear nearly worthless for purposes of cultivation. Some of the vast fountains in Florida were then and still are objects of wonder and admiration, large enough in some instances for several vessels to ride in,
hundreds of feet deep, filled with fish of various kinds, and the waters so transparent that a person floating across their calm bosom in some fragile skiff, with

the passing clouds and azure sky reflected as from a mirror with indescribable softness, would almost imperceptibly find himself wrapt in a pleasing sensation akin to dizziness or fancy himself suspended between two bright firmaments, enjoying the distant, mellowed prospects presented on either hand before him; or, peradventure, he might form the happy conception that he was partaking of the imaginary felicities of some fairy region—or the beatitudes of "the land of pure delight."[j]

But the almost interminable swamps and everglades, lagoons and hammocks, bull-frogs and alligators went far towards making up the general characteristics of the country, and these were far from being desirable to the Boones. Yet it must with truth be said that Daniel Boone was rather pleased than otherwise with Pensacola and its beautiful bay and even ventured to purchase a house and town-lot with the intention of settling there, though by no means well satisfied with the general appearance of the Floridas. Gladly did the explorers wend their way back to Carolina, which they at length reached after enduring over four months of incessant toils, hardships, and exposures. Slaughter, who was something of an adept in the games of chance, won enough where they tarried of night while journeying through the settled portions of their route, added to the few deer-skins secured by their skill, nearly to meet their entire expenses. In the wilds of Florida, their only subsistence was venison, wild fowls, and occasionally honey from a

31. Frontier Florida, with its diverse fauna and lush flora, was a true hunter's paradise, yet one that Boone and his comrades had trouble adapting to. "BLACK WOLVES OF FLORIDA," BY LLOYD JORDAN; COURTESY FRANK O. BELUE.

bee-tree; and oftentimes did they kindle their evening fire under the shade of some spreading oak or lofty palm or magnolia to dry or warm themselves or drive away gnats and mosquitos and extend their weary bodies upon the damp earth and go supperless to sleep.

Boone could have reached home a few days before the promised time, but as he neared the Sugar Tree settlement, he somewhat slackened his pace so that at noon on Christmas day he strode into his domicile, gave his "little girl," as he familiarly called his wife, and the children a greeting kiss, took his seat at the table, and joyfully partook with his family of the holiday repast which his good spouse had prepared for the occasion. And doubtless around that happy [wi] he spiced his conversation with striking contrasts of the comforts before him with the privations and sufferings he had experienced in Florida. But Mrs. Boone was unwilling to remove to Pensacola, so far distant from her relatives and friends; besides, from his own story, she was persuaded that there was nothing in all of Florida, with its interminable swamps, barren sand-hills, and scanty game, that should for a moment induce her good man to entertain the idea of moving there. He began to think so too, and the little town-lot in Pensacola was left to take care of itself; and henceforth Daniel Boone looked hopefully to the great Western Valley to find his long sought for ideal of a perfect country—one possessed of a rich soil, salubrious climate, good timber, extensive range, and game in great variety and profusion.[5]

At the close of the French War, there arrived in the Boone settlement a young man of Scotch-Irish descent of the name of Benjamin Cutbirth. He was born in the frontier county of Augusta, Virginia, about the year 1740. His father having died while the son was yet young, he grew up to manhood as the chief stay and support of a widowed mother and fatherless family, deprived of the opportunity of acquiring knowledge, save that which related to honest industry in securing a comfortable livelihood by the plow and hoe, with a perfect understanding of the ready use of the all important rifle. His mother having married again, young Cutbirth concluded to seek his fortune in the Yadkin country, of which he had heard many a good report. Once there, he encountered the bright eyes and rosy cheeks of the fair Elizabeth Wilcoxen, a niece of Daniel Boone's, and soon became inextricably entangled in the meshes of love that he wisely surrendered himself at discretion to the lovely charmer and never after had cause to regret his ready capitulation.

This marriage into the connection brought Boone and Cutbirth together. Their acquaintance soon ripened into friendship; and possessing a fellow feeling, they spent many a day and night happily together in the wilderness in the exciting pursuits of the chase. They ranged the forest far and wide and not unfrequently met parties of Indian hunters, who expressed much dissatisfaction on account of their intentions upon their hunting grounds and killing so much of their game. On one of their excursions, when they had had a very successful hunt and had dried and packed a large quantity of skins and furs in their camp on Roane's Creek, a north-easterly tributary of the Watauga, rising in the mountains of East Tennessee, a party of Cherokee Indians came upon them and robbed them of everything they possessed. There was no help for this mishap, and they had to submit to it with the best grace they could.

In Ashe County, in the extreme north-western corner of North Carolina, a rapid little stream takes its rise in the spurs and gorges of Rich Mountain and, running nearly an easterly course, flows into the South Fork of New River. Upon this secluded little mountain stream was a fine hunting range, particularly for bear, and a region too where ginseng grew plentifully and where Boone would sometimes gather *seng* for market as an interlude to a hunting expedition. Boone and Cutbirth made an excellent hunt in this region and pitched their camp on this creek. Discovering Indian sign, they resolved to lose no time in packing home their furs and peltry, of which they had a full load for their horses brought for this purpose, and erected a log-pen in which they deposited a large quantity of dried bear bacon which they had cured and wished to secure awhile beyond the reach of wild animals. But when they returned, the meat was all destroyed. From this circumstance, the stream had ever since been known as *Meat Camp Creek*. A number of families, chiefly from the banks of the Roanoke River, North Carolina, emigrated to Baton Rouge on the Mississippi.[6] In the following year, Benjamin Cutbirth, John Stuart, John Baker, and James Ward, all excellent woodsmen and all young married men, concluded to forego the happiness of home for a season and make an effort to penetrate the wilderness in a westerly direction to the Mississippi. At that day, the spirit of exploration—a longing for a better country— seemed to pervade the minds of the borderers to an uncommon degree. These four adventurous men plunged into the forest, and wending their toilsome way over the Appalachian mountain chain, descending to its western slopes, and passing through the wilds of what is now Tennessee, they finally beheld the majestic Mississippi. So far as can be ascertained, this was the first band of white men of whom we have any certain account that ever accomplished that great undertaking. It is very possible that some of the Indian traders may have done so before them, but reliable evidence of it is wanting.

Even at that early day, a large commerce was carried on with New Orleans. There, such commodities as lumber, pelts and furs, bear bacon and bear's oil, buffalo jerk and tallow, and dried venison ham found a ready market. Cutbirth and his Carolina friends, anxious to learn all about the country, its trade and productions, as well as its soil and climate, at once engaged in the business of hunting. In the fall of the year they would ascend the Mississippi some distance and then direct their cause up some one of its numerous tributaries till a good hunting ground was reached, establish a stationary camp for winter, and in the spring descend with the products of their hunt to New Orleans, where an ample remuneration awaited all their toils.

On one of these occasions, Cutbirth and his party met with great danger in endeavoring to enter the Mississippi during high spring flood, for the high-swelling waves from the main stream repeatedly drove them far into the back water and well-nigh engulfed their frail and heavily laden vessel. At another time, when conveying a boat load of lumber to New Orleans, they encountered a violent midnight storm upon the Mississippi. The angry waters soon filled their vessel, but the nature of the lading caused it to float, and by dint of hard rowing, they safely reached the shore, which at first they could only with great difficulty discern beneath the edge of a murky cloud. When standing on one bank of the Mississippi, Cutbirth once saw what he judged to be about three acres of the river bank fall into the stream on the opposite shore, "as quick," he said, "as the crack of a gun."

In this way Cutbirth and his Yadkin companions spent between one and two years and, by their industry and frugality, acquired quite a respectable property, when they were unexpectedly stripped of the whole and left destitute. James Adair, the Indian trader and subsequent historian of the Southern Indians, evidently mentions this very affair. Speaking of the period of about 1766 or 1767, he says a person from the Yadkin settlements came to view the Mississippi lands and was highly pleased with the soil, climate, and situation of the country. He related to Adair in a humorous manner that when at a Frenchman's house on the Spanish side of the river, a very lusty Choctaw Indian called there in company with others on a hunt. As the Choctaws generally were in the French interest, [and] he was desirous of ingratiating himself into the good graces of his host, he began to ridicule the Yadkin hunter with gestures and mocking language; and the more civilly the white man demeaned himself, so much the more impudently the savage treated him. At length, the sturdy Carolinian beginning to feel indignant at such uncalled-for treatment, suddenly seized him in his arms, carried him a few steps distant, and threw him headlong down the bank into the Mississippi. The laugh was now loudly turned against the jolly Choctaw by his Indian countrymen; for if the Indians were to see their grandmother break her neck by a fall from a horse or any other similar accident, they would nevertheless whoop and hallo in the wildest delight.

The drenched Indian came out of the water quite ashamed but appeared to be in very good humor after his purification, as he found he had not one of the French wood-peckers to deal with. However, one night when the Carolinian was on his return home through the Choctaw nation, the savages pursued and endeavored to kill him and actually seized his horses and baggage. He had a narrow escape with his life before reaching Quansheto, a Choctaw town, where he made his complaint to the head chief, which might have been expected to produce both pity and justice in any heart not callous to every feeling of humanity. But instead of endeavoring to redress his grievances and restore him his property, which he could easily have effected, he aggravated his suffering by the grossest abuse; and all this from the demagogue-motive of maintaining his popularity with his savage countrymen, leaving Truth and Justice to look elsewhere for friends and enforcers.[7] Cutbirth and his party now made the best of their way home through the Creek nation, experiencing many dangers and hardships.[8]

Among the Indian troubles of the period may be mentioned that of four traders and a half-breed child of one of them who were killed in the Cherokee country during the month of May 1766—some of whom, it was thought, in retaliation for a chief and four warriors of the Cherokee nation treacherously slain the previous year by a party of lawless Virginians on the frontiers of that province. Such crimes with their bloody retaliations rendered it dangerous for the white hunters to expose themselves too far upon the Indian hunting grounds; yet some more fearless than others, prompted by their passionate love of the chase, would make the venture.

It has already been mentioned that Linnville Creek, in the valley of Virginia, where the Boones probably tarried awhile on their way to the Yadkin country, was named after a noted border hunter—William Linnville. Among the pioneer settlers of that frontier region of Virginia, his name appears as a militiaman of Augusta County as early as 1742 and two years later as a captain. He early removed to the Yadkin Valley and perhaps with the Boone emigration. He married a sister of Joseph Bryan, who, be it remembered, was the father-in-law of Daniel Boone; and about 1763 George Boone, a younger brother of Daniel's, married Nancy, daughter of Captain Linnville. In the summer of 1766 Captain Linnville, being in bad health, thought a hunting trip among the mountains might prove beneficial. Accompanied by his son John and another young man, he passed far beyond the settlements over the mountain ranges at the head of the Yadkin River and pitched his camp upon a clear and rapid stream, a very considerable branch of the Catawba.

Awakening one morning just before daylight, Captain Linnville aroused his companions, telling them he had just vividly dreamed that they would all be killed by the Indians, and urged them instantly to escape and leave him to his fate—that he was not able to leave. He had scarcely finished his statement when they were fired upon and the old man wounded, when he again begged the young men to make their escape if possible. They sprang to their guns, when a second volley from the Indians killed young Linnville and badly wounded the other, having received a ball through the thigh, partially fracturing the bone. He, however, ran off in the dark without being discovered; but unfortunately, after having gone some distance, [he] trod on a stick, which, breaking, in some way caused him to fall and resulted in completing the fracture of his thigh. There he lay in agony, expecting as soon as light should appear to be tomahawked. But at daylight the Indians went to catching the horses and secured all but one, a wild young animal belonging to Captain Linnville, which he had brought out to break into use by packing with the expected proceeds of the hunt. Scalping the unfortunate Linnvilles, the Indians packed up what plunder they desired and left the camp, the young horse following the others.

The wounded young man discovering the departure of the enemy, crawled back to the camp to die beside his friends. He had not been long there when the wild horse returned, went kindly up to the prostrate sufferer, suffered him to put on an old bridle the Indians had left and then get him little by little to a suitable place, where he managed to mount and started for home, sixty miles distant. With his broken leg painfully dangling, when he had gone about a mile, the horse took fright from the broken limb or dripping blood and, throwing the poor rider, ran off. Despairing of reaching the settlements, he again crawled to the camp amid great suffering, his thigh having by this time become much swollen and very painful. He now discovered that the Indians during his absence had returned to camp, probably in quest of the young horse, and failing to find it, had taken off [with] what they previously left. So his absence had saved him from the toma-hawk and scalping knife. The wild horse again returned with the old bridle on and suffered the almost helpless cripple to remount and actually succeeded in reaching the settlements without even dismounting. He survived his singular ad-venture and in due time recovered and was presented by Mrs. Linnville with the noble horse which had brought him to the settlement from the scene of carnage. Relating upon his return the particulars of the attack upon the camp, the death of the Linnvilles, and his own remarkable escape, a party of friends went out and buried the dead; and none more likely than Daniel Boone to have headed a mis-sion of humanity like this.

The place where Captain Linnville and his son were unfortunately killed and their companion mortally wounded was on a clear and rapid mountain stream, a considerable branch of the Catawba of about fifty miles in length, in Burke County, North Carolina, which has ever since borne the name of Linnville River to perpetuate the misfortunes of these fearless border hunters. Their fatal camp, it is believed, was located not far from the bluff of the Short-Off Mountain, on the eastern bank of the river and about ten miles below the Falls, a beautiful cascade of from eighty to one hundred feet descent. This attack was made by a band of Northern Indian warriors.[k] Nor did the Cherokees fare any better, for a son of old At-ta-kul-la-Kul-la, together with seven of his relations, when engaged in picking berries, were about the same time fallen upon and slain by some of their Northern Indian enemies.[9]

Two causes contributed to induce Boone to move westwardly—the growing scarcity of game and the oppressive extortions of the clerks of courts, sheriffs, tax-gatherers, and lawyers of the province. Land agents would issue patents in behalf of Earl Granville, an extensive land-holder of that region, and afterwards pretend to have discovered a capital defect in the omission of Granville's titles of honor, which alarming discovery but too often had its intended effect of inducing the people to secure their lands by taking out new patents and paying their fees a second time. New frauds were constantly invented by these harpies. The deputy-surveyors, entry-takers, and other officers of inferior grade readily caught the cue and profited by the bad example of their superiors; and thus the most bare-faced impositions were everywhere practiced with perfect impunity. Goaded on almost to desperation by several years' continuance of the mal-practices, with their petitions to the proper authorities for redress of grievances rejected and their complaints treated with contemptuous scorn, the people at length rose in bodies under the name Regulators[l] but were defeated by Governor Tryon and his forces near Alawance Creek, May 16, 1771. The great principles of freedom, however, for which they contended survived their repulse and a few years later triumphed over all opposition.[10]

Anxious alike to escape these oppressions and locate in the midst of a better hunting region, Boone left the Sugar Tree Settlement and removed his family about sixty miles in a north-westerly direction, toward the head of the Yadkin, and settled upon a fine tract of land upon its northwestern bank some two hundred yards back from the stream and near the foot of the hills skirting the low grounds.[11] The spot where stood his primitive cabin is still pointed out, two hundred yards below Holeman's Ford and about seven and a half miles above Wilkesboro in Wilkes County. After awhile, Boone found another situation which pleased him better nearly five miles higher up the river on the southeastern side, on a beautiful low ground about a half a mile up Beaver Creek on its eastern side, where he erected his cabin and made his home for a season. At length he again changed his locality, choosing his final home on the Upper Yadkin, directly on its southern bank and just above the mouth of Beaver Creek.[12]

Beyond the greedy grasp of extortioners, Boone found a happy home in the quiet valley of the Upper Yadkin, with an agreeable diversity of hill and dale around him—"the hills gradually swelling into mountains, until the remote portions presented in all directions scenes of wild grandeur and sublimity, and were at last embosomed in the region that had been well called *The Switzerland of North America.*"[13] A hardy and rapidly increasing people, masters of their own free wills, lay scattered among these fertile uplands of North Carolina. There, through the boundless wilderness, hardy emigrants careless of the strifes of Europe, ignorant of deceit, free from tithes, answerable to no master fearlessly occupied lands that seemed without an owner.[m] Their swine had the range of the forest, the open greenwood was the pasture of their untold herds; their young men, disciplined to frugality and patient of toil, trolled along the brooks that abounded in fish and took their pleasure sleep under the forest-tree; or trapped the beaver; or, in small parties, roved the spurs of the Alleghenies in quest of marketable skins. How could royal authority force its way into such a region?[14]

Neither Daniel Boone nor his good wife, Rebecca, were the persons to be found complaining about their lot. They were always thankful for what they had rather than repining for imaginary wants, which, could they have been obtained simply for the asking, would in all probability never have added one iota to their happiness. With God's blessing of health, surrounded with a group of cherry-cheeked children, with a comfortable home and everything reasonably desirable to eat and wear as the fruit of their honest industry, and withal, a quiet conscience, this pioneer couple were contented and happy. They had some neighbors settled around them, and all cheerfully united their energies whenever occasion required it, at a cabin raising or log-rolling for a new-comer, meetings well calculated to promote social intercourse and interchange the passing news of the frontiers.

The spring of 1767 was signalized by the murder of five traders on the Cherokee or Tennessee River, said to have been committed by a war-party of Northern Indians.[15] During the month of June ensuing, Governor Tryon, with three commissioners, was engaged in running a boundary line between the back settlements of the province and the Cherokee hunting-grounds. The governor, having been bred a soldier, was fond of display and had a company of militia as an escort; and having met a few Cherokee chiefs, ran a portion of the line, and agreed upon the remainder, he returned with the honorable title conferred by the Cherokees of *The Great Wolf of North Carolina.* Beside the acquisition of this title and the marking of a few trees, this little expedition at a time of profound peace served to gratify the governor's vanity at the expense of an increase of the taxes which the province was illy able to bear. Whether Boone was employed as a guide to Tryon's party, for which he was so well fitted, we have no means of determining. The event, we may well conclude, was a subject of some interest to the border hunters as indicating the line of demarcation between the whites and Indians. Yet, after all, such lines were very little regarded by either party. On the 5th of September following, seven North Carolina hunters who had ventured into the mountain region some sixty miles beyond the boundary were fired upon in their camp about two hours after dark, as they were going to sleep, one of whom was killed on the spot and another mortally wounded. The others, having abandoned their wounded companion on the path, returned to the settlements.[16]

While residing upon the Yadkin, *fire-hunting* sometimes engaged Boone's attention. There were in vogue different modes of practicing it. One was to fire the dry leaves in a circle of several miles' circumference, which, burning inwardly, would drive all the game to the center, when huddled together where they were easily killed. Sometimes blinded and suffocated by the smoke and scorched by the fire, every moment approaching them nearer, they would force their way under the greatest trepidation and dismay through the flames but were no sooner once more in the open day-light than they were shot by the hunters who stood without in readiness to fire upon them. "It is really a pitiful sight," declared the elder Colonel Byrd, "to see the extreme distress the poor deer are in, when they find themselves surrounded with this circle of fire, they weep and groan like a human creature, yet cannot move the compassion of those hard-hearted people who are about to murder them. This unmerciful sport is called fire-hunting, and is much practiced by the Indians and frontier inhabitants, who sometimes in the eagerness of their diversion, are punished in their cruelty, are hurt by one another when they shoot across at the deer which are in the middle."[17]

Another custom, according to Flint, was for a person in the night to lead the way through the forest, generally mounted on horseback, carrying a blazing torch of pitch-pine or lightwood or a fire-pan full of burning pine-knots, which would quickly attract the wild gaze of the deer, as if spell-bound by the strangeness and brilliancy of the scene. The glare reflecting brightly from the eyes of the beguiled victim would make a distinct mark for the hunters in the rear to secure a fatal shot. This, in the hunter's parlance, was called *Shining the Eyes*. But Boone did not practice either of these modes of fire-hunting.[n] He had carefully studied the habits peculiar to deer and found that in the summer and early autumn they would nightly resort to the rivers and creeks, not for drinking only, but to eat a tender water-moss of which they were exceedingly fond, which grew plentifully in shoaly places, and also to avoid the flies and swarming insects so common to all forest regions and so annoying alike to wild and tame animals. If the stream was low or shallow, the fire-carrier would wade, followed by the hunters either in the water or along the bank, but more generally from the depth of the stream and the almost impenetrable thickets of cane-brake along the shore. All would avail themselves of canoes, floating down the stream, the fire of pine-knots blazing on the stone hearth in the prow and allowing the stupid gaze of the defeated animals. Experienced hunters would make as successful shots at night as by the ordinary mode of day-hunting, having the shining of the deer's eyes for a mark and the glaring light reflected from the sights of their rifles to enable them to take unerring aim. It was only upon the Yadkin that Boone ever practiced in this kind of hunting.[18]

As Boone's mind had been much exercised the past two years with the hope of finding a country more desirable than Carolina, and the Florida exploration had resulted so unfavorably, he now began to bend his thoughts seriously towards making a determined attempt to discover the fair region of Kentucky, so fascinatingly portrayed to him by Findlay a dozen years gone by. William Hill yet remained in the Yadkin country, and to him Boone fully made known his plans and wishes. Hill entered heartily into them, and preparations were made for the arduous enterprise. They started in the fall of 1767, perhaps accompanied by Squire Boone, and having crossed the Blue Ridge and Alleghenies and the Holston and Clinch near their sources, they fell upon the head waters of the West Fork of Big Sandy. Beautifully has the historian Bancroft declared that "the streams are the guides which God has set for the stranger in the wilderness." So Boone and Hill, concluding from its course that this stream must flow into the Ohio, pursued their journey along its banks, until, as they thought they had traveled well nigh a hundred miles and had penetrated considerably to the westward of the Cumberland Mountains, when probably striking a buffalo-path and pursuing it, they came to the salt spring which some twenty-eight years afterwards was known as Young's Salt Works, situated ten miles directly west of the present town of Prestonsburg on the Lick Fork of Middle Creek, a tributary to the west of Louisa Fork of Sandy in Floyd County, in the extreme eastern part of Kentucky.

Here they were caught in a severe snow storm which compelled them to camp, and they at length concluded to remain all winter. The salt spring which issued from the foot of a rocky bluff on the southern bank of the stream proved more valuable to them than [a] mine of the precious metals, for it was the means of enticing buffaloes and other animals there in great numbers to drink the waters or lick the brackish soil; and all Boone and Hill had to do, next to husbanding their ammunition, was, as Peter was commanded in the vision, "rise—kill and eat."° And here it was that Boone saw the first buffaloes he ever beheld and enjoyed many a delicious feast from the favorite rump of that animal or a tender loin of venison. As the country thus far had been forbidding, quite hilly, and much overrun with laurel, they became discouraged; and as winter passed away, they abandoned all hopes of finding Kentucky by this route and made the best of their way back to the Yadkin. Nor did Boone know until several years afterward the name of the stream near which he had wintered.[19]

Boone and Hill had become very much attached to each other and were often employed on hunting trips together. They entered into a solemn agreement that whichever of them should die first should, if possible, return and convey to the survivor intelligence from the spirit world. Hill was the first to enter upon that

32. *Buffalo roamed east of the Mississippi throughout the southeast to Florida, to western Pennsylvania and north to the Illinois country. Their paths—called "traces"—provided colonists and Indians with a network of early roads. Kentuckians followed this trace at the Battle of Blue Licks, August 19, 1782.* FILSON CLUB HISTORICAL SOCIETY.

untried state, but Boone used to pleasantly remark that the promised communications were never made.[p] Hill must have died shortly after returning from this trip to Sandy, for had he been living when Boone entered upon his subsequent great exploration of Kentucky, it is natural to suppose he would have taken part in an enterprise so consonant with his tastes and feelings.

Thus transcribed in the Cherokee country in the summer of 1768 a singular outrage which is best related in the touching narrative of Capt. John Stuart, southern superintendent of Indian affairs, in a letter to President Blair of Virginia: "I reproached the Cherokees severely," says Captain Stuart, "with the murder of five emigrants from your province who were going to the Mississippi which was committed in Summer last. They confessed it and said the perpetrators were a party of Chilhowie people who urged in their own defense that their relations had been killed in Augusta County in your province in 1765, for which they had never received any satisfaction, although repeated promises had been made either of putting the guilty persons to death, or making compensation in good from your province, which they believed because I had confirmed them. That they, nevertheless, were disappointed, and being tired with waiting, took that satisfaction which they could not obtain from our justice. All the warriors declared that they disapproved of the action, but the Chilhowie people were authorized by the custom of their country to act as they did and their plea of never having had any satisfaction was undeniable; that in any other instance, nothing should prevent their executing strict justice on offenders according to treaties. It is not only extremely disagreeable to myself, but very detrimental to his majesty's service to be obliged to fail in any promise made to Indians. The compensation of five hundred dressed deer skins value in goods for every person murdered, which, on the faith of Governor Fauquier's repeated letters, I engage they should receive in the spring, was extremely moderate; and this you will acknowledge, if you compare it with the sum expended by the province of Pennsylvania on a late similar affair; and I must confess, that this disappointment will render me extremely cautious in making promises on any future occasion."[20]

It was early autumn of probably this year that Boone, in company with others, was engaged in hunting in the Watauga region in what is now East Tennessee. They one day observed an unusually large bear, very poor and unfit for use, making his way across a deep gully branch upon a fallen tree which spanned the chasm only some twenty yards from the camp. Once over, his bearship followed down the stream, which ran southerly a little distance and then bore off westwardly, and maintained his general course in that direction. He had a singular white spot or stripe on his nose and a large white spot on his breast. A yellowish spot on the nose and a white one on the breast are not uncommon, but a white spot or stripe on the nose is very seldom to be found. The unusual size and marks of the bear were so remarkable as to attract the special notice of Boone and his companions.

Near the close of December, while still at the same camp, Boone and his party were surprised to discover the same bear, as they fully believed, returning on the very route he went out and crossing the gully branch on the same fallen tree, travelling eastwardly now in a well fattened condition. One of the party shot and killed him. Boone, in speaking of this circumstance, said that there was no mast that year such as bear were known to fatten on, short of the western part of the Cherokee country in the great bear masting region of the Tombigbee River and Bear Creek; and hence he concluded this animal by some peculiar instinct must have travelled that great distance for a supply of mast upon which to fatten before returning to his old haunt and denning up for his long winter sleep. Unless fat, this animal will not den up at all but keep rambling about, eating whatever he can. By watching closely the general direction of the bear in his autumnal journeyings, Boone soon learned to pursue the same course and was always sure of finding them in great abundance in the plenteous masting region.[21]

When once alone at a snowy time near where Jonesboro now is in East Tennessee, Boone laid himself down on a bed of boughs or cane and covered his blanket over him. In this situation and probably quite weary, he slept sweetly and soundly. A party of Cherokee Indians spying the solitary hunter, one of them crept up stealthily and, carefully raising the snow-covered blanket, exclaimed, "Ah, Wide-Mouth, have I got you now?" Boone, of course, took things calmly and expressed much pleasure at meeting his red brothers, and after a hearty shake of the hand all around, a general interchange of news and civilities followed. He was on this occasion either treated kindly and suffered to depart when and where he pleased, or if partly retained in surveillance, he had no difficulty in soon giving his brothers the slip and making a wide space as speedily as possible between him and them.[q]

DRAPER'S NOTES: CHAPTER 5

1. MS. notes of conversations with Col. Nathan Boone.

2. MS. letter of C. Harbin, Esq., who obtained the date of Squire Boone's death from the neatly finished soap-stone at the head of his grave, in the Joppa church yard, near Mocksville, Davie County, formerly a part of Rowan County, North Carolina. Joppa Meeting House was at this period free to all religious denominations. It will be remembered that Squire Boone was disowned by the Friends' Exeter Meeting, in Pennsylvania, for countenancing the marriage of his children out of the order. "So far as I can judge," says Thomas Pearson of Berks County, who has carefully examined the records, "Squire Boone was a respectable and orderly man, as he was appointed to perform services for the meeting several times, and no mention whatever of disorderly conduct." His widow

survived till 1776 or '77, when she died at their son-in-law, William Bryan's, in the Bryan settlement in the Forks of the Yadkin, upwards of seventy years of age.

3. MS. notes of conversation with Mrs. Nathan Boone.

4. Squire Boone was born October 5, 1744, and married August 8, 1765, to Miss Jane Van Cleve, whose parents were natives of New Jersey.

5. The facts connected with this Florida exploration have been chiefly derived from Col. Nathan Boone, the three surviving sons of John Stuart's widow, Mrs. Rebecca Boone Lemond, and Daniel Bryan—the latter of whom well recollected the time of the departure and returns of the parties.

6. Martin's *Louisiana,* i:349.

7. Adair's *Southern Indians,* quarto, London, 1775:296–297.

8. MS. statement of the late Elijah Callaway, of Ashe County, North Carolina, who married a daughter of Cutbirth's and learned these particulars of his history and adventures from his own lips. Cutbirth, like Boone, was a real good Leather-Stocking and lived mostly a hunter's life upon the frontiers; and finally settled with his wife on Duck River in Middle Tennessee, where, after having been a worthy member of the Baptist denomination about forty years, he died about the year 1817. He was a stout, square-built man, nearly six feet in height, with dark hair and rather dark complexion; possessed of singular courage and perseverance, and somewhat taciturn in his disposition.

Of Cutbirth's adventurous companions on his eventful trip to the Mississippi, Stuart subsequently joined Boone in his long exploration of Kentucky, during which he lost his life. Baker was one of Col. James Knox's party of celebrated *Long Hunters* in 1770–'71 and afterwards settled among the hills in the north-eastern part of Rockcastle County, Kentucky, where he died about 1820, fully eighty years of age. He was a handy, honest, good looking man, about middle size; and his sons and grandsons after him were unsurpassed hunters and woodsmen. It is related in Collins' *Kentucky* that the Big Cave in Rockcastle County "was discovered by John Baker, who, in company with his wife, commenced exploring it with a torch-light. At the distance of about three hundred yards, their light went out, and they were forced to crawl about in perfect darkness, for forty hours, before they found the place at which they entered." Ward also moved to Kentucky after it began to be settled and there died. He was not, however, the Capt. James Ward who lived and died in Mason County in that state.

Cutbirth's son-in-law, Elijah Callaway, was born in Bedford County, Virginia, October 12, 1769; and when he was five years old, his parents removed to the Upper Yadkin country, where he married Mary Cutbirth in 1789. He served many years as a justice of the peace and six years in each branch of the Legislature of North Carolina, and died at his residence at Walnut Grove, Ashe County, March 3rd, 1847, in his seventy-eighth year. He lived to do good and died firmly confiding in the Christian faith and hope.

9. *Pennsylvania Gazette,* August 14th and October 9th, 1766; MS. Preston Papers; MS. letter of Nelson P. Lindsey, Esq., of Linnville River, North Carolina; MS. statement of Samuel Boone, a grandson of Captain Linnville, who derived

the facts from Linnville's widow, his son and mother, and other family connections. Mrs. Linnville, after her husband's death, lived mostly with her son-in-law George Boone, went with him when he emigrated to Kentucky, and died there.

10. Unbroken in spirit, many of them gradually passed the Alleghenies and commenced the settlements of Tennessee and Kentucky. "Like the mammoth," says Bancroft, "they shook the dust from their feet and crossed the mountains."

11. Haywood's *Tennessee*; Martin's, Foote's, and Wheeler's works on North Carolina, Lossing's *Field Book on the Revolution.*

12. MS. statements of Elijah Callaway and his son Dr. James Callaway, mainly derived from an ancient woman, Mrs. Susanna Dula, whose father, William Ellison, lived on Beaver Creek when Boone resided there. See also Wheeler's *North Carolina,* ii:445.

13. Rev. F. L. Hanks' lecture before the New York Historical Society, December 1852.

14. Bancroft, iv:132, 133.

15. *Pennsylvania Journal,* July 30th, 1767.

16. *Pennsylvania Journal,* October 29th, 1767.

17. Byrd's *History of the Dividing Line,* 1728, p. 80, 81; Burnaby's *Travels in North America in 1759–'60,* p. 116, 117.

18. MS. notes of conversations with Col. Nathan Boone. It is stated also in the unedited manuscripts of the historian Kercheval that this mode of fire-hunting was practiced in early times in western Virginia.

TFB: *Draper's statement that Boone fire-hunted just in the Yadkin Valley may not be true. Boone was a market hunter and did what he had to do to provide for his ever-growing family. Peter Houston, a contemporary who lived in Bourbon County, Kentucky, and claimed to know Boone well, helped him "shine" and kill a treed panther. See Houston's memoirs in DM 20C:84(50–52). For a published transcription of Houston's entire narrative including the panther episode, see Peter Houston, A Sketch in the Life and Character of Daniel Boone, ed. Ted Franklin Belue (Mechanicsburg, PA: Stackpole Books, 1997).*

19. MS. statement and notes of conversation with Col. Nathan Boone, who, visiting Young's Salt Works in the winter of 1796–97 while on a hunt with his father in that region, received these facts from his father's own lips. At the salt spring called Young's Salt Works, settled by James Young in early times, some sixty years ago, the pioneers made salt; since then a well has been sunk at the same spot, where some salt is yet made. It is now known as the Middle Creek Salt Works and is situated in a wild, mountainous country, the settlements in its immediate neighborhood being sparse. MS. letters of Edwin Trimble, Esq., and John Howes, Esq., of Paintsville, Kentucky, March 1853.

20. Captain Stuart to Preston Blair, dated Hard Labour, 17th October, 1768, in the State Paper Office, London, a copy of which was adduced in the case of "Porterfield vs. Clark" and others, in the Supreme Court of the United States at its January term, 1844.

21. Conversations with Col. Nathan Boone.

EDITOR'S NOTES: CHAPTER 5

a. The picturesque and well-maintained Joppa cemetery is easily accessible off North Carolina's I-40 at the Mocksville exit. At the cemetery's gate a sign reads:

Daniel Boone's Parents
Squire and Sarah Boone are
Buried here. Daniel Boone, 1734–1820
lived many years in this region.

Vandals chipped away at the couple's soapstone headstones, and in the early 1900s caretakers removed them to a Mocksville bank vault. In 1922 brick masons inset the slabs in a concrete monument encased in red brick and reinstalled the protected headstones on their original site where they now sit. The inscription on the larger headstone, of Squire Boone, Sr., reads:

Squire Boone departed this life they sixty-ninth year of his age
in thay year of our Lord 1765. Geneiary Tha 2.

The following is inscribed on the smaller slab of Sarah Boone's:

Sah Boone desowned this life, 1777, aged 77 yars.

The remains of Morgan Bryan, grandfather of Daniel's wife, Rebecca Bryan Boone, are also interred at the Joppa cemetery.

b. Draper's excerpt of II Corinthians 9:7, King James Version, concerning the apostle Paul's teaching on the giving of alms: "Every man according as he purposeth in his heart, so let him give; not grudgingly, or of necessity: for God loveth a cheerful giver."

c. An excerpt from Jesus' well-known Sermon on the Mount, as found in Matthew 6:3, King James Version: "But when thou doest alms, let not thy left hand know what thy right hand doeth."

d. Five flags have flown over "La Florida." Though it was claimed by both France and Spain in the earliest days of European New World exploration, by the 1560s Spain reigned victorious over the land, establishing St. Augustine, near present-day Jacksonville, in 1565. In 1763, in the wake of the Seven Years' War, Spain relinquished Florida to England but regained it in 1783 after the American Revolution. In 1819 a provision in the Adams-Onis Treaty ceded Florida to the United States. In 1821 Florida gained statehood. The state seceded from the Union in 1861 to align with the Confederate States and rejoined the United States after the Civil War.

e. James Grant governed Florida from 1764 until 1771, when he returned to England. In Parliament, after the battle at Lexington and Concord, one MP heard Grant declare that "Americans could not fight and that he could march from one end of America to the other with just 5,000 men to quell the rebellion." Historians blame him in part for British defeats at Trenton (December 26, 1776) and Princeton (January 3, 1777). When Major General Grant allowed General

Lafayette to slip through his hands in Philadelphia in May 1778, his superiors shipped him to the West Indies to fight the French. After the war, he served in Parliament. Grotesquely obese, James Grant died on April 13, 1806, at age eighty-six.

f. Rolle's Town was founded on the St. John's River in 1765 by Denys Rolle, Esquire. Four hundred families were to colonize Rolle's 40,000-acre Florida claim, but the colony was mismanaged. During the 1770s the colonists migrated to the Carolinas and Rolle returned to England.

g. In 1763 Dr. Andrew Turnbull, at a cost of $166,000, founded an Atlantic coastal colony of Mediterranean indentured servants at New Smyrna, sixty miles south of St. Augustine, Florida. The colonists harvested sugar cane and indigo. William Gerard De Brahms, one of the Crown's surveyors, visited New Smyrna in the 1760s, observing "1,400 Minorcans, among whom were some French, and 75 Greeks. The Town has two Churches, one for English Protestants, and the other for Roman Catholicks." By 1770 Turnbull's 20,000-acre colony created tension with Indians, whom he placated with gifts. Arduous work conditions fueled resentment among New Symrna's residents, and by the mid-1770s most had migrated to St. Augustine.

h. The epic clash at Point Pleasant ended Lord Dunmore's War with a British victory. Col. Andrew Lewis commanded 1,500 Virginians as he marched from Fort Pitt into Indian country to camp on his 5,000-acre claim at the fork of the Ohio and the Great Kanawha (New River). At dawn on October 10, 1774, scouts informed him a war party of 1,000 Shawnee, Delaware, and Mingo had crossed the Ohio to surround his camp. The Indians attacked. By dusk the Virginians had suffered 75 dead and more than 100 wounded. Indian losses are unknown. As the Indians fled, Dunmore's 1,400 Pennsylvanians nearly intercepted them as they returned to their towns. Fearing the loss of their homes and people, Cornstalk, principal Makujay Shawnee chief, signed terms to open lands south of the Ohio to surveying, speculation, and settlement. On October 6, 1776, while under a flag of truce, a mob at Fort Randolph, Virginia, murdered Cornstalk, his son, Elinipsico, and two other Shawnee, Red Hawk and Petalla.

i. Draper's patronizing comments about Seminole life notwithstanding, it is plain that this "itinerant camp of Indians" saved the lives of Boone and his starving comrades, who lacked the woodsmanship to find game in Florida's vast seas of scrub, swamps, and palmetto-lined hummocks.

j. Today Florida is one of the world's vacation centers and the nation's fastest-growing state. Among its most popular natural attractions are its many magnificent, crystal-clear springs, which draw hundreds of thousands of tourists annually.

k. "Northern Indian warriors" is Draper's reference to the Shawnee who erected their towns north of the Ohio River but frequently crossed it to hunt or fight Kentuckians or to travel the Warrior's Path southward to raid Cherokee or Catawba villages.

l. For more on the Regulator movement, see chapter 11, note j.

m. These "lands that seemed without an owner" were Indian territory.

n. Boone may not have fire-hunted on any regular basis, but according to the memoirs of Peter Houston (recorded in DM 20C; published in 1996 by Stackpole Books as *A Sketch in the Life and Character of Daniel Boone,* edited by Ted Franklin Belue) in 1786 near Paris, Kentucky, Boone "shined the eyes" of a big panther and shot the beast.

o. Draper's paraphrase of Acts 10:13, King James Version: "And there came a voice to him, Rise; kill and eat." Draper is comparing Daniel Boone and Hill's first Kentucky foray to the apostle Peter's rooftop vision of Jehovah commanding his devout Jewish convert to Christianity to go and preach the Gospel to the Gentiles.

p. That Daniel Boone may have held a slight interest in Spiritualism must have intrigued Draper, who in 1869 left the Baptist church to fully convert to the belief. Squire Boone, Jr. (1744–1815), made a similar death pact. As his last hour loomed near, Squire, a lay Baptist minister, told his sons that if he could, three days after he died he would try to communicate with them. After his death his sons kept vigil at the appointed time and place but never sensed their father's presence.

q. Boone enjoyed a unique relationship with Indians, respected them as hunters, and enjoyed their company. He was influenced by his pacifist Quaker upbringing, and as a child he frequently saw Shawnee and Delaware hunters trading at his grandfather's Reading, Pennsylvania, outpost and there learned much about native diplomacy. To be sure, he did kill several warriors in self-defense, and he too suffered at their hands. In 1773 a Cherokee named Big Jim tortured Boone's sixteen-year-old son, James, to death; in 1780 the Shawnee shot and decapitated his brother Edward; another son, Israel, was shot and killed August 19, 1782, at the battle of Blue Licks. Boone could hardly mention these episodes without weeping, but he attributed such violence to border warfare and knew full well some whites committed acts as bad or worse. He bore Indians as a people no ill will and was often sympathetic to their plight. Indians knew he was no man of blood and no scalp hunter, which kept him from being killed in other encounters besides the one Draper relates here.

CHAPTER 6

1769–1770.—John Findlay.—His Early Trading Expedition to Kentucky.—Unites with Daniel Boone in a More Thorough Exploration of the Country.—Indian Troubles.—Boone and Stuart's Captivity and Escape.—Findlay and the Others Return, While Boone and Three Companions Remain, etc.

The memory of John Findlay, the precursor and pilot of Boone to Kentucky, merits a brighter page [in] western history than the meagre facts extant will possibly warrant. "Of all the pioneers," exclaims Ex-Governor Morehead in his Boonesborough Address, "the least justice has been done to Finley." The truth seems to be that such was the wandering character of his life, but little comparatively can be learned of him at this remote period. He appears to have been a native of the north of Ireland and early emigrated to the region of Carlisle in Cumberland County, Pennsylvania, which was almost wholly settled by a hardy race of Scotch-Irish Protestants.[1] As early as February 1752 we find Findlay engaged among the Shawanoes as an Indian trader and the following year with other traders was robbed and driven off.[2] The breaking out of the French and Indian War put a stop to the Indian trade for several years, during which he probably served on the Pennsylvania frontiers against the common enemy, for certain it is that Boone met him in 1755 on Braddock's fatal campaign, which both fortunately survived. We have already adverted to the casual meeting and how Boone first learned from Findlay something of the charming El Dorado of Kentucky. And during that meeting, Boone no doubt acquainted Findlay of the locality of his distant Yadkin home and of the many Pennsylvanians settled in that country.

During the winter of 1768–'9 Boone was agreeably surprised by the arrival of his old comrade Findlay at his rustic home on the Upper Yadkin. How Findlay succeeded in finding him after a lapse of over thirteen years since they had met amid the din and clangor of war, and since which Boone had removed sixty miles westward from his old home, we can only conjecture. Findlay was now employed with a horse as a peddler and had probably visited the Forks of the Yadkin; and there learning of Boone's removal, he was probably induced to follow him up from early attachment formed while mutually sharing the same martial toils and dangers; and very likely, moreover, Findlay thought his chances of driving a good trade in the sale of pins, needles, thread, and Irish linens would largely increase the farther he should go from Salisbury to the westward, even to the western confines of civilization, where Boone had erected his humble cabin and consecrated his home in the quiet valley and amid the rugged mountain scenery of the rapid-rolling Upper Yadkin. It is very possible, too, that in their early interviews about the Kentucky country, in which Boone evinced such uncommon interest, some agreement was made that Findlay after the war should join Boone and both go in search of the Eden of the West; and thinking perhaps that Findlay had forgotten his promise or, peradventure, had gone to his grave, Boone had attempted to reach the beautiful level of Kentucky by way of Sandy in 1767, which, as we have seen, proved a signal failure.

In the minds of both, the thought of Kentucky was uppermost. It was the last subject about which, thirteen long years before, they had held delightful converse and which they now gladly and eagerly renewed.[a] Boone narrated artlessly his fruitless attempt to discover the delectable land and how he had found and killed many a noble buffalo and wintered among the mountains of Sandy. Findlay too rehearsed his Kentucky knowledge and experience. He had in the autumn of 1752 descended the Ohio in a canoe with three or four assistant voyageurs and a cargo of goods suitable for the Indian trade in which he had been for some considerable time engaged. He went as far down as the Falls of the Ohio and was greatly pleased with the freshness and beauty of the country bordering upon the river. There were at that period not unfrequently camps of Indians temporarily sojourning at the Falls. He may have found none on this occasion and, returning, met a company of Shawanoes at the mouth of Big Bone Creek, who doubtless took him to view the wonderful mammoth bones only three miles distant. These Indians were going to take their fall and winter hunt in the interior of Kentucky where game was plenty, and they invited Findlay to go along with them, promising to assist him in transporting his merchandize to their hunting-ground and to trade with him as fast as they should succeed in obtaining pelts and furs—the common currency and medium of exchange with the Indian.

To this invitation he yielded a ready assent, and passing from Big Bone Creek through the rich lands of Kentucky along an Indian trail traced on Evans' old map, they arrived at an Indian settlement situated a mile west of the oil spring on Lulbegrud Creek, a northern tributary of Red River of Kentucky.[3] This town is evidently the one laid down on the Evans' map between Licking and Kentucky rivers, and called by the uncouth name of Es-kip-pa-ki-thi-ki.[4] It was directly on the route of the great *Warriors' Road* leading from the Ohio southward through Cumberland Gap and was doubtless the town alluded to by Franklin when he asserted that "in the year 1752, the Six Nations, Shawanesse and Delawares had a large town on Kentucke River."[5] The locality of the settlement on a small prairie was extremely beautiful, with a more level region adjacent and a better quality of land than was generally found in the country. "I do not know," said the late venerable pioneer Samuel Plummer, "but one other place to please the eye as well."

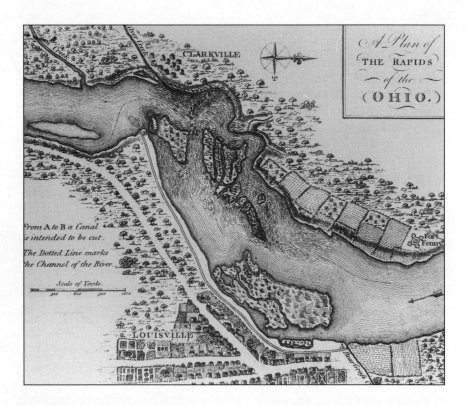

33. Falls of the Ohio, from Gilbert Imlay's Topographical Description of the Western Territory of North America *(1793).* COPPER ENGRAVING BY THOMAS CONDER.

Here Findlay came, erected a cabin for a trading house, and displayed his gaudy wares to the admiring gaze of the Indians. His tawny neighbors occupied a number of rude huts and had a growing crop of corn, beans, and pumpkins. Other traders also found their way there. Driving a brisk traffic awhile, disputes at length arose between the traders and a large party of the straggling Canadian Indians, when several of the traders collected here at Es-kip-pa-ki-thi-ki, or the Little Pick Town, were captured, some killed, their goods seized, while others, among whom was Findlay, decamped in safety to the settlements. This occurred, as has previously been stated, January 26th, 1753, and was another verification of the ominous name of the *Dark and Bloody Ground* and sometimes the Middle Ground, by which, as Findlay learned, the country was then only known to the Indians—where scenes of strife and carnage had long been familiar to the warlike sons of the forest.

Such was Findlay's auspicious advent to this western paradise and such its unhappy issue; and yet he loved Kentucky. He was not the man to get soured by misfortune. "This country," says Filson, "greatly engaged Mr. Finley's attention."

He looked more kindly upon the bright, rather than the dark, side of things; and thus it was that he dwelt so naturally and so particularly upon the real loveliness of the country, the richness of the soil, and the abundance of the game. Perhaps his enthusiastic love of nature occasionally betrayed him into descriptions that might seem to smack somewhat of extravagance, for he assured Boone that such was the strength of the current at the Falls of the Ohio and so plenty were wild geese and ducks there, they were continually drawn over the cataract, dashed against the rocks and killed, and a person had only to go in a canoe below and pick up as many of these fowls, fat and plump, as he wanted.[6]

Daniel Boone and his brother Squire, who was present, heard these recitals with feelings of peculiar delight. The subject for several years past had been one of unusual interest to them. Carolina was getting altogether too thickly settled and game so scarce as to render a roast wild turkey or venison steak quite a rarity. Florida had been tried and found wanting; the sterile hills and laurel mountains of Sandy were entirely uninviting; but the country which Findlay had seen and which he now so bewitchingly described seemed to fire their imaginations and promise to fulfill completely their long-cherished ideal of terrestrial beauty and perfection.

Men like the Boones and Findlay were probably not in the least influenced by the result of the Fort Stanwix treaty, if indeed, which is not very likely, they had heard a syllable of it. They had little studied the effect of treaties and perhaps had not much faith in an Indian's plighted word, even when solemnly backed by their customary hieroglyphics affixed to treaty papers. Such a glowing account of the country as Findlay gave was alone a sufficient inducement to a man of Daniel Boone's taste and temperament to eagerly desire to pay it a personal visit. Findlay at this period was somewhat advanced in years and made no pretensions to the skill of a woodsman. In his western journeyings, the streams and Indian trails had been his guides. He felt quite sure that there was a better route across the mountains than that which Boone had taken to reach Sandy, as war-parties of the Northern and Southern Indians frequently passed and re-passed along the great *Warriors' Road* through Kentucky; and he rightly conjectured that the only certain way of reaching Kentucky through the wilderness would be to penetrate farther to the westward than Boone had done, [wi] the Indian war-path should be gained, which would lead through the Ouasioto, or Cumberland, Mountains. If Boone thought from this vague information that he could pilot a party to the war-trace and gap in question, Findlay was ready and willing to attempt the daring enterprise.[7]

When the hope of discovering a new and desirable country was held out to Boone, he was emphatically a *minute-man;* his mind was always made up for such an undertaking. Boone and his brother at once resolved on the exploration. Their brother-in-law John Stuart, already much experienced in such matters and [wi] in the Bryan settlement in the Forks of the Yadkin, together with three of Boone's Upper Yadkin neighbors, Joseph Holder, James Mooney, and William Cooley, readily volunteered to share the dangers of the bold adventure.[8] Holden,

Mooney, and Cooley were employed by Boone to act as common hunters and camp-keepers. How Mrs. Boone acted on this occasion we do not exactly know; perhaps she kindly intimated a doubt of the wisdom of such trans-montane excursion, but her gentle nature would never have permitted her to throw any serious obstacles in the way. Let her good man and Findlay put in the spring crop and Stuart, Holden, and Cooley theirs, and the women and children could keep down the weeds and bestir the soil, and Squire could remain to aid all the respective families in gathering the harvest.[9] Findlay and Mooney, it is believed, were alone unblessed with wife or home. Such seem to have been their plans and arrangements. Winter soon glided away, and cheerful spring with its busy scenes came on; the seed was quickly sown and planted and the simple out-fit of the party speedily completed.

On the morning of the 1st of May, 1769, the adventurous band started from Boone's residence near the head of the Yadkin on their long and toilsome journey "in their quest of the country of Kentucke." They bade their wives, friends, and little ones adieu and, with alternate hopes and fears, turned their faces toward the great North-West. If a tear now and then stole unbidden down their manly cheeks, it was an indication that they were not destitute of the finer feelings of humanity. Each was equipped with a trusty rifle upon his shoulder; on his right side was his tomahawk with its handle thrust under the leathern belt that encircled his body, and on the left was suspended the hunting-knife in its sheath attached to the belt and a powder-horn and bullet-pouch of ample dimensions. They were attired in the simple, convenient, and beautiful hunting-shirt or loose open frock, generally made of dressed deer-skins, with leggings or drawers of the same material fastened to the body belt and tied around below the knee, and the usual deer-skin moccasins covered their feet.[b] An uncouth fur cap generally completed the equipage, but Boone despised the article and always wore a hat.[c] Each of the party was mounted upon a good horse, with a blanket or bear-skin fastened behind, together with a camp-kettle, a little stock of salt, and peradventure a small supply of provisions to last till the game region should be reached, when the wild woods alone would be relied on for subsistence alike for man and beast.

First scaling the lofty Blue Ridge, they soon reached the Three Forks of New River and then passed over the Stone Mountain at a place called "*The Stairs*," and thence over the Iron Mountain into Holston Valley; and continuing their course westwardly, they crossed the valley, passing through Moccasin Gap of Clinch Mountain, and crossing successively Clinch River, Powell's Mountain, and Walden's Ridge, they at length entered Powell's Valley.[10] This lovely vale must have elicited their admiration, and there too they must have fallen in with Joseph Martin's party, engaged in making their settlement and improvements. In Powell's Valley they doubtless struck *the hunters' trail,* which led them to the

34. American frontiersman, c. 1770. His hat is of fur felt; his caped "hunting shirt" is linen, as are his breeches. His moccasins and leggings are deerskin and he cradles a long rifle. The dogs are brindled Mountain Curs, a breed of the day. "THE LONG KNIFE" BY H. DAVID WRIGHT, GRAY STONE PRESS, NASHVILLE, TENNESSEE.

anxiously looked for Cumberland Gap.[11] That point reached, and finding the
Warriors' Road so distinctly marked, must have imparted new life and energy to
the fearless adventurers. A dozen miles farther along the same route probably
that [Dr. Thomas] Walker's party had pursued nineteen years before brought them
to Cumberland River, crossing which at the old Indian ford, they continued down
that stream a few miles to Flat Lick, where they left the Indian path and bore off
more to the left, crossing Stinking, Turkey, and Richland creeks and Robinson's
Creek of Laurel River, and thence across Rockcastle River and up its west branch,
or Round-Stone-Lick Fork, near to its head, where they encamped awhile.

Boone and Findlay began to think that the beautiful level of Kentucky could
not now be very far distant. While the rest of the party were encamped to recruit
themselves and horses and kill game and provide a supply of jerk, Boone, all
eager to catch a glimpse of Findlay's western paradise, shouldered his rifle and
directed his course to the distant ridge dividing the waters of Rockcastle and Kentucky and, ascending the highest knob, called the Big Hill,[d] obtained a fine view
of the gently undulating region which now comprises the counties of Garrard and
Madison and thought he could see still further beyond the level region to discover
which had so long been the darling object of his thoughts by day and his dreams
by night. With a gladdened heart, he returned to camp and related his discoveries. Once ready to renew their journey, they crossed the ridge near the knob
which Boone had ascended, which was not far from the head of Paint Lick Creek,
a small tributary of [the] Kentucky on the confines of the present counties of Garrard and Madison. They then bore more to the north-east, striking the waters of
Station Camp Creek, probably the Red Lick Fork, and made their Station Camp
from which circumstance the main creek derived its name.[12] This stream, which
must ever from this early historical association maintain a distinguished notoriety,
is chiefly in Estill County and flows into the Kentucky River from the south,
nearly opposite to Irvine.

It was probably owing quite as much to the weather, which had for sometime
been the most uncomfortable, as to the abundance of game that led at that time
and place to the location of the Station Camp. They soon erected a desirable
shelter, and while Boone and his companions were heartily engaged in hunting,
Findlay started off in search of his old trading-place on Lulbegrud Creek. He
could have had but little difficulty in finding it, for the *Warriors' Road* ran along
the western bank of Station Camp Creek to its mouth and, crossing the Kentucky
a short distance below, led directly to the old Indian town of Es-kip-pa-ki-thi-ki
on Lulbegrud. In about ten days Findlay returned, reporting that he had found the
place, and though the Indian huts were burned, some of the stockading and gate-
posts were yet standing.[13] Boone and Stuart now accompanied Findlay there,
which they reached on the 7th of June and found it precisely as he had stated,
which fully corroborated in their minds all that he had related of Kentucky, if they
had cherished a doubt of it before. Now returning to the Station Camp in high
spirits, all felt assured that Kentucky was really discovered.[14]

While the others continued in the exciting occupation of hunting, Boone and Findlay determined to make a more thorough examination of the country. They had not gone far when Findlay was taken sick, and though not dangerous, yet he felt himself unfit to undergo the hardships and exposures of the journey. So Boone, having provided him a comfortable shelter and a supply of meat, proceeded along on his course north of Kentucky River towards the garden spot of the west. At length he ascended an eminence and with joy and wonder beheld the beautiful landscape of Kentucky spread out invitingly before him.[15] Boone must have felt something as Moses did when he toilingly reached Pisgah's lofty summit and had a distant view of the promised land throughout its whole extent, with, however, this important difference, that the Lord's prohibition of Moses' ever going thither[e] did not happily apply in Boone's case.

That must have been a joyous day and a proud sight for Boone, looking out upon the broad vallies and fertile bottoms of Kentucky. "We have no doubt," exclaims the eloquent Simms, "he felt very much as Columbus did, gazing from his caravel on San Salvador; as Cortes, looking down from the crest of Ahualco, on the valley of Mexico; or Vasco Nunez, standing alone on the peak of Darien, and stretching his eyes over the hitherto undiscovered waters of the Pacific."[16] Having thus "proceeded alone to the heights," as Boone himself enthusiastically expressed it, "which overlooks this terrestrial paradise, so descended into those fertile plains which are unequaled on our earth, and laid the fairest claim to the description of the garden of God."[17] Returning to Findlay, who had measurably recovered, they made together a more thorough survey of the rich country in the Elkhorn region and, finally retracing their steps to camp, informed their companions of their discoveries.

The forests, prairies, and cane-brakes were all filled with game, and several months were now delightfully employed either in the pleasures of the chase or in sallying forth from their Station Camp to reconnoiter the country. Hunting, however, formed their chief occupation. The summer and fall hunt was necessarily confined almost exclusively to deer, whose skins were then in good condition, while the pelage of the furry tribe was not fit for use at that season of the year. The party paired off, each couple taking different directions and all returning to camp on a specific day. Boone and Stuart were hunting companions. Not infrequently, a couple would remain to keep camp and prepare the skins for packing and transportation.

Hunters, half inclined to indolence,[f] were fond of watching the salt-licks and there waylaying and killing the unsuspecting deer. But Boone preferred roaming without restraint through the noble forests. He would start at the peep of day, when the leaves were moistened with the night-dew and he could steal noiselessly upon his game. There are two periods during the twenty-four hours when deer are either feeding or walking around—about the rising of the moon and again early in the morning; and to these periods experienced hunters pay great attention. When on their feet and moving about, the deer are more easily discovered

35. Hunting pouch, c. 1775, made of sinew-sewn pigskin with French and Indian War era pow-derhorn, antler powder measure, and tomahawk. FROM *THE KENTUCKY RIFLE HUNTING POUCH* BY MADISON GRANT; PUB-LISHED BY JIM JOHNSON, GOLDEN AGE ARMS.

than when lying down; and although they were more particularly engaged in feeding at those respective periods, yet the hunters did not generally relax their efforts but with the expiring day.[18]

Preparing deer-skins for market was something of a labor. Both the hair and the outer grain in which the hair takes root were scraped off with a knife, as a currier dresses leather; and then, when dry, the skin was thoroughly rubbed across a staking-board until rendered quite soft and pliant, thus stripping it of all unnecessary weight and fitting it for packing more compactly. This process in hunter's parlance was denominated *graining,* and the skins were then pronounced *half-dressed;* and a horse, heavily-laden, could carry something like a hundred half-dressed deer-skins averaging two and a half pounds each, worth in market at that day about forty cents per pound.[g]

Instead of the *cache,*[h] or subterranean receptacle for skins so common in the Rocky Mountain region, it was customary with Boone and the hunters of his time to place their half-dressed skins across poles elevated several feet from the ground, with several layers upon each other and a pole fastened on top, and still another on each side suspended by tugs[i] to keep the skins closely together, covered with elk or other out-spread skins or peeled bark to protect them from the weather. When enough of these skins were thus collected to form a pack, they

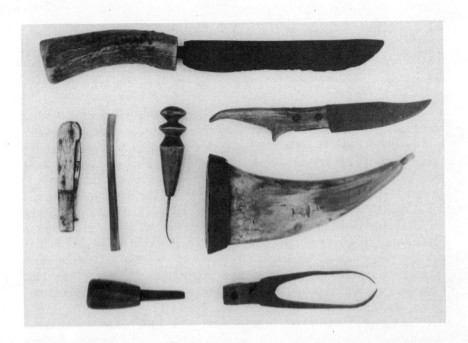

36. Eighteenth-century rifleman's accoutrements: antler-handled belt knife and patch knife, priming horn, bullet mold, rifle tampion, vent pick, turkey call made from turkey wing bone, and Barlow-style folding fork. FROM MADISON GRANT; COURTESY H. DAVID WRIGHT.

were nicely folded and packed into a bale, two of which, one swung on either side, would constitute a horse-load. The packs, until sent off, were placed on scaffolds protected from the weather and were thus elevated, as were those on poles, so as to be beyond the reach of hungry bears and ravenous wolves, who will not fail to eat, tear, and destroy them whenever an opportunity occurs.

No value was attached by hunters to buffalo, bear, and elk skins, as they were too bulky to convey so great a distance to market, and it is quite doubtful if they were then marketable at any price.[j] They were, however, killed in their season for meat. Buffalo were in the best order in the fall after feeding upon wild grass, buffalo clover, and pea vine, and to some extent also upon acorns, beech nuts, and chestnuts; the clover, a kind [*wm*] with a large, white blossom lasting the entire growing season, but the pea vine only affording sustenance in the latter part of summer and early autumn. The bear does not seem to lose flesh during his torpid state in winter, but coming out from his den in the spring and greedily devouring young nettles and other tender herbs, seldom any grass, which, acting as a cathartic, soon very much reduces him in flesh. During the early summer bears eat very little, and that chiefly worms and bugs which they paw out of the ground and scratch from decayed logs and trees, until berries and other wild fruits appear, and finally acorns, hazel, hickory, beech, and chestnuts, when they fatten very rapidly; and it is the quickness with which this flesh is acquired that gives wild bear meat in its appropriate season so sweet and tender a taste and renders it so incomparably superior to that of the tamed bear, as in the latter case, the animal is always kept in good order.

Elk meat was considered equal to venison and was used for variety or when buffalo, deer, or bear could not be obtained. The hunters occasionally killed elks to convert their hides into tugs or straps with which to pack their deer and other skins. Both elk and deer are fattest in the autumn and subsist upon the same kinds of food as the buffalo. About Christmas they all commence falling away in flesh and become extremely poor in the latter part of winter and early spring, and sometime in May they begin to improve again. Wild turkies, which make such excellent meat in the fall, winter, and spring, become very poor in summer in consequence of wood-ticks and scarcity of desirable food. A roasted buffalo marrow-bone or a choice cut from the buffalo hump was esteemed most delicious eating. Besides these rich and tempting viands which successively formed the hunter's repast, berries, plums, grapes, and nuts, towards the close of summer and during the autumn, added largely to the delicacies of the wilderness.[19]

There were then no bees in Kentucky, and so our hunters could not have had wild honey, for bees generally keep pace with and not much precede the advancing settlements. Hence originated the name of *English flies* bestowed upon them by the Indians, who used to say to each other when they saw a swarm of bees in the woods, "Well, brothers, it is time for us to decamp, for the white people are coming."[20]

So passed away, prosperously and happily, Boone's first summer and autumn in Kentucky. Numerous packs of skins were collected by the skill and industry of our sturdy hunters and secured upon scaffolds at the Station Camp and at several distant out-camps. The horses had regained their strength; a generous store of buffalo, bear, and elk meat, venison, and turkies had been provided when in the best condition in autumn and *jerked* for winter and spring supply. The arrival of Squire Boone was rather daily hoped-for than really expected, with supplies of salt, traps, and ammunition, and love-messages from their sweet-hearts, wives, and little ones, and to conduct on his return the loaded pack-horses to the Yadkin settlements. Never did Daniel Boone seem happier or his prospects more bright and hopeful. From June till December he had, in common with his companions, ranged the noble forests and prosecuted their sports without meeting a solitary Indian or discovering the least *sign* of any in the country. But a change was at hand— a storm portending, bading no good to these fearless hunters in the sequestered wilds of Kentucky.[21]

On the twenty-second of the latter month, Boone and Stuart again sallied forth, perhaps for the hundredth time, into the gorgeous forest, never once dreaming that danger lurked in their paths. We can almost forgive Filson for making Boone in his Narrative speak of gay blossoms late in December; for doubtless the day was a bright and beautiful one, peradventure the mellow Indian summer with brilliant parti-colored leaves and birds of gaudy plumage yet gracing the myriad of trees which over-spread the valley of [the] Kentucky River, while yet others were rich with over-hanging fruits—haws, grapes, and papaws, or custard apples. "Nature," exclaims Boone, "was here a series of wonders, and a fund of delight. Here she displayed her ingenuity and industry in a variety of flowers and fruits, beautifully colored, elegantly shaped, and charmingly flavored; and we were diverted with innumerable animals presenting themselves perpetually to our view." The perpendicular rocky precipices of [the] Kentucky River, oftentimes from three to four hundred feet high, are among the "series of wonders" to which Boone truthfully made allusion.

Near the close of this beautiful day, while roaming all unconcerned through a region of incomparable beauty near the Kentucky River, in ascending the brow of a small hill, a large body of Indians with guns, knives, and tomahawks rushed out from a thick cane-brake and made Boone and Stuart prisoners. The Indians were too near and the surprise too sudden to admit of the escape of our unwary hunters. The Indians proved to be a party of Shawanoes who were returning from a fall hunt on the Green River to their homes north of the Ohio. The leader's name was Captain Will. Finding men with guns and perhaps with skins packed upon their backs, the Indians sternly demanded them to shew their camps, threateningly intimating with their uplifted tomahawks the fatal consequences of tardiness or refusal.

Boone, like a true philosopher, invariably took things coolly, and never more so than when entrapped into difficulties and environed with dangers. An Indian in the ascendant is always proud and imperious; and yet, in his simple nature, he can oftentimes be immeasurably controlled in his actions, even by his own prisoner whom fortune has thrown in his way, if such prisoner only possess the requisite tact, shrewdness, and fearless independence—and these Boone possessed in an eminent degree. On this occasion, he readily consented to comply with all the whims and demands of his captors. But while he and Stuart were piloting them to the nearest camp, Boone's thoughts were busily employed upon the best course of procedure in these trying circumstances. Reaching the first camp and finding one of the camp-keepers there, Boone managed to start him off unnoticed by the Indians, who were busily engaged in securing the plunder, to give timely notice to the rest of the party quickly to remove from the Station Camp the packs of skins and everything of value beyond the grasp of the rapacious plunderers.[k]

Sad was the disappointment of Boone and Stuart, after leading the Indians with comparative cheerfulness to each successive camp, where the booty obtained was but trifling, and finally reaching the Station Camp, to find nothing whatever carried out of the reach of the Indians. "The time of our sorrow was now arrived," says Boone in his Narrative; all their horses, a large quantity of pelts of great value, guns, ammunition, and every article of comfort and convenience were all appropriated by this robber-band of Shawanoes. Whether Findlay and the camp-keepers were absent hunting and thus failed to receive the notification of the messenger or the craven spirit of fear had seized upon them, utterly paralyzing their efforts, is not now known, but they were, in all events, completely out of harm's way.

At no time had the Indians apparently designed keeping Boone and Stuart as prisoners of war, for it was then professedly a time of peace. Having gained their object, they dismissed their captives, presenting each with two pairs of moccasins, a doe-skin for patch-leather, a little trading gun,[1] and a few loads of powder and shot so that they might supply themselves with meat on their way back to the settlements, and then gave them this parting advice: "Now, brothers, go home and stay there. Don't come here any more, for this is the Indians' hunting ground, and all the animals, skins, and furs are ours; and if you are so foolish as to venture here again, you may be sure the wasps and yellow-jackets will sting you severely."

All this was said and done with a sober seriousness and according to the code of justice as regulated by the simple notions of the untutored Indian; and we must in truth say that Captain Will and party might have been far more rigorous in their exactions, for they certainly tempered their inflictions with a clever shew of mercy.[m] Boone, however, never once viewed the affair in this light. He and his companions had penetrated several hundred miles into the wilderness, where for seven long months they had toiled unceasingly to secure their skins, suffering meanwhile many privations and hardships; the deer they had killed belonged no more to the Indians than to themselves, and as for the horses, guns, and other articles, the Indians had not the shadow of a claim to them. However differently these things were considered by the respective parties, the red-men and pale-faces mutually shook hands and parted apparently in friendship.

Several days were consumed in going the rounds and sacking the hunters' camps. The Indians once on their way towards the Ohio richly laden with their ill-gotten spoils, Findlay and the others made their appearance. Gloom depicted every countenance save Boone's. His was always hopeful. He stoutly protested against letting the affair pass off without making a single effort to recover something of their losses. Findlay, Holden, Mooney, and Cooley were evidently bent on returning home and giving up the enterprise, so far at least as the peltries were concerned, as a bad job. Boone proposed that if they would remain at the camp, that he and Stuart would pursue the Indian trail, make a vigorous attempt to regain possession of some of the horses, and return to camp in the course of two or three days. Destitute of everything needful for the approaching winter, and plundered even of the goodly store of jerk, Boone keenly felt the need of securing at least one or two horses to enable some of the party to return to the Yadkin for supplies of ammunition and other necessaries. He was therefore willing to run some hazard with the hope of effecting an object so desirable. Nor was Stuart less anxious to engage in the enterprise.

When the Indians were thought to have advanced a sufficient distance towards home to feel themselves secure against pursuit, Boone and Stuart started, leaving the others at the Station Camp to await the result of their wild adventure. After two days, they overtook the Indians encamped at evening, and undiscovered, our sturdy soldiers secreted themselves in the cane or bushes and waited patiently the approach of denser darkness and the slumbers of the Indians to aid them in the accomplishment of their purpose. They permitted the night well-nigh to pass away, until they believed the Indians were profoundly locked in sleep, when they sallied forth from their silent covert. The horses were easily found not very far from the Indian encampment, some of them hoppled, and belled also—the later often practiced by frontier whites as well as by Indians, having a tendency to keep the herd together; and they succeeded in obtaining four or five horses. It was nearly day-light before they got started with their prize, as Stuart spent a considerable time unavailingly in search of his horse; and in default of which he had recourse to the law of retaliation and taken one of the Indians'; but Boone, more fortunate, had obtained his worthy nag.

The ensuing day and night, they kept up their flight on the return trail unremittingly and ventured to tarry a brief period early in the second morning to give the poor horses a momentary respite and enable them to refresh themselves on the wild grass, clover, and pea vine by the wayside. As the two weary adventurers were reclining upon the sunny side of a hill or sloping ground, Boone basking himself after a chilly night in the rays of the rising sun and Stuart at the moment engaged in tying his moccasins, the former thought with his ear to the ground that he heard something like a rumbling noise and, raising his head and casting a look behind, beheld with astonishment a party of Indians galloping on horseback over the crest of the hill with their guns glittering brightly in the sunbeams. This unexpected cavalcade was too near to allow Boone and Stuart the least chance of escape. So they wisely submitted themselves to their fate with the best grace they could.

Having quickly missed their horses, the Indians knew well enough where they had gone. So a dozen of the most active of their party, at the head of whom was Captain Will, mounted their fleetest animals and took [to] the trail in pursuit. When they came upon Boone and Stuart, some of the Indians appeared quite angry, shaking their tomahawks at the white men's heads; but generally evincing cheerful countenances, they whooped and laughed wildly, as though they were making sport at the expense of the re-captured prisoners for not having exhibited sufficient smartness in carrying out their bold design. Taking one of the bells from the horses and fastening it around Boone's neck, they compelled him to caper around and jingle it, chiding him every now and then in broken English with the derisive inquiry, *"Steal horse, eh?"* Satisfied with this sport, the Indians at length, with their captives and booty, set out leisurely on their return.

No uneasiness was betrayed, no murmur uttered by the undismayed prisoners. Boone felt an abiding consciousness that he and Stuart were superior in stratagem to their captors and that they needed only to put that cheerful philosophy to practice, which teaches a patient endurance of present evils, confiding hopefully in an early deliverance by their own well-directed exertions, eventually crowned with success by that over-ruling Power that shapes all our ends. Boone informs us in his Narrative that he and Stuart were treated with common savage usage and showed no desire to escape, which measurably warded off suspicion on the part of the savages. They, however, kept their prisoners under close surveillance by day without pinioning them, at night confining each between two Indians, perhaps fastened, or a tug stretched over the captives with each end attached to the body of the sleeping guards on either side to detect readily any movement that might be attempted looking towards an escape.

With a show of generosity, the Indians constantly intimated to Boone and Stuart that they should be liberated the next day and daily renewed the promise with all imaginable gravity. They probably only intended to keep their prisoners in durance until they should cross the Ohio, where they doubtless thought their horses would be beyond the reach of such enterprising spirits as Boone and Stuart; and once over the *Belle Riviere,* they could easily reach their towns in the Scioto Valley without any further annoyance. Boone became weary of these Indian promises made only to be broken. Seven days had now elapsed, and they were within a day's travel of the Ohio, over which he resolved he would not pass.

On the evening of the seventh day, Captain Will's party of Shawanoes pitched their camp beside a large, thick cane-brake in the primeval forests, when the last rays of sunset had departed.[22] This was probably at a point not very far east of May's Lick in Mason County, on the old *Warriors' Road* which led past the Upper Blue Licks to the mouth of Cabin Creek on the Ohio, a little above the present Maysville, Kentucky. In all that fertile region, cane-patches were frequent and of a luxuriant growth.[n] While the Indians were somewhat scattered, some engaged in hoppling the horses, some in gathering wood, and others in making a blazing fire, Boone gave a sign or hint to his companion which sufficed for a proper understanding between the captives. Casting a furtive glance around them, they each simultaneously seized a gun and some ammunition which had just been temporarily laid aside by the Indians—one of the party luckily obtaining his own, the other a poorer Indian gun; and dashing into the thick cane, they were out of the clutches of the savages before the latter had time to recover from the surprise caused by the celerity with which it was done. Going a little distance and the darkness becoming almost impenetrable, they hid themselves awhile, during which they inferred by the noise and evident movements of the Indians that some of them immediately commenced gathering up their horses lest they should lose them, while others seemed to hasten either way around the cane-brake, apparently intending to head [off] the fugitives should they attempt to emerge from it. So dark was it in the cane, and so difficult to make any headway in pursuit, that the Indians made no efforts to follow or search for them there. When the confusion was over and all was quiet again, Boone and Stuart ventured with the utmost circumspection to make their way through the tangled cane and, by dint of hard travelling, were soon beyond the reach of their inveterate foes.[23]

Guided by the light of the stars by night and the moss upon the northern side of the trees[o] by day, not daring, in all likelihood, to follow the old Indian war-trace, they returned "speedily," as Boone expressed it, to their old camp, having accomplished a journey probably within twenty-four hours on which the Indians had consumed seven days. They found, to their great grief, their camp abandoned and their companions gone; the dying embers of their camp-fire indicated but a recent departure. No time could be lost by our adventurers if they hoped to overtake Findlay and his party, so, weary as they were, they hurriedly pursued their outward trail and fortunately came up with the fugitives thirty-five or forty miles from the Station Camp on Rockcastle River. Here Boone, amid so much misfortune, was happily surprised to meet his brother Squire among the company. Having gathered the summer and fall crops, he had come out from Carolina with various supplies and also to explore the country, and when he reached the New River region, he had been joined by Alexander Neely. Following the hunters' trail through Powell's Valley and the *Warriors' Road* through Cumberland Gap, which led thence to Station Camp Creek, they accidentally found the camp of their friends of whom they were in search. Learning of the hazardous mission of Daniel Boone and Stuart, and drawing the worst apprehensions from their having so long overstaid their time, the whole company soon resolved in their disheartening situation on returning to Carolina. The mutual joy inspired by this auspicious meeting at Rockcastle may be readily inferred from Boone's account of that happy event. "Notwithstanding the unfortunate circumstances of our company," says he, "and our dangerous situation, surrounded by hostile savages, our meeting so fortunately in the wilderness made us reciprocally sensible of the utmost satisfaction. So much does friendship triumph over misfortune, that sorrows and sufferings vanish at the meeting not only of real friends, but of the most distant acquaintances, and substitutes happiness in their room."

That Mrs. Boone sent any complaining message about her husband's prolonged absence and urging his speedy return, we know from her amiable character could not have been true; but that she may have mildly expressed a hope soon to see him at home again is very probable. But if she did it, it made only a slight impression on the wanderer's mind, for while he really loved his wife and children, he did not yet care to go back to the plow so long as he could live comfortably by his rifle in the wilderness. And more than this, he had incurred no small expense and sustained no inconsiderable losses in the inception and prosecution of this enterprise; and now that Squire Boone had so opportunely arrived with more horses, traps, and a fresh supply of ammunition, he could not help thinking that it was his duty to remain and procure a load of valuable furs to pack home with which to wipe off all indebtedness against him. Stuart, always faithful to Boone's wishes and interests, thought so too; and Squire Boone and Neely concluded they would also like to remain and take a hand in hunting, trapping, and exploring the country.

The thing was soon arranged satisfactorily, these four resolving to continue in the wilderness, while Findlay and the others were equally determined on abandoning this Eden-land, which, though all beautiful to the eye, had been to them the scene of so much disappointment and misfortune. The parties respectively bid each other a hearty adieu and parted. No unusual event happened to the homeward-bound party until reaching Holston Valley, when Findlay took the left hand road, passing through the frontier settlements of Virginia, bending his course towards his home and kindred in Pennsylvania, while Holden, Mooney, and Cooley pursued more to the right over the mountains to the head of Yadkin. Thus were the Boones, Stuart, and Neely left alone in the forests and cane-brakes of Kentucky.[24]

DRAPER'S NOTES: CHAPTER 6

1. The Rev. Dr. Samuel Finley, president of Princeton College, and ancestor of Prof. S. F. B. Morse, the inventor of the electric telegraph, was a native of Armagh County, Ireland, to which his parents fled from Scotland on account of persecution, and he emigrated in 1734, at the age of nineteen, to Pennsylvania. He was one of seven brothers, some of whom settled in Cumberland County in that province, and the records of early settlers there show not less than half a dozen of the name of Finley or Findlay during the period of 1750 to 1757, some of whom bore the name of John, and one particularly, was many years a justice of the peace. From these Cumberland Finleys or Findlays descended the late Gen. Thomas Finley of Chillicothe and the Rev. J. B. Finley, of Columbus, Ohio; and on the authority of the latter, we state that John Findlay, the early Kentucky explorer, was related to the Findlays of Cumberland. The late Daniel Bryan, who remembered Findlay's visit to Boone in 1768–'9, was well aware that Findlay was from Pennsylvania.

There were other Findlays in Pennsylvania. A distinct family settled in Franklin County, from whom descended Gov. William Findlay of Pennsylvania, Gen. James Findlay of Cincinnati, and Thomas Finley, late post master at Baltimore. William Findlay, who served in the Revolutionary War and subsequently settled in Westmoreland County, and was a member of the Pennsylvania Convention of 1789 and afterwards of Congress, came directly from Ireland to this country; he was one of the old Scotch dissenters and was author of a work on the Funding System, and another on the Western Insurrection.

2. *Pennsylvania Colonial Records,* v:570.

3. The name of Lulbegrud was given to the stream by a party of early explorers encamped on its banks, who happened to have a copy of *Gulliver's Travels* with them, from which they derived the unpleasing appellation, but its original orthography, *"Lulbegrud, or Pride of the Universe,"* has become, in the course of time, somewhat metamorphosed [*wi*] in the manuscript letter of William Flanagan, Esq., of Winchester, Kentucky.

4. This Indian town was settled under the following circumstances. Peter Chartier, a half-breed Shawanoe and a trader of considerable influence, debauched a portion of the Shawanoes into the French interest; and after seizing a couple of Indian traders and plundering them of goods to the value of sixteen hundred pounds, they left the rest of their nation near the Forks of the Ohio early in 1745 and commenced the settlement of this town of Es-kip-pa-ki-thi-ki. Prosperity attended the colony for two or three years, but roving bands of Northern Indians

found out their new location and killed and harassed continually. The Shawanoes of the Forks of Ohio, hearing of the attack on their wayward brethren, and commiserating their misfortunes, urged their speedy return; but the disorganized Indians, with Chartier at their head, resolutely refused, believing that the injuries done them had been at the instigation of their brethren at the Forks of Ohio in order to dishearten them in their isolated home and compel their early return to the great body of the nation. The deprivations of their enemies—probably the Iroquois, who claimed the country by former conquest and hence warred upon all intruders—increasing, the Shawanoes, numbering about four hundred and fifty souls, abandoned Es-kip-pa-ki-thi-ki and, betaking themselves to their canoes, passed down Lulbegrud Creek and Red River into Kentucky Creek and up that stream thirty miles, where they left their canoes and commenced an unprovoked war upon the Chickasaws, killing several of that nation. This warlike people quickly resented this dastardly conduct, embodied and drove off this vagabond band of intruders, who retired among the Creeks and settled a town seventy miles above the French Alabama garrison and between the Creek towns of Ooe-asa and Coosa.

Several of the Shawanoe chiefs, with a band of followers, retraced their weary steps in 1748 to their brethren on the Ohio; and the others, after residing awhile among the Creeks and still restless, commenced their return northwardly. They tarried for a season on [the] Cumberland River, where several French traders located amongst them, and hence the locality subsequently became known as *the French Lick,* now the site of the city of Nashville. Here the Chickasaws found them rudely fortified and attacked them on the morning of the 5th of April, 1759, killing twenty of the Shawanoes and seizing two hundred and forty head of horses, [and] returned in triumph to their nation; and these were the first horses ever possessed by the Chickasaws. The Shawanoes, whose numbers were now estimated at two hundred and seventy, made their way down [the] Cumberland River, the women, children, aged, and disabled men in canoes and the warriors as guards along shore, intending to rejoin their brethren, who were now located on the Ohio, chiefly at the Lower Shawanoe Town, Shawanoe Town, at the mouth of the Scioto; but when they entered the Ohio, the heavy spring flood was rolling down, against which their progress was so slow and tedious that they stopped a few miles below the mouth of the Wabash at the present locality of Shawneetown, Illinois. Remaining there awhile, the French traders and Kaskaskia Indians invited them to take up their abode at Kaskaskia, which they did a couple of years, when a strong deputation of their Shawanoe brethren arrived, conducted them back by water to their kindred and friends, when a re-union was effected after an eventful separation of sixteen years. The distinguished Shawanoe chief, Catahecassa, or Black Hoof, then quite a young man, was with this clan in all their wanderings; and when he visited the Lulbegrud region in 1815 or '16, he could readily point out and accurately describe the ancient locality of Es-kip-pa-ki-thi-ki, and all the surrounding country.

After the departure of Chartier and the Shawanoes from Es-kip-pa-ki-thi-ki a few must have remained during each hunting season, or large hunting parties frequently resorted there, or more probably both, to have made it an object for so many traders to repair to that point at the time of Findlay's visit and decampment.—Evans' *Map and Analysis,* 1758; *Pennsylvania Colonial Records; Gordon's History of Pennsylvania;* Rupp's *History Western Pennsylvania;* Haywood's *Tennessee;* Adair's *Southern Indians,* 2, 3, 155, 156, 410; *Maryland Gazette,* July 5th and August 2, 1759; MS. statement of Joseph Ficklin, Esq., derived from Black Hoof; MS. letter of William Flanagan, Esq.

5. Franklin's *Ohio Settlement,* London, 1772, p. 44.

6. Filson, writing in 1784, says: "On these waters, and especially on the Ohio, the geese and ducks are amazingly numerous. . . . Of bears and buffaloes, elks and deer, their number was legion; and at many of the large salt-licks of the country, they congregated in such prodigious herds, that the sight was truly grand and amazing."

7. This account of Findlay's visit to Boone, his representations of Kentucky, and the project for attempting its discovery is made up from the MS. narrative of Daniel Bryan and notes of conversations with Daniel Bryan, Col. Nathan Boone and lady, Moses and Isaiah Boone, and the Hon. Edward Coles, who visited Boone in Missouri; together with Boone's Narrative, Filson's *Kentucky,* and the *Maryland Gazette.*

8. Filson's orthography is *Cool.* But it is the unanimous testimony of Daniel Bryan, Moses and Isaiah Boone, Col. Nathan Boone and lady, that Daniel and Squire Boone invariably pronounced the name Cooley. Probably Filson or his printer inadvertently dropped the final syllable.

9. Daniel Boone chiefly raised his nephew Jesse Boone, son of Israel Boone, and he was probably at this period a member of his family and aided in the labors of the farm during his uncle's absence. He was the grandfather of the late Hon. Ratliff Boone of Indiana and was always unfortunate in his younger days, first breaking a leg, then an arm.

10. MS. statement of Daniel Bryan, who had himself passed several times over the same route, the first time only eight years after this primitive adventure of Boone, Findley, and their companions.

11. The letter of Joseph Martin, which has already been given, dated in Powell's Valley, May 9th, 1769, probably about ten days before Boone and party passed along, speaks of *the hunters' trail* as a fixed fact anterior to that date.

12. Peck erroneously supposes this camp was "on the waters of Red River, and, so far as can now be ascertained, within the present boundaries of Morgan County." If Findlay's old trading-place is here alluded to by Dr. Peck, he still placed the locality a good many miles too far to the eastward. Boone's carelessly expressed Narrative does rather convey the idea that the main camp was located at the point where Findlay had formerly traded with the Indians; but Daniel Bryan, who was Boone's nephew, and went to Kentucky as early as 1777, [and] had a good opportunity of learning the facts, says it was "on the waters of Station Camp Creek." The venerable Samuel Boone, another nephew of the old pioneer, who resided many years in the region of Station Camp Creek, says it was on that

stream that Boone and Findlay had their main camp but does not know its precise locality. Spalding's *Sketches of Kentucky,* upon what authority we do not know, corroborates this visit. The very name of the stream carries with it evidence of the correctness of the position here taken; and the late Maj. Bland W. Ballard, who hunted upon Station Camp in 1779, well remembered it then bore its present name, the origin of which, however, he did not know. Col. Nathan Boone can only say that his father and Stuart's *subsequent* camp was on the north side of [the] Kentucky River but does not know where the first or Station Camp was located and would fully credit Daniel Bryan's statements on that stead. When one of the writers visited the venerable Daniel Bryan early in 1844, the particular spot where this famous camp was pitched was not a subject of thought or conversation; and since the passage of that old pioneer to the tomb, it can probably never be determined with more precision that here stated.

13. In the early settlement of the country, according to the statement of the late Samuel Plummer, there were some remains of huts still to be seen at the old Indian town on Lulbegrud, and a pair of cedar gate-posts, which one Webb cut down to get the iron hinges.

14. Bryan's MS. statement.

15. Filson's *Kentucky;* Boone's Narrative; Boone's Memorial to the Kentucky Legislature.

16. Simm's *Southern Magazine,* April 1845; also, Simm's *Views and Reviews.*

17. Boone's *Memorial.*

18. Conversations with Col. Nathan Boone.

19. These remarks on summer and fall hunting, graining and scaffolding skins, and the appropriate season for best securing pelts and wild meats are based entirely on notes of conversations with the venerable Col. Nathan Boone of Missouri.

20. Morse's *Kentucky,* edition 1794, p. 508; Kalm's *Travels;* Grahame's *Colonies,* Boston, ed., i:564; conversations with Col. Nathan Boone, who added that there were no bees in the woods of Missouri till the white settlements expanded.

21. In Perkins' sketch of the *Pioneers of Kentucky,* in the *North American Review* for January 1846, and republished in Perkins' *Memoirs,* it is suggested that Boone and Findlay must have been engaged in the Indian trade during all this period of over half a year, as such a party of half a dozen whites could hardly have so long scoured the choice hunting ground of the natives without discovery. But this volunteer guess-work cannot be suffered to over-ride Boone's own Narrative corroborated by Daniel Bryan's Narrative, and Daniel and Squire Boone's statements to their children.

22. Probably about the 4th of January.

23. The particulars of Boone and Stuart's first captivity and camp robbery are given mainly on the authority of Daniel Bryan, while the details of their excursion to recover their horses, their re-captivity and escape are partly from Bryan's statement, but chiefly from the recollections of the venerable Nathan Boone and

lady, who often heard Col. Daniel Boone rehearse them in their presence. Filson furnishes no minute narration of these events, except, by some unaccountable blunder, to make Boone and Stuart steal away from the Indians in the night when their captors were fast asleep; but such was not the manner in which Colonel Boone himself invariably related the incident to his family.

24. Bryan's MS. narrative; MS. notes of conversations with Daniel Bryan, and also with Col. Nathan Boone and lady.

Holden, Mooney, and Cooley never after, it is believed, returned to visit the West, this early adventure having proved too disastrous again to think of trying their fortunes in that quarter. Holden and Cooley were common neighbors of Boone on the Upper Yadkin and lived and died there. Poor Mooney was one of the morning hunters prior to the battle of Point Pleasant, whose companion Hickman was killed, and he himself fell during the contest of that memorable day.

The Boones never heard a word of Findlay afterward. But in the Upcott Collection of Newspaper Cuttings, in the New York Historical Society, is published [an] extract from a Philadelphian letter, dated January 3, 1772, evidently addressed to some London correspondent, containing the following intelligences: "Several Senecas have lately been killed by our people, and the Indians, in revenge, have murdered a whole family on Buffaloe Creek, and four farmers on Youghiogamy; and they have likewise killed Robert Parsons, the trader, and robbed John Findlay of above five hundred pounds' worth of goods." As this was nearly two years after Findlay had parted from the Boones in Kentucky, we may conclude that he at once re-engaged in the Indian trade upon his return to Pennsylvania, but with no better success in the sequel than formerly. And as we hear no more of him, save a vague tradition of the Rev. J. B. Finley, that he was lost in the wilds of the West not long after his Kentucky exploration with Boone, he probably did not long survive this last robbery, which occurred evidently towards the close of 1771; but whether this early and meritorious adventurer sickened and died alone somewhere in the fertile valley of the Ohio or fell a victim to savage cruelty remains a mystery and must unquestionably remain so forever.

EDITOR'S NOTES: CHAPTER 6

a. In the fall of 1851, during Draper's visit, Nathan Boone recalled to the historian a portion of these stories that John Findlay related to his father prior to their first Kentucky long hunt, stories sure to fire any hunter's blood. "Of bears and buffaloes, elk and deer, their number was legion; and at many of the salt-licks of the country, they congregated in such prodigious herds, that the sight was truly grand and amazing."

b. Draper's notions about Long Hunter dress are influenced by his interpretation of Rev. Joseph Doddridge's *Notes on the Settlement and Indian Wars of the Western Parts of Virginia and Pennsylvania, 1763–1783* (1824), a good proof text for anyone interested in mid-eighteenth-century trans-Allegheny frontier life.

c. Right. Daniel Boone did not wear a coonskin cap, and this is a good place to put down this bedraggled warhorse. (Nor, probably, did Alamo martyr and backwoods good-ole-boy Congressman David Crockett, unless doing so might pump a few more votes out of the folks back home in west Tennessee.) Boone called such fur caps—which were Indian wear—"uncivilized." But to this day, most folks envision Boone as tall and handsome, dressed in buckskin dripping with fringes, and topped with a coonskin cap with a bushy ring-tail bouncing from shoulder to shoulder, just like TV frontiersman Fess Parker, who portrayed Daniel Boone. (That Parker also portrayed Crockett from 1954 to 1956 in five Walt Disney episodes wearing a coonskin cap certainly adds to the Boone-Crockett iconographic confusion.)

d. Big Hill is east of Silver Creek's headwaters. Farther west is Paint Lick Creek.

e. It was from Mount Pisgah's lofty heights—the peak is identified both with Mount Nebo and with Ras es-Siaghah, about ten miles east of the mouth of the Jordan—that Moses viewed the Promised Land of Canaan, a land Yahweh did not permit him to enter. The story is chronicled in the Old Testament in the book of Deuteronomy 3:27; 34:1.

f. Ministers and the well-to-do often stereotyped frontier people as "border trash" and deemed market hunters slothful and lazy. Virginia aristocrat William Byrd II condemned borderland North Carolinians in biblical terms. "The men impose All the Work upon the poor Women," he observed. "Thus they loiter away their Lives, like Solomon's Sluggard, with their arms across, and at the Winding of the Year Scarcely have Bread to Eat." Rev. John D. Shane wrote that he never saw a hunter "make anything, or to do well hunting." Pastors warned their flocks that hunters were "always indigent, always ignorant, always idle. Their poverty . . . is their vice." A German visiting western Virginia in 1750 was shocked by people of the frontier who culturally were more Indian than white. Such folk seemed to be "a kind of white people . . . who live like the savages, having a half-Indian appearance" and were "nearly allied in disposition and manners to Indians."

Such comments reflect bias. Market hunters worked hard year-round to provide for their kin. Gender roles were well-defined: Hunting was man's work, tending hearth and home was women's work, and rarely did the two meet—very much like the gender roles of Woodland Indian hunting societies such Anglo-Americans lived near and adapted cultural traits from.

g. At 40 cents per pound and 100 pounds per load, each packhorse could carry $40 worth of skins to market. In the original transcript of "Life of Boone" (DM 3B:14–15), Draper alters the figure, noting that a packhorse could carry 200 pounds of peltry. Long hunters took furs to buyers in elm-bark canoes and in bateaux and dugouts. In 1747 Swedish botanist Pehr Kalm described "battoe" as flat-bottomed boats "made of boards of white pine. . . . They are sharp at both ends, and somewhat higher towards the end than in the middle. They have seats in them. . . . Usually they are three sometimes four fathoms long." The boat had a beam of four feet and its sides stood about twenty-four inches tall. Woodsmen preferred the more sturdy bateaux over canoes but also used dugouts shaped from the towering tulip poplars that lined riverbanks. One such leviathan floating the Tennessee in 1778 measured fifty-six feet long, three feet wide, and three feet deep and carried seven grindstones for ballast.

h. *Cache* as defined by author David J. Wishart in *The Fur Trade of the American West: 1807–1840:*

> The trappers dispensed with the burden of unnecessary transportation by caching furs, merchandise, and surplus equipment in the ground. The cache then became a base for trapping operations, a trading post without superstructure. The cache was generally made on a rise where the soil was dry. The trappers dug a deep pit, lined it with sticks and leaves, and carefully deposited the materials. The pit was then filled with soil and the surface of the ground restored to a natural condition in an effort to conceal the cache from Indians. The furs and goods were generally raised when the trappers repaired to the summer rendezvous.

i. "Tugs" served in place of rope. Indian and Anglo hunters sliced big-game hides into tugs, according to Daniel Boone's nephew Daniel Bryan, "by cutting hides round and round into long strips and twisting them." Although hunters also used deer and elk tugs, they favored tugs cut from the hide of a freshly killed buffalo. Cheap, quick, and easy to make, expendable, and workable, "buffler" tugs bound and knotted into place and left to dry wore like iron and remained virtually indestructible.

j. It is true that green (freshly skinned) buffalo, bear, and elk hides are bulky, and the difficulty of transporting and tanning them limited their marketability. A typical green buffalo hide in its winter prime weighs about 125 pounds, depending on the size of the animal and whether the skin is from a large bull or a smaller cow. Though it may be true in terms of money that "no value was attached by hunters to buffalo, bear, and elk skins," big-game hides were useful. Hunters laced such hides into pack coverings, used them in place of blankets, stretched them over a sapling frame for a lean-to or a hide boat, cut them into tugs, or sewed them into shoepacs and other heavy-duty winter garments.

Nor is it accurate that big-game hides were not "marketable at any price." That depended upon geography. On June 27, 1716, South Carolinian fur buyer Theophilus Hastings sent Lt. Gen. James Moore bundles of beaver pelts but complained, "I can get you no Buffalo skins as yet." On August 7, 1718, South Carolinian trader Robert Blakely received as a gift "one Buffaloe Skin." Farther west, French traders sold tanned buffalo robes from the rich Ouachita River basin for ten livres each. Listed in the inventory of the estate of Francois Bastien

(d. 1763), who lived near Fort de Chartres, Illinois, are "3 buffalo hides." In addition, there was a bustling Indian trade in buffalo robes from the Great Lakes to the Southeast.

k. Draper's Manifest Destiny bias and hero worship is showing badly in his high-blown Cooperesque rendering of this encounter. The fact was that Boone and his men were risking their lives and property by trespassing and poaching in Indian country. But the robbers got caught and had their stolen wares confiscated by the rightful stewards of Kentucky's game herds. Is it not fair to ask, in this case, who truly were the "rapacious plunderers"?

l. Draper means an Indian trade-gun. The study of Indian trade-guns is an arcane science worthy of several doctoral dissertations. Simply put, such trade-guns were cheaply made smoothbore long arms, iron-mounted, stocked to the muzzle in walnut or maple, fitted with octagonal to round barrels up to 48 inches long of large caliber (sixteen to twenty gauge), and used throughout the North American fur trade. Cheaply made means that makers built Indian trade-guns to sell at a lower cost than higher-quality arms; trade-guns were not poorly made junk pieces. Contrary to popular notions, Indians were conscientious consumers and traders, and European merchants catered to their demands. This was certainly true in the gun trade. Light, rugged, and versatile, a smoothbore handles many types of loads—shot, ball, or buck and ball. Indian trade-guns came from Europe in a variety of styles, grades, lengths, and calibers. In some Old World weapons factories, gunsmiths painted trade-guns in flashy floral motifs, Indian-style whorls and zigzags of blue, red, or yellow, or white with black spots, according to native tastes.

m. Boone's run-in with "the untutored Indian" could have been his last. Draper's dismissive comments bring even him to admit that the Shawnee showed mercy to the interlopers. In giving the hunters key tools of survival—a gun, ammunition, moccasins, a tanned deerskin to patch their moccasins—for their homeward journey, Capt. Will Emery and his warriors sought to accommodate rather than annihilate. Under eighteenth-century England's "Bloody Code," Old World judges dealt to poachers a far grimmer penalty—"hanged till dead,"

n. Cane *(Arundinaria gigantea)* is Kentucky's indigenous bamboo. Cane is a grass, aggressively spreading underground by a dense rhizome network that in the spring sprouts upward as shoots to form dense stands called canebrakes. During Boone's day, cane blanketed much of Kentucky, growing more than twenty feet tall, providing cover for man and beast, lessening erosion, and providing buffalo with winter feed. Today Kentucky's cane stands exist mostly along creek banks and in marginal, less arable soil, resulting in short, spindly brakes. Worse, relentless habitat destruction to feed industry is wiping out the shimmering grasslands that once provoked astonishment and wonder among early travelers.

o. This is an old myth. Depending upon the tree and amount of sunlight, shade, and moisture it receives, moss may grow on any side of a tree.

CHAPTER 7

The Hunting Seasons.—Habits of Beaver and Otter, and Modes of Taking Them.—Daniel Boone's Winter Camp.—Characteristics of Hunter Life.— Stuart's Mysterious Loss.—His Character.—Remains Subsequently Found.—Neely Returns Alone to the Settlements.—Hunters' Mode of Living.—Daniel and Squire Boone Alone in Kentucky.—Squire Boone Departs for Carolina.—Daniel Boone's Reflections.—His Wanderings.— The Beauty of the Country as Described by Filson and Imlay.—The Blue Licks.—The Buffaloes.—The Ohio.—Big Bone Lick.—Falls of the Ohio.— Boone's Adventure with an Indian.—His Cave on Shawanoe River.— Traditionary Adventure at Dick's River.—His Cautious Habits.—Squire Boone's Return.—Boone's Knob.—The Boone Brothers Ramble Through the Country.—Squire Boone Again Departs for North Carolina and Again Returns to Kentucky.

The checkered story of these solitary travails of the wilderness now claims our attention. Boone and Stuart led their new recruits back to the Station Camp, but since it was located so near the *Warrior's Road* and the Shawanoes had already learned its position, there is reason to believe that our hunters did not long venture to tarry there. They were now to commence their winter hunt, which was mainly trapping beaver and otters and occasionally killing game for food. As the bear had by this time entered upon his hibernation, and the buffalo, elk, and deer commenced falling off in flesh, and all the former generous store of jerk had been plundered and destroyed by Captain Will's vagabond depredators, it now became necessary to lay in immediately a new supply of jerked meat and select a new location for their winter's camp. But a single camp only was now requisite, as the furs of a winter's hunt were less in number and weight than a summer and autumn one and hence could be easily carried by the trappers to their head-quarters. Though less in quantity, they commanded a far better price, so that the winter and spring hunt, if at all successful, was deemed by far the most pecuniarily important to those who regularly led the rambling life of a hunter. Their new camp, so far as tradition can now inform us, was on or near the northern bank of the Kentucky and not very far from the mouth of Red River. In some secluded spot, with probably a gushing spring near by, they erected a little cabin to shelter them from the winter storms, laid in a stock of meat, and devoted themselves earnestly to the business of trapping.

We have already adverted to the fact that in the summer and autumn deer-skins were in the best condition, while the furs of the beaver and otter were unfit for use. Nature provides these animals with a warm covering to shield them from the severities of winter, which they shed as the heat of summer approaches. The long, gray hair or winter coat upon the deer takes deep root in the skin and thus nearly penetrates through the pelt, rendering it quite useless for purposes of leather. But in the month of May the deer shed their heavy coat of hair, which is succeeded by a thin, red coat, which takes slight root and leaves the hide in good condition for leather. Then the hunters turn their attention to hunting deer for their hides. This red coat gradually gives way in the fall to a short, blue one, which renders the skin less valuable in proportion to the time it has been taking root, and by Christmas the long gray fully appears, to prepare the animal for winter; and then, of course, the pelts are no longer sought by the hunter. Thus, in the nomenclature of hunters and fur-traders, deer skins are either in the red, short, blue, or gray, terms well understood by those engaged in such employments and fully indicative of the peculiar condition and value of skins as articles of trade and commerce.

When the deer-pelts, toward the close of December, become worthless, the beaver and otter fur is long and thick and in its best condition. In this case, the fur, not the skin, is the thing sought after; and until these furry animals shed their coat in the spring, they are trapped and taken with great avidity by the hunters. So when the trapping season closes, the deer-hunting period commences; and when the latter ends, the time for trapping again comes round. Thus the hunter has his routine of employment the whole year and is more busily engaged at some particular seasons than others, inasmuch as both skins and furs have their special seasons of being in the best order and consequently commanding the highest price.

No man ever possessed in a more happy combination than Daniel Boone those quiet, taciturn habits, love of solitary adventure, and admiration for the silent charms of nature which serve to make up the appropriate characteristics of a successful trapper. So much of his time was spent in this and kindred employments, which so peculiarly formed the passion of his life, that a faithful picture of the habits of the beaver and otter and the modes most commonly adopted to take them cannot be otherwise than regarded as eminently befitting the character of the man who has time and again been referred to as the great prototype of the hunters of Kentucky.[a]

The beaver is an amphibious quadruped, weighing when full grown from fifty to sixty pounds and measuring about four feet from the snout to the end of the tail, with a blunt nose, short ears and legs, small fore-feet, large hind feet with membranes between the toes to aid in swimming, with a flat, ovate tail a foot long, five or six inches wide, and about an inch in thickness. It is a peculiarity of this animal that although the body is so well covered with fur and hair, mostly of a chestnut brown colour, the tail has neither, except at its immediate connection with the body, and is covered with scales. "This tail," says one accurate writer, "serves for a rudder to aid the animal when swimming, in its changing and often rapid movement in the water. The fore part of the beaver has the taste and consistency of land animals, while the hind legs and tail have not only the smell, but the savor and nearly all the qualities of fish.[b] This peculiarity is thought by some to be accounted for by the habits of the animal, as when in the water its hind legs and tail are submerged and never seen; but it appears rather to be a connecting link between the inhabitants of land and water, its singularity in this respect being placed by nature beyond the control of mere circumstance."[1]

These sagacious animals are remarkable for their ingenuity in constructing their lodges or habitations. Dr. Godman has described with much care and accuracy the manner in which they conduct their architectural skill and labors. "They are not particular," says that able naturalist, "in the site they select for the establishment of their dwellings, but if in a lake or pond, where a dam is not required, they are careful to build where the water is sufficiently deep. In standing waters, however, they have not the advantage afforded by a current for the transportation of supplies of wood; which, when they build on a running stream, is always cut higher up than the place of their residence, and floated down.

"The material[s] used for the construction of their dams, are the trunks and branches of small birch, mulberry, willow, poplar, and etc. They begin to cut down their timber for building, early in the summer, but their edifices are not commenced until about the middle of latter part of August, and are not completed until the beginning of the cold season. The strength of their teeth, and their perseverance in this work, may be fairly estimated, by the size of the trees they cut down. These are cut in such a manner as to fall into the water,[c] and then floated towards the site of dam or dwelling. Small shrubs, etc., cut at a distance from the water, they drag with their teeth to the stream, and then launch and tow them to the place of deposit. At a short distance above a beaver dam, the number of trees which have been cut down, appears truly surprising, and the regularity of the stumps which are left, might lead persons unacquainted with the habits of the animals to believe that the clearing was the result of human industry.

"The figure of the dam varies according to circumstances. Should the current be very gentle, the dam is carried nearly straight across; but when the stream is swiftly flowing, it is uniformly made with a considerable curve, having the convex part opposed to the current. Along with the trunks and branches of trees, they intermingle mud and stones, to give greater security; and when dams have been long undisturbed and frequently repaired, they acquire greater solidity, and their power of resisting the pressure of water and ice, is greatly increased by the willow, birch, and etc., occasionally taking root, and eventually growing up into something of a regular hedge. The materials used in constructing the dams, are secured solely by the resting of the branches, etc., against the bottom, and the subsequent accumulation of mud and stones, by the force of the stream, or by the industry of the beavers.

"The dwellings of the beaver are formed of the same materials as their dams, and are very rude, through strong, and adapted in size to the number of their inhabitants. There are seldom more than four old, and six or eight young ones. Double that number have been occasionally found in one of the lodges, though it is by no means a very common occurrence. When building their houses, they place most of the wood cross-wise, and nearly horizontal, observing no other order than that of leaving a cavity in the middle. Branches which project inward, are cut off with their teeth and thrown among the rest. The houses are by no means built of sticks first, and then plastered, but all the materials, sticks, mud and stones, if the latter can be procured, are mixed up together, and this composition is employed from the foundation to the summit. The mud is obtained from the adjacent banks or bottom of the stream or pond, near the door of the hut. Mud and stones, the beaver always carries by holding them between his fore paws and throat.

"Their work is all performed at night, and with much expedition. When straw or grass is mingled with the mud used by them in building, it is an accidental circumstance, owing to the nature of the spot whence the latter was taken. As soon as any part of the material is placed where it is intended to remain, they turn round and give it a smart blow with the tail. The same sort of blow is struck by

37. Beaver pelts remained the staple of the American fur trade until the late 1830s, when silk hats became the fashion rage of the day. By then, beaver had been trapped nearly into extinction.

them on the surface of the water, when they are in the act of diving. The outside of the hut is covered or plastered with mud late in the autumn, and after frost has begun to appear. By freezing, it soon becomes as hard as stone, effectually [wm] their great enemy, the wolverine, during the winter. The habit of walking over the work frequently during its progress, has led to the absurd idea of their using their tail as a trowel. The habit of flapping with the tail is retained by them in a state of captivity, and, unless it be acts already mentioned, appears designed to effect no particular purpose. The houses, when they have stood for some time, and been kept in repair, become so firm from the consolidation of all the materials, as to require great exertion, and the ice chisel, or other instruments, to be broken open. The laborious nature of such an undertaking may easily be conceived, when it is known that the tops of the houses are generally from four to six feet thick at the apex of the cave."[2]

In its natural or forest life, where undisturbed by man, the beaver is social in its habits, often numbering twenty or more habitations in a single community, containing from two to twenty members each at some season of the year as circumstances warrant. Near their habitations, they establish magazines of green bark and soft wood for food, keeping them well replenished; and never do the members of one family plunder from the larder of another. A community of beavers, although it may consist of several hundred members, is seldom disturbed by domestic difficulties, peace and harmony being the bond which cements their union. If an individual is threatened with danger, it immediately takes measures to forewarn the whole village, which is done by striking the water furiously with its tail. Thus apprised of an enemy's proximity, the animals take shelter either in the water or their strong dwellings, which are very tidily kept in order. The entrance to a beaver's dwelling is by a small open door toward the water.[3]

A thorough knowledge of the signs of the haunts of beaver and otter is essentially necessary to enable the trapper to ascertain what water-courses they inhabit. They love secluded streams, floating along which or lodged on their shores [are] often seen bits of green wood, gnawed branches of bass-wood, slippery-elm, and sycamore, their favorite food. Their tracks or foot-marks betray their locality. They are often discovered by their ingeniously constructed dams and curious habitations. The trapper must avoid kindling a fire near their haunts, and shooting game, as the smell of smoke or report of a gun frighten[s] the timid animals which he hopes to entrap, alike by his stratagem and his thorough acquaintance with their habits and instincts.

Such is their sagacity and caution, and such the acuteness of their sense of smell, that particular care on the part of the trapper is requisite in his approach to their haunts to set his traps, that he leave on the ground or bushes that he may have touched no scent of his hands or feet. For this reason he generally approaches in a canoe or, if he has none at hand, enters the stream thirty or forty yards below, wades to the place for setting the trap, and returns in the same careful manner. The traps are set some three or four inches underwater and within half a dozen inches of shore, and always where the bank breaks off abruptly and

38. Trapper's water set on beaver slide. DRAWING BY E. KREBS, FROM *SCIENCE OF TRAPPING* (1935).

makes the water not very far from shore at least three or four feet deep. Sometimes the trapper, while sitting in his canoe, excavates with his paddle a hole in the bank of the stream of proper size to admit his trap, submerged the proper depth. To the trap is attached a chain, which, if not sufficiently long, is extended by an addition of cord made frequently of leatherwood bark varying from twelve to twenty inches in length; the other is fastened firmly to a submerged stake near shore. The iron portion of the fastening is connected with the trap to prevent the beaver, when caught, from gnawing it off, which he would do so if a cord and escape with the trap into deeper water, there drowning himself and losing the trap—an article of too great value to the trapper, far distant from smiths and settlements, to run the risk of losing.

The bait used is beaver musk or castor, taken from the cod in the groin of that animal, possessing rather a pleasant odor, and is often called by hunters barkstone.[d] This perfume is rubbed on the upper end of a small weight stick a few inches in length or in a small cavity there scooped out with the point of a knife, the lower end of which is slightly inserted in the ground near the edge of the water and directly abreast of the trap. To this scent stick is often attached a horsehair string leading to the trap and with [which] it is pulled into the water by the beaver that the stick may not remain, after the trap is sprung, to attract other beavers to the spot and thus prevent their journeying to some neighboring trap, all in readiness to give them a fatal embrace. When the proper bait is wanting, the trappers sometimes make use of the fresh aromatic roots of the sassafras or spice-bush, of both which the beaver is very fond. If the weather is inauspicious or threatening when setting the trap, a broad leaf, generally of sycamore, is so ad-justed over the top of the scent stick as to protect it from the rain or snow.

Sometimes bushes are stuck [on] each side of the concealed trap so that when the beaver come swimming along, they scent the musk and head towards shore, as they will invariably do, to smell it, imperceptibly allured on to destruc-tion, always paddling with their webbed hind feet, while upon their jaws rest their fore feet, which drop down to their natural position the moment their breast touches anything, and thus they are caught in the trap already sprung beneath them as they are in the act of snuffing delightfully their favorite musk. Once en-trapped, the poor victim generally swims out into deep water, hoping thereby to rid himself of this painful appendage, but the weight of the trap soon sinks and drowns him. Sometimes, however, the poor beaver failing thus to get clear of the terrible encumbrance will, before exhausted, return to shore and wring or gnaw off the skin of his imprisoned leg, the bones of which are usually broken by the force of the trap-spring, and makes his escape. In his agony, he generally hastens off several miles up or down the stream and then is quite as likely as others to get entrapped again, sometimes even within a day or two of the dismemberment of his limbs. The wound soon heals, and trappers not infrequently recapture the three-footed fugitive afterward.[4]

Though the otter somewhat resembles the beaver in size, their general habits are widely variant. The otter has a large, flattened head, short ears, webbed toes, crooked nails, and a tail slightly flattened horizontally. It usually feeds on fish, frogs, mussels, and other small animals; and when these cannot be obtained, it eats tender branches and bark growing in or near the water, and sometimes grass. Bad economists themselves, they often destroy the food which the more frugal beaver lays up in store. Less numerous than the beaver, their fur is more valu-able. They display sagacity in preparing their burrow, which is made upward under a bank starting beneath the water; and to prevent any accident of being drowned out by a freshet, they open an aperture to the surface, often concealed on top by leaves and bushes.

Otters live a more solitary and migratory life than the beaver, often changing their habitation, and hence are less frequently caught. The trap is set in the same manner for them as for beaver, except the bait, none at all being generally used or, if any, a fish or mussel placed on a stick in front of the trap. They have particular places along the shore of a stream or pond, not far from their burrows, where they go to roll, play, or slide down the bank; and these places are points of dirt or sand at the mouth of some gully or ravine. The beaten paths or slides at these places of frequent resort are called in hunter's parlance otter-slides; and where these start from the stream is the place for setting the trap. Their hide is tougher than the beaver's, and they very seldom when caught wring or gnaw off their feet.[5]

In skinning the beaver, the skin is cut from the under jaw down the neck and along the belly, ripped off, and then stretched within a hoop, generally of grape-vine, for drying. The otter skin is taken off cased or skinned whole and, being thus turned inside out, has a bow or drying board of full size inserted within. Preparing these skins was the work of bad weather or evenings when the trappers were not otherwise employed. From two hundred to two hundred and fifty pounds' weight of furs or peltry was considered a load for a horse.[e] The weight of a beaver skin averaging about a pound and a quarter, and an otter skin about a pound, a horse could pack near two hundred of them to the settlements. At the period when Boone hunted and trapped on the frontiers of Carolina and finally penetrated Kentucky, grained deer skins were probably worth about forty cents a pound or a dollar a skin, while beaver skins were worth about two dollars and fifty cents each, and otter skins from about three to five dollars. So that a horse load of furs, if all were beaver, was worth five times as much as the same weight of deer skins; and the value was increased if some of the valuable otter went to make up the fruits of a winter and spring hunt.[6]

Having thus given a somewhat minute account of the modes and customs of hunters and trappers, and the characteristics of the game they study so success-fully to secure, let us return to our little hunter band in their cabin on the northern bank of the Kentucky River. Winter was now upon them, but they were, in spite of all misfortunes, quite comfortably prepared for it. An abundant supply of var-ious kinds of jerk, bear's oil, buffalo tallow, dried buffalo tongues, fresh meat, and marrow-bones, which served to make up the store of the hunter's larder, had been secured; buffalo robes and bear skins liberally provided for purposes of bedding, and a goodly supply laid in of moccasins and patch leather. During cold weather, the hunters would stuff deer's hair in their moccasins, which kept their feet very warm; and at night during all seasons, both leggings and moccasins were taken off and, if wet, were well dried and rubbed until soft. The perspiration of the feet is peculiarly destructive to the moccasin; and to counteract this in part, this article was taken off nightly and dried, unless apprehensive of Indians, and even then the hunters would not infrequently tie them to their guns to have them in readiness to be caught up at a moment's alarm. To this habit of lying with their feet to the fire, thus always keeping their extremities warm, the old hunters mainly attributed their uniform good health.

To aid them in prosecuting their trapping operations, they made a small canoe.[f] It would appear that Squire Boone and Neely trapped in company, while Daniel Boone and Stuart, now so well acquainted with the country, agreed to di-vide their portion of the traps and visit different quarters, collect their skins, and meet at their camp on a certain day every two weeks. It was now probably the close of January or early in February 1770. Stuart took the canoe and crossed the Kentucky, while Daniel Boone remained on the northern side of that stream.

After their separation, it proved a very wet time in mid winter; the Kentucky became very much swollen and at the region of their camp had greatly overflowed its banks. Boone reached the camp at the appointed time and attributed Stuart's failure to the unusually swollen state of the river. When the flood subsided, Boone crossed the Kentucky, and nearly opposite to the camp, on the nearest high ground to where the backwaters had extended, found the remains of a recent fire which apparently had been used a couple of days and the initials of Stuart's name freshly cut in the bark of a tree near by. No further clue or evidence of poor Stuart's fate could then be found.

It was subsequently unkindly surmised by some that he had taken that occasion to run off and return no more to his friends and family. But Daniel Boone, and those who equally well knew Stuart's domestic relations, scouted the idea as preposterous. Stuart was then only about twenty-six years of age. He had been mostly raised on the Yadkin, where in 1765 he had married Boone's youngest sister, had two little daughters, and a third was born about the period of his death, who never saw her father's face. Of common stature and rather pale complexion, he possessed a pleasing countenance with a lively turn of mind. A man of warm and tender feelings, he was entirely devoted to his family and never had any difficultly with the companion of his bosom. Boone often said that he never had a brother whom he loved and respected more than he did John Stuart; that he had all the confidence in him that one man could repose in another and that he was strictly faithful in the fulfillment of his promises—a most essential requisite, as Boone always declared, in hunting companions, that they might mutually feel a strong assurance that some unusual misfortune only could cause a failure on the part of either to meet at camp at any given time. Boone therefore always thought that Stuart either got killed or sickened and died in the wilderness.

Let us lift the veil and partly dispel the mystery, even though it should involve a prochronism. When Boone and a party of road-cutters five years afterwards were engaged in marking the road from Powell's Valley to the Big Lick on the Kentucky, where Boonesborough was subsequently located, after taking up camp towards the close of the day at the old crossing of the Rockcastle, one of the party happened to discover on the bank of that stream the bones of a man in a standing hollow sycamore. Boone went with others to view the remains, and in taking out the bones, they found a powder horn, which Boone quickly recognized as that of his long lost friend; and upon a brass band encircling it was plainly engraven the initials of Stuart's name—a practice nearly universal with our hunter and soldier race along the western borders.[7] Boone thought that he could not be mistaken in beholding in the skull the general outlines of Stuart's well-remembered features. Upon a careful examination of the bones, that of the left arm between the elbow and shoulder was found to have been broken, and the discoloration produced by the leaden ball still distinctly discernible. There were no other

39. Entitled "The Attack on the Boones and John Stewart" and depicting long hunters, Woodland Indians, and a canebrake, this heroic engraving by an unknown hand was featured as the frontispiece in Humphrey Marshall's The History of Kentucky *(1812).*

evidences of injury; no cleaving of the skull by the Indian tomahawk or marks of the merciless scalping knife. No trace whatever of his rifle could be found.

Upon this singular discovery, Boone concluded that Stuart, when encamped on the southern bank of the Kentucky River, had for pastime cut the initials of his name on a tree and subsequently been fired on and wounded by the Indians and fled, perhaps leaving his rifle behind or dropping it from his disabled arm or, becoming weak in his flight from his enemies, have cast it away. Or apprehending a still further rise in the river, or discovering signs of Indians, he may have left his campfire, marked the tree to shew who had been there, and searched out a more suitable camping spot, where he was attacked by some straggling party of Indians. When perhaps wounded and beyond the immediate reach of his pursuers, yet fearful lest they should follow his trail; and fearful too of the uncertainty of he and Boone meeting very soon in consequence of the great flood, and apprehensive probably from their former as well as his present misfortunes, that Boone may have fallen by the vigilance of their lurking enemies; and moreover, his condition may have suggested forebodings that the unlucky bullet which had broken his arm or some other had penetrated his body and inflicted wounds still more dangerous, concluded that his wisest course would be to direct his footsteps as best he could to the nearest settlements, subsisting meanwhile on roots, herbs, and whatever else chance might throw his way.

And thus he had travelled in this languishing state till he had reached the Rockcastle, when finally [his] sinking nature could no longer bear up under the accumulated sufferings from his wounds and his wants, superadded to the over-tasked exertions he had made and the severities of the season, he had crept into the hollow sycamore, there to shelter himself from the pitiless peltings of the wintry storm. And there, alone and uncomforted, in the howling wilderness in mid-winter, perished the faithful friend and companion of Daniel Boone. Excepting the comrades of Findlay, killed probably at Lulbegrud seventeen years before, Stuart was, in the expressive language of Butler, "the first victim, as far as is known, in the hetacombs of white men, offered by the Indians to the god of battles, in their desperate and ruthless contention for Kentucky." It were needless to add how sincerely Boone deplored the loss of such a friend and brother. In proof of this, it is said that he resolved never to return home until he had learned, if possible, poor Stuart's fate.[8]

Squire Boone and Neely did not probably return from their trapping excursion until some little time after Stuart's mysterious disappearance. The effect of Stuart's uncertain fate upon Neely was apparently disheartening, for, as Daniel Boone informs us in his Narrative, "the man that came with my brother returned home by himself."[9] Though cast down, the Boones were not discouraged. They set themselves about making additional preparations for winter and particularly the erection of a better cabin, or "cottage" as Boone terms it, and devoted themselves entirely to trapping, keeping mostly in company that they might not get separated or lost. Having a generous supply of provisions in store, they seldom killed any fresh meat in winter except perhaps occasionally a turkey. Otter flesh was never eaten. Beaver meat, though not considered very good, was yet used to some extent by the trappers, particularly when busily engaged in trapping and not wishing to make any noise by shooting game. Beaver tails, which weigh from one to two pounds, are very oily and much relished by some; but Daniel Boone never esteemed them a delicacy, though preferable to any other portion of the body.[g]

Never did men stand more in need of the calm exercise of philosophy than the Boones. But they were practical philosophers. "We were then," says Boone in his Narrative, "in a dangerous, helpless situation, exposed daily to perils and death amongst savages and wild beasts, with not a white man in the country but ourselves. Thus situated, many hundred miles from our families in the howling wilderness, I believe few would have equally enjoyed the happiness we experienced." Though indeed a howling wilderness, it was not without its attractions for men endowed with such peculiar natures as theirs. "You see," sagely observed Daniel to Squire—"You see, brother, how little human nature really requires to be satisfied. Felicity is the companion of content, and is to be found in our own breasts, rather in the things around us. I firmly believe it takes but a little philosophy to make a man happy in whatever state fortune may place him.[h] It only asks a perfect resignation to the will of Providence; and a resigned soul finds pleasure in a path strewed even with thorns and briars."[i] There was no disputing this philosophy founded upon revealed wisdom and which was doubtless as sincerely cherished by the one as the other.

The close of winter and two of the spring months passed pleasantly away with no molestation on the part of the Indians. The trapping season now drew to a close, and success had crowned the efforts of our hunters. Their ammunition was now nearly exhausted. Under such circumstances, one would have thought both would unhesitatingly have started for home with the fruits of their toils and left in an open question whether again to return and prosecute hunting and trapping in Kentucky. But no such idea ever entered Daniel's brain, or if it did, he quickly banished such as an unwelcome intruder. Squire Boone was fitted for the journey, a supply of jerk provided, and the horses ladened with a couple of packs of furs swung across each [of] their backs; and on the 1st of May he took his departure for the Yadkin settlements to liquidate former debts incurred for the enterprise and procure a new recruit of horses and ammunition.

Daniel Boone was left alone in the wilderness, as he rather mournfully expresses it, "without bread, salt, sugar, without company of his fellow creatures, or even a horse or dog." He confessed that he never before was under greater necessity of exercising philosophy and fortitude to bear up against despondency. A few days he passed uncomfortably enough, a thousand vague apprehensions stealing into his mind which would undoubtedly have disposed him to melancholy had they been further indulged. "The idea of a beloved wife and family," observes the kind-hearted pioneer, "and the anxiety on account of my absence and exposed situation, made sensible impressions on my heart; for, as Childe Harold has it—

Thinking on an absent wife

Will blanch a faithful cheek."

But Boone was not the man to dwell long upon a train of reflections that could only lead him to become moody and dejected. Besides, he had really too many pleasures where he was. His life was one of excitements, and a certain sense of insecurity heightened his enjoyment. He lived in sight of loveliness but on the verge of danger. Beauty came to him with Terror looking over her shoulder. The wilderness was charming to the senses and the mind, but the thickets of green concealed the painted and ferocious savage; and he who hunted the deer successfully through his haunts might still, while keenly bent upon the chase, be unconscious of the stealthy footsteps which were set down in his own tracks. With the dawn of the day, he arose from his couch of leaves or rushes and started upon the chase. New groves and woods and hills and plains salute his vision with each returning dawn. He pursues no old paths but, reconnoitering the country, gathers a new horizon with every sunrise. He describes these wanderings as perfectly delicious. The swelling of the breeze, the repose of the leaf, the mysterious quiet of the woods, the chant of the birds, or the long melancholy howl of the wolf at evening—these are among the objects, the sights, and sounds which stir his sensibilities and move him to the happiest meditations. He tells of the delight which he feels as he ascends the great ridges and looks over the fertile vallies and the ample wastes before him. How he follows the Ohio—*la Belle Riviere* of the French—in all its silent wanderings—how he sits and studies the huge mountains as they cap their venerable brows with clouds. That he should find a pleasure in such contemplations declares for his superior moral nature. He was not merely a hunter. He was on a mission. The spiritual sense was strong in him. He felt the union between his inner [*wm*] and the nature of the visible world and yearned for their intimate communion. His thoughts and his feelings were those of a great discoverer. He could realize the feelings of a Columbus or a Balboa, and thus gazing over the ocean waste of forest which then spread from the dim western outlines of the Alleghenies to the distant and untrammeled waters of the Mississippi, he was quite as much isolated as was ever any of the great admirals who set forth on the Atlantic still dreaming of Cathay.[10]

That Boone's ammunition was nearly exhausted we have already mentioned. The scanty supply he had remaining required to be husbanded with the greatest care and only used when really necessary to provide himself with game for sustenance. Unable to make a business of hunting, he concluded to prosecute some further explorations of the country.[11] The region embracing from the Kentucky and Licking vallies, and the Ohio as low as the Falls, constituted the fine extent of country over which he now roamed. That he admired all these regions is sufficiently evidenced by the fact that at different times he lived in the Kentucky and Licking vallies and upon the banks of the noble Ohio. The homeland at that charming season of the year must have been a feast to Boone.

Filson, who wrote of Kentucky in 1784, thus glowingly described its primitive appearance: "This country is, in some parts, nearly level; and others, not so much so; and others, hilly, but moderately—and in such places there is most water. The levels are not like a carpet, but interspersed with small risings and declivities, which form a beautiful prospect. A great part of this soil is amazingly fertile; thus some not so good, and some poor. It is of a loose, deep black mold without sand, in the first-rate lands about two or three feet deep, and exceedingly luxuriant in all its productions. The country in general may be considered as well timbered, producing large trees of many kinds, and to be exceeded by no country in variety. Those which are peculiar to Kentucke are the sugar-tree, which grows in all parts in great plenty, and furnishes every family with plenty of excellent sugar. The honey-locust is curiously surrounded with large thorny spikes, bearing broad and long pods in form of peas, has a sweet taste, and makes excellent beer." The coffee-tree greatly resembles the black oak, grows large, and also bears a pod, in which is enclosed good coffee. The pappa-tree does not grow to a great size, is a soft wood, bears a fine fruit much like a cucumber in shape and size, and tastes sweet. The cucumber-tree is small and soft, with remarkable leaves, [and] bears a fruit much resembling that from which it is named. Black mulberry-trees are in abundance; and the wild cherry-tree is here frequent, of a large size. Here also is the buck-eye, an exceeding soft wood, bearing a remarkable black fruit; and some other kinds of trees not common elsewhere.

40. Despite its inaccuracies, John Filson's Map of Kentucke *(1784), which sold with his book, identifies many of Kentucky's landmarks to help guide settlers to the region.* FILSON CLUB HISTORICAL SOCIETY.

"Here," continues Filson, "is great plenty of fine cane, on which the cattle feed and grow fat. This plant in general grows ten to twelve feet high, of a hard substance, with joints at eight or ten inches distance along the stalk, from which proceed leaves resembling those of the willow. There are so many canebrakes so thick and tall that it is difficult to pass through them. Where no cane grows there is an abundance of wild-rye, clover, and buffalo-grass, covering vast tracts of country, and affording excellent food for cattle. The fields are covered with an abundance of wild herbage not common to other countries: the Shawanese sallad, wild lettuce, and pepper-grass, and many more, as yet unknown to the inhabitants, but which, no doubt, have excellent virtues. Here are seen the finest crown-imperial in the world, the cardinal flower, so much extolled for its scarlet colour; and all the year, excepting the winter months, the plains and vallies are adorned with variety of flowers of the most admirable beauty. Here is also found the tulip-bearing laurel-tree, or magnolia, which has an exquisite smell, and continues to blossom and seed for several months together. The reader, by casting his eye upon the map, and viewing round the heads of Licking, from the Ohio, and round the heads of Kentucke, Dick's River,[j] and down the Green River to the Ohio, may view, in that great compass of above one hundred miles square, the most extraordinary country that the sun enlightens with his celestial beams."[12]

Nor was Imlay,[k] who visited the country as early as 1783, less enchanted by its fascinating appearance. Landing at Limestone, now Maysville, in the spring of the year, he says: "Everything here assumes a dignity and splendor I have never seen in any other part of the world. You ascend a considerable distance from the shore of the Ohio, and when you would suppose you have arrived at the summit of a mountain, you find yourself upon an extensive level. Here an eternal verdure reigns, and the brilliant sun of latitude 39°, perceiving through the azure heavens, produces, endless prolific soils, and early maturity, which is truly astonishing. Flowers, full and perfect, as if they have been cultivated by the hand of a florist, with all of their captivating odors, and with all variegated charms which colour and nature can produce, here, in the lap of elegance and beauty, decorate the smiling groves. Soft zephyrs gently breathe on seats, and the inhaled air gives a voluptuous glow of health and vigor, that seems to ravish the intoxicated senses. The sweet songsters of the forest appear to feel the influence of this genial clime, and, in more soft and modulated tones, warble their tender notes in unison with love and nature. Everything here is delight; and, in that wild effulgence which deems around us, we feel a glow of gratitude for the elevations which our all bountiful Creator bestowed upon us. You must forgive what I know you will call a rhapsody, and what I really experienced after travelling across the Allegheny Mountain in March, when it was covered with snow, and after finding the country about Pittsburgh bare, and not recovered from the ravages of winter; there was scarcely a blade of grass to be seen; everything looked dreary, and bore those marks of melancholy which the rude hand of frost produces. I embarked immediately for Kentucky, and in less than five days landed at Limestone, where I found nature robed in all her charms."[13]

With trees of such exquisite beauty and stateliness, interspersed with patches of the slender, graceful cane or carpeted with wild grass, clover, or pea-vine, the surface level or slightly rolling, with springs gushing out from every hill-side and clear brooks rippling along every valley—such forest, the pride of the West, literally swarming with game of every kind, bird and beast, no wonder Boone thought Kentucky another Eden. He wended his way towards the Licking. Though the Licking Valley possessed none of the charms of that of the Kentucky, it contained an invaluable treasure in the mineral spring at the Blue Licks. The hills of the Licking are steep and rugged; near the Blue Licks, they are barren and strong, stripped of all herbage and of every bush and beaten to macadam by the tramping for all ages of immense herds of buffalo, elk, and mammoth. The spring itself is somewhat saline, that is, impregnated with common salt, but it also contains many other mineral ingredients. To the early settlers this spring had a thrice-fold value: It supplied them with salt, it was their grand medicine chest, and it attracted immense herds of game.[1] To it from various directions led great buffalo roads, sometimes worn several feet below the surface of the ground, along which the animals of the forest were ever coming and going, and some of which were large enough for the passage of wagons. It was by following one of these roads that Boone was led both to the Upper and Lower Blue Licks. About the latter particularly, at the two springs on either side of the river and in the open valley, he saw thousands of buffaloes and other animals resorting there to lick the ground impregnated with saline particles and drink the brackish water, producing no small confusion by their unceasing tramping, pawing, gamboling, and contention. One obstacle alone interfered with the enjoyment of this unlimited supply of game; in consequence of the bare character of the hills about the springs, it was impossible to approach the animals without exposing one's self to an enemy in the surrounding forest. But the nature of the hills and vallies, abrupt and varied, afforded excellent opportunities for concealment and for the exercises of that skill and cunning upon which the hunters prided themselves.[14]

We prefer to let Filson tell us something of the buffalo, their roads,[m] the licking and tramping operations as he himself either saw them or learned the facts from Boone and others. "The buffalo," says the primitive historian of Kentucky, "much resembles a large bull, of great size, with a large head, thick short crooked horns, and broader in his forepart than behind. Upon his shoulder is a large hump of flesh, covered with a thick boss of long wool and curly hair, of a dark brown colour. They do not rise from the ground like our cattle, but spring at once upon their feet; are of a broad make and clumsy appearance, with short legs, but run fast, and turn not aside for any thing when chased, except a standing tree. They weigh from five to ten hundred weight, and are excellent meat. I have heard a hunter assert, that he saw above one thousand buffaloes at the Blue Licks at once; so numerous were they before the first settlers had wantonly sported away their lives. The amazing herds of buffaloes which resort thither, by their size and number, fill the traveler with amazement and terror, especially when he beholds the prodigious roads they have made from all quarters, as if leading to some populous city; the vast space of land around these springs desolated as if by a ravaging enemy, and hills reduced to plains; for the land near those springs is chiefly hilly. These are truly curiosities, and the eye can scarcely be satisfied with admiring them."[15]

Passing down the Licking eight miles below the Lower Blue Licks, where an old Indian trail crossed the river, Boone struck across the country to the Ohio, which he reached some twenty or thirty miles above the mouth of the Licking, and thence followed down along its southern shore, everywhere admiring the pristine beauties of the wilderness and the grandeur of the scenes constantly presented to his view. "One day," says Boone, "I undertook a tour through the country, and the diversity and beauties of nature I met with in this charming season expelled every gloomy and vexatious thought. Just at the close of the day the gentle gales retired, and left the place to the disposal of a profound calm. Not a breeze shook the most tremulous leaf. I had gained the summit of a commanding ridge, and, looking round with astonishing delight, beheld the ample plains, the beauteous tracts below. On the other hand, I surveyed the famous river Ohio that rolled in silent dignity, marking the north-western boundary of Kentucky with inconceivable grandeur. At a vast distance I beheld the mountains lift their venerable brows, and penetrate the clouds. All things were still. I kindled a fire near a fountain of sweet water, and feasted on the loin of a buck, which a few hours before I had killed. The sullen shades of night soon overspread the whole hemisphere, and the earth seemed to gasp after the hovering moisture. My roving excursion this day had fatigued my body, and diverted my imagination. I laid me down to sleep, and I awoke not until the sun had chased away the night."[16]

He continued this tour and in due time explored a considerable part of the country, each day equally as well pleased as the first. Among other points of interest, he visited the famous Big Bone Lick and examined the wonderful fossil remains of the mammoth found there.[17] During this peregrination, Boone in two or three instances saw Indians at some distance from him sauntering along the northern bank of the Ohio, but his keen, wary eye beheld them first, which enabled him to withdraw without being in turn discovered. Near the foot of the Falls of the Ohio on the Kentucky shore, he found the remains of what he took to be a trading-house; a stone chimney three or four feet high and some of the surrounding picketing of split logs inserted end-wise in the ground were still remaining. It had apparently been occupied some twelve or fifteen years before.[18]

Having fully examined the Falls of which Findlay had told him so much and the rich lands on Beargrass, he struck across the country to the Kentucky River and probably reached it at a noted buffalo-crossing at Leestown,[n] a little above Frankfort, where he saw an Indian sitting up [on] the top of a fallen tree projecting partly over the water and intently engaged in fishing. Speaking of it in after years to his family, Boone used simply to say, "while I was looking at the fellow, he tumbled into the river, and I saw him no more." It was understood from the manner in which he spoke of it that he shot and killed the Indian; yet he seemed not to care about alluding more particularly to it. He probably felt in no friendly mood toward the whole race of red-skins. They had, within a few months, robbed him and his companions of all their peltry, furs, horses, and other valuables, had twice captured him and Stuart, threatening them ominously if they did not leave the country with a terrible "stinging" from the wasps and yellow-jackets, and had finally given poor Stuart a mortal wound; and no doubt Boone thought this fellow was one of a large party near by for whom he was fishing, and who might, very probably, discover him and thereby endanger his life, and thus, on the whole, he perhaps deemed it most prudent to have him out of the way. This act of Boone's, committed hundreds of miles from home or friends, he undoubtedly considered one of self-defense, and it may have been the means of preserving his life for great future usefulness to his family and country.[19]

Evading whatever enemies may have thirsted for his blood, Boone appears to have pursued his course up the Kentucky and sojourned awhile in a cave° situated in Mercer County on the waters of the Shawanoe Run, which flows into the Kentucky River. The cave at its entrance is about twenty feet wide and eight or ten high, over the mouth of which, on a high bank, is a tree still standing marked with Boone's initials, with the years of its occupancy indicated: *D.B.—1770.* It is still known as *Boone's Cave* and is now a good deal filled up, but on digging a few feet below the surface not many years since, coals and burnt chunks were found in a good state of preservation.[20] It was probably while still making his headquarters at this cave that he examined the fine country along Dick's River; and it is said, while [near] the forks of the Kentucky and Dick's rivers at a point somewhere about three-fourths of a mile above their junction, he unexpectedly found himself hemmed in by a party of Indians, leaving him the only alternative[s] of either surrendering himself into their hands or jumping down the precipitous heights of Dick's River to a second bank or bench below. Fearful to trust himself in the clutches of the Indians, he unhesitatingly made the leap and alighted, as he aimed, in the thick top of a small sugar maple, down which he slid to *terra firma,* and found himself comparatively unhurt some sixty feet below the elevation from which he had just taken his flight. We can well imagine how the astonished Indians, sure of the prey, witnessed this intrepid feat and peered over the cliff uttering an expressive *ugh!*—and perhaps pronouncing the solitary wanderer a charmed white man or some specter of the forest. But before his pursuers could pass around to a suitable place of descent, Boone had stolen off unseen beneath the overhanging bank and clustering trees and bushes, along the verge of the stream to its mouth, where he swam the Kentucky and happily eluded his enemies.[21]

Destitute of any further knowledge of events, which doubtless were almost of daily occurrence with our hunter during his sojourn at this sequestered retreat of Shawanoe Run or while exploring the surrounding country, silence alone seems befitting the faithful biographer, rather than too free an indulgence in vague, uncertain conjecture. At length, after various hair-breadth escapes, Boone safely returned to his old camp, which had not been disturbed in his absence. "I did not," says our cautious adventurer, "confine my lodging to it, but often reposed in thick cane-brakes, to avoid the savages, who, I believe often visited my camp, but fortunately for me, in my absence. In this situation, I was constantly exposed to danger and death. How unhappily such a situation for a man tormented with fear, which is vain if no danger comes, and if it does, only augments the pain. It was my happiness to be destitute of this afflicting passion, with which I had the greatest reason to be affected.

"The prowling wolves," continue Boone, "diverted my nocturnal hours with perpetual howlings, and the various species of animals in this vast forest, in the day time, were continually in my view. Thus I was surrounded with plenty in the midst of want. I was happy in the midst of dangers and inconveniences. In such a diversity it was impossible I should be disposed to melancholy. No populous city, with all its varied commerce and stately structures, could afford so much pleasure to my mind, as the beauties of nature I found here. Thus, through an uninterrupted scene of sylvan pleasure, I spent the time until the 27th day of July following, when my brother, to my great felicity, met me according to appointment at our old camp."[22]

How Squire Boone, with the proceeds of the furs he had taken to the Yadkin, had paid up the old debts contracted on his own and brother's account, procured new supplies, provided for the wants of their families, and now conveyed to Daniel the love and good wishes of his wife and children, with no material accident occurring by the way, was all soon told. Nor did the relation in the least lessen Daniel's felicity. Reserved as he naturally was, he now in turn no doubt unloosed his tongue a while, rehearsing his own adventures and discoveries, which were neither few in number nor wanting in interest.

Leaving their old camp shortly after, thinking it imprudent to linger there longer, there is reason to believe that they passed down the Kentucky River and selected a large cave near the mouth of Marble Creek, a small northern tributary of the Kentucky, in Jessamine County, where tradition relates that there Daniel Boone spent a couple of months, and then probably took up their abode in another cave near the mouth of Hickman Creek in the same county a few miles lower down the Kentucky. In this latter cave, the initials of Boone's name were for many years to be seen rudely carved on its rocky side with a date appended, but recently all, save the letter "D," have become obliterated by the lapse of time and dampness of the cavern. The one near Marble Creek, and that near Hickman, have each borne the name of Boone's Cave ever since that section of the country was settled. Near the latter is a noted elevation over three hundred feet high which for nearly seventy years past has been known as Boone's Knob. Situated immediately below the confluence of Hickman's Creek with the Kentucky, a striking and picturesque view of the diversified surrounding scenery is presented from its towering summit. Tradition also says that Boone spent a couple of weeks at this remarkable eminence engaged in fishing and hunting.[23]

In all their ramblings, the Boones seldom slept in their secluded and constantly changing camps. The forests among which they roamed furnished them daily food, and the blue-arched sky and expanded branches of the trees were most frequently their canopy by night. Constantly in danger, they as constantly were forced to be on their guard; but freedom to go where they pleased, the love of nature in all its magnificent wildness, the excitements attendant of their exposed situation, together with the unwearied pleasures of the chase appear to have fully repaid them for all their trials, toils, and vigilance. Once, returning to one of their cave-camps on the northern bank of the Kentucky, they discovered it had been visited during their absence, which at first somewhat alarmed them; their blankets, moccasins, leggings, and even camp-kettle were gone. Casting their weary eyes about for signs, they soon espied some wolf tracks and, trailing the plunderer, found their kettle well cleaned and the blankets torn to shreds, lining a comfortable bed beneath the root of an old up-turned tree in which was a litter of young whelps. The old thief was dispatched, and considerable pains were taken to tame the young brood, but without success; for, as Boone afterward declared, that after all his kind and patient efforts, they were wolves still.[24]

Winter was again approaching. It was needful that Squire Boone should once more pack in to the settlements the half-grained deer skins which he and his brother by their united industry had provided and obtain a new supply of ammunition and other necessaries. The long and tedious journey was at length effected by this faithful and energetic man, but not so soon, probably from autumnal rains and bad travelling, as was expected. As Squire Boone delayed beyond the allotted time for his return, Daniel became uneasy and started to meet his brother, determining if he failed to meet him, and uncertain as to his fate, to continue on home rather than remain alone the whole ensuing winter. On the way, Boone came across a lone aged Indian occupying a rude camp, who had apparently, perhaps in sickness, been abandoned and left to die as being too old to be of any further service to himself or others. Touched with his pitiable appearance and helpless situation, Boone went back half a mile, where he had killed a deer and appropriated only a small portion of it to his own use and carried the remainder to the old Indian, who, so far as looks and signs could express, evinced the sincerest gratitude for the kindness, when Boone left him to his fate. Pursuing on, Boone at length discovered at some distance ahead a large, dry tree on fire; and approaching it stealthily, lest he should unhappily encounter a party of Indians, he had the gratification to behold his brother there, who had stopped to kindle a fire by which to warm himself, for it was now early winter, probably December, with some snow on the ground. The meeting was mutually joyful.[25]

DRAPER'S NOTES: CHAPTER 7

1. J. R. Simms' *Trappers of New York,* 272.
2. Godman's *Natural History.*
3. J. R. Simms' *Trappers of New York,* 273, 277.
4. This account of the otter is made up from notes of conversations with Col. Nathan Boone; Dr. Hildreth's "Sketch of Isaac Williams," *American Pioneers,* 1: 348–49; and from Godman and Simms, as already cited.

5. MS. notes of conversations with Col. Nathan Boone; Simms' *Trappers of New York.*

6. Verbal statements of Col. Nathan Boone.

7. The venerable Joshua Pennington, a son of Stuart's widow by her second marriage, states that the remains of a saddle and bridle were also found in the trees and that Stuart's name was engraven in full upon them.

8. The particulars of Stuart's loss and the subsequent discovery of his remains are given from the oral statements of Daniel Boone to his children; Nathan Boone and lady; and also from the communications of Joshua and Daniel and Stuart Pennington, who derived the facts from their mother, who was Stuart's widow.

9. McClung states that this man was benighted on a hunting trip and, while encamped in the woods by himself, was attacked and devoured by wolves; and Peck declares with equal error that he was missing or lost in the wilderness and never heard of afterward, except that a decayed skeleton and some fragments of clothing were in after years found near a swamp, supposed to have been those of the unfortunate wanderer. We shall have occasion to speak again of Neely hereafter.

It is a curious anachronism of Simms that Neely returned to the settlements before Stuart's loss or death. And not less curious is the statement by the same accomplished author that the two Boones and Stuart were surprised by the fire of a party of Indians from a canebrake. "Stuart fell mortally wounded. The two Boones remained unhurt, but the Indians showing themselves numerously, with a shout, they were forced to precipitate flight, compelled from a distance to behold the savage as he stripped the fresh scalp from the bleeding skull of their comrade. These were only too well satisfied at being able to save their own." It seems almost a pity to spoil such precious bits of romance by the narration of unvarnished truth. Our beautiful writers are not always our most accurate historians.

10. Simms' "Sketch of Boone," *Southern Monthly Magazine,* April 1845.

11. MS. notes of conversation with Col. Nathan Boone.

12. Filson's *Kentucke,* original edition, 1784, pages 16, 21–24.

13. Imlay's *Western Topography,* 1st ed, London, 1792, 39, 40.

14. Perkins' "Pioneers of Kentucky," in *North American Review,* January 1846; Perkins' *Memoir and Writings,* ii:250. Conversations with Col. Nathan Boone.

15. Filson's *Kentucke,* 27, 32, 33.

16. Boone's Narrative, appended to Filson's *Kentucke,* 1784, 54, 55.

17. It is stated in Collins' *Historical Sketches of Kentucky* that there is no authentic account of Big Bone Lick having been visited by white men earlier than 1773, when James Douglas of Virginia visited it and found the ten acres constituting the lick bare of trees and herbage of every kind and large numbers of bones scattered upon the surface of the grounds; and that Dr. Goforth in 1803 made the first collection of these fossil remains. This statement needs correction. We have already mentioned the French visiting the lick in 1735 and finding "the skeletons of seven elephants"; Longueil's visit in 1739; and that in 1740 large quantities of the bones were taken to France. Three years afterward, Robert Smith and other

English traders visited the lick, as we learn from Christopher Gist's journal of his western mission and exploration of 1750–'51, and reported that some of the rib bones of three large animals found there were eleven feet long, a skull six feet across the forehead, and several teeth or "horns" five feet long, and one of which was as much as a man could carry; and Gist obtained from a trader a mammoth tooth weighing four pounds, which was presented to the Ohio Company. The French Academicians, Messrs. Buffon and D'Aubenton, wrote disquisitions on these Ohio fossil remains, which appeared in the eleventh and twelfth volumes of *Histoire Naturelle* and in the *Memoirs de l'Academe Roy des Sciences* for 1762. In 1765 George Croghan visited the lick and took away a tusk, as may be seen by his published journal of that year; and he again went there the following year, finding one of the buffalo roads leading to it from the Ohio wide enough for two wagons to go abreast; on which occasion he carried off a number of tusks and other remains and sent them to Lord Shelbourne and Dr. Franklin in London. Croghan's second visit and the mastodontoid remains he sent to England are noticed in the papers read before the Royal Society by Peter Collinson in 1767 and Dr. William Hunter in 1768, published in the transactions of that learned body as also in the *British Annual Register* for 1768 and 1769. Col. George Morgan of New Jersey, then engaged in the Indian trade, visited Big Bone Lick in 1766 and obtained nearly a complete skeleton with several jawbones in which the grinders were entire and several large tusks, one of which was six feet long; of which visit he gives some account, together with the Indian tradition respecting the mammoth, in a note appended to Morse's *American Geography,* 150, London, ed. 1794. In the same year, 1766, Capt. Henry Gordon descended the Ohio on his way to the Illinois and speaks of this lick in his journal annexed to Pownall's *Topography.* About this period, Dr. John Connolly also visited the lick; compare Burk's *Virginia,* iii:374 and Washington's *Diary of his Ohio Journey of 1770.* Of Boone's visit in 1770, we can give on the authority of his only surviving son, who derived the fact from his father. In 1773 the McAfee Company, with Capt. Thomas Bullitt, Hancock Taylor, and James Douglas, visited the lick; after which such visits became too common to deserve special notice.

18. In a manuscript paper on western antiquities, written by Gen. George Rogers Clark, occurs this remark, perhaps relating to the same remains which Boone saw: "The well in the ancient fortress at Louisville was filled up by Captain Patton, who made use of part of the old wall for that purpose." As Findlay is known to have visited the Falls, we have supposed it probable that he traded there in 1752, prior to going to Lulbegrud. Gist alludes in his Journal to a camp of French Indians at the Falls in 1751.

19. This adventure is stated on authority of Col. Nathan Boone and Isaiah Boone.

20. Gen. R. B. McAfee, in *Kentucky Yeoman,* September 18th, 1845; Collins' *Kentucky,* 452; Cramer's *Natural Wonders of North America,* St. Petersburg, 1837.

21   This tradition we heard from old settlers in the Dick's River region several years ago and since heard repeatedly by Isaiah Boone and Peter Wolf, of Indiana, and the late venerable Capt. Henry Wilson, of Bourbon County, Kentucky.

22.   Boone's Narrative in Filson's *Kentucke,* 1784, p. 55–56.

23.   The traditions of these caves and the Knob and the association of Boone's name with them have been handed down to us by William Hogan, an early Kentucky pioneer, John Woods, a venerable survivor of other days who knew both Boone and Hogan, and James Duncan, who settled in Kentucky about the year 1779 and was killed by the Indians in 1794. Samuel M. Duncan, a grandson of the latter, first visited these caves nearly fifteen years ago and states that the date in the one near Hickman's Creek was 1773, as does also the venerable Duke Hamilton, who had been acquainted with this cave from his boyhood. It is, therefore, quite probable that Boone occupied it both in 1770 and 1773. It was characteristic of him to cut either his name or its initials on trees or in caves, as was the case with the tree-memorial in East Tennessee where he killed a bear, and on the tree over the cave on Shawanoe Run; and we know that Boone in the summer and autumn of 1770 spent much time, either alone or with his brother, in this very region. We feel, therefore, pretty safe in venturing to assume that he occupied the two caves and visited the remarkable knob in the present county of Jessamine, Kentucky, which have borne his name for nearly three quarters of a century. To Samuel M. Duncan, Esq., of Nicholasville, Kentucky, are the authors indebted for the facts and traditions connected with those interesting localities and the view of Boone's Knob. While exploring the cave near Marble Creek in 1850, Mr. Duncan discovered, in a ledge near the mouth, about two pounds of lead, which, however, had lain so long exposed that it crumbled in pieces with a slight pressure between the thumb and fingers.

24.   MS. statement of the late Col. Boone Hays, eldest grandson of Daniel Boone, who learned the incident from his grandfather. Boone told another grandson, James, eldest son of Col. Nathan Boone, that on another occasion during his long Kentucky exploration, a passing wolf snatched up his hat where he had laid it for a few moments and made off with it, and Boone had to shoot the thief in order to recover the stolen article.

25.   Daniel Bryan, and Col. Nathan Boone and lady, are the authority for Squire Boone's second return alone to Carolina, the two latter relating the incident of the lone old Indian and the manner in which the Boones met on the way. Col. Daniel Boone gives us no details in his Narrative of this portion of his Kentucky adventures and slurs them over quite too rapidly to gratify curiosity or furnish desirable particulars for biography.

EDITOR'S NOTES: CHAPTER 7

a. In his Missouri years (1799–1820), Boone had an artificial pond dug near his home that he stocked with beaver and otter to keep as pets.

b. This is, of course, a lot of nineteenth-century "scientific" and culinary humbug.

c. More beaver balderdash. Beavers are instinctive creatures who fell trees randomly. Many times even the most industrious beaver cannot retrieve his chosen tree once it is severed from its trunk, as the falling tree may snag and hang on surrounding trees or limbs or in some other way fail to crash to earth with the precision Draper's "expert naturalist" so testifies. Alert eyes observing any bank bordering a well-populated beaver pond, creek, stream, or river will see that this is true.

d. Beaver musk—called "castors" in trapper slang and today known as castoreum—is exuded from a beaver's perineal scent glands and is used by these gregarious mammals to stake out territory in their watery abodes. Once thought to have medicinal value, castoreum makes deadly scent lure for beaver trapping, as well as for other trap sets, and is a base for many scent lures. To prepare, one cuts the pair of castors from between a dead beaver's hind legs to use the musk as is, or one dries the musk glands and grinds them up, mixing the aromatic, sweet-smelling brown powder with spices such as cinnamon, nutmeg, and cloves or with musk glands from other species of mammals. (Most trappers have their own time-honored "secret formulas.") Today, beaver trappers still collect and prepare castors to sell.

e. This figure does not agree with that in Draper's earlier account. See chapter 6, note g.

f. In the Ohio Valley and Cumberland watershed, native and white hunters cut and peeled wide sheets of green elm bark off trees to make bark canoes. The skill must have been common; most hunters, surprisingly, could build such a craft in less than a day, and often in just two or three hours.

g. There seems to have been no middle ground on roast beaver tail—frontier folks either gagged on the thick, whitish flaps of pungent steamed fat and gristle or devoured them with gusto. Hard-working market hunters enduring winter's cold needed the high caloric energy a daily dose of fat brings, and beaver tail certainly supplied that. Kentucky meat getter Hugh F. Bell relished the greasy things, and during his interview with Draper in the 1840s, he told how to cook them: "Take a large beaver tail, some 8 inches long and 4 broad, well-seasoned, and wrapped up in a coat of wetted oak leaves, and put into a bed of oak leaves and covered up overnight, would be elegantly cooked by morning."

Much better than eating a beaver's tail is the carcass. Draper's comments aside, a well-cleaned kit beaver of ten to fifteen pounds roasted whole in a big, deep pan with carrots, potatoes, and onions, topped with bacon strips, and basted in its own juice tastes like the tenderest of fine pork.

h. John Filson's soliloquy, supposedly via the mouth of Boone, shows the woodsman's amanuensis's perpetuating Rousseau's "Noble Savage."

Here and in many other passages, it is plain that Draper embraced Filson's portrayal of Boone as a "providential tool in the wilderness." And in Boone's own reflections as he began to number his days, he tended to define himself in this way too.

Boone's views on man—"I firmly believe it takes but a little philosophy to make a man happy in whatever state fortune may place him."—are vaguely reminiscent of Apostle Paul's words in Philippians 4:11: "I have learned, in whatsoever state I am, therewith to be content."

i.   Derived from Ezekiel 2:6: "And thou, son of man, be not afraid of them, neither be afraid of their words, though briers and thorns be with thee. . . . "

j.   Dick's River is a forty-five-mile-long branch of the Kentucky that flows through Lincoln, Boyle, Garrard, and Mercer counties. Cartographers have misspelled the river's name as "Dix" since about 1920.

k.   After serving a stint in New Jersey's Revolutionary Army, Gilbert Imlay (1754?–1828?) came to Kentucky in 1783 to speculate in land. Within two or three years, he attempted to purchase one tract from Boone and speculated on numerous other grants totaling more than 28,000 acres, but he was never able to make good his notes. Word got out, and a posse scoured the country for Imlay, but the glib talker fled to Virginia. In the early 1790s, he wrote *A Topographical Description of the Western Territory of North America* and a novel, *The Emigrants.* His books praised Kentucky in implausible purplish prose rivaling Filson's *Kentucke,* but the works sparked new waves of migration to the commonwealth.

In December 1786 Imlay wrote Boone claiming to be unable to pay his debt. In truth, Imlay had sold his claim to one of America's more intriguing rascals, James Wilkinson, who in turn sold it as a valued tract "located and surveyed by Col. Dan Boone." For whatever reason—was his conscience at work?—when a London house in 1793 released a second edition of *A Topographical Description,* Imlay added as an appendix John Filson's Boone Narrative.

In about 1794 Imlay's lover, author Mary Wollstonecraft, bore their daughter, Fanny, who in 1816 committed suicide. By 1796, after Imlay had abandoned Wollstonecraft, he vanishes from history. Some accounts say he died in 1828.

l.   Rich salt veins underneath Kentucky's sandstone base once resulted in an array of "salt licks"—broad spreads of salt-laden soil surrounding springs—that drew herds even in the prehistoric day of the great mammals. Besides its medicinal uses, settlers used salt as a preservative. Kentucky's major cities—Louisville, Frankfort, and Lexington—owe their origin in part to the availability of this precious commodity. Little wonder Boone and his men risked their lives to render salt in the winter of 1778. A lively commerce developed along the Salt River in Bullitt County, near Shepherdsville, and in other productive licks. By 1850 salt-making was a state industry, producing 246,500 bushels worth $57,825. A decade later, competition from Virginia and Ohio helped end Kentucky's salt trade.

m.   East of the Mississippi between the sixteenth and seventeenth centuries, buffalo paths, or traces, began to merge with extant Indian paths and mammal trails. The buffalo followed the same paths but widened and deepened them; a part of a buffalo trace surviving in Shelbyville measures about thirty feet across and three feet deep. "Lead traces" were major thoroughfares linking other traces, salt licks, canebrakes, and waterways; Indians and settlers used lead traces as a network of roadways. Portions of Kentucky's highways, secondary roads, and railroads follow the old buffalo traces.

   n.   In June 1775 Virginia surveyors Capt. Hancock Taylor and his cousin Willis Lee established Leestown, which by the mid-1800s merged with Frankfort. Leestown was actually down the river from Kentucky's capital.

   o.   According to my interview with Kentucky historian and writer Neal O. Hammon: "This so-called cave is a wide rock overhang and spring in a sink hole. The 'cave' faces south, thus it receives sun all day in the winter. As it is not noticeable from a distance, it would make a good, safe camping place."

CHAPTER 8

Explorations of the Taylors.—Of Stone and Others.—McColloch.—
Cleveland.—The Long Hunters.—The Boones Explore the Green River
Country.—Incidents.—Start for North Carolina.—Neely Gets Lost.—The
Boones Robbed by Indians.—Frontier Retaliation.—The Boones Arrive
Home.—Sketches of the Long Hunters.

A little digression from the main thread of our narrative now seems necessary. While the Boones and their companions were roaming through Kentucky during 1769–'70, other adventurers were not idle. In the spring of 1769 Hancock[a] and Richard Taylor,[b] accompanied by Abraham Hempinstall[c] and a person named Barbour, started from their residence in Orange County, Virginia, on an exploration of the country bordering on the Ohio and Mississippi rivers. From Pittsburgh they descended the river in a boat, stopping frequently to examine the country and procure game for their subsistence. On reaching the Mississippi, they ascended it to Fort Chartres,[d] then occupied by British troops; and after remaining there a few days, they descended the river to the Arkansas and went up that stream something like a hundred miles, a short distance above the ancient settlement called "The Post," where they encamped and hunted during the winter of 1769–'70.

In the ensuing spring Richard Taylor and Barbour, at the insistence of Hancock Taylor, separated from the others and, in company with an Indian trader whom they met on the Arkansas, passed from the mouth of the Yazoo through the Chickasaw, Choctaw, and Creek nations of Indians to Georgia, examining the country of east and west Florida, in which homes were then offered by government on liberal terms to attract settlers. From Georgia they passed northwardly to their home in Virginia. Hancock Taylor and Hempinstall descended the Mississippi to Natchez and New Orleans, thence to sail for New York. Finding no vessel up for that port, they passed up the Mississippi to Red River, which they ascended to the mouth of the Washita and up that stream some distance, where they finally encamped and hunted during the winter of 1770–'71. In the following spring they returned to New Orleans, sailed for New York, and thence proceeded to Virginia. Of all the regions explored by the Taylor party, they were decidedly best pleased with Kentucky.[1]

In the month of June 1769 a party of twenty or more adventurers was formed in the New River region for the purpose of hunting and exploring the western country. As Uriah Stone was one of the party who in 1766–'67 had penetrated through Kentucky and along the Cumberland Valley in company with Col. James Smith and others, it was unquestionably his glowing accounts of that region that gave rise to this expedition, with the assurance of his knowledge and experience as a pilot. Of this company were Casper Mansker, John Rains, Abraham Bledsoe, Isaac Bledsoe, John Baker, Joseph Drake, Obadiah Terrill, Robert Crockett, Henry Smith, Thomas Gordon, Humphrey Hogan, Castleton Brooks, Ned Cowan, and others. They started from Reedy Creek of New River, about eight miles below old Fort Chiswell, each of the party being equipped with horses, ammunition, and other necessaries for the adventure. [They passed] down Holston Valley, through Moccasin Gap and into Powell's Valley, and thence through Cumberland Gap to Cumberland River, down which they continued their journey to what has since been known as Price's Meadow or settlement, in the present county of Wayne, Kentucky.

Here, in a beautiful open country and near an excellent spring, they made their camp, which was designed as a place of general deposit for their skins and furs, agreeing to disperse in different companies and return to the main camp every five weeks with the fruits of the chase. Some of these parties directing their course to the south-west came to Obey's River, a southern tributary of Cumberland, which they so named after Obadiah Terrill, whose name "Obey's Mill" was found in after years cut upon a tree on the bank of that stream, and Robert Crockett, when returning to a temporary camp near the headwaters of Roaring River, was waylaid by a party of seven or eight Cherokee warriors on their way to war against the Shawanoes, and [they] left his body in the war-trace. Continuing down the southern side of the Cumberland, some of these hunting parties reached the Caney Fork. A few miles south of Roaring River, and between that stream and Caney Fork of the Cumberland in Flinn's Creek, in what is now Jackson County, Tennessee, a mile east of which on the road from that creek to Gainesboro is yet standing a large beech tree on which is cut, in ancient legible letters of over two inches in height, this inscription: *"Willia Wey, September 24th, 1769."*[2]

Leaving the main camp, our hunter-band at length appear to have crossed to the northern side of Cumberland and bent their course in a western direction until they struck Big Barren and thence up Drake's Creek to its head. The whole party then passed over the ridge dividing the waters of Barren and Cumberland, and travelled down Station Camp Creek within three miles of its junction with the river, when they came to a very plain buffalo path there crossing the stream. At this crossing place, they pitched their camp on a beautiful ridge making down from a pretty high bluff to the creek on its western bank and near a fine flowing spring. The locality of this camp was south of the main turnpike road leading from Nashville to Gallatin, and within the present county of Sumner, Tennessee. This circumstance originated the name of Station Camp Creek, which it has since retained.

Having camped the first night, Bledsoe and Mansker, concluding that so large a buffalo road as passed their camp must lead to important salt licks or sulfur springs, made an agreement that each should mount a horse next morning, and the one take a north-easterly and the other a south-westerly direction, going as far as they could that day and returning in the evening to report their discoveries. Bledsoe pursuing the well-beaten road about thirteen miles came to a large lick; and Mansker going about twelve miles the other way also discovered an important lick. Both returned in the evening with the intelligence, imparting great joy to their companions, when the names of the respective discoverers were bestowed upon Bledsoe's and Mansker's licks and the creeks flowing by them.

When Bledsoe came within about two miles of the lick he discovered, he experienced some difficulty in riding along the path, so crowded was it and on either side with buffalo; and when he reached the bank of the creek at the lick, he found the entire flat surrounding the lick of about one hundred acres covered with a moving mass of buffalo, which he not only estimated by hundreds but thousands. The space containing the sulfur springs was about two hundred yards across in which the buffalo and other animals had licked up the dirt to the depth of several feet, and within that area there issued from the earth about a dozen sulfur springs. So great was the crowd of animals in around the lick that Bledsoe was afraid to dismount lest he should be run over by them; and as he sat upon his horse, gazing at the scene before him, he shot down two deer in the lick, which, however, the buffalo so trampled in the mud that he could not skin them. These huge animals did not exhibit any signs of fear of Bledsoe or his horse, but when the wind blew from him towards them and they received the scent, they would dash wildly away in large droves and disappear.

Our adventurers now engaged in hunting and exploring the country, bestowing names on Drake's and other creeks flowing into the Cumberland on the north, and also on Drake's Pond and Drake's Lick. In the absence of the hunters, twenty-five Cherokees found the camp and carried off or destroyed about five hundred deer skins, some clothing, ammunition, pots, and kettles. Though the Indians made a plain trail in approaching, they so studiously avoided it in their departure, probably scattering or wading up the creek, that when the hunters returned and attempted to pursue them, they had soon to abandon all hopes of either recovering their property or chastising the insolent offenders. With but little ammunition left, and robbed of everything at their camp, the hunters knew full well that their hunting expedition would be broken up unless a reasonable supply of powder and lead could be obtained. In this emergency, Isaac Bledsoe and two others agreed to return to the settlements for the needed supply, leaving their friends, meanwhile, to use sparingly what little they had remaining for the purpose alone of procuring subsistence. In due time Bledsoe and his companions returned, when their hunt was renewed and completed.[3]

On the 6th day of April, 1770, half or more of the party returned to the settlements, while Stone, Mansker, Baker, Gordon, Hogan, Brooks, and four others built two boats, two trapping canoes, loaded them, together with a deserted boat they found, with furs and bear meat, and descended the Cumberland. Discovering at the French Lick, where Nashville is now located, an immense herd of buf-

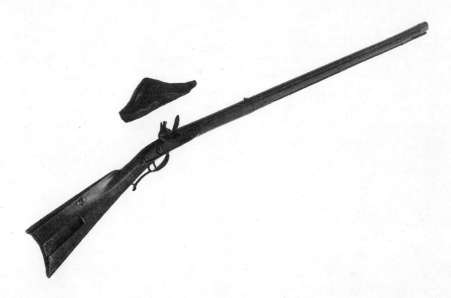

41. American long rifle, c. 1770s, once in the McAfee family of Kentucky. It features a curly maple full stock, brass nose-cap, front and rear sights, sliding patch box (lid missing), and two brass tacks hammered into the stock. Above the flintlock is a leather lock cover. FROM THE COLLECTION OF JIM AND CAROLYN DRESSLAR.

falo and other animals, they killed several buffaloes for their hides, with which to cover their boats. Reaching the mouth of Cumberland and finding their bear meat likely to spoil, they rendered it into oil and poured it into the lightest boat for market. And here also another misfortune befell them, in being robbed of two guns, some ammunition, salt, and tobacco by Piomingo, or the Mountain Leader, John Brown, and twenty-five Chickasaws on their way to war against the Senecas. The guns were the heaviest loss, for they soon replaced the other articles from some French boats they met and procured beside some taffia, a cheap kind of rum, which particularly proved most acceptable to the abstemious woodfarers. Descending the Mississippi to the Spanish Natchez, they disposed of their cargo, and most of them returned home. Mansker, however, was detained there awhile by sickness and then went with Baker to Ozark, where they met one Fairchild, a drover, with whom they passed through the southern Indian tribes to Georgia and thence back to New River, which they probably reached in the summer or early autumn.[4]

Maj. John McColloch, Sr., a native of New Jersey, but long a resident on the south bank of the Potomac, left his residence in or about 1769, accompanied by a white servant man and a Negro, and proceeded over the mountains to Pittsburgh, where, procuring a canoe, he descended the Ohio, viewing the country as he passed, which was the object of his journey. When on shore near the mouth of the Wabash, all were captured by Indians and separated. McColloch was conveyed up the Wabash to the present locality of Terre Haute and there detained in captivity four or five months, when he was given his liberty and directed to leave the country. Going to Vincennes, he took passage with some French voyageurs in a pirogue to Natchez and thence to New Orleans. There taking ship, he was during the voyage cast away on the island of Bermuda, where he remained several months before he obtained a passage for Philadelphia and at length reached the South Branch. Major McColloch subsequently settled on Short Creek above Wheeling, where his sons became famous for their exploits in the early settlement of that border region.[5]

Among the primitive settlers on the Yadkin, of a much later emigration, however, than the Boones and Bryans, was Benjamin Cleveland from Virginia. He was one of that hardy race reared on the frontiers of Orange County in that province who had grown to manhood familiar with the woods and rifle. Learning, probably, from Boone himself or some of his associates the existence of the Kentucky country, he resolved on making it a visit. He accordingly set out from the Yadkin in the summer of about 1772, in company with Jesse Bond, Edward Rice, and William Hightower, on a trip of hunting and exploration. When they had safely passed Cumberland Gap and entered upon the hunting grounds of Kentucky with bright prospects in advance, they were unexpectedly met and plundered by a party of Cherokees of all their guns, horses, peltry, and everything they possessed. A poor old shot-gun[e] was given them in turn, with a couple of charges of powder and shot, when they were ordered to leave the Indian hunting grounds. Their situation left them no alternative. On their way home, they killed a small deer with one of the husbanded charges, and this scanty supply was husbanded as long as possible; the other charge was spent ineffectually. They had the good fortune to catch a broken-winged wild goose and eventually had to kill their faithful little hunting dog for food, subsisting the whole while partly on berries, and finally, when well nigh famished, they reached the settlements.[6]

During the period of 1769–'70, settlements rapidly followed explorations in the upper Ohio Valley, and Washington again descended the Ohio as far as the Kenhawa to examine lands he had located in that region; and in his journal of the trip, he shows something of the growing impatience of the western Indians at the gradual encroachments of the whites on the lands south of the Ohio. But another band of adventurers, better known in border history as the *Long Hunters,* must now claim our special attention. Their long visit to Kentucky, hitherto so little known, shall be narrated with considerable minuteness as well on account of the prominence of that early event in the historical landmarks of Kentucky, as well as the interest inseparably connected with an enterprise so bold and perilous.

Tempted by the favorable reports of such men as Stone, Mansker, Rains, Drake, Bledsoe, Terrill, and other well-known woodsmen of the New River frontier, about fifty stout hunters, fired with a spirit of enterprise and prompted by an unconquerable love for a wilderness life, associated together for the purpose of hunting and trapping beyond the Cumberland Mountain. Some of the most noted and successful hunters of the New River and Holston country joined in this spirited undertaking, and Joseph Drake and Henry Skaggs, two of the oldest men and most experienced in wood-craft, were chosen leaders.[7] Equipped with three pack-horses for each man, rifles, ammunition, traps, dogs, blankets, and salt, dressed in hunting shirts, leggings and moccasins, they took their leave of friends and kindred early in the autumn of 1770, and pushing their way through the well-known gap in the mountain, they entered the Dark and Bloody Ground—"not doubting," adds Marshall, "that they were to be encountered by Indians and to subsist on game."

On an upper branch of Laurel River, within the limits of the present county of Laurel, Kentucky, and which they in consequence named Station Camp Creek, they erected their camp and hunted awhile. The stream is now known as

The Upper Ohio, Holston & Yadkin Rivers c. 1775

42. MAP BY NEAL O. HAMMON.

Robertson's Creek.[8] Continuing their course northwestwardly, some of the party pursued a buffalo to the mouth of Skaggs' Creek of Rockcastle and gave to the stream the name of one of their worthy leaders. While hunting on that stream, Charles Skaggs was one day busily engaged in skinning a deer when he unexpectedly discovered an Indian standing over him, and perceiving that one of his wrists was peculiarly crooked at the joint from some former injury, and remembering to have heard from James Knox or someone else that such was the fact with reference to the noted Cherokee hunter Captain Dick, he instantly arose and saluted him by name. The old Indian was evidently pleased to be recognized, and a friendly conversation ensued, Dick being able to speak some broken English. Learning that hunting was the chief object the whites had in view, he directed them to pass on northwestwardly over three ridges, and they would reach a fine river running towards the north, where was abundance of cane, and there they would fine game, particularly bear, in great plenty. He, however, cautioned the whites to be wary of Shawanoe war-parties who were then carrying on an irregular warfare against the Cherokees. Thus was Dick's River found and named in honor of the famous Cherokee hunter, who had a hunting camp on the stream and had often successfully followed the chase in that region. Drake's Creek, one of the northeastern tributaries of Dick's River, commemorates the name of one of the leaders of the Long Hunters.[9]

The Knob Licks were discovered by James Dysart and one of his comrades of the party, a few miles south of Dick's River, in the present county of Lincoln, a

43. In 1823 this illustration of Nathaniel Bumppo and his comrades appeared in James Fenimore Cooper's The Pioneers. *Cooper's best-selling "Leather-Stocking Tales" owed much to the deeds of Daniel Boone and his fellow long hunters.* DRAWING BY F. O. C. DARLEY, PUBLISHED BY H. C. CAREY & I. LEA.

noted locality, not producing salt water but simply a soft clay slate formation among the Knobs or detached hills, with the soil strongly impregnated with particles of salt and so eaten away as to present a singular basin of several acres in extent. While hunting, these two men came across a large buffalo path that appeared to be much used, and pursuing which a few miles, they were led to this celebrated place of resort for the tenants of the wilderness. Reaching the summit of one of the Knobs overlooking the Lick, some of which attained an altitude of two hundred feet, they beheld what they estimated at largely over a thousand animals, including buffalo, elk, bear, and deer, with many wild turkies scattered among them, all quite restless, some playing, and others busily employed in licking the earth; but at length they took fright and bounded away all in one direction, so that in the brief space of a couple of minutes, not an animal was to be seen. The hunters now entered the Lick and found that the buffalo and other animals had so eaten away the soil that they could in places go entirely underground.

At another time, Dysart was hunting alone when, coming to where a double or forked tree had fallen in opposite directions, leaving a passage between the sundered trunk and roots sufficiently large for an ordinary trail, he attempted to pass through; but just as he entered the narrow defile, he suddenly encountered a large bear. The bruin seemed determined not to turn his back upon his foe and, instantly raising himself upon his hind feet, seized hold of the breast of Dysart's coat. Dysart, possessing great muscular strength, made a violent push against the animal, when the coat gave way and the bear fell hurriedly backwards eight or ten feet; and recovering himself, he stood for a moment surlily eying the young hunter who had just handled him so roughly, which gave Dysart barely time to raise his rifle, at the crack of which the huge bear bit the dust and the lone hunter was happily relieved from his perilous situation.[10]

Our bold hunters did not long tarry in the region of Dick's River and the Knob Licks. Drake and Skaggs leading the way, the others followed, driving their team of pack-horses before them and directing their course southwestwardly to the heads of Green River, down which they pursued till they reached a beautiful stream on the south side called the Skin House branch of Caney Fork of Russell's Creek, which flows into Green River. This Skin House branch is about three miles in length, formed by ten or a dozen pure limestone springs, and glid[ing] through a charming valley then covered with sugar maple, beech, walnut, ash, and other timber, with a thick undergrowth of luxuriant cane. On this little crystal stream near the present village of Haskinsville, in Green County, the Long Hunters erected their Station Camp in the midst of a fine hunting region rich in mast for bear and turkies and plentifully supplied with cane and wild grasses for deer, elk, and buffalo.[11]

Success attended their industrious efforts, and a large number of deer skins were brought in to the Station Camp, the hunters being divided, as usual, into squads or parties who returned to camp at a given time with their skins and to learn each other's welfare and whatever discoveries of interest may have been made. But an apple of discord was now unhappily thrown among our adventurers. A

44. A hunter's camp in the lower Mississippi Valley, c. 1820. 1) lean-to; 2) blue stroud baby cradle; 3) log for pounding corn; 4) hid rack. Near the shelter's rear is a beaming log to dehair hides. The hunter is wearing a blue cloth turban and black breechcloth. BY FLEURY GENERALLY, LOUISIANA COLLECTION, TULANE UNIVERSITY LIBRARY, NEW ORLEANS.

jealousy is said to have arisen in the breast of Charles Ewing on account of the superior success of Henry Skaggs in the chase, which finally led to a separation, and Ewing either had the influence to lead off twenty-four or twenty-five of the party or they had become weary of the wilderness. There is also some reason to suppose that these separatists had well nigh extended their ammunition and had perhaps secured as many skins as they could well pack home on their horses. At all events, Ewing and his followers returned in safety to the settlements in Virginia.[12]

Among this band of adventurers was an old man of the name of Russell, who, probably before Ewing's departure, got lost on the main creek and was missing nineteen days in very cold weather before he was found by his companions. He was so dim-sighted that he was obliged to tie a piece of white paper to the muzzle of his gun to direct his sight at the game and thus killed a number of deer; and it was in consequence of the dim-sightedness that he got lost. When found, he was helpless and quite speechless, and so continued three or four days, but being kindly nursed by his comrades, he recovered and killed a number of deer afterwards. This circumstance gave name to Russell's Creek, on which the old hunter so long wandered and came so near losing his life.[13]

After Ewing's party had departed, fourteen of the original number yet remained. They were still successful and finally, in February 1771, concluded they had secured as much peltry as they were able to take home, and more than that would be a waste both of time and ammunition and a wanton destruction of game.[f] With some buffalo-skin tugs, they baled their skins into packs of suitable size. It was now suggested that some of the party should remain to keep camp, while the others should go out for the purpose of devoting a few weeks to a more thorough and extensive exploration of the country toward the north, east, and west, of which from the highest knobs and hills they had obtained some imperfect but favorable glimpses. Under this arrangement, Isaac Bledsoe, William Lynch, William Allen, Christopher Stoph, and David Hughes remained at camp, while Henry, Charles and Richard Skaggs, James Knox, James Dysart, Casper Mansker, William Miller, and two others started on their exploration, taking the most of their horses and ammunition with them and leaving their skins deposit in the skin-house and the remainder of their horses to range in the cane. They did not all keep together but seem to have formed themselves into three parties, one going north as far as the Ohio, another east and north to the Kentucky, and the third south and west, examining the barren country[g] down Green River.

At the designated day all returned. To their great sorrow and mortification, they found the camp robbed and destroyed and their comrades gone. Lynch had been taken sick with the shingles, an eruptive disease, and Bledsoe had gone in with him to the settlements; the other three had been discovered by a straggling party of Indians, probably composed of desperadoes of some northern and southern tribes headed by Will Emery, a half-breed Cherokee, and Stoph and Allen [were] captured, who were never heard of afterwards, while Hughes escaped towards the settlements.[14] Plundering the camp of such peltry, furs, and other articles as they chose, and stripping the skin-house of the bark covering, these marauders left the remaining portion of the skins to spoil by exposure to the weather. The horses had fortunately not been discovered by the Indians and, left to themselves, had rambled off and were traced twenty miles distant to a lick, where they were recovered. The dogs were found at the camp but quite wild; in a few days, however, they were as well-tutored as ever. Upon a large, spreading beech tree beside the camp, they rudely carved in the bark, *"Fifteen hundred skins gone to ruination,"* with the initials of the hunters' names appended.[15]

Regrets, if indulged, would have proved unavailing. Like men accustomed to meeting manfully the accidents of life, they held a consultation as to what, under the new aspect of things, was their best course of procedure. They were unanimous in the determination that if upon examination their ammunition should be found sufficient, to renew their hunt. By making an equal division, their ammunition was found ample for the purpose, and they recommenced their labors in great good earnest, resolving to do their very best; and thus, in due time they collected as much furs and peltry as they could convey home.[16]

The Boone brothers, after their reunion, probably returned and trapped awhile on the Kentucky. Discovering at length other signs than those of beaver and otter, they deemed it unsafe to remain there longer and proceeded to reconnoiter the country along the Green and Cumberland rivers. During the winter of 1770–71, when Mansker and some of his companions of the Long Hunters were engaged in hunting on the Green River, they one day towards evening heard a singular noise some distance from them. Mansker, brave and thoroughly experienced in wood-craft, bid the others remain quiet but ready to go to his relief should occasion require it, while he stole carefully from tree to tree, until finally approaching sufficiently near, he beheld, with mingled surprise and amusement, a man bare-headed, stretched flat upon his back on a deer skin spread on the ground singing merrily at the top of his voice! It was Daniel Boone. He had just pitched his camp for night and, probably awaiting his brother's appearance, was amusing himself with a song, for which he cherished a natural love with woodsmen generally; for with spirited songs of love and patriotism, interspersed with border narratives, Indian forays, and hunting adventures, would they while away many an evening before their cheerful campfires.[17]

Accompanying Mansker and his companions to their camp, the Boones spent some time with them. Returning to camp one evening, Daniel Boone and the others found that the two hunters left for camp-keepers that day had fallen into a belligerent mood and battered and bloodied each other at a shocking rate. Boone asked them what in the world two companions alone in the woods could possibly find to quarrel about. It provoked no small amusement at the expense of the pugilists when they related that their bloody game at fisticuffs had its origin in a trifling dispute respecting the natural history of the wood-tick, a pestilent little insect common in the wilds of the south and west.[18]

Some considerable time was now spent in hunting and trapping, reconnoitering the country, and giving names to the streams. Gasper's River, Drake's and Skaggs' creeks, all pouring their tributary waters into the Big Barren, were named in honor of three of the Long Hunters, and probably also Drake's Creek, still further west, flowing into Pond River. They at length crossed over the ridge and pursued down Bledsoe's Creek within four or five miles of the Lick, when the cane became so thick in the woods that they concluded they must have mistaken the place until coming to the Lick and discovering the cause. A party of French hunters from the Illinois country had been there, slaughtered the buffaloes simply for their tongues and tallow, loaded a keel boat which lay at the mouth of Bledsoe's Creek, and descended the Cumberland.[h] "Bledsoe told me," says General Hall, "that one could walk for several hundred yards in and around the lick on buffalo skulls and bones, with which the whole flat around the lick was bleached." This great slaughter of buffaloes sufficiently explained the sudden growth of cane within a few miles of the lick.[19]

Daniel Boone and his brother left the Cumberland Valley in March 1771 and, with horses laden with furs, set their faces homeward. On the ordinary occurrences of such a journey through a howling, inhospitable wilderness, it is not necessary to dwell. Reaching Powell's Valley perhaps in May, and tarrying to obtain a supply of meat, Squire Boone went out alone on horseback, as hunters often go, and espied at a distance a singular appearing being. Approaching him with caution, Boone soon recognized in him his old friend Alexander Neely. But how changed, how haggard his appearance! His simple story explained it all. He had come out with a party of hunters who camping in Powell's Valley, near Cumberland Gap, to hunt awhile, he had strayed off and got lost, and in his alarm had imprudently fired away all his powder, vainly hoping the report might reach the ears and attract the attention of his companions. He rambled about several days endeavoring to find the camp, but being a poor woodsman and half-bewildered, he did not succeed in his wishes. Failing in this, he next attempted to make his way back to the inhabited parts of the country and wandered, he knew not whither, for many a day without food or ammunition to obtain it, weary, clothes badly torn, limbs lacerated, and in a state of starvation bordering on despair.

While sitting down on a log to rest himself one day in this almost hopeless condition, a fat dog of ordinary size, probably belonging to some Indian hunter, ran up and jumped upon him as if glad to meet a human being. The cravings of hunger were too acute to admit of a moment's hesitation or to listen to the least whisperings of qualms either of the stomach or conscience, so he seized the devoted dog by the neck with one hand and drew his butcher knife from its sheath with the other and quickly cut the poor animal's throat, skinned the carcass, struck fire with the flint of his gun lock, roasted some of the meat, and feasted on it with the keenest relish. Jerking and packing the rest of his dog meat in his knapsack made of the dog skin, he trudged along with new hopes and brighter anticipations.

Thus hopeful, he unexpectedly met a few days after his old comrade Squire Boone. Neely inquired of Boone what he was doing in the wilderness and learned of his and his brother's camp, to which he desired to be taken. Boone was very willing to pilot him there, share freely with him all his hospitalities, and bestow upon him every possible attention upon a single condition. The poor lost hunter, ready to comply with any terms his old friend might see proper to exact, was now informed that he must pledge his honor to be contented with such small quantities of food at a time and at such intervening periods as the Boones should think prudent to give him. A too free indulgence at first of savory food in his weak condition might prove very injurious to him. To all this he readily agreed. "Then," said Neely, "I may as well throw away my dog meat." As he cast it upon the ground, Boone observed that both the meat and dog skin sack were not only fly-blown but quite alive with maggots. Mounting Neely upon his horse, Boone took him to camp, where he and his brother fed and nursed him with every possible care and cleansed and repaired his raiment. Through greatly debilitated, he soon sufficiently recovered to prosecute his journey. It is believed that he belonged to a party of adventurers under Isaac Bledsoe and had wandered from them while on their way with supplies for the Long Hunters; that they spent some time unavailingly in searching for him; and that the Boones were able so to direct him that he soon overtook his companions. For this kindness on their part, Neely ever felt deeply grateful to the Boones and urged them to visit him at his home on New River, which Squire Boone particularly failed not to do on several occasions.[20]

Bledsoe, Neely, and their companions meeting the Long Hunters on Big Barren River, Mansker and four or five others joined them, returned to the Cumberland Valley, and continued to hunt there several months. Among this band of Nimrods was John Montgomery. Having hunted awhile around Station Camp Creek and the neighboring licks, he concluded he would like to go alone and visit the French Lick region and informed his companions as he started not to be alarmed on his account should he be a week or two absent. He loitered around French Lick a day or so, and then went to what was afterwards called Robertson's Lick on Richland Creek, five miles west of the present city of Nashville. His object was not game but to view the country. Entering a thicket adjoining the lick, he lay down to take a nap and soon dreamed that if he did not take care, the Indians would kill him. So vivid was the dream that it alarmed and awakened him. While thinking of it, a gun was fired not apparently a hundred yards from him, and in a few moments a stricken deer came dashing through the bushes and fell dead almost at his feet. Knowing that Indians were close upon him, he hesitated whether to way-lay the fallen deer or retreat further into the thicket; but upon a moment's reflection he concluded that he had better quietly withdraw; for, should he wound or kill an Indian, he feared it would at least fill the minds of his hunting companions with apprehensions of retaliation, or even break up their hunting expedition with the loss of some of the party. Acting upon this discreet conclusion, he crept carefully away and returned to the Station Camp. It only remains in this connection to add that Knox, Dysart, and the most of the Long Hunters returned home about August 1771, well ladened with furs and peltry after an absence of eleven months. The party consisting of Bledsoe, Neely, Montgomery, and others appear[s] to have remained some considerable time longer, when they also returned to the New River settlements.[21]

Misfortunes were still in store for the Boones. The Great *Warrior's Road* leading through Kentucky and a portion of Powell's Valley was too frequently travelled by war parties both of the northern and southern Indians, who almost continually kept up an irregular warfare against each other, the Iroquois in antagonism with the Cherokees and Catawbas, and the Shawanoes and Delawares with the Cherokees, while the Chickasaws waged hostilities against the French of Illinois and their Indian allies. Under these circumstances, the Boones were met by a party of six or eight northern Indians near Cumberland Gap in Powell's Valley. Our returning hunters at the time were encamped and engaged in roasting some meat. The Indians at first assumed an air of friendship and shared the generous hospitality of the white strangers.

The next thing in order, as usual, was a proposal on the part of the Indians to swap guns—worthless ones, of course, offered in even exchange for good rifles, which the Boones refusing, they were taken by force, as well as their furs and horses. A small Indian then approaching Squire Boone demanded his shot-pouch, with which the owner showing no disposition to part, the Indian seized hold of the strap by which the pouch was suspended around Boone's neck, when quite a lively scuffle ensued, and Boone at length gave his nimble antagonist a violent whirl which sent him flying some distance, but with the Indian went also the strap, to which the fellow clinging firmly, it had broken by the propelling force that he had received from the powerful muscular exertion of the white hunter. So, after all, Squire Boone, though gaining the victory, lost his shot-pouch. His brother Daniel too had meanwhile been busy in some such similar manner; and so far as the spoils of war were concerned, both had come off only second best, the odds being too greatly against them. A large Indian now stepped up, shaking his tomahawk threateningly over their heads, and motioned to them to be off, probably not wishing the whites to witness the course of his own and companions departure. Disarmed and unable to cope with so large a party, the Boones went a few hundred yards, dodged behind a log, and watched the Indians till they left.

Now "forced to fly for their lives," as Daniel Boone expressed it, they hastened to the nearest frontier settlements, where a band of sympathizing borderers was quickly raised, equipped, and in pursuit. Passing a few miles beyond the camp where the robbery took place, a deer happened temptingly to cross the trail, when one of the whites shot it. This raised quite an angry contention, the most of the party severely reprimanding the incautious fellow for an act so highly imprudent, and especially as it had been discovered by the sign that the Indians who had plundered the Boones had been joined after that transaction by other squads of Indians who had been doing mischief along the frontiers, as well probably as annoying the Cherokees. The upshot of the matter was that the whole party returned to the settlements in a mood not altogether the most agreeable. But this circumstance of shooting the deer, as the Boones afterwards thought, proved most fortunate, if not providential, for it was subsequently ascertained that the Indians, constantly strengthened by accessions, had way-laid the trail in a very advantageous position not very far beyond the point where the whites had wheeled and returned. The superiority of this Indian party in numbers, with their admirably chosen ambuscade, would doubtless have proved them an over-match for the whites and added another fatal defeat to grace the pages of our early border annals.

When all the whites, save one, had returned home, the Boones and remaining borderers, all now well-armed, stopped for a rest at a deserted cabin, perhaps Martin's cabin in Powell's Valley or some other in that region, for there had been quite an alarm on that frontier in consequence of Indian depredations, perpetrated most likely by some of the squads of the main party who had plundered the Boones. Peering through the interstices of the cabin, the whites discovered a couple of Indians a short distance off, armed, finely dressed, and eked out with ornaments, when all three fired, and both the Indians fell dead. In the division of the spoils, Daniel Boone and the other man each shared a gun, while the silver trinkets fell to the lot of Squire Boone. So our unfortunate hunters, blending this act of self-defense with the severe law of retaliation, obtained in return a safe retreat with a moiety of their heavy losses. It is quite probable that these two Indians were also of the large party of northern warriors that had, in squads or collectively, done so much mischief and had detached themselves from their homeward-bound companions to secure more plunder and additional fame. Besides the death of these two fellows, it was afterwards learned that a number of others were drowned while attempting to cross a swollen stream on their way home.

At length our sturdy adventurers, after passing through so many dangers and hardships, reached their quiet homes upon the Yadkin. Though robbed and dispirited, it was something to get back in life and health to behold the faces and embrace the forms of their beloved wives and children. Boone declares that he was "cheered with the prospect of being enabled once more to re-visit his family and friends, and, from the peltry and furs which he and his brother had again an opportunity of taking with them, to recruit his shattered circumstances, discharge the debts he had contracted by the adventure, and shortly to return under better auspices to settle the newly discovered country. But how was this hope blasted, when they were once again surprised and attacked by the savages, forced to fly for their lives, and once more reached home after experiencing hardships which would defy credibility in the recital."

Boone's circumstances were not improved by this long Kentucky adventure, owing to the repeated robberies of the Indians. Some packs of furs and skins were also stolen by them from his camps while he was absent engaged in hunting, trapping, or exploring. So that, in the language of Isaac Shelby, he was "robbed of all the proceeds of this hunt of two years," and returned home poorer than when he departed. But he had seen *Kentucky*, which he "esteemed a second paradise," and that of itself was enough amply to repay him for all his toils, losses, and sufferings.[22]

With some condensed personal sketches of the Long Hunters, we shall close this varied chapter of mishaps and adventures. It is due to the memory and services of those brave and intrepid men that not only their names, but something of an outline of their lives and characters should be rescued from forgetfulness and placed upon the imperishable pages of the history of that border region which they so early explored, were so instrumental in bringing more fully to the notice and appreciation of their countrymen, and finally aided so effectually in accomplishing its permanent settlement.

Henry, Charles, and Richard Skaggs and three other brothers were grandsons of an Irishman who fled from Ireland of Londonderry in 1688–'89, when so many of the hardy Scotch-Irish race emigrated to the shores of the New World. We find his adventurous descendants, natives of Maryland, living on the frontiers of New River and sharing largely in the toils and hardships of the Long Hunters in 1770 – '71. In June 1775 we find Henry Skaggs aiding to pilot Col. Thomas Slaughter and others on an exploratory tour of the Green River country. Henry Skaggs and brothers were a noted family of hunters and nothing but hunters; and keeping pace with the advancing settlements, they pushed forward to Clinch River and were forting in 1777 at Shadrach White's Station in the neighborhood of the Maiden Spring Fork of the Clinch. In 1781 one of the family of Skaggs who had been residing in the Cumberland settlements removed to Kentucky. In 1779 Henry Skaggs, accompanied by upwards of twenty men, started for Kentucky, were attacked by Indians in Powell's Valley, lost part of their horses, when all had returned, save Skaggs, his son John, a mere youth, and a man named Sinclair. With eleven horses, they went to the Green River country to hunt, and during the succeeding hard winter, Sinclair got lost, probably drowned in the Green River, and young Skaggs sickened and died, and amidst the severities of the season, a hollow log was his burial place. His father was left alone to finish the hunt and return home with the horses, pelts, and furs. He settled on Pitman's Creek in the Green River country within present Taylor County, Kentucky, in 1789, with his children and connections around him sharing freely in the Indian difficulties of the times; and there he died in 1808 or '9, aged upwards of eighty years. Possessing a large and bony frame, he was bold, enterprising, and fearless. His brothers, Charles and Richard, who also settled in that region, lived to a good old age.[23]

Joseph Drake early settled on the frontiers of West Virginia [and] was one of the leaders of the Long Hunters. He served as a private in Colonel Bouquet's Ohio expedition in 1764 and married in 1773 Margaret, daughter of Col. John Buchanan, and served the next year in Christian's regiment on the Point Pleasant campaign. He visited Kentucky among the early adventurers in the spring of 1775 and in June aided to pilot a party to explore the region of Green River;[i] and the same year he settled on a tract of land six miles below Abingdon, Virginia, removed to Kentucky in March 1778, and was killed by the Indians in sight of Boonesborough in August following. He was a rough, fearless man, well-fitted for frontier life and hardships.[24]

John Knox, a native of Ireland,[j] obtained money enough when fourteen years of age from his two sisters by giving up all claim on his father's estate to pay his passage to America; and wending his way to the southwestern frontiers of Virginia, he there became attached to the woods and a hunter's life and, naturally enough, formed one of the Long Hunters. He served as a scout in Christian's regiment of the campaign of 1774 and headed a company in Morgan's riflemen at Saratoga and Stillwater, and elsewhere in the Revolution, and retired from that service with the well-earned rank of major. Settling in Kentucky, he became a colonel and served in the state legislature. He married late in life the widow of Gen. Benjamin Logan, was a man of worth and intelligence, and died at his residence in Shelby County, Kentucky, at an advanced age, December 23, 1822. A county in that state which he so early explored and in which he so long lived and finally died commemorates his name. Contrasting Boone and Knox, Marshall says, "the latter judiciously profited by the knowledge he acquired in his early excursions, became an early settler, and engrossed a competent share of the rich soil to render him independent. The former, possessing a different disposition, and taking another view of things, shared a different fate. Knox acquired affluence and ease, while Boone remained a hunter and poor."[25]

Of German parentage, Casper Mansker was born on board a vessel while his parents were crossing the Atlantic to Pennsylvania, whence they removed to the south branch of the Potomac, where their son grew up to manhood, when, wending his way to the head of the Holston, he engaged in his long hunts to the westward. Returning from Natchez with the proceeds of his first long hunt, he bought for his lady-love, a fair lass on the Clinch named Elizabeth White, a wedding dress; and though they were equally suited with each other, they had to make a runaway match, as her parents were opposed to her choice. Mansker again visited the Cumberland country in 1775, encountered and killed an Indian, and in 1799 was among the earliest of the permanent settlers there; and for fifteen years bore his share in the Indian warfare, having been wounded and having made many hair-breadth escapes, serving in the Nickojack campaign, and aiding the Chickasaws in repelling the Creeks. He died childless at his residence on Mansker's Creek, Sumner County, Tennessee, December 20, 1820, at the age of seventy-five, his widow surviving him till the 28th of April, 1841, when she died well-nigh one hundred years of age. Mansker was illiterate, brave, and generous, attained the rank of colonel in the militia, and freed by will his twenty slaves at his death. He was a man of middle size, possessing great muscular power, and was almost by instinct a woodsman.[26]

James Dysart was born in Donegal County, Ireland, in 1744, and his parents dying when he was an infant, he was raised by his grandmother and received the rudiments of a common English education. When seventeen years of age, he determined on visiting America, and his grandparents furnished him means to defray his expenses there on condition of his returning the next season. Landing at Philadelphia, and soon exhausting his means, he went to work and kept bending his course towards the southwest until he found himself on the head of the Holston and finally one of the Long Hunters. He married and settled in the Holston country, was a captain during the Revolution, served on Colonel Christian's campaign in 1776, and fought at the head of a company among Morgan's riflemen at King's Mountain. He afterwards rose first to a major and then a colonel, and one year represented his country in the Virginia legislature. In 1803 he emigrated to Kentucky and settled in the woods within the present limits of Rockcastle County, where he died May 26, 1818, at the age of seventy-four years, leaving a widow who survived him ten years, three sons, and three daughters. He was a large, square-built, coarse-featured man, weighing two hundred pounds, fond of books and newspapers, and a professor of the Christian religion.[27]

Valentine Harmon, another of the Long Hunters and a native of Germany, was among the first settlers of Kentucky, having been a member of the Transylvania Convention at Boonesborough in May 1775, and the next month aided in piloting Col. Thomas Slaughter and others on a tour of exploration to the Green River country. Settling first in Harrodsburg and then in Lincoln, he ultimately located himself in Rockcastle County, Kentucky, where he died about 1815, leaving behind him the reputation of a worthy pioneer and an honest man. He was large and fine appearing in his person but quite illiterate. Toward the Tories he bore no very amiable feelings; and in this his old fellow Long Hunter Colonel Dysart fully coincided with him. Meeting a person of that unfortunate character on some occasion long after the Revolution, he gave him a severe drubbing, Dysart, who was present, encouraging Harmon in inflicting the chastisement and preventing the bystanders from interfering. The poor Tory gladly made tracks and departed to parts unknown. Harmon, though married, left no descendants.[28]

John Baker, who accompanied Cutbirth and Stuart on their early trip to the Mississippi, and afterwards went with Mansker and others to the Cumberland country in 1769–'70, and then with the Long Hunters, eventually settled in Rockcastle County, Kentucky, where he died about 1820, leaving children as devoted as himself to the chase. He was a hardy, good looking man of middle-size and lived among the mountains. At an early day, he discovered the Big Cave, eight miles northeast of Mount Vernon, Rockcastle County. Accompanied by his wife, he commenced exploring it by torchlight, and when they had proceeded about three hundred yards, their torch unfortunately went out, when they had to grope about in perfect darkness for forty hours before finding their way back to the entrance. The arch is from ten to twenty feet high, and the main channel extends through a spur of the mountain, usually termed Big Hill, six hundred yards, through which carts and wagons pass without difficulty, the way being so level and straight that oxen are readily taught to pass through the pitchy darkness without a driver. Large rooms branch off several hundred yards long, some covering an area of several acres, and the end of one has not yet been reached. There is a fine, bold, running stream in the cave, and works have been constructed within for the manufacture of salt-peter by torch-light, which, before and during the last war with England, was carried on to a considerable extent.[29]

From England emigrated Thomas Bledsoe with a wife and two children about 1730 and settled in Culpeper County, Virginia, where his son, Isaac Bledsoe, was born in 1735. Early emigrating to the Fort Chiswell region on the New River, Isaac Bledsoe went out in 1769 with Stone, Mansker, and others, probably influenced by the example of his older brother, Abraham Bledsoe, a famous hunter, and in the autumn of the following year accompanied the Long Hunters. Afterwards settling in the Shelby neighborhood, in what ultimately became Sullivan County, east Tennessee, Isaac Bledsoe acted his part bravely during the Revolution. He commanded the escort to the commissioners who ran the western extension line between Virginia and North Carolina during the hard winter of 1779–'80 and the following year served under Col. Isaac Shelby in Carolina in taking the British post on Pacolet River and in the affairs at Cedar Spring and Musgrove's Mill. He shortly after removed to Boone's Station in Kentucky, where he remained two or three years, and then settled in the Cumberland country within half a mile of Bledsoe's Lick. Having for ten years successfully withstood the Indians, they at last killed him in his field near his residence, April 9, 1793, at the age of fifty-eight years. He was a colonel of the militia, as was also his brother Anthony, who fell a victim to savage cruelty before him, as did likewise at different times several of their children.[30]

Descending from Scotch-Irish parentage, John Montgomery was born in the Virginia Valley in 1748; and his parents had their frontier home broken up and had to flee from Indian ravages during the old French and Indian War. After which they resettled in the New River region, and there Isaac Bledsoe married one of their daughters. Returning from his trip with the Long Hunters, John Montgomery served on the Point Pleasant campaign of 1774 and in 1777 commanded a company to attend the treaty of the Long Island of Holston and to protect that exposed frontier, and the same year was ordered with his company to the relief of the infant settlements of Kentucky. Next year he joined Clark at the head of a company and shared largely in the celebrated conquest of the Illinois country, and was sent to Virginia to recruit, where in December 1778 he was promoted to the rank of lieutenant-colonel of Clark's regiment. Returning to the Illinois by way of the Holston and Tennessee, he was joined by Col. Evan Shelby and gave the rest of the Chickamaugas a severe chastisement when Shelby returned and Montgomery proceeded to the place of his destination.

Colonel Montgomery was at Cahokia with Clark in May 1780, when the British and Indians made a demonstration against that post and St. Louis, and the ensuing month carried on an expedition up the Illinois River to Peoria, suffering greatly for want of provisions. He settled in 1784 in the Cumberland country, distinguished himself on the Nickojack campaign, and shortly after went down the Cumberland River on a bear and buffalo hunt in company with several others. While encamped at Clay Lick, a few miles northeast of the Cumberland, about halfway between Eddyville and the mouth of the river, they were attacked by Indians on the morning of November 27, 1794, when Montgomery treed, shot an Indian, and received in turn a fatal ball and fell dead. The other hunters escaped, one of whom was wounded. The next day a party went from Eddyville and buried poor Montgomery's remains, scalped and partly stripped, near the road leading from the present village of Centerville to Salem in Livingston County, Kentucky. Colonel Montgomery left a widow, two sons, and two daughters, all of whom have since passed away. He served a term in the North Carolina legislature from the Cumberland settlements; and a county in Tennessee commemorates his name. He was brave to a fault, generous, and kind; six feet, two inches in height, with blue eyes, auburn hair, ruddy complexion, handsome features, possessing great strength and activity, and presenting altogether a real border war hero whose "lofty deeds and daring high" excite our liveliest admiration.[31]

A native of Culpeper County, Virginia, John Rains became an early settler in the New River region and went out with the adventurous party of hunters and explorers in 1769 led by Uriah Stone, Mansker, and others. In 1779 he was among the first band of whites who permanently settled the Cumberland country, served on the Coldwater and Nickojack campaigns, and was an efficient officer at the head of a company in the scouting service. Captain Rains contributed much information relative to Middle Tennessee for Judge Haywood's work and died near Nashville, March 26, 1834, at the advanced age of ninety-one.[32]

Among Stone and Mansker's exploring party of 1769, we find the names of Uriah Stone, the leader, Castleton Brooks, Humphrey Hogan, and Obadiah Terrill. All these names appear as witnesses or parties to a suit in July 1773 in Fincastle County, Virginia, so they were probably all living on the Holston. Of Brooks and Stone we have no further knowledge. Hogan was one of the early settlers and defenders of the Cumberland country and as such became entitled to a free grant of land from North Carolina in 1784. Terrill was a small, chunky man with a club foot and early settled in the Nashville region and finally died in the family of George Flinn, whom he had raised, above Ford's Ferry, Livingston County, Kentucky, about the time of the War of 1812. He was fond of speaking of his early explorations and border services and left no descendants.[33]

William Pitman and William Butler, both of whom eventually settled in the Green River country, are said to have been out with the Long Hunters; after the former, Pitman's Creek and Pitman's Station took their names, and he served on Clark's campaign of 1782; and the latter became a noted Indian fighter on the southern borders of Kentucky and served under Colonel Whitley on the Nickojack campaign.[34]

Of Irish parentage, William Miller was born in Virginia, March 30, 1747. Settling early on the southwestern frontier of Augusta County, in that colony, the father was killed by Indians while William was yet a mere youth. During his absence with the Long Hunters, he killed eighty-one deer and many other animals. He made a settlement on Paint Lick Creek, Kentucky, in 1776 and acted as a lieutenant under Capt. James Estill in March 1782, and Marshall blames him for a failure in the performance of his duty to that unfortunate officer, but which Miller and his friends always pronounced unjust.[k] He served on Clark's campaign of 1782, was subsequently a colonel of the militia, and died at his residence on the west side of Paint Lick Creek, Garrard County, Kentucky, August 30, 1841, in the ninety-third year of his age. He was six feet, two inches in height, fair complexion, sparse frame, and pleasing countenance, possessing a kind and benevolent disposition and an irreproachable character, and for many years was a member of the Presbyterian church. Colonel Miller was emphatically *the last of the Long Hunters.*[35]

DRAPER'S NOTES: CHAPTER 8

1. MS. statement furnished the author by the late President Zachary Taylor, son of Col. Richard Taylor. See also Bradford's *Notes on Kentucky,* Stipp's ed., 13; and Butler's *Kentucky,* 155.

Hancock Taylor was born in Orange County, Virginia, about 1735, and after this bold western adventure, engaged in surveying and was mortally wounded by the Indians in Kentucky in 1774. His brother, Richard Taylor, also a native of Orange County, took a prominent part in the Revolutionary War, first entering the service as a lieutenant under Patrick Henry in 1775 and attaining the rank of lieutenant colonel in the Virginia Line before its close, having participated in the battles of Brandywine, Monmouth, White Rains, and other less important actions, besides serving in the Pittsburgh country under Colonel Brodhead. In 1785 he settled near Louisville, Kentucky, was a member of the Kentucky Convention of 1792 and '99, and served frequently in the legislature and as an elector of president and vice president. He died at his seat near Louisville in 1839, in the 84th year of his age.

Abraham Hempinstall was a native of the state of New York, descended from Dutch parentage, and early emigrated to the Greenbrier country in western Virginia, where Hancock Taylor found him while on a hunt in that region about the year 1766 or '67. Finding him young and active and a capital woodsman, Taylor prevailed on Hempinstall to join him, which he did and remained almost constantly with him, not only during his Ohio and Mississippi adventures but his subsequent surveying trips in Kentucky, and was with Taylor when he received his mortal wound, and carried his friend a long distance on his back until he could be borne no longer and died in the wilderness. Hempinstall, as a guide or hunter, then aided other surveyors in locating lands in Kentucky. When the country became more quiet and established, he settled in what is now Woodford County, on a large, fine tract of land located for him by Hancock Taylor, but becoming dissipated and improvident, he soon squandered that and other lands away and died at the house of a friend in Shelby County, where he was well cared for, about 1810, fully seventy years of age, and though twice married, he died childless.

2. MS. notes of conversations with ex-Gov. William B. Campbell and the late Col. William Martin of Tennessee. David Harbert, an aged citizen of Jackson County, in that state, informed one of the authors in 1844 that he had at an early period seen a beech tree at the Three Forks of Cumberland and another at the Falls of Cumberland, on each of which was engraved the same name, coupled with the year 1769.

3. MS. statement of Gen. William Hall, who had the facts from Isaac Bledsoe; MS. notes of conversations with the late Col. Robert Weakley of Tennessee, Haywood's *Tennessee*.

4. Haywood's *Tennessee*. *Pamphlet Sketch of Tennessee*, 1810. Moses Fisk's "Summary Notes of the First Settlement of Tennessee," 1816, published in vol. iii, 2nd ser., *Massachusetts Historical Collection*.

5. MS. notes of conversations with the late Maj. David McColloch of Wheeling, a grandson of the old pioneer.

6. MS. statements of the late Col. William Martin, the late Elijah Callaway, and Hugh M. Stokes; also of Jeremiah Cleveland and Shadrach Franklin, nephews, and Gen. Benjamin Cleveland, who survived the hardships of this early

adventure, [and] distinguished himself often years afterwards at the front of a regiment of noblemen at King's Mountain.

7. MS. statement of James B. Dysart, a son of one of the Long Hunters.

8. MS. narrative of Hon. Robert Wickliffe of Kentucky.

9. MS. statements of Thomas Mitchell, who derived the facts from the late Archibald Skaggs, a son of Charles Skaggs; John B. Dysart's MS. correspondence; and conversations with the late venerable Israel Morrison of Lincoln County, Kentucky.

10. MS. statement of John B. Dysart of Missouri, a son of this early adventurer.

11. MS. statements of John B. Dysart, Thomas Mitchell, and Capt. John Barbee—the two latter obtaining their information from Henry Skaggs and brothers, and from their aged children.

12. MS. letters of Capt. John Barbee intimate that the larger party returned.

13. *Pamphlet Sketch of Tennessee,* 1810, p. 41; Haywood's *Tennessee,* 78; MS. statement of John B. Dysart.

14. "It was Will Emery, a half-breed Cherokee, who robbed Knox and Skaggs." MS. letters of Maj. Arthur Campbell and William Preston, October 6, 1774.

15. MS. statement of John B. Dysart, Capt. John Barbee, Thomas Mitchell, Col. James Davidson, and E. M. Leaville; conversations with Capt. Benjamin Briggs, Israel Morrison, and Joseph McCormick, who, collectively, obtained these facts from the Skaggs brothers, Colonel Knox, Colonel Dysart, Colonel Miller, and others of the Long Hunters. See also Haywood's *Tennessee,* 78. Captain Barbee and Joseph McCormick agree as to the number of skins lost; Thomas Mitchell thinks they were considerably more, perhaps twenty-five hundred or three thousand.

The first Baptist church organized in the Green River country was located on a beautiful eminence near a fine spring within a short distance of the old camp. At an association of that denomination held with this church in 1804, a shady grove near the spring was selected for the meeting; and the horses of those who came to attend the association were tied close together in the woods, and a large quantity of hair was pawed up by them. This led to the discovery of the inscription on the beech tree near by, identifying the precise locality of the skin-house; and Charles Skaggs, one of the Long Hunters subsequently visiting it, at once recognized the spot. A bar of lead of several pounds weight, probably lost when the Indians plundered the camp, was afterwards found there. The Baptist church here so early located was called Mount Gilead Church, after one of that name in Virginia, to which Colonel Haskins and some others of its constituent members belonged; and some twenty years since, when the Seceders or Campbellites withdrew from that church, they erected one of their own directly on the site of the old skin-house about one hundred and thirty yards from the other, and some of the ancient hair, the fruit of the blended toils and misfortunes of the Long Hunters, was used in the mortar in its erection. Vestiges of the hair are still found.

These churches are located on the eastern side and about midway of the Skin House branch. The main road leading from Greensburg to Columbia, after crossing the Caney Fork at the mouth of the Skin House branch, follows up this little branch to its source in a southeasterly direction, passing the new church on the right and the old one on the left. That spot will long remain memorable in the annals of early western exploration.

TFB: *The "Seceders or Campbellites" have their origin in the biblical doctrine of Alexander Campbell (1788–1866), whose energetic efforts to restore nondenominational New Testament Christianity in Kentucky caused him to sever ties with the Redstone Baptist Association in 1815.*

16. John B. Dysart MS. statement.

17. MS. notes of conversation with the late George Smith of Sumner County, Tennessee; MS. letters of E. P. Connell of Mansker's Creek, Tennessee; both of whom derived this anecdote from Colonel Mansker. E. M. Leavell of Kentucky states that his grandfather, Col. William Miller, one of the Long Hunters, often spoke of Daniel Boone visiting their camp on the Green River awhile before their return home; and the venerable Gen. William Hall, a meritorious pioneer of the Cumberland country, subsequently a brigadier-general in the Creek War, a member of Congress, and an acting governor of Tennessee, distinctly remembers to have heard Col. Isaac Bledsoe in his lifetime speak of himself and fellow Long Hunters meeting Boone somewhere on their route. And Col. Nathan Boone and lady have both often heard Col. Daniel Boone mention his falling in with the Long Hunters in the Green River country. It is, therefore, a mistake on the part of Marshall, Perkins, Peck, McClung, and Simms in stating that the Boones and the Long Hunters never met. Boone's silence in his Narrative with reference to it obviously led to the error.

18. Verbal statement to one of the authors by Col. Nathan Boone and lady, who learned the incident from Col. Daniel Boone.

19. Gen. William Hall's MS. letters; Boone's Narrative.

20. This narrative of Neely's getting lost in Powell's Valley has been derived from the life of the late Hugh F. Bell, who was a brother-in-law of Neely's; Gen. William Hall, who had the facts from Neely himself, and from the venerable Isaiah Boone, a surviving son of Squire Boone. After his trip with the Long Hunters, Neely returned to New River, from which, in 1785, he removed to the Cumberland country. In the spring of 1796 he and his son James had been out one day peeling bark and, returning home in the afternoon, stopped to drink at a spring near his own house about a mile from Bledsoe's Lick in now Sumner County, Tennessee, when two Indians in ambush fired upon and mortally wounded both father and son. Another son, William, ran out of the house with his loaded rifle, shouting at the top of his voice, when the Indians decamped. The two wounded men were conveyed to the house but lived only a few hours. Such was the untimely fate of poor Alexander Neely, a native of Pennsylvania, who left behind him four worthy sons and as many daughters.

21. MS. notes of conversations with H. F. Bell; MS. statements of Gen. William Hall, Hon. Robert Wickliffe, John B. Dysart, and E. M. Leavell; Haywood's *Tennessee,* 79.

22. MS. notes of conversations with Moses and Isaiah Boone, sons of Squire Boone's, and with Col. Nathan Boone of Missouri; Daniel Boone's Memorial to the Kentucky Legislature, 1812; Isaac Shelby in Bradford's *Notes on Kentucky,* Stipp's ed., 13.

23. MS. statements of Capt. John Barbee, derived from Thomas and Moses Skaggs, son of Charles Skaggs; MS. notes of conversations with Morgan Vardeman of Kentucky.

24. MS. statements of ex-Gov. David Campbell of Virginia; MS. Preston Papers; MS. notes of conversations with the venerable Capt. John Gass of Kentucky.

25. MS. statements of Mrs. Mary L. Smith, daughter of Gen. Benjamin Logan, and of Hon. Robert Wickliffe; Marshall's *Kentucky,* i:10; Wilkinson's Memoirs, i: table (in Appendix).

26. MS. narratives of Gen. William Hall, C. P. Connell, Mrs. Tabitha Moore, and the late Col. William Martin; Haywood's *Tennessee.*

27. MS. statements of John B. Dysart and ex-Gov. David Campbell of Virginia.

28. John B. Dysart's MS. letters to one of the authors.

29. MS. statement of John B. Dysart; Collins' *Kentucky,* 501.

30. MS. notes of conversations with the late Mrs. Sarah Shelby; the late Hugh F. Bell; Gen. William Hall; MS. journal of Gen. Daniel Smith; Haywood's *Tennessee.*

31. MS. statement of the late Col. William Martin; conversations with the late Hugh F. Bell and others; MS. Clark Papers, and documents from the archives of Virginia.

32. J. H. Rains MS. statement; Haywood's *Tennessee.*

33. MS. records of Fincastle County, Virginia; Haywood's *Tennessee;* conversations with Gen. Jonathan Ramsey of Missouri.

34. MS. statements of Capt. John Barbee and Thomas Mitchell; Virginia archives.

35. MS. statements of Mrs. Susan Brown and E. M. Leavell, a daughter and grandson of Colonel Miller; also of I. H. Spillman, Esq., and the venerable William Champ.

EDITOR'S NOTES: CHAPTER 8

a. In spring 1773 Capt. Thomas Bullitt led the first surveying expedition to Kentucky. Hancock Taylor was a member of Bullitt's forty-man party. By midsummer the McAfee brothers (see Introduction, note y) had hired Taylor to survey land tracts near present-day Frankfort and Harrodsburg. In 1774 Col. William Preston deputized Taylor, James Douglas, and Isaac Hite as surveyors and chose John Floyd to lead a new sixteen-man survey team to the Falls of the Ohio. There they staked claims covering 40,000 acres (about 65 square miles). On July 27, as Taylor and James Strother were paddling a pine dugout across the Kentucky River, a band of Shawnee fired on them, killing Strother and wounding Taylor, who died on July 29. Taylor's sleek long rifle, built by Virginia gunmaker Adam Haymaker, now resides in a private collection.

b. Richard Taylor was the father of Kentuckian Zachary Taylor (1784–1850), the twelfth president of the United States.

c. Abraham Hempinstall (also spelled Heptonstall or Hamptonstall) was a member of John Floyd's surveying team, which came to Kentucky in 1774.

d. This once formidable French fortress, named for the regent's son, Le Duc de Chartres, and built on the Mississippi floodplain near Prairie Du Rocher, Illinois (population now just over 400), went through several incarnations. Lt. Duque de Boisbriant erected the first Fort de Chartres in 1718. Built of logs, the complex housed 100 marines and had an officer's quarters, several storehouses, and a powder magazine. In 1753 engineer Jean Baptiste de Saucier began building on the site a massive limestone fort, with walls 18 feet high and 4 feet thick at the base, tapering to half that at the top and totaling 1,447 feet in total length. Towering bastions on the fort's corners guarded the fortress, and a dry moat encircled it. During Pontiac's Rebellion (1763), many of the fort's inhabitants fled.

That year, leading a British reconnaissance team along the Gulf coast and up the Mississippi, Capt. Philip Pittman viewed the fort and, in his journal (published as *The Present State of the European Settlements on the Mississippi*), left this description of this fortress that was never attacked and that some deemed "the Gibraltar of the West":

> The form is an irregular quadrangle, the sides of the exterior polygon are four hundred and ninety feet; it is built of stone and plastered over...the ditch [moat] has never been finished; the entrance of the fort is through a very handsome gate; within the wall is a small banquette raised three or four feet for the men to stand on when they fire through the loopholes. The buildings within the fort are, the commandant's and commissary's houses, the magazine of stores, corps de garde, and two barracks; these occupy the square. Within the gorges of the bastions are, a powder magazine, a bake house, a prison, in the lower floor of which are four dungeons, and in the upper floor two rooms, and an outhouse belonging to the commandant.

On October 10, 1765, the English occupied De Chartres, renaming it Fort Cavendish. But the rising waters of the Mississippi claimed it in the early 1770s, forcing the British to abandon it. As the fort languished, local farmers used its limestone blocks to build their homes and barns.

Today, part of the fort has been reconstructed at its original site—the stone powder magazine is the last vestige of the original fort's complex—but the Illinois State Parks system has never finished it, and the churning Mississippi still seasonally threatens in spite of the earthen dike surrounding the fort. The flood of 1993 that swamped much of the upper Mississippi basin inundated Fort de Chartres and denuded the site. Since then, the fort has been refurbished to it present state.

e. Another reference to a smoothbore gun.

f. Draper's labeling this gang of Long Hunters as proto-ecologists worried about "a wanton destruction of game" is laughable. Fur trade–era market hunters, Indian and white, annually slew hundreds of thousands of animals for profit, raping the land of its bounty.

g. Kentucky's Green River "barren country" once spanned present-day Hart, Metcalfe, Barren, Warren, Logan, Todd, and Christian counties. Here the landscape was a vast grassland because of the Indian practice of seasonally firing the dead grass to create lush, ever-spreading, near treeless pastures of fresh graze. Early settlers who customarily viewed towering timber stands as an indicator of fertile soil assumed these prairies were barren. But French botanist F. A. Michaux toured the barrens in 1802 and found such claims far from true: "I was agreeably surprised to meet with a beautiful meadow, the abundant grass of which was from two to three feet high, and afforded excellent food for cattle; amongst it I saw a great variety of plants....I collected and sent to France upwards of ninety species."

h. These "French hunters from the Illinois country" may have been Jacques Timothy Boucher de Monbruen and his men, who were scouring the Cumberland watershed as early as 1766.

i. In spring 1775 Joseph Drake came to Kentucky with John Floyd and for a while lived at Logan's Station (St. Asaph's).

j. By the 1200s the name Knox was well established in Scotland. John Knox, the famous post-Reformation Calvinist minister, was Scottish.

k. Attorney Humphrey Marshall was not the only Kentuckian to blame Col. William Miller for what Draper calls "a failure in the performance of his duty."

Controversy still shrouds Miller's role in The Battle of Little Mountain, which became known as Estill's Defeat, fought at Mount Sterling, Kentucky (Montgomery County). On March 22, 1782, Capt. James Estill's twenty-five Kentuckians clashed with a near equal force of Wyandots (descendants of the Iroquoian Petun-Huron) who had raided local forts. A hot, pitched battle raged over a sparse brake of a few acres. An hour into the fight, the Indians forded Little River Creek to attack the van. To counter, Estill split his forces into three units; Miller's men were to defend the left flank. As Miller's force moved out, a bullet slammed into his gun, knocking the flint from the jaws of the lock. His gun useless, Miller shouted that "it was foolhardy to stay and be shot down," then he and his men fled. Quoted in *The American Revolution, 1775–1783: An Encyclopedia,* s.v. "Battle of Little Mountain, Kentucky (March 22, 1782)."

Estill's left flank open, the Wyandots rushed in, killing Estill. The whites retreated, leaving seven dead. Six escapees were badly wounded. White captives later reported that the Wyandots had suffered twenty casualties.

William Miller became a scapegoat for the defeat. Even twenty years after the fight, one survivor, David Cook, still threatened to kill him. There is no record that Miller ever tried to vindicate himself or return to Estill's Station to face his accusers.

For the numbers of men and casualties, Estill's Defeat was one of Kentucky's bloodiest Indian fights. It is also one of the least known.

CHAPTER 9

Treaties at Fort Stanwix and Hard Labor.—Projected Ohio Colonies.—
Extortions of North Carolina Public Officers.—Regulators.—Daniel
Boone's Employments.—Hunts with Joe Robertson.—Meets Isaac Shelby
below Holston Settlement.—Settles on Watauga Awhile. —Makes a Trip
in 1773 with Benjamin Cutbirth to Kentucky.—Attempts to Remove There
and Heads a Large Party.—Repulsed at Walden's Creek, and Abandons
the Enterprise.—Indian Depredations on Simon Kenton and Others.—
Adventures of Gilbert Christian and Others.—Boone Retires to Clinch.—
Western Adventures of 1773.—Green's Bear Fight and Singular
Preservation.

During Boone's long sojourn and wanderings in Kentucky, several events elsewhere transpired, well calculated to exert no inconsiderable influence in hastening the inevitable settlement of that land of beauty and fertility. While Sir William Johnson was obtaining at the treaty of Fort Stanwix the cession of the right or claim of the Six Nations[a] to the West Virginia and Kentucky country as far as the Cherokee or Tennessee River, John Stuart, superintendent of the Southern Indian Department, at the same time held a treaty at Hard Labor, South Carolina, with the Cherokees and tacitly confirmed their claim to a portion of the same region extending from the Kenhawa to the Cherokee River by agreeing to a boundary line between the Cherokees and his majesty's subjects commencing at a point on Savannah River, and running nearly a direct northerly course by Tryon's Mountain to Chiswell's mine to New River, and thence on the easterly bank of that stream united with the Great Kenhawa in a straight line to its mouth. This would have cut off several quite flourishing Anglo-American settlements west of New River and along the Holston and invalidated large grants of land in that country made by the king and his legal representatives, yielding to the Cherokees a large tract to which they never laid any claim, though often in the settlements, until after the Royal Proclamation of 1763.

To obviate these causes of complaint and effect a change in the proposed line, Lord Botetourt, governor of Virginia, despatched Dr. Thomas Walker and Col. Andrew Lewis early in 1769 on a mission to John Stuart to make the necessary representations and prevail on him to postpone running the line till the king could be addressed on the subject. This ultimately led to the new treaty at Lochaber, South Carolina, in October 1770, between John Stuart and the Cherokees, Col. John Donelson being present as a Virginia commissioner by appointment of Governor Botetourt, when the Cherokees readily consented to a new boundary in accordance with the king's suggestions, beginning at Holston River, six miles above the Big Island, running thence in a direct line to the mouth of the Great Kenhawa. For this enlarged boundary, the Virginia Assembly voted £2,500 sterling to the Cherokees. In the fall of 1771 Alexander Cameron, deputy superintendent under John Stuart, with At-ta-kul-la-Kul-la, or the Little Carpenter, and other prominent Cherokee deputies, ran the line, Colonel Donelson being the principal surveyor. "In the progress of the work," says Colonel Donelson's affidavit, "they came to the head of Louisa, now Kentucky River, when the Little Carpenter (a Cherokee chief) observed, that his nation delighted in having their lands marked out by natural boundaries; and proposed that, instead of the line agreed upon at Lochaber as aforesaid, it should break off at the head of Louisa River, and run thence to the mouth thereof, and thence up the Ohio to the mouth of the Great Kenhawa." This boundary was accordingly agreed to, and this reason was assigned by the governor of Virginia to the Home Government for the change, and also that the ruggedness of the mountain region through which the treaty line would have led them would have required many months in the accomplishment. Colonel Donelson promised to send the Cherokees, the next spring, "a few presents for their generosity in extending the line to the Kentucky.[1]

An Ohio colony was an early and favorite measure. It virtually had its origin in Spotswood's scheme and in the subsequent Ohio Company of 1748. The idea was renewed by Samuel Hazard in 1755, who sent to the British Ministry a proposition for a new Protestant colony one hundred miles west of the western boundary of Pennsylvania and extend[ing] one hundred miles west of the Mississippi, to be separated "from Virginia and Carolina by the great chain of mountains," the Blue Ridge and Alleghenies.[2] Mr. Hazard made an exploratory trip in 1755 as far as the Great Kenhawa, travelling altogether eighteen hundred miles on the frontiers and engaging between four and five thousand men able to bear arms, including fifteen clergymen, to go and settle in the newly proposed colony. But the war then raging in Europe and America prevented any serious consideration of the subject.[3] A letter-writer from Fort Duquesne a few days after its capture in 1758 suggested that the king should grant charter for a western colony, "with a full liberty of conscience," and a separate governor; and another writer shortly after proposed for it the name of *Pittsylvania,* in honor of the distinguished head of the British cabinet, and that all Protestants who should come under the denomination of King David's soldiers, mentioned by the prophet Samuel, that every one that was in distress, every one that was in debt, and every one that was discontented, should be invited to settle in that "extraordinary good land."[4] [b] At the Peace of 1763 a pamphlet was published in London urging the "Advantages of a Settlement upon the Ohio in North America"; and the same year there appeared from Edinburgh a pamphlet recommending a new colony between the Mississippi, Wabash, and the lakes on the north to be called *Charlotiana,* in honor of the then queen of England. Col. Charles Lee, also, soon after peace, proposed two new colonies, one on the Ohio below the Wabash, and the other on the Illinois, but the proposal was rejected by the British Ministry.

In 1767 the British secretary of state[c] proposed three western colonies, one in the Detroit region, one in the Illinois, and the other "on the lower part of the River Ohio"; and the same year, as has already been mentioned, our own Patrick Henry and others also projected an Ohio colony. The year preceding, Gov. William Franklin of New Jersey and Sir William Johnson proposed a scheme for establishing a new colony on the south of the Ohio and wrote to Dr. Franklin, then in Europe, requesting his agency in procuring such grant. Thus originated the Walpole Company, of which Dr. Franklin was the most active member, and their petition was in May 1770 referred to a committee of the king's council and finally approved in August 1772 by the king in council, making a grant beginning opposite the mouth of the Scioto, extending southwardly through Cumberland Gap, and along the south-east side of Cumberland Mountain north-eastwardly to the junction of New and Greenbriar rivers, thence to the south-western corner of Maryland and thence by the lines of Maryland and Pennsylvania to the Ohio and down that river to the Scioto. This at the time was usually termed the Ohio Colony and excited no small interest along the western frontiers.[5]

So the speedy occupancy of the Ohio Valley was a subject rife in the minds of the people at the time Daniel Boone and his brother returned to the Upper Yadkin. Just at that particular juncture, however, that matter was perhaps less canvassed in North Carolina then elsewhere, as Governor Tryon and the Regulators had come to hard blows, producing great excitement in that colony; but probably the few scattered settlers on the Upper Yadkin where Boone resided were too remote from the scene of contention to have partaken very largely of the prevailing feeling of the times, yet [they] were not altogether ignorant of the growing expectations of wicked rulers of an arbitrary government. Boone was not the man tamely to submit to such oppression and seemed bent on further explorations and an early removal beyond the reach of the rapacious tax-gatherers and unlawful extortioners, who then lorded it with so high a hand over the poor border inhabitants of North Carolina.

How he spent the ensuing two and a half years after returning from his extended ramblings in Kentucky, his own scanty Narrative is entirely silent. He was, however, busily employed during the cropping season at home, assisted by his sons James and Israel, while the remainder of each year found him searching the western wilderness for game and a suitable country for a new settlement. During this period, one Joe Robertson, an old weaver who had a famous pack of bear-dogs and was devoted to the chase, often accompanied Boone into the Brushy Mountain and over to the Watauga, securing loads of bear-skins, which they packed to the settlements and sold.[d] On one of their adventurous trips, they penetrated as far as the French Lick on Cumberland and found several French hunters there.[6]

In May 1772 Isaac Shelby, then a young man, met Boone below the Holston settlement alone—such was his passion for adventure—and rehearsed to his new acquaintance the story of his former Kentucky exploration and robbery by the Indians.[7] There is also reason to believe that about the year 1772, Boone removed his family to the Watauga and there resided awhile; and then, from some cause, returned to his old place on the Yadkin.[8]

Early in 1773 Daniel Boone, Benjamin Cutbirth, and a few others explored Kentucky and were greatly pleased with the country. Boone then for a period reoccupied his old cave on the right bank of Little Hickman Creek, in what is now Jessamine County, Kentucky, in which he had, probably three years before, taken up his temporary abode; there he carved the initials of his name and the year on the side of the cavern—"D. B.—1773," and also in like manner on several beech trees near the mouth of the cave. Tradition has not preserved the particulars of this journey, and hence we may infer that only incidents of common occurrence attended the adventurers. So gratified were they with Kentucky that they resolved at once to remove and settle permanently in the country.[9]

It would appear that Boone on his way home made the acquaintance of Capt. William Russell, then residing near Castle's-woods on Clinch River, who entered so heartily into Boone's views with reference to settling Kentucky that he agreed to join him in the enterprise. Somewhere in this region, the McAfee company, on their way home from Kentucky, met Boone about the 12th of August, then making preparations to migrate to that country.[10] Returning to the Yadkin, Boone paid a visit to the Bryan settlement sixty miles south-east of his residence, where his brother-in-law William Bryan, several members of the Bryan connection, together with Benjamin Cutbirth and other hardy adventurers, consented to try their for-

45. Sword once owned by Isaac Shelby. FROM THE COLLECTION OF JIM AND CAROLYN DRESSLAR.

tunes in the wilderness. It was arranged that the Bryan party, who could cross the mountains more conveniently to the eastward of Boone's intended route, should join Boone's company in Powell's Valley on a specified day and pass the most dangerous part of the journey together. Hastening home, Boone sold his farm and such household goods, produce, and farming utensils as he could not well convey so great a distance when, joined by five other families, they "bade farewell to friends," as Boone tells us in his Narrative, and took their departure for Kentucky September 25th, 1773. Fifty-six years before, Squire Boone, with his parents, had bid adieu to friends and kindred in England and set sail for the New World; thirty-three years later, Squire Boone with his family, including his son Daniel, set out from Pennsylvania for the Yadkin country; and now, after a lapse of twenty-three years, we find Daniel Boone, true to the instincts of his family, at the head of a little band of poor but fearless, enterprising men seeking quiet homes in a distant wilderness. Such were the founders—and such the inception of the first earnest attempt at the settlement of Kentucky.

The Bryan party, numbering forty men, overtook the van as agreed on; those of them having families had left them at home, designing to commence a settlement and, should circumstances favor, remove their families and effects out afterwards. This re-enforcement was not exclusively composed of men from the Valley of South Yadkin, for several had joined them in the Fort Chiswell and Holston Valley regions, among whom were Michael Stoner, William Bush, and Edmund Jennings. They had successively passed Clinch Mountain and River, Powell's Mountain, and Walden's Ridge, and fairly entered Powell's Valley. Boone pronounced the aspect of those several mountain cliffs "wild and horrid." Yet it must be confessed that there is a grandeur in beholding the mighty growth of forest trees rising in gradual succession one above another from the base to the mountains' summits, their leaves presenting the varied tints of autumn, with here and there an old, gray rock jutting from the foliage or a bank of moss peeping through with the earth beneath covered with a luxuriant growth of herbs and wild grass.

Here, at or near the western base of Walden's Ridge, where Powell's River flows along a lovely vale, Boone and his party pitched their camp and awaited the arrival of the rear. James Boone and two brothers named John and Richard Mendinall, from Guilford County, North Carolina, had been despatched from the main company, probably at the Wolf Hill's, now Abington, across the country to Captain Russell's at Castle's-woods for the double purpose of notifying him of the advance of Boone's Kentucky adventurers and procuring a quantity of flour. Pack-loads of flour were provided, and Captain Russell sent forward his oldest son, Henry, a youth of seventeen, two Negroes named Charles and Adam, together with Isaac Crabtree and a youth named Drake, with several horses ladened with farming utensils, provisions, and other needful articles, and a few books. A small drove of cattle was also sent under their charge. Captain Russell himself remained behind to arrange his business and then with Capt. David Gass to hasten forward and overtake the others. His intention was to erect a comfortable domicile

46. This "D. Boon Cilled A. Bar on tree in the year 1760" carving on a beech tree in Carter County, Tennessee, was photographed in 1875. That Boone always spelled his last name with an "e" means that this relic of unknown provenance probably is a fake. STATE HISTORICAL SOCIETY OF WISCONSIN.

and open a plantation during the autumn and winter, put in a crop in the spring, and return for his family. Had these plans succeeded, William Russell would doubtless have become one of the most distinguished of the primitive settlers of Kentucky.

It was now the 9th of October, and little dreaming of danger, the party under young Boone and young Russell pushed on cheerfully and as rapidly as possible, endeavoring to reach the advance party that evening. Night overtaking them, and probably not aware that the company in front was only three miles distant, they encamped on the northern bank of Walden's Creek, at the old ford near the head of that stream—a southern tributary of Powell's River. Unknown to this little band, a party of stealthy Indians had that day dogged them a considerable distance; and during the evening, while young Boone and companions were seated around their blazing camp-fire, they heard the howl of wolves, or a successful imitation on the part of the Indians, when the Mendinalls, unused to such frontier serenades, dropped some expressions of fear. Crabtree, a regular backwoodsman, laughed heartily at their apprehensions and jeeringly told them that they would hear as well the bellowing of buffaloes as the howling of wolves in the tree-tops in Kentucky.

Locked in the sweet embrace of balmy sleep, all unconscious of danger, this little band of emigrants were attacked about day-break next morning by the Indians, who, creeping close to camp, fired upon their unsuspecting victims, killing some and wounding others. A heart-rending scene ensued.[11] Young Russell was shot through both hips and was unable to attempt an escape. As the Indians would run up with their knives to stab him, he would seize the naked blade with his hands and thus had them badly mangled and was finally tortured in a most barbarous manner. Young Boone was also shot through his hips, breaking them both and rendering him helpless. He recognized among the Indians Big Jim, a Shawanoe warrior who had often shared the hospitalities of his father's house. His unusually high cheek bones and broad face with a singularly peculiar chin rendered it almost impossible for any one who had ever known him to fail instantly to recognize his remarkable features. James Boone implored him by name to spare his life, but former friendship, past favors, nor present misfortunes made any sensible impression on the adamantine heart of the blood-thirsty warrior. The Indians tortured young Boone by pulling out his toe and finger nails, when he besought Big Jim at once to put him out of his misery. At the same time, young Russell was suffering similar tortures, when Boone remarked to him that he presumed his parents, brothers, and sisters were all killed by the Indians. At length, both the young sufferers were severely stabbed, and probably tomahawked, when death, like an angel of mercy, came to their relief.

Both of the Mendinalls and young Drake were among the slain, one of whom at the time ran off and was neither found nor heard of at that period; but many years after, some of the family of Mr. John Sharp, residing near by, found the bones of a man between two ledges of rocks about an eighth of a mile above the defeated camp which were supposed to have been those of the missing man, who had probably been mortally wounded in the attack, fled as far as he could, crawled between the ledges, and died. The Negro Adam fortunately escaped unhurt, hid himself in some driftwood on the bank of the creek close at hand, and was an unwilling spectator of the painful scene enacted at the camp. Crabtree, though wounded, also effected his escape and first reached the settlements; while Adam, getting lost, was eleven days in making his way to the frontier inhabitants. The other Negro, Charles, older and less active than Adam, was taken prisoner by the Indians, who carried him off with the horses and every article they esteemed of any value. When they had gone about forty miles, getting into a dispute about the ownership of the Negro, the leader of the party put an end to the quarrel by tomahawking the poor captive.

In the advance-camp was a young fellow who had been detected in pilfering from his comrades and had become the butt of contempt and ridicule of the camp to such an extent that he resolved secretly to abandon the party and return to the settlements. He took his silent departure awhile before day on the morning of the fatal 10th of October, and on the way, stole some deer skins which Daniel Boone had left hung up beside the trail for the rear to bring along. Reaching the ford at Walden's Creek when the Indians could have but a few moments before decamped, he came upon the mangled remains of the unfortunate slain, when, dropping the skins, he hastened back to the main camp, where he arrived about sun-rise with the unhappy intelligence. Fear, sorrow, and confusion more or less agitated every breast and could be seen depicted on almost every countenance. While a small party under Squire Boone was sent back to bury the dead, recover whatever property the Indians may have carried off, and ascertain their strength by their *sign*, Daniel Boone remained with the most of the men, ready to repel any attack that might be made on the main camp; and as they at first had no means of knowing the strength of the Indians who had made the fatal onslaught on the rear, they set themselves about making a rude fortification, probably by felling trees around their encampment.

When Squire Boone's burial party reached the defeated camp, they found Captains Russell and Gass already arrived there viewing the melancholy scene. In young Russell's body, which was mangled in an inhuman manner, was left sticking a dart-arrow; and beside all the bodies were left several painted hatchets and war-clubs—a sort of Indian declaration of war.[e] Mrs. Daniel Boone had sent sheets for shrouds, and young Boone and Russell were wrapped in the same winding sheet and buried together. Like Saul and Jonathan, they were lovely and pleasant in their lives, and in their death they were not divided.[f] The other two slain were also decently interred. The bodies of all were ripped open, but none of them were scalped, as the Indians would not venture to take white scalps to their towns in time of professed peace. The Indians had taken all the plunder, and the cattle were much scattered.

Squire Boone and party, with Captains Russell and Gass, returned to the main camp, when a general council was held. Though it was Daniel Boone's wish to continue the journey, the most of the emigrants were so much disheartened by

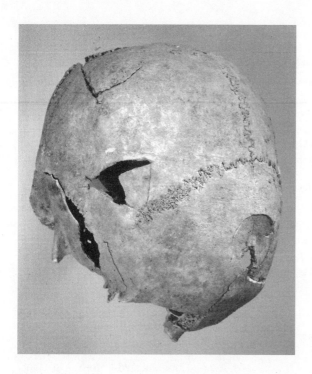

47a & 47b. Frontal (a) and right side (b) view of the skull of an American Revolutionary War soldier exhumed at Fort Laurens, near present-day Bolivar, Ohio, showing trauma caused from a ball-head war club. Simon Girty and British-allied Delaware and Shawnee attacked Fort Laurens the winter of 1778–79.
PHOTOS BY PAMELA SCHUYLER-COWENS; COURTESY DR. RICHARD M. GRAMLY.

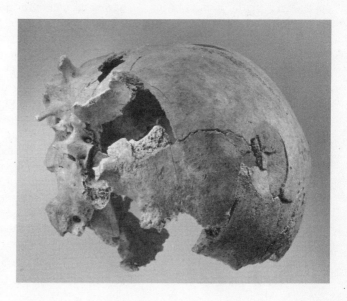

the check they had received, and thought that only repetitions of Indian cruelty could be expected should they persevere in their attempt, that it was deemed best to abandon the enterprise and return. By this time the cattle had become considerably dispersed, and when collected and the emigrants satisfied that the Indians who had done the mischief were only a small party and had departed, they commenced retracing their footsteps with indescribable feelings of sorrow and disappointment. With Boone the blow was doubly severe—the loss of his oldest son and the postponement, perhaps forever, of his darling plan of rescuing Kentucky from the grasp of the savage and the wilderness. Such a heavy loss sustained and such long and deeply cherished hopes deferred made him very heart sick. But while the others wended their way to their former homes in Virginia and Carolina, Boone accepted the invitation of Captain Gass to take up his temporary abode in a cabin on his farm, about seven or eight miles below Captain Russell's at Castle's-woods and a little south of Clinch River. Boone was, most likely, induced to this step by the hope of being joined the ensuing spring by Captains Gass and Russell in another attempt to permanently occupy Kentucky.

It was a matter of much public concern to learn with certainty to what Indian tribes the perpetrators of this Powell's Valley tragedy belonged and the causes that produced its commission. A considerable time elapsed before these facts were clearly ascertained. It then appeared that two Cherokee chiefs were concerned in it, and the others were Shawanoes. When Governor Dunmore made a demand upon the Cherokees for satisfaction, John Stuart, superintendent of Indian Affairs, despatched his deputy, Alexander Cameron, to Cho-tee, where he arrived in the beginning of September ensuing and succeeded, after much opposition from the young warriors, in having the chief principally implicated in the murder, named *Not-ta-wa-gua,* put to death. The executioners first appointed to carry the sentence into effect wounded the culprit in several places and left him for dead; but recovering and almost out of danger from his wounds, Mr. Cameron renewed his requisition and, with much difficulty and danger to himself, prevailed upon the principal chiefs to go in person and finish him, which they executed with much resolution, [wi] all the threats and opposition of his numerous relations and followers, and made several spirited harangues to their people on the occasion, warning them not to follow the example of Not-ta-wa-gua, lest they should meet the same disgraceful fate, and reprimanding them in sharp terms for their bad behavior on that and other occasions, which brought the young warriors to make their humble submission to their chiefs, and presenting as token thereof several strings of white beads.[g] The other Cherokee chief concerned in this tragedy was also condemned but found means to make his escape to the Chickasaws, but was not long after caught, confined, and ultimately paid the forfeit of his crime. Governor Dunmore, in a Proclamation issued shortly after, pronounced this conduct on the part of the Cherokees a "remarkable instance of their good faith and strict regard to justice."

In his speech at Fort Pitt, Dunmore charged the murder of young Russell and his companions as having been chiefly perpetuated by the perfidious Shawanoes and enumerated it among the chief causes that led to the Indian War of 1774. At Dunmore's treaty at Camp Charlotte, some of the plundered property belonging to Captain Russell, consisting of books and farming implements, was delivered up; but the horses, which had also been taken to the Shawanoe towns, had been sold to some Pennsylvania traders. How Big Jim, the hard-hearted Shawanoe warrior, met a merited fate thirteen years after the butchery of young Boone and his companions will be told in its appropriate place.[h] The cause of this cruel murder may unquestionably be found in the growing jealousy of the Indians in consequence of the rapid extension of the white settlements circumscribing the limits of their hunting grounds, pleading, in extenuation of the act, the permission or order of Cameron to rob all white intruders on their lands, by which the profligate portion of the savages became both their judges and executioners.[12] But this was not the only instance of Indian barbarity that occurred during the year. In the spring a hunting companion of Simon Kenton[i] was shot dead in their camp at the mouth of Elk River on the Great Kenhawa and their camp robbed. "This spring," said the Shawanoe chief Cornstalk in the summer of 1773 to Captain Bullitt, "we saw something wrong on the part of our young men: They took some horses from the white people, but we have advised them not to do so again." In July the Shawanoes killed a man named Richards on the Kenhawa; and in the same month a party of four men belonging to Capt. William Thompson's land explorers, who were passing by land through the Shawanoe country with several pack-horses loaded with goods and baggage, were attacked at a little Mingo village below the Shawanoe towns, one killed, another taken, together with the horses and plunder; the other two escaped.[13] About that time the same party of Mingoes seized a canoe ascending the Scioto loaded with goods belonging to one of the traders.[14] Not long after, the Shawanoes murdered on the Hockhocking[j] John Martin, a trader, and two of his men, named Guy Meeks and one Harkness, and seized Martin's canoe and goods exceeding £200 in value, assigning as a reason for the act that they were Virginians, and at the same time permitted a Pennsylvanian named Ellis to pass unharmed.[15] Sometime this year a party of Indians entered the cabin of one Martin, near Wheeling, killing him and all his family; and a small detachment while in pursuit of this marauding band was fired on, returned the fire, and dispersed the Indians.[16] Two men, named Cochran and Foley, were killed by the Indians about the time of the butchery of young Boone and his party.[17]

Shortly after, Gilbert and Robert Christian, George Anderson, one Hayes, and four or five others set out from the Virginia frontiers with a view of exploring Kentucky. Each of the party was provided with a pack-horse loaded with flour, ammunition, and other necessaries requisite for a long journey. Having passed Cumberland Gap and penetrated the wilderness within forty or fifty miles of the Crab Orchard, while encamped one Sunday, and all the party, save one, present, a band of fourteen Cherokees under Tom [Bob] Benge[k] made their appearance. Though they made signs of friendship, they were viewed with suspicion by the whites; and Gilbert Christian, in particular, objecting to their being allowed to advance to the camp, he and the men with him instantly betook themselves to the surrounding trees and stood on the defensive. Benge, who spoke quite good English, now called to the whites, declaring that they were all friends and brothers and that his party were Cherokees, between whom and the whites the most peaceable relations had for several years nominally existed. Gilbert Christian still opposed the propriety of permitting the Indians, double the number of the whites, to come up to camp but was over-ruled by the others, when the Cherokees advanced with many protestations of friendship and many a smirking attempt at brothering the white adventurers.

Having smoked, talked, and perhaps eaten awhile, Benge directed his attention to Gilbert Christian, who sat alone some distance off on a log with his rifle across his lap; and taking a seat familiarly beside him, asked to look at his gun. Christian, having unobserved thrown out the priming, handed the rifle to Benge, but not without apprehensions of evil. After examining it for sometime, Benge suddenly jumped to his feet uttering a signal yell and, presenting his gun, snapped it at Christian's breast. The Indians at the camp being too near and too much inter-mixed with the whites to use their guns, flew at Christian's party with their knives and tomahawks, when a severe struggle for life ensued—which, however, as there were two Indians to each white man, proved very unequal. It resulted in the death of Hayes and three others, when the survivors, among whom were the two Christians and Anderson, escaped, even after some of them had their hunting shirts stripped off by the grasping hold of the Indians. Their blankets and nearly everything else, except perhaps two of their horses, were lost by the whites. In consequence of their destitution, the severity of the weather with snow on the ground, they suffered almost incredibly; and though much scattered in disengaging themselves from the Indians, they got together again in the course of a few days on their return trail and at length reached the settlements.[18]

Boone, as we have seen, retired forty miles to Clinch River and made preparations for winter. For the support of his family, he must have relied mainly on his stock of cattle and his well-tried rifle. A living eye-witness thus describes his appearance at that time: "I have a distinct recollection of seeing Boone at my father's camp, on Reedy Creek of the Holston, in company with a tall young man named Crabtree, and some others—I think it must have [been] in 1773. Boone was dressed in deer-skin coloured black, and had his hair plaited and clubbed up,[1] and was on his way to or from Powell's Valley."[19]

Alas, exclaims a faithful writer on Western history—alas for our woodsman! Another year of quiet; stupid repose and farm labor seemed destined to try his patience. Dozing in security under his stoop by the westward flowing stream, he sighed for the howl of the wolf and the stealthy, scarce-leaf-rustling tread of the Shawanoese. He dozed, but dreamed not how rapidly, since he left them, his fellow white-men had desecrated the solemn forest-temples he had wandered and worshiped in. All that summer of 1773 had Mammon been sending his pioneers into the wilderness—surveyors and speculators. Washington descended the Ohio as low as Fishing Creek, where George Rogers Clark was already located; Capt. Thomas Bullitt, Hancock Taylor, James Douglas, the McAfee company, and others were all busily engaged in securing the choice lands of the country at the Falls of the Ohio and on the Kentucky and Salt rivers; while Capt. William Thompson and Col. Patrick Work of Pennsylvania led on a company of locators of military bounty grants, one of whom was the early western explorer James Smith.[20]

Simon Kenton also, with fourteen others, among whom were Capt. Hancock Lee, Dr. John Wood, and Michael Tygart, descended the Ohio to the Big Miami, explored the north-eastern portions of Kentucky, and returned by land to Greenbriar. Gallant men were many of these adventurers, and they loved dearly the life of danger they led; though some of them may have been superior to Boone in the power of planning, in grasp of intellect, in education, fortune, and demeanor, there were still few or none of them his equals in forest-craft and a simple love of forest-life. They measured out with cool, scientific, money-loving eyes the glorious vallies and greensward woods at sight of which Boone's lid had run over with tears of delight. They laid out towns where he had fancied the buffalo and deer would congregate forever; and though already the fierce mutterings of the tribes beyond the Ohio reached their ears and they knew a contest to be inevitable, they lingered, rod and chain in hand,[m] on the pleasant banks of the Elkhorn or by the carve-born rivulets that fed the Kentucky.[21]

How the winter of 1773–'4 passed away with Boone, we must leave the reader to judge. Hunting, however, must have been his chief occupation for the supply of his family with meat and the procurement of other necessaries by the sale or barter of pelts and furs. He used to relate this hunting adventure which occurred at that period and in the Clinch region with the parties to which he was well acquainted. One Green and a brother-in-law, who resided near Blackmore's on the Clinch, about fifteen miles below Captain Gass' place, where Boone was sojourning, went out some considerable distance among the mountains to hunt. They selected a good hunting range, erected a cabin, and laid up in store some jerked bear meat. One day, when Green was alone, his companion being absent on the chase, a large bear made his appearance near camp, upon which Green shot and wounded the animal, which at the moment chanced to be in a sort of sink-hole at the base of a hill. Taking a circuit to get above and head the bear, there being a slight snow on the ground covered with sleet, Green's feet slipped from under him, and in spite of all his efforts to stop himself, he partly slid and partly rolled down the declivity till he found himself in the sink-hole, when the wounded bear, enraged by his pain, flew at poor Green, tore and mangled his body in a shocking manner, totally destroying one of his eyes. When the bear had sufficiently gratified his revenge by gnawing his unresisting victim as long as he wished, he sullenly departed, leaving the unfortunate hunter in a helpless and deplorable condition, all exposed, with his clothing torn in tatters, to the severities of the season.

His comrade, at length returning, found and took him to camp. After a while, thinking it impossible for Green to recover, his companion went out on pretense of hunting for fresh meat and unfeelingly abandoned poor Green to his fate, reporting in the settlements that he had been killed by a bear. His little fire soon died away from his inability to provide fuel. Digging with his knife a hole or nest beside him in the ground-floor of his cabin, he managed to reach some wild turkey feathers which had been saved and with them lined the excavation and made himself quite a comfortable bed; and with the knife fastened to the end of a stick, he cut down from time to time bits of dried bear meat hanging over head, and upon this he sparingly subsisted. Recovering slowly, he could at length manage to get about. When spring opened, a party, of whom Boone is believed to have been one, went from Blackmore's settlement to bury Green's remains, with the brute of a brother-in-law for a guide; and to their utter astonishment, they met Green plodding his way towards home and learned from him the sad story of his sufferings and desertion.[n] The party were so indignant that they could scarcely refrain from laying violent hands on a wretch guilty of so much inhumanity to a helpless companion. Green, though greatly disfigured, lived many years.[22]

DRAPER'S NOTES: CHAPTER 9

1. Among Daniel Boone's MS. papers, it is mentioned that "Col. Donelson's line stopped at the lower end of a large bottom on the Kentucky River, at a large camp."

2. MS. Preston Papers; documents in the case of "Porterfield and others *vs.* Clark's heirs," Supreme Court, 1844; Charleston, South Carolina paper, December 3, 1771; Hall's *Sketches of the West,* i:248.

3. Almon's *Remembrances,* iii:131–35, 1776.

4. *Maryland Gazette,* January 12 and March 22, 1759.

5. *Maryland Gazette,* January 12th and March 22, 1759; Franklin's Ohio Settlement; MS. Fleming Papers; Sparks' *Life of Lee;* Sparks' *Washington;* documents in case, "Porterfield *vs.* Clark's heirs" in Supreme Court; *Documentary History of New York,* ii:998. "The increasing troubles," says Sparks, "between the mother country and the colonies prevented the ultimate completion of the project. But it was not abandoned till the beginning of the year 1776."

6. MS. notes of conversations with Col. Nathan Boone and the late Henry Rutherford of Tennessee. Soon after the Revolutionary War, Robertson resided in the family of Mr. Rutherford's father, Gen. Griffith Rutherford, of Rowan County, North Carolina, and used to speak of his hunting and exploring with Boone.

7. Bradford's *Notes on Kentucky,* Stipp's ed., 12–13.

8. Conversations with Col. Nathan Boone and lady; MS. letter of Daniel Pennington, a nephew of Daniel Boone; Haywood's *Tennessee,* 40.

9. MS. letters of Duke Hamilton and Samuel M. Duncan of Jessamine County, Kentucky, and of the late Elijah Callaway of North Carolina.

10. Gen. R. B. McAfee's *Sketches of the Settlement of Kentucky,* in the *Frankfort Commonwealth,* June 1, 1844.

11. A newspaper writer hailing from the Red Stone country in west Pennsylvania, whose article, published a year after the transaction and far distant from the scene of its occurrence, is copied into the 1st vol. [of] *American Archives,* 4th ser., folio 1015, indeed says that this tragedy happened on the 15th of October, 1773, and also makes other misstatements. We have preferred to follow the date in Boone's Narrative, corroborated by his original Family Record, now before us, in his own hand-writing, in which occurs this entry: James Boone, son of Daniel and Rebecca Boone, born May 3rd, 1757, was killed October ye. 10th., 1773, by the Indians."

12. The account of this Powell's Valley affair is made up from the following sources: Boone's Narrative; *Cape Fear Mercury,* Wilmington, North Carolina, December 1, 1773; Virginia *Gazette,* December 23, 1773; *American Archives,* 4th ser., 1, folios 278, 707, 873, 974, 1015, 1169; MS. letter of Gen. Hugh Mercer, January 8, 1774, and of Maj. Arthur Campbell, about June 20th, June 22nd, July 9th, and October 16th, 1774, in the Preston Papers; MS. statements of the late Daniel Bryan, Maj. Ben Sharp, and Elijah Callaway; MS. statements of and notes of conversations with Col. Nathan Boone and lady; Capt. John Gass; Mrs. Chloe Saunders, a daughter; Mrs. Tabitha Moore, a grand-daughter; and R. S. Russell, a descendant of Capt. William Russell; Rev. J. M. Allen; Willis A. Bush; the late Col. Robert Weakley, and others.

13. *American Archives,* 4th ser., i:873, 1015.

14. *Maryland Journal,* August 28th and September 9, 1773.

15. Jacob's *Cresap*[?], 44, 110; *American Pioneer,* i:312; *American Archives,* 4th ser., i:373.

16. *American Pioneer,* ii:382.

17. *American Archives,* 4th ser., i:707.

18. MS. statement of Col. George Christian of Tennessee, son of Gilbert Christian; *American Archives,* 4th ser., i:707.

19. MS. letter of the venerable Col. George Christian, August 25th, 1853.

20. *Maryland Journal,* August 28th and September 9th; and *New York Gazette,* September 2nd and 16th, 1773; copy of a MS. letter of Col. Patrick Work, written opposite the mouth of the Scioto, August 10th, 1773.

21. Perkins' *Pioneers of Kentucky,* in *North American Review,* January 1846, 81; Memoir and writings of Perkins, ii:255.

22. MS. notes of conversations with Col. Nathan Boone and the late Col. William Martin of Tennessee. The venerable Capt. John Carr of Sumner County,

Tennessee, writes that he has heard and known the story of Green's bear fight and desertion, and knew Green's son Zachariah, who settled in Sumner County and died there.

EDITOR'S NOTES: CHAPTER 9

a. The Iroquois Confederacy of New York originally called itself the Five Nations and was composed of the Mohawk, Onondaga, Oneida, Seneca, and Cayuga. In 1722 or 1723 the Tuscarora joined the league, which then became known as the Six Nations.

b. The Jewish leader King David in c. 1011 B.C.E. began his forty-year reign as Israel's second king. While in exile from his jealous predecessor, King Saul, David gathered a motley, mostly non-Hebrew army. Notes I Samuel 22:1–2, King James Version: "David therefore departed thence, and escaped to the cave of Adullam. . . . And every one that was in distress, and every one that was in debt, and every one that was discontented, gathered themselves unto him; and he became a captain over them: and there were with him about four hundred men."

c. This British secretary of state to the colonies was Lord William Petty Shelbourne, who in 1767 advocated pushing the Crown's colony-building schemes to the Mississippi River. In 1768 Lord Hillsborough succeeded Shelbourne.

d. This region of the Blue Ridge is still famous for its bear hunting and its championship bear dogs. Plott hounds, developed as a distinct breed by about 1780, originated and were first bred near this area.

e. For close combat, ball-head war clubs, also known as death mauls, death hammers, or tomahawks, were the Woodland Indian's arm of choice.

In 1764 Col. Henry Bouquet, a Swiss mercenary and Indian fighter, related to William Smith, author of *Expedition against the Ohio Indians* (1764), how his foes were armed for war: "Their arms are a fusil, or rifle, a powder horn, a shot pouch, a tomahawk, and a scalping knife hanging to their neck. When they are in want of firearms, they supply them by a bow, a spear or death hammer, which is a short club made of hard wood."

Lightweight and rock hard, a maple war club could stave in a skull with one quick blow. Warriors often inserted iron spikes or wooden pegs in the ball end to make their war clubs more deadly. Archaeologists have excavated war clubs that are elaborately carved or inlaid with white wampum and shaped like otter heads, human faces, and eagles. Warring Indians typically left bloodied war clubs beside their dead victims as a warning and as a show of bravado.

During Lord Dunmore's War, frontiersman James Robertson discovered one such club near some smoldering ruins in Kingsport, Tennessee. Robertson wrote in a letter (see DM 3QQ:73–73{1}) to Col. William Preston dated August 11, 1774, that Indians "left a War Club at one of the wasted Plantations well made and mark'd with the two Letters I G (well made) So that I think there is a White man with them." This club, now in a private collection, is maple, twenty-two inches long, and carved into the shape of an otter with the ball end, about three inches across, gripped in its jaws. A short wooden spike protrudes from the ball. The club shows slight wear and a warm patina but is in excellent condition.

f. Draper's rendering of the dual interment of James Boone's and Henry Russell's remains becomes a biblical allusion to the death of King Saul and his son Jonathan, killed c. 1010 B.C.E. while battling the Philistines. Saul's successor, King David, interred them in a common sepulcher (II Samuel 21:12–14). Draper's lyrical prose is taken from David's lament, found in II Samuel 1:23.

g. Grains of white shell wampum drilled from the shell of the quahog clam. See chapter 4, note g.

h. In 1851 Nathan Boone told Draper the details of James Boone's death. Big Jim met his end in 1786 during one of Col. Benjamin Logan's (1743–1802) two campaigns against the Shawnee towns on the upper Miami River. As Daniel Boone rode into the fray, he spied the notorious Shawnee and hollered out: "Mind that fellow. I know him. It's Big Jim who killed my son in Powell's valley!" At Boone's words, a band of Logan's scouts surrounded Big Jim and cut him down with guns and knives. Defiant to the last, Big Jim died fighting. Logan's men scalped and mutilated his corpse.

i. John Yeager, who was killed by Indians when they raided the whites' hunting camp on the Elk River in March 1773. Kenton and fellow hunter George Strader escaped into the night.

j. Near the present site of Hockingport, Ohio.

k. Capt. Bob (not Tom) Benge (1760?–94) remains one of the malevolent phantom enigmas of the eastern frontier. Of mixed Cherokee-Scots parentage, Benge was a stout, red-haired man, fluent in both English and native tongues. He was a formidable Cherokee leader with many American scalps to his credit, and on at least one occasion, he cannibalized the dead.

On April 8, 1794, Lt. Vincent Hobbs ambushed Benge's kidnaping party a day's journey west of the Clinch River near Stone Mountain. Benge died in the first volley as the Virginians routed his warriors. Hobbs scalped Benge and sent the scalp to the governor of Virginia, who repaid the gesture with a silver-mounted long rifle. One of Hobbs' soldiers, Samuel Livingston, lifted Benge's belt ax for a souvenir, and it remained in the family for several generations. Benge's hand-forged skull cracker is on permanent display at the Museum of the Cherokee Indian in Cherokee, North Carolina.

l. Clubbed hair was not exclusively an Indian fashion. It was a European male hairstyle in which the hair was braided into a long queue and folded under itself, the end tied with a leather thong or a ribbon at the top of the braid, thus keeping the braid out of the way. By all accounts, Boone wore his hair clubbed his entire life.

m. Draper's romantic gush notwithstanding, Boone, with "rod and chain in hand," surveyed much of Kentucky's land, owned about 30,000 acres, shot deer as rapaciously as any Long Hunter, and tried but failed at land speculation.

n. This bear-mauling incident is similar to another legendary episode that took place in the wilds of South Dakota. In 1823 a big she-grizzly protecting her cubs badly mauled mountain man Hugh Glass. Fearing Arikara attack, days later his comrades—allegedly a youthful Jim Bridger and John S. Fitzgerald—abandoned Glass to what they thought was sure to be a painful, delirious death. But Glass did not die. He half crawled, half walked 200 or so miles back to Fort Kiowa, reoutfitted, and hunted Bridger and Fitzgerald down; both were understandably stunned to see him alive. In 1954 Frederick Manfred immortalized Glass' epic saga in his famous novel, *Lord Grizzly.*

CHAPTER 10

1774.—Dunmore's War.—Daniel Boone's Services.—Atrocities and Hostilities on Both Sides.—Squire McConnell Incident.—Spies.—Yellow Creek Massacre.—Boone's Melancholia.—Captain Russell's Confidence in Boone and the Latter's Subsequent Tour of Kentucky with Michael Stoner.—Ordeal of the Fincastle Surveyors.—The Clinch Mountain Frontier.—Capt. John Logan, the Celebrated Mingo Chief.

A storm was now impending—the Indian outbreak of 1774 that boded no good to the border settlements. During the ten years of nominal peace, but in truth, of *quasi* war, succeeding Bouquet's treaty of 1764, more lives were sacrificed along the western frontiers than during the entire Indian War of 1774, including the battle of Point Pleasant. Indians had wantonly murdered whites, and whites as wantonly butchered Indians. Traders had been robbed and murdered, not infrequently superinduced by their over-grasping rapacity, and Indians, in turn, inveighed beyond human sight and treacherously slain. Crimination begat re-crimination, and Indians and whites alike looked with distrust upon each other. "Whoever," says Mr. [Johnn Jeremiah] Jacob in his *Life of Cresap*, "saw an Indian in Kentucky" or, indeed, anywhere in the great western valley, "saw an enemy—no questions were asked on either side—but from the muzzles of their rifles." Party quickly followed upon the heels of party with the significant chain and compass, and innumerable notched trees for landmarks as a sequence told but too plainly that the tide of emigration would still roll westwardly with its portentous volume constantly increasing. It is not strange then that the ever jealous Indians brooded with fearful apprehension over the accumulating evidences that they would soon have to give way before the progressive settlements.

The opinion has been advanced in the excellent work of Mr. Withers[a] that the war of 1774 virtually had its commencement in the attack on Boone's party in Powell's Valley and that, in the interval of time between that event and the opening of the ensuing season, nothing could perhaps be done by the Indians but make preparations for the hostilities in the spring. "Indeed it very rarely happens," continues Withers, "that the Indians engage in active war during the winter; and there is, moreover, a strong presumption, that they were for sometime ignorant of the fact that there were adventurers in the country, and consequently they knew of no object there on which their hostile intentions could operate. Be this as it may, it is certain that from the movements of the Indians at the close of the winter, the belief was general that they were assuming a warlike attitude and meditating a continuance of hostilities. War was certainly begun on their part, when Boone and his associates were attacked and driven back to the settlements; and if it abated for a season, that abatement was attributable to other causes than a disposition to remain quiet and peaceable while the country was being occupied by the whites."[1]

On the 25th of January, 1774, a party of militia who had been mustered by order of Dr. John Connolly fired upon some friendly Shawanoe Indians in their huts nearly opposite to Pittsburgh, who had come there on public business at the request of Col. George Croghan.[2] In the beginning of March quite a panic prevailed on the south-western frontiers of Virginia. "Capt. Russell from Fincastle," says the *Virginia Gazette* of the 17th of March, "brings the disagreeable intelligence, that a general discontent appears among the Indian nations; that the Cherokees and Shawanese have combined together; and that, in short, the frontier inhabitants are under the most dreadful apprehensions, from the ill-temper prevailing amongst these barbarians." "The people on this river," writes Capt. Daniel Smith, March 22nd, 1774, from Castle's-woods on the Clinch, "are much more fearful of the Indians than I expected to find them. The late reports alarmed them so much, that four families in my neighborhood moved over to Holston before I heard of their getting off; they went in such haste that they left all their stock, and the greatest part of their household furniture. When they got to Holston, they heard news that mitigated their fears a little, and they ventured back again to take care of their effects; then I saw them and prevailed on them to stay."[3]

A writer in the *Virginia Gazette* under date Williamsburg, March 24th, urges Governor Dunmore to call the Assembly together without delay to prepare to avert the blow the Indians were about striking on the frontiers, for, adds that writer, "some recent transactions of theirs, with which (if [the] report speaks the language of truth) your Lordship has already been made acquainted, leaves us no room to doubt that the storm which has been so long gathering, will, ere long,

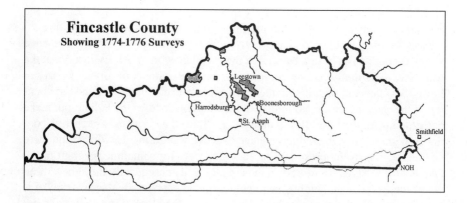

48. MAP BY NEAL O. HAMMON.

break forth in all its fury. * * * * Ten thousand incidents conspire to render a war at this time necessary, nay, inevitable; and the innocent lives of numbers might be saved by the timely proclamation of it. The very smiles of those faithless tribes ought to be considered as the harbingers of perfidy; but when they dare openly to annoy us with acts of hostility, surely a more solid resentment is due. Should an instance of any hostile act of theirs be demanded, I need only mention the un-happy murder of young Russell, committed not long ago, and, as has since been ascertained, was perpetrated by a Cherokee chief. Numberless other examples, of hostilities equally atrocious, might be adduced, were it not hoped that this of it-self is sufficient. Whether it would be prudent to wait for a second stroke, let the provident determine. The spring, it seems, is the stated period for an invasion; and, in all probability, the attack will be earlier on the more remote inhabitants."[4]

49. Lord Dunmore (John Murray), reproduced from an old engraving. STATE HISTORICAL SOCIETY OF WISCONSIN.

About the time of March, while Squire McConnell and six others were encamped down the Ohio, a party of Shawanoes came secretly to their camp by night; discovering whom, the whites jumped behind trees and placed themselves on the defensive, when the Indians professed to be friendly. Squire McConnell and one of his men, by invitation of the Indians, went with them to their town not far distant, when a council was held over them for three days, during which they were detained as close prisoners, having the war-dance performed around them and the war-club shaken fiercely over their heads. At length, when robbed of all their flour, salt, powder, lead, and such rifles as were of any value, they were severely threatened and sent off, the Shawanoes at the same time telling them that it was George Croghan's directions to them to kill all the Virginians they could find on the river and rob and whip the Pennsylvanians.[5] A company of emigrants had assembled early in April at the mouth of the Little Kenhawa, designing to descend the Ohio and make a settlement in Kentucky; and among them was George Rogers Clark, afterwards so celebrated in the annals of the west.[b] Some hunters of this party, ten miles below the main body, were fired on [by] Indians, who were beaten back when the hunters returned to camp.[6]

Other parties of whites on the river were robbed, some were driven off, and great apprehensions of danger were felt by all the adventurers and settlers along the Ohio.[7] Early in April Thomas Hogg and two or three others were killed near the mouth of the Great Kenhawa.[8] On the 16th of April a party of traders descending the Ohio in their canoe was fired upon near the mouth of Little Beaver by three Cherokees who waylaid the river, killing one man, wounding another, when the third made his escape, leaving the Indians to plunder the canoe of the most valuable part of the cargo, which was destined for the Shawanoe towns.[9]

To allay the fears of the people on the Clinch and Holston frontiers, Capt. William Russell, returning from Williamsburg to the Clinch River, employed, by order of Col. William Preston, Richard Stanton, Edward Sharp, Ephraim Drake, and William Harrod to proceed as spies on the 15th of April to the head of Powell's Valley, and there, on or near the *Warrior's Path,* to look out particularly for Indian sign; if they should discover any and the Indians should appear to be directing their course towards the settlements, then to return and give speedy notice; otherwise, to proceed along the boundary line between Virginia and the Cherokees as far as the water-course on which it terminated and ascertain whether that stream was the Cumberland or Louisa and, on their return, make out a report under oath for the use of the Assembly. "And," continues Captain Russell, "tho' we are apprehensive that the Cherokees and Northward Indians intend war, yet should you by accident fall in with any of their parties, you are to avoid acting towards them in a hostile manner, unless in cases of the last extremity, because the least hostility committed by you, at this time, when the Indians appear ripe for war, would not only blast our fairest hopes of settling the Ohio country, but be attended with a train of concomitant evils, and doubtless involve the Government in a bloody war."[10]

50a & 50b. Spontoon-style pipe tomahawk (a), c. 1750s; antler-handled hunter's knife (b). Both accouterments date from eighteenth-century Kentucky. FROM THE COLLECTION OF JIM AND CAROLYN DRESSLAR.

Such was the unhappy condition of the frontiers when Dr. Connolly issued a circular at Pittsburgh on the 21st of April, addressed to the people on the Ohio, informing them that an Indian war was inevitable and requesting Captain Cresap and party, who had retired to Wheeling, to cover the country with scouts until the people could fortify themselves. This message was taken as a signal for open hostilities, and on the 26th of April Captain Cresap and others attacked and killed two Indians in a canoe on the Ohio at Beach Bottom, a few miles above Wheeling, and the next day pursued another Indian party down the Ohio to the mouth of Pipe Creek, fifteen miles below Wheeling, where a skirmish ensued and a Shawanoe chief was killed and another wounded. On the 1st of May occurred the bloody tragedy at Yellow Creek, where some of Logan's relatives were among the slain.[c] The war was now fairly begun, and the Shawanoes and Mingoes residing with and near them sent forth their war-parties upon the Virginia borders, where the tomahawk and scalping-knife performed their horrid work. Of these numerous forays along an extended and exposed frontier of several hundred miles, we can only notice such as occurred in Boone's region on the Clinch River and that immediate neighborhood.

The remoteness of south-western Virginia from the hostile Indians exempted it for a period from the direful effects of the war. In May, before the news arrived on the Clinch of Connolly's semi-declaration of war and the consequent hostilities that followed, Daniel Boone started alone on a hunt in Powell's Valley and to visit the grave of his lamented son. Upon his arrival there, finding that the wolves had rolled off the logs that had been placed as a protection over the burial place and had scratched down some distance into the grave, Boone concluded to examine and see if the bodies had been disturbed. With the aid of a stick, he disinterred the remains of his son and young Russell, buried together; the wolves had not reached them. Fresh blood was yet visible upon their mangled heads—the hair upon both was plaited in accordance with the custom of that day. Boone could easily distinguish the two apart, though about the same age and both much disfigured; his son had fair hair, while young Russell's was decidedly black. He had barely re-adjusted the grave and replaced the logs upon it when there suddenly arose a severe storm, which lasted some considerable time. During its continuance, from the melancholy associations and gloominess of the place, mingled with the dismal howlings of the storm, Boone felt more dejected, as he used afterwards to relate, than he ever did in all his life.

As the evening shades drew near, the sky cleared up brightly, when he went a few hundred yards, hoppled out his horse, made a fire, and laid himself down beside it. But he could not sleep. After awhile he distinctly heard Indians stealthily approaching his camp, who had doubtless discovered both his trail and the fire. Boone, unseen, crept quietly away and carefully drove his horse before him, leaving the bell open to deceive the Indians until he had passed through a narrow defile on Walden's Creek, when he stopped the bell and decamped as rapidly as possible. He fortunately heard no more of the Indians. The storm very likely had delayed them in their course and thus perhaps saved Boone's life—if they were hostile, as the circumstances of their secret approach would seem plainly to indicate. He could never in after years speak of this affecting incident, even to his own family, without having his feelings deeply stirred within him.[11]

After an absence of three weeks, the four spies sent out by Captain Russell returned without having made any discoveries of Indians but [had] ascertained that the Cherokee and Virginia boundary line terminated on the Louisa or Kentucky River. When the intelligence reached south-western Virginia of the open rupture between the whites and Indians on the Ohio, Capt. David Gass and Michael Stoner were sent as scouts to Kentucky; they found some deserted cabins but seem not to have met any of the land adventurers in that country.[d] Near the present site of Stanford, they killed a bear and, making a tug of the skin, tied Captain Gass' horse with it, and smelling which, the animal became frightened and broke away. The horse was not recovered till the following year. Taking some traps with them, they caught a number of beaver and returned to the Clinch settlements. "I have had two scouts," writes Capt. Daniel Smith towards the close of June, "for some time past down a river called Louisa; they have been down there one trip, and brought word that there is no fresh sign of Indians."[12]

One Crabtree—perhaps the same who escaped the Powell's Valley massacre—was present about the middle of June at a horse-race on Watauga and there killed a noted Cherokee named Billy, a relation of old Ou-ta-ci-te.[e] It was a dastardly outrage and created no small fear lest a war with the Cherokees should be the consequence; but by the prudent management of the Watauga settlers in dispatching James Robertson[f] and William Fallin as messengers to the Cherokee towns to disavow the act in their behalf, together with the wisdom and forbearance of the old chiefs, peace was preserved. Efforts to bring Crabtree before the courts failed either in the prosecution or conviction.[13]

Governor Dunmore addressed a circular on the 10th of June to Col. William Preston and other commandants of the frontier counties, informing them that "hopes of a pacification can no be longer entertained" and ordering them to embody the militia and defend the country and to use their discretion in "providing extraordinary means for any extraordinary occasions." Energetic efforts were made to place the frontiers in some measure in a posture of defense by erecting and garrisoning forts and keeping out vigilant spies along the trails and streams of the wilderness. Colonel Preston on the 20th of June authorized Captain Russell to employ two faithful woodsmen to repair to Kentucky and notify the surveyors of their dangers. In reply, Captain Russell writes from the Clinch under date Sunday, June 26th, that the colonel's instructions had fortunately reached him on the morning of the previous day, which was the day appointed for the muster of his company. Boone was probably present. Captain Russell read to the people so much of the dispatch as was necessary for their satisfaction, when they voted to build the two forts on the Clinch in as convenient localities as could be selected, and, Captain Russell adds, "we shall begin instantly to erect them."

"I am sensible, good sir," continues Captain Russell, "of your uncommon concern of the security of Capt. Floyd and the gentlemen with him, and I sincerely sympathize with you, lest they should fall prey to such inhuman, bloody-thirsty devils as I have so lately suffered by; but may God, of his infinite mercy, shield him and company from the present impending danger! And could we, through Providence, be a means of preserving such valuable numbers, by sending out scouts, such a procedure could, undoubtedly, be of the most lasting and secret satisfaction to us, and the country in general. I have engaged to start immediately on the occasion, two of the best hands I could think of—Daniel Boone and Michael Stoner; who have engaged to search the country as low as the Falls, and to return by way of Gasper's Lick on Cumberland, and through Cumberland Gap; so that, by the assiduity of these men, if it is not too late, I hope the gentlemen will be apprized of the imminent danger they are daily in."[14]

Colonel Preston, on the 27th of June, ordered out one hundred and fifty men under Col. William Christian, assisted by Capts. William Campbell and Walter Crockett, to range along the frontiers. Captain Campbell with his company was dispatched to Moccasin Gap and the Big Island of Holston; Captain Crockett to the head of the Clinch and Blue Stone; and Colonel Christian to Castle's-woods on the Clinch. "When I got here," writes Colonel Christian from Captain Russell's at Castle's-woods, Tuesday, July 12th, "I found that Boone and Stoner had set off yesterday two weeks, in search of the surveyors: They were to go down the Kentucky to your salt lick; from thence across the country to the Falls of the Ohio, and from there home by way of Gasper's Lick on Cumberland River. If they find them on the Kentucky, they will be back in a few days; if not till they go to the Falls, it will probably be ten days from this time before they return. Captain Russell thinks they have passed the Falls some days ago, as Boone would lose no time if he could not find the people. This makes me think it unnecessary to send Drake, as I before proposed, until Boone's route is known." He then proposes an expedition of two hundred men directly across the country to the Shawanoe towns and adds: "I confess I want to delay sometime to see whether Boone returns, and by that time every thing could be well fixed."[15] This intended expedition ultimately gave place to the larger one under Col. Andrew Lewis to the mouths of the Great Kenhawa.

Captain Russell wrote Colonel Preston on the 13th of July that the people on the Clinch had altered their original design of only two forts on that river below Elk Garden and had erected three; one at David Cowan's in Castle's-woods, sometimes called Cowan's or Russell's Fort, but which Captain Russell named Fort Preston; a second, ten miles above, at Capt. Daniel Smith's, named Fort Christian; and a third, five miles below Castle's-woods at William Moore's, called Fort Byrd. Colonel Christian stationed ten men at Fort Preston and also at Blackmore's Fort near the mouth of Stony Creek, where four families had collected; the other two stations were very strong and well supplied with men. It was to Fort Byrd, or Moore's Station, that Captain Gass' and Daniel Boone's families, who lived but two miles off, repaired when it was made a place of rendezvous toward the close of June.

In this letter, Captain Russell thus speaks of Boone's mission and of the scouts in service. "I am in hopes, that in about two or three weeks from this time, Mr. Boone will produce the gentlemen surveyors here, as I can't believe they are all killed. Boone has instructions to take different routes till he comes to the Falls of the Ohio; and if no discovery there, to return home through Cumberland Gap, which will give them opportunity to discover if they are about the upper entrees on Salt Lick River, or have advanced towards Cumberland River, to make what few surveys were to be there—in which tour, if they are alive, it is indisputable but Boone must find them.[16] I have kept the other scouts out continually on duty, some to watch the head of Kentucky, and between that and Sandy Creek, and the others about Cumberland Gap and down Clinch River; and, as they are men that may be depended on, I hope the enemy cannot come upon us without being discovered before they make a stroke; if so, there is a probability of rewarding them well for their trouble between this and the Ohio."[17]

Of Boone and Stoner's tour to the Kentucky, we know comparatively but little. Boone kept a journal of that dangerous mission, which has long since been unfortunately lost. Having been employed for that service apparently at Captain Russell's muster on the Clinch on Saturday, June 25th, Boone received his instructions and returned home; and having respected the Sabbath, the two adventurers on Monday morning of the 27th of June plunged into the wilderness, relying for food and safety upon Divine Providence, their own sagacity, woodcraft, and well-tried rifles. They thus walked by faith, proving their faith by their works; and he who feeds the fowls of the air, and suffers not a sparrow to fall to the ground unnoticed,[g] watched over and protected these lone messengers of humanity.

An anecdote has been preserved of this tour coming from Boone himself, which strikingly displays to us how our pioneer fathers could heartily enjoy a joke or ludicrous accident, even among the countless danger to which they were constantly exposed. On their outward journey, they came to a remarkable horseshoe bend in some small stream, where the narrow neck or point between rose to quite an elevation. This narrow ridge, impregnated with particles of salt, had been gradually eaten away on both sides by the buffaloes until the cavities met. Entering the lick, Stoner discovered a buffalo through the aperture on the other side, when the honest German said to Boone, "Sthop, Gabtain, and we will have shum fun." He slipped forward and, taking off his cap, suddenly thrust it through the small aperture in the frail partition between the cavities, which was scarcely larger than the cap, into the very eyes and face of the buffalo, then busily engaged in licking the dirt. Instead of scampering back in terror, as Stoner had confidently expected, the spirited animal quickly resented this rude interruption and angrily forced his head and neck through the clay bank up to his shoulders, when poor

Stoner, alarmed for his own safety, wheeled and ran, bawling out at the top of his voice, *"Schoot her, Gabtain! Schoot her, Gabtain!"* Boone, so far from being in a mood to obey this injunction, threw himself upon the ground in a fit of convulsive laughter at Stoner's expense instead of the buffalo's, from the sudden and ludicrous turn the affair had taken. The surly animal, having caused the hasty retreat of the uncivil stranger, seemed satisfied with his success and pushed the pursuit no farther.[18]

On the North Fork of [the] Kentucky, they made a large encampment and probably rested themselves, when our adventurous woodsmen next visited the Big Lick on Kentucky River, where Boonesborough was subsequently located, and reached the camp at Harrodsburgh[h] previous to the 8th of July, where Capt. James Harrod and a party of thirty-four others were making improvements and laying off a town, granting to each settler a half-acre in-lot and a ten acre out-lot.[19] Boone obtained a lot adjoining that of one Evan Hinton, and a cabin was erected, long known as Boone and Hinton's cabin.[i] But town-making and cabin building came to a sudden termination. There was another camp three miles below Harrodsburg, at a large spring called Fontaine Bleu,[j] from which, on the morning of the 13th of June, Jacob Lewis departed to hunt and was never heard of after.[20] On the 8th of July, when James Knox and nine others were at that camp, some of whom were at the time drying papers in the sun, they were sur-

51. Michael Stoner was not the only woodsman to try his hand against America's wild cow; such foolhardy bravado nearly cost several Kentuckians their lives.

prised and fired upon by about twenty Indians, killing upon the spot James Hamilton from Fredericksburg, Virginia, and James Cowan from Pennsylvania; the Indians then rushing upon the survivors, they fled to Harrod's camp. The whole party, now numbering forty-three persons, went to Fontaine Bleu, buried the dead, and the next day set out for the settlements on the Clinch River, where they arrived on the 29th of that month, after making several discoveries of the enemy on the way.[21]

Boone and Stoner had probably left Harrod's settlement before this untoward disaster and pursued down the Kentucky to its mouth, and there scratched their names on a large rock.[22] Somewhere on this route, they evidently met Captain Floyd and three other surveyors and gave them notice of their danger.[k] Floyd and three others had parted on the 8th of July with fourteen men to go about twenty miles to finish home surveying; and all were by appointment to meet at a place on the Kentucky known by the name of *"The Cabin"* on the 1st of August in order to proceed together on their homeward journey. Floyd, with his three men, repaired to the place of rendezvous on the 24th of July and found the other party had previously assembled and gone off in the greatest precipitation, leaving him only this notice written upon a tree: "Alarmed by finding some people killed, we are gone down." He did not well understand by this notification whether a part had assembled there and gone down to the main camp to notify the others of the impending danger, or that the whole company had met and gone down the Ohio and Mississippi, as several had proposed returning home that way with a view both to see the country and avoid the fatigue of a land journey.

Captain Floyd and his companions immediately set out for the settlements, and after a painful and fatiguing journey of sixteen days through mountains almost inaccessible and ways unknown, they at last arrived near Captain Russell's fort on the Clinch. The party who left the notice for Captain Floyd on the tree of their "going down" proved to have been James Douglas, Capt. John Ashby, Jacob Sadowsky, Mordecai Batson, and probably Willis Lee and Isaac Hite and others, who had been surveying around the Falls of the Ohio, ascended the Ohio and Kentucky to Harrod's Landing on the latter, landed, and went in search of the parties at Fontaine Bleu and Harrod's camp, and finding the two men dead at the former and much fresh Indian sign, left the notice for Captain Floyd and descended the Ohio and Mississippi in a large pirogue to New Orleans, and thence made the best of their way, first to Pensacola, then to Charleston, and finally, to Williamsburg, Virginia, where they safely arrived in December following, after a long and perilous journey.[23]

From the mouth of the Kentucky, Boone and Stoner hastened to the Falls of the Ohio. There the water in the river was then so low that they went out quite a distance on the dry rocks in the bed of the stream, and Boone found some petrified buffalo manure attached to the rocks.[24] Three miles south-east of the Falls was still standing a few years since an ancient beech tree beside a slowing spring on which was cut, *"D. Boone, 1774"*—which serves as another landmark of the route of these faithful messengers.[25] At Mann's Lick, a few miles south of the

Falls, they found some surveyors with their attendants[1] and gave them notice of the hostile disposition of the Indians.[26]

The fate of Hancock Taylor's party of surveyors deserves particular notice. They were engaged in surveying on the Kentucky. While Taylor, James Strother, and Abraham Hempinstall were descending the river in a canoe to bring up some provisions and articles they had left where they had previously been at work, they were fired upon, below where Frankfort and Leestown were subsequently located, by a party of Indians concealed on the bank of the stream; Strother was shot dead in the canoe, and Taylor received two balls in his body, one of which eventually proved mortal. Hempinstall and Taylor evaded the Indians and, being joined by John Bell, John Green, and another person, commenced their return by land to Virginia, Taylor travelling two or three days, when Hempinstall and his companions carried him by turns on their backs two days more. But failing rapidly, they could convey him no farther, when Green copied off and reduced Taylor's field notes to surveys, which Taylor signed and thus authenticated. He died and was buried on the 1st of August on the bank of Taylor's Fork of Silver Creek, within the present county of Madison, Kentucky, and rough stones were placed at his grave, on one of which his initials, *"H. T.,"* were rudely hacked with a tomahawk. The survivors soon reached the settlements with the record of the surveys and tidings of their misfortunes.[27]

After an absence of sixty-one days, Boone and Stoner returned to the Clinch on the 26th of August, having travelled eight hundred miles and passed through many difficulties in their various peregrinations. Finding that Captain Russell had just started with a company of men from the Point Pleasant campaign, Boone immediately dispatched an express to overtake Captain Russell with information of his return and expressing a desire to go on the expedition. "Capt. Floyd seems very uneasy," writes Maj. Arthur Campbell on the 28th of August, "at the way Drake has used him, as he now plainly discovers that he was expecting to be appointed to a separate command. For this reason, and to relieve Floyd's anxiety, I wrote pressingly to Mr. Boone to raise men with all expedition to join Capt. Floyd; and I did not doubt but you would do everything in your power to encourage him. And what induced me particularly to apply to Mr. Boone, was seeing his Journal last night, and a letter to Capt. Russell, wherein he professes a great desire to go on the expedition, and I am well informed he is a very popular officer where he is known. So I hope Capt. Floyd will still succeed, as I have good reason to believe. Mr. Boone will get all in Capt. Looney's company that intended to go with Bledsoe, and perhaps you can assist a little out of Waggoner's recruits, as I have heard today he is likely to get some men. I have been informed that Mr. Boone tracked a small party of Indians from Cumberland Gap to near the settlements. Upon this intelligence, I wrote pressingly to Capt. Thompson to have a constant lookout, and to urge the spies strictly to do their duty."[28]

Captain Floyd also wrote to Colonel Preston about securing Boone's assistance in completing his company for the expeditions and, at the same time, in simple yet touching language, expressed his gratitude in view of Boone's generous self-denial and exposure in going to Kentucky to notify him of the outbreak of the Indians. "You will hear," says Floyd, "of Mr. Boone's return, and desire of going out. If Mr. Drake gets a berth down there, and does not immediately return to me and assist according to your instructions, pray let Boone join me and try. Capt. Bledsoe says Boone has more influence than any other man now disengaged; and you know what Boone has done for me by your kind directions—for which I love the man. But yet do as you think proper in everything respecting me."[29]

Boone had actually started, perhaps with a party of recruits, to join the troops already on their march to the rendezvous at the Great Levels of the Greenbriar but was met or overtaken in a day or two with orders to return to the Clinch and aid in defending that exposed frontier.[30] During his absence in Kentucky, the enemy had committed some depredations. Capt. John Dickinson had a skirmish with a party of them on the Greenbriar about the 28th of June; and on the 31st of July an attack was made on the Kelley's on that river, when Col. John Field narrowly escaped by flight. On Sunday, the 7th of August, a straggling party of two Indians and a white renegade attacked several persons, mostly children, near the residence of Balser Lybrook, where two other families had also collected on Sinking Creek of New River in what is now Giles County, Virginia. Old Lybrook was wounded, and three of his children, one of whom was an infant, were killed, together with a young woman named Scott and a child of the widow Snydoe, nearly all of whom were in a camp at the time of this tragic occurrence. Three boys were captured, and several other children narrowly escaped. Two of the little captives, sons of John McGriff and the widow Snydoe, stole off from the Indians while encamped near the Clover Bottom of Blue Stone River about midnight of the Tuesday succeeding and were found in the woods by some scouts on the ensuing Friday morning.[31]

"Sundry other people," writes Colonel Preston on the 13th of August, "have also been murdered along the frontier parts of the neighboring counties. The inhabitants of Fincastle, except those on Holston, are chiefly gathered into small forts, also great numbers in Botetourt; as Indians are frequently seen, and their sign discovered in the interior parts of both counties.[32] Such is the unhappy situation of the people, that they cannot attend their plantations, nor is it in the power of the scouts and parties on duty to investigate the inroads of the enemy, as they come in small parties, and travel among the mountains with so much caution."[33] The reader may thus form some idea of the circumstances by which Boone was surrounded when he returned from Kentucky and engaged in the defense of the Clinch settlements. The Fincastle regiment, comprising about two hundred and seventy rank and file, all prime frontier riflemen, had marched towards the mouth of the Kenhawa under Colonel Christian and Captains William Russell, William Campbell, Evan Shelby, John Floyd, Walter Crockett, William Herbert, and

James Harrod—the latter with a company of twenty-two who had retired from Kentucky. Thus were the frontiers left quite weak, relying mainly upon the hope that the Indians, learning that a large army of *Long Knives,* as they termed the Virginians, was preceding to invade their country, would find quite enough to do in defending their own wigwams, corn-fields, and families.

September proved a month of unusual activity, alarm, and danger along the Clinch frontier. The depredations committed were not on a large scale but were, nevertheless, sufficient to keep the people in constant apprehension and the scouts in diligent search of the inroads of the enemy. On the 8th of that month Samuel Lammey was taken prisoner on the North Fork of Holston, and at the same time the families of John and Archibald Buchanan narrowly escaped.[34] Early in the morning of the same day a party of twelve or fifteen Indians fired upon John Henry, while standing in his own door, four miles from Capt. Daniel Smith's, or Fort Christian on the Clinch, and dangerously wounded him, when he fled to the woods, leaving his wife and three children, who were yet in bed, to be captured by the enemy. Henry fortunately soon met an old man whom he knew, named John Hamilton, who concealed him in a thicket until he could go and alarm the fort and bring him assistance, when the wounded man was taken to a place of safety, but did not long survive. As soon as this intelligence reached the Rich Valley settlement, the principal part of the people fled to Maj. Arthur Campbell's at the Royal Oak on the Middle Fork of the Holston. Great fear was entertained at this time for the safety of Captain Smith's fort, as he had only eight men for its defense, while the stations of Glade Hollow, Elk Garden, and Maiden Spring above him were in a much better condition to resist an attack. A scarcity of ammunition was everywhere keenly felt and deplored by a suffering people.[35]

On Tuesday, the 13th of September, three Indians attacked one of Captain Smith's soldiers about half a mile from the Maiden Spring Station, when he returned the fire and brought one of the Indians to the ground. The soldier escaped without injury. A party of whites, who happened to be within three hundred yards when the guns were fired, hastened to the spot and gave the two surviving Indians a smart chase. Quite a quantity of blood was found where the Indian fell, and a large cave or pit was discovered into which he had crawled or been thrown within seventy or eighty yards of the place where he was shot. A plug[m] which had burst from the fellow's wound was picked up a few steps from the tree behind which he stood wounded, and no doubt was entertained that his death speedily followed. "The pit is to be searched," writes Major Campbell, "by means of letting a man down by ropes, with lights, as our men are anxious to get his scalp." Whoever could truthfully assert that he had "killed an Indian and *got his hair*" was certain to be regarded as a man of uncommon prowess and worthy of all the praise a grateful frontier people could bestow.

Captain Smith's scouts discovered the same evening the tracks of a party of the enemy going off with horses and, as was supposed, with the prisoners they had previously taken. Captain Smith immediately set out with a party of twenty-one men in pursuit, but after several days, two Indians, probably the surviving two who had attacked the soldier, discovered the whites, alarmed the main party ahead with the prisoners, and all escaped. So Captain Smith returned unsuccessful. Signs of this party of Indians had been seen by the scouts at the pass at the Sandy River, which, with several other passes, they were ordered to watch; but these passes were so distant from each other that it took several days to perform the tour, and the marauders had gone by sometime before the spies discovered their tracks; and the scouts, moreover, had thirty miles to go to give notice of their approach. But before they could arrive, the mischief was already done and the birds flown.[36]

During these times of peril, Boone was not idle. In a memorandum book kept at the time by Capt. Daniel Smith is this brief yet significant record: "Sept. 22nd, Lieut. Boone, fourteen men, four days, three pounds of beef per day"; and as Major Campbell wrote a few days before that meat was scarce on the Clinch and mostly kept in reserve for the use of the spies[n] and parties in pursuit of Indians, we may safely conclude that Boone headed his fourteen men on a four days' scout after the enemy. When there was anything to be done in the line of active service, he was never found among the drones or laggards. The danger too was rapidly approaching his own more immediate neighborhood, as we shall now have occasion to mention, when he had consequently to double his diligence to protect the weak and helpless and, if possible, to punish an unpitying foe.

In July the celebrated Mingo chief Capt. John Logan captured a prisoner on the West Fork of the Monongahela of the name of William Robinson, who[m] he conveyed to the Indian towns. The helpless captive was doomed to the stake. Logan's eloquence failing to save the prisoner's life, he boldly cut the cords with his tomahawk and rescued the intended victim from the impending flames. Three days after this occurrence, Logan approached Robinson with a piece of paper and, making some gun-powder ink, ordered him to write a message, which he designed to leave at some house whose inmates would fall before his deadly rifle and bloody tomahawk. Thrice did Robinson attempt to put Logan's imperious dictation to paper before he could get the phraseology sufficiently strong to satisfy the fastidious chief. With this gun-powder missive and a band of chosen savage warriors whose hearts, like his own, were rankling with enmity and burning with hate, Logan sallied forth from New Comer's Town on the Muskingum in quest of scalps and prisoners.

He first made his appearance, it would seem, among the Cherokees, endeavoring to embroil them in the war, but the stern opposition of O-con-nos-to-ta, and At-ta-kul-la-Kul-la, or the Little Carpenter, scarcely restrained the hot-blooded young warriors from taking up the hatchet and joining actively in the fray. As it was, perhaps a few of them clandestinely joined Logan as he and his desperate band started upon the war-path, breathing out vengeance and slaughter upon the devoted Long Knives. On Friday, September 23rd, Logan's party appeared before Blackmore's Fort on the Clinch, some seventeen miles below Fort Byrd or Moore's Station, where Boone commanded. Finding some Negroes without the fort, they succeeded in capturing two of them and Logan gave chase to another, who was relieved by the timely aid of Mr. John Blackmore. A considerable number of cattle and horses were now wantonly shot down, and the Indians several times cursed one of their Negro captives for the space of a quarter of an hour within full view of the fort. But the garrison was too weak to resent the insult or dare venture out to meet the haughty foe. So Logan and his warriors departed, leaving a war-club behind as an emblem of defiance.[37]

Within the present county of Sullivan, in East Tennessee, near King's Mill on Reedy Creek, which flows from the north-east into the South Fork of Holston, and something like thirty or forty miles south of Blackmore's Fort, resided with his family a lonely forester of the name of John Roberts. In his region the people had not yet taken refuge in forts and were consequently more exposed to danger from Indian forays than the inhabitants of the Clinch River Valley. Logan, hastening over mountains and rivers, suddenly fell upon poor Roberts and his family, "sparing neither women nor children." On the evening of Saturday, the 24th of September, all were indiscriminately slaughtered, Roberts, his wife, and several children, excepting only the oldest son, James, a youth about ten years of age, who was made prisoner. About sun-rise the next morning, hallooing and the report of many guns were heard at several houses from which the people had fled to the woods; and the attack on Roberts' family was ascertained and rapidly heralded throughout that region, when Capt. William Cocke raised a small party and vainly pursued the savages, while John Anderson, James Clendenin, and another person collected together the families of Clendenin, Gilbert Christian, who was himself absent at the time at one of the stations on [the] Clinch, and a few others also on Reedy Creek below Roberts' place, numbering in all nearly twenty persons, all of whom marched on foot fully four miles to King's Fort.[38] "It was a skittish time with the women, you may be sure," writes an aged surviving participator and eye-witness of that affecting scene.[39]

When this party of fugitives reached the fort, they found Roberts' second son, a bright little lad, had just been brought in, who had been badly tomahawked and scalped. Though left for dead by Logan and his murderous band, he had so far recovered his senses that when his uncle made his appearance near the scene of this savage tragedy, the little fellow, whose imagination probably pictured an Indian in every bush and tremulous thicket, ran off. His uncle called him by name, when he instantly recognized his voice, turned and ran to him [and] rejoiced. When questioned by his uncle, he returned sensible answers and pointed out his murdered parents and sisters, but his brother not being found, it was conjectured, as it afterwards turned out, that he had been captured. The little sufferer "received but one tomahawk blow on the back of his head," wrote Major Campbell, "which cut through the skull; but it is generally believed his brains are safe, as he continues to talk sensibly, and being an active, wise boy, what he relates is credited. For my part, I don't know as I ever had tenderer feelings of compassion for any of the human species. I have sent for him, and employed an old man that has some skill to attend him. I wish I could get Dr. Lloyd to him; if he cannot come, please try if he cannot send me up some medicine with directions. I have been too tedious and circumstantial in relating the little hero's story, but as it seems to be a singular instance, I am persuaded you will not be displeased with it." A few days later, Major Campbell apprised Colonel Preston that "the boy that was scalped is dead. He was an extraordinary example of patience and resolution to his last, frequently lamenting that 'he was not able to fight enough to save his mamma.'"[40]

It was at Roberts' forest-cabin that Logan left a war-club, to which was attached the celebrated missive which he had forced Robinson to write at his own dictation. Both the club and the note were sent first to Major Campbell at the Royal Oak on the Middle Holston, who wrote to Colonel Preston on the 12th of October and added in a postscript, "I have sent you enclosed Logan's original letter, which came to hand this day." Appended to the same sheet and in Colonel Preston's hand-writing is the following:

The words of the original letter:

To *Captain Cresap:*

Why did you kill my people on Yellow Creek for? The white people killed my kin at Conestoga, a great while ago, on Yellow Creek, and took my cousin prisoner. Then I thought I must kill too; and I have been three times to war since;—but the Indians are not angry—only myself.

Captain John Logan.

"July 21st day, 1774"

"This is a document," as Mr. Mayer justly observes, "savagely circumstantial and circumstantially savage;—cool, deliberate, and bloody, even to the date,—and left as this sentimental Indian's apology—not as his challenge,—in the desolated dwelling and amid the reeking bodies he had butchered."[41] Logan once declared that he had two souls, the one good and the other bad; that when the good soul was in the ascendant, he was kind and humane; but when the bad soul ruled, he was perfectly savage and delighted in nothing but blood and carnage.[42] Of this latter trait, his cruel butchery of the Roberts family was a striking exemplification. But this Indian hero, in whose character there is so little beside his pathetic eloquence to admire, had not yet "fully glutted his vengeance"; so, with the reeking scalps of his victims and his little broken-hearted prisoner, he hied away to Moore's Fort on the Clinch, where Boone was in command. "Mr. Boone is very diligent at Castle's-woods"—so wrote Major Campbell on the 29th of September—"and keeps up good order: I have reason to believe they have lately been remiss at Blackmore's, and the spies there did not do their duty."[43]

But the very day Major Campbell was thus writing from the Royal Oak, Logan and his forest blood-hounds stole something of a march even upon the

52. *Representative maple ball-head war clubs (also called "death mauls").
From top to bottom: 22-inch-long otter effigy club collected in 1774 by frontiersman James Robertson near Kingsport, Tennessee; 24-inch-long club, c. early
1700s; 17-inch-long club; 23-inch-long Kickapoo club; eastern Sioux club, c.
1820, ball carved as a man's face.* FROM THE COLLECTION OF JIM AND CAROLYN
DRESSLAR.

cautious Boone. Between sun-set and dark, three men, who went about three
hundred yards beyond the fort yet in plain view to examine a pigeon-trap, were
waylaid and shot at, and one of them, John Duncan, was killed on the spot,
scalped, and a war-club left beside the mangled body. Though Boone and a party
of men instantly ran from the fort to the place of ambuscade when the report of
the guns was heard, the Indians escaped unpunished. Early the next morning
Boone sent an express to Major Campbell with the news of the enemies' appearance in his quarter and prepared to go immediately in search of them. Of the result of that pursuit we have no knowledge but presume the wily Logan kept out of

the way of Boone and his vigilant riflemen. In addition to the untimely fate of Duncan, Major Campbell has given us the substance of the remaining portion of Boone's letter, despatched by the express. "Mr. Boone also informs me," says Major Campbell, "that the Indians have been frequently about Blackmore's since the Negroes were taken, and Capt. Looney having only eleven men cannot venture to go in pursuit of them. Mr. Boone has sent me the war-club that was left; it is different from that left at Blackmore's, and Boone thinks it is the Cherokees who are now annoying us. I rather believe it is some of Major McDonald's desperate fugitives that have taken refuge somewhere on the Ohio back of us, and would willingly deceive us into the belief that it is the Cherokees, that they may thus succeed in creating a misunderstanding between us and the old chiefs."[44]

Previous to this, "the murder of Russell, Boone and Drake's sons was in every one's mouth," casting much of the blame upon the Cherokees.[45] Now it is ascertained that two parties of their warriors had left their towns, either to join the Shawanoes or fall upon some of the border settlements, and that the Cherokees appeared in very bad temper. The consternation into which the late attacks had thrown the inhabitants on the Clinch and Holston rivers it is almost impossible to conceive; and the more so as many of their choice men were absent on the expedition, and the few remaining were almost entirely destitute of ammunition. "Two of these people," writes Colonel Preston, "were at my house this day, and, after travelling above an hundred miles, offered ten shillings a pound for powder, but there is none to be had for any money. Indeed it is very alarming; for should the Cherokees engage in a war at this time, it would ruin us, as so many men are out, and ammunition so scarce. Add to this the strength of those people, and their towns being so near our settlements on Holston."[46]

Whether some of the insubordinate Cherokees really aided Logan and his desperate band does not clearly appear. New outrages, however, speedily followed upon the heels of those already related; and we have to record two attacks on the same day, at places nearly forty miles apart, indicating that Logan had, very likely, been reinforced and divided his dusky warriors into two parties. He probably headed in person the one destined to act against Capt. Evan Shelby's settlement between the North and South Forks of the Holston, while the other was directed to strike yet another blow at Blackmore's on the Clinch. "On the last Thursday evening, ye 6th instant," writes Major Campbell on the 9th of October, "the Indians took a Negro wench prisoner, belonging to Capt. Shelby, within three hundred yards of his house. After they took her some distance, they examined her, asking how many guns were in the fort, and other questions relative to the strength of the place. They also asked if the store was kept there now. After they had carried her off about a mile, they saw or heard a boy coming from [the] mill; they immediately tied the wench, and went off to catch the boy; while they were gone the wench luckily got loose and made her escape. She says they knocked her down twice when she refused to tell in what situation that fort was; and she says one was a large man much whiter than the rest, and talked good English; it was the same kind of person Mr. Blackmore saw in pursuit of the

Negro he relieved. Some think Capt. John Logan is about yet; others, that it is Will Emery, a half-breed Cherokee, as he was one mentioned in Shoat's deposition as being out, and he is known, for some time past, to be in the Shawanoe interest; he was the interpreter when Donelson run the line, and it was he who robbed Knox and Skaggs."[47]

In this foray against Shelby's Fort and neighborhood, Logan seems to have failed in securing the substantial results usually attending his hostile enterprises. Nor was the other part of his plan executed with much more success. Approaching Blackmore's Fort, which was situated on the northern bank of the Clinch, the Indians evidently perceived that the people were chiefly some distance away from the gate and therefore concluded to make a bold push to enter the fort and take it by a *coup de main.* Creeping silently along the bank of the stream, completely out of the view of the garrison, everything promised favorably until one Deal Carter, who happened to be some fifty-five paces from the fort, discovered them and immediately commenced hallooing murder! One of the Indians fired at and missed him, but a second shot passed through his thigh; and though the wound was not mortal, it yet rendered him powerless to escape when one of the Indians more bold than the rest soon ran up, tomahawked, and scalped his fallen victim. Two of the garrison, one of them whom was named Anderson, who were either just outside the fort or quickly ran there, now fired upon the Indians—Anderson, at the fellow in the act of scalping poor Carter, while the other man shot at another Indian. What was the effect of these shots is not known, but the Indians all scampered off about a hundred yards' distance, when they fired several shots at Anderson and his companion, some of the balls striking into the stockade a few inches only from Anderson's head. By this time several of the garrison had hastily mounted the bastion nearest the scene of action and fired upon the enemy, when they decamped to the adjacent woods and mountains. For a few moments it was an exciting time. Though Carter, by the timely discovery of the Indians, lost his own life, yet he was probably instrumental under Providence of saving the fort from a bloody tragedy.

When this attack was made, there were but sixteen men in the fort, and Captain Looney, who had been ordered there for its defense, happened to be about on a visit to his family, who resided in the neighborhood of Reedy Creek, where the Roberts family had so recently fallen before the ruthless foe, while Lt. John Cox and twenty-four men from the Upper Holston, though on their way, had not yet arrived there.[48] "It is remarkable," observes Major Campbell, from whose letter to Colonel Preston these details are derived, "that Capt. Shelby's wench was taken the same day, and about the same time of the day, that this affair happened on Clinch. So many attacks in so short a time, give the inhabitants very alarming apprehensions. Christian's fine stock of cattle and horses is missing, and a number of cattle and horses about the fort are either killed or carried off. Want of ammunition and scarcity of provisions are again become a general cry. Since I began this, I am mortified with the sight of a family flying by. If ammunition does not come soon, I will have no argument that will have any force to detain them; and if our army is not able to keep a garrison at the Falls the ensuing winter, I expect we shall be troubled with similar visits the greatest part of the coming season."[49]

Shortly after this second Indian attack on Blackmore's, Capt. Daniel Smith, in connection with Boone, arrived there with a party of thirty men. The night afterwards they had six out of seven of their horses stolen by the Indians from a small enclosure of which the stockading one side of the fort made part. Early the next morning, Smith and Boone set out in quest of the enemy with twenty-six choice men all greatly anxious to overtake the Indians. They found some Indian and horse tracks not far distant from the fort but soon lost all trace of them. "I am this far," wrote Captain Smith from Castle's-woods the 13th of October to Colonel Preston, "on my return from the lower settlements to the head of the river. Mr. Boone can inform you of the bad success we've had after the inhuman savages—the murders they've committed, and the mortification we've suffered of putting horses into a pen adjoining the fort for the Indians to take away, and whose trace we could by no means discover. I shall be as expeditious as possible in getting to the head of the river, lest they should invade those parts that are particularly under my care."[50] The late Col. William Russell, of Kentucky, a son of Captain Russell of Clinch, then a youth of sixteen, is believed to have served on this scouting expedition under Smith and Boone; and his comrades, from his tender age, were compelled to relieve the weight of his rifle by carrying his portion of baggage and provisions—thus commencing a soldier's career which subsequently shone with such distinguished luster at King's Mountain, on Wayne's Indian campaign, and during the late war with England.[51]

This was the last disturbance on the south-western frontier during that brief but bloody Indian outbreak. Logan and his "inhuman savages"—as Captain Smith not inaptly termed them—returned to the Shawanoe towns of the Muskingum eleven days after the memorable battle of Point Pleasant—in which conflict he could have taken no part, though repeatedly asserted by writers on border history.[52] "Last Friday was two weeks"—so wrote Colonel Christian to Colonel Preston on Tuesday, the 8th of November, 1774—"Logan, a famous chief, went home, with a little boy, a son of Roberts on Holston, and two of Blackmore's Negroes. He said he had taken them on the frontiers next [to] the Cherokee country, and had killed, I think, either five or seven people. The boy and Negroes will be soon in." Within two or three days after his return, Logan delivered his pathetic speech to John Gibson to be conveyed to Lord Dunmore, which has given him so undying a notoriety throughout the civilized world.° Young Roberts safely reached the Holston country and grew to years of manhood and usefulness.

Though there is some reason to believe that Boone may have served as a militia captain on the Upper Yadkin, and was sometimes so denominated prior to actual service in the Indian War of 1774, yet up to this period he never really ranked in that conflict higher than a lieutenant. But his neighbors, who best could judge of his merits and efficiency, deemed him worthily entitled to the notice and promotion of his country. The movement originated entirely in the hearts and affections of the people. The only documents handed down to us throwing light upon the subject are the following, both of which were addressed to Colonel Preston:

"Whilst I was in the lower settlements," says Capt. Daniel Smith from Castle's-woods, "I was shown a petition signed by many of the inhabitants, representing their situation to be dangerous because they have been so irregularly supplied with the number of men allotted to the district; and also requesting you to appoint Mr. Boone to be a captain, and to take charge of these lower forts, so that he may be at liberty to act without orders from the Holston captains, who, by their frequent absence, leave the inhabitants sometimes in disorder. Instead of signing this paper, I chose to speak my sentiments to you concerning Mr. Boone and the paper which I suppose he will shew you. As to the paper, I believe it contains the sense of a majority of the inhabitants in this settlement. Mr. Boone is an excellent woodsman. If that only would qualify him for the office, no man would be more proper. I do not know of any objection that could be made to his character, which would make me think him an improper person for that office. There may possibly be some impropriety in it because of Capt. Russell when he returns, but of this you are much the best judge."[53]

"As Mr. Boone," writes Major Campbell, "is to be the bearer hereof, he can inform you particularly of the news this way. You will see by the enclosed, that your old acquaintance, William Poage, wants a commission. He now acts as sergeant at Fort Preston. I believe he is a fit man enough, on many accounts, to be an officer, and I would be glad could you gratify him with a commission, should it not interfere with others already appointed, which I am afraid will be the case, as either Vance, or Capt. Looney's ensign, is intended for that station. I wish Mr. Boone's application, or rather ye people's for him, may not have a similar tendency. I think it is men, and not particular officers, they stand in most need of. Of this I am informed, that it was not proposed by Mr. Boone to petition you as they do; but it arose from a notion that a distant officer would not be so particularly interested for their safety, as he who lives among them; and some disgust at Capt. Looney for being away at home the time of the late alarm, which he pleads, in excuse, that he wanted to see the safety of his own family, when Roberts' was killed in his neighborhood."[54]

It is scarcely necessary to add that a captaincy was bestowed upon Boone by Colonel Preston, who had blank commission for that purpose from Governor Dunmore, and the three lower forts on Clinch, Blackmore's, Moore's, and Cowan's, were assigned to his command.[55] Some few alarms yet followed, and continued vigilance was requisite, but in the course of a few weeks the war happily terminated. The Cherokees had inflicted capital punishment upon those of their nation who had been concerned in the murder of young Boone, young Russell, and their hapless companions, and the signal defeat of the Shawanoes and their confederates at Point Pleasant disposed the Southern Indians to heal all differences and live on terms of friendship with their white neighbors.

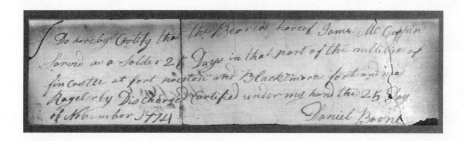

53. Daniel Boone wrote this discharge for James McCushin on November 25, 1774, during Lord Dunmore's War. It is the earliest known example of Boone's handwriting. FILSON CLUB HISTORICAL SOCIETY.

Peace was made with the humbled Shawanoes. They threw themselves upon the governor's mercy and told him to make the terms and they should be complied with. They stipulated for the return of all prisoners, horses, and other plunder taken from the whites, offering even to give up their own horses. They agreed to relinquish all lands and hunt no more south of the Ohio; to molest no passengers on that river, but render them every assistance and protection; to be governed in their trade by such regulations as should be dictated to them, and never more take up the hatchet against the English. For the fulfillment of these stipulations, they gave six hostages—two of whom were to be chiefs, and the others either chiefs or their sons. The treaty was to be formally ratified at a meeting at Pittsburgh the ensuing spring, where all the Ohio Indians, for greater solemnity, were to be present. Twelve refractory Mingoes, who refused to accede to the peace, were conveyed as prisoners to Pittsburgh. Leaving about one hundred men under Captain Russell to maintain Fort Blair at the mouth of the Great Kenhawa, twenty-five to garrison Fort Fincastle at Wheeling, and seventy-five more to garrison Fort Dunmore at Pittsburgh, all to protect the frontiers and keep the Indians in awe, the troops under Dunmore and Lewis were disbanded and returned to their respective homes. During the winter, the Indians brought in and delivered up their prisoners and plunder, and evinced so sincere a disposition for peace that these posts were, by Governor Dunmore's orders, evacuated and the men discharged.[56]

That portion of the Fincastle troops comprising the companies of Captains Shelby and Russell had determined on returning home by way of Kentucky, in order to examine that attractive country, while others, perhaps, would pursue their homeward course up Sandy River. It was arranged that Capt. Daniel Smith should go early in November with a small party down the Sandy to meet any troops who might take that route; and should he meet none, then to *mark* his way back, provide barbecued or jerked meat upon scaffolds at conspicuous passes with written directions how the troops should proceed should they yet march that way, and where to find good hunting grounds. Upon Captain Smith's return and failure to meet the troops, he was immediately to join Captain Boone and go with forty or fifty men and a number of horses to the mouth of Dick's River on the Louisa or Kentucky—"but twice that number," adds Major Campbell, "would go, at their own cost, to meet their friends." Boone, in the meantime, was ordered to send two or three trusty scouts down the Louisa and return by way of Cumberland Gap. But Captain Russell having been assigned to the command of Fort Blair and the season far advanced, this plan was abandoned and the Fincastle troops returned by way of the Kenhawa. So there was no occasion for Boone's intended detour to Kentucky. During November the surviving Fincastle men reached their homes, and by the 20th of that month the men under Boone's immediate command, as well as all others in service on Clinch and Holston, were discharged.[57] [p]

Thus ended the war which cost the people of Virginia about one hundred thousand pounds, many valuable lives, and incalculable amount of individual suffering and privation along the exposed frontiers.[58] Boone was most actively engaged during the whole contest and had, in all situations and under all circumstances, proved himself equal to the trust reposed in him. With this consciousness of having done his duty, he rejoiced like Logan, "at the beams of peace," when the hardy settler could once again retire from the pent-up fort and in safety re-occupy his isolated cabin-home, and the fearless hunter could once more roam the bewitching forest with the wild freedom he loved so well.[59]

DRAPER'S NOTES: CHAPTER 10

1. Withers' *Chronicles of Border Warfare*, 110, 111.

2. *American Archives*, 4th ser., i:468, 484.

3. MS. letter of Captain Smith to Col. William Preston, in the Preston Papers.

4. *American Archives*, 4th ser., i:278.

5. MS. letter of Captain John Floyd to Col. William Preston, dated Little Gantt, April 26th, 1774, Jacob's *Cresap*, 45.

6. Letter of Gen. G. R. Clark, in the "Louisville Literary News-Letter," January 1839, *Hespenian* magazine, February 1839.

7. Captain Floyd's letter of April 26th; MS. letter of Alexander Spotswood Dandridge, May 15th, 1774, in the *Preston Papers*.

8. *American Archives*, 4th ser., i:707, 1015.

9. *American Archives*, 4th ser., i:345, 468; Jacob's *Cresap*, 4, 6, 107, 140.

10. MS. instructions, April 15th, 1774, in the Preston Papers.

11. MS. notes of conversations with Col. Nathan Boone and lady.

12. MS. letter of Captain Smith, in the Preston Papers; and notes of conversations with Capt. John Gass.

13. MS. letters of Maj. Arthur Campbell and Col. William Christian, in the Preston Papers; Haywood's *Tennessee*, 43, 44.

14. MS. letter of Captain Russell, June 26th, 1774, in the Preston Papers.

15. MS. Preston Papers.

16. The primitive name for Licking River, Kentucky.

17. MS. letter of Captain Russell among the Preston Papers.

18. MS. notes of conversations with Col. Nathan Boone.

19. "The first corn ever planted in Kentucky," says Bradford's *Notes on Kentucky,* "was planted in the year, 1774, at *Fontaine Bleu,* near Harrodsburg, by David Williams, John Shelp and James Sadowsky." But this is not strictly correct, for Dr. Walker and party had twenty-four years previously planted corn and peach-stones on the northern bank of [the] Cumberland River, a few miles below the present town of Barboursville, Knox County, Kentucky.

20. Col. Daniel Boone MS. Papers.

21. MS. records of Mercer County, Kentucky; MS. notes of conversations with the late Capt. Ben Briggs of Kentucky; *American Archives,* 4th ser., i:707; newspaper sketches of the late Gen. R. B. McAfee and Col. Nathaniel Hart, Sr., of Kentucky.

22. Conversations with the late Capt. Benjamin Briggs, who had this fact from Michael Stoner.

23. MS. letter of James Douglas, December 14, 1774; *American Archives,* 4th ser., i:707; Butler's *Kentucky,* 155; *American Pioneer,* ii:326; Bradford's *Notes on Kentucky,* 20; McAfee and Hart's newspaper sketches.

24. Conversations with Col. Nathan Boone.

25. MS. notes of conversations with Col. Isaac Clark, near Linnville, Kentucky, in 1846, who had seen the tree and inscription.

26. Conversations with Col. Nathan Boone.

27. MS. letter of Capt. William Russell, in the Preston Papers, August 28, 1774; MS. statement of the late President Z. Taylor, a nephew of Hancock Taylor; conversations with Capt. John Gass; *American Archives,* 4th ser., i:787; Sketches by the late Col. Nathaniel Hart, Sr., of Woodford County, Kentucky.

28. MS. Preston Papers.

29. MS. letter of Capt. John Floyd to Colonel Preston, August 28th, 1774, which, with other ancient papers, have [been] copied from the originals in possession of the present Col. Nathaniel Hart of Kentucky.

30. Conversations with Col. Nathan Boone.

31. MS. letter of Maj. Arthur Campbell, August 9th and 10th, and of Capt. James Robertson of Virginia, August 12th, 1774; Kercheval MS.; Howe's *Virginia,* 278; *American Archives,* 4th ser., i:707.

32. Fincastle County was formed out of Botetourt in 1772 and embraced all of Virginia west of Botetourt; and hence Colonel Preston, who was both county lieutenant and surveyor of Fincastle, extended his authority over the Kentucky country, both as chief surveyor and in sending scouts to the Louisa or Kentucky River. In 1776 Fincastle was divided into the counties of Montgomery, Washington, and Kentucky, and the name of Fincastle as a county became extinct.

33. *American Archives,* 4th ser., i:707.

34. MS. letters of Maj. Arthur Campbell, September 17 and October 6, 1774; *American Archives,* 4th ser., i:808.

35. MS. letters of Maj. Arthur Campbell, September 9th, and En. William Doack, September 22nd, 1774; *American Archives,* 4th ser., i:808.

36. Maj. Arthur Campbell's letters of September 17th and 23rd, 1774, in MS. Preston Papers; *American Archives,* 4th ser., i:808.

37. Letter of Maj. Arthur Campbell, September 26th and 29th and October 1st, 6th, and 9th, 1774, in the MS. Preston Papers; *American Archives,* 4th ser., i:808.

38. Captain Cocke's MS.

39. Col. George Christian of Tennessee to one of the authors, August 15th and 25th, 1853.

40. MS. letters of Maj. Arthur Campbell, September 26th, 29th, October 3rd, 6th, and 12th; Capt. William Cocke's, September 25th, and Capt. Anthony Bledsoe's, October 15th, 1774, all among the Preston Papers; conversations with the late Mrs. Sarah Shelby of Tennessee; MS. letters of Col. George Christian, August 15th and 25th, 1853; *American Archives,* 4th ser., i:808; *American Pioneer,* i:208.

41. Discourse on Logan and Cresap, delivered by Brantz Morgan, delivered before the Maryland Historical Society, May 9th, 1851; of which it is small praise to say that it is a learned and able production.

42. *American Pioneer,* i:359.

43. Major Campbell to Colonel Preston, in MS. Preston Papers.

44. In July preceding, Maj. Angus McDonald had, with four hundred men, attacked the Wappatomika towns on the Muskingum, killed a few Indians, dispersed others, burned half a dozen villages, and destroyed a considerable quantity of corn; Major Campbell's MS. letter to Colonel Preston, October 1, 1774.

45. Major Campbell's letter, in the MS. Preston Papers; without date, but written about June 20th, 1774.

46. *American Archives,* 4th ser., i:808.

47. Maj. Arthur Campbell to Colonel Preston, October 9th, 1774, in the MS. Preston Papers.

48. Major Campbell, in a letter of the 6th of October, furnishes the following table of the strength of the forts on the Clinch, with their distances from each other and the names of their respective commandants—beginning at Blackmore's, the lowest on the stream. The distances are not, probably, so reliable as those we have already, in part, indicated: *Blackmore's* sixteen men, Sergeant Moore commanding; *Moore's,* twenty miles above, twenty men, Lieutenant Boone commanding; *Russell's* four miles above, twenty men, Sgt. W. Poage commanding; *Glade Hollow,* twelve miles above, fifteen men, Sgt. John Dunkin commanding; *Elk Garden,* fourteen miles above, eighteen men, Sgt. John Kinkead commanding; *Maiden Spring,* twenty-three miles above, five men, Sgt. Joseph Cravens commanding; *Whitou's Big Crab Orchard,* twelve miles above, three men, Ens. John Campbell of Rich Valley commanding.

49. MS. letter of Major Campbell to Colonel Preston, October 12th, 1774.

50. MS. letters of Major Campbell, October 12th, and Capt. Daniel Smith, October 13th, 1774, in the Preston Papers.

51. Collins' *Kentucky,* 502.

52. By some readers, this notice may be deemed an undesirable exposition of the Indian hate that rankled in the bosom of Logan. The more his true character is studied, the more readily will the "romantic illusion which used to hang about this celebrated chief" be partially dissipated, if not entirely destroyed, as the accomplished editor of the *Virginia Historical Register* frankly admits. We are told in the *Life of Dr. Wheelock* by a missionary who saw Logan repeatedly in the Pittsburgh County in 1772 that he was then informed that during the preceding French and Indian War, Logan was an active leader of a band of savages who desolated the defenseless frontiers, killing, scalping, and captivating a number of poor men, women, and children; and that after the war, a murder and robbery of a white man were committed on the Allegheny Mountain, and from circumstances, suspicion fixed the crime on Logan, though no positive proof could be had to convict him. "There are two young men now in my company," writes Capt. Anthony Bledsoe from Camp Union, on the Greenbriar, October 15th, 1774, to Colonel Preston, "who say they knew one Logan, a mixed-breed in the Shawanoe nation—one of whom I can depend on, the other is a stranger; they both agree in sentiment as to Logan's being a notorious villain." Dah-gan-on-do, or Captain Decker, a venerable Seneca who resided all his eventful life of over one hundred years on the Allegheny, informed one of the authors that Logan, whom he knew well, "was a very bad Indian."

It has been customary to point to Logan's speech as the production of a pure blooded Indian. Captain Bledsoe's MS. letter shows us that he was only "a mixed breed." His father was Shi-kel-la-my, and dwelt at the "charming plain of Shamokin," on the noble Susquehanna. In John Bartram's *Travels to Oswego,* a rare work published in London in 1751, our Quaker traveller, under date July 10th, 1743, in noticing his visit to Shamokin, thus speaks of Shi-kel-la-my's origin—and the authority, it must be conceded, is beyond all cavil or dispute: "July 10. We departed in the morning with Shickalamy and his son, he being the chief man in the town, which consisted of Delaware Indians; he was of the Six Nations, or rather a Frenchman, born at Montreal, and adopted by the Oneida after being taken prisoner; but his son told me he was of the Cayuga nation, that of his mother, agreeable to the Indian rule *Partus sequitur ventrem,* which is as reasonable among them as among cattle, since the whole burthen of bringing up falls upon her; therefore in case of separation the children fall to her share." p. 17. Strictly speaking, Logan was therefore a half-breed, though by habit and education a thorough Indian.

TFB: Partus sequitur ventrem *means, idiomatically, "Once born, a man follows his stomach."*

53. MS. letter of Captain Smith, October 13th, 1774, in the Preston Papers.

54. Maj. Arthur Campbell, without date, but evidently about October 17th, 1774, in Preston Papers.

55. This commission having Dunmore's signature was preserved by Boone and sent, some sixteen years ago, by his descendants accompanying a memorial to Congress for remuneration for his services.

56. MS. letters of Col. William Christian, November 8th, and Capt. William Russell, November 12th, 1774, in the Preston Papers; *American Archives,* 4th ser., i:1013, 1014, 1169; ibid., 4th ser., ii:1189; Withers' *Border Warfare,* 137.

57. MS. letters of Major Campbell, October 9th, November 4th, and November 21st; Colonel Christian's, November 8th, and Captain Russell's, November 12th, 1774.

58 *American Archives,* 4th ser., ii:92.

59. And among Boone's MS. papers, we find evidence that he soon plunged deep into the wilderness, for in January ensuing he was encamped on [the] Kentucky River—probably silently enjoying one of his highly praised hunts. For sketches of Col. William Preston, Col. Arthur Campbell, Gen. William Russell, and Gen. Daniel Smith, whose names are so frequently associated with Boone's in the transactions of 1773 and 1774, see Appendix.

EDITOR'S NOTES: CHAPTER 10

a. Draper's appreciation for Alexander Scott Withers' *Chronicles of Border Warfare* (1831) seems to have undergone a radical transformation. In chapter 3, n. 4, he deemed Withers' work "bungling and unreliable."

b. Regarding George Rogers Clark, see chapter 12, note 1.

c. Draper glosses over this tragic affair in one sentence. On May 15, 1744, Jacob Greathouse and his band of frontier rogues, perhaps at the instigation of Col. Michael Cresap, lured the family of Mingo chieftain Capt. John Logan to Yellow Creek, a narrow stream flowing into the Ohio fifty miles south of Pittsburgh, got them drunk, shot them, and scalped and mutilated their corpses. Logan and his avenging warriors rose up against the whites scattered along the desolate ridge of the central Appalachians, running from southwestern Virginia to northeastern Tennessee. This violence helped ignite Lord Dunmore's War. In 1786 Logan was assassinated, perhaps by order of the Iroquois Confederacy; he had become, his nephew declared, "too great a man to live." But the Indians never forgot Greathouse's treachery and in March 1791 commandeered his flatboat while en route to Limestone (Maysville), Kentucky. Greathouse and his wife were tortured to death and his crew killed.

d. If true, Stoner must have returned in time to accompany Daniel Boone on his trip to Kentucky, making it two trips to Kentucky for Stoner before August 1774. It would be interesting to know who had built the cabins they found.

e. Ou-ta-ci-te (or Mankiller), who lived in the region of the headwaters of the Savannah River, was a prominent Cherokee chieftain during the French and Indian War. In 1762 he was part of a three-man Cherokee delegation that traveled to London under the auspices of Lt. Henry Timberlake. At the outbreak of the Revolutionary War, he allied himself with Dragging Canoe's anti-American Chickamauga band and relocated at the headwaters of the Coosa.

f. For James Robertson, see chapter 16, note r.

g. Based on the scriptures II Corinthians 5:7, James 2:18, Mathew 6:26, and Mathew 10:29.

h. Draper used "Harrodstown" and "Harrodsburg" interchangeably to refer to the settlement of Harrod's Town. I have standardized his usage to Harrodsburg.

i. Kentucky historian Neal Hammon wrote the following to me in a letter dated April 1, 1992, regarding the Boone-Hinton cabin, allegedly built in June or July 1774: "This is very unlikely for several reasons, the primary one being the time element. Boone did not leave Castlewood, Virginia, until 26 June, and Harrod and his men abandoned Harrodsburg shortly after an Indian attack on 8 July. It is approximately 300 miles from the Clinch settlements to Harrodsburg, and most of the route was through mountainous country. Another important point is that Daniel Boone never claimed he visited Harrodsburg in 1774. He stated that when he arrived in central Kentucky, he found the surveyors 'drove in by Indians,' and so he proceeded to survey some land for James Hickman on what is now Hickman Creek [deposition of Daniel Boone in "Boofman's Heirs *vs.* James Hickman," *Fayette County Kentucky Complete Book A,* pp. 604–42]. The so-called Boone-Hinton cabin was probably built by Squire Boone and his good friend Evan Hinton in the latter part of 1775 or early 1776. Hinton never claimed to have been in Kentucky in 1774."

j. The proper spelling is Fountainbleau.

k. Firsthand evidence is lacking that Boone ever saw John Floyd in Kentucky; he probably did not. The journal of Thomas Hanson, one of Floyd's assistants in the summer of 1774, does not mention such a reunion. Historian Neal Hammon asserts in his unpublished manuscript, "Into Western Waters": "The fact that Harrod and his men panicked after the Indian attack and fled from Kentucky without warning the surveyors of their danger has never been mentioned by historians. Instead, most accounts state that Boone arrived at Harrodsburg before it was abandoned, implying that everyone knew that it was his mission to find the surveyors and lead them home."

l. This is unlikely. Daniel Boone later deposed that when he arrived in Kentucky, he found the surveyors "well drove in by the Indians."

m. Woodland Indians plugged bullet wounds with wads of goose down or beaver fur to stop the blood flow.

n. "Spies" is an eighteenth-century term for scouts. In 1860 John Cuppy, the last living scout of frontier leader Samuel Brady (1756–95), described to Draper the "Dress of Spies" operating in the Pittsburgh region, c. 1780: "Spy dress—a handkerchief tied around the spy's head of any color, sometimes a capeau (shorter than a hunting shirt) of cloth or a hunting shirt, and moccasins; and thick, loose woolen leggings reaching above the knee, so thick that a rattlesnake could not penetrate through with their fangs." (See DM 9S:36–37.) Such woodland dress was a practical mix of Indian and Anglo garments.

o. Capt. John Logan's famous speech has long been lauded as an example of Native American eloquence, but controversy surrounds its true authorship and the literal interpretation of its message. Supposedly, Logan dictated the plaintive message, which Simon Girty translated to Col. John Gibson, who wrote it down. The speech is found in many sources and is here excerpted from C. Hale Sipe,

The Indian Chiefs of Pennsylvania, 2nd ed. (Lewisburg, PA: Wennawoods Publishing, 1995), 443–44:

> I appeal to any white man to say if ever he entered Logan's cabin hungry and I gave him not meat; if ever he came cold or naked and I gave him not clothing.

> During the course of the last long and bloody war, Logan remained idle in his tent, an advocate for peace. Nay, such was my love for the whites that those of my own country pointed at me as I passed and said, "Logan is the friend of the white man." I had even thought to have lived with you, but for the injuries of one man. Colonel Cresap, the last spring, in cold blood and unprovoked, murdered all the relatives of Logan, not sparing even my women and children. There runs not a drop of my blood in the veins of any living creature. This called on me for revenge. I have sought it. I have killed many. I have fully glutted my vengeance.

> For my country, I rejoice at the beams of peace; but do not harbor the thought that mine is the joy of fear. Logan never felt fear. He will not turn on his own heel to save his life.

> Who is there to mourn for Logan? Not one.

p. Not true. Forts Blair and Dunmore were still occupied by militia troops in the spring of 1775.

CHAPTER 11

Aboriginal Claim to Kentucky.—Shawanoes.—Henderson and
Company's Purchase by Daniel Boone's Advice.—Treaty of Watauga.—
Boone's at the Treaty, and Then Heads a Party and Goes to Kentucky and
Erects Fort Boone.—Henderson Brings Up the Rear Party.—Various
Troubles.—Plan for Government Formed.

Before adverting to Henderson and company's celebrated *Purchase* from the Cherokees, a rapid notice of aboriginal claims to Kentucky and the successive treaties by which the Indian title became extinguished seems peculiarly necessary. There is some reason to suppose that the Catawbas may once have dwelt upon the Kentucky River—that stream, on some of the ancient maps published a hundred years ago, was called the Cuttawa or Catawba River. But that tribe of Indians so far as we know never laid any claim to that territory.

It would appear from the historical evidences extant that the Shawanoes were the earliest occupants of Kentucky of whom we have any certain knowledge. Colden,[a] the primitive historian of the Iroquois Confederacy, informs us that when the French commenced the first settlement of Canada in 1603, the Five Nations, who then resided near the present locality of Montreal, were at war with the powerful Adirondacks, who at that time lived three hundred miles above the Three Rivers in Canada. The Iroquois found it difficult to withstand the vigorous attacks of their enemies, whose superior hardihood was to be attributed to their constant devotion of the chase, while the Iroquois had been chiefly engaged in the more peaceful occupation of planting corn. Compelled to give way before their haughty foes, the Confederates had recourse to the exercise of arms, in order, if possible, to retrieve their martial character and prowess. To raise the spirits of their people, the Iroquois leaders turned their warriors against the Satanas, or Shawanoes, "who then," says Colden, "on the banks of the Lakes"—or, as other historians assert, in western New York and south of Lake Erie—and soon subdued and drove them out of the country.[1] The Shawanoes then retired to the Ohio, along which and its tributaries they planted numerous settlements. Some of them, however, when driven from western New York, seem to have located somewhere on the Delaware, for De Laet in 1624 speaks of Sawanoos residing on that river.[2]

The *Jesuit Relations of 1661–'62* allude to their residence in the West under the name of Ontouagannha or Chaouanons, and seem to have been the same as well called Tongorias, Enighecks, Erieehonons, Eries, or Cats by the early missionaries and historians;[b] and the same, moreover, known in the traditions of the Senecas as Gah-kwahs, who resided on Eighteen Mile Creek a few miles south-west of Buffalo in western New York, which the Senecas still call *Gah-kwah-gig-a-ah Creek,* which means *the place where the Gah-kwahs lived.*[3] In 1672 the Shawanoes and their confederates in the Ohio Valley met with a disastrous overthrow by the Five Nations[c] at Sandy Island, just below the Falls of the Ohio, where large numbers of human bones were still to be seen at the first settlement of the country.[4] The surviving Shawanoes must then have retired still farther down the Ohio and settled probably in the western part of Kentucky; and Marquette in 1673 speaks of their having twenty-three villages in one district and fifteen in another, all lying quite near each other. At length, the Shawanoes departed from Kentucky and seem to have gone to the upper part of the Carolinas and to the coast of Florida and ever after proved a migratory people. They were evidently "subdued," as Colden, Evans,[d] and Pownall[e] inform us, and the decisive battle was fought at Sandy Island, when a vital blow was given to the balance of power on the Ohio, which decided finally the fall of Kentucky with its ancient inhabitants.

It was this conquest that gave to the powerful Iroquois all the title they ever acquired to Kentucky. At the peace of Ryswick in 1697,[f] their right to their western conquests was fully acknowledged; and at the treaty of Lancaster in Pennsylvania in 1744, they ceded to Virginia all their lands west of that colony. In 1752 the Shawanoes and other western tribes at Logstown on the Ohio confirmed the Lancaster treaty and sold their claim to the country south of the Ohio; and at the treaty of Fort Stanwix in 1768, the Six Nations made a new cession of their claim to Kentucky as low as the Cherokee or Tennessee River.[5] Up to this period, the Cherokees never so much as thought of contesting with the Iroquois their claim to the Kentucky country; for some of the visiting Cherokees, while on their route to attend the Fort Stanwix treaty, killed game for their subsistence and on their arrival at Fort Stanwix tendered the skins to the Six Nations, saying, "They are yours—we killed them after passing the Big River," the name by which they had always designated the Tennessee.[6] But probably discovering that other Indian nations were driving a good business by disposing of their distant land rights, the Cherokees managed to hatch up some sort of claim which they in part relinquished to Virginia at the treaty of Lochaber in 1770; and when Colonel Donelson ran the line[g] the following year, the boundary was fixed at the suggestion of the Cherokee deputies on the Kentucky River as the south-western line, as they delighted, they said, in natural landmarks. This considerably enlarged the cession, for which they received an additional compensation.

In 1772 the Shawanoes made no claim to Kentucky; and at the treaty of Camp Charlotte in October 1744, they tacitly confirmed their old sale of that country in 1752 by agreeing not even to hunt south of the Ohio.[7] Thus, then, we see that the Iroquois had twice ceded their right to Kentucky as low as the Tennessee River and twice received their pay; the Shawanoes had disposed of their claim, such as it was, and received for it a valuable consideration;[h] and the Cherokees, finding it profitable to lay claim to some valuable unoccupied region, sold their newly assumed right to the country south and east of the Kentucky River. Their claim—if indeed it rises to the dignity of a claim—south and west of the Kentucky was fairly purchased by Henderson and Company, as we shall now proceed to notice—and thus, with the subsequent purchase by treaty of the Chickasaws of the strip between the Tennessee and the Mississippi, the Indian title[i] to the whole Kentucky country was fully and fairly extinguished.[8]

In introducing a character so prominent in the colonization and settlement of Kentucky as Col. Richard Henderson, something more than merely the mention of his name is demanded. His great paternal grandfather was an emigrant from Scotland, and his grandmother, whose maiden name was Williams, came from Wales, and both settled in Hanover County, Virginia, where Richard, son of Samuel Henderson, was born on the 20th of April, 1735. His father removed to Granville County, North Carolina, about 1745 and was subsequently appointed sheriff of that county; and so sparse was the population at that early period that the only opportunity then existing of giving his children an education was by employing a family instructor. Young Richard was soon able to engage in the practical duties of his father's office, which gave him that enlarged knowledge of men and things for which he became so eminently distinguished in after life.

Upon the expiration of his father's term of service, he read law for twelve months with his cousin, the late Judge Williams, and applied to the chief justice of the colony for an examination, and for his certificate to the governor, who issued the license to practice. The judge asked how long and what books he had read. When frankly told the brief period and few books, the judge said it was useless for him to go into an examination, for no man in that period of time and [with] the books he had specified could be qualified to obtain a license. With great promptness and firmness, young Henderson replied: "Sir, I am an applicant for examination, which it is your duty to give me; and, if found worthy, to grant me a certificate—if otherwise, to refuse one." A most searching examination followed, which resulted in a presentation of the certificate, with many encomiums upon his talents and qualifications. His license was readily issued by the governor, when he entered upon a successful professional career.[9]

In 1767 he was appointed one of the two associate justices of the Superior Court of the colony; and during the troubles with the Regulators, he was once in September 1770 rudely driven from his court at Hillsborough.[j] Having served six years upon the bench of the highest judicial tribunal of North Carolina, he retired from that dignified position by the expiration of the limitation of the court. In every situation, he proved himself an eminent scholar and jurist, possessing versatile talents and commanding influence. He was considered the Patrick Henry of North Carolina.

Such was Colonel Henderson, who had heard the report of Boone's wanderings in Kentucky and his representation of the loveliness of that distant country.

Colonel Henderson had doubtless heard these reports during his professional visits at Salisbury, as well as through the brothers Nathaniel, David, and Thomas Hart[k]—the latter of whom subsequently declared that he "had known Boone of old, when poverty and distress held him fast by the hand; and, in those wretched circumstances, he had ever found him of a noble and generous soul, despising every thing mean."[l] Confiding implicitly in Boone's representations of the beauty, extent, and fertility of Kentucky, these men, with Henderson at their head, resolved at once to secure it for effecting the settlement of the country.[10] Henderson possessed much of the real spirit of enterprise so necessary for the founder of a colony and was thus happily adapted to enter upon their new and hopeful experiment.[m]

In the autumn of 1774 Colonel Henderson and Capt. Nathaniel Hart visited the Cherokee nation to ascertain if they would sell the Kentucky country. The result was favorable. The preliminaries were arranged, and the ensuing February or March was agreed on as the time for the Cherokees to meet Henderson and party at the Sycamore Shoals on the Watauga River, to enter upon a formal treaty. Meanwhile, At-ta-kul-la-Kul-la, or the Little Carpenter, a young Indian man, and an Indian woman accompanied Henderson and Hart on their return home, which was in November, to see and examine the goods offered as the consideration. These goods were purchased at Cross-Creek, now Fayetteville, North Carolina, on the 6th of December and were soon after sent forward in wagons to the Watauga settlement. Over twelve hundred Cherokees, nearly one half of whom were warriors, were collected at the Sycamore Shoals by the assiduity of Daniel Boone, who was employed for that purpose. On the 14th of March, 1775, the treaty was regularly opened after the usual Indian ceremonies. The Cherokees proposed selling the country above Kentucky River as far as the Great Kenhawa, averring that Colonel Donelson had not paid them a portion of the promised consideration for their cession of that country to Virginia; but Colonel Henderson told them he would have nothing to do with that tract, as Virginia claimed it; that he wished the country below the Kentucky and would not part with his goods for any other.

When Henderson renewed his suit on the following day, Dragging Canoe,[n] an influential chief, spoke decidedly against selling the region between the Kentucky and the Tennessee, as the Cherokees wished to retain that country for hunting grounds; that they regarded the buffalo and other game as quite beneficial to them as the tame cattle were to the whites. Henderson told them plainly if he could not have the tract he sought, he would keep his goods; whereupon the Dragging Canoe went off displeased and, the others following, broke up the conference that day. But the next day, the 16th of March, the Indians again met and during that and the ensuing day came to terms; not, however, without feelings sensible that the goods were too insignificant for the extent of country desired, but the young warriors, who had been tantalized with a sight of the goods, were now clamorous for them.[11] Thus influenced, probably, the Dragging Canoe seems to have acquiesced in the cession but informed Colonel Henderson that the country below the Kentucky was the *Bloody Ground,*[o] that a black cloud hung over it, and it would be found dark and difficult to settle; that the Northern and Western Indians were bad people and when passing through Kentucky on their way to war against the Southern tribes, they would be apt to kill any of Henderson's settlers whom they might meet; but should Colonel Henderson persist in making such settlement, the Cherokees would no longer hold him by the hand, nor could they be held responsible for any mishaps or evil consequences that might ensue.

Thus, on the 17th of March, 1775, O-con-nos-to-ta, or the Great Warrior, At-ta-kul-la-Kul-la, or the Little Carpenter, and Savanookah, or Covonok, commonly called the Raven, signed the deed in behalf of the nation and with the assent of the warriors present, granting to Henderson and company the tract of country from the mouth of the Kentucky or Louisa River to the head spring of its most northerly fork, thence south-easterly to the top of Powell's Mountain, and thence, first westerly, and then north-westerly to the head spring of the most southerly branch of the Cumberland River, and down that stream, including all its waters to the Ohio and up the Ohio to the mouth of the Kentucky.[12] This was denominated "The Great Grant." One of the Indian signers, an old chief, probably At-ta-kul-la-Kul-la, taking Boone by the hand when the deed was delivered, said, "Brother, we have given you a fine land, but I believe you will have much trouble in settling it"—the same ominous apprehension that Dragging Canoe had expressed to Colonel Henderson.

When the deed was signed and delivered, Colonel Henderson stated that he wished a path from Holston River to the purchase he had just made and offered there for "the value of two thousand weight of leather" in goods and to pay their indebtedness to John Carter, which amounted to six or seven hundred pounds sterling. This was accepted by Dragging Canoe on the part of the Cherokees, and a deed [was] given the same day as the other, usually called "The Path Deed,"[p] but which it is impossible from its vague description to trace with any degree of certainty. Neither whites nor Indians seem at the time to have had any definite understanding as to its width or extent, except that it was to reach the Kentucky country; the purchasers, however, we infer, construed it to embrace Carter's and Powell's vallies, while the Indians apparently intended it only as a narrow travelling path, and yet they spoke of the country through which it passed as almost valueless for hunting purposes.

Though the goods "filled a house," and were estimated as worth ten thousand pounds sterling,[q] yet when they came to be distributed among upwards of twelve hundred Indians, all greedy for their share,[r] it might well be asked, what were they among so many? Much dissatisfaction ensued, particularly among the young warriors, one of whom received only a shirt for his portion, who declared that he could have killed in one day on the land sold more deer than would have purchased such a paltry garment. The treaty closed with an entertainment given by Henderson and company, for which several beeves were killed and roasted, when the destructive rum, so fatal to the Indian race, passed around freely, which was quaffed with many a wry face and swaggering word in its praise.[13]

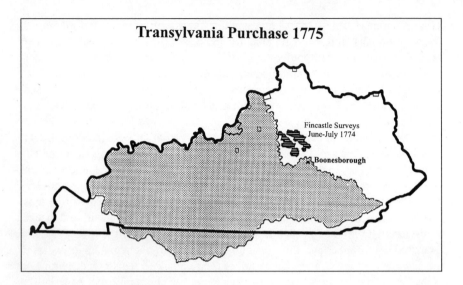

Transylvania Purchase 1775

Fincastle Surveys
June-July 1774

Boonesborough

54. MAP BY NEAL O. HAMMON.

As early as the 10th of February, more than a month before the consumma-
tion of the treaty, Governor Martin of North Carolina issued his proclamation
against the legality of the purchase, alleging it to be a violation of the Royal
Proclamation of October 7, 1763, as well as contravening an act of the Provincial
Assembly; and declaring that in payments of which, among other goods, a quantity of ammunition had been promised the Cherokees which was regarded as dangerous to the safety of the frontiers. It was furthermore proclaimed—the evidence
of the truth of which, however, no where appears—that the company had issued
advertisements inviting debtors, fugitives from justice, and all persons in desperate circumstances to repair to the new acquisition, where assurances of an asylum
were held out.[14]

Governor Dunmore of Virginia quickly caught the news and spirit of Martin's proclamation and issued a similar one on the 21st of March against the "pretended purchase" of "one Richard Henderson and other disorderly persons, his
associates," who were commanded in his majesty's name forthwith to depart and
relinquish the possession so unjustly obtained in pain of being immediately fined
and imprisoned. He also gave notice in his proclamation that the king had ordered
all the country, as far west as the Kentucky River acquired by the Lochabar treaty
of 1770, as extended by Donelson's line of 1771, to be surveyed into lots from
one hundred to a thousand acres and sold at public auction to the highest bidder,
subject only to an annual quit-rent of one half-penny sterling per acres, and a
reservation of all mines of gold, silver, and precious stones. But the Assembly of
Virginia then in session six days afterward appointed Patrick Henry, Richard

Bland, Thomas Jefferson, Robert Carter Nicholas, and Edmund Pendleton [to] a committee to inquire whether the king had a right to advance the terms of granting lands in the colony, and at the same time recommended all persons to forbear purchasing or accepting land-grants on the conditions proclaimed by the governor.[15]

A large number of frontier people attended the treaty who had not the fear of royal governors before their eyes. Among those present beside Daniel Boone,[s] were such prominent border men as James Robertson, John Sevier, Isaac Shelby, the Bledsoes, Richard Callaway, William Twitty, Nathaniel Henderson, William Cocke, and many others. All seemed delighted with the vigor and extent with which the company gave promise of prosecuting their enterprise, and not a little of this confidence resulted from the high character of the men composing the company. All were eager to learn upon what terms lands would be granted in the new Kentucky colony. This was promptly determined upon the spot and proclaimed by the company at Watauga that all such persons as would go out, settle the country, and raise a crop of corn that year should have five hundred acres of land for five pounds sterling clear of all charges; but it was at the same time expressly stated that they would not make grants at so low a rate to any who did not assist them in their first settlement.[16]

"At least five hundred people," writes Colonel Preston to Lord Dunmore, "are preparing to go out this spring from Carolina, beside great numbers from Virginia, to settle Kentucky; and the company intend to have a treaty with the Wabash Indians and give them a considerable present to permit the settlement on those lands. Numbers have already removed, and are about to remove, there this spring to plant corn, let the consequences be what they will. Upon the whole, my Lord, it appears to me, that the country will very shortly be inhabited by numbers of industrious people who cannot be prevented from going there."[17] The fearless frontier men, like Boone and his sturdy compeers, conscious of their own rectitude of purpose, heeded not the royal fulminations of Martin and Dunmore, and probably regarded them only as the expiring throes of tyranny in the New World.

Boone, whose knowledge and suggestions had been so influential in bringing about the treaty and purchase, and who had been present by request of the purchasers to collect the Indians and designate the boundaries, was all in readiness by their directions to head a party of pioneers to mark the road to the Kentucky, who, to the number of twenty, all well armed, started immediately on this service. Under Boone's command were enlisted such experienced backwoodsmen as Squire Boone, Benjamin Cutbirth, Michael Stoner, David Gass, Col. Richard Callaway, William Bush, Edmund Jennings, John Kennedy, John Vardemen, and James Hall.[18] They rendezvoused at the Long Island of Holston, where they were overtaken by Capt. William Twitty, Samuel Coburn, James Bridges, Thomas

Johnson, John Hart, William Hicks, James Peeke, and Felix Walker, all from Tryon, afterwards Rutherford County, North Carolina, who had also attended the Watauga treaty.[t] They now numbered nearly thirty persons under the same management and control of Boone, "who," says Felix Walker, "was to be our pilot and conductor through the wilderness to the promised land; and perhaps no adventurers since the days of Don Quixote, or before, ever felt so cheerful and elated in prospect; every heart abounded with joy and excitement in anticipating the new things we would see, and the romantic scenes through which we must pass; and, exclusive of the novelty of the journey, the advantages and accumulations ensuing on the settlement of a new country was a dazzling object with many of our company. Under the influence of these impressions we went on our way, rejoicing, with transporting views of our success, taking our leave of the civilized would for a season."

Leaving Long Island, "we marked," says Walker, "our track with our hatchets." Yet theirs was a difficult and dangerous task. "The Northern Indians," says Perkins, "were still smarting under the injuries which had caused the war of the year previous, and though the pipe of peace had been smoked with the Long Knives, it was no reason why their hunting-grounds should be invaded. As for the purchase from the Cherokees, what was it worth? The Cherokees never owned the land. Boone understood all of this, and went upon his way with armed men and muffled footsteps. Over the mountains, across the vallies, through the tangled thickets, round the rough knobs, silently and safely the road-markers, blazing the trees as they went, passed along; and at length the levels they were seeking came in sight."[19]

The remains of John Stuart, Boone's faithful companion who had so mysteriously disappeared over five years before, were accidentally discovered in a hollow sycamore at Rockcastle River, as has been already anticipated. "Once," says Felix Walker, "we killed a fine bear on our way, camped all night, and had an excellent supper." Thus far our road-markers had encountered no unusual obstacle, but toils and dangers now began thickly to beset their path. "On leaving the Rockcastle," says Walker's Narrative, "we had to encounter and cut our way through a country of about twenty miles, entirely covered with dead brush, which we found a difficult and laborious task. At the end of which we arrived at the commencement of a cane country, travelled about thirty miles through thick cane and reed, and as the cane ceased, we began to discover the pleasing and rapturous appearance of the plains of Kentucky. A new sky and strange earth seemed to be presented to our view. So rich a soil we had never seen before; covered with clover in full bloom, the woods were abounding with wild game—turkies so numerous that it might be said they appeared but one flock, universally scattered in the woods. It appeared that nature, in the profusion of her bounty, had spread a feast for all that lives, both for the animal and rational world.

"A sight so delightful to our view and grateful to our feelings, almost inclined us, in imitation of Columbus, in transport to kiss the soil of Kentucky, as he hailed and saluted the sand on his first setting his foot on the shores of America. The appearance of the country coming up to the full measure of our expectations, seemed to exceed the fruitful source of our imaginary prospects. We felt ourselves as passengers though a wilderness just arrived at the fields of Elysium, or at a grandeur where was no forbidden fruit. Nothing can furnish the contemplative mind with more sublime reflections, than nature unbroken by art; we can there trace the wisdom of the Great Architect in the construction of his works in nature's simplicity, which, when he had finished, he pronounced all good. But alas! fond man! the vision of a moment made dream of a dream, and shadow of a shade! Man may appoint, but One greater than man can disappoint. A sad reverse overtook us two days after, on our way to Kentucky river."

While encamped near the head of Taylor's Fork of Silver Creek, about four miles in a southerly direction from the present town of Richmond, Madison County, Kentucky, and fifteen miles only from the Big Lick on the Kentucky, about half an hour before day on the morning of March 25th, a party of Indians crept up and fired upon the whites while asleep, badly wounding Captain Twitty through both knees and his Negro servant fatally, who jumped up with a spasmodic effort, but instantly fell dead into the fire. Some Indians now rushed

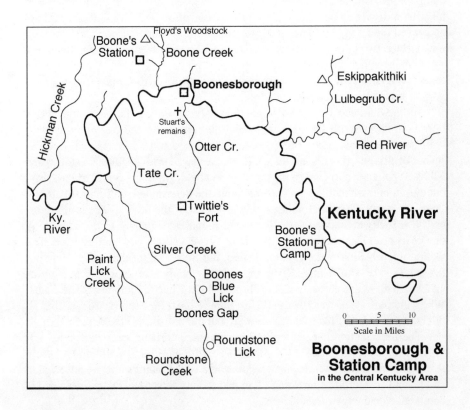

55. MAP BY NEAL O. HAMMON.

forward to scalp Twitty, when his faithful bull-dog[u] seized one of them by the throat and threw him down; his cries brought one of his tawny companions to his relief, who tomahawked the dog, when all precipitately retreated.

At the first fire, Felix Walker was also severely wounded but fled with the other survivors from the camp into the surrounding bushes.[20] It was very dark. Squire Boone escaped with scarcely any clothing on, which was also probably true of the others; for he had seized only his gun, which laid by his side, and, as he thought, his shot-pouch and powder-horn, but which he discovered when he reached the adjacent thicket was only his jacket. Once at a convenient distance from the fatal camp, he called out in an under tone for his brother Daniel, who readily responded when they got together; and Daniel gave his brother some balls and powder, of which he was deficient. The remainder of the party soon collected and, hearing nothing of the Indians, concluded to advance carefully to the camp with their guns ready for use; but the enemy had fled, without having taken any of the baggage. Some of the horses, however, which had been hoppled out near by, were carried off by the marauders.[21] Boone's party guarded the camp till day-light and gave the best attention they could to their unfortunate wounded companions. Boone confessed that he and his comrades were "surprised and taken at a disadvantage" but claimed the honor of having "stood their ground" and saved their baggage. For the protection of the wounded, Boone and his men now erected two or three small cabins some four or five feet high, but without any stockading, which they dignified with the name of Twitty's Fort; and here the road-markers tarried until death relieved poor Twitty from his sufferings and Walker was able to be carried on a litter.[22]

An incident occurred of so singular a character during their stay at Twitty's Fort as to deserve a brief relation. When all were encamped one night, a rabid wolf crept stealthily among the men and attempted to bite James Nall but was scared or driven off. This after a while was renewed with a similar result, when Nall was persuaded to change his position and lie down in the center of the party; but even there, when all again became quiet, the determined wolf jumped among them and bit Nall on the forehead, when several of the others seized their guns and shot, partly at random, at the retreating animal. One ball took effect, breaking one of its hind legs above the joint, when it gave a single howl and expired. The wound upon Nall's forehead soon healed, but in the fall of that year, while out fire-hunting on the Clinch River in company with a brother-in-law, he was attacked with hydrophobia, when his brother-in-law had to jump out of the canoe. When the paroxysm was over and Nall taken home, he expressed fears that he might injure some of his friends, was tied, but did not survive the next fit.[23]

The introduction here of a sensible and characteristic letter of Boone,[v] addressed to "Col. Richard Henderson—these with care," and written just before leaving Twitty's Fort, will further explain some of the matters already adverted to and give us in addition something of an insight into the pioneer's feelings and his commendable energy of character:

April the first, 1775.

Dear Colonel,

After my compliment to you, I shall acquaint you of our misfortune. On March the 25th, a party of Indians fired on my
company about half an hour before day, and killed Mr. Twitty
and his Negro, and wounded Mr. Walker very deeply, but I
hope he will recover. On March the 28th, as we were hunting
for provisions, we found Samuel Tate's son, who gave us an account that the Indians fired on their camp on the 27th day.[24] My
brother and I went down and found two men killed and
sculped, Thomas McDowell and Jeremiah McFeeters. I have
sent a man down to all the lower companies in order to gather
them all to the mouth of Otter Creek.[25] My advice to you, Sir,
is, to come or send as soon as possible. Your company is desired greatly, for the people are very uneasy, but are willing to
stay and venture their lives with you; and now is the time to
flusterate their [the Indians'] intentions, and keep the country
whilst we are in it. If we give way to them now, it will ever be
the case. This day we start from the battleground, for the mouth
of Otter Creek, where we shall immediately erect a fort, which
will be done before you can come or send; then we can send
ten men to meet you, if you send for them.

I am, sir, your most obedient,

Daniel Boone

N.B.—We stood on the ground and guarded our baggage till
day, and lost nothing. We have about fifteen miles to Cantuck,
at Otter Creek.

Walker's Narrative furnishes us some additional facts. "Captain Twitty was
shot in both knees, and died the third day after; an active and enterprising
woodsman, of good original mind and great benevolence, and although a light
habited man, in strength and agility of bodily powers was not surpassed by any
of his day and time, well calculated for enterprise. A black man, his body servant, was killed dead; myself badly wounded; our company dispersed. So fatal
and tragical an event cast a deep gloom of melancholy over all our prospects;
and high calculations of long life and happy days in our newly-discovered country were prostrated; hope vanished from the most of us, and left us suspended in
the tumult of uncertainty and conjecture. Colonel Boone, and a few others, appeared to possess firmness and fortitude. In our calamitous situation, a circumstance occurred one morning after our misfortunes, that proved the courage and
stability of our few remaining men—for some had gone back. One of our men,

who had ran off at the fire of the Indians on our camp, was discovered peeping from behind a tree, by a black woman belonging to Colonel Callaway, while gathering small wood. She ran in, and gave the alarm of 'Indians!' Colonel Boone instantly caught his rifle, ordered the few men to form, take trees, and give battle, and not to run till they saw him fall. They formed agreeably to his directions, and I believe they would have fought with equal bravery to any Spartan band ever brought to the field of action, when the man behind the tree announced his name, and came in. My situation was critical and dangerous, being then a youth, three hundred miles from white inhabitants. My friend and guardian, Captain Twitty, taken dead from my side, my wound pronounced by some to be mortal, produced very serious reflections. Yet withal I retained firmness to support me under the pressure of distress, and did not suffer me to languish in depression of mind.

"But where shall I begin, or where shall I end, in thanks and grateful acknowledgments to that benign and merciful Providence who spared and preserved me in the blaze of danger and in the midst of death! I trust I shall remember that singular and protecting event, with filial sensations of gratitude, while I retain my recollection. We remained at the same place twelve days; I could not be removed sooner without the danger of constant death. At length I was carried in a litter between two horses, twelve miles, to Kentucky River, where we made a station, and called it Boonesborough, situated in a plain on the south side of the river, wherein was a lick with two sulphur springs strongly impregnated.[26] On entering the plain we were permitted to view a very interesting and romantic sight. A number of buffaloes, of all sizes, supposed to be between two and three hundred, made off from the lick in every direction; some running, some walking, others loping slowly and ceaselessly, with young calves playing, skipping, and bounding through the plain. Such a sight some of us never saw before, nor perhaps ever may again."[27]

Though Boone had hoped to have left Twitty's Fort at the battle ground on the 1st of April, yet it would seem from Walker's Narrative that his wounds were so dangerous and painful, the party were unable to convey him to the Big Lick a little below the mouth of Otter Creek before the 6th of that month; and once there, they immediately commenced the erection of Fort Boone.[28] Its locality[w] was sixty yards south of the Kentucky and a little below the Lick near the present ferry; and the few cabins erected were strung along, fronting the river. The whole party appear to have been careless—had, probably, become callous to fear and kept watch only the first night after their arrival. Perhaps the men had become weary of their labors and exposures, and Boone had little or no control over them. However it may have been brought about, it was lamentably too true; and no wonder Boone has recorded that "on the fourth day, the Indians killed one of our men." Leaving Boone and his party hard at work on their new fort, let us return to Colonel Henderson and note his progress as his manuscript journal and published letters inform us.

Having concluded the Watauga treaty on the 17th of March, and immediately despatched Boone and his pioneers to open the way, Henderson followed on the 20th, more leisurely, at the head of a band of thirty men with several wagons loaded with articles needful for the new settlement. With Henderson were Colonel Luttrell and Capt. Nathaniel Hart. Reaching Capt. Martin's Station in Powell's Valley on the 30th, they were detained there awaiting the arrival of the wagons, erecting a house there in which securely to lodge them, until the 5th of April, when they again set forward; but the straying of horses so retarded them that on the 7th, when only ten miles from Martin's, Boone's letter came to hand with the disagreeable and even alarming intelligence of the murderous attacks of the Indians. On the next day, April the 8th, Colonel Henderson addressed a letter to his partners in North Carolina, some extracts from which will best exhibit some of the difficulties and vexatious delays attending the expedition:

"Few enterprises of great consequence continue at all times to wear a favorable aspect; ours has met with the common fate, from the incautious proceedings of a few headstrong and unthinking people. On the 25th of March last, the Indians fired upon a small party of men, in camp, near the Louisa, killed two and put four others to the rout; and on the 27th did likewise on Daniel Boone's camp, and killed a white man and a Negro on the spot, but the survivors maintained their ground and saved the baggage.[29] But for a more particular account I refer you to Mr. Boone's original letter on that occasion, which came to hand last night. You scarcely need information that these accidents have a bad effect with respect to us. * * * * You observed from Mr. Boone's letter the absolute necessity of our not losing one moment, therefore don't be surprised at not receiving a particular account of our journey with the several little misfortunes and cross accidents, which have caused us to be delayed so that we are still one hundred and thirty or one hundred and forty miles from our journey's end. We are all in high spirits, and on thorns to fly to Boone's assistance, and join him in defense of so fine and valuable a country. My only motives for stopping are, first, that you should receive a just representation of the affair, and secondly, to request your immediate assistance; for want of workmen our wagons are laid aside at Captain Martin's in the valley, the chief of our salt and all our salt-peter and brimstone are left behind."

From Colonel Henderson's manuscript journal, we shall make a short extract, commencing on the day when the preceding letter was written:

"Saturday, April 8th.—Started about 10 o'clock. Crossed Cumberland Gap; about four miles [beyond] met about forty persons returning from the Cantucky on account of the late murder by the Indians; could prevail on one only to return. Memo. Several Virginians who were with us returned.

"Sunday, 9th.—Arrived at Cumberland River, where we met Robert Wells and his son returning.

"Monday, 10th.—Dispatched Capt. Cocke to the Cantucky to inform Capt. Boone that we were on the road. Continued at camp that day on account of the badness of the weather."

"No doubt," wrote Colonel Henderson from Boonesborough to his North Carolina partners, "no doubt but you have felt great anxiety since the receipt of my letter from Powell's Valley. At that time things wore a gloomy aspect; indeed it was a serious matter, and became a little more so after the date of the letter than before. That afternoon I wrote the letter in Powell's Valley, in our march this way, we met about forty people returning, and in about four days the number was a little short of one hundred. Arguments and persuasions were needless; they seemed resolved on returning, and travelled with a precipitation that truly bespoke their fears. Eight or ten were all that we could prevail on to proceed with us, or to follow after; and thus, what we before had, counting every boy and lad, amounted to about forty, with which number we pursued our journey with the utmost diligence— for my own part, never under more real anxiety. Every person, almost, that we met, seemed to be at pains to aggravate the danger of proceeding; and had we given them all a fair hearing, I believe they would, in return for this favor, have gotten all our men. Many seemed to be of the opinion (who had been with Boone) that the men assembled at the mouth of Otter Creek, would get impatient and leave him before we could possibly get there, if no other accident befell them; and, with me, it was beyond a doubt, that our night, in effect, depended on Boone's maintaining his ground—at least until we could get to him. Here, gentlemen, your imagination must take the burden off my hands, and paint what I am unable to describe. You need not be afraid of giving scope to your fancy; it is impossible to make the picture worse than the original. Every group of travellers we saw, or strange bells which were heard in front, was a fresh alarm; afraid to look or inquire, lest Captain Boone or his company was amongst them, or some disastrous account of their defeat. The slow progress we made with our packs, rendered it absolutely necessary for some person to go on and give assurance of our coming, especially as they had no certainty of our being on the road at all; or had ever heard whether the Indians had sold to us or not.[30] It was owing to Boone's confidence in us, and the people's in him, that a stand was ever attempted in order to wait for our coming. The case was exceedingly distressing: we had not a fellow that we could send on a forlorn hope in our whole camp: all our young men had sufficient employ with the pack-horses; and, the truth is, very few would have gone, if they had been totally idle. Distress generally has something in store when it is least expected; it was actually the case with us. Mr. William Cocke (with whom some of you are acquainted), observing our anxiety on that account, generously offered to undertake the journey himself, and deliver a letter to Captain Boone, with all expedition in his power. This offer, extraordinary as it was, we could by no means refuse—it was not a time for much delicacy; a little compliment and a few sincere thanks, instantly given, preceded a solemn engagement to set off next morning; and if he escaped with his life, to perform the trust.

"The day proved dark and rainy; and I own, Mr. Cocke's undertaking appeared a little more dangerous than the evening before—in spite of affectation, it was plain he thought so—whether it was from the gloominess of the weather, or the time of setting off being actually come, or what, I cannot tell; but perhaps a little of both. Indeed I rather suspect there is some little secondary mischievous passion, personating courage, hankering about the heart of man, that very often plays him a double game, by causing him to view dangers at a little distance, through the wrong end of the glass; and as soon as cool deliberation, by the help of caution, has shifted the telescope, and brought the object home to a nearer view, and perhaps the dangerous features a little magnified, this monkey passion most shamefully deserts, and leaves the affair to be managed as it can. Be that as it may, in these cases we are not always without a friend. *Pride* will, if possible take up the cudgels; and let the world say what it will of her, she answers the end of genuine innate courage (if there be such a thing), and for aught I know, it is the thing itself.

"But to return to our subject. No time was lost; we struck whilst the iron was hot, fixed Mr. Cocke off with a good Queen Anne's musket, plenty of ammunition, a tomahawk, a large cuttoe knife, a Dutch blanket, and no small quantity of jerked beef. Thus equipped, and mounted on a tolerably good horse, on the 10th day of April, Mr. Cocke started from Cumberland River, about one hundred and thirty miles from the place, and carried with him, besides his own enormous load of fearful apprehensions, a considerable burden of my own uneasiness. The probability of giving Mr. Boone and his men word of our being near them, administered great pleasure, and we made the best of our time, following on.

"The general panic that had seized the men we were continually meeting, was contagious; it ran like wild-fire; and, notwithstanding every effort against its progress, it was presently discovered in our own camp; some hesitated and stole back, privately; others saw the necessity of returning to convince their friends that they were still alive, in too strong a light to be resisted; whilst many, in truth, who have nothing to thank but the fear of shame, for the credit of intrepidity, came on; though their hearts, for some hours, made part of the deserting company. In this situation of affairs, some few, of genuine courage and undaunted resolution, served to inspire the rest; by help of whose example, assisted by a little pride and some ostentation, we made a shift to march on with all the appearance of gallantry, and, cavalier-like, treated every insinuation of anger with the utmost contempt. It soon became habitual; and those who started in the morning, with pale faces and apparent trepidation, could lie down and sleep at night in great quiet, not even possessed of fear enough to get the better of indolence. Then in a mistaken notion amongst the vulgar, with respect to courage, which cannot be eradicated but by dint of experiment; all watching, when it comes to be put in practice, has to them the appearance of cowardice; and that it is beneath a soldier to be afraid of any thing, especially when a little fatigued. They would all agree in the morning, that it would be highly prudent, and necessary to keep sentinels around our camp at night; but a hearty meal or supper (when we could get it), and good fires, never failed putting off the danger for at least twenty-four hours; at which time it was universally agreed, on all hands, that a watch at night would be indispensably necessary. Human nature is eternally the same; a death-bed repentance and a surprised camp are so nearly assimilated, that you may safely swear they arise from the same cause. Without further speculation, we have been so fortunate, hitherto, as to escape both. I wish, from my soul, that they may not be in league to come together. Never was fairer opportunity, as to the one, and you may form a tolerable judgement as to the other; the western waters having, as yet, produced no visible altercation with respect to morals or Christian charity amongst us."[31]

Such was the fickle feeling of fear and hardihood that alternately possessed our forest adventurers. But they pushed forward. Once they met a party of ten men "on their return from Louisa," who "had well nigh turned three or four of our Virginians back"; and then, among their little mishaps, when camped north of the Rock-Castle River, they "lost an axe"—a misfortune of no small moment at a time when such articles were in so great demand. On the 16th of April, it is recorded, they "met James McAfee with eighteen other persons returning from Cantucky; travelled about twenty-two miles and camped on the head of Dick's River, where Looney, from McAfee's camp, came to us, resolved to go to Louisa." Two days afterward, no doubt much to their joy, they "met Michael Stoner with pack-horses to assist us; camped that night in the edge of the rich land. Stoner brought us excellent beef in plenty." Sending Stoner with this timely relief was kind and thoughtful in Boone. The safe arrival and flattering reception of the way-farers at Fort Boone in the land of promise is thus noted in the ancient journal:

"Thursday, 20th of April.—Arrived at Fort Boone, on the mouth of Otter Creek, on Cantucky River, where we were saluted by a running fire of about twenty-five guns—all that were then at the fort. The men appeared in high spirits, and much rejoiced on our arrival."

56. Belt ax once owned by Isaac Shelby. FROM THE COLLECTION OF JIM AND CAROLYN DRESSLAR.

"Here I must beg the favor," observed Colonel Henderson in his letter to his North Carolina partners, "of your turning back with me to Powell's Valley. Our anxiety at that time is now of very little concern to you; but the impressions still remain on my mind, and indeed I would not wish to get clear of them in a little time. It learnt me to make an estimate of the probable value of our country; to see the imminent danger of losing it forever, and presented me with a full view of the ridiculous figure we should cut in the world, in case of failure. With respect to the real consequence of such a disappointment, I could not so well judge for the company in general, as for myself, but thought it too serious an affair with respect to us all, to be tamely given up without the fire of a single gun, or something like an attempt to take possession and defend our rights, so long, at least as we should find our posts tenable.

"Though the danger Mr. Cocke exposed himself to in rendering this piece of service to the company, dwelt on me for some time, yet having despatched a messenger to Captain Boone was a matter of such consolation, that my burthen from that time was much lightened. We soon found, by his letters on the road, that he had a companion, and went on very well—with a small stoppage by waters excepted. On Thursday, the 20th April, [we] found him with Captain Boone and his men at the place appointed, where he had related the history of his adventures, and come in for his share of applause; here it was that the whole load, as it were, dropped off my shoulders at once, and I questioned if a happier creature was to be found under the sun. Why do I confine it to myself; it was general; the people in the fort, as well as ourselves, down to an old weather-beaten Negro, seemed equally to enjoy it. Indeed it was natural for us, after being one whole month, without intermission, travelling in a barren desert country, most of the way our horses packed beyond their strength; no part of the road tolerable, most of it either hilly, stony, slippery, miry, or bushy; our people jaded out and dispirited with fatigue, and what was worse, often pinched for victuals. To get clear of all this at once, was as much as we could well bear; and though we had nothing here to refresh ourselves with but cold water, and lean buffalo beef, without bread, it certainly was the most joyous banquet I ever saw. Joy and festival was in every countenance, and that vile strumpet, Envy, I believe, had not found her way into the country."

What, on this memorable day, must have been Boone's exultant feelings when viewing the little settlement planted under his auspices, and greeting the arrival of Henderson and his reinforcement rendering certain permanent occupancy of Kentucky—for so many years the darling object of his heart!

As Henderson's manuscript journal is the only account preserved of the daily transactions of the first three months of the settlement of Kentucky, and that withal is so full of curious incident, no apology need be made for drawing freely upon a document of such intrinsic value and interest. It serves to make us better acquainted with the common occurrences of every-day wilderness life in the incipient stages of a colony destined in the course of time to become a prominent member of a powerful confederacy playing well its part in the eventful scenes of the world's history.

"Friday, April 21st.—Viewing the fort, and finding the plan not sufficient to admit of building for the reception of our company, and a scarcity of ground suitable for clearing at such an advanced season—was at some loss how to proceed. Mr. Boone's company having laid off most of the adjacent good lands into lots of two acres each, and taking them as they fell to each individual by lot, were in actual possession and occupying them. After some perplexity, resolved to erect a fort on the opposite side of a large lick, near the river bank, which would place us at the distance of about three hundred yards from the other fort—the only commodious place where we could be of any service to Boone's men, or *vice versa*. On communicating my thoughts to Mr. Luttrell on this subject with my reasons for preferring this place to a large spring over a hill about three quarters of a mile from Fort Boone, he readily gave his assent, and seemed pleased with the choice. Mr. Hart said, in a very cold, indifferent manner, 'he thought it might do well enough.' Accordingly 'twas resolved, that a fort should be built at said place. Moved our tents to the ground—i.e. Mr. Luttrell and myself and our particular companies lodged there Saturday night. Proceeded with Capt. Boone and Col. Callaway to laying off lots; finished nineteen, besides one reserved round a fine spring.

"Saturday, April 22nd.—Finished running off all the lots we could conveniently get—to wit fifty-four, and gave notice of our intention of having them drawn for in the evening. But as Mr. Robert McAfee, his brother Samuel, and some others, were not well satisfied whether they would draw or not, wanting to go down the river about fifty miles, near Captain Harrod's settlement, where they had begun improvements, and left them on the late alarm; and being informed by myself, in hearing of all attending, that such settlement should not entitle them to lands, and etc., from us, and appearing much concerned and at a loss what to do—on which the lottery was deferred till next morning at sun-rise, thereby giving them time to come to a resolution.

"Sunday, April 23rd.—Remained at camp—drawed lots, and etc. Spent the day without public worship—nothing of that kind having been put in practice before, and ourselves much at sixes and sevens, and no place provided for that purpose.

"Monday, April 24th.—Employed in viewing the respective lots, and endeavoring to satisfy the drawers by exchanging my own and those over whom, of our company, I had any influence, to give entire satisfaction.

"Tuesday, April 25th.—As there were fifty-four lots, and not so many drawers by thirteen, some of the best lots were left,—therefore had a second lottery, at the end of which every body seemed well satisfied. I had been able by one way or other to obtain four lots for the fort garden, and etc.; and in these lotteries our particular company had such luck in drawing as to enable me to give in exchange lots which gave entire satisfaction.

"Wednesday, April 26th.—Other people coming, employed in showing lots for their use. Sowed small seed, planted cucumbers, and etc.

"Thursday, April 27th.—Employed in clearing fort lot, and etc.; Mr. Luttrell, Nathaniel Henderson and Samuel Henderson, all that assisted me. Mr. Hart having made [the] choice of a piece of ground for his own and people's cultivation, adjacent to the town lands, did not come near nor offer assistance, though I had often mentioned to him the necessity of building a magazine, our powder being exposed in tents, and the weather somewhat rainy. Mr. Luttrell reported to me, that Capt. Hart said he would have nothing to say concerning the fort, things were managed in such a manner; though I cannot guess the reason of his discontent.

"Friday, April 28th.—Mr. Luttrell chose a piece of ground about three quarters of a mile from the fort, and set three of his people to work; two remained with me to assist in clearing about where the fort is to stand. He, on all occasions, is exceedingly obliging and good-natured, and seems desirous of promoting the company's interest.

"Saturday, April 29th.—Built, or rather begun, a little house for a magazine, but did not finish it. Mr. Hart told me in the morning, that he would assist, but never saw or heard of him this day more.

"Sunday, April 30th.—No public worship.

"Monday, 1st. May.—Continued to work on the magazine.

"Thursday, May 2nd.—Continued same work and working on our lots.

"Wednesday, May 3rd.—Finished the magazine. Capt. John Floyd arrived here, conducted by one Js. Drake from a camp on Dick's River, where he had left about thirty men of his company from Virginia; and said he was sent by them to know on what terms they might [settle] our lands. That if they were reasonable, they would pitch on some place on which to make corn, or otherwise go on the north side of the river. Was much at a loss on account of this gentleman's arrival and message, as he was surveyor of Fincastle under Colonel Preston, a man who had exerted himself against us, and said and did every thing in his power or invention, as I am informed, to defeat our enterprise and bring it into contempt. 'Tis said, that he not only had our case represented, or rather misrepresented, to Lord Dunmore, but actually wrote to Governor Martin on the subject. This man—Capt. Floyd—appeared to have a great share of modesty, an honest, open countenance, and no small share of good sense; and petitioning in behalf of himself and his whole company, among whom were, one Mr. Dandridge (son of Nathaniel West Dandridge, of Virginia), and one Mr. Todd, two gentlemen of the law in their own parts, and several other young gentlemen of good families—we thought it most advisable to secure them to our interest, if possible, and not show the least distrust of the intentions of Capt. Floyd, on whom we intended to keep a very strict watch.

"Accordingly, though the season was too far advanced to make much corn, yet we promised them land, and etc.—one thousand acres to the principal gentlemen, on the terms—per hundred, and etc. This we would not have done, but for the scarcity of men, and the doubt with respect to the Virginians coming into our measures, acknowledging title, and etc. We restrained these men to settle somewhere in a compact body for mutual defense, and to be obedient to such laws as should, from time to time, be made for the government of all the adventurers on our purchase; and gave the leave to made choice of any lands not before marked by any of our men, or a certain Capt. Harrod and his men who were settled somewhere about fifty miles west of us, on the head of Salt River, and of whom we could form no conjecture, but thought it best to prevent any interruption to him or his men till we should know what he intended with respect to us and our title.[x]

"The day before this, one Capt. Calames[y] and Mr. Berry, with five other men, arrived here from Frederick or somewhere in the north-west frontiers of Virginia. They had heard nothing of our purchase when they left home, but merely set off to view the country, and etc. Hearing of us and our pretensions they thought it proper to come, though they seemed not very conversable; and I thought I could discover, in our first intercourse, a kind of sullen dissatisfaction and reserve, which plainly indicated a selfish opinion to our disadvantage. This, after some time, wore off, and they gladly treated with us for lands, and other indulgences, which we granted.

"Thursday, May 4th.—Capt. Floyd returned home; seemed highly pleased with gaining his point of settling, and etc. I must not omit to mention here, that Mr. Floyd expressed great satisfaction on being informed of the plan we proposed for legislation, and said he must most heartily concur in that and every other measure we should adopt for the well-governing or good of the community in general. This plan is exceedingly simple, and I hope will prove effectual. 'Tis no more than the people's sending delegates to act for them in General Convention.

"Friday, May 5th.—Nothing material. Let Mr. William Cocke have five yards and a half osnaburg off my old tent, for which I drew him five shillings and sixpence Virginia money.

"Saturday, May 6th.—Lived on as usual. Very little of Mr. Hart's company; he keeps much to himself—scarcely social.

"Sunday, May 7th.—Went into the woods with my brothers Nathaniel and Samuel, and Capt. Boone, after a horse left out on Saturday night. Staid till night, and on our return found Capt. Harrod and Col. Thomas Slaughter, from Harrodsburg on Dick's River.[32] Colonel Slaughter and Harrod seemed very jocose, and in great good humor.

"Monday, May 8th.—Rainy. Was much embarrassed with a dispute between the above mentioned gentlemen. Capt. Harrod, with about forty men, settled on Salt River last year; was driven off; joined the army with nearly thirty of his men; and being determined to live in this country, had come down the spring from the Monongahela, accompanied by about fifty men, most of them young persons without families. They came on Harrod's invitation. These men had got possession sometime before we got here, and I could not certainly learn on what terms or pretense they meant to hold land, and was doubtful that so large a body of lawless people, from habit and education, would give us great trouble, and require the utmost exertion of our abilities to manage them; and, not without considerable anxiety and some fear, wished for an interview with Capt. Harrod, who, I understood, was chief, and had all the men in that quarter under his absolute direction and command—but was soon undeceived as to this point.[33] Though these gentlemen were friendly to each other, and open in all their conduct, they were warm advocates and champions for two different parties. A schism had raised between Harrod's men, whom he brought down the Ohio with him, and those from divers parts of Virginia and elsewhere, amounting to about fifty in number on both sides. Harrod's men being first on the spot, claimed a priority of choice; and had they have stopped there, the dispute would scarcely ever had existed, for the others seemed willing to yield to such a preferences.

"But the complaint laid before us by Colonel Slaughter, in behalf of the other men, and on which we were to decide, was, that Harrod's men had not contented themselves with the choice of one tract of land apiece, but had made it their entire business to ride through the country, mark every piece of land they thought proper, built cabins, or rather hog-pens, to make their claims notorious at the place, and by that means had secured every good spring in a country of twenty odd miles in length, and almost as broad. That, though it was in those parts one entire good tract of land, and no advantage in choice except as to water, yet it was unjustly depriving them of a very essential inducement to their settling in the country; that, for their own part, after giving up that Capt. Harrod should, as to himself, have an indulgence, that his men might each make a choice for himself first, and then that *they* might come in for the second choice: This was strenuously urged by their advocates, Colonel Slaughter, a sensible and experienced old gentleman—a man of good family and connections, and a great friend to our country, and with this farther in his favor, that the men he appeared for, had, from their first assembling together at Harrodsburg, in obedience to our written declaration respecting encouraging settlers in our country, industriously employed themselves in clearing land and making ready for as large a crop of corn as possible, depending on a punctual performance on our part. That Capt. Harrod's men had totally neglected to do any thing that way, there being at this time at Harrod's settlement at the Boiling Spring, six miles from Harrodsburg, not more than three acres cleared and ready to be planted, and that for the Captain only; whilst, in less time, with the same number of hands, they had somewhere between sixty and eighty.

"Fair and clear as this case was in favor of Slaughter's men, upon every principle of justice and our own express declaration in writing, we were afraid to determine in favor of the right side; and not being capable, if we could have wished it, to give a decree against them, our embarrassment was exceedingly great. Much depended on accommodating the matter, which we dare not offer. The days favored us, being rainy, and caused them to spend it with us, by which means we had it in our power to get better acquainted with the opposite gentlemen, and give a turn to the dispute for the present, trusting to a future day, and hoping that some conciliating measures would be offered and agreed to by themselves.

"To divert the debate on the foregoing occasion, and draw them a little off so disagreeable a subject, the lawless condition we were in, and the want of some such thing as legislation, made the subject of conversation, mixed with occasional matters. It answered the end. Our plan of legislation, the evils pointed out, the remedies to be applied, and etc., were acceded to without hesitation. The plan was plain and simple—'twas nothing novel in its essence; a thousand years ago it was in use, and found by every year's experience since to be unexceptionable. We were in four distinct settlements. Members of delegates from every place, by free choice of individuals, they first having entered into writings solemnly binding themselves to obey and carry into execution such laws as representatives should, from time to time, make, concurred with by a majority of the proprietors present in the country. The reception this plan met with from these gentlemen, as well as Capt. Floyd, a leading man in Dick's River settlement, gave us great pleasure; and, therefore, we immediately set about the business, appointing Tuesday, the 23rd instant, at Boonesborough, and accordingly made out writings for the different towns to sign, and wrote to Capt. Floyd, appointing an election, and etc. Harrodsburg and the Boiling Spring settlement received their summons verbally by the gentlemen aforesaid.

"Tuesday, May 9th.—Col. Slaughter and Capt. Harrod took their departure in great good humor and apparently well satisfied. Our plantation business went on as usual, some people planting, others preparing, and etc. We found it very difficult at first, and indeed yet, to stop great waste in killing meat. Many men were ignorant of the woods, and not skilled in hunting, by which means some would get lost; these and others—and, indeed, at all times, would shoot, cripple and scare the game, without being able to get much, though always able to keep from want, and sometimes have a good store by them. Others of wicked and wanton dispositions would kill three, four, five or half a dozen buffaloes, and not take half a horse load from them all.[z] These evils we endeavored to prevent, but found it not practical, many complaining that they were too poor to hire hunters; others loved it much better than work; and some who knew little of the matter, but conceit, from having a hunting-shirt, tomahawk and gun, thought it was an insult to offer another to hunt for them, especially as pay was to be made, and etc.[aa]

"For want of a little obligatory law or some restraining authority, our game soon, nay, as soon as we got here, if not before, was driven very much. Fifteen or twenty miles was as short a distance as good hunters thought of getting meat— nay, sometimes they were obliged to go thirty, though by chance, once or twice a week, a buffalo was killed within five or six miles. This method of destroying game, was from our first coming, kept a secret from us as much as possible, and indeed we did not wish to be informed of it. The strictest inquiry was made into every hunter's conduct. It would not do to have it in our power to convict a man of the fact we had highly censured, and spoken of as a thing to be taken notice of, and let the culprit pass unnoticed. 'Twas some pleasure to find they were afraid of discovery, and I am convinced this fear saved the lives of many buffaloes, elks, and deer. As to bear, nobody wasted any that was fit to eat, nor did we care about them.

"Mr. Hart continues to keep himself much retired on his hill, and unless urged, does not give himself any pains about our public affairs. I wish it may not be owing to discontent with something done, or supposed to be done, by Mr. Luttrell or myself, or both.

"Wednesday, May 10th.—Nothing remarkable.

"Thursday, May 11th.—Common occurrences.

"Friday, May 12th.—Old story.

"Saturday, May 13th.—No washing here on this day; no scouring of floors, sweeping of yards, or scalding of bedsteads here.

"Sunday, May 14th.—No divine service, our church not being finished—that is to day, about fifty yards from the place where I am writing, and right before me with my face to the south of the river, behind my camp, and fine spring a little to the west stands one of the finest elms that perhaps Nature ever produced in any region. This tree is placed on a beautiful plain, surrounded by a turf of fine white clover, forming a green to its very stock, to which there is scarcely any thing to be likened. The trunk is about four feet through to the first branches, which are about nine feet from the ground; from thence above it so regularly extends its large branches on every side, at such equal distances, as to form the most beautiful tree that imagination can suggest. The diameter of the branches from the extreme end is one hundred feet; and every fair day, after the sun has risen fifteen degrees above the horizon, and when at the same height at evening, it describes a semicircle on the heavenly green around it, of upwards of four hundred feet in circuit. At any time between the hours of ten and two, one hundred persons may commodiously seat themselves under its shadowy branches. This divine tree or rather one of the many proofs of the existence from all eternity of its Divine Author, we came time enough to redeem from destruction—not owing to its beauty, that was unnoticed; the leaves were not yet out, and the lazy could find no pleasure in basking under it; 'twas too big to cut down without labor, and it would not die for betting ('twas said) the first year. The claimant of the lot in town on which it stood would have wished it in the Red Sea, at the devil, or any where, to have got clear of it; and, I believe, 'twas owing to the dread of cutting this tree, that made my way easy in endeavoring to obtain the lot for the purpose of building a fort.

"Thank God! the tree is mine, where I often retire, and oh! were my family and friends under it with me, it would be a heavenly tree indeed—but that is not the case. This same tree is to be our church, state-house, council-chamber, and etc. Having many things on our hands, have not had time to erect a pulpit, seats, and etc., but hope by Sunday sennight to perform divine service for the first time in a publick manner, and that to a set a scoundrels who scarcely believe in God or fear a devil, if we were to judge from most of their looks, words, and actions.

"Monday, May 15th.—Omitted to mention the receipt of a packet of letters, by express, from Col. Hart, Messrs. William Johnston and James Hogg, as also two from Capt. Russell with some enclosures; was much disappointed in not receiving accounts from my family and friends. It seems these gentlemen of the company were strangely transported with the news of a few men being killed, and my writing pressingly for ammunition and a supply of salt. They had not even given themselves times to think, but sent off an express with little more advice than that my last letter had come to hand, they were sorry for the accident; prayed fervently against such evils for the future; damned the Indians for rascals; commended our courage in going on, notwithstanding the mischief; hoped that we were forted and able to resist a little; gave us very good advice, and left us to our own discretion.

"These letters bear dates from the 20th to the 23rd of April. I must not omit to mention a most friendly letter accompanying these, from Col. Fanning, dated the 10th this over and above the satisfaction of perusing the most cordial declarations of friendship, and etc.[34] He, by the by, gave me some satisfaction as to my wife and family. A true friend cannot omit offices of friendship; so he did not fail to state about his stay at Col. Williams' a few days before, and that all were well at my house. A word from Col. Hart, which he got from Mr. Bullock must have been longer from home than 'tis presumable he was.

"With this express arrived here ten men—eight from Dunmore County, Virginia, and the express and another man from Powell's Valley. Major Bowman, Capt. Bowman, and one Capt. Moore, were the principal men; and with these we had no difficulty. They seemed to be well pleased with the country; offered to buy lands, and were willing to settle on our terms; were prepared to make corn, but asked to be indulged, having come at so late a season, which we granted readily, as they seemed like very good people, and said they imagined that one hundred families at least would be out with them before spring. They seemed desirous of being in Harrod's neighborhood, and there was some degree of friendship and acquaintance among them—therefore sent them off in great good humor, and etc.

"Tuesday, May 16th.—Continued eating meat without bread, and should be very contented were it not for the absence of four men who went down the river by land, on Friday sennight, to bring up the goods left by Capt. Calames at the mouth of Elkhorn, about fifty or sixty miles below. These men were expected on Tuesday or Wednesday last at farthest, and having no news of them is a matter of great concern to Capt. Calames, and is not a little alarming to ourselves.

"Wednesday, May 17th.—Hunters not returned. No meat but fat bear, and a little spoiled buffalo and elk, upon which, with a little coffee, we made out pretty well, trusting to luck for dinner, and depending on amendment to-morrow. Am just going to our little plant-patches, in hopes the greens will bear cropping—if so, a sumptuous dinner indeed. Capt. Calames grows very uneasy on account of his men, and applies to me for six men and nine horses to go in search; gave my promise to do what was in my power. Proposed it at dinner to Mr. Luttrell, who denied having horses fit to go, and thought footmen would answer. In short, Mr. Luttrell was unwell, and seemed in ill-humor with every thing about him, or I don't think he would have refused doing a thing in which not only the honor of the company was so much concerned, but 'twas refusing to the calls of humanity itself. He is, at some times, thoughtless, but I think means, when serious, to act as well as may be for himself and company. This evening wrote a line to Col. Callaway at the fort (Mr. Boone being away), and another to Capt. Hart, stating the case and desiring assistance, and withal asking them to come to my camp in the morning to determine on something, and etc.

"Thursday, May 18th.—Col. Callaway and Capt. Hart came early—Mr. Callaway could raise three men and one horse, Capt. Hart one horse. Mr. Luttrell was in bed, and not in good humor; the bells made too much noise—this I suppose from hearing him quarreling with the horses in the night, and his lying later than usual. Had only two mares and one stallion; the mares in the plow—the one very poor, with a sore back, and the other not much better, but willing she rode. My horse was * * * * running in the woods, very poor, and I believe would not go a journey of twenty miles without giving out.[35] However, the day proving dark, and no good woodsmen to be gotten—our hunters, Mr. Squire Boone and Michael Stoner being still out, as also Capt. Boone and some others, all of whom were by promise to have returned last night, and on whose account, as they were gone over and down the river, I was a little uneasy—went about a mile to Capt. Calames' camp, stated the case, and etc. He seemed of my opinion, that it was best to wait this day and try to get more men and horses, which we hoped to effect—especially some good woodsmen. 'Tis now twelve o'clock, and no news of the hunters or absentees.

"Three o'clock, hunters came in—no news of the lost men.

"Friday, May 19th.—Sent off Mr. Stoner with Capt. Calames and some of his men in search of those persons above mentioned. On this occasion no person turned out except John McMillen, and no person offered, or could be prevailed upon to lend a horse, though many fat idle ones were about the town every day, and at this time more than twenty were in sight, save Capt. Cocke, Capt. Hart, Nathaniel Henderson, and myself—and mine, indeed, was one of the Company's. P.S. Calames returned, one Hogan going in his place.

This evening Mr. Matthew Jouitt arrived here from Capt. Floyd, whom, with six other men, he says, he left about ten miles off on the No. side of the river, looking lands, and etc. By him heard that Capt. Floyd was not at St. Asaph at the return of Col. Slaughter and Mr. Harrod, and being afraid that the town, on that account, had not proceeded to elect delegates to meet in Convention.[36]

"Saturday, May 20th.—The election for Boonesborough was had this afternoon with great regularity, when Squire Boone, Daniel Boone, William Cocke, Samuel Henderson, William Moore, and Richard Callaway were elected.

"Wrote to Mr. Todd and sent William Bush to St. Asaph, directing an election, in case it was not done, with orders to be in on Tuesday evening at farthest.[37]

"Monday, May 22rd.—One Capt. Thomas Gist arrived from above Pittsburgh with six or seven men.[38] Their business was to survey eight thousand acres of land by officers' claims on the north side of Kentucky. Brought news that the Lees, surveyors for the Ohio Company, were at Wheeling as they passed and talked of coming down the river."

DRAPER'S NOTES: CHAPTER 11

1. Colden's *Five Nations,* London, 1755, i:21–23.

2. New York Historical Society Collections, new series, i:303.

3. Shea's *Discovery and Exploration of the Mississippi Valley,* note 41; Colden, i:260; General Cass' Discourse, in which occurs this sentence: "Father Sagard, in 1632, called the Eries the 'nation du chat,' or the raccoon, on account of the magnitude of these animals in their country and that is the soubriquet, which, to this day, is applied by the Canadians to the Shawanese"; MS. notes of conversations with the venerable Seneca chief, Gov. Black Snake, and Dah-goh-no-deh or William Patterson, and Soh-so-wah or Buck-tooth.

4. Charlevoix, 4th ed., 1744, i:443; Gallatin's *Synopsis,* port folio, 1816; Haywood's *Aboriginal History of Tennessee,* 218; McMurtrie's *Louisville,* 89, 104; letter of the late Col. Joseph H. Davies to Gen. G. R. Clark, in MS. Clark Papers.

5. MS. Preston Papers; case of "Clark's heirs *vs.* Porterfield's," in the Supreme Court, 1844; Sparks' *Washington;* Preston was secretary to the commissioners at the Logstown treaty.

6. Haywood's *Aboriginal History of Tennessee,* 231, 232. Twenty years prior to the treaty of Fort Stanwix, the Cherokees acknowledged that the river bearing their name was the northern extent of their [*wi*]—see ii:941. The MS. Preston Papers show conclusively that the Cherokee claim north of the Tennessee was but a simple afterthought. Yet they turned it decidedly to their advantage.

7. Letter of Sir William Johnson, April 4th, 1772, in *New York Documentary History,* ii:992.

8. The Cherokees could never have lived in Kentucky, except perhaps a temporary colony of them planted [*wi*] by the Six Nations. George Croghan stated in January 1756 "that a party of the Six Nations had brought some of the Cherokee from their country, and settled them on the Ohio at Kentucky River about one hundred miles from the Lower Shawanoe towns, where they [*wi*]." *Pennsylvania Records,* ii:733–34.

9. MS. memoir of Richard Henderson by his brother, the late Maj. Pleasant Henderson, kindly communicated by the Hon. H. C. Jones of North Carolina, whose lady is the only daughter of Major Henderson.

10. "My brother, Richard Henderson, was induced to attempt the purchase of Kentucky from the Cherokees, through the suggestions and advice of the late Col. Daniel Boone, who then resided in Rowan County, North Carolina, and had hunted in and explored the country as early as 1768 or '69." MS. narrative of the late Maj. Pleasant Henderson. Filson, the late Col. Nathaniel Hart of Kentucky, and the venerable Col. Nathan Boone fully corroborate this statement.

11. When Governor Dunmore issued his Proclamation against the Henderson purchase, a copy, together with a message, was despatched to the Cherokees. Andrew Boyd was the messenger. Upon his return, in June 1775, Colonel Preston thus wrote his Excellency: "The answer of the Cherokees, signed by the warriors present, and attested by the interpreter and some traders, Mr. Boyd will deliver your Lordship, together with what information he could gather at the place, by

which it plainly appears that those people have been deceived into a sale of lands they had no claim to. I had a letter from a considerable trader amongst these Indians who says, that they were deluded into the treaty; that when the young men saw the goods, they insisted on having them on any terms, which their great men were obliged to comply with, otherwise lose their authority in the nation, as they hold it on no other foundation than the love of the people, which a refusal would have forfeited. Tho' he declares that they never, for the fourteen years he has been there, claimed any lands in that quarter farther than the waters that empty into their own river."—i.e. the Cherokee or Tennessee.—MS. Preston Papers.

12. Among others at the treaty, there was a distinguished chief called At-ta-kul-la-Kul-la, the Indian name known to the white people by the name of the Little Carpenter—in allusion, say the Indians, to his deep, artful, and ingenious diplomatic abilities, ably demonstrated in negotiating treaties with the white people and influence in their national councils; like a white carpenter could make every notch and joint fit in wood, so he could bring all his views to fill and fit their places in the political machinery of his nation. He was the most celebrated and influential Indian among all the tribes then known; considered as the Solon of his day. He was said to be about ninety years of age, a very small man, and so lean and light habited that I scarcely believe he would have exceeded more in weight than a pound for each year of his life. He was marked with two large scores or sears on each cheek, his ears cut and banded with silver, hanging nearly down on each shoulder, the ancient Indian mode of distinction in some tribes and fashion in others. In one of his public talks delivered to the whites, he spoke to this effect: He was an old man, had presided as chief in their council and as president of his nation for more than half a century; had formerly been appointed agent and envoy extraordinary to the king of England on business of the first importance to his nation; he crossed the big water, arrived at his destination, was received with great distinction, had the honor of dining with his majesty and the nobility; had the utmost respect paid to him by the great men among the white people; had accomplished his mission with success; and from the long standing in the highest dignities of his nation, he claimed confidence and good faith in all and everything he would advance in support of the rightful claims of his people to the Bloody Ground, then in treaty to be sold to the white people.—*Narrative of a Kentucky Adventure in 1775,* by the late Hon. Felix Walker, in *De Bow's Review,* February 1854.

13. Beside Colonel Henderson, there were present at the treaty Thomas and Nathaniel Hart, John Williams, John Luttrell, and perhaps other partners of the company. The chief details of the treaty are collated from copies of the manuscript depositions in the archives of Virginia of several persons who were in attendance.

14. *Pennsylvania Gazette,* March 22nd, 1775; Martin's *North Carolina,* ii:339; Jones' *Defense,* 151.

15. *American Archives,* 4th ser., ii:171, 174.

16. MS. deposition in the archives of Virginia.

17. MS. letter of Colonel Preston, March 10th, 1775.

18. Daniel Bryan, in his MS. narrative, gives the following names of persons as also accompanying Boone on this service: William Moore, William Miller, Reuben Searcy, Bartlett Searcy, Edward Bradley, Samuel Tate, John King, Oswell Towns, Captain Crabtree, and William Hays, who was Boone's son-in-law; and Bryan further adds that Mrs. Susan Hays accompanied her father and husband and was thus the first white woman who stood [on] the soil of Kentucky. A Negro woman accompanied Colonel Callaway.

19. *North American Review,* January 1846, p. 84; Perkins' *Memoirs and Writings,* ii:258.

20. Felix Walker [*cut off on microfilm; picks up on DM 3B:177{1}*] in 1689. His grandfather emigrated to America in 1720 and settled on Appoquinimink Creek in Delaware. His youngest son, John Walker, emigrated after his majority to the South Branch of Potomac, in now Hampshire County, Virginia, and served on Braddock's campaign. He married Elizabeth Watson, and of their seven sons, only three arrived at man's estate—Felix, the eldest, was born on the South Branch July 19th, 1753. When, after Braddock's Defeat, the defenseless frontiers were overrun by the enemy, Mr. Walker removed with his family to the western borders of North Carolina, settling on Leeper's Creek about ten miles east of the present village of Lincolnton. The Cherokees becoming hostile, he served on Grant's campaign against them in 1761. In the fall of 1763 he settled near King's Mountain, and a few years later, first at the mouth of Cane Creek of Broad River, and finally at the junction of the Green and Broad rivers, where he died January 25, 1796, in his 68th year. He was the first signer to articles of association in his county, in 1775, pledging assistance by force to the tyrannical measures of Great Britain, and was the same year elected as a member of the North Carolina Convention, having previously resigned his civil commissions under royal authority. During the same year also, he was chosen by the Continental Congress a captain in Col. Robert Howe's regiment of regulars and took an active part in the Revolutionary struggle. He also served as colonel commandant and judge of Rutherford County for many years.

Reared on the frontier, Felix Walker had not the best educational advantages but at the age of sixteen was placed in the employ of George Parker, an English merchant of Charleston, South Carolina, with whom he remained some considerable time, and was then sent to Dr. Dobson's school in what is now Burke County. In February 1775 he solicited permission to visit the Kentucky country, then about to be settled under the auspices of Henderson and company. The grievous wound he received from the Indians has already been mentioned; and he was the first person wounded on the soil of Kentucky in the long struggle with the Indians who recovered from his wounds. Once restored to health, he visited Harrodsburg and other portions of the country and, in July of that year, returned to Carolina—tarrying awhile, however, with Col. Charles Robertson on Watauga, with whom he had taken up his quarters during the treaty in March preceding. Returning to Watauga a few months after, he was in

November 1775 appointed clerk of the commissioners who then governed that little trans-montane republic. We find him the next year an officer in the army at Charleston when the British were repulsed in their attack on Fort Moultrie; but the Cherokees soon after breaking out, he returned to Watauga and commanded a company stationed on the Nolachucky for the protection of the frontiers.

Early in 1778 he married a daughter of Col. Charles Robertson, and she dying a few months after, he returned to North Carolina, and when Rutherford County was organized in the fall of 1779, he was appointed clerk of the court. In 1780 he married Isabella, daughter of William Henry, and thence forward to the end of the war he was much engaged in the sanguinary warfare against the British and Tories. He was in 1792 elected a member of the House of Commons of North Carolina and was on six different occasions again chosen to fill the same position; and for three successive terms, 1817 to 1823, he represented his district in Congress. About 1825 he wrote a brief narrative, which has been recently published, of his Kentucky adventure in 1775, and some family sketches, and we cannot but recognize in these writings evidence of that cheerful piety so characteristic of many of the noble pioneers of the West. Removing in his old age to Mississippi, he died near Clinton. He was rather below the middle stature, with blue eyes, and in his advanced years, his hair, perfectly white, was formed into a cue. His son, the late Gen. William Watson Walker, was second in command of Long and Walker's expedition to Mexico, mentioned in Foote's *History of Texas;* and to Samuel R. Walker, Esq., a son of the latter, we are mainly indebted for the facts used in this sketch, as well also for the likeness of his worthy grandsire, Felix Walker.

21. A conjoint letter written at Boonesborough July 18th, 1775, by Colonels Henderson and Luttrell states that it was a party of Cherokees, headed by the notorious Will Emery, who attacked Boone's and Tate's camps and took the plunder and horses to the Shawanoe towns, and the Shawanoes "described the horses as well as the owners could have done." Capt. William Russell, in a manuscript letter to Colonel Preston dated at Fort Blair, mouth of the Kenhawa, June 12th, 1775, states on the authority of Cornstalk, head chief of the Shawanoes, that it was the Cherokees who attacked Tate's camp and the Picts, or Miamies, who fired on Boone's party: "The Cornstalk," says Russell, "brought me two of the horses taken by that party of Cherokees who murdered the people on Kentucke in March; the Shawanoes took the rascal who had them, but he made his escape from them, and it is supposed he is returned to the Cherokee Nation. It appears to have been the Picts that fired on Boone's camp, when the two men were killed out of his party."

22. Boone's Narrative; Boone's letter of April 1st, 1775, to Colonel Henderson, in Hall's *Sketches of the West;* Felix Walker's Narrative; Bradford's *Notes on Kentucky;* MS. notes of conversations with Capt. John Gass and Isaiah Boon; Captain Gass, who first went to Boonesborough in 1776, remembers to have seen Twitty's rude fort at an early day.

23. MS. notes of conversations with Capt. John Gass, Col. Nathan Boone, and the late Col. William Martin.

24. Perhaps on Tate's Creek, between Silver Creek and Boonesborough, and so named in consequence of this attack on Tate's camp upon its waters.

25. These companies were doubtless Harrod's at Harrodsburg and Boiling Spring, the McAfees on Salt River, and perhaps McClelland's at the Royal Spring on Elkhorn, and Hinkson's on Licking.

26. Placing one horse directly before the other some seven or eight feet apart, a couple of poles were adjusted on either side of them, supported by straps across the horse's backs; and several straps or tugs were stretched across the poles between the horses, and over them spread a blanket or skins. Upon this horse-litter, as it was termed, the patient was placed and the horses led with care. Such litters were easily constructed and often called into requisition by the pioneers. "A spring at Boonesborough," says Filson, "constantly emits sulphurous particles, and near the same place is a salt spring." They were greatly resorted to by buffalo, deer, and other wild animals when the country was first explored.

27. Mr. Walker, in his Narrative, pays this just tribute to the great Kentucky pioneer: "Colonel Boone conducted the company under his care through the wilderness, with great propriety, intrepidity, and courage; and were I to enter an exception to any part of his conduct, it would be on the ground that he appeared void of fear, and, of consequence, too little caution for the enterprise. But let me with feeling recollection and lasting gratitude, ever remember the unremitting kindness, sympathy, and attention paid to me by Colonel Boone in my distress. He was my father, physician, and friend; he attended me as his child, cured my wounds by the use of medicines from the woods, nursed me with paternal affection until I recovered, without the expectation of reward. Gratitude is the only tribute I can pay to his memory. He is now beyond the praise or blame of mortals, in that world unknown from whose bourn no traveller returns. I also was kindly treated by all my companions, particularly John Kennedy. From Captain Cocke I received kind and friendly attentions."

28. Compare Walker's Narrative and Colonel Henderson's letter of June 12th, 1775.

29. During the period of 1774–'75, the Kentucky was most generally called the Louisa, sometimes the Levisa. It seems clearly to have been mistaken at this early date for the Louisa of Dr. Walker's discovery in 1750—which was the main East Fork of Big Sandy, as Dr. Walker himself informed the late Hon. John Brown of Kentucky but which, probably by mistake, has since been applied to the West Fork. The late Col. William Martin, of Tennessee and a native of Orange County, Virginia, and a most intelligent pioneer, informed one of the authors that he remembered that anterior to the Revolution, Louisa County, adjoining Orange, was vulgarly called Levisa. Hence, doubtless, the corruption of Louisa into Levisa as early applied to both the Kentucky River and the Kentucky country. Col. William Whitley gave the name of Levisa to his first daughter, born in the Levisa country at Harrodsburg February 25th, 1777, now the venerable widow of Maj. James

McKinney, whom one of the authors visited in Missouri in October 1851; Colonel Henderson has here committed a palpable anachronism.

TFB: *"One of the authors" is a recurring phrase Draper uses to refer to himself.*

30. This intimation that Boone left before the conclusion of the treaty does not seem to correspond with Boone's Narrative, and particularly towards its close, when Boone introduces the remark of the old Cherokee chief to himself when signing and delivering the deed. The statements of the late Daniel Bryan, the late Col. Nathaniel Hart, of Kentucky, whose father was at the treaty, the late Maj. Pleasant Henderson, a brother of Col. Richard Henderson, and of the present Col. Nathan Boone all go to confirm the opinion that Boone was not only at the treaty but aided in fixing the boundaries of the purchase. As Henderson's letter, from which we quote, was written nearly three months after the treaty, he may have thoughtlessly said what was not in this particular strictly correct; and he may only have intended to say that though Boone left the treaty-ground after the conclusion of the purchase, yet perhaps before the grand entertainment and final departure of the Indians. The deeds were signed on the 17th of March, and Henderson did not leave till the 20th, when, as he records it, "having finished the treaty at Watauga, set off for Louisa." Boone could not have started before the signing of the deeds on the 17th; and it would hardly be supposed, that Henderson would have sent forward Boone and his party of pioneers to mark the road and commence the settlement before a certainty of obtaining the grant. It is, moreover, certain that Captain Twitty, Felix Walker, and their companions remained till the conclusion of the treaty and overtook Boone, who had preceded them a little, at the Long Island of the Holston some thirty miles from the treaty-ground; and the fact that this party was with Boone is another evidence of the thoughtlessness of Henderson in penning the remark upon which we here correct.

31. Colonel Henderson's letter, Boonesborough, June 12th, 1775, in the appendix to the second volume of Hall's *Sketches of the West.*

32. Harrodstown or Harrodsburg was on the waters of Salt River, and placing it on Dick's River must have been a slip of the pen on the part of Colonel Henderson.

33. "They were chiefly raised on the Monongahela, where no law had ever extended, or the right to the soil been determined."—Note by *Colonel Henderson.*

34. Edmund Fanning was a native of New York and graduated in 1757 at Yale College. His exertions had a powerful influence in producing the war of the Regulators in North Carolina, during which he was whipped severely by the enraged populace and had his house destroyed in Hillsboro. He retired with Governor Tryon to New York, raised a regiment of Tories, at the head of which he served during the Revolution. In 1782 he was surveyor general of New York but was soon forced to Nova Scotia. In 1786 he was appointed governor of Prince Edward Island, which he held for nineteen years, and also a general in the British Army. He died in London in 1818, leaving a widow who was but recently living, a son,

and three daughters. General Fanning was talented, haughty, supercilious, and unscrupulous.

35. TFB: *Ellipsis by LCD.*

36. St. Asaph was at a large spring, near where Benjamin Logan subsequently located his fort a mile from the present village of Stanford, Kentucky. It was doubtless originally so named after the celebrated Bishop of St. Asaph. The Hon. W. C. Rives, in his discourse before the Virginia History Society in 1847, thus speaks of him: "An able and eloquent prelate, the Bishop of St. Asaph, whose name Americans must ever recall with the profoundest veneration and gratitude, as one of the earliest and more powerful champions of American rights, declared, in 1774, that 'he looked upon North America as the only great nursery of freemen then left on the face of the earth.'" This speech—adds Mr. Rives in a note—"was intended to have been delivered in the House of Lords, the 11th of May, 1774, on the third reading of the Bill for altering the charter of the colony of Massachusetts Bay. Though not actually delivered on the occasion referred to, it was composed and published at the time by the venerable Bishop. It is one of the noblest pieces of eloquence and wisdom in the language, and strongly recalls to the mind of the reader, by the similitude of its character, inspiration and power, the great speech of Milton for the liberty of unlicensed printing."

37. This was John Todd, a distinguished pioneer of Kentucky, and in the sequel killed at the fatal battle of the Blue Licks.

38. He was a son of Christopher Gist so distinguished for his early and adventurous explorations of the West.

EDITOR'S NOTES: CHAPTER 11

a. Cadwallader Colden, author of *The History of the Five Indian Nations of Canada, Which Are Dependent on the Province of New-York in America, and Are the Barrier between the English and French in That Part of the World* (1747) and *The History of the Five Indian Nations Depending on the Province of New-York in America* (1727).

b. Calling the Erie the "Cats" is a common misinterpretation. The French called the Erie "la nation de Chat"—the nation of the cat, "cat" actually meaning raccoon, not some sort of feline. French interpretations of Huron renderings of the name Erie include, among others, Rhiierrhonons, Eriehronon, Erieehronons, and Ehriehronoms. The Erie spanned several Iroquoian-speaking native groups culturally and linguistically related to the Huron, Neutral, and other Iroquoians. They established villages as far south of Lake Erie as Toledo and Pittsburgh. Catholic missionaries made numerous references to them, which have been compiled in *Jesuit Relations and Allied Documents.*

In late 1654 the Iroquois began attacking the Erie deep in their own territory and continued raiding them for at least the next decade. By 1680 the Erie had surrendered to the Five Nations. Western Seneca towns soon had disproportionately large numbers of Erie living among them. Because of the Eries' early disappearance as a distinct people, little is known about them.

c. During this era of Iroquois wars upon Ohio Valley Algonquins, the well-armed Five Nations not only preyed on the Shawnee, but also fought the Wyandot, Ottawa, Miami, Illinois, Ojibwa, and Mesquakie (Fox). It was fur, beaver mostly, that the Iroquois craved, not land; they justified their depredations in their claim that the western tribes were overhunting. As the numbers of furbearers declined in the East, war intensified in the West. Worse, fighting instead of hunting led to smaller peltry harvests, forcing the Five Nations to depend less upon gathering their own peltry and more upon stealing furs from their foes.

d. Lewis Evans, *Analysis* (1755). See Introduction, note i.

e. Thomas Pownall, author of *A Topographical Description of Such Parts of North America as Are Contained in the (Annexed) Map of the Middle British Colonies, &c., in North America* (1776).

f. The Treaty of Ryswick, signed on September 30, 1697, ended King William's War (War of the League of Augsburg), 1689–97.

g. Virginian Colonel John Donelson's "Donelson Purchase" in 1771 claimed about 10 million Cherokee acres in the middle Ohio region as far west as the Kentucky River. This bit of Anglo perfidy is enlightening. Principal Cherokee chieftain At-ta-kul-la-Kul-la (Little Carpenter) initialed the treaty, assuming the western border was to be the Louisa River ("discovered" in 1756 by Dr. Thomas Walker), which empties into the western branch of the Big Sandy. That the treaty neatly confused Walker's Louisa with the Kentucky (the 44-mile-long Louisa then went by the same name) and more than doubled the size of the agreed-upon claim never bothered Lord Dunmore's land speculators who negotiated the deal. It was an error, perhaps an intentional deception, that the aggressive treaty makers let stand.

h. Shawnee claims to the region go back to antiquity, the earliest occupation site probably being the Fort Ancient Hopewellian complex near present-day Xenia, Ohio. Such a definite link of the historic Shawnee to the Hopewell culture has yet to be established.

i. Draper's deft rendering here of American Indian history and treaty making is strong testimony to his own Manifest Destiny leanings, as is his justification of the subsequent illegal shenanigans of Col. Richard Henderson and his fellow Transylvania Company stockholders. In a larger sphere, such an articulate apologia for stripping the Indians of lands they had occupied for millennia sheds much light on nineteenth-century Anglo-American thought; by then the insidious taproot feeding present-day Native American injustices was firmly in place.

j. In 1770 anger over taxes spawned the Regulator movement in Orange County, North Carolina, at the county seat of Hillsborough. Incensed at the Crown's levy upon settlers and at unfair political appointments in the Colonial Assembly, several hundred Regulators stormed Judge Richard Henderson's court that September, demanding redress of their grievances. Henderson fled as the

Regulators dragged several officials out by their heels and flogged them. That night and on into the next day, Regulators prowled streets smashing windows and torching barns, stables, and Henderson's home. The local militia defeated the Regulators on May 6, 1771, at the Battle of Alamance. Officials hanged six of the leaders and imprisoned many more, ending the movement.

k. North Carolinians Nathaniel, David, and Thomas Hart were members of the Transylvania Company.

l. This fragment of Thomas Hart's letter to Nathaniel Hart, dated August 3, 1780, was written to absolve Boone of a large debt he owed Thomas Hart after thieves robbed Boone at a Virginia inn in February 1780.

m. More truthfully, Henderson the land speculator devised an illegal, hare-brained scheme to make Transylvania stockholders rich feudal barons, complete with fief and quitrent-paying tenants to lord over.

n. The charismatic Dragging Canoe ("Tsi-yu Gansi-ni"), unlike his father, At-ta-kul-la-Kul-la, O-con-nos-to-ta, and the Raven, all of whom signed the Sycamore Shoals Treaty, was no accommodationist to these colonials. Breaking ranks with the elders, he challenged Henderson's "purchase," and his efforts divided the Cherokee into neutral and militant wings. In 1776 the insurgents joined "the Northerns" (including longtime Shawnee enemies) to fight their common American foe, siding with the British in the Revolution. By mid-1777 the dissidents were a secessionist faction calling themselves Ani-Yuniwiya—"the Real People"; settlers called them "Chickamaugas" because they built their towns on Chickamauga Creek, as well as at Muscle Shoals and on the Tennessee in north Alabama. Besides Dragging Canoe, Chickamauga leaders like Bloody Fellow, Double Head, Pumpkin Boy, Will Weber, and John Watts worked to establish a pan-Indian alliance to keep encroaching Anglo-Americans at bay. Dragging Canoe died on March 1, 1792, predicting long before the Trail of Tears the Indian removal policies of the American government. Two years later the Chickamaugas made peace but continued in the nineteenth century in their role as Cherokee leaders.

o. It is thought that Dragging Canoe's words—"Kentucky was the *Bloody Ground*"—is the origin of the phrase "Dark and Bloody Ground" as a reference to frontier Kentucky. For Draper's exegesis of the phrase, see chapter 16, note 4.

p. After his purchase, Col. Richard Henderson told the Indians that "he did not love to walk on their land. That he had some Goods, Guns and Ammunition which they had not yet seen." With Henderson was John Carter, an Indian trader. That the Cherokee could not pay off their sizable debt to Carter became a bargaining chip for both the Indians and the Transylvania Company. Carter at first offered to absolve the debt in exchange for "the Path Deed." Instead, the Indians struck a much better deal with Henderson—the Path Deed in exchange for more trade goods and leather, plus extinguishing their debt to Carter.

In 1776 Dragging Canoe's Chickamaugas attacked a string of colonists who had built their cabins on the land deemed ceded to whites by terms of the Path Deed.

q. Were Henderson's goods, which "filled a house," worth "ten thousand pounds sterling," as Draper asserts? In 1784 Dubliner J. F. D. Smyth wrote there were "only ten waggons loaded with cheap goods, such as coarse woolens, trinkets, and spirituous liquors." Contemporary observers were more specific, listing, besides rum, livestock, guns, powder and ball, corn, flour, calico shirts, trade silver, ribbons, blankets, salt, and bearskins.

The figure "ten thousand pounds sterling" is suspect; the original Treaty of Watauga says the land was to be deeded to Henderson and Company "in consideration of the sum of *two* thousand pounds of lawful money of Great Britain."

r. Draper's diatribe, "twelve hundred Indians, all greedy for their share," is a bit much in view of the facts. It is plain who the money mongers were.

s. Tradition, probably based upon Draper's manuscript, has long held that Daniel Boone was with Henderson at the Sycamore Shoals Treaty on March 17, 1775. Was he? Woodcutter Felix Walker states in his lucid journal that on March 10 Boone and his team of axmen left from Long Island on the Holston River to begin their historic trail-blazing exodus. Draper attempts to resolve this in note 30 of this chapter.

t. Daniel Boone's firstborn daughter, Susannah Boone Hays (1760–1800), had married one of the woodcutters, William Hays (1754–1804), weeks earlier at Fort Blackmore, Virginia. She and Col. Richard Callaway's African slave woman cooked and tended to the woodcutters' needs during the epic journey.

u. The American bulldog was a direct descendant of his true English cousin and first bred in the American colonies in the mid-1700s. Other men, like Daniel Trabue, used bulldogs on Kentucky's frontier to hunt bear and buffalo. Trabue's bulldog had such a fine reputation as a tenacious fighter that hunters at Logan's Station (St. Asaph's) regularly borrowed the fierce canine.

v. True to form, Draper has rewritten Boone's missive, correcting the woodsman's rough spelling and punctuation.

w. According to historian Neal Hammon, a building housing the restrooms in the Boonesborough State Park now stands about on the original Fort Boone site. The later Boonesborough fort site is properly located by the historical marker.

x. Henderson's land grab was doomed before he signed its papers. Hearing rumors of what was afoot, on February 10, 1775, the governor of North Carolina, Joseph Martin, issued a royal proclamation condemning the actions of "Richard Henderson and his Confederates." Critical to Transylvania's success was the willingness of James Harrod and his men at Harrod's Town (established June 16, 1774, north of the Kentucky) to agree to Henderson's mandates. At first they did. But by 1776 John Gabriel Jones' opposition forced a rift in the settlement's unity and led to dissension. Worse for Henderson, anti-British forces driving the Revolution were suspicious of such huge land acquisitions by possible Tory land barons.

And there were other issues: Virginia claimed Kentucky as her own; colonial officials questioned the validity of the Sycamore Shoals treaty; and military leaders like George Rogers Clark declared that Transylvanians were unable to defend their claim from Indian attack, and most of the settlers agreed. In December 1776 Virginia incorporated "the County of Kentucky" into her commonwealth and two years later declared Henderson's purchase "null and void."

y. In the various compilations of Kentucky land records, Capt. Marquis Calmes' name is also spelled Callimes, Calmer, Calmers, and Calmis. In the original transcription of this entry of Richard Henderson's journal, he spells it "Collomes."

z. For a thorough account of the extermination of the eastern buffalo, see Ted Franklin Belue, *The Long Hunt* (1996).

aa. For the significance of a "hunting-shirt" as a badge of manly valor, and especially in this context, see chapter 1, note n.

CHAPTER 12

May 23rd. to December 31st, 1775.—Representatives from the Four
Kentucky Settlements Assemble at Boonesborough.—Col. Richard
Henderson Conducts Official Proceedings.—Bills and Amendments.—
Livery of Seizin.—Of the Convention's Compact.—Colonel Henderson's
Diary.—Land Title Problems.—Frontier Life.—Indian Raids.—Growing
Crisis over Land Claims and the Slaughter of Game.—Meeting of
Transylvania Proprietors in North Carolina.—More Indian Troubles.

O n Tuesday, the 23rd of May, 1775, eighteen delegates from the four Kentucky settlements assembled at Boonesborough. The next day they met in conventions in the rear of Henderson's camp under the "divine elm" and formed the first legislative assembly west of the Alleghenies. The respective settlements were represented as follows:

For *Boonesborough*—Squire Boone, Daniel Boone, William Cocke, Samuel Henderson, William Moore, and Richard Callaway.

For *Harrodsburg*—Thomas Slaughter, John Lythe, Valentine Harmon, and James Douglas.

For *Boiling Spring* settlement—James Harrod, Nathan Hammond, Isaac Hite, and Azariah Davis.

For the town of *St. Asaph*—John Todd, Alexander Spotswood Dandridge, John Floyd, and Samuel Wood.[1]

Having unanimously chosen Col. Thomas Slaughter, chairman, and Matthew Jouitt, clerk, the Rev. John Lythe, one of the delegates, "performed divine service," which we suppose means that he offered a prayer, when the Convention sent a message to the proprietors acquainting them of their choice of officers: Colonel Henderson, in behalf of himself and the rest of the proprietors, opened the Convention with an address, a copy of which has been preserved among the proceedings and is a sensible and judicious production.

"You are called and assembled, at this time," said President Henderson, "for a noble and honorable purpose—a purpose, however ridiculous and idle it may appear at first view to superficial minds, yet is of the most solid consequence; and if prudence, firmness, and wisdom are suffered to influence your councils and direct your conduct, the peace and harmony of thousands may be expected to result from your deliberations. In short, you are about a work of the utmost importance to the well-being of this country in general, in which the interest and security of each and every individual is inseparately connected."

"You are placing," he continued, "the first corner stone of an edifice, the height and magnificence of whose superstructure are now in the womb of futurity, and can only become great and glorious, in proportion to the excellence of its foundation. These considerations, gentlemen, will no doubt animate and inspire you with sentiments worthy the grandeur of the subject. Our peculiar circumstances in this remote country, surrounded on all sides with difficulties, and equally subject to one common danger, threatening our common overthrow," and suggested that such a consideration should "secure to them a union of interests, and consequently that harmony of opinion, so essential to the forming of good, wise and wholesome laws."

"If any doubt remain against you," he continued, "with respect to the force and efficacy of whatever laws you now or hereafter make, be pleased to consider that all power is originally in the people; make it their interest, therefore, by impartial and beneficial laws, and you may be sure of their inclinations to see them enforced." He proceeded to add: "As it is indispensably necessary that laws should be composed for the regulation of our conduct,—as we have a right to make such laws, without giving offence to Great Britain, or any of the American Colonies,—without disturbing the repose of any society or community under heaven;—if it is probable, nay, certain that the laws may derive force and efficacy from our mutual consent, and that consent resulting from our own virtue, interest and convenience, nothing remains but to set about the business immediately, and let the event determine the wisdom of the undertaking."

He then called their attention to specific objects requiring legislation and suggested "as the first in order, from its importance, the establishing of Courts of Justice, or tribunals for the punishment of such as may offend against the lands," and then proposed the adoption of "some plain and easy method for the recovery of debts, and determining matters of dispute in respect to property, contracts, torts and injuries." "These things," he declared, "are so essential, that if not strictly attended to, our name will become odious abroad, and our place of short and precarious duration. It would give honest and disinterested persons cause to suspect, that these was some colourable reason, at least, for the unworthy and scandalous assertions, together with the groundless insinuations, contained in an infamous and scurrilous libel lately printed and published concerning the settlement of this country—the author of which avails himself of his station, and under the specious pretense of a proclamation, pompously dressed up and decorated in the garb of authority, has uttered invectives of the most malignant kind; and endeavors to wound the good name of persons, whose moral character would derive little advantage by being placed in competition with his, charging them amongst other things equally untrue, with a design "of forming an asylum for debtors and other persons of desperate circumstances"—placing the proprietors of the soil at the head of a lawless train of abandoned villains, against whom the regal authority ought to be exerted, and every possible measure taken to put an immediate step to so dangerous an enterprise.[2] I have not the least doubt, gentlemen, but that your conduct in the Convention will manifest the honest and laudable intentions of the present adventurers, whilst a conscious blush confounds the wilful calumniators and officious detractors of our infant and yet little community."

He next recommended "establishing and regulating a militia," which he justly regarded as "of the greatest importance." "It is apparent," he said, "that without some wise institution respecting our mutual defense, the different towns of settlements are every day exposed to the most imminent danger, and liable to be destroyed at the mere will of the savage Indians. Nothing, I am persuaded, but their entire ignorance of our weakness and want of orders, had hitherto preserved us from the destruction and rapacious hands of cruelty, and given us at this time an opportunity of forming secure defensive plans, to be supported and carried into execution by authority and sanction of a well-digested law."

"There are sundry other things," he finally said, "highly worthy your consideration, and demanding redress; such as the wanton destruction of our game, the only support of life among many of us, and for want of which the country would be abandoned ere to-morrow, and scarcely a probability remain of its ever becoming the habitation of any Christian people. This, together with the practice of many foreigners, who make a business of hunting in our country, killing, driving off, and lessening the number of wild cattle and other game, whilst the value of the skins and furs is appropriate to the benefit of persons not concerned or interested in our settlement—these are evils, I say, that I am convinced can't escape your notice and attention." And he concluded with the customary assurance of the cheerful concurrence of the proprietors in every measure, which could, "in the most distant and remote degree, promote the happiness, or contribute to the grandeur, of the new-born country."[3]

A courteous response was made to the address of the president, drawn up by Mr. Todd, promising their early attention to several matters suggested to them. The business of legislation now proceeded with earnestness and parliamentary regularity—were introduced, referred to appropriate committees, reported back and, having had their three several readings, were passed and approved by the lords-proprietors of the soil. Mr. Robert McAfee was appointed sergeant-at-arms and was speedily ordered "to bring John Gass before the Convention to answer for an insult offered Col. Richard Callaway"; and the same day the offender "was brought before the Convention and reprimanded by the Chairman."[4]

Mr. Todd and Mr. Harrod were appointed a committee to wait on the proprietors to know what name for the colony would be agreeable and reported that it was their pleasure that it should be called *Transylvania.*

Messrs. Todd and Dandridge, the two lawyers in the convention, were appropriately placed on the committee "to bring in a bill for the establishment of courts of judicature, and regulating the practice therein"; also "to bring in an attachment bill" and "a bill for the punishment of criminals." Upon the committee "to bring in a bill for establishing and regulating the militia" were very properly placed Mr. Floyd as chairman, Mr. Harrod, and Mr. Cocke, all three of whom had been captains in service during the Indian war of the preceding year. Mr. Lythe, very naturally, while faithful to his sacred calling, upon leave introduced "a bill *to prevent profane swearing and Sabbath breaking,"* which, when read the first time, was ordered "to be re-committed, and that Mr. Lythe, Mr. Todd, and Mr. Harrod, be a committee *to make amendments."*

We cannot but note with interest the part acted by Daniel and Squire Boone in this primitive legislative assembly of the Ohio Valley. It is recorded "on motion of Mr. Daniel Boone, leave is given to bring in a bill *for preserving the game,* and etc. Ordered, that Mr. Boone, Mr. Davis, Mr. Harrod, Mr. Hammond and Mr. Moore, be a committee for that purpose." Accordingly, the same day, a bill for this object was reported by the committee, of whom Daniel Boone was chairman, and read the first time. Previous leave having been granted. "Captain Boone brought in a bill *for improving the breed of horses";* and Squire Boone, on leave, introduced "a bill *to preserve the range."* It was, furthermore, "ordered, that Mr. Harrod, Mr. Boone, and Mr. Cocke wait on the proprietors and beg that they will not indulge any person whatever in granting them lands on the present terms unless they comply with the former proposals of settling the country, and etc."

The eight laws specified were all enacted and approved; and one other, relating to clerks' and sheriffs' fees, passed the Convention but in some way was

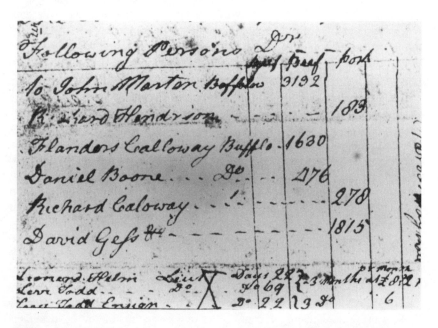

57. Receipt, c. 1775, from James Harrod to John Martin, Flanders Callaway, and Daniel Boone for buffalo meat—called "wild beef"—totaling 5,238 pounds. Richard Henderson, Richard Callaway, and David Gass sold 2,276 pounds of pork. STATE HISTORICAL SOCIETY OF WISCONSIN.

omitted to be handed in by the clerk for the signature and approval of the proprietors and hence failed to become a law. During the last day's session of the Convention, May the 27th, President Henderson sent in a message desiring to exhibit the title deed from the aborigines and first owners of the soil of Transylvania and requesting that the boundaries of the same might be entered upon their record. This request being complied with, Colonel Henderson personally attended the Convention with John Farrar, who, having been specially appointed by the Cherokees at the Watauga treaty for that purpose, now, in their name, performed the ancient but now obsolete custom of *Livery of Seizin*[a] and thus, in the presence of the Convention, made a formal transfer of the country to the Transylvania Company. Colonel Henderson then produced the deed, the metes and bounds of which were entered on the journal.

Before the adjournment, a solemn compact between the proprietors and the people of the colony, declaring "the powers of the one, and the liberties of the other," was entered into, signed, and sealed by Henderson, Hart, and Luttrell on the part of the company and by Col. Thomas Slaughter, chairman of the convention, in behalf of the colonists. This interesting compact, alike so creditable to the knowledge of republican government possessed by our backwoods legislator and to the liberal principles which actuated the proprietors, deserves a place in this connection:

"Whereas, it is highly necessary for the peace of the proprietors, and the security of the people of this colony, that the powers of the one, and the liberties of the other, be ascertained,—we, Richard Henderson, Nathaniel Hart and J. Luttrell, on behalf of ourselves, as well as the other proprietors of the colony of Transylvania, of the one part, and the representatives of the people of the said colony, in Convention assembled, of the other part, do most solemnly enter into the following contract and agreement, to wit:

"1st. That the election of delegates in this colony be annual.

"2nd. That the Convention may adjourn, and meet again on their own adjournment—provided, that in cases of great emergency, the proprietors may call together the delegates before the time adjourned to; and, if a majority does not attend, they may dissolve them and call a new one.

"3rd. That, to prevent dissention and delay of business, one proprietor shall act for the whole, or some one delegated by them for that purpose, who shall always reside in the colony.

"4th. That there be perfect religious freedom and general toleration—provided, that the propagators of any doctrine or tenets, evidently tending to the subversion of our laws, shall, for such conduct, be amenable to, and punished by, the civil courts.

"5th. That the judges of the Superior or Supreme courts be appointed by the proprietors, but be supported by the people, and to them be answerable for their mal-conduct.

"6th. That quit-rents never exceed two shillings sterling per hundred acres.

"7th. That the proprietors appoint a sheriff, who shall be one of three persons recommended by the court.

"8th. That the judges of the superior courts have, without fee or reward, the appointment of the clerks of this colony.

"9th. That the judges of the inferior courts be recommended by the people, and approved by the proprietors, and by them commissioned.

"10th. That all civil and military officers be within the appointment of the proprietors.

"11th. That the office of Surveyor General belong to no person interested, or partner in this purchase.

"12th. That the legislative authority, after the strength and maturity of the colony will permit, consist of three branches, to wit: the delegates or representatives chosen by the people; a council, not exceeding twelve men, possessed of landed estate, residing in the colony, and the proprietors.

"13th. That nothing with respect to the number of delegates from any town or settlement shall hereafter be drawn into precedent, but that the number of representatives shall be ascertained by law, when the state of the colony will admit of amendment.

"14th. That the land offices be always open.

"15th. That commissions without profit, be granted without fee.

"16th. That the salaries of all officers appointed by the proprietors, be settled and regulated by the laws.

"17th. That the Convention have the sole power of raising and appropriating all public moneys, and electing their treasurer.

"18th. That, for a short time, till the state of the colony will permit to fix some place of holding the Convention which shall be permanent, the place of meeting shall be agreed on by the proprietors and the Convention.

"To the faithful, and religious, and perpetual observance of all and every of the above articles, the said proprietors, on behalf of themselves as well as those absent, and the chairman of the Convention on behalf of them and their constituents, have hereunto interchangeably set their hands and affixed their seals, the twenty-seventh day of May, one thousand seven hundred and seventy five."

After a harmonious session of four days, the convention adjourned on Saturday, May 27th, to meet again the first Thursday of the following September at Boonesborough. Colonel Henderson, in his manuscript journal, testifies that "the delegates were very good men, and much disposed to serve their country"; that they "finished the Convention in good order," and "every body was pleased" with the result. Such was the first legislative convocation in Kentucky, and such the fruits of its deliberations. These ancient records prove that the pioneers were very far from being a lawless band; order was heaven's first law with them, and they were even anxious to make and enforce laws for the preservation of the game and range of the country. Boone was fully sensible of the necessity of these legal regulations and gave his efficient influence in procuring their enactment.[5]

Let us resume the story of the founding of the young republic in the wilds of the West as recorded in his diary at the time by Col. Richard Henderson and now copied from the ancient manuscript document. Though sometimes minute and even apparently trivial, the narrative is nevertheless one of abiding interest and we do not feel at liberty to omit any portion of it.[b]

"Sunday, May 28th, 1775.—Divine service for the first time by the Reverend John Lythe, minister of the Church of England. Most of the delegates returned home.

"Monday, May 29th.—Capt. Gist and Capt. Harrod set out on the north side of [the] Kentucky to look for land whereon to lay officers' claims to the amount of 8,000 acres. Five or six persons, in company with Mr. Lawrence Thompson and [*wm*] Thompson, arrived from Orange. No letters from our friends. Letter with an account of the battle of Boston.[6]

"Tuesday, May 30th.—Nothing uncommon.

"Wednesday, May 31st.—Mr. Hoy and Capt. [*wm*] arrived from P.D. [*wi*] News that Governor Martin turned Regulator, joined by Jno. Colson and a number of other scoundrels.

"Thursday, June 1st.—Jesse Oldham arrived from the Co. [Company] with letters—mixed news.

"Friday, June 2nd.—Hunters returned—very good meat, and etc.

"Saturday, June 3rd.—People arrived from St. Asaph; had wantonly broke up, hid their tools and on their way home.

"Sunday, June 4th.—Whitsunday—rainy; divine service by Mr. Lythe. Capt. Harrod returned.

"Monday, June 5th.—Made out commissions—to wit, for Harrodsburg, Boiling Spring settlement, and St. Asaph, both military and civil. Samuel and Nath'l [Henderson] went out to see the mouth of Muddy Creek.

"Tuesday, June 6th.—Capt. Harrod went down the river home, accompanied by Mr. David Wilson and Alexander from McLenb'g [*wi*], who arrived here last week. Mr. Hart talks of going next Monday. Abundance of people going away, selling their lots, and etc. and will not be detained. Offered several young men, to admit them to enter lands as if they were working corn, and etc., rather than they should go; they seemed determined on going, and accordingly went in the evening. This afternoon, Capt. Hart entered 1,000 acres of land on Salt River, including the salt springs. His reason for doing so, as Mr. Luttrell informed me— and said that Mr. Hart seemed much disturbed—was that I had intended for myself the mouth of Salt Lick Creek, including a salt spring.[7] Mr. Luttrell entered 1,000 acres adjoining Mr. Hart's entry at Salt Lick.

"Wednesday, Thursday, Friday and Saturday, nothing extraordinary.

"Sunday, June 11th.—Daniel Goodman went away with Jno. Looney, Wm. Wilson and Page Portwood. Divine service by Mr. Lythe. Wrote by Daniel Goodman to my wife, Daniel Williams, and Jno. Christmas.

"Monday, June 12th.—People going away—Mr. Hart, and etc. Wrote constantly till 3 o'clock in the morning."

By Captain Hart, Colonel Henderson sent to the proprietors in North Carolina a letter under date Boonesborough, June 12th, 1775, giving a clear account of the condition of men, matters, and things at that time in Kentucky. We shall break the thread of our journal-story for a season in order to introduce to the reader an extract from the colonel's graphic narrative:

"It will, no doubt," says Colonel Henderson, "surprise you, but it is nevertheless true, that we are in no posture of defence or security at this time; and, for my own part, do not much expect it will ever be effected, unless the Indians should do us the favor of annoying us, and regularly scalping a man every week until it is performed;[c] if the intervals should be longer, the same spirit of indolence and self-security, which hath hitherto prevailed, would not only continue, but increase. To give you a small specimen of the disposition of the people, it may be sufficient to assure you, that when we arrived at this place, we found Captain Boone's men as inattentive on the score of fear, (to all appearances) as if they had been in Hillsborough. A small fort [that] only wanted two or three days' work to make it tolerably safe, was totally neglected on Mr. Cocke's arrival; and unto this day remains unfinished, notwithstanding the repeated applications of Captain Boone, and every representation of danger from ourselves. The death of poor Twitty and the rest, who at the time you were informed, became sacrifices to indiscretion, had no more effect than to produce one night's watching after they got to Otter Creek, not more than ten days after the massacre. Our plantations extend near two miles in length, on the river and up a creek. Here people work in their different lots, some without their guns, and others without care or caution. It is in vain for us to say any thing more about the matter; it cannot be done by words. We have a militia law, on which I have some dependence; if it has no good effect, we must remain for sometime much at the mercy of the Indians. Should any successful attack be made on us, Captain Hart, I suppose, will be able to render sufficient reasons to the surviving company, for withdrawing from our camp, and refusing to join in building a fort for our mutual defence.

"This representation of our unguarded and defenseless situation is not all that seems to make against us. Our men, under various pretenses, are every day leaving us. It is needless to say any thing against it; many of them are so much determined, that they sell their rights for saving land on our present terms, to others who remain in their stead, for little or nothing; nay, some of them are resolved to go, and some are already gone, and given up all pretensions for this season, and depend on getting land on the next fall's terms. Our company has dwindled from about eighty in number to about fifty odd, and I believe in a few days will be considerably less. Amongst these I have not heard one person dissatisfied with the country or terms, but [they] go, as they say, merely because their business will not admit of longer delay. The fact is, that many of them are single, worthless fellows, and want to get on the other side of the mountains, for the sake of saying they have been out and returned safe, together with the probability of getting a mouthful of bread in exchange for their news.

"Having given you a slight view of one side of the question, it may not be amiss to turn the subject over, and see what may be said on the other hand. Notwithstanding all our negligence, self-security, scarcity of men, and whatever else may be added against us, I cannot think but we shall carry the matter through, and be crowned with success. My reasons for this opinion, call for in you, a kind of knowledge of the geography of our country. Those who have no idea of the matter may be aided by Captain Hart. We are seated at the mouth of Otter Creek, on the Kentucky, about 150 miles from the Ohio. To the west, about 50 miles from us, are two settlements, within six or seven miles one of the other.[8] There were, some time ago, about 100 at the two places; though now, perhaps, not more than 60 or 70, as many of them are gone up the Ohio for their families, and etc.; and some returned by the way we came, to Virginia and elsewhere. These men, in the course of hunting provisions, lands, and etc., are some of them constantly out, and scour the woods from the banks of the river near forty or fifty miles southward. On the opposite side of the river, and north from us, about forty miles, is a settlement on the crown lands, of about nineteen persons; and lower down, towards the Ohio, on the same side, there are some other settlers, how many, or at what place, I can't exactly learn.[9] There is also a party of about ten or twelve, with a surveyor, who is employed in searching through that country, and laying off officers' lands; they have been more than three weeks within ten miles of us, and will be several weeks longer ranging up and down that country.[10]

"Now, taking it for granted, that the Cherokees are our friends, which I most firmly believe, our situation exempts us from the first attempt or attack of any other Indians. Colonel Harrod, who governs the two first mentioned settlements (and is a very good man for our purpose), Colonel Floyd (the surveyor), and myself, are under solemn engagements to communicate, with the utmost dispatch, every piece of intelligence respecting danger or sign of Indians, to each other. In case of invasion of Indians, both the other parties are instantly to march and relieve the distressed, if possible. Add to this, that our country is so fertile, the growth of grass and herbage so tender and luxuriant, that it is almost impossible for a man or dog to travel, without leaving such sign that you might, for many days, gallop a horse on the trail. To be serious, it is impossible for any number of people to pass through the woods without being tracked, and of course discovered, if Indians, for our hunters all go on horseback, and could not be deceived if they were to come on the trace of footmen. From these circumstances, I think myself in a great measure secure against a formidable attack; and a few skulkers could only kill one or two, which would not much affect the interest of the company.

"Thus, gentlemen, you have heard both sides of the question, and can pretty well judge of the degree of danger we are in. Let your opinions be as they may on this point, by no means betray the least symptom of doubt to your most intimate friends. If help is ever wanting, it will be long, before succor can come from you, and therefore every expense of that kind is superfluous and unnecessary. If we can maintain our ground until after harvest, in Virginia, I will undertake forever after to defend the country against every nation of red people in the world, without calling on the company for even a gun-flint. * * * * [11]

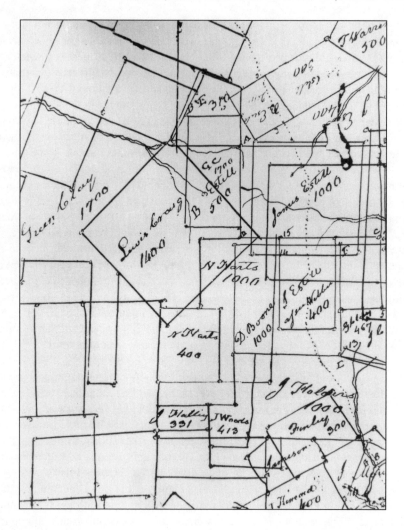

58. *Confusion over boundaries marking land claims led to overlapping or "shingled maps" such as this one from Madison County, Kentucky, which features the names of Boone and many well-known contemporaries.*

"With respect to the country, Mr. Hart, who brings this, will give you ample satisfaction. All that I shall say about it is, that it far exceeds the idea which I had formed of it; and indeed it is not surprising, for it is not in the power of any person living to do justice to the fertility of the soil, beauty of the country, or excellence of its range; let it suffice, that we have got a country of good land, with numberless advantages and inducements to a speedy population; that this country is large enough, and surely will be settled immediately on some principles or other: the grand affair on our part, is to manage matters so as to have our rights acknowledged, and continue lords of the soil. Every thing has succeeded to my wish with respect to title. The torrent from Virginia appears to be over, and gentlemen of considerable fortune, from thence, are some of them come, and others coming, with design to purchase under us, as they cannot come within the indulgences to adventurers of this season; and applications are daily making for the next year's price. Many of them are daily returned home, and would have been much dissatisfied, if I had not promised them, on my word and honor, that the terms should be published in all the Williamsburg papers."

Colonel Henderson's diary resumed:

"Tuesday, June 13th, 1775.—Col. Boone set off for his family, and the young men went with him for salt, and etc.

"Wednesday, June 14th.—Made a list of what men we had left at the camp, and found them to amount to [*wm*].

"Thursday, June 15th.—Things as usual.

"Friday, June 16th.—Fine rain.

"Saturday, June 17th.—Fine rain. A muster of the men at the fort by Capt. Moore; thirty-two men appeared with arms, in bad order, weather wet.

"Sunday, June 18th.—Fine growing weather. Corn planted the 26th and 27th of April was tasselled and shot. Had a mess of snap beans; peas ripe, and cucumbers set. Michael Stoner, our hunter, not returned—was expected yesterday. No meat. Two men from Virginia found bacon, on which with the beans aforesaid we had an excellent dinner.

"Monday, June 19th.—Fair, and fine growing weather. Hunters not returned; grow very uneasy on their account.

"Tuesday, June 20th.—Went a hunting. Hunters returned just as we were ready to set out.

"Wednesday, June 21st.—Returned home late at night with a load of buffalo meat, and found two gentlemen with Col. Harrod and some young men at our camp. These gentlemen, Mr. Nourse[d] and Mr. Johnston were from Virginia; Nourse from Berkley and Johnston from Frederick County. Both had called on Capt. Russell[e] at Pt. Pleasant, who had tempered them well. We found them clever and as much in our interest as we could wish. They were then on their way to the North of the Kentucky, to survey officers' claims. They seem resolved on purchasing, and becoming settlers with us. Mr. Johnston made application to have about 10,000 acres of land granted to him as officers' claims, though not more than 1,000 surveyed, the rest only entries in Col. Preston's books. On being refused, or what amounted to the same, advised to survey on Crown Lands, lest he might fail; went over to lay his claims on the other side.[12] Seemed satisfied with our reasons for giving no encouragement.—N.B. One piece of 1,000 acres, surveyed near the Falls, we gave him some encouragement about.[13]

"Thursday, June 22nd.—Col. Harrod, with the other two gentlemen, crossed the river.

"Friday, June 23rd.—Nothing extraordinary. Discharged Mr. Stoner and Mr. Jackson, our hunters, for a while. Stoner engaged to go after my brother Samuel's horses. Samuel Henderson and two others set off down the river in a canoe to hunt elks, our horses being too much fatigued with constant riding.

"Received a letter by Mr. Johnston from Rev. Charles Mynn Thruston, advising of the proceedings in the Virginia Convention, and desiring to make a large purchase in partnership with Johnston and Edm.d Taylor.[14]

"Saturday, June 24th.—Things as usual.

"Sunday, June 25th.—Mr. Nourse and Mr. Johnston arrived from the woods much pleased with the lands, but complained for want of water.[f] Hunters returned— good luck.

"Monday, June 26th.—Nothing extraordinary.

"Tuesday, June 27th.—Mr. Nourse, Mr. Wilson, Mr. Alexander, and Jonathan Jennings, set off for Virginia. Col. Harrod and Mr. Benj.m Johnson set off just before them for Harrodsburg. In the afternoon, two very good fellows, to wit, Sigismund Striblin and Daniel Hollenbeck, who had been with us, off and on, upwards of a month, set off for Pittsburgh. They took with them in their canoes two young men, to bring up two canoes from down the river about seventy miles, belonging to Capt. Calames and Mr. Benj.m Perry, for which we were to give £3.10 s., in case they brought them up safe. Striblin and Hollenbeck left us 93 [pounds] of flour, 20 of which was for Mr. Luttrell, the rest for my two brothers and ourselves. This day settled all accounts with Abraham Mitchell, and allowed him £6 for his trouble in coming out, and having assumed to pay Ralph Williams £5 for him, am more indebted 20s. Va. money, which is in full.

"Wednesday, June 28th.—Things as usual, only scarcity of meat; and Thursday, 29th, same case.

"Friday, June 30th.—Meat plenty, and many joyful countenances.

"Saturday, 1st July, 1775.—Dry weather. People going away. Mr. Luttrell and myself set off for Harrodsburg, to meet Col. Slaughter, who has been about four weeks viewing Green River.

"Sunday, Monday, Tuesday, and Wednesday, were bogging in the woods, seeking the way. Went too near the river, and was much plagued with the hills, cane and bad ways. Wednesday morning, 5th July, arrived at Capt. Harrod's and found all well.

"Thursday, July 6th.—Went to Harrodsburg; saw Col. Tho. Slaughter and others from Green River.[15] Accounts something different, Col. Slaughter seemed well pleased in general, but could not find a spot on which to locate his 10,000 acre tract, but said there was a fine country; others spoke indifferently, and thought otherwise.

"Friday, July 7th.—Set off back in company with Mr. Slaughter and about twelve others, who were going in [to the settlements] to bring out their families or stock. Harrodsburg seemed quite abandoned; only five men left on the spot to guard the crop. Came on to St. Asaph, where we lodged that night. On our way, saw the Knob and Flat licks, the former of which is a great curiosity, containing within the *lick* and *stamp*ᵍ near 100 acres of land. Saturday, Sunday, Monday and part of Tuesday, on our way home. 'Twas our intention to have hit *Boone's Trace*ʰ about twenty miles south-west of Boonesborough, but crossed it inadvertently, and got out of our way. We suffered in this journey a little for want of provisions. The weather was very dry, and the springs being scarce, water was rarely to be gotten. Buffalo had abandoned their range, and were gone into other parts. When we got to this place, we found all well, but a scarcity of meat. Sunday people gone since we left home, and more going.

"Wednesday, July 12th.—Horses being almost worn out, my brothers, Nathaniel and Samuel, with some others, went up the river in a canoe, to get meat if possible. Our salt quite out, except about a quart which I brought from Harrodsburg. The men sent for salt not yet returned, nor any news from the East. Times a little melancholy; provisions very scarce; no salt to enable us to save meat at any distance from home. Weather very dry, and we [are] not able to raise ten or fifteen fighting men at any one time, unless they were all summoned, which could not easily be done without long notice, they being much dispersed, hunting, and etc.

"Thursday, 13th July.—Things as usual. Meat a little difficult to get.

"Friday, 14th, Saturday 15th, Sunday 16th, Monday 17th, Tuesday 18th, and Wednesday 19th, nothing uncommon, more than that three men arrived, to wit, Capt. Linn, Mr. Crittenden, and one Thornton Farrar from Monongahela, intending to settle on the No. of Kentucky. No news.

"Thursday, July 20th.—My brother Samuel, Joel Walker, Val. Harmon, John Harmon, and their boys, set off for Carolina; and Capt. Linn and his company set off down the river for Lee's settlement, with whom I sent two men for a little salt, our men being not yet returned.[16]

"Friday, July 21st, Saturday 22nd, and Sunday 23rd, nothing uncommon, more than that a fellow called Grampus, belonging to Mr. Luttrell, ran away on Thursday, which was thought nothing of at first, supposing he would return; but on Saturday it was discovered that he had stolen Mr. Luttrell's mare (his only riding beast), and was totally gone, supposed to be countenanced by the Ralstons who went away a day or two before my brother, and were to wait.

"Monday, July 24th.—Mr. Luttrell took a resolution of following his man, and immediately set off with Capt. Benning, Mr. Hoy and one William Bush—I believe with an intent of not returning till he goes home, though he declared he would not go farther than the settlement, or where he could get his man, till I should overtake him, as I have intentions of going home as soon as a sufficient number of people come to defend the fort.

"Tuesday, July 25th.—Things as usual. Weather dry, and indeed has been so most of the summer; we had a little rain on Sunday and Monday was a sennight, but are still in great want. One Thomas Carlen, from Col. Floyd's camp, informs me that all is well there. By Capt. Linn we are informed that five or six men were gone down the Ohio to the Falls, by order of Capt. Bullitt. Mr. Bullitt's orders and his men's resolutions were, to pay no regard to our title, but settle the land, *nolens volens*. They also inform that Major Connolly is resolved on the same conduct."[17]

The desultory attacks of the Indians portending a general outbreak had no small effect in retarding the settlement of Kentucky. Captain Russell, commanding at the mouth of the Great Kenhawa, after a four days' conversation with *King Cornstalk* of the Shawanoes from whom he received visit, "discovered that it was the intention of the Pick[i] tribe of Indians to be troublesome to our new settlements, whenever they can; and he farther assured me, that the Mingoes behave in a very unbecoming manner, frequently upbraiding the Shawanoes in cowardly making the peace, and call them Big Knife people,—so that Cornstalk cannot well account for their intentions.[18] If this be true, and a rupture between England and America has really commenced, we shall certainly receive trouble at the hands of those people in a short time, as they got news of the battles in the Shawanoe towns eight or ten days before the Cornstalk came here."[19]

During the month of May, one Barton was killed or lost in Kentucky, and in June further mischief followed in Powell's Valley, which, though trivial in itself, had a most unfavorable effect upon the Transylvania settlements. The following letter, written by Colonel Henderson and Luttrell, July 18th, 1775, and addressed to their North Carolina associates, throws much light upon these Indian disturbances and other matters of that period pertaining to Kentucky:

"We are informed," say Messrs. Henderson and Luttrell, "that a party of Indians (not more than five or six) fired on four men at camp down the Valley, about twenty five miles below Capt. Joseph Martin's house, wounded two men, but were repulsed. This was on the 23rd of June, in the afternoon. The next morning, they were pursued by five white men, who, in a short distance, found one dead, and think there were more wounded, by the quantity of blood they discovered on the ground.

"This affair has a good deal alarmed the people there, and caused them to build a fort at Capt. Martin's, and work in companies. We wish that this may not be the beginning of a very troublesome affair, as well as an immediate prejudice to us. You know it is right in the way, and such reports are very terrifying to pusillanimous travelers; and I believe there are as many of that sort as any: though *Tristan Shandy*,[j] for what reason I know not, omitted them in his catalogue. This is not all that we apprehend may be the consequence. We are much afraid there is not a just representation of the matter, and that our people were the aggressors. These are only apprehensions of our own, and most surely we wish our apprehensions may be groundless.

"To give you a just notion of the matter, we are under the necessity of beginning our story again. You must know, the particulars were not communicated to us by Capt. Martin, but from Capt. Cocke, who was on his way from this place to

Virginia, and was at that time in the Valley. In short, they both wrote, and both about Indians; but to distinguish the one account from the other, so as to make you understand what we mean, we find it indispensably necessary to quote each man's intelligence; and then, by throwing in a few anecdotes, and some of our opinions, leave you to work the matter as you can. Don't be surprised that Capt. Martin gave no account of this in his letter; it was written the 22nd [of] June, a day before the engagement, and the bearer, (a little crazy creature), came away afterwards, without Martin's knowledge.

"After some other things of no consequence, Capt. Martin says: 'Six of the Northern Indians have undoubtedly been with the Cherokees, in order to get them to join with them against the white people; but the Cherokees refused. Dunmore and Col. Byrd have sent two expresses to the Cherokees, to your prejudice; one to get the Cherokees to meet the Six Nations of Indians, and hold a treaty concerning the boundary—they make no doubt that the Cherokees will give up all the land north of the Cumberland; the other to get the Cherokees to be off the bargain with you, at any rate, and they will get properly authorized from his Majesty, and purchase the same of them, and give more, running at the same time the risk of displeasing his Majesty.

"'There have been,' continues Capt. Martin, 'Eleven Indians in the Valley. They seemed much alarmed when they found it settled below Cumberland Gap. They immediately returned home, after promising to come up to one of the cabins to get some bread, etc. The white people went to see them a second time—found they had taken their back tracks. They followed them several miles; found they had gone on as fast as possible towards the Cherokee Nation; which promises something not very agreeable. I dread the consequences, as there will not be, for three weeks, more than seven or eight in the Valley, but I am determined to brave it out; have had thoughts, several times, of going to the Nation, only don't know how you would approve of it. I am very happy in settling the Valley. There are seventy-two tytheables making corn, but are chiefly obliged to go home, some to move their families, some to get provisions, and some for ammunition. We are in great distress for powder; several people will be obliged to break up shortly for want of it, being out of powder to supply them.'

"Capt. Cocke's intelligence, June 25th, 1775:

"On the 23rd instant, a party of Indians fired on Mr. Davis' camp, which consisted of four men. They shot Mr. Shoemaker through the head, who fell, but instantly rose to his feet again and shot an Indian. They also wounded Mr. Davis with a spear, though but slightly. The men fought with the utmost bravery, and kept their camp.[20] A boy got off, and ran about two miles to Mr. Newell's, where I was; and in a few moments the men came themselves. Our party was then eight; and, as it was then night, and Mr. Newell had his wife with him, we judged it impracticable to follow the Indians till morning. In the morning we concluded to leave three men with Mrs. Newell, and five of us to follow the Indians, whose number was judged to be five or six. When we came to the battle ground, we saw a great quantity of blood; followed until we found one dead, which I scalped. It is judged to be a Cherokee, and it is expected that more got wounded in the attack. One left his gun and spear in the time of the battle, and we got a tomahawk, scalping knife, powder-horn, shot-bag, and spear.

"'The next day the people in the Valley seemed animated with success. Capt. Martin takes particular care to spirit up the people, and by his example every one seems inspired with fresh courage. This morning they unanimously joined in a re-solve to stand by and support each other, and build a fort at Capt. Martin's for the reception of their families. The Indians, if Cherokee, will endeavor to screen themselves from fault, by laying the blame on the whites. I think it prudent to ac-quaint the heads of the Nation with a just state of the affair.

"'Some days before the attack, seven or eight of the white people came on a camp of Indians, whose number was eleven—six fellows, and the rest wenches and children. The whites discovered them first; rode up to them; the Indians seemed very friendly, told them they were Cherokees, and complained of their want of powder. The whites gave them powder, and they parted friendly, with a promise to go to the white people's camp; but they never went, unless it was that party that made the attack.'

"This, sirs, is the whole account respecting that affair from Powell's Valley, which, when we come to consider, we are far from being satisfied with in many respects. To us it seems improbable that five or six Indians should have the ad-vantage of the onset against four men only, and be put to the rout in the manner described—not only to fail killing, but to be so much disconcerted as to drop a spear on the spot, and run away in confusion; and when one of their company died of his wounds, to take no steps to carry off or secrete his body—a circum-stance they seldom fail attempting, at the utmost hazard of their lives.

"There is but too much reason to doubt, that Mr. Cocke's apprehensions were not without foundation—that the Indians would strive to fix the blame on the whites. He was on the spot, as it were, and we don't doubt but he might hear from the guilty expressions of the same kind, or we don't think such a thought would have entered his head. And what is more, it is most probable it was some of the Indians they gave an account of having seen before; and no man in his senses would believe their intentions hostile against the whites, or any others, when they were clogged in the manner they represent, with their wives and children, and subject to be over-taken with the greatest ease.

"Those Indians were acquainted, that twenty or thirty men belonging to those white people's camps and those adjacent, and would not think of destroying the four then present without being immediately pursued. The presumption is strong, that they came in consequence of the friendly invitation they had; and that the four white men perfidiously fell on them, and perhaps have murdered several, while the survivors will give but a poor account of our friendship and humanity to their nation.

"Another circumstance which much inclines me to this opinion, is, that it was one in day-light. Few instances can be produced where Indians have premeditat-edly entered on an engagement, when numbers were nearly equal, without the advantage of an ambuscade, or beginning their assault in the dark. What is more, they were Cherokees, undoubtedly; and, if they had succeeded, dare not avow the act in their nation. And if it was plunder they wanted, the woods were full of houses, and therein they might have succeeded without involving their lives in mutual danger.

"Upon the whole we shall be agreeably undeceived, if it should turn out otherwise, and should think nothing of the matter if we were sure it was a deliberate act of that party of Indians. In that case the presumption would be, that they were the same Indians that fired on Tate and Boone, this spring, and are of no consequence. It is now reduced to a certainty, that they were Cherokees, a parcel of banditti that you have all heard us often mention, and on whom my suspicions immediately fell, on the first information of the mischief. We say reduced to a certainty,—we think our authority good. Our hunters have, at two different times, met with some Shawnese, at a salt-lick about forty miles from this place, who informed them 'twas Cherokees—Will Emery and his party. They say that they brought the scalps to their nation; and described the stolen horses as well as their owners could have done,—and do not omit a rifle-gun which they got from Inman, without a ramrod, and carried here in that condition to the nation. Cornstalk, their chief, was much dissatisfied, and consulted with his own warriors and some traders about the matter, and talked about taking and delivering them up to the whites, lest his own people might be unjustly blamed. The Cherokees got wind of something to their disadvantage, and ran off to the Mingoes, since which we have heard nothing from them. The Shawnese were so desirous of vindicating their innocence, that they obtained certificates from their chief traders of the truth of these facts, before they would venture into our neighborhood. 'Tis true, our men did not see their letters, because the Indians were not at camp, and our men had not time to go with them; though much importuned for that purpose.

"We are also credibly informed that King Cornstalk went to see Capt. Russell, at Point Pleasant, as soon as the Cherokees left his town, in order to acquaint him of the particulars, and moreover remove suspicion with respect to his people. If these accounts of the friendly and cautious demeanor of the Shawnese be true,— and we verily believe they are,—you will be at no loss in determining on that part of Mr. Martin's intelligence respecting the six Northward Indians. 'Tis possible that the Mingoes might make such application, but the Shawnese are far from it, and we do not believe it of the others. These, and such like falsities, are easily and very often, manufactured, and ought to obtain no kind of credit.

"Whether Lord Dunmore and Col. Byrd have interfered with the Indians or not, R. Henderson is equally ignorant and indifferent. The utmost result of their efforts can only serve to convince them of the futility of their scheme, and possibly frighten some few faint-hearted persons, naturally prone to reverence great names and fancy every thing must shrink at the magic of a splendid title.

"Matters of more importance to the Company demand our more immediate attention. To spirit up the people, and convince them of the goodness of our country, and that the Indians in general are friendly, would be of real service and cause them to venture out. Our enterprise has now come to a crisis, and a few weeks will decide in the matter. Harrodsburg and the Boiling Spring settlements, which sometime ago could have armed and turned out seventy or eighty men at a short warning, are almost abandoned. On the most emergent occasion they could not rally twenty men; and the better half of them are in the woods on the north side of [the] Kentucky, and perhaps could not be summoned to our assistance in less than a fortnight. Boonesborough to-morrow night will not be able to muster more than ten or twelve men.

"The news of the small skirmish in the Valley, we suppose, will keep back the people from the frontiers a short time; and we have already sensibly felt the effects of that little disaster, and may probably have cause of complaint a considerable time.

"Our salt is exhausted, and the men who went with Col. Boone for that article are not returned. We are informed that Mrs. Boone was not delivered the other day, and therefore do not know when to look for him; and, until he comes, the devil himself can't drive the others this way.[k] David Johnston, one of the men who undertook this business, has, we are also informed, taken a small trip to Orange, and can best inform you of the particulars, and how he has disposed of the horses under his care.

"These things with respect to us are of no moment, and are no more than little disasters, which, amongst other things, serve to diversify life for the present, and will pass off with the next change of fortune. As the Indians cannot be acquainted with a true state of our weakness, nor, do we believe, have thoughts of forcing the settlement, we hope that in a little time the people on the other side of the mountains will take courage and venture out. Harvest is now over, and as soon as the affair in the Oie Valley has been talked and fought over half a dozen times, we shall have men enough to answer every purpose.

"On considering the several reports and occurrences between us and the Indians, we have thought it proper to write to the chiefs of the Cherokee Nation, informing them of the mischief done this spring, as well as that attempted the other day in the Valley, together with our reasons for suspecting some of their people. This letter is conceived in terms, that, we think, will be approved of by the company; as it has a tendency to convince the Indians of our friendly intentions, and sacred regard to the solemn engagements entered into at Watauga, as well as a just sense of the infraction of that treaty.

"As we have thought it unnecessary to be at the expense of an express, this letter and its answer must run the risk of a passage by the way of Watauga.

"And now, dear sirs, which of you all are willing to exchange berths with us? Is this matter settled, and the person ready to start with a sufficient stock of resolution to remain here five or six months, if required? We cannot doubt but some of you have undertaken this business, and will be on the spot by the end of August. The country might invite a prince from his palace, merely for the pleasure of contemplating its beauty and excellence; but only add the rapturous idea of property, and what allurements can the world offer as an equivalent for the loss of so glorious a prospect? Our crop of corn is beyond all description, and will scarcely admit of a deduction for untimely planting, cultivation, and being somewhat pinched with a dry season. In short, a description of our country is a vain attempt, there being nothing elsewhere to compare it with, and therefore can be only known to those who visit it."[21]

It was now indeed a crisis for Kentucky. There were a few really valuable acquisitions to the new settlers during the season, among them George Rogers Clark,[1] Simon Kenton,[m] Benjamin Logan,[n] and William Whitley,[o] who were destined to exert a powerful influence on the growth and history of the country. The great mass, however, were of a different class, roving, restless, and transient; traversing the country, some selecting their future homes, and others admiring the beauties of the wilderness or indulging in the pleasures of the chase. The countless herds of buffalo had already begun to recede from the new settlements, and the scarcity of other game now began to be so sensibly felt that hunt or starve was the only alternative.[22] The Powell's Valley skirmish and the consequent departure from Kentucky of many of the adventurers were events of the most inauspicious character. Captain Floyd at the close of May estimated the number of settlers in the country at about three hundred, when three months [later] there could scarcely have been fifty remaining—not reckoning "a great many land jobbers[p] from towards Pittsburgh, who go about on the north side of [the] Kentucky in companies, and build forty or fifty cabins a piece on lands where no surveying has yet been done."[23]

About the 10th of August, Colonel Henderson took his departure for North Carolina, leaving Captain Floyd to attend to the business of the land office. The families of Hugh McGary, Richard Hogan, and Thomas Denton arrived in Powell's Valley from the Upper Yadkin in North Carolina; and after tarrying three months, having sent one John Harmon before them to raise a crop of corn at Harrodsburg, they were joined the latter part of August by Daniel Boone and family and twenty young men all destined for Kentucky. Arriving on the head of Dick's River up towards the Crab Orchard, our adventurers departed; the Boone party consisting in the language of the times of twenty-one guns—equivalent to twenty-one fighting men—bore a more northerly direction for Boonesborough, while the McGary party kept on down Dick's River for Harrodsburg. Though Boone had never been that route to Harrodsburg, he gave McGary's party such directions as were deemed necessary; and when they reached the mouth of Gilbert's Creek on the east side of Dick's River, becoming somewhat bewildered as to their way, the three youths, James Ray,[q] who was McGary's step-son and then fifteen years of age, John Denton, and John Hays, were left behind to take care of the stock, while the others hastened forward to find their way to Harrodsburg. Again becoming embarrassed by the lofty precipitous cliffs [wi] the mouth of Dick's River, McGary went on alone and, striking a path, followed it to Harrod's camp or station at the Boiling Spring and obtained Silas Harlan as a guide to conduct

59. Simon Kenton (1755–1836), friend of Boone and one of Kentucky's most stalwart frontiersmen. Illiterate, Kenton could write no more than to sign his name. Line-and-stipple engraving by James B. Longacre, from National Portrait Gallery of Distinguished Americans (1835).

the families to Harrodsburg. Harlan was then sent to pilot in Ray and his companions with the stock, and instead of remaining only three days as promised, these youths had taken up their quarters under a shelving rock two weeks before they were relieved.

Boone and his party arrived at Boonesborough on the 6th or 7th of September without having experienced any other difficulties than those common to a journey through the wilderness; and "my wife and daughters," exclaims Boone, "were the first white women that ever stood on the banks of Kentucky River";[r] while Mrs. McGary, Mrs. Hogan, and Mrs. Denton, who reached Harrodsburg on the 8th of September, were the first white women in that settlement.[24] The crisis had now evidently passed. This new acquisition of twenty-seven able men, with Boone among them, and several families of women and children, gave to the settlements a prestige of permanency they never exhibited before. On the 8th of September, Boone stands [wi] indicative of an early hunt to supply his larder with meat.

Boone brought with him orders from Colonel Preston to Captain Floyd, interdicting him and others "from stretching a chain" under Governor Dunmore's Proclamation of March 1775, which provided for the surveying the vacant lands on the western waters into lots from one hundred to a thousand acres, to be sold at auction to the highest bidder, subject to an annual half-penny quit-rent, with a reservation to the Crown of all gold and silver mines and precious stones. Prior to May 1774 Dunmore received instructions from the British ministry upon what conditions to dispose of the vacant lands in the colony. At first the governor made "several judicious and diverting remarks" on the orders and "seemed but little inclined to carry them into execution."[25] These instructions were suspended awhile, until at length the Proclamation was issued, when Colonel Preston—the county surveyor of Fincastle, then including Kentucky—was expressly notified by Dunmore of the new arrangement. Preston hesitated—consulted friends, and awaited the action of the Virginia Convention, which finally resulted in the advice of that body to the surveyors "to pay no regard to the Proclamation."

"The people in general," wrote Floyd from Powell's Valley, April 21st, 1775, to Colonel Preston, "seem not to approve of the governor's instructions with regard to settling the lands." They were, almost to a man on the frontiers, unable to bid off lands and promptly pay the amount; and they wished to enjoy, as they had done in West Virginia, settlement rights and pre-emption privileges. Receiving letters upon this subject from Maj. Arthur Campbell and Capt. William Russell, the people of Kentucky "would not suffer Capt. Floyd to survey under the Proclamation."[26] "Not an acre," declares Preston, "was surveyed under the Proclamation"; and now that Floyd received orders through Boone not to stretch a chain[s] on such surveys in Kentucky, together with the tottering condition of royal power in the Colonies, put an end to any further attempted innovations and experiments upon the land established land usages of the Virginia frontiers.

The time of Boone's arrival at Boonesborough, the attention of the eastern patriots and legislators was directed to the "new settlement of Virginia, on Kentucky."

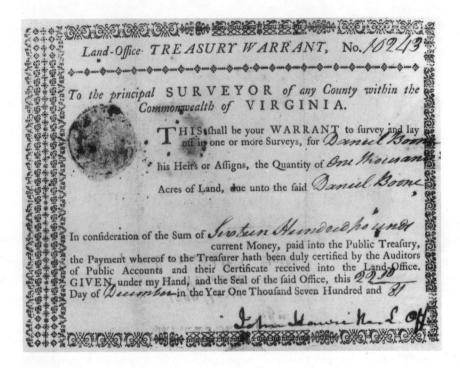

60. Virginia "Treasury Warrant No. 10243," entitling Daniel Boone the right to invest in Kentucky lands. But the scrupulously honest Boone failed in land speculation. FILSON CLUB HISTORICAL SOCIETY.

Among the proceedings of the Pennsylvania Committee of Safety, upon whom Benjamin Franklin was one, September 7th, 1775, occurs the following:

"The Board being informed, by inquiry of the Hon. Peyton Randolph, Esq., that the application of Colonel George Slaughter for leave to purchase gunpowder, for the use of the New Settlement in Virginia, on Kentucky, is founded in necessity, for the protection of a number of families; they not being able to furnish themselves elsewhere, have agreed to permit their purchasing one hundred pounds weight at Yorktown, in the Province, if the Committee of that place think fit to spare the same." A minute of this transaction was signed by President Franklin and furnished to Colonel Slaughter.[27] It is most probable that this powder was designed by Col. George Slaughter for his brother Col. Thomas Slaughter of Culpeper County, Virginia, who was chairman of the Transylvania Convention and had returned to Virginia to procure a number of families to settle in Kentucky as a condition of his receiving ten thousand acres of land from Henderson and Company; but from some cause, he failed to carry out his purposes, and this precious supply of powder in all probability never reached Kentucky.

Thursday, the 6th of September, was the day to which the Transylvania Convention stood adjourned to meet at Boonesborough. Many of the members of the May convention had left the country; and Messrs. Henderson, Hart, and Luttrell, three of the proprietors who were then present, were all now absent, and we may safely conclude that the convention failed by default to re-assemble at the time appointed.

There was a meeting, however, of the proprietors of Transylvania at Oxford, Granville County, North Carolina, Colonel Henderson presiding. Col. John Williams was appointed agent for the company to repair, as soon as possible, to Boonesborough and remain there till the 12th of April next ensuing, voting him one hundred and fifty pounds proclamation money of North Carolina for such services, and empowering him to appoint surveyors, and officers in the land office; and that in granting deeds, the agent shall reserve to the proprietors one half of all gold, silver, copper, lead, or sulphur mines. It was also voted "that a present of two thousand acres of land be made to Col. Daniel Boone, with the thanks of the proprietors for the signal services he has rendered to the company";[28] and "that the thanks of this company be presented to Col. Richard Callaway, for his spirited and manly behavior in behalf of the said Colony; and that a present of six hundred and forty acres of land be made to his youngest son." A [wi] of six hundred and forty acres was also made to Rev. Henry Patillo of North Carolina on condition of his settling in Transylvania—which, however, he did not do.

James Hogg was delegated to represent the colony in the Continental Congress then sitting at Philadelphia, and a memorial was prepared by the proprietors to be by him presented to that body. After alluding to their purchase from the Cherokees "for a large and valuable consideration," they proceeded to observe:

"They will not trouble the honorable Congress with a detail of the risks and dangers to which they have been exposed, arising from the nature of the enterprise itself, as well as from the wicked attempts of certain governors and their emissaries; they beg leave only to acquaint them, that through difficulties and dangers, at a great expense, and with the blood of several of their followers, they have laid the foundation of a Colony, which, however mean in its origin, will, if one may guess from present appearances, be one day considerable in America.

"The memorialists having made this purchase from the aborigines and immemorial possessors, the sole and uncontested owners of the country, in fair and open treaty, and without the violation of any British or American law whatever, are determined to give it up only with their lives. And though their country be far removed from the reach of ministerial usurpation, yet they cannot look with indifference on the late arbitrary proceedings of the British Parliament. If the united Colonies are reduced, or will tamely submit to be slaves, Transylvania will have reason to fear.

"The memorialists by no means forget their allegiance to their sovereign, whose constitutional rights and pre-eminences they will support at the risk of their lives. They flatter themselves that the addition of a new Colony, in so fair and equitable a way, and without any expense to the Crown, will be acceptable to his most gracious Majesty, and that Transylvania will soon be worthy of his royal regard and protection.

"At the same time, having their hearts warmed with the same noble spirit that animates the united Colonies, and moved with indignation at the late ministerial and parliamentary usurpations, it is the earnest wish of the proprietors of Transylvania to be considered by the Colonies as brethren, engaged in the same great cause of liberty and of mankind. And, as by reason of several circumstances, needless to be here mentioned, it was impossible for the proprietors to call a convention of the settlers in such time as to have their concurrence laid before this Congress, they here pledge themselves for them, that they will concur in the measures now adopted by the proprietors.

"From the generous plan of liberty adopted by the Congress, and that noble love of mankind which appears in all their proceedings, the memorialists please themselves that the united Colonies will take the infant Colony of Transylvania into their protection; and they, in return, will do everything in their power, and give such assistance in the general cause of America, as the Congress shall judge to be suitable to their abilities.

"Therefore, the memorialists hope and earnestly request, that Transylvania may be added to the number of the united Colonies, and that James Hogg, Esq., be received as their delegate, and admitted to a seat in the honorable the Continental Congress."[29]

Nothing particularly favorable resulted from Mr. Hogg's mission to Congress. Upon sounding the leading members, it was found advisable not to present the memorial. Congress had petitioned the king for accommodation, and to take Transylvania under their protection might embarrass the prospect of reconciliation, especially as the purchase was made and settled in defiance of the king's proclamations. The Virginia delegates were opposed to recognizing Transylvania, except with the consent of the Virginia Convention, as it was an infringement upon their charter limits. John and Samuel Adams, and Silas Deane, of New England, took an especial interest in all that related to the new colony. "You would be amazed," wrote Mr. Hogg to his associates, "to see how much in earnest all the speculative gentlemen are about the plan to be adopted by the Transylvanians. They entreat, they pray that we may make it a free government, and beg that no mercenary or ambitious views in the proprietors may prevent it. Quit-rents, they say, is a mark of vassalage, and hope they shall not be established in Transylvania. They even threaten us with their opposition, if we do not act upon liberal principles when we have it so much in our power to render ourselves immortal. Many of them advised a law against Negroes."[30]

It will be remembered that Colonel Henderson had in June pledged his honor that the next year's terms and inducements to settlers should be published in the Williamsburg, Virginia, papers. That promise was fulfilled by the appearance of the following publication on the 30th of September, 1775, and which doubtless had a favorable influence in directing the attention of adventurers to Kentucky during the autumn and the spring ensuing.

"A company of gentlemen, of North Carolina, having, for a large and valuable consideration, purchased from the chiefs of the Cherokee Indians, by and with the consent of the whole Nation, a considerable tract of their lands, now called Transylvania, lying on the rivers Ohio, Cumberland and Louisa; and understanding that many people are desirous of becoming adventurers in that part of the world, and wish to know the terms on which lands in that country may be had, they therefore hereby inform the publick, that any person who will settle on and inhabit the same, before the first day of June, 1776, shall have the privilege of taking up and surveying for himself five hundred acres, and, for each tithable person he may carry with him and settle there, two hundred and fifty acres, on the payment of fifty shillings sterling per hundred, subject to an [*sic*] yearly quit-rent of two shillings, like money, to commence in the year 1780.

"Such persons as are willing to become purchasers may correspond and treat with Mr. William Johnston, in Hillsborough, and Colonel John Williams, of Granville, North Carolina, or Colonel Richard Henderson, at Boonesborough, in Transylvania.

"This country lies on the south side of the rivers Ohio and Louisa, in a temperate and healthy climate. It is in general well-watered with springs and rivulets, and has several rivers, up which vessels of considerable burden may come with ease. In different places of it are a number of salt springs, where the making of salt has been tried with great success, and where, with certainty, any quantity needed may be easily and conveniently made. Large tracts of the land lie on limestone, and in several places there is [an] abundance of iron ore. The fertility of the soil and goodness of the range almost surpass belief; and it is at present well stored with buffalo, elk, deer, bear, beaver, and etc., and the rivers abound with fish of various kinds. Vast crowds of people are daily flocking to it, and many gentlemen of the first rank and character have bargained for lands in it, so that there is a great appearance of a rapid settlement, and that it will soon become a considerable Colony, and one of the most agreeable countries in America."[31]

Boone's attention was now divided between attending to his stock, harvesting corn, providing wild meat [for] his family, exploring the country, and naming the confluent streams with the Kentucky in the region of Boonesborough. Boone and his fellow pioneers were but too happy for an occasion to erect a cabin for a new comer. The latter part of September the Boonesborough settlement received a valuable accession by the arrival of Col. Richard Callaway and William Poage, with their families, from Virginia. There were then not more than half a dozen cabins in Boonesborough; others were in [the] process of erection, and among them one of pretty fair size for Colonel Callaway, whose son Caleb and nephew Flanders Callaway had spent the season there and raised a crop of corn; and these young men now met Callaway's and Poage's party a day's journey before reaching Boonesborough and assisted in driving the cattle, hogs, some ducks, and chickens were also brought out by this party of emigrants and were probably the first introduced into the country. Mrs. Boone and her daughter, Mrs. Hays, must have been gratified with the addition of Mrs. Callaway and Mrs. Poage, with their young daughters, to the domestic circle of Boonesborough; and that gratification was increased by the arrival about the same time of Squire Boone and family. It may be added as illustrative of the friendly disposition of the Cherokees at that period that when the Callaway company was near [the] Cumberland River, a party of ten Cherokees and a squaw came up to them in a friendly manner and, having killed a small buffalo, kindly divided it with the white adventurers. While on their journey in the wilderness, the Callaway company was passed by Hugh Wilson and family, who went on to Harrodsburg.[32]

About this time, that noble pioneer Simon Kenton, who had been spending the season near where the village of Washington, Kentucky, has since sprung up, found his way to Boonesborough, where they soon learned how to appreciate his worth as a man and his fine qualities as a hunter, scout, and intrepid Indian fighter. During the autumn, quite a number of persons arrived in Kentucky to examine the country; some remained, while others returned to the old settlements for their families. Of this latter class was Boone's brother-in-law, William Bryan, and his four brothers from the Yadkin, at the head of about thirty men; and having explored the country and penetrated westwardly as far as the Green and Barren rivers, they returned to Carolina.[33] Another party consisting of Col. Abraham Hite, Jr., Isaac Hite, Joseph Bowman, Ebenezer Soverein, Nathaniel Randolph, Peter Casey, Peter Higgins, and Moses Thompson were examining the country along the southern shore of the Ohio above the Falls, killing game and locating land as late as the middle of December.[34] During the autumn, John McClelland and family, Robert Patterson, and six other young men from the frontiers of Pennsylvania descended the Ohio and settled McClelland's Fort at the Royal Spring on Elkhorn, now Georgetown, Kentucky. In the course of the season, Capt. Willis Lee surveyed a large tract of land for the Ohio Company; and Capt. George Rogers Clark also surveyed several thousand acres on the Licking and Kentucky and returned in the autumn to Pittsburgh.

Near the close of November Col. Richard Henderson [and] Col. John Williams, with about forty men, arrived at Boonesborough, and in the party came Col. Arthur Campbell of Holston.[35] A convention of the representatives of the Transylvania settlements was called to meet at Boonesborough on the 21st of December to recommend a suitable person for principal surveyor of the colony. From the dispersed situation of the people and the extreme badness of the weather, a majority of the delegates failed to assemble; but those who met unanimously united in recommending Capt. John Floyd for that responsible station, who was commissioned accordingly. Colonel Campbell had desired the place, but Captain Floyd, being an old surveyor thoroughly acquainted with the people and the country, gave him the decided advantage of his competitor. Nathaniel Henderson was selected as entry-taker in the land office, and Richard Harrison as secretary. Captain Floyd, having appointed six deputies, took his departure on a visit to Virginia.[36]

On Saturday afternoon, the 23rd of December, Colonel Campbell, with a couple of lads named Sanders and M'Quinney, crossed the river at Boonesborough and parted. Campbell went up the river about two hundred yards and then up a bottom, while the lads, without a gun, went up the hill. About ten minutes after they separated, the report of a gun and the cry of distress were heard and the alarm given that Colonel Campbell had been shot by the Indians. Several persons crossed the river and hastened to his assistance and met him running to the landing with one shoe off, who said that three hundred yards from there, he had been fired on by a couple of Indians, who missed him. A party of men under the command of Captain Boone was immediately dispatched but made no discoveries other than two moccasin tracks, but whether Indians' or not could not be determined. At that time there were ten or a dozen men in different parties hunting over the river, part or all of whom, it was feared, would be killed if what Colonel Campbell said was true, which, however, many doubted. Night came on; several of the hunters returned but had neither seen nor heard of the lads or Indians.

On Monday following, a party out in search found poor M'Quinney killed and scalped in a cornfield about three miles from Boonesborough on the north side of the river, but nothing could be discovered relative to young Sanders. On Tuesday a party of fifteen or twenty men was despatched, under the command of Jesse Benton, to scour the woods for twenty or thirty miles around and discover, if possible, whether the Indians had really gone or were still lurking about to do more mischief before their departure.[37] These rangers were to receive two shillings a day for this service, and £5 for every scalp they should produce. During their absence, the few missing hunters one by one returned till all came in safe, young Sanders only excepted.[38] The rangers returned on Sunday, the 31st of December, convinced that the Indians had immediately, on committing their depredation, run off for the northward, as their tracks were discovered thirty or forty miles towards the Ohio, making in that direction.

This little attack produced its natural consequences. Many people who were ashamed to confess themselves afraid found out that their affairs over the mountains would not permit of their longer remaining in the country. It was, however, well-known at Boonesborough that King Cornstalk said at the Indian treaty at Fort Pitt in October that some half a dozen of his wayward warriors had set off from the Shawanoe towns, with the intent, as they termed it, of taking a look at the white people of the Kentucky, and he was apprehensive that they might do some damage; and if any of them should get killed by the whites, no notice should be taken of it. This was believed to have been the party that committed the mischief, and particularly as about that number of Indians had been seen near the old War Path about fifteen miles east of Boonesborough two or three days before the attack.[39] The Transylvanians soon relapsed into their former security as though nothing had happened.

We must now chronicle the arrival in the country of William Whitley and George Clark with their families. Whitley was of Irish descent—his father was Solomon Whitley, his mother Elizabeth Barnett; and he was born in what is now Rockbridge County, Virginia, August 14th, 1749. Reared to labor on the farm, without any educational advantages whatever, he grew to manhood; at twenty-one he married Esther Fuller, who was born May 10th, 1755, and was admirably fitted to be his companion. They commenced house-keeping in a small way, but after a while, early in 1775, Whitley said to his wife one day, "Esther, I have heard a fine report of Kentucky, and think we could get our living there, with less hard work than we can here."[40] "Then, Billy, if I were you, I'd go, and see," was her prompt and encouraging reply. In two days he was on his way with ax, and gun, and kettle, accompanied by his brother-in-law, George Clark.[41] They made a location at the spot five miles north-west of the Crab Orchard subsequently known as Whitley's Station on the Walnut Flat and returned the same season to Virginia for their families.

When migrating in the fall with their wives and children to Kentucky, they left their cattle at Walden's Creek in Powell's Valley and hastened forward, lest winter should overtake them on the way. Mrs. Whitley was mounted on horseback, with her eldest child, Elizabeth, about three years old, fastened behind and the youngest in her lap; and when little Elizabeth would fall asleep, Mrs. Whitley would take the little one's head under her arm to prevent the child from falling off— for one falling, as was sometimes the case, all, tied to each other, would necessarily go together. On one occasion, in descending the steep bank of a creek, the horse, having caught one of his feet under a root, stumbled, pitching them all into the stream below. Clark's children, being much older, were less troublesome. On Yellow Creek of the Cumberland, Colonel Henderson's party passed them, and shortly after, hearing the report of several guns ahead, Clark and Whitley's families were greatly alarmed, thinking the Indians had attacked Henderson's party; but Colonel Henderson was so considerate in anticipating the fear the circumstance would produce as to send back a runner with the explanation that they had fired at a bear and presented a piece of meat for the acceptance of Whitley's company. Many a time Whitley and Clark had to unpack and sometimes leave their families, go ahead, and search out a suitable way. In this inclement season of the year, with rain, hail, and snow, and frequent large cane-brakes through which to pass, after thirty-three days spent in traversing the wilderness, they at length reached the place of their destination early in December and commenced the settlement of Whitley's Station on the waters of Dick's River.[42]

Such were the principal events connected with the first year's settlement of Kentucky. Probably not less than five hundred people from the frontiers of Pennsylvania, Virginia, and North Carolina had, during the season, visited and explored the country; and now, at the close of December, the population of all the settlements could not have exceeded two hundred people. Capt. Floyd had, the preceding April, correctly anticipated the result of the adverse influences at work calculated to retard the settlement of the country—"I think," wrote Floyd from Powell's Valley to Colonel Preston, April 21st, "there will be but small improvements made this year, as many seem confused, and numbers are leaving the country." The clashing of the interests of the Transylvania Company with the proclamations fulminated by Governor Martin and Dunmore, the uncertainty as to a general Indian war, the rupture of the Colonies with the mother country, together with a general scarcity of provisions and ammunition in Kentucky, all conspired to unsettle the minds of the people and postpone with many of them a permanent settlement until a more favorable period.

Yet upwards of nine hundred entries had been made in the Transylvania land office at Boonesborough, embracing 560,000 acres of land, and most of the purchasers were waiting to have it surveyed.[43] About two hundred and thirty acres of corn had been raised;[44] horses, cattle, hogs, and poultry [had been] introduced into the country; and Capt. Nathaniel Hart had brought and planted at Boonesborough a nursery of five hundred apple scions, which unfortunately were subsequently destroyed by the Indians. The McAfee company had also planted apple-seeds and peach-stones at their settlement on Salt River below Harrodsburg. The germ of a permanent colony had been planted, laws made, the militia organized, civil and military officers commissioned; the first slight Indian attacks had been repelled and the country successfully maintained. There were, moreover, twelve women, heads of families, settled in the country.[45]

In justice to Colonel Henderson and his associates, it must be observed that they furnished all the supplies of gunpowder and lead with which the inhabitants not only defended themselves and families but provided them with wild meat. Indeed, the books of the company exhibit accounts for these articles with all the inhabitants of the country in the years 1775-6; while they are credited with various items, such as cutting the road to *Cantucky,* hunting and ranging. The prices of articles in these accounts afford some curious comparisons with those of the present time. Powder was charged at $2.66 per pound and lead at $16^2/3$ cents, while labor was credited at thirty-three or fifty cents per day for ranging, hunting, or working on roads. These accounts remain unclosed upon the books in every instance, showing a condition of no little indebtedness for the colonists of Transylvania to the great proprietors.[46]

The people of Kentucky were from the first truly patriotic. The proprietors had declared that their "hearts were warmed with the same noble spirit that animated the united Colonies," the people had evinced their fearless patriotism by not suffering lands to be surveyed under the proclamation of the royal governor, and there was not, so far as we can learn, a Tory in all the Transylvania Colony.[t] Many of the settlers were either of Irish or Scotch-Irish descent—such were the Lewises, Campbells, Christians, Prestons, McDowells, and others of the Virginia Valley; and such also were Logan, Todd, Whitley, Kenton, McClelland, Patterson, the McAfees, and others of the Kentucky pioneers. At this period, this hardy, brave, and enterprising class of people formed a strong if not predominating element in the population of West Virginia and Kentucky; and during the course of the war now opening, they were destined powerfully to contribute toward the downfall of British power in America. Corroborative of these views, a paragraph from an unpublished letter of that period may here be appropriately cited:

"The spirit of opposition to ministerial measures seems to gain ground in the back country as the people become by degrees better acquainted with the cause. Their ideas of allegiance to their Sovereign are very high. They have also the highest conceptions of Liberty; and could they once be convinced that obedience to the Ministry ceases to be a duty when tyranny begins, and that some tyrannical, or at least unconstitutional steps, have been taken to enslave the people, there would be no doubt of their most hearty concurrence. Many of them are descended from those brave men who so nobly defended their religion and liberty in Ireland during a late inglorious and despotic reign, and were so instrumental in supporting the Revolution in that kingdom. Those transactions almost every descendant from the Protestant Irish is well acquainted with, either by history or tradition. Therefore they cannot bear the thought of degenerating from their worthy forefathers, whose memory is, and ought to be, held very dear to them. Upon the whole I am persuaded that the cause of Liberty, in which the Colonies are engaged, will find almost as many friends as there are inhabitants in the back country."[47]

DRAPER'S NOTES: CHAPTER 12

1. "Captain Harrod," remarks the late Col. Nathaniel Hart of Kentucky, "occasionally camped or resided at the Boiling Spring during the season of 1775, though he neither built cabins nor a fort there until 1779 or 1780." Corn was raised there in 1775.

So at St. Asaph, on the big Buffalo Spring, no permanent settlement was made in 1775; it was only a temporary camp where some corn was planted and raised. In March 1776 Benjamin Logan settled within a short distance of the Big Buffalo Spring but abandoned his settlement in the summer when Miss Boone and the Miss Callaways were captured and repaired to Harrodsburg; and in February 1777 [he] permanently re-settled his old place, which thence forward became conspicuously known as *Logan's Fort*.

2. The proclamation of Governor Martin of North Carolina of February 10th, 1775, which was much more severe in its charges than Governor Dunmore's of the 21st of March following.

3. Felix Walker, who served seven years in the North Carolina Legislature and six years in Congress, remarks in his Narrative in reference to this Boonesborough assembly or convention: "In justice to Colonel Henderson, it may be said, that his message or address to the assembly was considered equal to any of like kind ever delivered to any deliberative body in that day and time."

4. This John Gass was a cousin of the person of the same name who has been cited as authority in this work and still [*rest of line cut off*].

5. The journal of the Convention may be found at length in the appendix to the second edition of Butler's *Kentucky;* Hall's *Sketches of the West,* i:264–275; *Louisville Literary News-Letter,* June 6th, 1840; Hazard's *United States Register,* iii:25–28; and abridged in Morehead's Boonesborough Address of May 25th, 1840. Henderson's MS. Journal, from which these were taken, is still extant.

For sketches of the members of the Transylvania Convention, see Appendix.

6. This must have been the battle of Concord and Lexington, April 19th, 1775, and had certainly reached Kentucky in a very brief period, in view of the slow process of travel at that day, and that the news came via Orange County, North Carolina.

7. Licking River, Kentucky.

8. Harrodsburg and Boiling Spring settlement.

9. Capt. John Hinkson's settlement, subsequently known as Ruddel's Station; probably Willis Lee's settlement on the Kentucky, about a mile below the present town of Frankfort.

10. This party was under the leadership of Capt. Thomas Gist.

11. TFB: *Ellipsis by LCD.*

12. The country north and east of the Kentucky was denominated the *Crown Lands* because the Indian *title* had been extinguished—at Fort Stanwix treaty in 1768, by the Six Nations; and by the Cherokees at the treaty of Lochaber in 1770, and by agreement with Col. John Donelson in 1771; and thus that region became the property of the Crown.

13. Falls of Ohio—now Louisville.

14. Charles Mynn Thruston was a native of Gloucester County, Virginia; he served on Forbes' campaign in 1758; afterwards studied for the ministry and settled in Frederick County; he served with much distinction during the Revolutionary War at the head of a regiment and was known as the warrior parson. After the war, he filled the office of judge and representative to the legislature. In his old age he removed to the West, and died in 1812, and was buried where the battle of New Orleans was afterwards fought.

15. There are some memorials yet extant of this early Green River exploration. On the north bank of Big Barren River, about three miles from Bowling Green, Kentucky, and about a quarter of a mile above Van Meter's Ferry, are three beech trees indicating one of the camping grounds of this party. The most conspicuous tree has engraven in its bark on the north side the names of thirteen persons, handsomely cut; the highest name being about nine feet from the ground, and the lowest, four and stand in the following order, beginning with the uppermost and descending to the lowest, to wit: *"J. Neavell, E. Bulger, I. Hite, V. Harmon, J. Jackson, W. Buchanan, A. Bowman, J. Drake, N. Nall, H. Skaggs, J. Bowman, Tho. Slaughter, J. Todd, 1775, June the 13."* About five steps south of the principal tree and near the verge of the riverbank stands a beech marked on the north

side with the name of *"William Buchanan, June 14th, 1775";* and on the south side of the same tree, there is the name *"J. Todd, June 17th, 1775."* About twenty steps north of the first tree, there stands a third beech with the inscription of *"J. Drake, Isaac Hite, June 15th, 1775";* and above the names is this additional date, *"June 23, 1775."* All the marks are apparently old enough to correspond with the dates and show that the party must have camped there ten days: *MS. letter of Hon. J. R. Underwood, of Bowling Green, Kentucky, November 1, 1843;* Collins' *Kentucky.*

These men were exploring the country. Slaughter, Todd, Hite, and Harmon had been members of the Transylvania Convention; and Colonel Slaughter, upon condition of bringing a certain number of settlers to the country, was to have a grant of 10,000 acres of land. Skaggs, Drake, and Harmon had been among the *Long Hunters* and now probably came out as pilots to the others. Abraham Bowman was a colonel in the Virginia line during a part of the Revolution and subsequently settled in Kentucky, and died at the good old age of 88, in 1837. *"J. Bowman"* was probably either John or Joseph Bowman, most likely the latter, who was, with Isaac Hite, exploring the country shortly after the same year. Bulger was a useful pioneer, rose to the rank of major, and was killed at the battle of the Blue Licks; and Capt. William Buchanan, who was in the siege of Boonesborough in 1778, was killed in Holder's Defeat in August 1782. Of Nall, James Neavell, and John Jackson, nothing is known; the former was probably a brother to James Nall, one of Boone's road-markers who was bitten by a mad wolf, and the other two were with Abraham Bowman exploring Dick's River region.

16. Lee's settlement, or Leestown, was on the Kentucky just below the present Frankfort, where was a noted buffalo crossing place.

17. This ends Henderson's Journal, with this note: "The occurrences of tomorrow and so on, you'll find in another stitched book, covered with brown paper, and begins with Wednesday, 26th July, 1775. Of that "stitched book," we regret to say, we have failed to get any tidings.

18. Peace resulting from the treaty of Camp Charlotte, between Governor Dunmore and the Shawanoes, in the autumn of 1774.

19. Concord and Lexington; MS. Preston Papers.

20. In his MS. narrative, Captain Cocke conveys the idea that the party attacked consisted of James Davis, Peter Shoemaker, William Griffith, and one Campbell; that Shoemaker received several shots through the back of his neck, who fell, and to all appearances seemed past recovery, but suddenly recovering, shot an Indian with his own gun, and seizing Campbell's gun that lay near him, shot a second Indian. Campbell appears to have been the boy alluded to and probably casting away his gun, ran off to Samuel Newell's. The good conduct of the others intimidated the Indians, who fled. "We sustained no other loss," says Cocke, "than that of Shoemaker's losing an ounce or two of blood, and the inconvenience of a few days unpleasant feelings with the wounds."

21. *Louisville Literary News-Letter,* May 9th, 1840.

22. "But I must drop my pen, for it is too dark to write, and I have no candle, and, as soon as it is day, I am obliged to go and hunt or starve." Captain Floyd to Colonel Preston, Boonesborough, September '83.

23. Floyd's correspondence, May 30th, 1775; MS. letter of Captain Floyd, September 1st, 1775.

24. MS. notes taken from the lips of Gen. James Ray by Mann Butler, the historian of Kentucky, and the late Col. Nathaniel Hart.

25. MS. letter of Thomas Lewis, county surveyor of Augusta, June 19th, 1775, to Colonel Preston.

26. MS. Preston Papers.

27. Force's *American Archives,* 4th ser., iii:860.

28. Though the proprietors *intended* to be generous to Boone for the "signal services" he had performed for them—giving them their information concerning the country—attending the Watauga treaty, and defining the boundaries of the purchase—heading the pioneers in marking the road to Kentucky, and founding Boonesborough—yet when Virginia asserted her right, and the company filed to maintain their claim to the country, Boone troubled himself no more about his "present." It remained an unfulfilled promise. As the company afterward received two hundred thousand acres of land from Virginia and the same from North Carolina for the losses they had sustained by the enterprise, a strict [*wi*] to [*wi*] would have prompted a remembrance of the "signal service" of their early settlement.

29. Hall's *Sketches of the West,* ii:221–228.

30. Hall's *Sketches of the West,* ii:248–254.

31. Force's *American Archives,* 4th ser., iii:847.

32. MS. notes of conversations with Mrs. Elizabeth Thomas; McAfee's Sketches. Mrs. Thomas was a daughter of William Poage and was born in Rockbridge County, Virginia, September 4th, 1764, and died near Harrodsburg, Kentucky, October 8th, 1851, in her 88th year. Going to Kentucky when she was eleven years old, and having a retentive memory, she was a living chronicle of the events of that period.

33. MS. Narrative of Daniel Bryan.

34. MS. Journal of Col. Abraham Hite, Jr.

35. Captain Floyd's MS. letters; MS. Narrative of Col. William Whitley.

36. Floyd's MS. Correspondence; Hall's *Sketches,* ii:241–242.

37. Jesse Benton, the father of present Hon. Thomas Hart Benton, was a native of Granville, North Carolina, and settled prior to the Revolution in the frontier county of Surry as a young lawyer, where he was appointed clerk of the court. Thence, in the fall of 1775, he accompanied Colonel Henderson to Kentucky and the next year raised a crop of corn in the country. He became connected by marriage with the Harts; and settling in Hillsborough, Orange County, he was in 1781 chosen to a seat in the House of Commons and subsequently died in Hillsborough.

38. Colonel Boone in his Narrative says one man was killed and another wounded; and Mrs. Thomas simply spoke of one person having been killed. Captain Gass, however, distinctly states that it was never known whether Sanders was killed or taken, but he never returned.

39. Hall's *Sketches,* i:259–260; ii:246–247; and conversations with the late Mrs. Elizabeth Thomas, who was at Boonesborough when this occurrence took place.

40. Reports about Kentucky were then rife among the people of the Virginia Valley. Harrod, Floyd, and Drake, and many others who had visited Kentucky in 1774 and returning, went on the Point Pleasant campaign; and much being said among the men about the new country, hundreds resolved, if peace was made, to visit Kentucky the ensuing spring. The campaign over, the men spread the intelligence in their respective neighborhoods. "What a buzz is this," exclaims the Rev. John Brown of Rockbridge, May 5th, 1775, to Col. William Preston, "what a buzz is this amongst the people about Kentucky! To hear them speak of it, one would think it was a new-found paradise; and, I doubt not, if it is such place as represented, but ministers will have their congregations."

TFB: *Brown did not use the word* buzz *in his letter to Preston; Draper modified this and other nuances of Brown's letter. Brown actually wrote, "What a Buzzel is amongst People about Kentuck?" Compare Draper's version with the original in Reuben Gold Thwaites and Louise Phelps Kellogg, eds.,* Revolution in the Upper Ohio, 1775–1777, *(Madison: State Historical Society of Wisconsin, 1908), 10.*

41. On page 55 of Peck's *Memoir of Boone,* this worthy pioneer is mistaken for his more distinguished namesake, George Rogers Clark. George Clark married a sister of William Whitley and shared largely with him in early Kentucky adventure; he was in Logan's Fort during the attacks in 1777; and the next year, having served in the conquest of the Illinois country, he went with Kenton on his horse-stealing expedition, when Alexander Montgomery was killed, Kenton captured, but Clark escaped. Following Kenton, he settled Clark's Station in Mason County, Kentucky, and in 1790 removed to Nashville, Tennessee, where he died of fever in 1792.

42. MS. Narrative of Col. William Whitley; notes of conversations with his children, Mrs. Levisa McKinney, the late William Whitley, Jr., and with the late Solomon Clark, son of George Clark; Marshall's *Kentucky,* i:41.

43. MS. letter of Captain Floyd, December 1, 1775; Hall's *Sketches,* ii:242.

44. MS. Floyd correspondence.

45. Mrs. Daniel Boone, Mrs. Hays, Mrs. Squire Boone, Mrs. Callaway, and Mrs. Poage, at Boonesborough; Mrs. McGary, Mrs. Denton, Mrs. Hogan, and Mrs. Wilson, at Harrodsburg; Mrs. McClelland, at McClelland's Station; and Mrs. Whitley and Mrs. Clark, at Whitley's Station.

46. Butler's *Kentucky,* 2nd ed., p. 31-32.

47. MS. original copy of a letter from Colonel Preston to Edmund Pendleton.

EDITOR'S NOTES: CHAPTER 12

a. *Livery of Seizin* (from the French *saisie,* "seizure") is a feudal ceremony of great antiquity invoking seizure of the soil as a powerful metaphor to demonstrate formal transfer of title and possession of land. During the speech making at Boonesborough on May 23, 1775, Indian agent John Farrar, who had presided at the Sycamore Shoals treaty two months before, cut a thick piece of sod and handed it with great solemnity to Col. Richard Henderson, and as the two men clutched the turf, Farrar read aloud the terms of the deed, transferring title to Kentucky to Henderson's Transylvania Company.

b. This statement shows perfectly the struggle Draper had in distinguishing the significant from the banal. His lack of historical perspective and his desire to be encyclopedic were two of the stumbling blocks that hampered him in his writing.

c. Kentuckians scalped their share of Indians in return. And worse. That year at Harrod's Town, Hugh McGary's stepson was shot by a Shawnee. McGary shot a Shawnee wearing his boy's shirt and axed the corpse into a bloody mess of entrails and flesh to feed to his dogs. Settlers drew the battle lines by their actions: lust for land; relentless market hunting, which led to the slaughter of buffalo, deer, and elk; unwillingness to accommodate Indian hunters; and willingness to shoot Indians on sight. Many whites refused to work toward a communal effort, seeking rather to stake land claims or hunt. In turn, Ohio Indians took up the hatchet to prey on encroaching whites.

d. Few journals of Kentucky's frontier history are so rich a trove as those of James Nourse and Nicolas Cresswell. Nourse worked as a draper in London for fifteen years. On March 6, 1769, he sailed with his family for Virginia, arriving on May 10. He lived in Hampton for a year, then bought a plantation near the Potomac River in Berkeley County. In April 1775 Nourse left for Kentucky to claim land for himself and his brother. Joining Nourse at Fort Pitt on his Kentucky adventure was the young Englishman Nicholas Cresswell, age twenty-four, who had just arrived in America to speculate in land. Also with them were George Rice, Edmund and Reuben Taylor (cousins of Hancock Taylor), Benjamin Johnston, who was going to Harrod's Town, Tom Ruby, and George Nolan.

Stylistically, the journals of Nourse and Cresswell are strikingly dissimilar, even though the two are often describing the same day's events. Straightforward and modest, Nourse's memoirs are somewhat laconic, whereas Cresswell's flamboyant narrative is more revealing, written with humor, candor, and verve. For Nourse's unpublished journal and the extent of his Kentucky claims, see "Journey to Kentucky in 1775: The Diary of James Nourse," *The Journal of American History* 29.2 (1925): 121–38; 29.3: 251–60; 29.4: 351–64. Also see Nicholas Cresswell, *The Journal of Nicholas Cresswell, 1774–1777.* 2nd ed. (New York: Dial Press, 1928).

e. Capt. William Russell, commandant of Fort Blair's 100-man garrison in 1775 following the Battle of Point Pleasant at the site the previous year.

f. James Nourse's journal entry of the same day reveals an interesting slice of Boonesborough life: "Johnston and Harrod went out to look at the land[.] [T]alks of laying an order of Council he has for some gentlemen in Virginia for 10000 acres here. Killed a fatt buffalo and bro't the best of it into Boonsburg; last night cold; the day cool—arrived about 12 o'clock having traveled all the way due north. Johnston found the land he was about to take, already surveyed. (Nourse Diary) 29.4: 352.

g. "Lick" and "stamp" are frontier terms referring to salt licks (see chapter 7, note j) and stamping grounds, a spring-fed barren region of many acres where buffalo herds had so stamped down the vegetation that the region was as pocked as a moonscape. But as settlers discovered, the heavily manured stamps made ideal pastureland. Speculators coveted stamps and fought over them in court to gain the rights to them. Kentucky settlers named three different sites Stamping Ground, but the name survives only in Scott County. There, road marker 217 on State Road 227 near Stamping Ground reads: "This area first explored April 1775 by William McConnell, Charles Lecompte and party from Penn. Buffalo herds had stamped down undergrowth and ground around spring—origin of town's name. McConnell and Lecompte in Blue Licks, 1782."

h. In 1775 Daniel Boone and his woodcutters blazed the buffalo path that he named Boone's Trace. Boone's Trace began at Hazel Patch, led to the Rockcastle River, passed near present-day Berea to near Richmond, where the Indians attacked Boone's party, then followed Otter Creek to the Kentucky to the site of Boonesborough. That Henderson and his men got lost following Boone's Trace confirms sworn testimony that the path was a poorly marked buffalo trail. As Samuel Estill deposed in a court case involving land claims, "Boone's Trace was a marked trace but it was pretty difficult to follow through the thick cane, though I have followed it."

i. The Piqua (alternately, Pekowi, Pekowitha, Pec-u-we, Pickaways, or Picaway) is one of five Shawnee tribal divisions. The other four divisions, spelled, translated, and pronounced a myriad of ways, are Chillicothe, Mequache, Kispokogi, and Thawikila. James H. Howard's *Shawnee!: The Ceremonialism of a Native American Tribe and Its Cultural Background* (Athens, OH: Ohio University Press, 1981) is a definitive work on the Shawnee.

j. An English novel written by Laurence Stern (1713–68), first published in 1760.

k. A testimony to Boone's capable frontier leadership.

l. George Rogers Clark (1752–1818) was one of the major Virginia frontier leaders, whose near mythic exploits place him in the annals of America's heros. Clark served as captain in Lord Dunmore's War (1774). He first came to Kentucky in 1775 to establish claims near present-day Frankfort. In 1777 Gov. Patrick Henry promoted him to lieutenant colonel, and by 1779 his ragtag forces had seized the British-occupied French towns Kaskaskia, Vincennes, and Cahokia. Clark, made brigadier general by Gov. Thomas Jefferson in 1781, built several Kentucky forts, led "scorched earth" type raids against Ohio Valley Indian towns, and in 1784 established Clarksville, Indiana. An inveterate Indian hater, George Rogers Clark was a complex, learned man whose efforts did much to open Kentucky and the Old Northwest to Anglo-American settlement. He died, unmarried and childless, of a stroke on February 13, 1818, at his sister's home near Louisville.

m. Simon Kenton (1755–1836) was literally one of Kentucky's pioneering giants—he stood at a raw-boned six-foot-four—whose exploits rivaled Daniel Boone's. In 1775 Kenton fled to Kentucky as a fugitive from law, wronglfully believing that he had beaten to death a love rival, William Leachman, and he took the name Simon Butler to mask his identity. In 1779 he learned that Leachman was alive, so he resumed the use of his real name. When they first encountered each other in the wilds surrounding the Lower Blue Licks in 1775, Kenton and Boone distrusted each other. Boone found Kenton brusque and evasive and suspected he was a British spy; Kenton, wary of Boone's quiet, almost taciturn manner, feared he knew about his supposed murder. But both became lifelong friends. Kenton served as a scout, helped establish Limestone (Maysville) and Washington, and in 1777 saved Boone's life during a Shawnee raid on Boonesborough. A modest, gentle man, Kenton died impoverished in 1836 in Zanesville, Ohio, and is now largely forgotten by his countrymen, who are ignorant of his valorous role as a protector and guardian of the West's borders,

n. Virginian Benjamin Logan (1743–1802) fought in Lord Dunmore's War as a captain. In 1775 he came to Kentucky to establish St. Asaph (Logan's Station) at Buffalo Spring, west of present-day Stanford (in Lincoln County). Promoted to colonel, Logan by 1780 was second in command to George Rogers Clark and leading forays from the Bluegrass to attack the Ohio Indians. He had a long, distinguished political career, serving terms in the Virginia Assembly prior to Kentucky's statehood (1792) and in Kentucky's General Assembly after statehood. Twice he attempted to gain the governor's seat.

o. William Whitley (1749–81), born in Augusta County, Virginia, was one of Kentucky's best-known Indian fighters. In 1775 Whitley claimed land at Crab Orchard on the Dix River and moved his family there in 1776. Indian wars drove them to Logan's Station, and Whitley lent a strong hand in defending the settlements. In 1792 he was appointed a major in the Kentucky militia; four years later his 6th Regiment defeated the Chickamaugas along the Tennessee. He served a term in the state House of Representatives. Devoutly anti-British, he raced horses on his oval clay track counterclockwise (opposite the British style), setting the precedent for American horse races. On October 5, 1781, at the Battle of the Thames, he led a charge against the British-allied pan-Indian forces of Tecumseh, the Shawnee chieftain. Although both men fell, William Whitley, dead at age sixty-three, became one of the four or five men credited with the dubious honor of killing the great Tecumseh. His fortified home at Sportsman's Hill (Lincoln County) was one of the first brick homes in the commonwealth and today is surrounded by a state park. Whitley's Station was approximately two miles north-west of Sportsman's Hill.

p. Land jobbers and outliers staked western land claims to sell to eastern buy-ers by roaming the countryside erecting roofless huts (called "pigsty cabins") to show ownership.

q. James Ray's involvement in this episode may be misdated. On October 29, 1777, Ray received a Kentucky land tract from Virginia commissioners. Under Virginia law, only men twenty-one years or older before 1778 could apply for grants.

r. This claim may not be true. In July 1755 Shawnee warriors attacking the Draper's Meadows village on the New River kidnaped Mary Ingles and her two sons and took them 300 miles west to their towns on the Scioto. Three months later she escaped from an encampment at Kentucky's Big Bone Lick and fol-lowed the river back to Draper's Meadows—a grim, forty-day trek with no fire, no shelter, and no food save what she could grub with her own hands.

s. This is eighteenth-century surveying jargon. A surveying team was made up of four to six men, one of whom was "chain carrier." Carriers "stretched their chains" to measure linear distances and mark boundaries. A survey chain was made of hand-forged sixteen-inch rods linked together like hooks and eyes and measured forty-four yards, or one "pole," long. Surveyors measured and recorded their land lines in poles.

t. Draper's bold assertion regarding Toryism may reflect his own nationalis-tic bent. Kentuckians were representative of other colonials. Though few avowed Tories may have been in the Transylvania colony, many, including Boone and his kinsmen, were charitable toward the British and were not rabid secessionists. Even in 1778, while parleying prior to the siege of Boonesborough, Kentuckians sought accommodation with the Crown.

CHAPTER 13

1776.—Life at Harrodsburg.—Conflicting Land Claims.—Emigrants to the Far West.—Indian Wars and Rumors of War.—Jack Jones' Treachery and the Transylvania Convention.—James Cooper Killed by Shawanoes.—Indians Capture Jemima Boone and Fanny and Betsy Callaway While Canoeing on the Kentucky River.—Daniel Boone Heads Rescue Party.—Salvation of the Girls.—Indian Raids on Kentucky Settlements.—First Kentucky Wedding.—George Rogers Clark Conveys Gunpowder to Kentucky Inhabitants.—The Formation of the County of Kentucky.

With the opening of the New Year, we find Daniel and Squire Boone engaged as assistants or hunters to a party of surveyors in the employ of Henderson and Company, and passing down the Kentucky to the region around the Falls of the Ohio, they were absent several weeks. No special incident transpired. No Indians were encountered during this service; lands were surveyed and game killed to supply the wants of the party in their temporary camps, which were seldom occupied more than a single night. James Galloway, a young, enterprising Pennsylvanian who had joined this surveying expedition, had just arrived at Boonesborough, where he found about a dozen cabins and six women, Mrs. Daniel Boone, Mrs. Squire Boone, Mrs. Hays, and three others.[1]

During the winter, the Kentucky rose from heavy rains, ran round the cabins at Boonesborough next [to] the river hill, and great fears were entertained that the water would enter the cabins; but fortunately it did not. In February William Poage and family removed from Boonesborough to Harrodsburg—the intrepid youth James Ray coming from the latter place to pilot them there. Shortly after starting, a heavy storm came on, which compelled them to camp a day or two, during which Ray killed a buffalo and supplied them with meat. On Gilbert's Creek of Dick's River they overtook Samuel Coburn, James McDaniel, [and] Julius Saunders with their families, camped, all destined also for Harrodsburg. Arriving there, they learned the interesting fact that Mrs. Hugh Wilson had a month or two before given birth to the first child born in Kentucky, who was named Harrod Wilson and grew up to be a worthless man.[2]

The cabins erected at Harrodsburg [in] 1774 were along the branch on the low ground. When McGary's party arrived in September 1775, they selected an eminence about three hundred yards farther west as a more suitable location, on account of a spring which issued from the foot of a rocky bluff on the north side. There McGary, Denton, Harrod, and three others erected cabins; so when the

61. Early engraving of Boonesborough. The fort, completed during the summer of 1778, was said to have been 260 feet long by 150 feet wide. Wood engraving from Lewis Collins' Historical Sketches of Kentucky *(1847).* ENGRAVED BY CHARLES W. THOMSON, CINCINNATI, FROM A DESIGN BY COLLINS.

Poage party arrived in February 1776, Hugh Wilson's was the only family residing in the old cabins.[3]

The inhabitants, particularly those about Harrodsburg, were not without a
subject to excite their attention during the winter. Incensed against the Transylvania Company for having risen in the price of their lands, they entered into a confederacy not to hold lands on any other terms than those of the preceding year.
They complained also that the proprietors, with a few other persons, had engrossed all the land at and near the Falls of the Ohio—a point which was even
then looked upon as destined to become a considerable mart in the western country, from its natural position as well as the rich and fertile region with which it
was surrounded, "which," observes Colonel Williams, "occasioned many people
to fix their affections on that place." Colonel Harrod and Abraham Hite, Jr., were
at the head of this party.

To check these claims, Colonel Williams, the agent of the company, endeavored to conciliate matters by solemnly declaring that no large bodies of land contiguous to the Falls should be granted to any person whatever. Upwards of twenty
thousand acres had been entered there for the proprietors and from forty to fifty
thousand more in large tracts by a few other gentlemen—hence the complaints.
To pacify the people, Colonel Williams pledged himself to grant to no person
within a certain distance of the Falls more than one thousand acres, and that of all
grants already made exceeding that quantity, the excess should revert to the company; and furthermore, that a town should be immediately laid out at the Falls in
which a lot should be reserved to each of the proprietors and then the first settlers
to choose their lots and improve them within a specified time or forfeit their
claim. These proposals, so far as they went, appeared at least for a while to give
satisfaction; but hearing no more about the proposed town at the Falls of Ohio,
which was to have been laid out in March, we think it more than likely that the
scant and precarious supply of powder at that period prevented the undertaking.[4]

With the dawning of spring, new comers everywhere appeared. On the 8th of
March Benjamin Logan arrived from the Holston with his family at his old camp,
better known as St. Asaph or Logan's Station.[5] We find the Transylvania land office, in the latter part of that month, opened at Harrodsburg, probably designed as
a conciliatory measure to accommodate the people.[6] During that month also, a
Canadian Frenchman named Loramie,[a] in the employ of the British government
as an Indian interpreter, left Montreal in company with a fellow emissary and
went to Detroit to stir up the Indians to war against the Americans—thus carrying
out the inhuman policy of Lord Dartmouth of the previous year.[7] This betokened
no good to the frontier settlements, as the sequel too clearly proved.

Among the rolling tide of emigrants for April came Levi Todd, a younger
brother of John Todd, a young man of much enterprise who became a prominent
actor in the subsequent events of the country. The Bryan company, to the number
of twenty-eight, returned from the Yadkin early in April and commenced a settlement on Elkhorn, where Bryan's Station was afterwards located, erected two half-

faced camps about thirty yards apart, and put in sixty-six acres of corn, enclosing it with a good fence.[8] Again were hundreds of persons who descended the Ohio engaged in ranging the country north of the Kentucky, building pens or cabins; and in many instances, after remaining not over three weeks and having selected as many as twenty settlement rights and erected a cabin on each, they would return home to sell them. These improvements would frequently be made upon land previously surveyed, to satisfy officers' claims for services in the old French and Indian War, and oftentimes too on tracts of other locators, and thus were quarrels without number engendered.[9] "I'm afraid," declared John Todd, "to lose sight of my house lest some invader should take possession. But why do I preach politicks? 'Tis a country failing, and not one *Mac* from Conococheague but would make a fool of Waller himself in talking landed politicks.[10] I'm worried to death almost by this learned ignoramus set; and, what is worse, there are but two lawyers here, and they can't agree."[11]

Old settlers and newcomers alike wearied in roaming the charming forests and glades of Kentucky. The face of the country at that time was beautiful beyond conception. Nearly one half of it was covered with cane, while between the canebrakes were frequently fine open grounds, as if expressly intended by nature for cultivation. Nor was the country destitute of the finest timber—which was happily distributed for the wants of man. The soil was extremely fertile, producing in its untamed state amazing quantities of weeds of various kinds, wild grass, rye, and clover. The dews were very heavy, which rendered the nights cool and refreshing. The land then appeared more level than when subsequently cleared and settled, as the thickness of the growth prevented the early explorers from discovering the diversities of the surface. Every person then expected that the country would always furnish a sufficient supply of iron, sugar from the maple, and salt from the springs for home consumption; and all seemed to think that springs of water were scarce, that the country would be but thinly inhabited, and that the cane and other range would remain plentiful and exhaustless.[12]

"Our time," says Nathan Reid in his recorded conversations, "was mostly spent in locating and surveying lands, or in hunting the buffalo and deer, of which there were vast herds. Sometimes we extended our excursions far into the country— and what a country it was at that day! It would be difficult for the most fertile imagination to draw an exaggerated picture of its then lovely appearance. The soil was black as ink, and light as a bank of ashes. A person passing through the woods might be tracked almost as easily as through the snow. Often from many days together have Capt. Floyd and myself wandered in various directions through the land, sometimes tearing our way through thick cane-brakes, not knowing at what moment we might be shot down by the Indians, or fall into their hands to suffer a more cruel death. Whenever night overtook us, there we laid down and slept, if sleep we could. Sometimes strange sounds and noises, to which we were unused, broke from the solemn wilderness; then again the screams of night birds, and the squalls of wild beasts in their distant lair, made us feel very sensibly that we were in a strange land, and caused us many times to turn uneasily upon our leafy bed. At other times, on awaking in the morning after a night's sound sleep, and hearing the buffalo bulls lowing in all directions *around* us, it was difficult to resist the impression that we were not in an old settled country.

"We lived, meanwhile, entirely on the flesh of wild game—such as turkies, deer, bear, and buffalo, which we ate without bread or salt. The hump of the back of the buffalo was regarded by us as a great delicacy. It consists of a streak of fat and a streak of lean, and when properly cooked would be considered [*wm*] by a city epicure.

"Strange as it may appear, it is nevertheless true, that amid all the dangers, privations and exposures of our situation, a very considerable portion of our time was spent in real enjoyment. The abundance and variety of the game—the pleasure of hunting—the novelty of the life we led—the dreams we indulged of better days to come, all combined to keep up our spirits, and banish uneasiness from our thoughts. Frequently have [John] Floyd, and I sat down on a log, or at the foot of a tree, and giving a free rein to our heated imaginations, constructed many a glorious castle in the air. We would, on such occasions, contrast the many discomforts that then beset us, with the pleasures we would one day enjoy in the possession of boundless wealth. Spread out before us lay the finest body of land in the world, any quantity of which, with but little exertion, we could make our own. We clearly foresaw that it would not be long before these lands would be justly appreciated, and sought after by thousands. Then we should be rich as we cared to be. These golden visions of the future, however, so far as I was concerned, were never realized."[13]

Other troubles than those relating to the conflict of title and jurisdiction were in reserve for the people of Kentucky. The Cherokees, incited by British emissaries, broke out in open war against the colonies and sent messengers with the battle-axe and scalping-knife to the Northern Indians. A *dark cloud,* as had ominously been foretold at the treaty of Watauga, now hung loweringly over the settlements of Kentucky. "Those settlements, meanwhile," says Perkins, "were with open eyes watching the movements of their Indian neighbors. All along the border the impression grew daily more and more definite, that the savages, instigated and backed by the British, would suddenly swoop down as in the time of Pontiac and lay all waste. The hated race of 'cabiners,' those speculators who came out to obtain a pre-emption right by building a cabin and planting a crop; the wretched traders who were always wandering about the frontier; the hunters who were revelling among the countless herds of game now for the first time seen,—all began, during the winter and spring of 1776, to draw closer to the stations, men sat round the fire with loaded rifles, and told their tales of adventure and peril with new interest, as every sound reminded them how near their deadly enemies might be. And from hour to hour scouts came in with rumors of natives seen here or seen there, and parties of the bold rangers drew their belts, and left the protection of their forts to learn the truth of these floating tales.

"But there was one who sat at such times silent and seemingly unheeding, darning his hunting-shirt, or mending his leggings, or preparing his rifle-balls for use; yet to him all eyes often turned. Two or three together, the other hunters started by day-light to reconnoitre; silently he sat working, until the day had drawn herself into the shadow of the earth, and the forest paths were wrapped in gloom. Then, noiselessly as the day had gone, he went; none saw him go,—he had been among them a moment before, and then was missing. 'And now,' said the loiterers by the smoldering logs, 'we shall know something sure; for old Daniel's on the track.' And when, by and by, some one yet wakeful saw the shadow of Boone, as he reentered the cabin unheard as a shadow, he found, as usual, that the solitary scout had learned all that was to be known, and the watchful slept in peace. We know nothing more characteristic than this habit of his, so quietly, alone and in the darkness, to undertake the searching of the forest infested by Indians."[14]

The restless and treacherous Mingoes were the first that year to commit hostilities in Kentucky. Some time in April Willis Lee, an enterprising Virginia surveyor who had visited the country in 1774 and the next year effected a settlement on the eastern bank of the Kentucky, a mile below the present town of Frankfort, was killed; and at the same time, or not very long after, two youths, twin sons of Andrew McConnell, who had migrated the preceding winter from Pennsylvania and settled at Leestown, were captured by a party of Mingoes within a few hundred yards of that place. Learning the circumstance, Col. George Morgan,[b] who was then in the Shawanoe towns as an agent of Congress to invite the western Indians to a treaty, prevented, with the aid of King Cornstalk, the usual custom of requiring the prisoners to run the gauntlet as they entered the town and finally procured their liberation, took them to Pittsburgh, and delivered them to their uncle residing in the adjoining county of Westmoreland. This mischief created great alarm, causing many to abandon Kentucky, not a few of whom Captain Floyd met in Powell's Valley the last of April and first of May, spreading the most exaggerated reports wherever they went.[15]

During the months of April and May, Congress took into consideration the property of an expedition for the reduction of Detroit and endeavored to devise a plan for its execution. Happy would it have been for Kentucky had this scheme been carried into effect and a long and sanguinary Indian war thus checked in its incipiency; but the poverty of the country and the increasing troubles on the Atlantic border interposed inseparable obstacles, and nothing was effected.[16]

It was no easy manner to quiet the uneasiness of the people in the Harrodsburg region. A mutual arrangement was made that the proprietors should not require any money for lands already sold till the ensuing September in order to give the people time to enquire more fully into the validity of the Company's title; but meanwhile, surveys should proceed so that all might know the bounds of their purchases and that new settlers might learn what lands were subject to entry.[17]

Sometime in April, and probably anterior to this arrangement, the malcontents had drawn up a petition to the Virginia Convention, signed by Capt. James Harrod, Abraham Hite, Jr., and eighty-six others, stating that they had been at a great expense and many hardships in settling the country; that the Transylvania Company, who had promised them an indefeasible title, had lately, to the alarm of the petitioners, advanced the price of the purchase money from twenty to fifty shillings sterling per hundred acres and at the same time had increased the fees of entry and surveying to a most exorbitant rate; and by the brief period fixed for taking up lands, even on those extravagant terms, the proprietors plainly evince, as the petitioners assert, their intentions of rising in their demands as the settlers increase or their insatiable avarice should dictate. And the petitioners further stated that they were still more alarmed, as they had lately learned from a copy of the deed of the Six Nations given at the treaty of Fort Stanwix in 1768, that all the Kentucky country as low as the mouth of the Cherokee or Hogohegee, or, as now termed, Tennessee River, was embraced in that cession to the Crown for a valuable consideration and that the Six Nations declared the Cherokee River to be their true southern boundary; and under these circumstances, they presume that the king will vindicate his title to the country. They say that they would cheerfully have paid the consideration at first stipulated by the Transylvania Company whenever their grant had been confirmed by the Crown, or otherwise authenticated by the supreme legislature, but regard the increased demands of the company as injurious, impolitic, and unjust in the present infant state of the settlement. They closed with expressing their anxiety to concur with their brethren of the united Colonies for their just rights and privileges, as far as their infant settlement and remote situation would admit, and implored the Convention to take them under its guardian care and protection, but should the Convention conclude that the petition would more properly come before congress, the petitioners begged them favorable recommendation to the Virginia delegates in that body.

About the 1st of May Colonels Henderson and Williams left Kentucky on a mission to the Virginia Convention and thence, if need be, to Congress to endeavor to secure a confirmation of their claim.[18] On the 18th of May the Kentucky memorial was presented to the Virginia Convention;[19] and on the 30th of that month John Craig of Augusta County sent in a petition setting forth that he had visited Transylvania the preceding autumn with some stock in order to settle there; but finding, in order to enter land, it was first necessary to sign a paper declaring that an assembly should be chosen by the freeholders who should make laws as nearly similar to those of England as the circumstances of the country would admit, that a governor should be chosen from time to time from among the proprietors who should have a negative on all laws, and also to elect a member to the General Congress; that there should be only one religion tolerated and that conformable to the church of England; the petitioner declared he did not subscribe to the paper, while others who signed entered for the best lands he himself had chosen.[20]

Scarcely had Colonels Henderson and Williams taken their departure when most of the settlers about Harrodsburg re-assumed their former resolution of not complying with any of the Transylvania land-office rules whatever; "Jack Jones," wrote Captain Floyd, "it is said, is at the head of the party, and flourishes away prodigiously."[21] Having given five weeks' notice, an election was held at Harrodsburg commencing on the 8th and continuing till the 15th of June, when Capt. John Gabriel Jones and Capt. George Rogers Clark were chosen delegates to the Virginia Convention, with a petition praying to be considered as citizens of Virginia and organized into a new country, pledging themselves to furnish their quota of men and means in supply of the common cause of liberty. This petition bore [the date] the 15th of June and was signed by Abraham Hite, Jr., as clerk in behalf of the people. At this election, twenty-one persons were chosen as a general committee, or Committee of Safety, of whom fourteen, namely John Gabriel Jones, chairman, John Bowman, John Cowan, William Bennet, Joseph Bowman, John Crittenden, Isaac Hite, George Rogers Clark, Silas Harlan, Hugh McGary, Andrew McConnell, James Harrod, William McConnell, and John Maxwell, met on the 20th of June and also prepared a petition to the Virginia Convention stating their grievances, recommending a list of persons for civil magistrates and mentioning that they had received a message from the Delaware Indians residing near the mouth of the Wabash with information that the British had invited the Indians to a treaty at O'Post, or Vincennes; and upon their return, they would send the whites the result, which they feared would be hostilities on the part of the Kickapoos, and wished the whites to send messengers to receive the information. The committee appointed James Harrod and Garret Pendergrast to visit the Delawares for that purpose.

In a few days the delegates with the petitioners were on their way to Virginia. Meanwhile, Colonels Henderson and Williams arrived at Williamsburg and presented to the Convention on the 15th of June a lengthy memorial of themselves and associates, setting forth their claim and endeavoring to justify their general conduct in Transylvania—averring that they had accommodated all adventurers with lands on moderate and easy terms, observing the strictest justice and impartiality, without respect to persons or the different sects or persuasions of religion.[22]

On the 24th of June the Convention resolved that the inhabitants settled on the western frontiers ought to hold their lands without paying any consideration to private persons until the validity of the title under the Cherokee purchase shall have been considered and determined by the legislature; that all persons then actually settled on unlocated lands in Virginia to which there should be not other just claim should have a pre-emption right to the same; and furthermore, that no purchase of lands within the chartered limits of Virginia should be made under any pretense whatever from any Indian nation without the approbation of the Virginia legislature[23]—and this latter prohibition was shortly after incorporated into the Constitution of Virginia, limiting such purchases exclusively in behalf of the public.[24]

Two days after this tacit decision of the Virginia Convention, the Henderson company issued at Williamsburg a sort of manifesto that until the disputed title to the Transylvania lands would be determined, they earnestly desired no person to take possession of any entered or surveyed lands in that country, as all such lands ought of right to be granted only to the respective persons in whose names they were entered; and also desiring that no encroachments might be made on the company's reserved lands below the Green River and as high up the Cumberland, on both sides, as Mansker's Lick.[25] And on the 4th of July the Virginia Convention appointed commissioners in eleven frontier counties of that state to collect testimony against the validity of the Henderson purchase;[26] and thus the matter rested quietly for a considerable period, leaving the claim of the proprietors of Transylvania in a tottering and precarious condition.

On the 7th of July, in view of an impending Indian war, Col. William Russell wrote from the Holston country, advising the immediate abandonment of Kentucky;[27] and on that very day, James Cooper and a Dutch-man started from Hinkston Station on the Licking to visit a buffalo lick to kill game, when they were fired upon by a party of Shawanoes returning from the Cherokee country and Cooper [was] killed on the spot.[28] The Dutch-man's horse, becoming frightened, threw his rider, whose foot was caught in the stirrup, in which situation one of the Indians ran up, evidently to tomahawk him, when the Dutchman, who had retained his gun, had the presence of mind to aim it so well as to shoot the Indian dead. Observing another Indian at this moment making towards him, he fortunately disengaged himself from his own unmanageable horse and, mounting Cooper's, made his escape to the station. A party went in pursuit of the enemy and killed another of the marauders.[29] On the 14th of the same month a man was killed at the Blue Licks on the Licking; and several others who were engaged in land hunting, surveying, and improving were missing, most of whom were believed to have fallen prey to the wily Indians.

While the Continental Congress, from the pressing exigencies of the times, was in session on Sunday, July 14th, 1776, providing for re-inforcements for General Washington and supplies of money, flour, canteens, camp-kettles, powder, lead, and "musket cartridges well balled" for the use of the flying camp[c] and militia ordered into service—the people of Boonesborough, with no Sabbath to call them to divine service, no man of God to proclaim to them the glad tidings of the gospel, were listlessly loitering about the place, little expecting that [a] party of dusky warriors were skulking on the bank of the river within view of the settlement, ready, like so many tigers, to pounce upon their prey. A golden opportunity too soon presented itself. Jemima Boone, the second daughter of Daniel Boone, then in her fourteenth year, having previously received a *cane-stab* in her foot, which was quite painful, asked Elizabeth and Frances Callaway—familiarly known as Betsy and Fanny Callaway—daughters of Col. Richard Callaway, the former about sixteen, the latter fourteen years of age, to accompany her on a little excursion on the river, where she might plunge her foot in the water to ease the pain. They readily consented. Nathan Reid, a young Virginian who had arrived in the country in May preceding with Captain Floyd, was invited to join them to paddle the canoe, which he promised to do.[30] But when they were ready to start shortly after, he was just then engaged, and they went without him; Elizabeth Callaway had become somewhat experienced in using the paddle, and they never for a moment apprehended the least danger. The afternoon was now pretty well spent, the weather pleasant, and nature robed in her most attractive charms. They soon found themselves the sole occupants of the only canoe, or *dug-out*, belonging to the place, gliding gently down the stream, the two Miss Callaways each using a paddle while Jemima Boone sat in the stern holding the steering oar, with her sore foot dangling over the side of the boat in the cooling, comforting element. The rugged banks of the river, the projecting cliffs and towering trees with patches of graceful cane and gaudy flowers here and there to the very verge of the water attracting their attention, they descended the stream, keeping up a sprightly, careless conversation, and spoke of visiting a little island below where wild onions grew—perhaps with a view of procuring some for a poultice for Jemima Boone's foot.

About a quarter of a mile below Boonesborough was a prominent rocky cliff on the northern shore, towards which the current had naturally drawn them. One of the Miss Callaways carelessly proposed going ashore and getting some flowers and young cane, but Jemima Boone slightly opposed the idea of touching on the Indian shore, saying she was afraid of the *Yellow Boys*.[d] Without, however, any real intention of carrying this proposition into effect, our fair voyagers concluded to turn about, but not being very skillful with the oars, and the current here setting in pretty strongly towards the cliff, they found their canoe, contrary to their wishes and despite all their expectations, almost upon the northern shore.

Suddenly five Indians rushed out from a thicket of cane and bushes where they had been concealed, and one of them, more impatient than the rest to secure the prize, dashed into the water waist deep and, seizing hold of the buffalo tug at the prow, with which the boat was fastened when not in use, attempted to draw the canoe ashore. When Fanny Callaway, though the smallest of the three, yet fearless of danger, commenced plying her paddle pretty freely over the Indian's head and shoulders, until she broke it by the operation. Her sister joining her in this demonstration, and other Indians now coming to the relief of their half-discomfited fellow and making motions toward upsetting the canoe, the girls desisted from their belligerent attitude, were hurried ashore uttering piercing screams, the canoe upset and sent adrift, when all quickly disappeared.

So constant and loud were the shrieks of the girls, made more with a view to give alarm to their friends than to express their own terrors, that the Indians threateningly flourished their knives and tomahawks; and seizing Elizabeth Callaway by the hair, they plainly intimated that if she did not instantly cease her screams, her scalp would be the forfeit. Upon ascending the river hill and reaching the level ground, Jemima Boone refused to proceed, declaring that she had rather die than suffer as she did with her wounded foot. One of the Indians

62. *"The Abduction of the Daughters of Boone and Callaway" (1852) by
Jean-François Millet and Karl Bodmer. The episode formed the nucleus of
James Fenimore Cooper's* The Last of the Mohicans *(1826). Chromo lithograph
published by Goupil, Paris.* WASHINGTON UNIVERSITY GALLERY OF ART; GIFT OF
MRS. CHARLES W. BRYAN, JR.

endeavored to alarm her fears by threatening to kill her unless she went on; but
still persisting in her determination, her captors gave her and Fanny Callaway,
who was also without shoes, each a pair of moccasins; [the Indians also] cut off
their dresses and petticoats at their knees to facilitate their march through the
woods and bushes, the girls making use of the detached strips for leggings. Now
all hurried on as rapidly as possible, the Indians generally keeping [to] the ridges,
which, being more barren of herbage, left less trail than the rich, low grounds
covered with cane, wild clover, and pea-vine.

The Indians consisted of three Shawanoes and two Cherokees—one of the
latter was the Hanging Maw, a well known chief of his nation whom Jemima
Boone well remembered having seen at her father's—probably on Watauga. He
could speak very good English, and when she told him who she was, he enquired
if the others were her sisters. Thinking Hanging Maw would be more likely to
spare and treat them well if he thought them to be the children of his old friend
Boone, she replied, "Yes." The old chief laughingly responded, "We have done
pretty well for old Boone this time."

They camped that night about six miles from the river and about three miles south-west from where Winchester now stands, the chief town of Clark County. As soon as they stopped, the captors were pinioned at their elbows so that their hands could not touch each other; each of the captives [was] placed beyond the others' reach, with one end of the tug with which they were tied made fast to a tree, while the other was lain upon by one or more of the Indians, who sprawled themselves upon the ground in a circle around their prisoners. Thus, without sleep, the girls sat with their backs against a tree, weary and anxious during the tedious vigils of the night—the dull monotony of chirping insects occasionally relieved by the howling wolves or hooting of owls. Jemima Boone, remembering that she had a pen-knife in her pocket, made an effort to reach it that she might cut herself and companions loose and make their escape, for the Indians appeared to sleep soundly; but so closely was she pinioned that she could not effect her object.

Early Monday morning the Indians resumed their hasty journey. The girls felt a strong confidence that they would be pursued and rescued. To guide their friends, they broke twigs and bushes as they marched along, discovering which, the Indians asked what they did it for. The girls replied that they were tired and caught hold of the branches to pull themselves along. Betsy Callaway particularly was so bold and persevering in making these *signs* and tearing off and dropping shreds of her white linen handkerchief, one fragment of which had "E. Callaway" worked upon it, that the Indians more than once shook their tomahawks threateningly at her; and per-emptorily bade her and the other girls [to] desist from breaking the bushes, which they had more particularly observed and seemed to fear the consequences. Though they had to be more cautious, they still sought opportunities to leave behind memorials of their route and actually blistered their hands and fingers in breaking twigs and bushes. Betsy Callaway, who wore a pair of high, wooden heeled shoes, in passing over damp or mellow ground, particularly fresh buffalo wallows, would leave her heel-marks pretty strongly imprinted in the soil; observing which, the Indians took the precaution to knock off the heels of her shoes, but this did not restrain her from making not a few impressions with the entire sole of her shoe. Another device practiced by our captives, and especially by Jemima Boone, whose sore foot was plead in excuse, was to seek favorable opportunities to tumble down, accompanying the fall with a loud scream—this with the double object of retarding their progress as also to give their friends notice should they be within hearing distance. If the Indians did not suspect the design, they at least feared the effect of the noise and would again angrily and threateningly brandish their knives and tomahawks.

During the forenoon of Monday the Indians came across an old white poney of little value which had probably strayed from one of the stations or been lost by some of the hunters. Jemima Boone, on account of her lameness, was first placed upon the animal, and then Fanny Callaway with her, and sometimes all three together, the Indians evidently hoping thereby to expedite their retreat. But their captives were full of inventions and managed by some adroit contact of their heels with the poney's flanks to cause him to be fractious, when the mischievous girls found no difficulty in tumbling off, only to re-mount and renew the farce. The poney acted precisely as though he fully understood his part of the performance, exhibiting a cross disposition, trying to bite the girls as they mounted, and once bit Betsy Callaway quite sharply on the arm, the scar of which remained visible ever after; but some knocks and bruises the girls received in their falls they bore with becoming patience and even thankfulness, so long as they were conscious of retarding the retreat. The Indians witnessed these scenes with mingled feelings of laughter and vexation; one would mount the poney in a triumphant manner, give him a few smart blows with his tomahawk handle to shew how little vicious he really was and how little inclined to kick or cut up his pranks. At length the Indians began to discover that they were gaining nothing by the help of the poney and abandoned him in the course of that day.

Monday at length wore away, the Indians all the while urging forward their prisoners and frequently breaking their trail to prevent successful pursuit. Smoked buffalo tongue was their only food, and this was shared with the captives, but it was so hard and, not being salted, was so unpalatable that they ate but sparingly. The girls were sometimes honored by their savage captors with a shew of kindness and affection and generously complimented as being "pretty squaws," but no improprieties were attempted—which, to the honor of the Indian race be it spoken, are seldom if ever committed upon their helpless female captives. The others, as well as Hanging Maw, could speak pretty good English, and all evinced a disposition to be social and communicative; [they] said they were going to the Shawanoe towns; that the Cherokees had killed or driven all the people from Watauga and thereabout and that a party of fourteen Cherokees were then on the Kentucky waiting to do mischief. The girls retained several words of their language, which were known to be Shawanoese. During the march, the Indian upon whom Fanny Callaway had laid the canoe-paddle with so much spirit was greatly joked by his companions. That night their camping-ground was a few miles south of the crossing of Hinkson's Fork of the Licking, and the night was spent by the captives as unpleasantly as the first—pinioned as before, still hopeful of deliverance; and while they were probably watchful for the approach of their expected deliverers, they were yet sufficiently weary, we may well conclude, by turns to take some sleep. Betsy Callaway had been particularly assiduous in encouraging the younger girls and keeping up their flagging spirits.

Tuesday morning the 16th of July at length dawned, when the march, or rather flight, was renewed. Though the Indians continued expeditious in their retreat, they seemed to act as if they felt themselves pretty safe beyond the reach of pursuers. About nine o'clock that morning they crossed Hinkston's Fork within about thirteen miles of the Upper Blue Licks; and a few miles beyond Hinkson, the Indians for the first time during the retreat concluded to venture killing some game and soon shot down a buffalo. Cutting out a portion of the delicious hump, they pushed on for the next stream, there intending to stop and cook the first meal since they had taken their prisoners.

We must now return to Boonesborough and trace the vigorous and unremitted pursuit on the part of the whites. When the terrible shrieks of the girls were heard by their parents and friends, Daniel Boone leaped from his bed in his cabin, on which he had been reclining, seized his rifle, and ran to the river with others without stopping even for his moccasins. At the moment of the alarm, Captain Floyd and Nathan Reid, who had strolled down to the Lick, were conversing under the shade of an elm and did not happen to hear the screams of the captives; when they saw a lad, Caleb Callaway, running rapidly towards them, who soon told the sad tale of the capture of Jemima Boone and his sisters. Hastening to the cabins, Floyd and Reid found the preparations already making for immediate pursuit; Colonel Callaway was loading his gun, while Boone and the others were running down the river to stop the canoe, which the Indians had turned loose. Samuel Henderson, who was then the affianced of Betsy Callaway, was in the act of shaving and dropped his razor when only half done and hastened to join the others with agonized feelings, which it were in vain to attempt to portray. There too was Flanders Callaway, who loved the rosy-cheeked Jemima Boone, young as she was; and he too pressed forward to rescue if possible his young lady-love and fair cousins. Boone was cool and determined—Colonel Callaway much more excited, and both, like tender parents, were filled with anxious solicitude for the safety of their children. The reader can but faintly imagine the aching hearts and wringing hands of the mothers, brothers, sisters, [and] friends left behind in Boonesborough.

When Boone, Floyd, Reid, Henderson, William B. Smith, John Gass, and others reached the point below, opposite to which was the canoe floating down the stream, the anxious inquiry arose, "Who will swim over after the canoe?" There was no other; but to venture for it might be attended with great peril, for perhaps the Indians were numerous and secreted in the cane and bushed to pick off any who might be so bold as to attempt a pursuit. John Gass, a young man of much fearless enterprise and a nephew of Capt. David Gass, plunged into the water and swam the stream while Boone and those with him guarded the bank, watching closely to give a long shot to any Indian who might shew himself to molest young Gass; but none appeared, and Gass soon returned with the canoe, receiving great applause for his bold adventure. Some little time was thus consumed in recovering the canoe. The sun was now about an hour and a half high when Boone with five others crossed the river, while Colonel Callaway, Capt. Nathaniel Hart, Capt. David Hart, Capt. David Gass, Flanders Callaway, and five or six others who were mounted on horseback dashed down the stream something over a mile below Boonesborough, where they easily forded.

On ascending the river bank, Boone directed his party to divide in order to discover as soon as possible the course the Indians had gone. Boone, John Gass, and Henderson went down the river, while Floyd, Reid, and Smith went up.[31] Colonel Callaway's mounted party soon came up to Boone and his companions, who by this time had bent their course up stream and struck the trail in the rear of

Floyd's party. Colonel Callaway at first insisted upon following directly on the Indian trail, to which Boone objected, explaining the danger of the girls being tomahawked by the Indians the moment they should hear the noise of the approaching mounted men. It was then arranged that Colonel Callaway with his horsemen should follow the path that led to the Lower Blue Licks and endeavor to cut off the retreat of the Indians at their customary crossing of Licking at that point, while Boone and the footmen should pursue the trail or its general direction more cautiously.

Floyd's party, the first to find the trail, pushed on as rapidly as they could about five miles, when, night approaching, they halted. At that moment, Boone and his men came up, and consulting what was best to be done, their attention was arrested by the barking of a dog. Marking the place where they left the trail, they moved forward with great caution towards the spot whence the noise proceeded, thinking it might be the Indian camp; they soon, however, discovered a party of men, nine in number, who had been engaged in building a cabin. Here they concluded to tarry all night and despatch one of their number back to Boonesborough for ammunition, provisions, and breech-clouts[e]—for it being Sunday, the men had on pantaloons, which somewhat impeded their movements. John Gass was the one selected for this night errand—who, by his knowledge of woodcraft and his fearless perseverance, might well be denominated a *Knight-Errant* of the primitive and chivalrous days of Kentucky.[32] He reached the settlement in safety, obtained the articles desired, including Boone's moccasins, with some jerked venison, which was the only article the women could supply from their scanty larders. With these desirable supplies, young Gass wended his way silently back to the cabin, which he reached before day; how he could have succeeded so well with no trail he could follow at night is passing strange.

As soon Monday morning as they could see to follow the trail, Boone and his companions set off with a full determination to accomplish their object, joined by three of the cabin-builders, John McMillen, William Bush, and John Martin—a most welcome accession of experienced woodsmen.[33] They soon [came] upon the spot where the Indians with their captives had encamped the preceding night. Boone and his followers now experienced great difficulty in keeping the trail, as the Indians had walked a considerable distance apart through the thickest cane they could find, and much precious time would be wasted in tracing their several routes until they should again unite. Life or death, captivity or freedom was the stake at issue and was to be determined by the right use of every moment. Boone, well understanding all of this and observing by the general course the Indians had taken that they were aiming for the Shawanoe towns on [the] Scioto, stopped and remarked that it would never do to follow them in that way, for they were making tracks faster than their pursuers; and moreover, until the Indians should become less cautious of pursuit, it would not be safe to keep upon the trail if they could, lest the whites should be first observed by the sentinel the Indians usually keep in their rear on the back track and the captives tomahawked rather than suffer them to be re-taken.

Paying therefore no further attention to the trail, they struck off somewhat to the right of the route of the Indians and, taking a straight course, hurried on with all possible speed and silence. They frequently fell in with the trail and discovered that the girls were thoughtful enough to leave sign behind them to indicate their course, bending and breaking twigs [and] dropping shreds of cloth; and in the course of that morning, in crossing a buffalo wallow, of which there was many, quite soft and entirely destitute of grass, [they found] the prints of the heels of Betsy Callaway's shoes where she had twisted them in the soft ground to make as much sign as possible to aid pursuit, should any be attempted. Boone and his companions well knew the object of these efforts, and they tended to cheer them in redoubling their exertions.

Night came once more and stopped them in their eager course. After refreshing themselves as well as they could upon a small allowance of jerked venison, with their thirst slaked at some convenient spring or stream, they threw themselves upon the ground to sleep. By Tuesday morning's dawn they were up and pushing on with all their might. By ten o'clock in the forenoon they reached Hinkson's Fork of the Licking, there a small stream. Boone, pausing a moment, observed to his followers that from the course the Indians pursued, he was confident their trail would be found crossing the stream but a short distance below; and sure enough, they had not gone down over two hundred yards before they struck the trail. Here their tracks were quite fresh, and the water at the place they had passed over was still quite muddy, They had now pursued the Indians upwards of thirty-five miles and supposed they would be less cautious in travelling, and hence Boone thought it would now be best to follow on their trail again.

After crossing the Hinkston, they entered the great War Path leading from the Cherokee to the Shawanoe nation, and running parallel with it were a great many well-beaten buffalo roads leading to the Upper and Lower Blue Licks, which were greatly visited by these and other animals to drink the brackish waters. The Indians would frequently break out of the War Path into a buffalo road, pursue it a short distance, and then diverge into some other or into the War Path again to elude pursuit should any be made. They little knew the man who headed the advancing whites, for he had an eye as keen as any Indian's and at once comprehended all their wiles and stratagems.[f] Boone and his party now set off at a long trot, and after going some eight or nine miles, they came upon a freshly slaughtered buffalo, the hump of which the Indians had skinned and taken a choice cut. The blood was yet trickling from the carcass, and Boone remarked that he was certain the Indians would stop to cook at the first water.

Pursuing on warily, they soon came across a small snake the Indians had "scotched," yet writhing in death. Ten miles from the Hinkston's Fork, they came to a small stream where the trail entirely disappeared, and no sign of it could be found on either bank. The Indians with their prisoners had waded along the bed to the creek, as they were accustomed to do when desirous of eluding pursuers. It was now about mid-day. Boone knew full well the Indians were close at hand and probably engaged in preparing their repast. His study had been how to get the prisoners without giving the Indians time to murder them after they should discover the whites. It was therefore necessary to use the greatest caution—the safety of the girls required it—one imprudent step might cost the captives their lives. The greatest possible silence was enjoined, and when within striking distance, no man was to touch a trigger until he had received the signal from Boone.

They silently crossed the stream and divided. Henderson, Reid, and some others went below, while Boone, Floyd, and the rest proceeded cautiously up the creek to the right and had gone but two or three hundred yards when, descending a slope, the Indians were descried kindling their fire in the glen below, near a small branch. The man of Boone's party in advance—probably William B. Smith— first discovered the camp only thirty yards distant and waved his hand for the others to hasten on, but before they could reach him, he raised his gun and delivered an aimless fire—and missed! His excuse for this premature discharge was that the Indians had discovered him and he fired to prevent giving them time to tomahawk the prisoners. Boone and Floyd, who had now got within shooting distance, hurriedly discharged their rifles as the Indians were moving off, each mortally wounding his man. One other gun was fired—a long shot—probably by John McMillen, but without effect. The Indians were kindling their fire; one had been posted on the elevated grounds a little distance behind to act as sentinel, and as the smoke ascended from the camp-fire, he left his gun and ran down to the fire to light his pipe and procure the necessary articles for mending his moccasins and was busily engaged in overhauling his budget. At the moment the whites fired upon the camp, one of the Indians was picking up wood, another preparing the meat for cooking, a third was in a reclining posture near the captives, apparently as a guard over them, while the old Cherokee chief Hanging Maw had just gone to the branch with a kettle for some water. It was the sentinel examining his budget near the fire whom Floyd wounded; he tumbled into the fire but, instantly recovering, ran off. Another, as he ran, sent his tomahawk flying at the head of Betsy Callaway, which barely missed its aim, and then, with the others, dashed into the cane and disappeared.

The girls had ventured as far back on their trail as they dared, which was but a short distance from the fire, still faintly hoping that deliverance might come, but they had become quite dispirited that day. They were sitting down on a log, Fanny Callaway on one side of her sister and Jemima Boone on the other, and both reclining their heads in her lap for rest. At the crack of the guns, the men rushed toward the camp with a loud yell, which gave the Indians no time either to kill their captives or save scarce an article of their baggage—"we sent them off," says Floyd dryly, "almost naked." The girls jumped instantly to their feet, Jemima Boone wildly exclaiming, *"That's daddy!"*—and with screams of joy were rushing towards their deliverers, when Boone commanded them to throw themselves flat on the ground lest the Indians should fire from their covert. This was momentarily obeyed, but they soon again bounded to their feet, when one of the whites coming up, mistaking Betsy Callaway, with red bandanna handkerchief around her head [and] with her dress cut off short, for a wounded Indian, in the excitement of the moment clubbed his gun and was in the act of striking her perhaps a death-blow, when his arm was fortunately arrested by Boone, who

63. *"The Deliverance of the Daughters of D. Boone and Callaway" (1852) by Jean-François Millet and Karl Bodmer. Center frontiersman's dress shows the influence of Benjamin West's "The Death of General Wolfe" (1770), suggesting that Millet studied the work for detail. Chromo lithograph published by Goupil, Paris.* WASHINGTON UNIVERSITY GALLERY OF ART; GIFT OF MRS. CHARLES W. BRYAN, JR.

exclaimed, "For God's sake don't kill her when we have travelled so far to save her from death!" The man, upon discovering his error, wept like a child.

"The exultation of the poor girls," said Nathan Reid, one of the rescuing party, "cannot be described." For a little period the rescued prisoners were so excited, particularly the two youngest, and so full of gratitude in embracing their friends and deliverers, that could the Indians have returned and renewed the contest, the whites would have been in a poor condition to have maintained their ground.[g] "The place," says Floyd, "was covered with thick cane, and being so much elated on recovering the three poor little heart-broken girls, we were prevented from making any further search."

As it was, the Indians were contented to seek their own safety and had gone off with a single shotgun, without ammunition, knife, or tomahawk, and some even without their moccasins—which, when they stop, they generally take off to dry for their longer preservation. Boone quaintly observed, "At yonder bush," pointing to one, "I fired at an Indian." Some of the men went and examined the spot and there found a rifle, which its owner, when wounded, had dropped or thrown away. Drops of blood were found here and also at the fire. The Indian wounded by Captain Floyd had no gun in his hand; he had left it at the tree where he stood sentry, and the girls did not think to mention it till they were some dis- tance on their return journey. Both Indians shot were Shawanoes and did not go very far before death claimed them as his victims.[34]

Among the plunder was the rifle found at the bush, knives, tomahawks, and other articles. Two small shotguns[h] were also obtained, which were broken over a tree as worthless. A war-club left by the Indians was like those Captain Floyd had seen of the Shawanoes. When the two girls were sufficiently recovered to speak, they told what they had learned of their captors about the Cherokee disturbances on Watauga and of the Cherokee war-party on the Kentucky ready for mischief; and that it was only three miles from the camp to the Upper Blue Licks and that their captors represented that a large number of Indians were assembled there. No time was lost in commencing the return march. We may well conclude that the slaughtered buffalo killed only two or three hours before was now drawn upon for rations for the weary and hungry party; or, failing in this, that Daniel Boone's trusty rifle brought down a buck, a loin of which served for their evening meal.

The girls were all much jaded, and particularly Betsy Callaway, who had not been relieved in the rapid journey by riding the poney, except to mount and go through the farce of tumbling off again. But their joyous spirits gave them new strength, and their whole return trip was replete with pleasantry and good cheer. Samuel Henderson, with his half-shaved face, came in for his share of jokes, which he and Betsy Callaway bore with a happy grace. The abandoned poney, when reached, was again called into requisition and served a good turn for the weary girls to ride awhile alternately, which they had not the least difficulty in doing without receiving a single kick or bite or having a solitary antic played upon them—a change of circumstances had effected quite a happy reformation! Reach- ing the hill skirting the river opposite to Boonesborough without accident, they were that moment overtaken by Colonel Callaway's party of horsemen, who had just returned from near the Lower Blue Licks, where they had discovered the tracks of a retreating Indian and concluded the girls had been retaken; the Indians routed and the happy meeting here and that after they had crossed the river we must leave for the reader's imagination to supply. This seventeenth of July, after all had safely returned, was a joyous day at Boonesborough. And strange to say, Jemima Boone had, by the exercise consequent upon her romantic adventure, nearly recovered from the effects of the cane-stab in her foot. The whole nar- rative of the captivity and rescue goes to prove that truth indeed is stranger than fiction.[35i]

During the absence of the pursing parties, few were left for the defense of the little settlement of Boonesborough; but they were so vigilant that the party of fourteen Cherokees mentioned by Hanging Maw and his associates as loitering upon the Kentucky for an opportunity to commit mischief were only able to burn the cabin of David and Nathaniel Hart, which was located between a quarter and a half mile distant from the station, where was a garden and nursery, the latter of which they cut down.[36] Boone states in his Narrative in a vague, general way that "a great deal of mischief" was done and "several forts attacked"; which alludes in part to the acts of hostility already recorded and others yet to be noticed committed at the close of the year and early the ensuing season. There were no other attacks in Kentucky during the summer or autumn of 1776, except perhaps that some few straggling hunters or land-jobbers may have been cut off. Congress was then endeavoring to pacify the western tribes, while the Cherokees, who had broken out in open war, had business enough nearer home to demand their attention.

The successive depredations committed by the Indians had a disastrous influence upon the feeble Kentucky settlements. Huston's Station,[j] located upon the present site of Paris, was the first to break up, the people taking refuge at McClelland's;[k] and this was quickly followed by the abandonment of Hinkson's[l] on the Licking, Bryan's[m] on Elkhorn, Lee's Town[n] on the Kentucky, and Harrod's Station,[o] or the Boiling Spring settlement.[37] Hearing of the captivity of the girls at Boonesborough, the few settlers at Whitley's Station[p] abandoned their homes and ten acres of corn; and reaching Logan's Station,[q] Captain Logan endeavored to prevail on Whitley's party to make a stand with him at that place, but failing in this, he was compelled for the safety of his family to join the others and remove to Harrodsburg. The people of Hinkson's Station, nineteen in number, with Capt. John Hinkson at their head, reached Boonesborough on their way to Virginia and Pennsylvania. "They all seem deaf," wrote Captain Floyd at the time, "to any thing we can say to dissuade them. Ten, at least, of our own people, are going to join them, which will leave us with less than thirty men in this fort. I think more than three hundred men have left the country since I came out, and not one has arrived, except a few *cabiners* down the Ohio.

"I want to return," continued Floyd, "as much as any person can do; but if I leave the country now, there is scarcely one single man who will not follow the example. When I think of the deplorable condition a few helpless families are likely to be in, I conclude to sell my life as dearly as I can in their defence, rather than make an ignominious escape. I am afraid it is in vain to sue for any relief from Virginia, yet the Convention encouraged the settlement of the country, and why should not the extreme parts of Fincastle be as justly entitled to protection as any other part of the country? If an expedition were carried on against those nations who are at open war with the people in general, we might be in a great measure relieved, by drawing them off to defend their towns. If any thing under Heaven can be done for us, I know of no person who would more willingly engage in forwarding us assistance than yourself. If so, at the request and in behalf of all the distressed women and children and other inhabitants of this place, implore the aid of every leading man who may have it in his power to give us relief cannot write. You can better guess at my ideas from what I have said that I can express them."[38]

Seven stations had broken up—but three remained occupied: McClelland's, Harrodsburg, and Boonesborough. The people at these places set themselves immediately about surrounding their cabin-groups with palisades. At Boonesborough they commenced erecting a new fort just above the Lick branch on the bank of the Kentucky and three hundred yards above Fort Boone, where Colonel Henderson in April 1775 had cleared a spot and built a magazine; and there, too, John Gass found Henderson and his particular friends living in a few cabins when he first arrived at Boonesborough in January or February 1776. Up to this period not one of the Kentucky stations was fortified or even partially protected. Fort Boone, as it was originally called, wanted two or three days' work to make it tolerably safe when Captain Cocke arrived there in April 1775, and it remained unfinished in June following;[39] and when Callaway and Poage's families arrived in September, there was yet no picketing.[40] So Fort Boone could never have consisted of more than a few scattered cabins, which two or three days' work would have connected with palisades and rendered pretty secure.

Amid these scenes of danger and excitement, little Cupid deigned to visit two kindred hearts in our far-off frontier settlement. Elizabeth Callaway, the eldest of the captive girls, and Samuel Henderson, one of the rescuing party, were the first couple married in Kentucky. The wedding took place in Boonesborough on the 7th of August, 1776, when Daniel Boone, officiating as a magistrate under Transylvania authority, solemnized the rites of matrimony, for which a license had been previously issued by the clerk or secretary. The dress of the bride and groom would not at this day be thought altogether suited for such an occasion. A plain Irish linen dress adorned the modest bride, while Henderson's hunting-shirt having become quite thread bare by time and rough usage, he borrowed Nathan Reid's, in which he was married. Watermelons, probably, formed the only delicacy of the bridal feast. It may be added, as indicative of the doubts of the settlers at this period of the stability of the government founded under the auspices of the Transylvania proprietors, that Colonel Callaway, in consenting to the match, required a bond of Henderson that the marriage should be again solemnized by authority less doubtful at the earliest opportunity—which pledge was sacredly fulfilled.[41]

The partial panic created in the country by the Indian depredations in the spring and early summer, after a while measurably subsided. But the *hegira* had greatly weakened the country, having carried off, as stated by Captain Floyd, fully three hundred people, among whom, according to another reliable authority, were several women and children.[42] The fort at McClelland's Station appears to have been promptly prosecuted to completion, while those at Harrodsburg and Boonesborough, as the alarm subsided, dragged along slowly, if not entirely abandoned. The attention of the northern Indians was now turned for awhile to another quarter, for in the autumn they were invited to a treaty at Pittsburgh to make solemn promises of peace and neutrality in the unnatural contest waging between the Colonies and mother country, receive a few presents and much good advice, and then return to their wilderness homes to do as British emissaries with alluring gifts should tempt them. Cornstalk among the Shawanoes and White-Eyes[r] among the Delawares were sincerely devoted to peace, but their good intentions availed but little among their bribed and turbulent countrymen. Probably, too, the fact that the Indians had learned from sad experience that the people of Kentucky were real *Sharp-Shooters,* their equals in their own peculiar modes of warfare, had something to do in producing the calm that ensued.

Though the enemy kept aloof, ammunition was yet needed for the defence of the settlements and procuring wild meat for their subsistence. It was everywhere a very scarce article. Little powder was yet made in the Atlantic states, and that was in pressing request there, while the Chiswell lead mines in Virginia were vigorously worked to obtain supplies of lead for the American armies as well as for the defence of the western frontiers. The Transylvania Company had furnished much of the ammunition used the first year in the country; and Maj. Arthur Campbell of Holston had sent a limited supply of powder and lead to Captain Boone, which the latter reported on the 7th of September, 1776, he had disposed of to the people, the powder at six shillings per pound and the lead at ten pence, except one pound of powder and two pounds of lead, which had been delivered to the scouts.[43] So scarce had become the article of lead that Captains Harrod and Logan were deported to go for a supply to Holston; they went on horseback, taking a pack-horse with them, and returned after an absence of twenty days with a quantity for the defence of Kentucky.[44] This was procured at the Long Island of the Holston, where Colonel Christian was then organizing for his campaign against the Cherokees.

About the 8th of September, Captain Floyd took his departure from Boonesborough for the old settlements;[45] and with him went Capt. David Gass, Nathan Reid, John McMillen, and others to join Colonel Christian's Indian expedition. While McMillen was in advance as a spy, he was killed in Big Moccasin Gap, near the North Fork of [the] Holston.[46] Captain Gass had not yet moved his family to Kentucky, and probably those who accompanied him had also other business beside serving on the campaign to call them to the Holston country. Many of the young men who first visited Kentucky were in the habit of returning to the old settlements each successive autumn, some to visit or bring out their connections, some for farming utensils, and others to replenish their tattered wardrobes.[47]

Large crops of corn were raised in the country this season and generally cribbed in the fields where they were raised.[48] In the autumn Thomas Denton put in an acre and a half of wheat at Harrodsburg, which was the first sown in Kentucky.[49] During the months of November and December several people left the stations and returned to their deserted camps, as there had been no body of Indians in the country, and it was thought doubtful whether any Indian nation really intended to wage open war against the Kentucky settlements.[50] Notwithstanding the desultory hostilities of the Indians in the spring and early summer, there were more cabin improvements made in 1776 than in any other year, as shown by the records of the commissioners for granting settlement rights and pre-emptions.[51]

Captains Clark and Jones, the delegates chosen to represent the western part of Fincastle in the Virginia Convention, learned upon their arrival in Botetourt County that body had adjoined after having formed a constitution for the new state, chosen Patrick Henry the first governor, and set the new government in operation. Jones tarried on the Holston, while Clark proceeded on his mission, visiting Governor Henry at his residence in Hanover County, and thence journeying to Williamsburg; and at length, after considerable hesitation on the part of the Executive Council, obtained from them on the 23d of August an order for 500 lbs. of gunpowder to be conveyed to Pittsburgh, subject to Clark's order, for the use of the "inhabitants of *Kentucki.*"

The first session of the new republican legislature of Virginia met on the 7th day of October, when Captains Clark and Jones laid the Kentucky memorial before that body, and though they were not admitted to seats, the enactment of a bill was procured for the erection of the *county of Kentucky,* despite the opposition of Colonel Henderson and some obstructions in the process of legislation which delayed its passage till the 7th of December. On the 23d of that month David Robinson was appointed county lieutenant, John Bowman colonel, and Anthony Bledsoe lieutenant-colonel, and George Rogers Clark major of the new county; Benjamin Logan was commissioned the first sheriff and John May surveyor, while David Robinson, George Rogers Clark, Isaac Hite, Benjamin Logan, Robert Todd, and five others who never became inhabitants of Kentucky were appointed justice of the peace.[52] This legislation organizing Kentucky into a separate county was emphatically a repudiation of the claim of Henderson and company and virtually the downfall of the Transylvania government.[53]

In drawing to a close the events of the year, it remains to notice that Major Clark and Captain Jones, with their precious cargo of powder and other stores, descended the Ohio from Pittsburgh late in the season; and having only seven men, they had to hide their cargo and set their boat adrift as they neared Limestone, and thence went across the country to the nearest settlements. Meeting with a few land explorers at Hinkson's deserted settlement, Jones and some of the men agreed to remain, while Clark should proceed directly to Harrodsburg for a party to join them and go after the ammunition. After Clark's departure, Jones was joined by Capt. John Todd and others, and now numbering altogether ten men, they concluded they were sufficiently strong to convey the stores from the Ohio to Harrodsburg. They accordingly started, and when proceeding along the trail on the ridge, five miles north-east of the Lower Blue Licks, they were ambushed and defeated by a party of forty or fifty Indians, chiefly Mingoes under the noted Captain Pluggy; Captain Jones and William Graden were killed, Joseph Rogers and Josiah Dixon taken prisoners, while the rest escaped. This occurred on the 25th of December.

Four days afterwards, on Sunday the 29th, Captain Pluggy and his party attacked McClelland's Station; Major Clark had just arrived there with a small party from Harrodsburg destined to bring in the hidden stores, and the Indians were finally repulsed with the loss of their distinguished leader and some others, while the whites had four wounded—Capt. John McClelland, Charles White, Robert Todd, and Edward Worthington, the two former mortally. McClelland was a man of wealth and influence, and his loss was sensibly felt. The Indians, having wantonly shot down the cattle and stolen the horses around McClelland's, sullenly retired from the country; but their two prisoners proved faithful to their countrymen and did not divulge the secret of the hidden stores.[54]

DRAPER'S NOTES: CHAPTER 13

1. James Galloway's MS. Narrative, written in 1832 at his dictation by his grandson, Albert Galloway, of Greene County, Ohio; Hall's *Sketches*, ii:243.

2. As there have been conflicting claims to the honor of *first born* of Kentucky, we have taken much pains to learn the following facts: The birth of Harrod Wilson is given upon the respectable authority of Mrs. Elizabeth Thomas, corroborated by others. Elizabeth Hays, eldest grandchild of Daniel Boone and the first white female native of Kentucky, was born at Boonesborough June 12th, 1776, became the wife of Maj. Isaac Van Bibber, and died in Missouri August 3rd, 1828. William Logan, son of Benjamin Logan, was born at Harrodsburg December 8th, 1776, was a member of the Convention that formed the constitution of Kentucky in 1799, afterwards a judge of the Court of Appeals of that state and a senator in Congress, and died on the 9th of August, 1822. About the close of 1776, John Anderson was born at Boonesborough, and Elizabeth, daughter of William Manifee—she married Jonathan Ridgeway. Levisa, daughter of William Whitley, was born at Harrodsburg, February 25th, 1777, married Maj. James McKinney, and is yet living in Missouri; and shortly after her birth was that of Ann, daughter of William Poage at Harrodsburg, who became the wife of Gen. John Poage, who commanded a regiment at the battle of the Thames. Frances Henderson, daughter of Samuel and Elizabeth Henderson, was the first child of parents married in the country and was born at Boonesborough May 29th, 1777, became the wife of Rev. James J. Gillespie, and died in Franklin County, Tennessee, May 7th, 1841. Enoch, son of Squire Boone, was born at Boonesborough October 16th, 1777, and is yet living in Kentucky. After this period, births of children were of too frequent occurrence for us to attempt to trace.

3. MS. notes of conversations with Mrs. Thomas; General McAfee's correspondence, also his newspaper "Sketches."

4. Hall's *Sketches*, ii:243–245, 248.

5. Bradford's *Notes on Kentucky*; Marshall's *Kentucky*.

6. Col. Nathaniel Hart, in Lit. News-Letter, May 23rd, 1840.

7. *American Archives*, vol. v, 4th ser., 417, 468.

8. MS. letter of Captain Floyd, May 19, 1776; and Daniel Bryan's MS. Narrative.

9. Floyd's MS. letters to Colonel Preston, May 19th and 27th, 1776.

10. The Conococheague settlements, on a stream of that name in Pennsylvania, were chiefly inhabited by Scotch-Irish; a noted lawyer in Virginia.

11. Referring to himself and John Gabriel Jones; John Todd's letter, June 22nd, 1776, in MS. Preston Papers.

12. Levi Todd's Narrative, in MS. Clark Papers; conversations with the late Capt. Henry Wilson.

13. MS. notes of conversations with Major Reid, by his son Nathan Reid, Jr.

14. *North American Review,* January 1846; Perkins' *Memoir and Writings,* ii:265.

15. Letter of Captain Floyd, May 1st, and of Col. William Fleming, August 2nd, 1776, in *MS*. Preston Papers.

16. Journal of Congress, April 29th and May 3rd, 1776.

17. Captain Floyd's MS. letter, May 19th, 1776.

18. Floyd's MS. letter, May 19th, 1776.

19. *American Archives,* 4th ser., 1528.

20. *American Archives,* 4th ser., 1543.

21. MS. letter of Captain Floyd, 19th May, 1776, to Colonel Preston.

22. *American Archives,* 4th ser., 1573–1575.

23. Ibid., 1044.

24. Almon, iv, 69.

25. *American Archives,* 4th ser., 1079.

26. Ibid., 1610.

27. MS. Preston Papers.

28. It may be added of Cooper that he was charged in connection with Capt. John Hinkson with wantonly killing Wipey, a friendly Delaware Indian, in Westmoreland County, Pennsylvania, in May 1774; and now, in turn, fell by the hands of the savages.

29. Pennsylvania Packet, August 20th and September 10th, 1776; Almon, iv, 53; Floyd's letter to Colonel Preston, July 21st, 1776.

30. Nathan Reid was born on Rockfish River, in what is now Nelson County, Virginia, on the 3rd of March, 1753—the youngest son of Irish parents, who, migrating from the north of Ireland, settled first in Pennsylvania and then on Rockfish. With a limited education, he followed the fortunes of an elder brother as a trader to the Holston country in 1774; and there became acquainted with and warmly attached to John Floyd, whom he accompanied in 1776 to Kentucky and aided in rescuing the captive girls. Returning in the fall to the old settlements, he joined Colonel Christian on his campaign against the Cherokees. In January 1777 he received a captain's commission in the Continental army and participated in the battle of Brandywine and but for sickness would have played his part in the battle of Germantown. He was in 1778 in Monmouth battle and in 1779 shared in the taking of Stony Point and Paulus-Hook. In 1780 he visited Kentucky on business and in January 1781 assisted in repelling Arnold's invasion of Virginia. He served till the end of the war, having attained to the rank of major. Shortly after the war, he married Miss Sophia Thorpes and settled on Goose Creek, in Bedford County, Virginia; and a few years later, he purchased a farm near New London in the same county, where he continued to reside until his death, which occurred on

November 6th, 1830, after a week's illness from a severe attack of pleurisy. He was buried with military honors. Major Reid was a man of great energy, probity, and benevolence of character, nearly six feet in height, of great muscular powers, ruddy complexion, black hair, grey eyes, which, when excited, were exceedingly bright and piercing. Among his sons was Maj. John Reid, a young man of uncommon promise who served with great distinction as General Jackson's aid in his campaigns against the Indians and at New Orleans, and who died under the paternal roof January 18th, 1816, at the early age of thirty-one years.

31. Boone gave Reid this piece of advice. "In your tramps," said he, "through the country, never look for the Indians, but keep a sharp lookout for their guns lying across logs or fallen timber."—*Reid's MS. Notes.*

32. John Gass was wounded in the little battle at Harrodsburg in March 1777 and aided in the defense of Boonesborough during the big siege of September 1778. He settled in Clark County, Kentucky, where he died about 1825, at the good old age of about seventy-seven years.—*Correspondence of Capt. John Gass, his cousin.*

33. John McMillen was a young Virginian and, not long before the captivity of the girls, went out hunting, accompanied by John Gass, son of Capt. David Gass, then a youth in his twelfth year. At Harrod's Lick, on the north side of Stoner's Fork of the Licking, McMillen wounded a buffalo bull and was following on the trail. The weeds and bushes were so thick that he came close upon the wounded animal before seeing him, when the buffalo, smarting under his wounds, turned upon McMillen and ran furiously over him, breaking his gun and badly wounding him. Aided by young Gass, he got back to Boonesborough and had so far recovered when the girls were taken as to be able to assist the cabin-builders and aid in the rescue of the captives. In the fall of 1776 a small party of men left Boonesborough to join Colonel Christian on his Cherokee campaign, when McMillen went along; and, acting as a spy in advance of his party, was killed in Moccasin Gap, near the North Fork of Holston.—*Correspondence of the venerable Capt. John Gass,* who was with McMillen on his buffalo hunt.

William Bush was born in Virginia about the year 1747; he was one of Boone's adventurers in 1773 when defeated in Powell's Valley and again advanced with the road-markers that led the way in settling Boonesborough early in 1775. He acted well his part in the rescue of the captive girls. He participated in the skirmish at Boonesborough April 24th, 1777, and was in the big siege of September 1778, as well as in many other contests with the Indians. In 1790 he commanded a company of Kentuckians on General Harmar's campaign. He settled on his pre-emption about a mile and a half from Boonesborough on the north side of the Kentucky, in what is now Clark County, where he died July 25th, 1815. His wife, whose maiden name was Frances Burrows and to whom he was married in Orange County, Virginia, about the year 1780, survived till 1828; they left numerous respectable descendants. Captain Bush was about five feet, eight inches in height, rather heavily formed, possessing great energy, perseverance, and benevolence, with little or no avarice or show of ostentation.

John Martin was born near Goshen, Orange County, New York, in the year 1736. He served one year in the New York provincials on the northern frontier during the French war and saw active service in the field. Early in 1775 he went down the Ohio with Capt. John Hinkson and others to Kentucky and raised a crop of corn that year on the South Fork of Licking; aided in 1776 in rescuing the captive girls; and the next year he was one of two spies employed at Logan's Station and took part in the defense of that station when attacked in May 1777 by a large body of Indians. In June 1778 he was wounded in a skirmish with the Indians at or near the present town of Washington, Kentucky. When Boonesborough was attacked in September 1778, a report reached Logan's Station, where Martin then was, that Boonesborough had been taken, when Martin hastened alone to the Holston settlements and procured re-inforcements of 150 men for the defense of Kentucky. During the winter 1779–'80, he erected Martin's Station, a mile below the present town of Paris, on the Licking, but was not there when it was captured the ensuing June. He served on Clark's Indian campaign of 1780; and in 1781 we find him in service as a captain building boats for Clark's intended Detroit expedition. He aided Logan in burying the dead at the Blue Lick defeat in August 1782 and again led forth his company on Clark's Shawanoe campaign in the fall of that year, as well also on Logan's campaign in 1786. He was a member of the Danville, Kentucky, Convention of May 1785. He settled in Lincoln County, Kentucky, where he died April 28th, 1821, at the age of eighty-five years. Captain Martin was a man of large frame and was familiarly known in early times as *the big Yankee.* He deservedly ranked among the most efficient and meritorious of the early pioneers of Kentucky.

34. William Wilson, a messenger then in the Indian country to invite the Wyandotts to a treaty at Pittsburgh, heard "that the white people over the big river had fired on a party of Shawanoes and Cherokees; that one of the party had got into the Shawanese towns, who said that one of the Shawanoes was certainly killed, and he did not know but more of them were, for there were a great many guns fired at them." Wilson subsequently learned, as may be seen in Hildreth's *Pioneer History,* p. 99, 100, that the surviving Indian confessed that his party had been doing mischief when the whites pursued them, "Killed two of the Shawanoes, and rescued the prisoners, that the Cherokees had sent a tomahawk-belt, with two scalps tied to it, to the Shawanoes, informing them that they had struck the white people," and invited them to join in the war. "This day," writes Captain Arbuckle from Point Pleasant, August 15th, 1776, to Col. William Fleming, "my messengers returned from the Shawanoe towns, with one of the Shawanoe chiefs and brother of Cornstalk's, who informs me that after the Shawanoe and Cherokee party had taken three women prisoners from Cantuckee, the whites followed and retook the prisoners, and killed two of their men." *MS. Fleming Papers.*

35. This narrative has been drawn up, with great care, from Captain Floyd's letter, July 21st, 1776; MS. letter of Capt. Matthew Arbuckle, August 15th, 1776; a series of detailed MS. notes dictated by the late Maj. Nathan Reid, the last survivor of the pursuing party, kindly furnished for this work by Nathan Reid, Jr.,

Esq.; MS. notes of conversations with Capt. John Gass, who was a youth at Boonesborough at the time of the captivity; also conversations with Col. Nathan Boone and lady, who often heard Col. Daniel Boone and Jemima Boone relate the particulars of the adventure; Isaiah Boone and the late Judge Moses Boone, who were youths in Kentucky in 1776, and Mrs. Elizabeth Bryan, daughter of Jemima Boone and Flanders Callaway; correspondence with Alfred Henderson; Mrs. Catherine Williams and Mrs. Frances Wall McGuire, daughters, and Richard P. Holder and W. D. Holder, grandchildren of Frances Callaway and John Holder; MS. statement of the late Daniel Bryan, Col. William Martin, Maj. Bland W. Ballard, Col. Richard Callaway, Jr., David Henry, Maj. John Redd, and Capt. Henry Wilson; the present Joseph McCormick, Sr., Maj. John L. Martin, Willis A. Bush, Morgan Bryan, and others. Also MS. Narratives of Maj. Pleasant Henderson, who visited Boonesborough shortly after the captivity and rescue; and the late Mrs. Lucy Brashear, who went to reside at Boonesborough shortly after the occurrence and whose statement was kindly furnished by Thomas Turner, Jr., Esq., of Kentucky. The published works consulted were Bradford's *Notes on Kentucky,* Hildreth's *Pioneers History,* Perkins' article on the pioneers of Kentucky in the *North American Review,* and the late Nathaniel Hart's newspaper sketches. Flint is replete with error, as also are articles upon the captivity in Hunt's *Western Review* for January 1820 and Hall's *Western Monthly Magazine* for September 1833. Boone himself had told the story in less than half a dozen lines, while Marshall and McClung were unable to add anything to it; and Hale, in his sketches of the West, but re-vamps the unreliable narrative in Hunt's *Review.*

36. The late Col. Nathaniel Hart's newspaper sketches.

37. The Bryan party having *laid by* their corn crop, and left two men to keep up the fence, returned to North Carolina to move out their families in the fall, but the Cherokee war prevented [it].

38. Captain Floyd to Colonel Preston, July 21st, 1776.

39. Colonel Henderson's letter, June 12th, 1775.

40. MS. notes of conversations with the venerable Capt. John Gass and the late Mrs. Elizabeth Thomas; MS. statements of the late Col. Richard Callaway, Jr.; McAfee's newspaper sketches.

41. MS. notes of Maj. Nathan Reid; MS. letter of Alfred Henderson and Mrs. Elizabeth Dixon, surviving children of Samuel and Elizabeth Henderson.

42. MS. narrative of Levi Todd, who arrived at Boonesborough in April 1776 and remained a permanent settler in the country.

43. MS. letter of Daniel Boone to Colonel Preston, September 7th, 1776.

44. MS. records of Lincoln County, Kentucky.

45. Captain Boone's MS. letter, September 7th, 1776, to Colonel Preston.

46. Notes of conversations with Capt. John Gass; Major Reid's MS. Narrative.

47. Levi Todd's MS. Narrative.

48. Todd's Narrative, in MS. Clark Papers.

49. Gen. R. B. McAfee's MS.

50. MS. Narrative of Gen. Levi Todd.

51. Marshall, i:45.

52. The county lieutenant had the command of all the militia of his county, whether in one or more regiments. Col. David Robinson, a native of Ireland, was born in 1730 and early migrated with his parents to the Augusta Valley in Virginia. Having received a fine classical education, he spent many years of his life as a teacher of youth in the higher branches of education. In 1755 he was appointed a lieutenant in Capt. William Preston's company of rangers and served on the Shawanoe expedition under Maj. Andrew Lewis in 1756, when the men nearly starved. He also served as a lieutenant in Capt. John Dickinson's company of rangers from 1757 to May 1759 and commanded a company in Colonel Lewis' regiment on Bouquet's Indian campaign of 1764. For some cause he declined the appointment of county lieutenant of Kentucky. He never was married and died at the residence of Maj. Alexander Montgomery, whose lady was his niece, in Fayette County, Kentucky, in 1807, at the age of seventy-seven years. He was a good classical and scientific scholar and a man of talents and worth.

Colonel Bledsoe was a native of Culpeper County, Virginia. He became a prominent pioneer on the frontiers of Virginia and Tennessee; but never removing to Kentucky, he did not accept the appointment of lieutenant-colonel of that county. He was killed at his residence in what is now Sumner County, Tennessee, in July 1788, at the age of fifty-five years.

MS. Journals of the Virginia Council; MS. letter of Capt. John Floyd, December 16th, 1776; MS. Papers of Gen. Simon Kenton; Introduction to Butler's *Kentucky,* 2nd ed., lxx.

53. It was not till November 1778 that the Virginia Legislature formally voted the claim of Henderson and company null and void; but as the company had been at great expense in extinguishing the Cherokee title, such as it was, and in effecting the settlement of the country, it was resolved that a just and reasonable compensation should be allowed them—which eventuated in a grant of 200,000 acres of land at the mouth of the Green River on the Ohio, and a similar grant by North Carolina as a compensation for that part of the company's purchase within the limits of that state. Thus their golden dreams of wealth and empire vanished. For brief notices of the members of this company, so intimately associated with the early history of Kentucky, see Appendix.

54. Clark's MS. Memoir and Diary; MS. Memorial of Hugh McGary, chairman of the Kentucky Committee to the Governor and Council of Virginia; Levi Todd's MS. Narrative; MS. Statement of the late Capt. Henry Wilson; MS. correspondence of the Hon. David Todd of Missouri; McDonald's *Kenton;* Bradford's *Notes on Kentucky.*

EDITOR'S NOTES: CHAPTER 13

a. Louis Lorimier (1748–1812), one of the more intriguing, colorful, and influential traders of the Middle Ground. Lorimier, reed thin and four feet, six inches tall, was fluent in native dialects. His honesty at his outpost at Piqua (in northern Ohio) put him in good stead with the Indians. Gen. George Rogers Clark's and Col. Benjamin Logan's campaigns in Ohio against British-allied Indians left Lorimier's post sacked; in 1786 he moved to Illinois and married Charlotte Pemanpieh Bougainville, the mixed-blood Shawnee daughter of Louis Antoine de Bougainville. In 1793 he established a post at Cape Girardeau, Missouri, and helped settle that community. Lorimier was of a unique caste—a white man whose life, marriage, decorum, and dress reflected a dual Gallic-Indian status. Artist John James Audubon, who met him in 1811, left this vivid description:

> His hair was plastered down close to his head with a quantity of pomatum; it ended in a long queue rolled up in a dirty ribbon that hung below his waist. The upper part of his dress was European, once rich but now woefully patched and dilapidated with shreds of gold and silver lace here and there. . . His waistcoat . . . had immense pocket flaps that covered more than half his tight buckskin trousers that were ornamented with big, iron knee-buckles to support Indian hunting gaiters long past their prime. His moccasins . . . were of the most beautiful workmanship.

City officials erected a large monument over the graves of Lorimier and his wife at the Old Lorimier Cemetery in Cape Girardeau. See Alice Ford, ed. *Audubon, by Himself* (New York: Natural History Press, 1969).

b. George Morgan (1742–1810) in the 1760s was a co-partner in the Philadelphia-based trading firm Baynton, Wharton, and Morgan. As an Indian agent at Fort Pitt in 1776, Morgan treated Indians fairly, and the Delaware honored him with the name Taimenend ("Affable One"). After the Revolution, he settled his family in New Jersey, where he became a landowner and trustee of Princeton University.

c. The notion of a "flying camp" originated with George Washington in 1776 during the New York campaign. Washington expected to muster 10,000 militiamen from Pennsylvania, Delaware, and Maryland to assist the New Jersey forces as a mobile reserve unit. The flying camp had several duties: to help guard the Jersey coast; to keep supply lines open for American traffic; to protect the Jersey forces from Tory attack; and to provide a buffer zone for Continental forces marching from New York. In theory, on paper, and in Washington's mind, the concept was an excellent idea. But high desertion rates, epidemics, provincial conflicts, poor discipline, and low morale plagued the flying camp, and by November 1776 the system had broken down and the novel idea was abandoned.

d. Frontier slang for Indians, whom whites also called Injuns, reds, redskins, red devils, red rascals, various permutations of "red sons of bitches," and savages. Indians in turn called Kentuckians whites, white men, white eyes, English, Big Knives, Long Knives, "white sons of bitches," or any number of profane terms learned from whites.

    e. For white hunters, wearing breechcloths and adapting other such items of Indian clothing was a logical, pragmatic approach to backwoods dress. See chapter 4, note b.

    f. Actually, Hanging Maw and the other warriors well knew that Boone would be the one man hottest on their trail, hence they moved with secrecy and made haste.

    g. According to Draper's correspondence with Evira L. Coshow, granddaughter of Jemima Boone Callaway and great-granddaughter of Daniel Boone, after the three girls were safe, Boone said: "Thank Almighty Providence, boys, we have the girls safe—let us all sit down by them and have a hearty cry." Grandmother Jemima told Evira that "there was not a dry eye in the company—a cry for joy." See LCD to Evira L. Coshow, March 14, 1885, DM 21C:29.

    h. Most likely smoothbore Indian trade guns.

    i. Yes it does. The "savage Indians capturing the helpless white girls" is a time-honored American motif in literature, art, and film. A much embellished version of the kidnapping episode appears in James Fenimore Cooper's *The Last of the Mohicans* (1826). Since then, novelists, artists, and Hollywood have exploited the theme many times over, perhaps most recently in Michael Mann's lush 1992 Twentieth Century Fox remake of Cooper's *Mohicans.*

    j. According to Peter Houston's memoirs (written in 1842), Houston's Station was built by him and his brothers James and Robert in 1780 in what is now Paris. These dates cannot be reconciled. Perhaps whoever built the earlier settlement of Huston's Station was not related to the Houston brothers, who came to Kentucky in 1779. For a published transcription of Peter Houston's memoirs, which offer eyewitness glimpses of Boone and frontier life, see Ted Franklin Belue, ed. *A Sketch of the Life and Character of Daniel Boone: A Memoir by Peter Houston* (Mechanicsburg, PA: Stackpole Books, 1997).

    k. McClelland's Station, founded in 1775 by John McClelland north of the Kentucky in the area of present-day downtown Georgetown (Scott County). By 1776 McClelland's Station sustained a population of about thirty families in a region notorious for Indian raids. In an attack that December 29th, Indians killed McClelland; in turn, the fort's defenders shot and killed Pluggy, an infamous Mingo chief. After McClelland's death, his stockaded station fell into disrepair. The definitive work on forts in the Bluegrass is Nancy O'Malley's *Stockading Up: A Study of Pioneer Stations in the Inner Bluegrass Region of Kentucky.* Archaeological Report 127. (Frankfort, KY: Kentucky Heritage Council, 1987).

    l. In its earliest incarnation (1775), John Hinkston's barely defensible station, built in what is now Harrison County, consisted of about fifteen cabins. Frontiersman Simon Kenton and others helped add a blockhouse the winter of 1776–77, but fearing attack, the settlers abandoned Hinkston's for neighboring forts. By 1779 Isaac Ruddell led a team of pioneers to reoccupy, rebuild, and fortify the site, and the name was changed to Ruddell's Station. In 1780 British Capt. Henry Bird and a war party of Ohio and Great Lake Indians attacked Ruddell's. After the fort's capitulation, the Indians fell on the thirty to forty Pennsylvania German families, murdering twenty of the defenseless settlers with tomahawks, knives, and war clubs. Bird marched the survivors to Detroit, where they were held as prisoners of war until the end of the Revolution. See O'Malley, *Stockading Up,* 241–44.

m. Bryan's Station was built in 1779 by brothers Joseph, James, William, and Morgan Bryan southeast of what is now the Lexington-Maysville Road in Fayette County. Bryan's (sometimes called Bryant's) was an imposing log fort. Forty-four cabins were built into its parallelogram perimeter of twelve-foot-high walls that ran 200 yards long and 50 yards apart; the walls were fortified with gun loops and topped on the corners by two-story blockhouses. On August 15–16, 1782, British Indian agents Simon Girty, Alexander McKee, and Capt. William Caldwell led more than 300 Indians against Bryan's. Indians killed two men in the two-day siege and were repulsed, but the raid on Bryan's was the prelude to the devastating Battle of Blue Licks on August 19, frontier Kentucky's darkest hour.

n. In June 1775 brothers Capt. Hancock Lee and Willis Lee from Virginia founded Leestown, the second fort on the Kentucky (the first was Boonesborough). Threats of attack caused the site to be briefly abandoned, and in time Leestown merged with Frankfort, Kentucky's state capital. See chapter 7, note 1.

o. Frontiersman James Harrod established the Boiling Springs settlement (Boyle County) in 1774, six miles south of Harrod's Town (also known as Oldtown or Harrodsburg) in Mercer County. Harrod lived at the well-watered site from 1775 until 1792, when he went on a hunting trip and was never again seen, dead or alive. His fate remains a mystery.

p. For Whitley's Station and the career of William Whitley, see chapter 12, note o.

q. In 1775 Benjamin Logan and John Floyd erected Logan's Station west of present-day Stanford in Lincoln County. Firsthand accounts describe it as a typical log fort of the day, but with one difference: Logan's Station had a well-buttressed, camouflaged trench that ran to a nearby spring. This proved a great advantage when Indians besieged the fort for thirteen days in May 1777. With the close of the Indian wars, settlers left the station, and the fort fell into disrepair.

r. White Eyes (?–1778) was a well-known, pro-American Delaware chieftain who worked hard to keep his people neutral during the Revolutionary War. White Eyes encouraged accommodation between Americans and Indians and allowed Moravian missionaries to preach and convert many Delaware to that belief. In 1778 American soldiers murdered him and, to hide their grievous act, reported that White Eyes had died from smallpox. When the truth became known, many Delaware defected to the Crown's cause.

CHAPTER 14

1777, or "The Year of the Three Sevens."—Indian Attacks.—James Ray Outruns a Band of Seventy Shawanoes.—Indians Attack Boonesborough and Daniel Boone Wounded.—Simon Kenton Saves Boone's Life.—Death of Ens. Francis McConnell.—Kentucky Census and the Mustering of the Militia.—Squire Boone Badly Wounded.—Barney Stagner Killed and Beheaded Near Harrodsburg.—First Court for Kentucky County.—Battle of Cove Springs.—Reinforcements from Virginia and the Yadkin Arrive in Kentucky.

In consequence of the attack on McClelland's Station, the death of their noble leader, Captain McClelland, the loss of their cattle and horses, the people of that fort abandoned the place in a body on the 30th of January, 1777, and removed to Harrodsburg. It was a melancholy occasion on the part of the settlers; it seemed a point gained by the enemy when another of the strong-holds of the whites had been broken up. Boonesborough and Harrodsburg were the only settlements that remained occupied—except perhaps Price's Settlement on the Cumberland.[1] About this time, a party of thirty men went to the Ohio and brought in the secreted ammunition without molestation.

Capt. Hugh McGary,[a] as chairman of the Kentucky Committee of Safety, sent a memorial to the governor and Council of Virginia, dated Feb. 27, 1777, praying for aid and relief in their distressed situation. "We are surrounded," says the ancient manuscript document, "with enemies on every side; every day increases their numbers. To retreat from the place where our all is centered, would be a little preferable to death. Our fort is already filled with widows and orphans; their necessities call upon us daily for supplies.[2] Yet all this would be tolerable could we but see the dawn of peace; but a continuance of our woes threaten us— a rueful war presents itself before us. The apprehension of an incursion the ensuing spring fills our minds with a thousand fears. The brave despise danger, even death, on their own account; it is the state of weak infancy and helpless widowhood that sets heavy on us."

As attacks upon the infant settlement now began to thicken, some account of the Indian mode of warfare may now properly be introduced; and we accordingly quote from the early Kentucky historian Marshall:[b] "The Indian manner of besieging a place is somewhat singular; and will appear novel to those who have derived their ideas of a siege from the tactics of regular armies. It is such, however, as the most profound reflection, or acute practical observation, operating upon existing circumstances, would dictate or approve. They have not great armies with which to make war; neither have they cannon nor battering engines; nor have they even learned the use of the scaling ladder. Besides caution, the natural offspring of weakness, is even more inculcated than courage. To secure himself, is the first— to kill his enemy, the second, object of the Indian warrior.

"These sentiments, the results of the principle of self-preservation, are common to all the tribes; and their practice is conformable to their utmost variety and extent—with the exceptions common to general rules. The Indians, in besieging a place, are hence but seldom seen in force upon any quarter; but dispersed, and acting individually, or in small parties. They conceal themselves in the bushes or weeds, or behind trees, or the stumps of trees; or waylay the path, or field, and other places, to which their enemies resort; and when one or more can be taken down, in their opinion, they fire the gun, or let fly the arrow, aimed at the mark. If necessary, they retreat—if they dare, they advance upon their killed or crippled adversary, and take his scalp, or make him prisoner, if possible. They aim to cut off the garrison supplies by killing the cattle; and they watch the watering places for those who go for that article of primary necessity, that they may, by these means, reduce the place to their possession, or destroy its inhabitants in detail.

64. This earliest known depiction of a raid on Kentuckians shows the massacre of Thomas Baldwin's family. Baldwin lived near Boonesborough and lost his wife and three children in the 1783 attack. FROM NARRATIVE OF THE MASSACRE BY THE SAVAGES OF THE WIFE AND CHILDREN OF THOMAS BALDWIN (1835).

"In the night, they will place themselves before themselves near the fort gate ready to sacrifice the first person who shall appear in the morning. In the day, if there be any cover, such as grass, a bush, a large clod of earth, or a stone as big as a bushel, they will avail themselves of it to approach the fort, by slipping forward on their bellies, within gun-shot; and then, whosoever appears first, receives the first fire, while the assailant makes his retreat behind the smoke. At other times, they approach the walls or palisades with the utmost audacity, and attempt to fire them, or to beat down the gate. They often make feints to draw out the garrison on one side of the fort, and, if practicable, enter it by surprise on the other. And when their stock of provision is exhausted, this being an individual affair, they supply themselves by hunting, and again frequently return to the siege, if by any means they hope to get a scalp.

"Such was the enemy who infested Kentucky, and with whom the early adventurers had to contend. In the combat they were brave; in defeat they were

65. Anglo-European scalp on bone hoop. FROM THE COLLECTION OF JIM AND CAROLYN DRESSLAR.

dextrous; in victory they were cruel. Neither sex nor age, nor the prisoner were exempt from their tomahawk or scalping-knife. They saw their perpetual enemy taking possession of their *hunting ground,* to them the source of amusement, of supply, and of traffic, and they were determined to dispute it to the utmost extent of their means. Had they possessed the skill which combines individual effort with a concerted attack; and had they directed their whole force against each of the forts, then few and feeble, in succession, instead of dissipating their strength by attacking all at the same time, they could have easily rid Kentucky of its new inhabitants, and again restored to it the buffalo, and the Indian—the wild game, and its red hunters."

During January and February the Indians remained quiet and the Kentuckians enjoyed a temporary rest. In the latter month, Captain Logan with his own and some half a dozen other families left Harrodsburg and reoccupied Logan's Station or

Fort, as it was indiscriminately called.[c] About the 1st of March William Bush and a few others arrived from Virginia, bringing public despatches and the military and civil commissions for the officers of Kentucky county—to George Rogers Clark as major, Daniel Boone, James Harrod, John Todd, and Benjamin Logan as captains. Prior to this, every fort and every camp had its own selected chief, with but little order or subordination. On the 5th of that month the militia of the county were embodied and organized at Boonesborough, Harrodsburg, and Logan's Station, as spring was now dawning and troubles from the Indians anticipated. The very next day, while James Ray, William Coomes, and Thomas Shores were at work clearing land at the Shawanoe springs, about four miles north-east of Harrodsburg, for Hugh McGary, young Ray's step-father, Ray and Shores left their chopping and visited a neighboring camp, where Ray's brother William was engaged in sugar-making, to slake their thirst with the sugar-water. A party of about seventy Shawanoe warriors under the noted war-chief *Cot-ta-wa-ma-go,* or Black Fish, came unexpectedly upon the sap-drinkers, killed and scalped William Ray, captured Shores, when James Ray, by his uncommon fleetness, though long and hotly pursued, escaped.[3] Black Fish afterwards remarked that there was a boy at Harrodsburg who out-ran all his warriors. Coomes hid near by in a tree-top and witnessed their wild orgies over the dead body of young Ray and around their captive, gurgling the syrup at the camp, singing their war-songs, and dancing their war-dance. Towards evening a party of thirty mounted men went from Harrodsburg under Captain Harrod and McGary in search of their missing friends; and coming upon Ray's mangled remains, at the sight of which McGary turned pale and was near falling from his horse, one of the men shouted out, "See there! They have killed poor Coomes!" Coomes, who hitherto lurked in his hiding place, now sallied forth, triumphantly exclaiming, "No, they haven't killed me, by Job! I'm safe!" Having buried Ray and rescued Coomes, they returned to Harrodsburg about sun-set.[4]

After the captivity of the girls, and again when McClelland's Station was attacked, the people of Harrodsburg gave some attention towards fortifying the place, but it was yet incomplete. They now immediately and earnestly set themselves about the matter and worked hard all night in endeavoring to put the fort in a state of defense; and the next morning, the 7th of March, the Indians appeared about sun-rise and set fire to one of the old cabins, when the men sallied forth from the fort, and a skirmish ensued in which four of the whites were wounded, one of whom, Archibald McNeal, died twelve days after; and of those who recovered were Captain McGary and John Gass, the latter of whom had performed so noble a part in the rescue of the captive girls the previous year. Benjamin Linn particularly distinguished himself in this affair by killing an Indian and securing his scalp at great risk of losing his own by the adventure. Several of the Indians were wounded, as was indicated by the signs of blood on the trail of their retreat. The whites lost quite a number of cattle killed by the enemy and a few horses carried off.[5]

Captain Boone and his men at Boonesborough, who had commenced building a new fort soon after the rescue of the captive girls, by dint of hard labor, had completed it during the winter, and the spring of 1777 found them occupying their new and improved quarters. On the 7th of March, the very day of the skirmish at Harrodsburg, a party of Indians, probably detached from Black Fish's main body, appeared at Boonesborough, and managed to kill a Negro in the field at work and wounded another person. This induced those who had scattered out in camps in that region to take refuge in Boonesborough while Captain Boone was diligent in instructing and directing his men, constantly keeping sentinels at the fort and scouts ranging the country.[6]

The next day after the affair at Harrodsburg, the people at that place ventured out and brought in from the cribs corn raised the previous year, and were thus employed ten days. But they had no meat except such as the hunters obtained by cautiously leaving the fort before the break of day, going many miles, killing their game, and returning stealthily by night with their pack loads of meat on horseback, not unfrequently being shot at on their departure or return. James Ray, then but a youth of seventeen, was the boldest and most successful of these solitary hunting adventurers, in the prosecution of which he had a faithful old nag, not exactly fitted to run the gauntlet through the forest, but it was the only one left of a drove of forty horses brought to the country by the settlers. The gratitude and admiration of men, women, and children were deservedly bestowed upon young Ray, who well merited the character of possessing all the peculiar qualities requisite for a superior woodsman.[7]

The Indians scattered over the country but seemed to pay their especial respects to Harrodsburg during the month of March. On the 18th, near night, they killed and scalped Hugh Wilson within a half a mile of the fort and escaped, and on the 28th attacked the stragglers outside the fort, killing and scalping Garret Pendergrass within a hundred yards of the fort, his family witnessing the affecting scene. Peter Flinn was either killed or captured—probably the former, as he never returned, while John Haggin was at the same time intercepted and fled though the woods to Boonesborough, and every one at Harrodsburg thought him killed, when, two weeks afterwards, he returned and, carelessly entering his cabin like one risen from the dead, coolly saluting his wife as though [nothing] specially had happened, "How are you by this time, Nancy?"[8]

Though the Indians still lurked about, they did but little mischief till towards the close of April. The whites at this period made it a point, as their numbers were few and provisions scarce, to act on the defensive, except where some decided advantage should offer or necessity compel them to act otherwise. On the 19th of the month Col. Richard Callaway and Capt. John Todd were chosen the first burgesses to represent Kentucky County in the Virginia Legislature; and the same day, by way of variety, a wedding occurred at Harrodsburg, uniting James Berry to the widow Williams, who had been in her weeds[d] just a month and a day. The next day, April 20th, Lt. Ben Linn and Samuel Moore, two active woodsmen, started from Harrodsburg on a secret mission to the Illinois country, the nature of which is best explained by Clark's expedition to that region the following year.[9]

Boonesborough now came in for its share of Indian attention. Early on Thursday morning, the 24th of April, Daniel Goodman and another man left the fort and went into a field some four hundred yards distant to drive in some horses. They were fired upon by four or five Indians, but not being wounded, they fled and were pursued to within sixty or seventy yards of the fort, where an Indian overtook Goodman and killed him with his tomahawk and commenced the operation of taking off his scalp. By the time the Indian had secured this bloody trophy, Simon Kenton, who with two others had been standing at the fort gate ready to start out on a hunt, ran to the relief of his friends and, when within a few yards of the bold scalper, shot the fellow down; and then Kenton in company with his hunter-companions gave chase to the others, pursuing them to the edge of the field.

Hearing the reports of the first guns fired on Goodman and his comrade, Boone with ten or a dozen men rushed out of the fort with their rifles and joined Kenton and the others in the lane, which was skirted with a field on either side. The Indians, to the number of about one hundred, who were here secreted in the fence-corners, behind stumps, and other hiding places, were completely succeeding in drawing the whites into a fatal ambuscade. While Boone and his party were yet advancing, Kenton, casting his eye to the left, discovered an Indian about to fire upon them, when he adroitly got the first shot, and the savage smote the earth in death. By the time Kenton had reloaded and Boone's men came up, they heard a rush of footsteps on their left and, turning, discovered that a large number of the enemy had jumped into the lane between the whites and the fort to cut off their retreat.

Seeing the perilous situation of himself and friends, Boone exclaimed, "Boys, we are gone—let us sell our lives as dearly as we can!"—and gave orders to charge through the Indians, which was quickly obeyed by first firing upon the enemy and then beating down with clubbed guns all that stood in their way. The whites succeeded in their object, but they had to fight hard for it. Stephen Hancock killed an Indian, shooting him in the head. During the melee, Captain Boone received a ball in his left ankle, which broke the bone and threw him on the ground; and when the tomahawk was uplifted to despatch the fallen captain, Kenton, like an angel of mercy, came to his rescue, discharged the contents of his gun through the body of the Indian, when, another warrior appearing with knife in hand to take Boone's scalp, Kenton clubbed his gun and knocked him down, and then ran with Boone in his arms to the fort. The women in the fortress were anxiously watching the issue of this sudden and exciting contest, and seeing her father approaching wounded, Jemima Boone rushed out of the fort and met him several rods from the gate and assisted him in.

Three others were wounded, Captain Todd, Isaac Hite, and Michael Stoner— either Todd or Hite was shot through the hand. Stoner had advanced some distance down the lane ahead of the others and raised his gun to fire at an Indian and, while taking aim, was himself shot through the right wrist, which caused his gun to fall from his hands. Attempting to regain it, and finding himself unable to grasp it with his disabled hand, he was again wounded, the ball penetrating his hip, which now laid him prostrate on the ground. An Indian now ran up apparently confident of a scalp, but just as he reached Stoner, some of the whites shot him dead, and another Indian renewing the attempt met a similar fate. The whites now approached and assisted Stoner to his feet and, finding he was able to walk, bade him make the best speed he could to the fort and they would endeavor to keep the enemy at bay till he and the other wounded men were beyond danger.

Before starting, however, our cool and considerate German snatched his gun from the ground and, presenting it to one of the men, said, "If I leave you, I will leave my gun wid you; she pe vell loaded, and if you hold her on one of tem Cot tam Yellow rascals, I vill varrant you'll fetch him." William Bush, to aid his friend Stoner to hasten his retreat, caught him by the arm or around the waist as they were crossing the Lick Branch, and the wounded soldier [was] showing signs of becoming exhausted, but Stoner, fearing that two together would make too prominent an object for the enemy's aim, desired Bush to let go of him, exclaiming, "O Pilly Push, Dey vill schoot us; we are too pig a mark—we are too pig a mark, Pilly Push!" So Bush desisted and shared, as he had done before, in checking the pursuit of the Indians by every now and then suddenly stopping and presenting his rifle, which would set them to jumping and capering about most violently to prevent aim being taken at them; and in this would they would be momentarily checked, while the wounded men would gain a little distance to be overtaken by their protectors. Jacob Starnes, Joseph Kennedy, and William Cradelbaugh also figured like good soldiers in this affair, and all at length reached the fort.[10] At least six Indians were killed, and probably many more, for several of the whites fired three times during the continuance of the contest, and the Indians themselves subsequently acknowledged that twenty-two of their number fell on this occasion.

After the whites had all got into the fort and the gate was closed, the wounds of the disabled were dressed. The ball that penetrated Captain Boone's ankle was extracted on the side opposite to its entrance and was found completely flattened by the force with which it came in contact with the bone which it fractured. Boone now sent for Kenton and said, "Well, Simon, you have behaved like a man to-day; indeed you are a fine fellow." It was a compliment richly deserved. The Indians continued hovering around the deserted cabins formerly known as Fort Boone, or the little Fort, when they withdrew. Boone had a painful time with his disabled limb; he had it placed in a sling as he lay in bed during his recovery. There was no physician in the country, but the frontiersmen were familiar with the treatment of wounds by poultices. Ever after, from much fatigue or in consequence of the effect of the weather, he suffered more or less from this old injury.[11]

Though this large party appeared at Boonesborough, others still remained lurking around Harrodsburg. On the 25th of April, the day after the skirmish at Boones-borough, Indians were heard around Harrodsburg imitating owls, turkies, and other game, but their decoys were too well understood by the whites to be entrapped by them. On the morning of the 29th of that month, while Ens. Francis McConnell and James Ray were a hundred yards south of the fort shooting at a mark, some Indians stole sufficiently near that one of them, shot at and mortally wounded McConnell, who fell behind a log, when Ray dashed towards the assailant, thinking there was but one, and was soon attacked by a large body whose shots did not take effect. He retreated one hundred and fifty yards to the fort and, finding the gate closed, took refuge behind a stump seven steps from the fort walls, where for about four hours the bullets of the enemy knocked up the earth around him. All this while, his mother was a painful spectator from the portholes of his dangerous situation; but Ray at length bethought himself of an expedient and exclaimed, "For God's sake, dig a hole under the cabin wall, and take me in!" It was speedily done, when Ray darted through the aperture and was safe. Towards evening, Silas Harlan, James Ray, and others opened the fort gate, raised the yell, and ran out and brought in McConnell, who had during the day repeatedly waved his hand for assistance; and to favor this sortie, several men got upon the cabin roofs and fired in the direction where the Indians were hallooing, which, with the yells of Harlan's advancing party, caused the Indians to scamper away like so many partridges. McConnell died shortly after he was brought in and was buried in an unoccupied bastion in the south-west corner of the fort.[12]

On the 1st of May a census was made of the people at Harrodsburg—showing men fit for duty, 84; do. unfit, 4; women, 24; children over ten years, 12; do. under ten, 58; slaves over ten, 12; do. under ten, 7—total, 201.[13] At this time there were twenty-two men at Boonesborough and fifteen at Logan's Station; making the whole number of men fit for service in Kentucky one hundred and twenty-one, the number of families about forty, and the total population about two hundred and eighty.[14] To attempt successfully to resist hordes of savages with such a mere handful of men appeared indeed hopeless odds; three isolated forts in the wilderness two hundred miles from the nearest settlements in Virginia, to which imploring appeals for relief had been sent, but none came; their cattle were mostly killed and horses stolen; no corn planted at Harrodsburg, the largest settlement, and wild meat difficult to be procured. Under these desponding circumstances, Captain McGary and John Haggin were sent on the 18th of May to Fort Pitt to learn the prospects of peace and of recovering the horses stolen by the Indians.

At this period each of the stations furnished two good spies or scouts selected by their captains for the payment of whose services Major Clark pledged the faith of Virginia; Simon Kenton and Thomas Brooks were chosen on the part of Boone; Samuel Moore, except when absent on his mission to Illinois, and Bates Collier, by Harrod; John Kennedy, John Martin, and sometimes John

Conrad, by Logan. These scouts ranged the country as high as the Three Islands above Limestone on the Ohio and as low as the mouth of the Licking and were generally able by their skills and vigilance to detect the advent of bands of the enemy and give timely notice of their approach. But when the Indians were once in the country and scattered in squads, sometimes watching a station and then hunting for supplies, the scouts were too few in number always to keep pace with their designs and movements.

The people at Boonesborough were divided by Captain Boone into two companies, one of which, day about, was to act as guards and spies, while the other endeavored to plant and cultivate some patches of corn. Soon after Colonel Callaway and Capt. John Todd had taken their departure on the morning of Friday, the 23d of May, to attend the Virginia Legislature as the representatives of Kentucky, a party of about two hundred Indians made their appearance near the corn-field where the men were at work and were first seen by a man at the fort seeing the reflection of the sun upon an Indian's gun, when he gave the alarm and they were fired upon by the guard, but being greatly out-numbered, the whites were forced to fly to the fort, and on the retreat, Joseph Kennedy was badly wounded with three balls—one of the shots supposed to be mortal. He escaped with the others to the fort. During the flight or in the subsequent attack, two others were wounded. The Indians kept up a warm and constant fire upon the fort until eleven o'clock at night, which they renewed the next morning and continued hotly till midnight, boldly attempting several times to fire the fort, but they were gallantly repulsed by the fearless few within. Michael Stoner, still suffering from his wounds, was placed where he could watch the close approach of the enemy and shot down a warrior attempting to fire the fort who wore a silver moon on his breast, at which Stoner took deadly aim. Though Boone was not yet recovered, he could direct and encourage his men, but such skillful Indians fighters as Kenton and Stoner and their brave companions really needed no special instructions how to watch at the port-holes and send their bullets flying after any Red Skin who might dare show himself with the reach of their rifles. Boone informs us that seven of the Indians were slain, while Major Clark and Captain Cowan assert that "the enemy suffered considerable loss." On Sunday morning the 25th they retired after having, as usual, destroyed what cattle they could find. Kennedy in due time recovered from his grievous wounds and long lived to serve his country.[15] We must not omit to record that during this attack, or possibly the preceding one, William Bailey Smith was let out of the fort by night, who went to Boone's old acquaintances on the Yadkin for relief.[16]

[With] Indians still harassing the fort at Harrodsburg, a party consisting of Squire Boone and several others went out on the 26th of May in search of the enemy. Passing through some small glades south-east of the fort, the men in advance called out, *"Boone, come on!"* Boone was lingering behind, examining for fresh moccasin tracks, when he heard some little distance [to] one side of him the single exclamation "Boone!"—and stopping to look, received a shot in his left side, breaking one of his ribs in two places. The Indians, probably few in number, escaped unseen.[17]

John Kennedy and a fellow scout from Logan's Station, while in the performance of their round of duty, discovered the Indians near Boonesborough, who, evidently despairing of success in that quarter, were bending their course with a portion of their number towards Logan's. It became something of a contest of speed and stratagem who should reach Logan's Station first, but the scouts succeeded. Early on Friday morning, the 30th of May, though confident that Indians were about, Mrs. Ann Logan, Mrs. Whitley, and a Negro woman ventured out of the fort to milk the cows, guarded by William Hudson, Burr Harrison, John Kennedy, and James Craig. There were fired upon by their stealthy foe and Hudson shot through the head and killed instantly, while Harrison was shot down, and Kennedy, though wounded with four balls, reached the fort, as did also Craig and the women uninjured.[18] The Indians were fifty-seven in number, who kept up a constant fire on the fort until evening, screened behind trees and banks while the twelve uninjured men in the garrison made such a defense as deterred the enemy from too near an approach to the stockade. Among those brave defenders, the names of Benjamin Logan, William Whitley, John Martin, Benjamin Pettit, James Craig, George Clark, William Manifee, Azariah Davis, James Mason, and James Hawkins, a free mulatto, stand conspicuous. The wives of Logan, Whitley, Clark, Pettit, and Manifee were learned [in] the use of rifles, and the two former during the siege melted down their pewter plates and converted them into bullets.[e]

As the Indians ceased firing just at evening, Whitley observed Harrison, who had lain all day where he fell and [was] supposed by all to be dead, slightly move his head; and this fact was quickly communicated to Captain Logan, who hallooed to the wounded man, "If you are in your senses, move your foot." Harrison did as requested. Logan then exclaimed, "Lie still—don't be discouraged, and I will bring you in at the risk of my life." A bag of wool was produced, which Logan carefully rolled before him as a protection against bullets until he reached Harrison, whom he grasped in his arms and ran to the fort.[19] The Indians did not observe Logan till he reached the fort, when they fired a single gun, the ball of which entered the corner of the house near the gate. The Indians now renewed the attack and continued it until sometime in the night, during which they killed all the cattle and hogs they could find. They hovered around the fort, though kept quiet, till Sunday morning, when they departed. Before their departure, the intrepid Logan again ventured out and brought in the dead body of Hudson, scalped and mangled, "surely a sight alarming," says Whitley's Narrative, and buried him within the station.[20]

It is quite evident that the Indians attacked the three forts almost simultaneously, expressly to prevent their extending relief to each other. And such was the weakness of his fort and the pressing want of ammunition that the heroic Logan concluded to go to Virginia for relief and started alone on the 6th of June, travelling almost day and night till he had accomplished the object of his mission.[21]

66. *Cranial fragment excavated at Logan's Fort, Stanford, Kentucky, showing cut marks from scalping. Archaeologists suspect the remains to be of William Hudson, killed May 30, 1777.* DR. NICHOLAS HERRMAN, UNIVERSITY OF TENNESSEE, AND KENTUCKY ARCHAEOLOGICAL SURVEY, LOGAN-WHITLEY CHAPTER NSDAR, AND LOGAN'S FORT FOUNDATION.

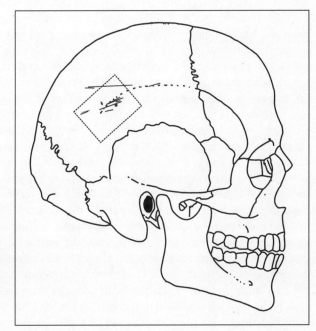

67. *Diagram showing placement of cranial fragment.* DR. NICHOLAS HERRMAN, UNIVERSITY OF TENNESSEE.

Early in June Daniel Lyons, returning from the Cumberland River, was supposed to [have] be[en] killed in endeavoring to enter Lyon's Fort—a part of a
leather hunting-shirt thought to have been his was afterwards found. On the 3rd
of that month an express from Harrodsburg to Boonesborough, arriving within a
mile and a half of the latter place, discovered a large party of Indians, when the
express returned. Lieutenant Linn and Samuel Moore returned to Harrodsburg
June 22nd from the Illinois country with favorable accounts; and half a mile from
Harrodsburg, Barney Stagner, an elderly man, was killed and beheaded, and the
same day a few guns were fired at Boonesborough without effecting any thing
save the killing of some cattle. Captain Logan returned to his fort on or about the
23rd of June with high hopes of the early arrival of men for the defense of the
country and reported that [he] had seen the *sign* of about thirty Indians crossing
Cumberland Mountain and directing their course toward the old settlement.[22]

July was comparatively a quiet month. On the 6th, as an incident of the
times, a buffalo bull returned up to the fort at Harrodsburg and was killed. How
indifferent people can become to danger when killing, scalping, and beheading
were things of frequent occurrence may be inferred from the following entry in
Clark's Diary—"July 9th, Lieut. Linn married—*great merriment.*" The bride was
Hannah Soverens, and the wedding took place in Harrodsburg. And in those trou-
blous times, it is pleasing to note the first harvest in Kentucky—"July 14th, and
15th, reaped wheat" at Harrodsburg. On the 26th Hugh McGary returned from
Fort Pitt and reported no prospect of peace or of recovering their stolen horses
from the Indians.[23]

Besides petitions, expresses had been repeatedly sent to the older settlements
for aid to assist in repelling the vigilant foe: McGary and Haggin to Fort Pitt,
Captain Smith to the Yadkin, Logan to Holston, and twice had Captain Harrod
gone to meet the expected troops. The news had spread among the frontier settlements that "Boone was badly wounded" and "the people of Kentucky were
penned up in forts," and a general anxiety was felt to send adequate relief;[24] but
the pressing wants of the main army under Washington, the poverty of the country, and the unsettled state of the western frontiers of Virginia and North Carolina
all conspired to retard the arrival of the long expected reinforcement. At length
Colonel Bowman reached Boonesborough on the 1st of August, to the great joy
of the people, bringing with him from Virginia two companies under Capts.
Henry Pawling and John Dunkin, who was succeeded soon after his arrival by
Isaac Ruddell, the two companies numbering one hundred men. He was ordered
to protect the people of Kentucky if his force was sufficient; if not, to "export
them into some interior and secure parts of the country."[25]

An event occurred at Harrodsburg on the 5th of August of rather an unusual
character. A party of ten or twelve Indians had secreted themselves near a turnip
patch close to the fort, and the alarm shown by the cattle indicated the presence
and hiding place; when Major Clark with a number of men crept out of the fort,
got into the rear of the Indians, and killed four of them and wounded others, and
took plunder which sold for upwards of £70. On the 11th of that month John Higgins died at Harrodsburg of a lingering disease—the first natural death probably

that occurred in Kentucky; and on the 25th, while six of Colonel Bowman's men had nearly reached Logan's Fort, they were waylaid and Ambrose Grayson killed and Jonas Manifee and Samuel Ingram wounded. The Indians escaped, leaving on Grayson's dead body several proclamations from Gov. Henry Hamilton of Detroit, addressed to Major Clark and Captain Logan in person and the Kentuckians in general, offering pardon to all who would repair to the British standard with their arms and use them, promising them good fare and, at the close of the war, two hundred acres of land to each man; and that all who held commissions from the state should have equal rank and be taken into British pay. Captain Logan wisely kept these proclamations for many years concealed from the people, lest the more thoughtless might perhaps, in a time of much public suffering and distress, be tempted from the path of rectitude and patriotism.[26]

On the 2nd of September the first court for Kentucky County convened at Harrodsburg. George Rogers Clark, Isaac Hite, Benjamin Logan, Robert Todd, Richard Callaway, John Kennedy, Nathaniel Henderson, Daniel Boone, James Derchester, James Harrod, and others not named were the justices of the peace, the first four having been appointed the previous December and the others in June in place of those first appointed who did not settle in the country. Levi Todd was chosen clerk of the court, and the officers of the county severally took their oaths of offices. In June preceding, Richard Callaway was commissioned colonel of the county in place of John Bowman, who had been promoted to county lieutenant, made vacant by Col. David Robinson not settling in the country.[27]

The Indians did not abate their vigilance but constantly watched the paths leading from Harrodsburg; they were often seen by the whites, and shots were sometimes exchanged. It has already been noted that in consequence of the continued annoyance of the Indians, the people at that station were unable to plant any corn in the spring. They were, therefore, the more assiduous as autumn approached, to save what little yet remained cribbed of the previous year's crop which the Indians had not discovered and destroyed; or if discovered, was purposely spared in order to waylay any who might venture after it. On the 11th of September a party of thirty-seven men under Colonel Bowman went to Capt. Joseph Bowman's settlement at the Cove Spring, five miles south-east of Harrodsburg, to shell corn and convey it to the fort. While thus engaged in shelling, a party of Kickapoos[f] stole up through a cane-brake and fired upon the whites. Bowman gallantly hallooed to his men, "Stand your ground!—we are able to beat them, by the Lord!"

Squire Boone was one of the party, and having a small three-edged sword by his side, he had previously drawn it half out of the scabbard to have it convenient for use in case of need. Upon the first alarm, he jumped behind a tree and shot at the Indians and then squatted in the weeds to load his gun; and while engaged in loading, an Indian shot Eli Gerrard dead, who had partly sheltered himself behind the same tree, and his body fell on Boone. The Indian who had shot Gerrard ran up with his tomahawk in hand to finish the work of death and secure the trophy of a scalp, and not knowing that Boone was there, approached within ten feet of him before a mutual discovery took place. The Indian thus meeting an unexpected foe, exclaimed *Waugh!*—raised his tomahawk, and gave Boone a cut across the fore-head two or three inches in length; the blow, however, [had] been near partially broken, for the tomahawk was knocked in some way from the Indian's grasp. Boone by this time had dropped his gun and thrust his sword into the Indian's ab-domen with one hand, while with the other he seized the Indian's belt and, pulling his antagonist towards him, shoved the sword completely through the fellow's body, the point protruding some fourteen inches. The Indian now made several ef-forts to draw Boone's knife from its sheath, which was attached to his shot-pouch strap, but the blood from Boone's forehead falling upon the handle made it so slippery that the Indian could not draw it. Failing in this, the Indian now began with a desperate effort to back off towards a low fence close at hand, Boone still holding on till they reached the fence, when he released his grasp and the Indian threw him-self over the fence, fell upon his back, and broke off the point of the sword and soon died.[g] Another was killed; and beside the loss of Gerrard, six others, including Boone, were wounded, one of whom died that night. The Indians retreated, leaving signs of blood on their trail, and Major Clark soon came up with a reinforcement from town and conveyed the wounded to the station. This spirited little affair was known among the frontiersmen of that day as the battle of *Cove Spring.*[28]

Captain Smith had been successful in raising a company of forty-eight men among Boone's old friends and kindred on the Yadkin—some of the Boones and several of the Bryans being among them; John Holder was lieutenant, and all were enlisted to serve six months. They reached Boonesborough on the 13th of September, all mounted men marching into the fort in single file with a space of six feet between the horses, thus presenting quite an imposing appearance. While they were received with great joy by the inmates of the fort, half a dozen Indians who were secreted on the hill overlooking the station immediately decamped and reported to their friends the arrival of two hundred white warriors.[29]

By the arrival of Bowman and Smith's men, the people of the country as-sumed an entirely new attitude. When ever a party of Indians were known to be in the country, they were sought for by the whites rather than avoided; and the Indi-ans in the turnip-patch affair at Harrodsburg at the Cove Spring engagement and on other similar occasions were boldly met and "out-generaled," as Boone as-serts, "in almost every battle"; and instead of denominating the Virginians by the *soubriquet* of *Long-Knives,*[h] as they had formerly done, and whose superiority they now began to learn from sad experience, they now spoke of them as the *Close* or *Sharp Shooters.* The Indians were in a great measure disheartened and were compelled to give up all hopes of taking any stations until they could greatly augment their dusky forces. The Kentuckians, on the other hand, were greatly elated with their little successes against their enemies and the arrival of the mili-tary companions from Virginia and North Carolina; and Captain Smith brought intelligence of one hundred and fifty more men on their march for Kentucky and that Washington had defeated Howe—and Clark adds in his diary of this latter item, *"Joyful news, if true!"*[i] Though it did prove incorrect, it goes to evince the warm sympathies of the backwoodsmen of Kentucky for the patriots and the pa-triot cause under the banner of the great and good Washington. "Our affairs," declares Boone, "began to wear a new aspect, and the enemy, not daring to venture on open war, practiced secret mischief at times."[30]

On the 1st of October Major Clark left Harrodsburg for Virginia, accompanied by twenty-two men, and was joined at Logan's Fort by Captain Pawling[j] and his company of fifty-four men and some women and children. The people of Kentucky were loath to part with Clark even for a brief period, but he assured them he was going to promote their highest interests and should early return to devote himself to the defense and prosperity of the country. While so many men were thus leaving, others arrived to supply their places; on the 2nd Capt. John Montgomery[k] reached Logan's with thirty-eight men from the region of Fort Chiswell in West Virginia, and about a dozen days later Capt. Charles G. Watkins[l] arrived at Boonesborough with a company of fifty men from Bedford County, Virginia. And late in the autumn Captain Logan went alone on horseback to the Holston, obtained four kegs of powder and four horse loads of lead for the use of the Kentucky stations, and safely returned, accompanied by a guard of twelve men, one of whom was Benjamin Briggs, Mrs. Logan's nephew, then only in his thirteenth year.[31]

The year 1777 was one of constant anxiety and watchfulness in Kentucky; the Indians were unusually vigilant, and but little corn was raised at Boonesborough and Logan's Fort and none at Harrodsburg. "We were but a handful," says Boone, "to the numerous warriors that were every where dispersed through the country, intent upon doing all the mischief that savage barbarity could invent. Thus we passed through a scene of suffering that exceeds description." But the year closed, as we have seen, with brighter prospects dawning upon the infant settlements of Kentucky, and Boone partook largely of the general feeling of joy and hope pervading all classes of people.

The following letter of Colonel Bowman addressed to General Hand,[m] then in command at Pittsburgh, furnishes some hints rather than details of the condition of the country at that period:

Harrodsburg, December 12th, 1777

Sir.—We received yours by Mr. John Haggin, dated Fort Randolph, 19th November, 1777, which news gives great satisfaction to the poor Kentucky people, who have these twelve months past been confined to three forts, on which the Indians have made several fruitless attempts. They are left almost without horses sufficient to supply the stations, as we are obliged to get all our provisions out of the woods. The Indians have burned all our corn they could find the past summer, as it was in cribs at different plantations some distance from the garrisons, and no horses on which to bring it in. At this time we have no more than two months bread—near 200 women and children, and not able to send them to the inhabitants; many of those families left desolate widows with small children destitute of necessary clothing.

Necessity has obliged many of our young men to go to the Mo-non-ga-hale, their former place of abode, for clothing, intend-ing to join their respective companies as soon as possible, and as there will be a sufficient guard, I think it proper to order some corn to this place for our support. We intend to keep pos-session of the country, and plant crops the ensuing spring, as we have no other place from which to expect relief. If we are denied this request, we must do without bread till we can get it from what we intend to plant. I find it difficult to keep the gar-risons plenty in meat, and if we have no bread we must at any rate suffer.

Your humb. serv't,

John Bowman[32]

Flavored[n] by Lieut. Linn.

In this time of threatened scarcity, the pioneers at Boonesborough had another source of in part supplying the deficiency. In the fields where a crop had been raised the previous year, and where ears and kernels had fallen scatteringly upon the ground, many a bag-full was gathered which had grown spontaneously and produced in some instances seven or eight bushels to the acre. This circumstance, or one like it, gave rise to the answer of Gen. Charles Scott some years afterwards when asked upon his return from Kentucky as to the productiveness of the coun-try: "If planted," said he, "and cultivated as you Virginians do yours, twenty bushels would be an ordinary yield; if planted, and not cultivated, ten barrels; *and if not planted at all, seven barrels!*"[33]

The provident supply of ammunition secured by the intrepid Logan rendered the prospect fair for obtaining a sufficiency of wild meat from the woods. Game was plainly dressed and served up on wooden platters or pewter plates with corn bread and hominy. Corn was then ground with great difficulty on the laborious hand-mills or pounded in the cavity of a stump by means of a pestle attached to a sweep, for water and horse mills were then and for some years afterwards un-known in Kentucky. When the Indians were not too troublesome, cows were kept to some extent and milk used for food and culinary purposes. The tallow and marrow from buffaloes were important articles in cooking; and parched corn pounded into meal sweetened with maple sugar furnished an admirable substitute for the most delicious coffee.[o]

Many of the young men, as already indicated, returned each successive au-tumn to their original homes in the old settlements to provide themselves with a new supply of clothing. Those who remained had necessarily to rely upon the

68. *Until the early 1800s, when the eastern buffalo were exterminated and the last remnants of their habitat cleared, fenced, and farmed, America's wild cow provided Indians and settlers with food and an array of useful items.* PHOTO BY MARCUS COPE.

skins of wild beasts for raiment, together with the homely product of the wild nettle and buffalo wool. The wild prickly nettle is a plant of luxurious growth in the rich lands of the West, attaining a height of three to four feet, with a bark of fibre somewhat resembling that of flax and hemp or rather of a character between the two; the stalk falls when touched with frost, and when the fibre matures or rots by the rains or snows, it is separated from the stalk and spun. A coarse article of cloth was manufactured from it; and sometimes it was combined with the coarse wool or hair from the buffalo, the nettle being used as warp and the buffalo wool as filling. For the manufacture of socks, buffalo wool alone was used, which was quite soft and wore very well.[34]

In drawing to a close the events of the year, we shall relate a hunting adventure which occurred about this period in the Boonesborough region. William Bush and Michael Stoner had gone from the fort on a bear hunt and had toiled nearly all day without success. When night was fast approaching, they discovered much bear sign on and around a tree which had a large cavity in it some thirty feet from the ground, with a limb extending to it from the other tree. Stoner proposed to climb the tree with the extending limb and see what discoveries he could make; and, carrying his plan into execution and reaching the hole, he enquired in a familiar way, "Who keeps de 'ouse?" It turned out that a she-bear with her cubs had there made their den for winter, and not relishing this intrusion, the old bear advanced upon Stoner in a hostile manner. He retreated as well as he could, calling out, "Vy don't you shoot, Pilly Push!—Vy don't you shoot, Pilly Push!" When Bush could shoot, after a hearty laugh from the ludicrous turn the affair had taken, the bear was wounded and turned and held to the limb with her fore feet, when Stoner, quick as thought, drew his knife and cut off her claws, when she fell to the ground—Stoner remarking at the same time that he "tid not like sich company."[35]

DRAPER'S NOTES: CHAPTER 14

1. The only written evidence extant of this settlement is found in the manuscript records of the Virginia commissioners granting John South, Sr., a settlement right and pre-emption "for raising a crop of corn in Price's Settlement on Cumberland in 1776, and removing up to Boonesborough on the 1st. of April, 1778." The venerable Col. James Davidson of Lincoln County, Kentucky, states that such an early settlement existed. It was located south of [the] Cumberland River, within the present county of Wayne, Kentucky.

2. Harrodsburg.

3. Ray placed their numbers at forty-seven, but Coomes, who had a better opportunity of counting them, declared there were about seventy in all; and Levi Todd's Narrative conveys the idea of a larger hunting party than Ray supposed it was.

4. Coomes was a native of Maryland of the Catholic faith, and removed to Kentucky with his family in the spring of 1776 and located at Harrodsburg, where he shared the dangers of a protracted Indian war. He subsequently settled near Bardstown, Kentucky, where he lived to a good old age. Mrs. Coomes probably taught the first school opened in Kentucky at Harrodsburg in 1776. It may be added that Shores, who was captured by Black Fish's party, joined the British stand at Detroit and never returned.

5. MS. diaries and statements of G. R. Clark, John Cowan, Levi Todd, James Ray, Mrs. Thomas, and others.

6. MS. diaries and statements of Clark, Cowan, Todd, Robert Hancock, Joseph Kennedy, and William Cradlebaugh—the two latter then at Boonesborough.

7. MS. Ray notes; MS. statements of Levi Todd, Dr. John Ray, and conversations with Mrs. Thomas.

8. Clark's and Cowan's MS. Diaries; conversations with Mrs. Thomas.

9. Diaries of Clark and Cowan; Bradford's *Notes on Kentucky*.

10. William Cradlebaugh was born in North Carolina in 1744; went to Boonesborough in 1776 and was there through all the troubles of 1777 and 1778; served

on Bowman's campaign of 1779, Clark's of 1780, and Logan's of 1786; and once went as an express to Kenhawa, swimming creeks and rivers and procuring his food by the way. He settled near Boonesborough in Madison County, Kentucky, received a pension, and died in 1833 at the advanced age of eighty-eight years.

11. Clark's and Cowan's MS. Diaries; Todd's MS. Narrative; MS. statements or notes of conversations with William Cradelbaugh, Joseph Kennedy, Capt. John Gass, Col. Nathan Boone, Daniel Bryan, Robert Hancock, Dr. G. W. Stoner, and Willis A. Bush; newspaper sketch of the late Col. Nathaniel Hart; McDonald's *Kenton;* and Bradford's *Notes on Kentucky.*

12. Clark's and Cowan's MS. Diaries; Todd's MS. Narrative; MS. Notes of conversations with Mrs. Elizabeth Thomas; Mann Butler's MS. notes of conversations with Gen. James Ray; Butler's *History of Kentucky.* An instance of the exaggerated character of the reports that reached Virginia of the troubles this spring in Kentucky is found in a MS. letter written by Rev. John Todd of Louisa County, Virginia, May 16th, 1777, to Col. William Preston: "We hear that a large body of Indians attacked the Kentucky people lately, to cut them off; and that seventy at least of our men were killed and missing, and one hundred Indians were left dead upon the field. If this be true, the balance will no doubt be cut off."

13. Cowan's MS. Diary and Todd's MS. Narrative, which fully agree, except that Cowan gives but eighty-one men fit for duty.

14. Levi Todd's and William Whitley's MS. Narrative; Boone's published Narrative.

15. Joseph Kennedy came to Kentucky from North Carolina in the spring of 1776 at the age of sixteen and made Boonesborough his home. Recovering from the wound he received on there on the 23rd of May, 1777, he returned to North Carolina in the fall of that year and served against the Tories. Coming again to Kentucky in the spring of 1779, he located himself at Logan's Fort and engaged first as a scout, and then went to Vincennes to join Colonel Clark in an intended expedition against Detroit. The next year, he served as an ensign on Clark's campaign against the Shawanoes and returned in the fall to North Carolina. At the foot of Cumberland Mountain, on his way to Kentucky, three of his party were killed by the Indians on the 26th of December, 1780, and he himself taken prisoner. He was conveyed to Augusta, in Georgia, and there delivered to the British but was liberated by Colonel Lee's capturing that post on the 5th of June, 1781. The ensuing winter again found him in Kentucky, where he was appointed a lieutenant and engaged in the ranging service; and was with Colonel Logan's men who buried the dead killed in the fatal Blue Lick defeat in August 1782; and in the autumn of that year served on Clark's campaign against the Shawanoes. Again, at the head of a company, he followed Clark on his Wabash expedition in 1786. He rose to the rank of major of militia. Among the many civil offices he filled, he served as a member from Madison County in the Convention of 1792 that formed the first constitution of Kentucky. He continued to reside in Madison County, greatly honored and respected, till his death November 30th, 1844, at the good old age of eighty-four years.

16. Clark, Cowan, and Todd Mss.; MS. Statements of Joseph Kennedy, William Cradlebaugh, Samuel Boone, Daniel Bryan, and Tobias R. Stoner; Boone's Narrative.

17. Clark and Cowan's Diaries; MS. notes of conversations with Moses and Josiah Boone and Mrs. Thomas.

18. Kennedy recovered from these grievous wounds. He came to Kentucky with Boone's company of road-markers in the spring of 1775; and ever [wi] his full share in the dangers and contests incident to the times and country. He was appointed one of the justices of the peace for Kentucky in 1777 and commanded a company on Clark's campaign against the Shawanoes in the summer of 1780; and soon after this service, he visited North Carolina, and returning to Kentucky, was killed with two of his companions at the foot of Cumberland Mountain December 24th, 1780, and his brother Joseph Kennedy at the same time taken prisoner by the Indians. Captain Kennedy was unmarried.

19. Harrison died of his wounds on the 13th of June ensuing.

20. Whitley's MS. Narrative; Clark and Cowan's MS. Diaries; MS. notes of conversations with the late Capt. Benjamin Briggs.

21. Whitley's MS. Narrative; Cowan's MS. Diary.

22. Clark and Cowan's MS. Diaries.

23. Clark and Cowan's MS. Diaries.

24. MS. letter of Isaac Shelby, June 20th, 1777, to Capt. Joseph Martin.

25. Clark's Diary; Marshall's *Kentucky;* MS. notes of conversations with the late Capt. Henry Wilson, one of Bowman's relief party; and MS. Virginia Archives.

26. Clark and Cowan's Diaries; Whitley's MS. Narrative; Marshall's *Kentucky;* Bradford's *Notes on Kentucky;* Littell's *Political Transactions in Kentucky.*

27. Clark and Cowan's Diaries; MS. Virginia Archives; Marshall's *Kentucky.*

28. Clark and Cowan's MS. Diaries; General Ray's and Daniel Bryan's MS. Narratives; and MS. notes of conversations with Moses and Isaiah Boone.

29. Clark's MS. Diary; MS. Statement of Daniel Bryan, who was one of Smith's company. It may with propriety be added that the Indians were not only frequently deceived in this way, but were fond of exaggerating their exploits, and sometimes relating pure fiction and palming them off for truthful narratives. Of this latter character the following may be considered, communicated in a letter from the Moravian missionary David Zeisberger, then residing among the Delawares on the Muskingum, dated September 23rd, 1777, and addressed to Gen. Edward Hand, commanding at Fort Pitt:

"Captain *White-Eyes* desired me to inform you, that it was reported that some Tawas and Chippewas had been to war and returned, who related that they had attacked a fort at Kentucky, where they fought awhile till a number were killed on both sides, when the white people hailed the Indians, and desired them to come nigh and speak with them, and told them that they were sorry to see the dead bodies of both parties lying there; but neither the Tawas and Chippewas nor the white people were the cause of it, but their father, the Governor over the lake, was the cause, and they should blame him for it. That after this, the white people invited them to the fort, treated them handsomely, and let them go in peace."— *MS. Hand Papers.*

30. Clark's Diary; Boone's Narrative; Bradford's *Notes on Kentucky.*

31. Clark's MS. Diary; MS. notes of conversations with Joseph Jackson and Capt. Benjamin Briggs, the former of Watkins' company and the latter of Logan's guards.

32. *MS. Hand Papers.*

33. MS. statement of Willis A. Bush, derived from Daniel Bryan.

34. MS. statement of Hon. David Todd; conversations with Col. Nathan Boone.

35. MS. Correspondence of Willis A. Bush and John R. Stoner. In the services and memory of that honest and fearless pioneer Michael Stoner, let us attempt to pay a slight tribute. We have already remarked that he was born of German parentage on the Schuylkill near Philadelphia in 1748, and his parents dying when he was four or five years old, he was early apprenticed to learn the trade of a saddler in Lancaster; and when about sixteen, from some cause or other, he left and wended his way to New River, in Virginia. Subsequently going to Fort Pitt, he joined Samuel Harrod in 1767 and explored the Illinois country, Kentucky, and Tennessee, when he returned to the south-western frontiers of Virginia. In 1773 we find him associated with Boone in his abortive effort to move to Kentucky; and in 1774 [Stoner] was selected for his intimate knowledge of the West to accompany Boone to Kentucky to notify the surveyors of the Indian war. And again the following spring he was among the pioneers and road-makers that followed the fortunes of Boone and laid the foundation of Boonesborough; and [he] was in 1775 and 1776 mostly employed as a hunter to supply that station with meat, and also made an improvement, and raised a crop of corn on Stoner's Fork of Licking.

In April 1777 he was wounded at Boonesborough, and the next month we find him taking an active part in the defense of that station against the Indians. He discharged and gave name to Stoner's Lick in the Cumberland country in 1780; and in 1781 he was connected with Pettit's Station in Kentucky. He served as a spy on Clark's campaign of 1782 and was again with Clark on his Wabash campaign of 1786, and once served on an expedition under Colonel Hardin. He loved hunting to the last and, in his old age, indulged this passion by taking a trip to Missouri, where he spent nearly two years hunting and trapping. On that jaunt he visited his old friend Daniel Boone and was finally induced, only by some finesse, to return home. He died in Wayne County, Kentucky, September 3rd, 1813, at the age of sixty-five years. He was a short, heavy-formed man of great powers and endurance. His companion in life, who was a daughter of Andrew Tribble and came to Kentucky at the age of fifteen in 1784, survived till 1852, when she died in Bath County, Kentucky. There are several descendants of these worthy pioneers who reside in Kentucky and rank among the most respectable citizens of that noble commonwealth.

EDITOR'S NOTES: CHAPTER 14

a. Rightly or wrongly, Hugh McGary is immortalized as the hothead who, on the morning of August 19, 1782, spied Indians above the banks of the Licking, wheeled his horse across the branch shouting, "All who are not cowards follow me!" and led Kentuckians straight into the jaws of death, igniting the Battle of Blue Licks. McGary and his wife had come to Kentucky the fall of 1775 by way of the Yadkin Valley of North Carolina. In 1777 he served as captain at Harrod's Town and established his own station at Shawnee Springs (Mercer County); in 1778–79 he fought alongside George Rogers Clark at Vincennes and Kaskaskia and was promoted to major of the militia by 1782; in 1787 he earned the rank of colonel. Despite his infamous reputation after Blue Licks, McGary was a courageous defender of Kentucky. He died in 1808 in Shawneetown, Illinois. See chapter 12, note c.

b. Humphrey Marshall (1760–1841), married to Mary Marshall, sister of U. S. chief justice John Marshall, came to Kentucky by way of Virginia in 1782. Well educated, well heeled, and a devout atheist who wielded a formidable pen, Marshall enjoyed a long but controversial political and legal career. In 1812 he wrote the seminal *History of Kentucky,* a near best-seller for its day and from which Draper quotes extensively. He is buried in Frankfort.

c. The terms stations and forts were used indiscriminately and often interchangeably, but actually the two differ. Frontier stations tended to be smaller, perhaps originating with several cabins and one blockhouse circled by a palisade, and identified by a family name, such as Boone's Station. Forts tended to be more spacious, better fortified and garrisoned, and more permanent.

d. A reference to the archaic term "widow's weeds"; a woman's wearing of black clothing to signify mourning for her deceased husband.

e. For too long, the role of frontier women has been overshadowed by the exploits of their trailblazing counterparts, a wrong today's historians are righting. Women drove oxen and cattle and tended the beasts, tilled the soil, harvested the fields, did the cooking and sewing, swept the dirt floors of their overcrowded one-room cabins, split kindling, lugged firewood and wooden noggins of water, tended the sick and wounded, birthed and nursed babies, defended their homes with gun and ax, and comforted children and the bereaved.

In times of war, in forts and stations, frontier women often stood at the log palisades with their men to shoot, loaded guns, cut and greased ticking patches, poured molten lead from hot ladles into bullet molds, wiped sweaty or bloody brows, carted off the wounded and dying, doled out dipper gourds of water, and donned hunting shirts and hats and breeches to fool Indians into thinking a fort was better manned than it really was.

Women did all these things and more to aid in frontier life, bringing with them to the border a sense of order and domesticity in an often unruly man's world. To his credit, Draper interviewed and gathered the recollections of many such women, Native American, Anglo-American, and African-American alike.

f. The Kickapoo (meaning unknown) were Algonquins of Indiana, Illinois, and Wisconsin whose nomadic travels took them as far as Texas and Mexico. The Kickapoo share many cultural and linguistic traits with the Shawnee, causing many anthropologists to speculate that these two tribes were once more closely related. According to Kickapoo oral tradition, the Shawnee and the Kickapoo were once one people, but an argument over a bear's foot caused a split. French Jesuits were the first to mention the group. During the era of colonialism and conquest, much of the Kickapoo nation was absorbed by the culturally similar Mascouten (Fox), which in turn, after the French Beaver Wars of the 1720s, sought protection through alliance with the Sauk.

g. Squire Boone, Jr. (1744–1815), was a woodsman's woodsman, an adventurous, hard-fighting Baptist preacher whose worthy exploits and many skills will forever remain in the shadows of those of his famous older brother. He took to his grave the deep scar left from this tomahawk gash, which cut into his skull. Of his epic *mano a mano* grapple at Cove Spring, Squire declared it was "the best little Indian fight he ever was in. Both men stood and fought so well."

h. Some frontier histories assert that Indians called Virginians Long Knives because of the swords some of the border militiamen carried into battle.

i. News of Gen. William Howe's (1729–1814) defeat at the hand of Gen. George Washington was not true. Several times between 1776 and 1777, Howe's forces hemmed in Washington's Continentals and could have crushed them, which might have led to a total British victory. But Howe, rather then risk his men, chose to let the Americans escape and ever afterward suffered blame for his actions.

j. Virginia militia captain Henry Pauling was a veteran of Lord Dunmore's War; his efforts in Kentucky supplemented those of Col. John Bowman.

k. Virginia militia captain John Montgomery was Colonel Montgomery by 1779, when he was with George Rogers Clark at the capitulation of Vincennes commanding a detachment. Montgomery made Kentucky his home after the war and turned market hunter. Indians killed him near Eddyville (Lyon County) on November 27, 1793.

l. Born in Scotland, Charles Gwatkin (1741–1806) filled numerous military offices in Bedford County, Virginia, during his lifetime, including justice of the peace (1777), lieutenant colonel of the militia (1778), sheriff (1788), militia colonel (1790), coroner (1792), and colonel of regulars (1793). Gwatkin married Mary Callaway, daughter of Col. Richard Callaway of Boonesborough.

m. Gen. Edward Hand (1742–1802), a Continental officer born in Ireland who studied medicine to pursue a medical career. On April 1, 1777, George Washington appointed him brigadier general and commandant of Fort Pitt. A good leader respected by his troops and Washington's trusted friend, Hand died of cholera at his home in Lancaster, Pennsylvania.

n. "Flavored" means that the correspondent's assistant drafted and corrected the original letter.

o. In hard times parched cornmeal might have been used in place of coffee, but it is doubtful if it was an "admirable substitute." On April 25, 1849, Gen. Robert Orr explained to Draper (DM 6NN:179ff) how to make the sustaining mix used by Indians and frontier whites alike: "When Indians go to war [they] prepare a mixture of parched corn pounded fine and mixed with sugar and sometimes chestnuts and beans. Each one will have a small bag of this mixture with a little dry venison—it is palatable and strengthening and is used very sparingly and lasts them a long time as they only use it when within our borders and afraid to shoot."

CHAPTER 15

January to June 20th, 1778.—Captivity of Daniel Boone and His Salt-
Boilers.—Death of Cornstalk.—Black Fish Seeks Revenge.—Boone's
Men and Their Capture.—Boone Travels to Detroit.—Sheltowee and
Shawanoe Life.—Escape of Andrew "Pe-cu-la" Johnson.—Pe-cu-la's
Revenge North of the Ohio River.—Escape of Boone and His Subsequent
Return to Boonesborough.—The Fate of Boone's Salt Boilers.—
The Coming Storm.

'Twas then in the hour of utmost need
He promised his courage, art and speed.
Now slowly stalked with stealthy pace,
Now started forth in rapid race,
Oft doubling back in mazy train,
To blind the trace the dews retain,
Now clombe the rocks projecting high,
To baffle the pursuers eye,
Now sought the stream, whose brawling sound
The echo of his footsteps drowned.—*Rokeby.*[1]

The early settlers of Kentucky had generally to accustom themselves to the use of food unsalted, as the article of salt could but very seldom be obtained and then only in small quantities.[a] As the government of Virginia had, upon Colonel Bowman's solicitation, with parental care and kindness, sent for the benefit of the Kentucky garrisons a number of pans or large kettles[b] suitable for making salt, and Captain Watkins' company of men were wintering at Boonesborough, it was thought advisable to undertake during the winter to manufacture salt at the Lower Blue Licks for the use of the several stations. It was a season of the year when the Indians generally remained quiet in their towns or were engaged in hunting. It was therefore agreed that Captain Boone should take the command of a party of men and repair to that place, work a month at salt-making, and then be relived by Captain Watkins with a similar party.

In accordance with this arrangement, Boone started for the Blue Licks about the 8th of January, 1778, with thirty men under his command, conveying on horses the necessary kettles for the operation. They camped on the southern bank of the Licking and made salt from the spring on the low ground on that side of the river, near the old ford and just above the bridge which spans the stream at that famous modern watering-place. So weak was the water that eight hundred and forty gallons were necessary to make a bushel of salt.[2] The first small sack of salt made was sent by Jesse Hodges to Boonesborough, as the people there had long been without any. While the salt-boilers were at work, two or three of the men were constantly employed in the double capacity of scouts and hunters,[c] Boone himself being generally one of the number. Thus the month during which Boone's party work[ed] before being relieved had nearly worn away and nothing remarkable happened. Jesse Hodges, with another man, was again despatched with some pack-loads of salt to Boonesborough, while Thomas Brooks and Flanders Callaway were out spying in one direction and Boone in another.[3] Having to make a circuit of several miles on these tours, Boone was in the habit of taking some beaver traps with him and, having found beaver sign pretty plenty on the Licking a few miles below the Lower Blue Licks, set his traps and gave them some attention.[4]

The Indians on the 1st of September preceding had made a warm attack on Wheeling, and on the 27th of that month a party of Wyandots had defeated Capt. William Foreman and a company of men at the Grave Creek Narrows. King Cornstalk of the Shawanoes used every effort to keep his people quiet, but Black Fish, the head war-chief with many of the nation, seemed determined to go upon the war-path. On a mission of peace, Cornstalk, his son, and two other noted men of the Shawanoes visited the fort at Point Pleasant and were there treacherously and brutally slain by some of the lawless soldiery on the 10th of November.[d] This roused the whole nation and was unquestionably the spring that set in motion a winter war-expedition against Boonesborough. They had been too severely beaten at Point Pleasant in 1774, and the fort there was now too strong and too well guarded to think of successfully wreaking their vengeance upon that garrison; and moreover, according to the law of Indian nations, it mattered not where the revenge was obtained, [just] so that it was meted out upon the heads of the hated race of pale faces. The weakest point, and where an attack would be least expected, would be the one selected against which to direct their operations. The British leaders at Detroit and their emissaries in the Indian towns, taking advantage of the outraged feelings of the Shawanoes for the cold blooded murder of their distinguished chieftain, encouraged the enterprise, and several of their retainers connected with the Indian department accompanied the expedition.

On Saturday morning, the 7th of February, Boone started out with his packhorse for a supply of meat. During the warm season, the buffaloes subsisted mainly on wild grass and visited the licks and salt springs in vast numbers to lick the dirt and drink the mineral waters; but in cold weather they seldom resorted there, confining themselves to the cane region for their winter range;[e] and at the period of which we speak, there was no cane of any consequence within five or six miles of the Lower Blue Licks, so it became necessary for Boone to take something of a wide circuit to find game. In the afternoon, when the sky was dark and snow had commenced falling, he was about ten miles below the Lower Blue Licks on [the] Licking. He had given his beaver traps the necessary attention and, having killed a fine buffalo, had packed the choicest of the meat upon his horse, fastening the load securely with strips of the green hide of the buffalo encircling the animal, and was wending his way back, leading his horse along the buffalo trail on the eastern bank of the river. Such loads of meat often consisted of three or four hundred pounds' weight.

Passing some narrows where the high land crowded in closely upon the river and where a large tree had fallen transversely on the buffalo road, with its top up the ridge, leaving barely room for the path between the root of the upturned tree and the stream, his horse evinced signs of fright soon after emerging from the narrow pass, when Boone, turning, discovered four Indians who had been concealed behind the fallen tree and had suffered him to go by, thinking probably to capture him more easily by approaching him from the rear and without exposing themselves to a shot from his rifle. His first thought was to throw off the load of meat, mount his horse, and escape, but the green buffalo tugs with which the load was fastened were frozen and could not be loosened; and then, instantly attempting to draw his knife from the scabbard to sever the tugs, he found it had been thrust into its sheath all bloody and had frozen fast, which, together with the handle being greasy, as were his hands also, entirely defeated his object.

This was all the work of a moment, and as the Indians were now close upon him, he had no alternative but tamely to surrender without making a further effort or betake himself to his heels. Though now in his forty-fourth year and less active than formerly, he did not hesitate. An animated chase commenced. One of the Indians remained behind, perhaps to take charge of their game; two of them aimed to out-flank him, while the third quickly stripped the horse and, mounting, followed rapidly on Boone's trail, which was easily pursued in the newly fallen snow, then one or two inches deep. His pursuers, who were probably active young warriors, proved to be fleet of foot, and in a race of something like a half a mile, they approached so near as to fire at him, some of the balls striking on either side of him and knocking up the snow; and when within eight or ten paces, they again fired, when a ball cut loose the strap of his powder-horn. These shots, Boone always thought, were not made with a view of killing, but only of intimidating and causing him to surrender. Finding himself getting exhausted and the Indians rapidly gaining upon him, he saw it was impossible to escape; so he dodged behind a tree and stood his gun against the tree so his pursuers could see it as a token of submission. The Indians now came up, whooping and laughing in great good humor in view of their success, shook him heartily by the hand, and took possession of his gun, knife, and ammunition.

Boone was soon made acquainted with the fact that there was a large Indian encampment near by, for which his captors were probably seeking supplies of meat, and thither they conveyed him. This encampment was on an old Indian war trace that crossed the Licking eight miles below the Lower Blue Licks and a few hundred yards north or north-east of the river. Boone was soon ushered into the presence of no less than one hundred and twenty new brothers—among whom were Laramie[f] and Baubee,[g] two Frenchmen in the employ of the British, and Pompey,[h] a Negro, who had long lived with the Indians and was well versed in their language. James and George Girty were likewise of the party, dressed and painted Indian style, but were apparently ashamed of their company and mission, as they did not for that, or some other reason, choose to reveal their renegade character.[i] The Indians had a long fire built upon the ground by which to warm and cook, though they had but little shelter from the inclemency of the season.

Mun-see-ka, the successor of Cornstalk as king of the Shawanoes, and *Cot-ta-wa-ma-go,* or Black Fish, were the commanders of the party, which, with the white and black exceptions mentioned, was composed exclusively of Shawa-

69. Simon Girty and brothers James and George, like Matthew Elliot and Alexander McKee, were white partisans who chose to "go Indian" and were uniquely valuable to their native allies, offering insights into Anglo culture, technology, and tactics. ILLUSTRATION BY H. DAVID WRIGHT.

noes.[5] The leading chiefs gathering around the new comer, the customary act of Indian politeness followed, namely, shaking hands, accompanied with the "How d' do, brodder?"[j] On these occasions only the chiefs and principal warriors take part, nor do the common warriors venture to speak at treaties without special permission, and then are often laughed at for their bold assurance. Among the last of the chiefs who approached and shook hands, Boone recognized his old captor of 1769 and frankly accosted him, *"How d' do, Captain Will?"* All appeared surprised at this, and none more so than Captain Will himself, who asked Boone where he had known him. "Don't you remember," enquired Boone, "taking two prisoners eight years ago on Kentucky river?—I am one of them." The Indian captain needed only half a hint to remind him of his wily captive who had so adroitly escaped from him, and seemed pleased to renew their old acquaintance and renewed the shaking of hands with increased cordiality. Those who had once given the prisoner this Indian greeting now followed Captain Will's example, as they too had previously known him. It was a most ludicrous scene of mock friendship and civility conducted with all apparent sincerity and gravity on the part of these stoics of the woods, and which Boone bore with all the grace and politeness of which he was a master.

This introduction once over, Black Fish, with Pompey as interpreter, freely related to Boone that he and his warriors were then on their march against Boonesborough, which was particularly the object of their expedition; and then, in the presence of the other leading chiefs, enquired what men those were at *Pe-me-mo Lick*—the general name in Shawanoe for salt springs but alluding, in this instance, aided by the proper gesticulations, to the Lower Blue Licks. Boone at first evaded a direct reply by asking how he knew there were any white men there. It was promptly replied that some of the Indian spies had been there and seen them. Boone then acknowledged that they were his men, when Black Fish said he was going to kill them. Boone's study now was how to divert the attention of the Indians from Boonesborough, as one side of the fort was not enclosed with palisades, and in the midst of winter the people there would not be on the watch, and consequently the place could in all probability be easily taken either by surprise or a vigorous attack; and in that case, even if the lives of all the women and children were spared, they would experience incalculable suffering in being compelled to march at that inclement season to the Indian towns, and once there they would have to suffer all the horrors of a prolonged Indian captivity. As there was snow upon the ground and the Indians were nearly five times the number of the salt-boilers, the latter, ignorant of their discovery, would find it quite impossible to escape, and their captive leader looked upon their case as hopeless.

Boone concluded that some finesse under the circumstances would be perfectly justifiable and, therefore, represented to Black Fish that he was very willing to go and live with his red brothers and take all his people there also; but his young men were nearly all at the Blue Licks making salt, and only the women and children, with some old men and a few warriors, were left in the fort at Boonesborough; that the fort was strong and could not be taken, and if it could the Indians very well knew that the weather was so cold and inhospitable the women and children would inevitably perish if then attempted to be removed to the Shawanoe towns. He then added that he would persuade his men to surrender themselves peacefully to the Indians as prisoners of war, provided Black Fish would promise them good treatment and an exemption from running the gauntlet;[k] and that when the weather became mild in the spring, the Indians could go against Boonesborough with an increased force and, by taking horses, easily and comfortably convey the women and children to their towns over the Ohio, Boone promising to accompany the expedition and prevail on his white friends to acquiesce in this measure. All this seemed perfectly fair to the unlettered Indian diplomats, and Black Fish and his chiefs fully agreed to the arrangement. Boone, however, was given to understand that should his salt-boilers refuse to give themselves up peacefully, his own life would be in jeopardy. He knew full well he had yet a difficult and trying service to perform, but it seemed necessary to meet it manfully, and he felt consoled with the reflection that if he succeeded, he should thus be instrumental in sparing the effusion of blood and warding off untold suffering and distress from the unsuspecting garrison and, in the end, best subserve the highest dictates of humanity.

On Sunday morning, the 8th of February, with the snow five or six inches deep, the Indians commenced their march for the Blue Licks. About noon they arrived within view, and when they had surrounded the place, they sent Boone ahead, followed at a short distance by a few of their number. The men for some days had not been making salt, in consequence of the spring being inundated by the swollen state of the river, and were encamped on the point on the southern bank of the river immediately adjoining the ford. When they discovered Boone on the river hill just south of them, they were lying about on their blankets, apparently sunning themselves and whiling away the time, and at first thought Captain Watkins was at hand with his relief party, for whose arrival they were anxiously looking; but the next moment, seeing Indians, they jumped to their feet, seized their arms, and were ready for battle. Boone soon came near enough to exclaim, *"Don't fire!—if you do, all will be massacred!"* He then briefly but forcibly explained to them his captivity, the strength and original destination of the Indians, that they were surrounded and escape was impossible, the nature of the capitulation he had made with the Indians, the promise of good treatment, the necessity of a ready compliance on the part of his friends, and closed by begging them not to resist but peacefully surrender themselves to the enemy.

Confiding in Boone as a father, the men promptly obeyed.[l] They found themselves in a circle and stacked their arms in the center when the Indians approached, formed a line around the whites, and ordered them to sit down. The number of prisoners, including Boone, was twenty-seven, the two scouts and two salt-packers being absent.[6] A council was held in which it was proposed to kill all the prisoners except Boone and compel him to lead them to Boonesborough and prevail on the people to accompany the Indians to their towns. After the engagement entered into with Boone, such a cruel and treacherous proposition seems scarcely possible; but it should be borne in mind that on this particular occasion, the Shawanoes were smarting under the unprovoked murder of their noble chief, Cornstalk, and his three companions by the whites at Point Pleasant and had in the midst of winter carried forward this expedition for the special purpose of seeking revenge—and revenge, in the Indian's moral code, is one of the most exacted of virtues. One Indian after another spoke, until about two hours were consumed, and the speakers were about equally divided on the question. Neither Baubee, Laramie, nor the Girtys spoke in the council, though the latter at least were believed to have cast their influence on the side of mercy. During the solemn deliberations, Pompey sat beside Boone, interpreting all that was said but in a voice so low that none of the other prisoners heard what he said. At length Boone was permitted to make the closing speech and spoke in substance as follows, as remembered by one who was present and heard it:[7]

"Brothers!—What I have promised you, I can much better fulfil in the spring than now. Then the weather will be warm, and the women and children can travel from Boonesborough to the Indian towns, and all live with you as one people. You have got all my young men; to kill them, as has been suggested, would displease the Great Spirit, and you could not then expect future success in hunting nor war. If you spare them, they will make you fine warriors, and excellent hunters to kill game for your squaws and children. These young men have done you no harm, they were engaged in a peaceful occupation, and unresistingly surrendered upon my assurance that such a course was the only safe one for them; and I consented to their capitulation, on the express condition that they should be made prisoners of war and treated well. I now appeal both to your honor and your humanity; spare them, and the Great Spirit will smile upon you."

Pompey interpreted these remarks sentence by sentence to the Indians. This was the first speech which Boone's fellow prisoners understood and which conveyed to them the first certain intelligence that the subject under deliberation was one of life or death to them; and under such circumstances, it is not strange that they caught with eager solicitude every word that dropped from their leader's lips and awaited with painful anxiety the result of the earnest, impassioned appeal made in their behalf. The vote was taken and announced, fifty-nine for sacrificing to sixty-one for sparing the prisoners—two majority in favor of mercy.[m] From the fact that Black Fish permitted Pompey to interpret to Boone the deliberations of the council and allowed Boone to make the closing speech, it is presumable that he and the leading chiefs were opposed to the bloody proposal, which seems to have been brought forward and urged by the younger and more hot-headed portion of the warriors; but Boone's energy and faithfulness defeated their murderous intentions. It was thought at the time by his fellow prisoners that but for Boone's influence, they all would have been massacred, Boonesborough taken, and its helpless inmates left at the cold mercy of the conquerors.

Within a few minutes after the decision of the council, preparations were made for marching; all the salt was wasted[n] by being scattered about, when the Indians picked up and adjusted their knapsacks and divided the plunder, consisting of kettles, guns, and axes, among the prisoners and themselves to carry. A large brass kettle was pointed out to Boone as his burthen, but he gave the Indian so ordering him to understand that he would have nothing to do with it. The Indian then, with an angry, intimidating look, thrust the kettle at him, when Boone gave him such a violent push as sent both the Indian and kettle whirling some distance from him. At this juncture, Black Fish stepped up and put an end to all further altercation and took Boone under his special care and protection.

The Indians marched a few miles that afternoon, proceeding down the Licking to the mouth of Johnson's Fork, which they crossed in a canoe they had used on their way out to the Blue Licks and probably reached their old encampment. They took up camp a little before night, and soon after, Boone's wary eye was attracted to several Indians who were clearing away the snow and making an unobstructed path of perhaps a hundred yards in length. Suspecting the object, Boone enquired its meaning of Pompey, who replied that it was for running the gauntlet. Taking Pompey with him, Boone went to Black Fish and gently chided him for not fulfilling his promise that the prisoners should be exempted from running the gauntlet. "O Captain Boone," replied the chief archly, "this is not intended for your *men,* but for *you;* by our agreement your men were exempted from this custom, but you made no such stipulation for yourself." Taken literally, this was too true to be denied, and Boone concluded to make the best of it. Black Fish gave him his choice whether to go through the ceremony there or at the Indian towns in the presence of the women and children. Boone said if he must run it, he would much prefer to do so there, where the ranks would be filled with *men* and *warriors.*

Running the gauntlet oftentimes resulted fatally, and particularly if the poor prisoner happened to evince a timid disposition or endeavored piteously to beg to be excused, as was frequently the case.[8] The two lines were formed five or six feet apart on either side of the path; and once at the end, the runner was safe. The Indians were variously armed with tomahawks, clubs, sticks, and switches, and Boone stripped to his breech-cloth, leggings, and moccasins. The race commenced, when the Indians made very violent gestures as if they would knock his brains out but, after all, really appeared to show him favor, for he received only a few slight strokes from the switches. But his own shrewd management had something to do with the result, for he purposely ran in a very zig-zag manner, first making a dash so close to one side of the line as to cause the Indians suddenly to give way, and then as unexpectedly to dart in the same way to the opposite side, giving but few of them an opportunity to inflict a blow. Seeing Boone in a fair way to pass the ordeal comparatively unscathed, one fellow nearly at the farther end of the line threw himself partly within the race-path, with a view the better to give the prisoner a home thrust, but Boone appeared not to observe this maneuver and, just before reaching him, bending his head forward and increasing his speed, struck the Indian full in the breast, prostrating him instantly and running over him unharmed. This incident gave the *coup de grace* to the exciting ceremony and caused a perfect shout of laughter along the lines at the poor Indian's expense, when all came up to shake hands with Boone and congratulate him on his success, complimenting him as a "vel-ly good so-jer"—and at the same time pointing to their discomfited fellow and denouncing him as a "squaw," with a degrading prefix intended to give increased force to the epithet.[o]

During that evening a council was held, when either Laramie or Baubee, probably at the instigation of the young warriors, proposed that inasmuch as the prisoners were to be spared and converted into Indians, their ears should be trimmed—that is, to slit the rim of the ear nearly its whole length, and when healed, to suspend ear-bobs from them and thus greatly elongate these partially detached rims.[p] The two Frenchmen got into quite an animated dispute about the matter, the one urging and the other as warmly opposing the measure; and finally they became so excited as to draw their swords on each other and were only prevented from bloodshed by the timely interference of Black Fish and other influential chiefs. As the ear-trimming proposition was now dropped, and the controversy respecting it had been carried on in the French language, Boone, upon inquiry, learned of Pompey the subject which had given so violent a discussion and which had so nearly involved the respective disputants in a bloody, if not fatal, affray.

When packing up for departure the next morning, an Indian who had been carrying one of the salt-kettles on his back ordered James Callaway to carry it, who flatly refused to do so. The Indian still insisting, and Callaway as obstinately declining the service, the former drew his tomahawk and raised it in the attitude of striking, when Callaway, nothing daunted, bent forward his head as if to receive the blow and at the same time taking off his hat and patting the crown of his head with his hand, saying, "Here, strike!—I would as lief lie here as go along; but I *won't* tote your kettle!" Seeing the resolute character of the man with whom he

70. An extraordinary example of detached earlobes stretched in copper ear ornaments are seen on this Shawnee. "Paytakootha, or Flying Clouds" by Charles Bird King, c. 1820, from McKenney and Hall's History of the Indian Tribes of North America (1836).

had to deal, and not wishing to lose the British bounty of one hundred dollars paid at Detroit for prisoners, while scalps commanded only half that sum, the Indian turned away with a dry smile, put up his tomahawk, and carried the kettle himself. Callaway did, however, so far yield to the wishes of his captors as to consent to carry a gun and auger for them, but under this specious concession a malicious spirit lurked, for he soon sought an occasion while trudging along beside a deep stream to stumble and fall, pitching the load as if by accident into the water, and thus relieved himself and the Indians of any further trouble on account of the gun and auger.

In the evening of the very day the Indians left the Blue Licks with their captives, Thomas Brooks and Flanders Callaway, the hunter-scouts, returned; and seeing the men and kettles were gone, they thought at first that the party, weary of waiting for Captain Watkins, had started for Boonesborough and kindled a fire to camp for the night. They soon happened to find an Indian bow and some arrows, and then discovered the wasted salt mingled with the snow, and a little further observation revealed a multitude of moccasin tracks, and too well did they now understand the sad misfortune which had befallen their companions. Hastening that very night towards Boonesborough, they met Captain Watkins and party encamped on their way to Blue Licks to take their turn at salt-making, but the sad tidings brought by the scouts induced all to return to the fort, where they arrived early the ensuing day bearing the melancholy intelligence which overwhelmed many a heart with deepest sorrow. The salt scheme was abandoned. Kenton, Haggin, and a few others anxious for their captured friends started for the Blue Licks, pursued the trail of the Indians to where they crossed the Ohio some distance above the mouth of the Licking, and then returned.

The Indians probably followed on the trail which crossed the Licking eight miles below the Lower Blue Licks, leading towards the Shawanoe towns on the Little Miami; and reaching the Ohio, they crossed in a large boat made of four buffalo hides with a rude frame-work fitted within and which carried about twenty persons.q This was their outward route, and this boat was there kept secreted for several years, ready for use whenever they had occasion to cross the Ohio on their way to war against the Kentuckians. When Indians journeyed in small parties, it was quite common for them to carry along a large dried or tanned deer or elk skin with holes plentifully inserted along the edge through which, with leather strings, to fasten it on to a hoop and use as a canoe in which to place their guns, budgets, and clothing and swim over streams pushing their frail vessel before them. The same skin also served the purpose of a blanket at night.

Boone informs us in his Narrative in a very general way that both whites and Indians, on this march to the Shawanoe towns which lasted ten days, experienced "an uncomfortable journey, in very severe weather," and that he and his companions "received as good treatment as prisoners could expect from savages." While this was any thing but such as was desirable, it was nevertheless quite as generous on the part of the Indians as their straitened circumstances would allow. Of nights the prisoners were made fast and closely watched at their dreary encampments;

the weather was cold and snowy, so much so that some of the Indians had their ears frozen; and worse than all, no game of any kind happened in their way. In consequence of the depth of the snow and the plunder the party had to carry, their progress was necessarily slow and tedious, which was greatly aggravated by the pinching of hunger. It is related that the Indians killed and ate their dogs. Then both whites and Indians subsisted for several days on slippery elm bark, the tendency of which was to relax the bowels, which effect was counteracted either by chewing the inner bark of the white oak, which, possessing a stringent quality, was denominated *oak-ooze,* or using a decoction made from the oozings of this bark, when, Boone used to say, he could travel with the best of them. At length, the Indians shot a deer and boiled its entrails to a jelly, of which they all drank, and it soon acted freely on their bowels. They gave some to Boone, but his stomach refused it. After repeated efforts, they forced him to swallow about half a pint, which he did with wry faces and disagreeable retchings, much to the amusement of the simple savages, who laughed heartily. After this medicine had well operated, the Indians told Boone that he might eat but that if he had done so before, it would have killed him. They then all fell to and soon made amends for their long fast.[9]

At length, on the eighteenth of February, the Indians arrived with their prisoners at Little Chillicothe on the Little Miami—so called in contradistinction to old Chillicothe on the Scioto. It was situated on the eastern bank of the river, immediately below the junction of Massie's Creek and about three miles north of the present town of Xenia, Ohio, and was then the chief town of the Shawanoes. Their arrival was warmly greeted by the entire population—scarcely, since the memorable defeat of Braddock, when Boone and his fellow prisoner, John Holley, escaped the general slaughter and captivity, had the Shawanoes at one time conducted so many prisoners to their towns. It was a memorable evening and was becomingly celebrated by a grand war dance—preceded by requiring the prisoners to run the gauntlet, notwithstanding the express stipulation to the contrary. Boone, we believe, was not again compelled to go through this ordeal. James Callaway, whose undisguised contempt of the Indians sought every occasion to give vent to his feelings, knocked two or three down a bank at the very commencement of the race, which so amazed and put the others off their guard that he passed through without injury. William Hancock was the last to pass the trial, the others having met with varied results, several having been severely whipped and cudgeled. When Hancock ran, an Indian had prepared himself by infringing upon the race-course to give him a heavy blow, which Hancock perceived in good time to avert as Boone had done on a similar occasion, by knocking the fellow down, to the great amusement of the Indians, squaws, and children. The next day, Ansel Goodman was brought in by two Indians who had not travelled as rapidly as the others, when he had to try his luck at the gauntlet; being expert on foot, he escaped unhurt.

Boone and sixteen of his companions were now adopted; among them are known the names of Joseph Jackson, Micajah Callaway, William Hancock, John Dunn, George Hendricks, Benjamin Kelly, Ansel Goodman, John Holley, Andrew Johnson, John Brown, and Richard Wade. Those chosen for this purpose were generally selected for their presumed good qualities and general adaptedness to their new position. It was Boone's good fortune to be adopted by Black Fish as his son and had conferred upon him the Indian name of *Shel-tow-ee,* or *Big Turtle,* when he was formally introduced to his Indian mother, two little sisters, and his new Indian home.[10] Such adoptions were regarded by the Indians with great affection, and no partiality was shown between their natural and adopted children when the latter had passed through the process of having had "all the white blood washed out" by a strong rubbing ablution.[r]

On the 10th day of March, ten[s] of the captives who had not been adopted started for Detroit, conducted by forty Indians, at the head of whom was Black Fish, who took along his newly adopted son, Boone. Of these ten, we know the names of eight, namely Samuel and William Brooks, Bartlett Searcy, Jesse Cofer, Nathaniel Bullock, William Tracy, Daniel Asbury, and James Callaway—the latter of whom the Indians seemed particularly anxious to take to Detroit and sell as a prisoner, as he possessed so intractable a temper.

71. *"Boone's Indian Toilette." Frontispiece in Cecil B. Hartley's* Life and Times of Daniel Boone: The Great Western Hunter and Pioneer *(1859).*

Accompanying the Indians was an old hag of a squaw, for whom her red friends appeared very solicitous to secure a companion—perhaps for the hundredth time; and on this trip, she was given successively to two of the prisoners, neither of whom could discover anything attractive about her or the least pleasure in carrying her luggage; and each, in turn, weary of the burthen, was beaten by the Indians and the squaw-wife bestowed upon another. Nathaniel Bullock was the last unlucky wight to receive this intended favor, who inwardly cursed his ill fortune in having an incubus in every way so undesirable fastened upon him. Having fallen some little distance behind while carrying her burthen, and in no very good humor, with his ungracious spouse hanging lovingly upon his arm, Bullock seized the occasion to trip her up and plunge her into an air-hole in the frozen stream over which they were passing and, giving her a push with his hand, thrust her completely under the ice.

After a while, when asked by the Indians about his squaw, he said she had stepped [to] one side—but did not add that she probably shuffled off this mortal coil by the operation. He feared the stake and faggot might be his portion, but little else was said about the squaw, the Indians probably thinking she had returned to their towns or tarried awhile by the way to pay her Wyandot, Delaware, Mingo, or Ottawa friends a visit. Arriving at Detroit on the 30th of March, Bullock got into difficulty with an Indian [and] knocked him down, when several others came to the relief of their fallen companion, seized Bullock, and carried him upon their shoulders around the camp, crying out *"So-jer!—So-jer!"* They were glad to sell him to a Frenchman residing there. The other captives were also sold, either to citizens of Detroit or delivered up to Governor Hamilton as prisoners, claiming their reward of one hundred dollars, which was generously paid in goods from the public store.

Speaking of this journey and visit to Detroit, Boone has left but this simple record: "During our travels, the Indians entertained me well; and their affection for me was so great, that they utterly refused to leave me there with the others, although the Governor offered them one hundred pounds sterling for me, on purpose to give me a parole to go home. Several English gentlemen there, being sensible of my adverse fortune, and touched with human sympathy, generously offered a friendly supply for my wants, which I refused, with many thanks for their kindness; adding, that I never expected it would be in my power to recompense such unmerited generosity."

Upon the first arrival of Black Fish and his party at Detroit, Governor Hamilton, learning the name and character of Boone as the principal prisoner, sent for the *loan* of him, wishing to take him in charge that night, obtain from him what intelligence he could, and safely return him the next morning. Boone appeared in the governor's room, when Boone answered that officer's inquiries concerning Kentucky in such a manner as made him more the wiser for the interview. Among other inquiries, Boone was asked if he had heard any thing of Burgoyne's army.[1] "Yes," replied Boone, "it was a well-known fact in Kentucky before I was taken, that Burgoyne and his whole army had surrendered to Gen. Gates." The governor then called to his private secretary, Jehu Hay, in an adjoining room, saying, "Hay, the report of Burgoyne's disaster is, I fear, too true; Capt. Boone says it was well known in Kentucky before he was taken." Turning to Boone, his excellency requested him not to mention it to the Indians, as it would do no good. "You are too late, Governor," he answered, "I have already told them of it." The governor then added that he would feel greatly obliged to him if he would endeavor to speak slightingly of the affair as if it were merely a vague report unworthy of credence and what he had said of it formerly was only intended as a joke.

On this occasion there is little doubt but [that] Boone used some duplicity with the governor as he had previously done with the Indians. Black Fish had doubtless related the details of the capture of Boone and his salt-makers and the arrangement with reference to the future surrender of Boonesborough. Boone is said to have adroitly exhibited to Hamilton his old commission of captain from Lord Dunmore, which he carried about his person, and promised to be friendly to the British cause; and furthermore, agreed to give up the people of Boonesborough to be conducted to Detroit and there live under British protection and jurisdiction. In this way he very much ingratiated himself into the governor's good graces, who made warmest endeavors to purchase him of Black Fish, offering nearly four and a half times the usual reward for prisoners, in order to send him home, probably by way of Niagara and Montreal, on parole. That he had adopted him as a son was a sufficiently weighty reason with Black Fish against the tempting offer; but a yet more powerful objection was that he wished him to accompany the intended Indian expedition against Boonesborough, there to be instrumental in effecting the peaceful surrender of the garrison, in accordance with the arrangement which he and Boone had made when the latter was first captured and in duress—as the renowned Santa Anna,[u] in later years when similarly circumstanced, acknowledged the independence of Texas.

72. *Great Lakes Indian woman, showing clubbed hair wrapped with either ribbon or gartering, seven strands of beads, white linen European trade shirt, and blue stroud skirt.*

Finding his efforts to redeem Boone unavailing, the governor gave him an order on the king's commissary, Captain McGregor, for a horse, saddle, bridle, and blanket, together with a supply of silver trinkets to use as currency among the Indians. These he accepted. He doubtless concluded that he was indebted to Governor Hamilton and the emissaries of King George for setting on the Indians who captured him and caused him indescribable sufferings of body and mind, though he took good care never to betray any such feelings; and consequently he deemed it but just to himself to avail himself of any articles from the British public stores that would tend to render his captivity less painful and distressing; while at the same time, he felt constrained to decline similar favors from individuals who would have expected some day to be reimbursed for all such advances to him. So Boone could truly say that he and his fellow captives "were treated by Governor Hamilton with great humanity"; policy dictated such a kind and conciliatory course toward Boone and his Kentuckians if they were ever to be won over to the British interest. It was but seldom, however, that an American prisoner ever joined the enemies of his country, however hard his fate or how seductive soever might have been the temptations held out to effect that object.

During Boone's sojourn at Detroit, he astonished the governor by making gun-powder, he having been shut up a portion of the time in a room with all the materials necessary for its manufacture. Finally, on the 10th of April, he took his leave of his fellow captives and started with Black Fish and party on their return to Chillicothe. Boone found his poney quite serviceable to him on his journey. They passed down the southern shore of the lake, up Huron River, and then fell upon the heads of Scioto and down that stream, visiting a number of Delaware, Mingo, and Shawanoe villages, notifying their warriors to assemble at Little Chillicothe at the specified time for the grand expedition against Boonesborough. Speaking of this circuitous return trip from Detroit, Boone says: "This was a long and fatiguing march, through an exceedingly fertile country, remarkable for fine springs and streams of water." Such a country could not well escape his keen observation, for he loved to feast his soul upon nature in all her beautiful varieties. On the 25th of April they returned to Chillicothe.[v]

While Black Fish was absent, an event occurred that gave him some concern. It was the escape of Andrew Johnson, one of the captive salt-makers. From his first captivity, Johnson had impressed the Indians with the belief that he was but little better than a fool. He would feign to be afraid to leave camp alone, and when set to practice at shooting, he would evince great shyness of the gun and ludicrously dodge at the flash and report, making awkward shots, widely missing the mark even when a large tree [was] near by. Though the Indians usually exercise great compassion toward a fool, they could not well help amusing themselves with Johnson; and being small in size, they gave him the name of *Pe-cu-la,* or *the Little Duck.* He was really an admirable woodsman and seized an early occasion to take French leave, which he effected without the least difficulty, as he was thought by the Indians to possess too little intellect to know enough to attempt an escape or, if attempted, to succeed in it and hence was not watched as were the other prisoners.

He soon re-appeared in Kentucky, the first man who escaped from Indian captivity, and gave information of the distance and locality of the towns of the Shawanoes and of some of the neighboring tribes. As all the stations had been almost entirely stripped of their horses by the stealthy Indians, and the weary hunters had to pack in the fruits of the chase upon their backs, a retaliatory expedition was set on foot with Johnson to act both as commander and pilot. In the month of May William Whitley and Nehemiah Pore went from Logan's Fort to Harrodsburg, where they were joined by Johnson, John Haggin, Samuel Pickings, and John Sovereins and started on their enterprise. Ten days before, the Indians had captured one Lee while fishing in the Salt River.ᵂ Near the Big Bone Lick, Johnson's party heard the report of guns and waylaid the path until dark, but no enemy appeared. They afterwards learned from Lee, when he returned from captivity, that it was the Indian party who had taken him that shot the guns and killed a buffalo and were detained in jerking the meat.

Supposing they had gone by some other route, our adventurers pushed on to the Ohio, which they crossed on rafts hastily constructed for the purpose, and about fourteen miles beyond the river, they discovered some Indian sign. Proceeding on, they came to a camp about three o'clock in the afternoon which the Indians had just left; and carefully pursuing, they came within hearing of them about an hour before sundown. Johnson and his five brave and persevering comrades now secreted themselves and that evening advanced cautiously and viewed the enemy's camp and found their number too strong to attack openly. It was then determined to postpone the attack till just before day and take them by surprise. But in the course of the night, the Indian dogs set up a furious baying at them, when an old Indian arose and set them on. This forced the whites to fire, killing two of the Indians and a dog, besides wounding two warriors. The Indians were twenty-five in number, but presuming from their boldness that their assailants were numerous, they fled, when the victorious Kentuckians secured seven good horses and returned safely home after an absence of fourteen days. When Boone got back to Kentucky, he reported the name of the old chief who encouraged on the dogs as *Long King* and also gave the number and loss of the Indians in this affair.

This routed Indian party under the Long King appear to have been Shawanoes. As soon as Black Fish heard of the disaster, he asked Boone who he thought it could possibly be that had done this bold act, as he and the Indians generally thought none of the Kentuckians knew the locality of the Shawanoe towns or geography of the Indian country. Boone replied, more to vex the old chief than really thinking it was so, that it was Pe-cu-la. "No," answered Black Fish, "it could not have been him, for he was a fool, and could never have reached Kentucky." "He was no fool," said Boone, "but a man of good sense, and a fine woodsman." "Then why," enquired Black Fish, "did you not tell me so before?" "Because," responded Boone, "you never asked me; and you were contented to use him for a laughing-stock." This little expedition, unimportant as it was, gave the Indians much real concern that the Kentuckians had learned the way to their towns; and it was, moreover, the first evidence to them that the captivity of the large party of salt-boilers was in a fair way to result as disastrously to the Indians as advantageously to the whites.

Black Fish and his tawny countrymen were speedily startled with another evidence of the enterprise of the Kentuckians. Early in June a party of Shawanoes stole several horses from Boonesborough, when Maj. William B. Smith, Capt.

David Gass, John Martin, Ephraim Drake, John Pleak, and thirteen others mounted on horseback started in pursuit; and reaching the Ohio at the present locality of Maysville, they found Indians crossing the stream and succeeded in killing one of their number. Returning in the evening along the old buffalo and Indian trace leading to the Lower Blue Licks, when four miles from the river where the town of Washington now stands, they discovered, by hearing a loud laugh, another Indian party encamped, consisting of about thirty warriors who proved to be the very marauders of whom they were in search. Smith's men fell back, tied their horses, and while one half remained there as a guard with directions to mush forward if they heard an attack, Smith with the others crept along nearly to the Indian encampment and placed themselves in the cane on either side of the buffalo road.

At length, one of the Indians, hearing a noise which he thought indicated the proximity of a fox, walked forward towards the whites, leisurely smoking his pipe, armed only with a bow and arrows. He was suffered to pass all the men except the last, Ephraim Drake, who knew if the Indian was permitted to advance any farther, he would discover the horses; when Drake shot him through the head, the Indian, uttering a dying yell and leaping up some distance, fell dead in the path upon his face. His companions at first raised a hearty laugh, thinking probably he had taken a gun and filled the fox of which he had gone in pursuit; but as if suspicious that all might not be right, they seized their guns and advanced, when several of the whites fired generally at random, except John Martin, who, within about five paces of an Indian, fired simultaneously with his foe, both being at the same time wounded. In the midst of this firing, the reserve, rushing up, aided in routing the savages. The wounded Indian dropped his gun and fled with the others, leaving a trail of blood, and Martin, though badly disabled in the left shoulder, picked up his adversary's gun before the smoke had left the touch-hole. This incident was long remembered among his pioneer associates as *Martin's Shawanoe duel.* Several horses were recovered from the Indians, and all their budgets fell into the hands of the victors. Martin was conveyed to Boonesborough, where his wounds were many times dressed by Jesse Hodges and in due time recovered.

Let us now return to Boone and see how he fared and how he employed himself during his captivity. "At Chillicothe," says he, "I spent my time as comfortably as I could expect; was adopted, according to their custom, into a family where I became a son, and had a great share in the affection of my new parents, brothers, sisters, and friends. I was exceedingly familiar and friendly with them, always appearing as cheerful and satisfied as possible, and they put great confidence in me. I often went a hunting with them, and frequently gained their applause for my activity at our shooting matches. I was careful not to exceed many of them in shooting; for no people are more envious than they in this sport. I could observe, in their countenance and gestures, the greatest expressions of joy when they exceeded me; and, when the reverse happened, of envy. The Shawanese king took great notice of me, and treated me with profound respect, and entire friendship, often entrusting me to hunt at my liberty. I frequently returned with the spoils of the woods, and as often presented some of what I had taken to him, expressive of my duty to my sovereign. My food and lodging was in common with them, not so good indeed as I could desire, but necessity made every thing acceptable."

In the spring, as the grass was getting up nicely, Boone asked permission of Black Fish to hopple and turn out his poney in the prairie. "Yes, after a little," replied the chief. In half an hour after, he came to Boone and told him he could go and turn out his horse. Boone went and soon discovered several Indians secreted in the old grass, dry weeds, and bushes with their guns, plainly enough placed there by Black Fish's orders to watch the prisoner and see if he evinced any disposition to run away. Boone, feigning not to see them, turned out his poney and went whistling back as unconcernedly as if nothing had happened. He was thus watched two or three times and, having inspired confidence in the Indians, was finally permitted to go at liberty.

When first allowed to go out hunting by himself, he was entrusted with but a single charge for his gun, lest, if too well supplied, he should be encouraged to run away; and this he was unusually careful not to shoot until he was perfectly confident of bringing down his game and return home with his load of meat, much to the satisfaction of Black Fish and his family. The next time he had two charges assigned him and so gradually increased, and he managed by light loads to save some of the powder and oftentimes recovered the ball shot away; and in this manner, he succeeded in secreting several charges of ammunition in one corner of his hunting shirt, still making bountiful returns of the spoils of the chase. In these hunting excursions, he viewed with pleasure the beautiful country for many miles around and looked forward to the day when, in the order of Providence, it would be dotted with the dwellings of the white man and temples would be reared for the worship of the Almighty. The Little Miami Valley yet presents to the eye of the lover of nature many a charming scene. Thus invested with freedom, Boone might much sooner have effected his escape than he did, but he deemed it wisest to delay until he could learn with more certainty the time for the departure of the expedition against Boonesborough.

The Indians had a custom of *borrowing* and using articles from each other without asking the owner's consent; and others, knowing to the fact, would not betray the transgressor. Missing his poney, Boone went to Black Fish with his loss, who simply replied that he was probably somewhere in the range and reckoned he would come back again. Boone knew full well his poney had been *borrowed* by some lawless fellow and only feared he might not be brought back in time to serve him in his premeditated escape. After three or four weeks, Black Fish came one day and notified Boone that his poney had returned. He was found to have been badly used, his back being very sore, but by good care and attention he was soon restored. Nothing was further said about this Indian borrowing.

On one occasion, Black Fish sent Boone to fell a tree and cut a series of small troughs along the surface, holding something like a quart each, in which to salt the horses. As he had been somewhat unaccustomed to using the ax, he blistered his hands by the operation and, exhibiting them to Black Fish, remarked feelingly: "See, you are making a slave of me; you don't treat me like a son, for men, warriors and hunters never should be made to perform such menial services; in Kentucky I had servants[x] to do such work." The old chief readily acknowledged the force of what he said and told him he need not work. Both Black Fish, who was then well nigh fifty years of age, and his kind hearted squaw became greatly attached to their new son; the readiness with which he adapted himself to his new position tended to endear him to them and frequently elicited their warm approval. They always addressed him with the affectionate title of son and in every thing proved that they truly regarded him as sustaining that relation to them.[y]

Whether the old couple had any sons does not clearly appear, though Boone speaks of his "brothers and sisters." They had two little girls, named *Pom-me-pe-sy* and *Pim-me-pe-sy,* the former, ill-tempered and hateful, some four or five years of age, while the latter, whom Boone used frequently to nurse, was perhaps about two years old and quite amiable.[z] With his silver trinket currency obtained at Detroit, he would purchase maple sugar and give [it to] the children, who would receive it smilingly, calling [it] in their native tongue *me-las-sa.* By way of illustrating Black Fish's kindness, as well as instancing an Indian's idea of politeness, Boone used to relate that many a time after Black Fish had sucked a lump of maple sugar awhile, he would take it from his mouth, sometimes presenting it to him and at times to his squaw or children.

An Indian's cabin exhibited but few evidences of taste or comfort.[aa] If it was so large in size as a dozen or fifteen feet square, the owner felicitated himself and family upon possessing so spacious a domicil constructed with a few dozen poles with the interstices but imperfectly filled. The most of the year it was well lined with strings of corn in the ear braided together by the husks and thickly suspended from wooden pins on every side and from the roof-poles overhead. The fire was built either in the center or against a rude stone back at one end of the cabin, the smoke finding egress through an aperture in the roof; and the inmates slept before the fire rolled up in skins or blankets or in rude beds made on poles fastened to one side of the cabin. A few wooden dishes, spoons, and brass or iron kettles comprised the culinary department, while meats, corn, beans, pumpkins, and hominy formed the daily fare—and these oftentimes all cooked together. Simple as was this mode of living, Boone could have borne it like a philosopher but for the filthy manner in which the cooking was done. He could not relish the housewifery of his Indian mother. She allowed her chickens to roost on the lubber-pole, as it is termed, from which the hooks are suspended on which to hang the pots over the fire; and Boone could not help thinking that such was not a very cleanly place to hang the dinner kettle.

Sometimes, to while away the time, Boone would go out into the field and voluntarily assist in planting or hoeing corn; observing which, Black Fish would remark: "My son, you need not work; your mother can easily raise corn enough for my family, and yours also when they come from Kentucky."[bb] The old chief would sometimes smooth over the fresh soil and carefully mark out the geography of the country, all apparently to instruct and entertain Boone; while the latter, in turn, took great pains to enlighten Black Fish in the principles of civilization and what great comforts would accrue to his people if they would more nearly conform to the mode of living among the whites, cultivating the soil more extensively, raising cattle and sheep, manufacturing cloth, and constructing more commodious and comfortable houses.[cc] Black Fish and many of his people seemed greatly interested in these teachings of Boone, which so strongly commended themselves to their good sense; but the Shawanoes had suffered themselves to be dragged into a war which had already deprived them of their noble old King Cornstalk and was soon to take from them their wise old chief, and by long years of hostilities, they were destined to become much weakened and debased.

On the first of June Black Fish with his squaw, with a party of Indians, went to the Salt Springs of Scioto to make salt, taking Boone along. These noted springs were located some twelve or fifteen miles south-east of the present town of Chillicothe, on Salt Creek, an eastern tributary of the Scioto.[11] The early western explorer Gist, who visited them in 1751, describes them as being situated not very far above the mouth of Salt Lick Creek, "on the south-side of which," says Gist's ancient journal, "is a very large salt lick; the streams which run into this lick are very salty, and, though clear, leave a bluish sediment: The Indians and traders make salt for their horses of this water, by boiling it; it has, at first, a bluish colour, and somewhat bitter taste, but upon being dissolved in fair water, and boiled the second time, it comes out to tolerably pure salt." The water was very weak, requiring from ten to fifteen gallons to make a pound of salt; and at the latter rate, eight hundred and forty gallons were necessary for a bushel of salt, being the same as at the Lower Blue Licks.

The route to the Salt Springs led them by Paint Creek, long known as Old Town, on the North Fork of Paint Creek and now the site of the village of Frankfort, eleven miles north-west of Chillicothe. Here lived a white man named Jimmy Rogers, who had become domesticated with the Indians, who got Boone to exercise his skill in stocking a gun for him.[12] He took it with him to the Salt Springs, and while there engaged upon it, with the Indians from curiosity crowding around him, he would pretend to be so much absorbed in his work that in dodging about with his gun-stock in hand, he would manage to knock the Indians about at a lively rate without ever once himself seeming to notice it, greatly to the amusement of the fortunate few who escaped the raps and thumps so prevalent all around them. Boone accomplished this piece of mechanism in a plain, substantial manner. The salt-making operation lasted ten days. "During this day," says Boone, "I hunted some for them, and found the land, for a great extent about this river, to exceed the soil of Kentucky, if possible, and remarkably well watered."

While yet at the Salt Springs, a large Indian army arrived there, composed mainly of Wyandots and Mingoes with a few Shawanoes, under the command of Half King of the Wyandots, now on their return from an unsuccessful expedition against Fort Randolph at Point Pleasant and Donnelly's Fort on the Greenbrier, from which latter place they had been repulsed with considerable loss on the 29th of May. A portion of these warriors, intending to join the grand expedition against Boonesborough, hastened the return of the Indian salt-boilers. Again reaching Paint Creek Town, and the gun Boone had stocked for Rogers giving so much satisfaction, he was there importuned to stock a lock and barrel for an Indian who had obtained them from a captured boat of unfortunate white adventurers descending the Ohio who had broken two of their guns in a vain effort at defense. Boone consented to stock this gun also in consideration of a few charges of ammunition and a flint, ostensibly to try it when completed, but really to hoard away for his intended escape, promising to have it in readiness for the owner when he should shortly march to Chillicothe at the rendezvous of the Boonesborough expedition, with the assurance that it should carry a ball one hundred yards and place it within the circle of a dollar.

As they reached an old Sugar Camp at the head of Gladys Run, three miles south of Chillicothe and a mile and a half south-west of the present town of Xenia, the Indians scared up a flock of wild turkies, and after chasing them about three quarters of a mile, they flew into trees.[13] While busily engaged in shooting them, and out of sight of Boone, the squaws, and children, who had under their charge the horses packed with salt and kettles, Boone concluded that as the grand army was then assembling to march against Boonesborough, he would have no better opportunity to escape to Kentucky; so calmly drawing his knife, he cut the lash-ropes and tumbled the brass kettles from his poney. His Indian mother, alarmed at these demonstrations, asked him, "My son, what are you going to do?" "Well, mother," he replied calmly, "I am going home; I must go and see my squaw and children, and in a moon and a half I will bring them out here to live with you." "You must not go," she said, "for your father, Black Fish, will be angry and will catch and bring you back; besides, if you could get away, you have no gun nor ammunition, and would perish." Boone then said that the Indians couldn't catch him and reminded her of his gun-barrel and lock and gave her to understand that he had a flint, some balls, and powder; and then bidding them farewell and mounting his poney, he laid on the whip, leaving the squaws raising an intermingled cry and yell, to give the alarm to the Indians, which served as an additional impetus to Boone to urge his poney forward at his very best speed. He was soon beyond the hearing of the squaws or the reach of pursuers. The Indians followed the trail some distance but soon returned, saying he would get lost. But when Jimmy Rogers heard of his escape, he said he was sure Boone would go to Boonesborough "as straight as a leather thong."

It was near night, on Tuesday the 16th of June, when Boone took leave of his Indian mother and her attendants. He rode hard that evening and kept on, slackening his pace somewhat all night and till about ten o'clock the next day, when his poney gave out. He had stopped only a few moments when the poor creature's legs became so stiffened he could scarcely move them. Taking off the saddle, bridle, and horse-blanket, Boone hung them up in a tree the better to preserve them from the weather, thinking they might be discovered and prove serviceable to some one. He now pushed ahead on foot, frequently breaking his trail by running upon trees fallen transversely across his route in order to thwart his Indian friends should they attempt to follow him. He reached the Ohio before the close of that day, and in the bottom, close to the river, he found a dry poplar sapling nearly rotted off at the ground and leaning against a large tree; this he succeeded in pushing down, which fortunately broke into three pieces of about equal [size]. Fastening them together with grape vines, he soon had a raft on which he placed his gun barrel, lock, and clothing, [and] he swam the stream, pushing his little craft before him.

His clothing readjusted, he now thought himself safe from re-capture but pressed forward till evening, when, wearied as he was, he thought he might venture to take some rest; so taking off his moccasins and spreading his blanket upon the ground with the tree-tops to shield him from the night dews, he soon fell into a profound sleep, from which he was suddenly awakened by something seizing one of his toes. The first thought was that he was again in the hands of the Indians, but jumping to his feet, he judged it was a wolf or fox by the noise it made in scampering away. He then completed his night's repose without further disturbance. His feet getting *scalded,*[dd] in frontier parlance, by heat in walking, he peeled some oak bark, jammed it into an ooze with which he rubbed his feet, and renewed his journey. He concluded to stock his gun. Finding a sour-wood sapling of the proper size, with a natural crook for the breech, he cut it down with his knife and made a groove in which he placed the barrel and fitted on the lock, fastening both firmly in their places with the strings he had used in *hoppusing*[ee] on his blanket to his back.[14] Putting in his flint and trying his gun he found it made an excellent fire. On the 19th he passed the Forks of Johnson Creek.[15]

Owing to the soreness of his feet, he did not make so good progress as he wished and killed nothing till he had passed the Blue Licks, when he brought down a buffalo with his new gun, struck fire, cooked and ate a delicious meal, and reserved the buffalo tongue to carry and present to his son Daniel,[ff] then ten years of age, whom he hoped, with the rest of his family, soon to greet at Boonesborough. Speaking of his gun and the circumstances under which he had fitted it for use, he often remarked afterwards: "You may depend upon it, I felt proud of my rifle; it had the very best lock I ever had in my life."[gg] He safely reached Boonesborough on Saturday, the 20th of June, having performed a journey, as he estimated the distance of hundred and sixty miles, in less than four days—"during which," he adds, "I had but one meal."

But where was his wife and why did she not rush to see him? "Bless your soul," said his old companions as they hailed him like one risen from the dead and shook his hand till it fairly tingled, "She put in to the settlements long ago; she thought you was dead, Daniel, and packed up and was off to the old man's in Carolina." We may safely conclude that he was sadly disappointed to find all his family gone to the Yadkin, except his daughter Jemima, who had been married to Flanders Callaway not long before his captivity; and going to his old cabin, the old family cat that had not been seen there since the departure of Mrs. Boone and the children now re-appeared and, evidently recognizing him, jumped fondly into her old master's lap.

Though he had undergone many sufferings and privations during his four and a half months' captivity and now found his family gone to Carolina, he was yet not without the inward satisfaction of having rendered some useful services to his country. Upon a public mission for providing salt for all the Kentucky garrisons, he had fallen into the enemy's hands, and though compelled to surrender his fellow salt makers as prisoners of war, he proved himself so successful a diplomatist as to induce Black Fish with his army, though specially destined against Boonesborough, to relinquish the enterprise and return to their towns. Had the Indians, after making Boone and his twenty-six companions prisoners, instead of returning home with their captives, continued on to their original destination, they might have either taken Boonesborough in its then unprepared condition by surprise or, threatening to burn their captives in view of the fort, compelled the surrender of the garrison to save their dearest friends from a fate so horrid. And acting progressively on this plan, it is highly probable that similar success would have attended them at Logan's Fort and Harrodsburg. But to Boone's happy address must be ascribed under God the salvation of the Kentucky settlements. Nor should it be forgotten that the most of Boone's men returned in due time and served as pilots to expeditions against the Indian towns north of the Ohio. "Never," Boone used to say, "did the Indians pursue so disastrous a policy, as when they captured me and my salt-boilers, and learned us, what we did not know before, the way to their towns, and the geography of their country; for though at first our captivity was considered a great calamity to Kentucky, it resulted in the most signal benefits to the country." So what is designed for evil, a wise Providence often over-rules for the good[hh] of the weak and the oppressed.[16]

The varied fortunes attending Boone's fellow prisoners shall now be briefly noticed. William Hancock, who had been adopted by Captain Will, was the next after Boone to effect his escape. He was a poor woodsman[ii] and greatly discontented with the savage life he led; and used afterwards to say that he could not understand how Boone could go whistling about apparently so contented among a parcel of dirty Indians, when he (Hancock) was constantly melancholy. Recovering from a severe spell of sickness, and learning from Captain Will that the Indians were soon to march against Boonesborough, he resolved at all hazards to attempt his escape. He procured three pints of raw corn, and one night early in July, when his Indian mother was absent, he sought an opportunity to run away, but Captain Will, from some cause, suspected his prisoner's intention and sat up and watched him all night. Just before day he called out "Wil-lum," when Hancock, feigning sleep, did not answer. The old chief then said "Wil-lum" was asleep and he too would take some rest; so saying, he laid himself upon the floor, placing his head against the door to prevent its being opened without his knowledge.

When Captain Will fell asleep, Hancock, taking his corn, cautiously opened the door sufficiently to crawl out without wakening the sleeping sentinel and started in an almost naked condition, as his clothing was purposely hid from him to prevent his running away. Proceeding but a short distance, he fell over a tug which fastened a horse to a tree, and mounting the horse, he rode nearly to the Ohio, when the animal gave out. Upon a couple of logs tied together with grape vines, he attempted to cross the Ohio, but the river was quite swollen, his raft got entangled in some drift-wood and was carried down the stream, he supposed, twenty miles before he reached the southern shore. There were several successive days of cloudy weather, and not having sun, moon, or stars for his guide, he made but slow progress, and his scanty supply of corn became exhausted. At length he gave himself up to despair as not only lost but nearly starved and nature well nigh exhausted, when he lay himself down to die; he fell asleep for the last time, he thought, but soon awoke somewhat refreshed and happened to observe a tree within view with some marks upon it and upon examination there found the name of his brother, Stephen Hancock, plainly cut in the bark and the remains of a fire nearby where they had both camped when out hunting several months before. He instantly recognized the spot as only four miles from Boonesborough north of the Kentucky, and with renewed energy, he soon reached the river opposite the fort, where, hailing the garrison, his voice was known, and all went out to meet him. He was nine days performing his toilsome journey and was so exhausted that Captain Boone, Colonel Callaway, and Stephen Hancock nursed him three days, when he began to mend and rapidly recovered.[17]

While the Indians were absent on their expedition against Boonesborough, in September 1778 Ansel Goodman, George Hendricks, and quite a youthful fellow prisoner[jj] attempted to run away to Kentucky but unfortunately met the Indian army returning, when the young man was killed, Hendricks retaken by some Wyandotts, Goodman from his fleetness escaping his pursuers. Hendricks, after a while, was sold at Detroit and, finally, it is believed that he as well as Goodman safely reached Kentucky. Jack Dunn also ran away, but destitute of good principles, he subsequently deserted from an army of Kentuckians and gave the Indians notice of their approach, and nothing definite is further known of him. Such a deserter from Clark's army in 1780 reporting to the Indians that Colonel Logan's regiment only was approaching, and when they subsequently had to encounter three times as many after all the Kentuckians had united, they burned the white deserter under the impression that he had deceived them, and this may have been Jack Dunn. A renegade left Colonel Logan's men on his Indian expedition of 1786 against the Mackacheck towns[kk]

James Callaway, having been purchased from the Indians by Governor Hamilton, remained in Detroit without having much to do except to attend roll-calling every Sunday morning, until sometime in November 1778, when he was employed by a resident merchant to go on service for him some distance from the place; but when ready to depart, he was required to take the oath of fidelity to the king, which he peremptorily refused. He was at once thrown into prison. About the same time, Samuel Brooks and some fellow prisoner, starting from the Detroit region, attempted to return to Kentucky. While descending the Detroit River in a canoe and groping along a thick fog, they found themselves, when the fog cleared away, close to an Indian village on the bank of the stream and were retaken. They were made to run the gauntlet, in which the squaws and youths are frequently more unmerciful than the warriors; both passed through a severe ordeal, and Brooks, particularly, when struck would stop and pay his tormentor in kind and during the race got his arm broken. They were sent back to Detroit and put in confinement in the same apartment with James Callaway, where, from Brooks' loud speaking, as Callaway was hard of hearing, they were detected in planning an attempt to escape, at the time when Governor Hamilton was about starting on an expedition against Vincennes, and fearing they might escape and give intelligence of [*wm*] William Brooks first to Niagara, then Buck Island, and finally, some other prisoners were sent to Quebec and confined till near the close of the war, when Brooks returned to Kentucky.[18] Callaway, after being confined about two years in Quebec, was sent to St. Paul's Bay[ll] in the fall of 1780 and kept there as a prisoner for twelve months, and sent thence by sea to New York and up the Hudson to Dobb's Ferry, and there exchanged, and went immediately to Bedford County, Virginia, where he arrived on the 24th of December, 1781.[19] Samuel Brooks, probably from his broken arm, was unable to be sent off and died in prison. Boone gave it as his opinion that Brooks would have recovered but for irascible temper constantly getting him embroiled in difficulties.

Jesse Cofer and Nathaniel Bullock ran away from Detroit in company with Simon Kenton in June 1779 and safely reached Kentucky by way of the Wabash.[20] Kenton had been over the Ohio on a foray of horse-stealing in the autumn of 1778 and [was] captured by the Indians and narrowly escaped the stake.[mm] Richard Wade had a severe spell of seven weeks' sickness, his fellow prisoner John Brown taking care of him; and when he recovered, they both ran away from the Indians in the night and pursued this plan until beyond danger of recapture. Wade settled first in Madison, and then in Wayne County, Kentucky, and with him Brown, who was unmarried, made his home as long as he lived. United in captivity and escape, they never separated afterwards.

Benjamin Kelley was adopted into the same family in which young Tecumseh was raised, and in the fall of 1782, when the British and Indians marched to attack Wheeling, Colonel McKee having given him a horse, saddle, and bridle, he accompanied the expedition, determined to seize that opportunity to escape. Reaching Wheeling, Kelley, with a fellow prisoner also along, both painted and dressed in Indian style, left the Indian camp in the night and attempted to crawl to the fort gate and beg admittance but were fired upon and driven back, when they professed to have been making demonstrations against the garrison, which pleased the Indians. One of the white British leaders had hinted to Kelley the direction of the nearest white settlements, and he and his companion again started and, after meeting various adventures, finally reached a frontier station, rested a few days, and went on to Virginia. Returning to Kentucky, Kelley [became] a Baptist minister and died at a good old age in Ohio County in that state.

John Holley, who had served on Braddock's campaign, remained in captivity till Clark's Shawanoe campaign in the fall of 1782,[nn] when he escaped, joined the whites, and returned to Kentucky. We are ignorant of the fate of William Tracy and Daniel Asbury; Bartlett Searcy escaped and safely reached Harrodsburg and eventually settled, it is believed, in the Cumberland country. Joseph Jackson continued to live with the Indians till 1799, when, on a trading visit to Detroit, he heard of his brother living in Kentucky and went to see him. After awhile he became downcast and said the Indians had ruined him and he must go back and get some satisfaction. He returned the next spring with fur enough to purchase a well improved farm in Bourbon County and two Negro men, married well, and became a good citizen.[21] Micajah Callaway was kept five years and five months in captivity, moving from place to place with his tribe, when, in July 1783, going to the Falls of the Ohio with a party to effect an exchange of prisoners, he was released by the execution of General Clark in his behalf.[22]

DRAPER'S NOTES: CHAPTER 15

1. TFB: *This poem, transcribed by Draper, and the note, "Boone's Escape from Chillicothe—or near there—July, 1778," precede chapter 15.*

2. This statement of the strength of the water is made upon the respectable authority of Joseph Ficklin, who was a youthful defender of Bryan's Station when attacked in 1782. Forty gallons of water at Onondaga were formerly required for a bushel, but by sinking their wells deeper, stronger water was obtained and thirty gallons was sufficient, and from sixty to ninety gallons as required at the Kenhawa salines.

3. Jesse Hodges was born in Goochland County, Virginia, in November 1760 and came to Kentucky in Captain Watkins' company in the fall of 1777. He was in the big siege of Boonesborough in September 1778 and served on Bowman's expedition in 1779 and on Clark's of 1780 and 1782, and was for many years engaged in the defense of the country. He enjoyed a pension and died in Madison County, Kentucky, in 1838, leaving behind him the fragrance of a good name.

Thomas Brooks, as well as his brothers Samuel and William, was born on the Appomattox River in Virginia and migrated to Kentucky as early as 1777, and was that year engaged in the spy service. He doubtless bore his full share in the Indian fights and campaigns of that day. Having married at Boonesborough Sarah, daughter of Thomas Boone, a cousin of Daniel Boone, he early settled on the bank of the Ohio a mile above Limestone, now Maysville, where he died in the spring of 1800, leaving several children. He lived freely and [though] with many faults, he [also] had virtues. In height he was about five feet, seven inches, with a stout muscular form, dark hair and eyes, and weighed well nigh two hundred pounds.

4. Flint, copied into Uncle Philip's (Dr. Hawkins') *Life of Boone,* introduces as an imaginary exploit of Boone meeting two Indians drawing their [*wi*], then shooting one and knifing the other, as represented by Causici in sculpture in the rotunda of the capitol at Washington.

TFB: *Iconographic "Booneiana" forever crops up in story, song, and film. Mythic Boone images also appear in sculpture. In 1826 Jacksonian Democrats commissioned artist Enrico Causici to sculpt* The Conflict between Daniel Boone and the Indians *for display in the capitol rotunda to symbolize the nation's aggression toward Indians and its Manifest Destiny land dealings. It is a bizarre, awkward-looking thing—a derrick-size Romanesque fellow wearing a Trojanlike helmet straddling a dead Indian and stabbing another. Whatever its artistic merit, Causici, as Draper observes, based his work on a woodcut featured in Timothy Flint's* Biographical Memoir of Daniel Boone. *On page 5 of* Life of Daniel Boone, the Pioneer of Kentucky *(1847), Rev. John M. Peck disputes the mythic Indian-killing image of Boone. Causici's sculpture, Peck declares, "represents a brawny white man in deadly conflict with two Indians. One lies at his feet in the agonies of death; the other, with uplifted tomahawk, is about to give the final stroke, when he is paralyzed by the hunter's knife. This was intended to represent an incident in the life of Boone, but unfortunately, it is wholly fictious."*

Peck is correct. But that the image is "wholly fictious" meant little to the band of Kentuckians who in 1845 went to Missouri to exhume Daniel and Rebecca Boone's remains for reinterment in Frankfort; in the 1860s cemetery officials commissioned a sculptor to rerender Causici's mythic "Boone as Indian slayer" image for one of the four bas-relief side panels inset in the fifteen-foot monument they erected on the Boones' new grave. Thus, Boone's grave marker symbolizes the old hunter as a heroic Indian fighter, an image he despised. For the definitive treatise on such iconographic myth making, see J. Gray Sweeney, The Columbus of the Woods: Daniel Boone and the Typology of Manifest Destiny *(St. Louis: Washington University Gallery of Art, 1992).*

5. Mun-see-ka appears to have been the same as Nim-wha—change of names in Indian nomenclature being of very frequent occurrence. The former name was the one known to Joseph Jackson, one of the captured salt-boilers, who lived many years among the Shawanoes; and the latter is the one frequently mentioned in the MS. Papers of Col. Daniel Brodhead, long the American commandant at Pittsburgh. Nim-wha figured in the old French and Indian War, took part in the treaty of Fort Pitt in 1768, and doubtless fought with his people at Point Pleasant in 1774; succeeded Cornstalk as king of the Shawanoes, headed his warriors at the capture of Boone and his salt-boilers, marched against Fort Laurens and besieged it some time in 1770, and died early in 1780. Moluntha was his successor.

6. We can give the names of twenty of them, derived from Joseph Jackson, one of the number, Col. Nathan Boone, Capt. John Gass, and Robert Hancock: Daniel Boone, Joseph Jackson, William Hancock, George Hendricks, Benjamin Kelly, Nathaniel Bullock, John Holley, James Callaway, Micajah Callaway, Daniel Asbury, William Tracey, Ansel Goodman, Jesse Cofer, William Brooks,

Samuel Brooks, John Dunn, Bartlett Searcy, Andrew Johnson, John Brown, and Richard Wade.

7. Joseph Jackson, who related it to one of the authors in April 1844, then in his eighty-ninth year.

8. Heckewelder furnishes us an instance which had nearly proved fatal, which he witnessed at Lower Sandusky in April 1782. Three prisoners were brought in, two of whom ran the gauntlet and escaped unhurt. But woe to the coward who hesitates or shows any symptoms of fear! He is treated without much mercy and is happy, at last, if he escapes with his life. Such was the character of the third, who, frightened at seeing so many men, women, and children with weapons in their hands ready to strike him, kept begging the Indian captain to spare his life, saying he was a mason and would build him a fine, large, stone house or do any work for him that he should please. "Run for your life," cried the chief to him, "and don't talk now of building houses!" But the poor fellow still insisted, begging and praying the captain for an exemption, but the chief finding his exhortations vain, fearing the consequences, turned away, refusing longer to hear him. Our mason now began to run but received many a hard blow, one of which nearly brought him to the ground, which, if he had fallen, would at once have decided his fate. He, however, reached the goal, not without being badly bruised, and he was, besides, bitterly reproached and scoffed at all around as a vile coward, while the others were hailed as brave men and received tokens of universal appreciation.

9. This statement of the use and effect of the deer entrails was related by Boone to Joseph Wood, a venerable pioneer of Marietta, Ohio, who furnished it to Henry Howe for his work on Ohio. Col. Nathan Boone adds that the Indians have what they term *black drink*, a soup made of herbs, of which they drink freely when they have overloaded their stomachs at a dog-feast, when they have striven to out-eat each other and find it necessary to disgorge the unnatural quantity.

TFB: *Black drink was made by southeastern Indians by drying, roasting, and then boiling the prepared, crushed leaves of the yaupon holly* (Ilex vomitoria) *in water. The resulting dark brown tea was strained before drinking. Black drink contains a large amount of caffeine and was drunk for pleasure or for "spiritual purification," was used as a diuretic, and sometimes was quaffed in large quantities as an emetic. Tribal custom permitted only older men to drink the brew, never young boys or women.*

10. So named, perhaps, with reference to his strong, compactly built appearance.

11. Chillicothe, the flourishing seat of justice of Ross County, Ohio, is here alluded to, which does not occupy the site of any old Indian town. Old Chillicothe was located on the western bank of the Scioto, just above the mouth of Lick Run, where Westfall, in Pickaway County, is now situated. Removing to the Little Miami, the Shawanoes founded New, Big or Little Chillicothe, or Old Chillicothe, as Boone calls it, just below the mouth of Massie's Creek; and when this was burned by the Kentuckians in 1780, they located another town of that name

on the western bank of the Big Miami, from which, two years later, they were driven away by the Kentuckians, when they [the Shawanoes] established another bearing their favorite name on the Maumee. The name Chillicothe means, as the aged Shawanoe chief Black Hawk related to Joseph Ficklin, *Fire that won't go out*—hence, the town of the sacred council fire.

12. Rogers, a few years after, removed with a portion of the Shawanoes to Missouri, had an Indian wife, and raised a family of children, some of whom were educated.

13. Boone, many years after, suggested to a friend the location of land at that spot, as it was very beautiful, and said it was three miles from Chillicothe, describing its locality at the head of a run. It was located accordingly and found, upon measurement, to be three miles and twenty poles from Chillicothe.—Notes of conversations with the late Maj. James Galloway of [*wi*].

14. An Indian word in quite common use among the frontier men of that day, simply meaning to fasten in knap-sack style one's budget to his shoulders.

15. MS. Deposition of Daniel Boone in the Mason County Records.

16. TFB: *Draper's paraphrase of Genesis 50:20.*

17. William Hancock was born in Goochland County, Virginia, in 1738, and served on Colonel Byrd's Cherokee expedition near the close of the old French and Indian War, and first visited Kentucky in 1775. Returning to Virginia in the fall of that year, he removed to Boonesborough early in 1777 and took part in the contests there that season with the Indians. Escaping from his captivity, he shared in the long siege of Boonesborough in September 1778 and served on Clark's campaigns of 1780 and 1782, and in the battle of Blue Licks. After the Indian wars, he settled out on a farm in Madison County in Kentucky till 1797 [1799?], when he removed to Missouri, and died in St. Charles County in that state in 1821, in the eighty-third year of his age. He was a man of medium height, about five feet, eight inches, straight as an Indian, and for many years was an exemplary member of the Baptist denomination.

18. William Brooks was born on the Appomattox River, Virginia, about 1761, and went to Kentucky with his brothers Samuel and Thomas Brooks early in 1777. Returning from captivity, he early settled on the bank of the Ohio about three miles above Limestone, now Maysville, married Elizabeth Grimes, and raised several children. He was a captain of the militia and died in November 1816, at the age of fifty-five years. He died very poor and dissipated; he was kind and benevolent to a fault. When he died, his body was attached and kept several days unburied to extort from his children the payment of some old debt of their father, but the scheme failed. He was five feet, nine or ten inches, raw boned, [with] black hair and eyes, straight nose, rather a large mouth, and weighed about 175 pounds. He could barely read and write.

19. James Callaway was born in Bedford County, Virginia, in 1756. He went to Kentucky in Captain Pawling's company of Col. John Bowman's regiment in 1777. After returning from captivity, he married and settled in Kentucky, and in 1820 removed to Howard County, Missouri, where he died in July 1835, at the

age of about seventy-nine years. He enjoyed a pension from his country in his old age; several children survived him.

20. Jesse Cofer was a native of Virginia and went to Kentucky as early as 1777. Returning from captivity, he visited his friends in Virginia and came again to Kentucky in the fall of 1780, and the ensuing winter married a daughter of George Boone, a brother of Daniel Boone. He lived at different times in Madison, Fayette, and Clark counties, Kentucky, and removed in 1819 to Boone County, Missouri, where he died while sitting in his chair in 1822. He was about six feet in height, having blue eyes, a fair complexion, with a pleasing countenance; was worthy and patriotic and for many years a member of the Baptist church. His wife survived him two or three years.

Nathaniel Bullock was born in Virginia in 1757 and early ventured to Kentucky. After returning from his captivity, he engaged in the defense of the country and rose to the rank of captain. He married the widow Baughman, settled near Boonesborough, and died in June 1820, at the age of sixty-three—his wife surviving him a year. In height he was six feet, had high cheek bones, blue eyes, and fair skin.

21. Joseph Jackson was born in Bedford County, Virginia, December 15th, 1755, and went to Kentucky in Captain Watkins' company in the fall of 1777. One of the authors of this work visited this venerable pioneer at his residence near Jacksonville, Bourbon County, Kentucky, in April 1844, and though he retained some Indian characteristics, he was kind and intelligent. He was of a large, commanding appearance, light complexion, and died the following winter. His descendants are highly respectable. He received a pension from his country.

TFB: *Like many such multi-ethnic individuals, Joseph Jackson—who fought against his fellow Kentuckians at Blue Licks in 1782; the forces of Col. Josiah Harmar in 1790; Gen. Arthur St. Clair in 1791, and Gen. "Mad" Anthony Wayne at Fallen Timbers in 1795—was a tormented man who lived on the fringes of two cultures, truly belonging to neither. Shortly after his interview with Draper, Jackson hung himself. He was eighty-eight years old.*

22. Flanders, James, and Micajah Callaway were sons of Col. James Callaway and nephews of Col. Richard Callaway and were all born in Bedford County, Virginia. Micajah Callaway went to Kentucky in Captain Pawling's company in 1777; and returning from captivity, he served as an interpreter at various Indian treaties and conferences and acted for four months as a spy under General Wayne on his campaign against the Indians. He enjoyed a pension and died at his residence in Washington County, Indiana, April 11th, 1849, at the age of ninety-one years, emphatically the last of Boone's old salt-boilers.

The authorities consulted in drawing up this detailed account of the captivity of Boone and his party are—MS. notes of conversations with Joseph Jackson, one of the captives; Col. Nathan Boone and lady, Moses and Josiah [Isaiah?] Boone, Capt. John Gass, Capt. Henry Wilson, Zachariah Holliday, and Benjamin Briggs, all aged and intelligent pioneers; MS. statements of Micajah Callaway, one of the captives; his wife and children; Daniel Bryan; Morgan Bryan; Boone

Hays; Robert Hancock; Rev. Carter J. Kelley; N. S. and J. C. Bullock; MS. Virginia Archives; MS. Clark Papers; MS. Hand Papers; MS. Trabue narrative; Boone's published Narrative; Capt. John Carr's published statement; Gen. R. B. McAfee's newspaper sketches; Howe's *Ohio;* Marshall's *Kentucky; American Pioneer;* and Perkins' *Pioneers of Kentucky.*

EDITOR'S NOTES: CHAPTER 15

a. See chapter 7, editor's note l, regarding the importance of salt on the frontier.

b. Such kettles used for salt boiling typically had a twenty- to thirty-gallon capacity. In 1780 at Boone's Station, Peter Houston used thirty-gallon malt kettles for salt production as well as tanning deer and buffalo skins. See Belue, *Sketch,* 16, 18–21.

c. William Cradelbaugh, Jesse Hodges, and Stephen Hancock were the salt packers and couriers. Thomas Brooks and Flanders Callaway were the hunter-scouts. For an overview on the fate of Boone's men after their capture on the Lower Blue Licks in February 1778, see Ted Franklin Belue, "Terror in the Canelands: The Fate of Daniel Boone's Saltboilers," *Filson Club History Quarterly* 68 (1994): 3–34; also see William Dodd Brown, ed., "The Capture of Daniel Boone's Salt Makers: Fresh Perspectives from Primary Sources," *Register of the Kentucky Historical Society* 83 (1985): 1–19.

d. For the death of Cornstalk, see chapter 5, note f.

e. Besides offering protection from biting cold winds and ice and snow-storms, cane was the buffalo's winter fodder. But when the canelands sleeted over, buffalo could not eat the tall grass and starved.

f. Louis Lorimier (see chapter 13, note a).

g. Charles Beaubien, a French trader and British Indian agent.

h. The role of blacks in frontier history has been long overlooked. Such men were of great use to Indians, often providing insights into white culture and white military strategies hitherto unknown to warriors. Many blacks came to Indians with valuable skills, such as blacksmithing or the ability to make gunpowder. Others, like Pompey, were bilingual and served as mediators. Draper believed the Shawnee had kidnaped Pompey as a youth and raised him to be a warrior. See Ted Franklin Belue, "Did Daniel Boone Kill Pompey, the Black Shawnee, at the 1778 Siege of Boonesborough?" *Filson Club History Quarterly* 67 (1993): 5–22.

i. The Girty brothers—George, Thomas, James, and Simon—were some of the most despised white men on the frontier. In 1756 Shawnee and Delaware Indians killed their stepfather and kidnaped the youths. British mediators secured the release of Thomas, but James stayed with the Shawnee, George lived with the Delaware, and Simon became brother to the Seneca. Of the three, Simon was the most infamous, emerging in the early 1800s as the archetypal "white savage renegade"—a mythic stereotype that Draper accepted but one that stands in need of scholarly revision. Simon Girty was a complex man deeply imprinted by Indian life who played a pivotal role as mediator and agent for the British Indian

Department. He saved the lives of many American hostages in Indian villages, was a blood brother to Simon Kenton and kept him from a slow, painful death at the stake; and befriended Daniel Boone during his Shawnee captivity.

j. "How d' do, brother" was a common Indian pidgin English greeting, often shortened to "Howdy." West of the Mississippi, the greeting became "How!" and was typically accompanied by the bold show of a raised right hand with open palm forward to show one was unarmed.

k. Running a gauntlet was serious business, though gauntlets varied in kind and severity. Typically, Indians stripped the runner and might paint his face and shoulders black—the mark of doom. Warriors (or an entire village, if done at an Indian town) lined up in a parallel row that might extend more than a hundred yards, all brandishing war clubs, switches, or pipe tomahawks, primed for a chance at the runner. On signal, the runner dashed through the human chute, getting pommeled on his way. Should the victim grovel, stop, or get knocked down or fall, he might get brained. But the goal was to stay alive and reach the line's end. Once there, the runner was safe. At best, a gauntlet tested the mettle of a man and might be an obligatory prelude to an adoption rite; at worst, it was a hideously slow death sentence.

l. The men knew they had no choice. From their later actions, it appears that many of the captives, notably James Callaway, Andrew Johnson, and Nathaniel Bullock, felt betrayed and would rather have fought than surrendered.

m. Several biographers have theorized that Boone voted in this crucial exchange. That is unlikely. Boone was a hostage and as such was entitled to few if any rights and had little clout in tribal law.

n. One captive, Joseph Jackson, reported that the Indians wasted 300 bushels of salt by dumping it in the snow.

o. In other words, "damn squaw!" Draper avoided profanity, and it is rarely found in his writings.

p. Ear slitting was a custom among mid-eighteenth-century Eastern Woodland Indians. One stuck a knife in the apex of the ear's rim and slit the ear down to the lobe, stuck a wad of beaver hair or buffalo wool into the wound to staunch the blood, then bathed the cut in a gel of pounded slippery elm bark or bear oil to promote healing. Once the ear healed, the warrior distended the detached lobe with lead weights pounded flat until the lobe stretched, sometimes to the shoulder, and after binding it with brass wire for reinforcement, added sterling silver earrings, turkey spurs, rings, bells, tufts of swan down, or whatever else might grab one's fancy. Elongated ears that bounded and undulated wildly as one walked marked a man as a valorous warrior, but the slender appendages were fragile, susceptible to frostbite and getting caught in branches.

The painful practice began to die out toward the end of the 1700s, but it was common enough that many observers mentioned the unusual custom in their memoirs. While among the Choctaw, Indian trader and adopted Chickasaw James Adair observed in *The History of the American Indians, Particularly Those Na-*

tions Adjoining to the Mississippi, East and West Florida, Georgia, South and North Carolina, and Virginia (c. 1740s):

> He had been among Indians at a drinking match, when several of their beaus have been humbled as low as death, for the great loss of their big ears. Being so widely extended, it is as easy for a person to take hold of, and pull them off, as to remove a couple of small hoops were they hung within reach; but if the ear after the pull, stick to their head by one end, when they get sober, they pare and sew it together with a needle and deer's sinews. . . . It is not deemed a scandal to lose their ears by any accident, because they become slender and brittle, by their virtuous compliance with that favorite custom of their ancestors.

q. Indians stretched freshly skinned buffalo hides, skin side out, over a wattle of hickory, white oak, or willow to sun dry until taut as a drumhead. One bull hide made a coracle that could float an 800-pound burden. Indians sewed several hides together and caulked the seams with tallow and ashes to make a larger, water-resistant hide craft. By day, buffalo boats functioned on water; by night, Indians hauled the soggy crafts ashore to dry them out and used them for huts by flipping them over and propping up one end on forked sticks. Boone learned the art of buffalo-hide boat making from Indians, and in 1851 Nathan Boone described to Drapter how his father made them (Draper's Notes, 6S): "Get poles a little larger than a man's wrist and split them and bend them over . . . for the ribs of a boat, making the boat 8 or 10 feet long according to the size of the skin, and four or five or six feet wide. . . . Lay the skin (of the buffalo) down with the hair next [to] the ribs and stretch it down to the whaling or rib which forms the gunwale of the boat, trim off the edges and cut loops through it and lash it along."

r. Indian adoption ceremonies of white captives are well documented and interesting. Many times the captive took the place of a son killed in war, a native custom known as "covering the dead." Indians chose adoptees with care, and history is replete with the stories of white captives who, in the prose of the day, "turned Indian" in mind and spirit and evinced no wish to return to white society. Micajah Callaway and Joseph Jackson, two of Boone's captured salt boilers, converted to Algonquin life; a short time after being taken hostage, both were reported seen fighting with their native brothers against their white Kentucky kinsmen—Callaway in Lochry's Defeat (1781) and Jackson at the Battle of Blue Licks (1782). Early Boone biographers ignored the fact that as a white Shawnee and son to Black Fish, Boone found much to enjoy and admire about Indian life.

s. This may not be true. The Indians might have marched as many as fourteen captive Kentuckians to Detroit to sell. See my essay in the *Filson Club History Quarterly* cited in note c.

t. On October 17, 1777, at Bemis Heights, New York, the British forces of Maj. Gen. "Gentleman Johnny" Burgoyne (1722–94) playwright, playboy, theater devotee, and officer, formally surrendered to Maj. Gen. Horatio Gates (1728–1806) and his New England troops.

u. Antonio Lopez de Santa Anna Perez de Lebron (1794–1876), Mexican military leader and five-time Mexican president, gained his most notorious fame on the morning of March 6, 1836, by attacking the Alamo, the American-held mission in San Antonio, Texas, and killing all of its 180 plus defenders. On April 21, 1836, American forces led by Sam Houston captured him at the Battle of San Jacinto. The self-styled "Napoleon of the West" was exiled to Cuba but was permitted to return to his native Mexico.

v. On April 9, 1797, English traveler Francis Baily had a chance encounter with Daniel Boone on the Ohio River. Boone recounted to Baily this Upper Ohio portion of his Shawnee exodus, which Baily recorded in his memoir, *Journal of a Tour in Unsettled Parts of North America in 1796 and 1797*: "He [Boone] made us follow his narration, how he was taken prisoner by Indians and carried on a tour around the Great Lakes with them....He took (in truly Indian style) a drop of water, and on a board he marked out the whole course of his travels."

w. The Salt River of north-central Kentucky is the commonwealth's fifth largest watershed and was once a primary supplier of salt for the region. See chapter 7, editor's note l.

x. Here Draper inserts the word *servants,* a reference to Boone's African slaves. In all other accounts, and many times in his correspondence, Boone, a small-time slave owner, used *Negroes*—the favored term of his day.

y. By all accounts, this is true. Boone was no man of blood and, unless under threat, was kind to Indians. In his Missouri years, in an interview with biographer Rev. John Mason Peck, the old hunter, who was fast becoming a legend in his own lifetime, declared that the popular notion that he had slain "hecatombs" of Indians was wrong; he despised the myth that he was a mighty Indian killer. And though Dr. Robert Spencer Cotterill's remarks in *The History of Pioneer Kentucky* (1917, p. 131) may have been tinged with wistful romanticism reflecting Boone's celebrity, what he says is indeed true: "They [the Shawnee] had known Boone ever since they had taken him and Stewart in Central Kentucky. He was known to them personally and by reputation. But they were far from feeling toward him the animosity usually displayed to their white foes. . . . History, in fact, has no stranger anomaly than the relations of Boone and the Shawnee."

z. At times during Col. Nathan Boone's military career, his wife and daughters would accompany him on his travels to western Missouri and eastern Kansas. One daughter, Draper records (DM 16C:29; see also DM 21:15{6}; 21:61; 21:63{1}), at Fort Leavenworth, was startled by an elderly Shawnee woman who showered her with affection upon hearing that her grandfather was Shel-tow-ee —Daniel Boone. The old woman claimed to be one of Black Fish's daughters— one of the very ones that Boone looked after in 1778—and proudly proclaimed that she was Shel-tow-ee's adopted sister during his captivity.

aa. Though a bark wigwam was not as substantial a shelter as a Swedish-style log cabin, Shawnee and other Ohio Indians adopted the use of cabins for permanent settlements. Many times these Indian log houses were more comfortable, less crowded, better outfitted, and cleaner than their Anglo-made Kentucky counterparts.

bb. Boone, probably unknowingly, was trespassing on well-defined gender roles by assisting the women in hoeing or planting. In Shawnee culture, field work, except under duress or other extraordinary circumstances, was no work for a warrior and made one seem less a man.

cc. When Black Fish first captured Boone, they conversed through the African ex-slave interpreter, Pompey. During Boone's captivity, he must have learned some Shawnee and Black Fish some English. Such cross-cultural influences were common. But more revealing here are the two leaders' actions: By discussing their lifestyles and the advantages each would bring the other, it is clear that Black Fish and Boone sought accommodation, not war, to bridge the gulf between their people, locked in a duel for land and home.

dd. "Scalded" feet meant one's foot soles had stayed wet for so long that the many-layered, shriveled flesh peeled off in thick hunks that tore deeply into the tender sole. For militiamen or a colonial army that traveled on its feet, scalded feet could abruptly end a foray.

ee. "Strings" refers to rawhide thongs known as "tugs." See chapter 6, note i.

ff. Daniel Morgan Boone (1769–1839), Daniel and Rebecca Boone's third son.

gg. That Daniel Boone, running for his life, could stop to stock a gun from scratch and kill a buffalo with it is a tribute to the man's patience, ingenuity, and gunsmithing skill.

hh. Draper's paraphrase of Genesis 50:20.

ii. Though Draper calls Hancock a "poor woodsman," this brave fellow escaped from Capt. Will Emery's wigwam at the Shawnee town of Old Chillicothe with no horse, no weapon, little food, and nearly naked but managed to evade his trackers, cross the Ohio at flood stage, and return 160 miles to Boonesborough in nine days.

jj. Aaron Ferman, whom the Indians captured when he got lost from Simon Kenton during a horse-stealing raid.

kk. The village sites of the Makujay (Mequache) division of the Shawnee. Col. Benjamin Logan's 1786 Shawnee campaign took him as far north as the upper Miami River, in what is now Logan County, Ohio.

ll. Baie-St.-Paul, on the western end of the St. Lawrence River near present-day St.-Siméon, Quebec.

mm. Unlike Boone's, Simon Kenton's Indian captivity was a cruel, grim one. Barely missing death at the stake, and forced to run a total of nine gauntlets, Kenton suffered broken bones, deep cuts, multiple scars, a cracked skull, and many other injuries before escaping from Detroit to return to Kentucky. (See chapter 12, note m.)

nn. Brig. Gen. George Rogers Clark's November 1782 Ohio campaign was the Kentuckians' retaliatory strike in the bloody wake of their defeat in the Battle of Blue Licks the previous August 19. Clark led more than 1,000 well-armed militiamen up the Miami into north Ohio to Alexander McKee's Town, the troops expending much of their efforts in torching the towns and crops and killing the livestock of the Shawnee, who were marginally involved in the Blue Licks massacre. Clark's forces raiding McKee's Town gave salt boiler hostage John Holley diversion enough for him to devise an escape, according to Draper (DM 11C:62{31}): "Holley had tied his horse and was rummaging in a cabin, some Indians in company, when whites, came into sight. The Indians with him dashed him off, and he pretended to be bothered in untying his horse, thus delay[ing] till the whites came up."

CHAPTER 16

June–October 1778.—Daniel Boone Makes Ready for the Coming of Black Fish and His Warriors. —Escape of William Hancock from the Shawanoes and His Ill Tidings.—Boone Leads Party of Spies on Paint Creek Foray.—The Shawanoes Arrive within Sight of Boonesborough.—Negotiations, Intrigue, and Subterfuge.—The War Clouds Burst.—The Siege of Boonesborough.—Pompey the Black Shawanoe Killed.—The Siege Lifted.—Of the Court Martial of Boone.— Boone Returns to the Yadkin.

During Boone's captivity, the usual amount of Indian troubles had been experienced in Kentucky. On the 28th of March, Col. Alexander McKee,[a] Capt. Matthew Elliot,[b] and Simon Girty[c] fled from the Pittsburgh region and joined the Indians and thence forward were untiring in their efforts to urge the savages of the North-West to war against the feeble frontiers. "The Indians have pushed us hard this summer," wrote Colonel Bowman to Col. George Rogers Clark; but the latter enterprising officer had gained important advantages for Kentucky by procuring from Virginia a few troops, descending the Ohio, and joined by a few Kentuckians, boldly pushing forward with about one hundred and seventy five men, capturing Kaskaskia, Cahokia, and Vincennes and putting an end to British rule and influence in the Illinois country.[d]

Boone, upon his return, found the fort at Boonesborough still in a bad state of defense. The announcement of the speedy approach of a larger Indian army awakened the garrison to the necessity of immediate preparations; and they proceeded at once, animated by the presence and energy of Boone, to repair the palisades enclosing the fort, those on one side of which being almost entirely wanting, to strengthen the gates and posterns, to enlarge the upper end of the fort and form double bastions, as Boone calls them—that is, on the south-east and south-west corners new bastions were built, the second story of which was made as high as a man's head, time not permitting to roof them. The second story of these bastions, as well as Henderson's kitchen and Phelps' house occupying the two river corners, projected several feet outwardly beyond the first story, so as to give the garrison [the] chance to shoot any person who might venture close up to the fort on any side or beneath the bastions, as apertures were left for shooting through the projecting floor. All these improvements, by dint of vigorous application, were completed in the course of ten days. The old well nearly in the center of the fort furnishing but a scanty supply of water, a new one near it was commenced but not finished. It was now the first of July, and though spies were

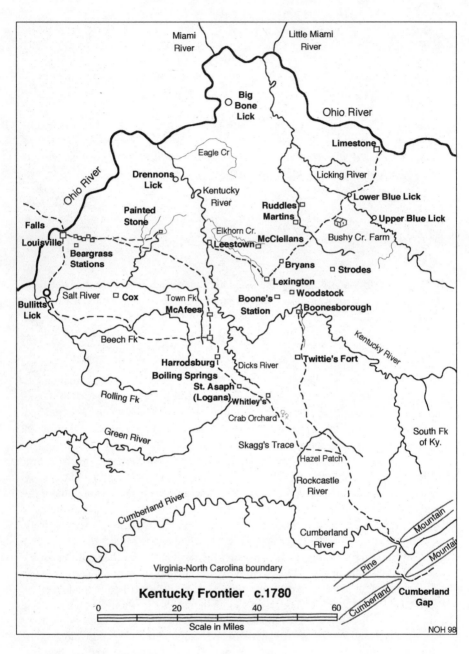

Kentucky Frontier c.1780

Miami River

Little Miami River

Big Bone Lick

Ohio River

Ohio River

Eagle Cr

Limestone

Licking River

Drennons Lick

Kentucky River

Lower Blue Lick

Painted Stone

Ruddles Martins

Upper Blue Lick

Falls

Elkhorn Cr.

McClellans

Bushy Cr. Farm

Louisville

Leestown

Beargrass Stations

Bryans

Strodes

Bullitts Lick

Salt River

Cox

Town Fk

Lexington

Woodstock

McAfees

Boone's Station

Boonesborough

Beech Fk

Kentucky River

Harrodsburg

Dicks River

Twittie's Fort

Boiling Springs

St. Asaph (Logans)

Whitley's

Rolling Fk

Crab Orchard

South Fk of Ky.

Green River

Skagg's Trace

Hazel Patch

Rockcastle River

Cumberland River

Mountain

Mountain

Cumberland River

Pine

Virginia-North Carolina boundary

Cumberland

Cumberland Gap

0   20   40   60

Scale in Miles

NOH 98

73. MAP BY NEAL O. HAMMON.

constantly sent out by day and sentinels kept vigilant watch by night, momentarily expecting the arrival of the enemy, none came. Sending to Logan's Fort and Harrodsburg for reinforcements, about fifteen men came from the former and a few from the latter—Harrodsburg having at that time about forty men.

This state of suspense was not broken till the arrival of William Hancock on the 17th of July, who reported that in consequence of Boone's departure, the Indians had postponed their expedition three weeks, nine days of which had already expired; [and] that, puzzled as to the course they should pursue, they had sent runners to Governor Hamilton at Detroit, apprizing him of Boone's escape and asking his advice under this new position of affairs. He determined at every sacrifice to escape and notify the Boonesborough people of the postponement of the attack, that they might prepare themselves to meet it. The two documents which follow will further explain Hancock's intelligence: It is to be regretted that Boone's deposition referred to has not been preserved.

Boonesborough, 18th July, 1778

Dear Colonel:

Enclosed is my deposition with that of Mr. Hancock, who arrive here yesterday. He informed us of both French and Indians coming against us to the number of near four hundred, whom I expect here in twelve days from this. If men can be sent to us in five or six weeks, it would be of infinite service, as we shall lay up provisions for a siege. We are all in fine spirits, and have good crops growing, and intend to fight hard in order to secure them. I shall refer you to the bearer for particulars of this country.

I am, & etc.

Daniel Boone

To Cols. Arthur Campbell or Evan Shelby.[e]

Kentucky SS. Boonesborough, 17th July, 1778

The deposition of William Hancock being first sworn on the Holy Evangelists, is as follows: This deponent saith, that the 5th of this instant he was in company with twelve Frenchmen in Big Chillicothe Town, at which time there was a Grand Council held with the principal Indians from different nations. There were considerable presents made them by the French from Detroit, two of whom were a Captain and an Ensign, and that they informed him they were coming at least two hundred men strong against this garrison. This deponent saith, that the Indians informed, they should come four hundred strong, and offer the English flag to the inhabitants, and if the terms were rejected, they intended to batter down our fort with their swivels,[f] as they are to have four sent them from Detroit, which will be conveyed up the Maumee river, and down the Great Miami to the Ohio, and thence up the Kentucky to Boonesborough. This deponent further saith, that the French and Indians intend to lie around our fort, and live on our stock, till they starve us out. Further this deponent saith not.

Sworn before me. Richard Callaway[1g]

Such was the nature of the intelligence and request for relief despatched by a special messenger on the 18th of July to Col. Arthur Campbell, the county lieutenant of Washington County on the Holston. This done, the fort repaired, crops maturing, and a good lookout kept up, they had only to await the event and meet it manfully. Towards the close of August, some corn was gathered and garnered in the loft of their cabins. Boone informs us that "the Indians had spies out reviewing our movements, and were greatly alarmed with our increase in number and fortifications. The grand councils of the nations were held frequently, and with more deliberation than usual. They evidently saw the approaching hour when the Long Knife would dispossess them of their desirable habitations; and anxiously concerned for futurity, determined utterly to extirpate the whites from Kentucky. We were not intimidated by their movements, but frequently gave them proofs of our courage."

These Indian spies, Boone began to suspect, could have reported nothing favorable—and hence the delay, perhaps abandonment, of their enterprise. Weary of this unpleasant suspense, Boone proposed toward the very close of August to head a party to surprise the Paint Creek Town of Scioto, with a view of taking prisoners in order to discover the intentions of the enemy with respect to Kentucky; and such a bold attack might put the Indians on the defensive and avert the intended expedition against Boonesborough. To encourage volunteers to join him, Boone told them he thought they might secure a sufficient number of Indian horses and furs to pay them well for their time and trouble and, meanwhile, render the country an essential service.[h]

Captain Callaway warmly opposed the scheme, but Boone's influence prevailed. Thirty persons volunteered and started on the last day of the month; when they reached the Blue Licks, eleven of the number who had families behind now began to consider the force too small to accomplish the object in view and returned to the fort. Boone was nothing daunted, for such valiant men as Simon Kenton, Alexander Montgomery, John Holder, Pemberton Rollins, and Jesse Hodges yet remained faithful, and he heroically persevered. They crossed the Ohio on rafts and, painted in Indian style, advanced rapidly towards the Paint Creek Town.

When within four miles of that place, and Kenton was some distance ahead as a spy, he heard the tinkling of a bell and soon discovered approaching an Indian riding on a poney without a bridle and another Indian skulking along behind, who suddenly bounded upon the horse behind the other with his back to the other, greatly to the rider's surprise, when both set up a loud laugh. Kenton, who had secreted himself, drew up his rifle and shot, when both fell off, one dead and the other wounded, the poney scampering off into the cane. Kenton now ran up to take his scalps, supposing he had killed them both, but found one not yet ready to part [with] that article and gave him a severe kick.

Other Indians, hearing the report of the gun and seeing the frightened poney, now advanced, and two ahead of the others, rustling through the cane, attracted Kenton's attention, who perceived them taking deliberate aim at him and sprang aside just in time to see the flash of their guns and hear their balls whistle close to his ears. He made off and took shelter behind a tree, when several other warriors appeared, some on horseback; at this critical moment Kenton was relieved by the rapid advance of Boone and his party, and quite a skirmish ensued, which lasted some little time. At length the savages gave way, leaving behind them the Indian whom Kenton had shot, whose scalp Kenton now secured. Two of the Indians, at least, were wounded, and three horses, with all the Indian baggage taken. The whites sustained no injury whatever.

This Indian party, which Boone thought numbered thirty warriors and Kenton estimated at forty, were on their way to join the gathering of Indian forces destined against Kentucky. Kenton and Montgomery were now sent forward to spy [on] the town and soon reported the apparent absence of the warriors, when Boone concluded that the expedition against Boonesborough was being carried into effect. Since crossing the Ohio, Boone and party had been so wary and cautious as not to shoot any game and were now very hungry; and seeing some buffaloes, they killed one, concluding they would run but little additional risk, since their presence was already known to the Indians. They hastily cooked and ate a hearty meal and discovered as they departed where two Indians had been posted behind a tree evidently watching their movements, attracted probably by the report of the guns in killing the buffalo. They now returned with all possible speed, except Kenton and Montgomery, who resolved to remain and try their hand alone at getting horses and perhaps securing a prisoner. Boone and his party discovered the Indian army at the Lower Blue Licks, and making a circuit to avoid them, they safely reached Boonesborough on the 6th of September after an absence of seven days. During this rapid march by day and night on the return, Holder's feet gave out, when he remained and Rollins with him, but they got in during the ensuing night.[2]

Thus the main object Boone had in view was attained—learning the intentions of the enemy. They were now close at hand, but being generally tardy in their movements, in consequence of having their food to procure by the way, and late in cooking their morning repast enabled Boone and his men to out-strip them and reach Boonesborough in good time to put every thing in proper order to give them a warm reception. The night succeeding Boone's return was one of anxiety and withal of steady preparation; guns were examined and, if necessary, cleaned and repaired, bullets molded and trimmed, vegetables brought in, and such vessels as they had were filled with water.

Monday morning, the 7th of September, dawned beautifully. The Indian army crossed the river about a mile and a half below the fort, at a ford which has ever since borne the name of *Black Fish's Ford,* and marched along the elevated ridge south of the river and about ten o'clock came in view of the fort. Captain Boone happened at the time to be outside the fort with his rifle in hand expecting their arrival; and his brother Squire Boone's sons, Moses and Isaiah, respectively in their tenth and seventh years, were at the same moment watering some horses and, thinking as some others did that it was the expected reinforcement approaching, were on the eve of riding out to meet them, when their Uncle Daniel admonished them that they were Indians and they had better ride into the fort. The enemy, some on horseback, were strung along scatteringly in Indian file[i] displaying both English and French flags. Their number was about four hundred Indians, chiefly Shawanoes, with some Wyandots, Cherokees, and others, and forty Frenchmen and Canadians, presenting a very formidable appearance, all under the chief command of Black Fish, aided by Moluntha, Black Hoof, Black Beard, and other chiefs.[3] Capt. Isadore DeChaine, a Frenchman, who was British interpreter to the Wyandots; Peter Druillier, a British Indian trader; and the Negro Pompey were prominent personages in the Indian army. They marched down the hill and halted about three hundred yards from the fort, a little above where there was a cornfield and a nursery of pretty good sized peach-trees, the tops of which they cut off, leaving the trunks for posts to support poles, using the tops for a covering. This rude arbor formed their encampment, and there they planted the British standard.

Pompey soon advanced with a white flag within one hundred and fifty yards of the fort, got upon the cornfield fence, and enquired in a loud voice if Captain Boone was there. Boone replied yes. Pompey announced that Black Fish had letters for him from Governor Hamilton and that the governor and Indians expected him to fulfill his promise of peaceably surrendering the fort and garrison. A hurried council was held in the fort, when it was concluded not to go for the letters and Pompey was told to return and bring them. Black Fish, though considerably farther distant than Pompey, called out to Boone by his adopted name of Sheltow-ee to come out to him. Boone determined, with the approbation of his friends, to venture out and designated a certain stump where he would meet Black Fish and receive the letters. Boone went forth fearlessly to Pompey, and both went together and met Black Fish. After a friendly shake of the hand and a few common-place inquiries between Boone and the old chief as to their health since they had last seen each other, Black Fish chidingly asked: "My son, what made you leave me in the manner you did?" "I wanted," replied Boone, "to see my wife and children so bad, that I could not stay any longer." "If you had only let me known," said Black Fish, "I would have let you gone at any time, and rendered you every assistance."

Black Fish, reminding Boone of his promise to surrender the fort and people, demanded its fulfillment and presented Governor Hamilton's letters and Proclamation. In these Boone was advised to give up the fort in accordance with his pledge; that it would be folly for him and his friends to attempt defending themselves against so powerful a force; and should they have the temerity to resist, the undistinguished massacre of men, women, and children would be the probable consequence. [The letters also said] that the people should be taken to Detroit, become British subjects, and be treated well; that such of them as held offices should be continued in the same rank, and should any suffer loss of property by the change, it should be made good. When Boone had perused the letters, Black Fish asked him how he liked them. To this Boone replied that the Indians had kept him so long a prisoner that other commanders had been appointed to fill his place in his absence; that he could only counsel with the others and must consult them, which he would go and "let Black Fish know the result." Black Fish said that his warriors were hungry and had nothing to eat, when Boone, knowing full well they would take what they wanted, and thinking it wisest to make a merit of it, replied: "There, you see plenty of cattle and corn; take what you need, but don't let any be wasted." Both parties now retired; and the Indians immediately commenced whooping and yelling, some shooting down cattle and others gathering corn.

Boone submitted the letter to the people within the fort. As for himself, he said that he never had the remotest idea of surrendering; that what he had said to the Indians and British on that stead, when a prisoner, was only to curry favor and fool them; and that he was for resistance; but if the people thought it best to give up, he should be compelled to yield to the wishes of the majority. Squire Boone said warmly that "he would never give up; he would fight till he died." Callaway, Smith, Gass, Holder, and all the leading men were decidedly opposed to the proposition of a trip to Detroit or yielding to the enemy in any particular. "Well, well," said Daniel Boone, "I'll die with the rest." It was now agreed as a stroke of policy to amuse the Indians as long as possible, with a hope thereby of gaining time for the arrival of the expected reinforcement from the Holston. So Boone and Major Smith[j] were appointed to go out and hold an interview with Black Fish and consult more fully about the letters and proposition to surrender and ask for further time for the people to deliberate upon so important a matter.

The ambassadors went forth and were met by Black Fish, Moluntha and another chief, and about twenty warriors, a part of whom laid down their arms. Much formal parade ensued, as is usual among Indians, in shaking hands and in renewing professions of friendship. A panther skin was spread on a log for a seat for the white diplomats, while a couple of Indiana held bushes over their heads to protect them from the rays of the sun—and perhaps too as emblematic of peace, for many tribes make use of a bunch of bushes for that purpose. Black Fish now arose and addressed them for about five minutes, referring to Governor Hamilton's letter and proclamation and again earnestly urging the speedy compliance of Boone with the former promise he had made to surrender. He then exhibited a wampum-belt, upon which were black, white, and red rows of beads—the black indicative of a warning against evil or an earnest reproof; the white emblematic of the olive branch of peace; and the red or colour of blood, with generally the accompanying figure of a hatchet, declaration of war and indicating in this instance that should Boone and the garrison resist, no mercy need be expected.[k] One end of the belt, Black Fish said, represented Detroit and the other Boonesborough; now which row would they choose, that of peace and friendship or blood and carnage? These, he continued, were his orders, and he must faithfully execute them; and looking Boone earnestly in the face, added: "Brother, there is a heavy cloud hanging over this country—this is called *The Bloody Land,* you know—we have had much war, and whoever gets the first fire always beats.[4] Now I am come to take you away easy." Then Moluntha spoke and, referring to Boone's Scioto expedition, said: "You kill my son the other day over the Ohio River." Boone answered, "No, I have not been there"; when Moluntha replied, "It was you— I tracked you here to this place."

Smith remarked that the governor's proposition to remove to Detroit was doubtless intended to be kind but that it would be very difficult to effect the removal of so many women and children. "I have brought forty horses," exclaimed Black Fish, "on purpose for the old people, women, and children to ride"; and again pressed the delivery of the fort. Boone asked for that and the following day to enable the people to consider the matter fully, as there were so many commanders and counsellors in the fort. This was at length granted and a line thirty yards from the fort agreed upon over which the Indians were not to pass, and the whites were not to carry arms outside of the garrison, nor the Indians near the fort. The interview closed with a present of seven jerked buffalo tongues from Black Fish to the women in the fort as a token of good faith—which were at first suspected to be poisoned, but they were not. Smoking together in friendship, with an assurance on the part of Black Fish that no cattle or hogs should be wantonly killed, they parted, the white ambassadors being accompanied by twenty Indians as far as the limit agreed on. This ended the events of the first day.

A night of vigilance ensued, but the Indians remained quiet. The next day they appeared quite friendly and, getting water at the spring there, met some of the women also procuring water and complimented them as "pretty squaws." Pompey that day twice rode up on an indifferent poney, proposing to exchange him for a gun; but no one felt disposed to trade with him, for there were no guns to spare and none at any rate for Pompey. As he was very officious, embittered feelings were cherished towards him by many of the garrison; and some even declared that if he appeared again, they would shoot him, let the consequences be what they might. During the day the Indians sent word to the women and children not to be alarmed, as they were going to shoot some beeves; and whenever the garrison could coax any of the cattle into the fort, they did so. Altogether, old and young, white and black, there were sixty persons in the fort capable of bearing arms, but only about forty of them were really effective.[5] To make an impression on the minds of the Indians of the great strength of the garrison, the women were dressed up in the surplus hats and hunting shirts and, with guns in hand, marched and counter-marched within the fort with the big gate open so the Indians at a distance could witness them, while the men mounted the walls and cabins in every quarter.

"It was now," says Boone, "a critical period with us. We were small in number in the garrison. A powerful army [was] before our walls, whose appearance proclaimed inevitable death, fearfully painted, and marking their footsteps with desolation. Death was preferable to captivity; and if taken by storm, we must inevitably be devoted to destruction. In this situation we concluded to maintain our garrison, if possible. We immediately proceeded to collect what we could of our horses and cattle, and bring them through the posterns into the fort."

Towards evening the Indians called for Boone to receive from him the final answer to the summons to surrender and march to Detroit. Captain Boone, Callaway, Major Smith, Squire Boone, and a few others went out some thirty yards within the protection of the guns of the garrison and there met Black Fish and an Indian deputation; both parties were unarmed, as they had previously agreed to be at their interviews. Boone now informed the Indians that the people would not consent to go to Detroit and added, "We are determined to defend our fort while there is a man living." "Now," he continued, addressing Black Fish, who stood attentively hearing his speech, "we laugh at all your formidable preparations; but thank you for giving us notice and time to provide for our defense. Your efforts will not prevail; for our gates shall for ever deny you admittance."

Boone could not tell whether this answer affected their courage, but they were evidently disappointed and looked quite surly. Black Fish, particularly, appeared surprised and said Governor Hamilton's expectations would be thwarted. Observing, as he must have done, that the new palisades and bastions would render the fort difficult to be taken, Black Fish thought it the wiser course to resort to stratagem. So he declared that Governor Hamilton's orders were to take them captives and not destroy their lives; and since they did not like to go to Detroit, if nine of the whites would come out and hold a treaty, he would enter into friendly negotiations, withdraw his forces, and return home peaceably. "This," observes Boone, "sounded grateful to our ears, and we agreed to the proposal." The fact that the Indians in the Illinois country had just entered into treaties of peace with Colonel Clark gave Boone and his companions some reason to hope that Black Fish might be sincere. At all events, the commencement of the attack would be delayed and more time given for the arrival of the expected reinforcement from the Holston.

Some difficulty ensued in selecting a place for holding the treaty, the Indians at first proposing to have it in the fort, perhaps with a view of surprising the garrison by some *coup de main* as had been successfully practiced a few years before at Mackinaw and attempted by Pontiac at Detroit;[1] but Boone told them the women and children were afraid of Indians and it must not be held there. The Indians then suggested that it be held at their camp, where, beyond the reach of the guns of the fort, they could seize the commissioners with impunity, but Boone and Callaway both strenuously objected to it. The place finally selected was the green plat about sixty yards directly in front of the big gate and near the Licks; chosen, says Boone, "on purpose to divert them from a breach of honor, as we could not avoid suspicions of the savages." During the conference, which lasted a considerable time, Squire Boone took occasion to remark that an army under the command of Col. George Rogers Clark was then on its march from Virginia, which information, though not strictly true so far as Clark was concerned, produced manifest uneasiness in the minds of the Indians.

The council at length closed with the understanding that the treaty should be holden the next morning and that Black Fish should be accompanied by eighteen Indian deputies, as that number, he said, was necessary in order that each town or village to which his warriors respectively belonged might be represented. This inequality Boone and his friends combated, viewing it as a plan to entrap the whites, but they could not venture to risk any more of their men out of the fort on so perilous an experiment. Black Fish could not be prevailed upon to lessen the number of his Indian deputies, as he contended that his people would not consider the treaty binding unless each town should be represented in making it.

Boone was well convinced that the excuse was a mere subterfuge, but he relied upon the superior energy of the nine white commissioners to extricate themselves from any difficulty into which they might be thrown. He returned to the fort more confident than ever that treachery was brewing and that the attack would commence the next day; but he was cool and had no doubt as to the result, for he knew the Indians had no cannon, that the fort was in good condition for resistance, the garrison well supplied with ammunition and provisions for a long siege and had a larger number of men for its defense than at any former attack. He did not overlook the fact that the Indians were now far more formidable in point of numbers than ever before and had British officers with them to aid in directing their operations. Black Fish was seen that evening walking around the fort and carefully viewing it; and soon afterwards, the Indians were observed holding a council and performing the war-dance. Boone remarked that these were additional evidences of the hostile designs of the Indians.

The next morning, Wednesday, September 9th, the strange contest was renewed—the Indians maturing their wiles and stratagems and the whites gladly resorting to any expedient *to gain time.* That morning the cattle were hovering around the fort, exhibiting signs of uneasiness as usual when Indians were about; and when the Indians were told that the "white squaws" were afraid to venture out to milk them, they had the gallantry to aid in driving them into the fort—and once there they were of course retained; and altogether about sixty head were secured. Two objects were thus gained—the cattle saved from wanton destruction and from furnishing support to the enemy while additional subsistence was provided for the garrison.

But few Indians were anywhere to be seen, which Boone regarded as ominous of the expected attack. The forenoon was consumed in preparing the dinner for those who should take part in the treaty. Some tables were carried out and others formed for the occasion by driving forked sticks in the ground and placing slabs on them; chairs were carried from the fort, with pewter plates, knives, and forks; then came the nicely cooked deer and buffalo tongues and other viands, with such additional dishes as the good housewives of the garrison could provide, the aim being to make as favorable an exhibition of plenty as possible and in the style that Indians might infer that the whites had an abundance for a siege. At noon the dinner was eaten with an evident relish on the part of the Indians, after which the furniture was taken back to the fort.

Associated with Boone in making the treaty were Colonel Callaway, Major Smith, Capt. William Buchanan, Squire Boone, Flanders Callaway, John Smith, Sr., Edward Bradley, and a person named Crabtree, who far surpassed common men in size, strength, and action. As the day was warm, all unnecessary clothing was carefully avoided that they might be better prepared to meet any emergency that might arise; and though viewing the whole thing as a mere trick, yet they wished on their part to conduct the treaty fairly, as the Indians might possibly be forced into sincerity from a conviction of their inability to take the fort. Before leaving the fort, Boone had given the most explicit order that every part should be strictly guarded and the port-holes in the bastion nearest the treaty-ground should be manned with twenty-five of the very best marksmen with their rifles ready, loaded, and primed, their eyes on the sights and fingers on the triggers, specially charged the moment the Indians should betray the least treachery "to fire at the lump," white and red, as they would be more likely, two to one, to hit an Indian than a white man and thus cover the retreat of the commissioners. These orders, as will presently be seen, were strictly obeyed.

Boone, now observing two or three Indians hanging about whom he was persuaded could not be chiefs, pointed them out to Black Fish, saying, "These are no chiefs, and have no business here!" Black Fish appeared surprised that they were there and ordered them away. Other young warriors were discovered to have been substituted for some old chiefs at the council board, and Black Fish was asked the reason of it, when he assured his white brothers that the change had been made to gratify the young men who were anxious to witness the proceedings of the treaty. While all were seated, each white man between two Indians, and the pipe of peace had passed around, Black Fish arose and said that "he wished to make a lasting peace and forever bury the tomahawk, and live as brothers should live." Boone very tersely replied that he "was willing" and asked the old chief upon what terms he wished to make peace. Black Fish said that as the Indians regarded Kentucky as their hunting ground, he would therefore propose that the people of Boonesborough should have six weeks in which to abandon the country and retire to the old settlements. Boone and his friends said they could not agree to such a stipulation.

Black Fish then enquired, "Brothers, by what right did you come and settle here?" He was answered that Col. Richard Henderson and company had purchased all the country between the Kentucky and the Cumberland rivers from the Cherokees and paid them satisfactorily for it. Turning to a Cherokee Indian present, Black Fish asked him if his people had sold the country as stated to the whites. The Cherokee promptly confirmed it. After making a little pause, as though somewhat disconcerted at this turn in the discussion, he added, "Friends and Brothers, as you have purchased this land from the Cherokees and paid them for it, that entirely alters the case; you must keep it, and live on it in peace." He then proposed that the Indians should return home; that Boone and his friends should remain unmolested, retaining all their property, taking the oath of British allegiance, and submitting to the authority of Governor Hamilton of Detroit; that the Ohio should be the boundary between the Kentuckians and Indians, not to be passed in a hostile manner by either party; that, after the treaty should be ratified by the British and Virginian authorities, both parties might peaceably hunt on either side of the Ohio, that the Indians might trade with the whites, that there should be no robbery of hunting camps or stealing of horses, but all should [wm] and act like brothers. After a considerable discussion, these terms were mutually agreed to, Black Fish declaring that the treaty should be alike binding on both parties as long as the trees should grow or water run down [the] Kentucky River.

A good deal of ceremony was used, as is generally the case in Indian treaties, shaking hands and smoking pipes; and one of the whites acted as clerk, putting the articles in writing, which were formally signed. Black Fish, who was the guiding spirit of his people and took the entire lead of the Indians in this treaty, now remarked that but one thing remained to be done—that he must step aside a little distance and "give out the big talk to his young men that they might fully understand that a firm peace had been made." Taking his position, he made quite a lengthy speech in his native language in a very loud, impassioned manner, as if addressing his warriors at a great distance from him, but a few of whom were not anywhere to be seen during the treaty. He spoke with a fine voice, exhibiting much of the grace and ease of an accomplished orator.

Then, returning to the commissioners, he desired them and the Indian deputies to rise up and cautioned the whites not to be afraid, that it was usual with the Indians when making friends to shake hands singly, but when they concluded a treaty designed to be long and lasting, as an evidence of entire friendship, they shook *long hands*—two Indians embracing each white man and bringing their hearts closer together. So saying, Black Fish and another Indian advanced with extended arms towards Boone, who evinced no distrust, and while the old chief inter-locked his right arm in Boone's left and with his left hand seized Boone's left one, the other Indian did the same on Boone's right; and thus were all the whites embraced or attempted to be embraced in this singular mode of confirming the treaty. As this instant, Black Fish exclaimed "Go!"—when an Indian rose up at some little distance beyond the treaty ground and, drawing a gun from under his blanket, fired it in the air as a signal. All the Indians now immediately grappled and attempted to drag the whites down the clay bank a few steps off, under the cover of which they would be protected from the guns of the fort; but in this attempt, they were completely foiled.

The moment the perfidy was apparent, the marksmen in the bastion fired a volley at the Indians, which prostrated with a mortal wound one of the savages, who had hold of Major Smith, and had its evident effect of disconcerting the others. Colonel Callaway was the first to break loose from the Indians. Boone, in the excitement of the moment, threw Black Fish flat upon the ground, and pretty hard at that, when the other Indian left go his hold; and at this instant, a disengaged Indian, who had carried around the pipe-tomahawk for the treaty-makers to smoke in council and had been assigned no special part in the ceremony of shaking *long hands,* as there were two Indians to each white man without him, now standing in front of Boone, aimed a blow at Boone with his pipe-tomahawk, which partially missed its object, as he was in a posture bending forward ready to run, and the handle struck across the back of his head, cutting a gash through the skin over two inches in length, while the tomahawk edge inflicted a lesser wound between the shoulders. A second blow aimed at him he dexterously avoided, and Major Smith, at that instant passing rapidly by, received it, the force of which, however, being almost spent, caused but a slight wound.

Old John Smith, who was a large, fleshy man and past middle age, came very near being hauled into a ditch or gut leading to the Lick Flat, but with a powerful effort, he sent one of the Indians whistling fully a rod from him down

74. Pipe tomahawk made by Squire Boone, a skilled woodsman, silversmith, blacksmith, and lay Baptist preacher whose legacy is forever overshadowed by that of his more famous older brother. FROM THE COLLECTION OF JIM AND CAROLYN DRESSLAR.

the descending ground and escaped. Crabtree, Squire Boone, and the others, nerved by the unusual excitement of the occasion, shook off the Indians as easily as though they had been so many little children, and thus extricated, they quickly escaped to the fort. When some fifteen paces from the council table, Squire Boone received a ball, grazing one shoulder and the back-bone and lodging in the other shoulder; he was knocked down, falling partly on the fort side of a small hickory tree, but instantly jumped up and ran for the gate through which all had passed except himself and South and which was now closed. They quickly repaired to the door of a cabin between the gate and the bastion nearest the treaty ground, which had been previously designated in case the gate was shut, and there they were admitted.

As the parties to the treaty were precluded from carrying arms there, Boone had instructed his fellow commissioners to leave their guns loaded close to the gate, where they could conveniently be caught up as they returned to the fort, so well persuaded was he of the hostile result of all these anxious efforts. He always declared it as his opinion that it was the timely volley from the fort and seeing their old war chief fall to the ground, probably supposing him killed, that so confused and dismayed the Indians that the whites were enabled to so easily extricate themselves from the grasp of their enemies and escape without receiving a single fatal wound, though not less than two hundred shots were discharged at them by the Indians who were concealed behind the clay bank skirting the Lick Flat, bushes, logs, fences, and stumps in every direction, where they had carefully secreted themselves the preceding night. And the few Indians who had been seen loitering about at some little distance now seized their arms, which had also been conveniently deposited the previous night, and instantly took part in the contest. Under all these circumstances, with such fearful odds against them, the escape of Boone and his fellow treaty-makers was wonderful. It was evidence of God's providential care for the feeble band in the wilderness environed with dangers and threatened with merciless destruction.[6]

The first gun fired after the Indians' treacherous signal was by William Stafford. He was posted in the south-west bastion and had his gun ready and pointing at an Indian sitting on a log some little distance beyond the treaty council, witnessing the proceedings and awaiting the denouement, well bedecked with brooches, half-moons, and other silver ornaments; and while taking sight at the fellow and thinking what a fine mark he would make, the signal-gun fired, and the yell attending the attempted seizure of the white commissioners followed, when he discharged his rifle, instantly killing the chief, for such his appearance proclaimed him. His body lay where he fell till carried off by his companions the ensuing night. At the moment of the first firing, Ambrose Coffee lay stretched at full length on the upper log of the outside of the south-east bastion carelessly viewing the progress of the treaty and at the same time was unawares that he was a target for the concealed Indian marksmen; and at the first fire, no less than fourteen bullet holes were made in his clothes, when he tumbled down into the bastion unhurt and was afterwards no little jeered for his folly in exposing himself with so little concern.

Soon after the attack commenced, Pemberton Rollins had one bone of his arm broken above the elbow,[m] the ball having first passed through the thin part of the two adjoining pickets, which had not in this instance been sufficiently protected by a third one overlapping the joint. The attack was so sudden, the firing on both sides so constant and deafening, three of the treaty commissioners coming in wounded, while Rollins had his arm broken; all these and the roar of musketry mingled with the fearful yells of the savages, answered by the shouts of the men within, greatly alarmed some of the women and children at first, who cried and screamed, expecting the fort would be stormed and taken; and withal, the dogs raised a furious baying, while the cattle in the fort ran about in wild confusion. Such, with the constant anxieties of the mind, formed some of the troubles and dangers incident to an attack so vigorous on the part of the savages.

Captain Boone, upon reaching the fort from the treaty so suddenly broken off, at once went around encouraging the men. All had had their places in case of an attack previously assigned them, and in accordance with this arrangement, Squire Boone, who had seized his loaded gun as he entered the fort, ran to his place in the south-west bastion and soon embraced an opportunity of firing at some Indians he saw dodging about; and re-loading, he found his shoulder hurt him so much in trying to push down the ball that he got his brother Daniel, now coming into the bastion, to ram it down for him. Having again discharged his gun, he went to his cabin, when his wife, who was his only surgeon in all such cases, examined his wound and thought it was only a slight one; he returned to his place in the bastion, but the painfulness of his shoulder increasing, he discovered that the ball was lodged there. When the Indians slacked their fire a little, his brother Daniel Boone, by making quite an incision, cut out the bullet; and in consequence of the wound, which proved a bad one, he had to retire to his house but had a light broad-ax placed beside his bed, declaring that he would use it as long as he could in case the Indians should break into the fort. Captain Boone had his own wounds dressed as soon as he had gone the rounds of the garrison and, by his cool intrepidity, had served to re-assure all classes.

During the afternoon the Indians made a rush towards the fort as though they designed attempting to scale the pickets but were soon beaten back to their lurking places. Proper care had not been taken to cut down all the trees and bushes within shooting distance and burn up the stumps and logs. There were a few sycamores along the Lick Branch just above the treaty-ground, and above the south-east bastion of the fort about forty yards stood the "divine elm," and other trees beyond it in the same direction were quite numerous, as they were also on the hill-side to the south-east and along the river bank opposite the garrison. The abrupt clay bank skirting the Lick Branch next [to] the fort was some half a dozen feet high and afforded ample concealment for the Indians, extending almost from the Indian encampment circling partly around the fort to the river, and the river bank also furnished a place of convenient shelter. The locality of the fort was injudiciously chosen, as the enemy, from the hills on either side of the river, could command a full view of what transpired within the garrison. The fort was a parallelogram containing fully three fourths of an acre, located on a second bank something like sixty yards from the river, and the river was about one hundred yards wide; so from the high bluff on the northern bank of the river, with no intervening bottom as on the south side, the Indians could send an occasional ball into the fort, as they could also from the hill beyond the Lick, which was a somewhat longer shot than the other.[n]

Among the inmates of the fort was an old Dutchman named Mathias Prock, usually called Tice Prock, who was a potter by trade. He could not bear the smell of gunpowder, and the moment the attack commenced, he hid himself under a bed at Colonel Callaway's, and when the good and courageous Mrs. Callaway discovered the trembling coward so ingloriously skulking from his duty, she quickly ousted him from his hiding place with her broom-stick; he then ran into Squire Boone's gun-smith shop adjoining and crept under the bellows, and from this too he was speedily driven by the persevering woman. Tice now took refuge in the new well near the old one and which had been dug only a few feet deep. At this juncture in the affair, Boone and Callaway came up and severely reproached him for his cowardice, but poor Tice frankly confessed his constitutional failing and plead his occupation as an excuse: "Be sure," said he, "I was never made for a figh-der; I ish a bot-ter." He was then told if he would not aid in defending the fort, he should dig in the well, and he worked with considerable zeal so long as he thought he was in the least exposed to the shots of the enemy, then took it quite easy, and finally, when the firing slackened, he ventured to leave the well, declaring he would not work while others were doing nothing. Colonel Callaway again ordered him to his task, when Tice took occasion to demur, whereupon the colonel drew his tomahawk, which he always carried in his belt at his side, and gave chase to the delinquent, who, true to his non-resistant principles, betook himself to his heels and, running to the well, jumped into it at a single leap, then some ten or twelve feet deep, and there kept at work a considerable time.[7]

The first day and night and the second day of the attack, the enemy kept up a warm and steady fire on the fort with but few and brief intermissions. As no sensible effects were produced, new schemes were devised on the part of the Indians and their white and black allies. The Boonesborough people had that year raised some flax, which was stacked near by; this the Indians in the night scattered along a fence running from the lower part of the Lick Flat near the river to Henderson's kitchen, which formed the north-west corner or bastion of the fort, and set it on fire, expecting it would communicate to the buildings; but a hole was dug under the outer wall of the kitchen through which several men crept, pulled down that end of the fence connecting with the fort, and returned in safety. Thus that hopeful design of the enemy proved a failure.

On Friday, the 11th of September, the river below the fort for some distance was discovered to be quite muddy, and a noise was heard under the river bank like the cutting of roots, while the end of a cedar pole was seen moving as if used to loosen the dirt. The garrison at once suspected that the Indians, led on by their French assistants, were pushing a mine from under the river bank, where their operations were concealed, and were throwing the dirt into the stream. Their aim was a matter of various conjecture. Some thought a gun-powder plot was forming to blow up the fort, while others surmised that a wide passage was designed through which to march a large body of warriors into the fort. Two plans were immediately set on foot to frustrate the enemy's design, whatever it might be; one was to erect a battery on the top of Henderson's kitchen for the double purpose of observing these new operations of the enemy and try to dislodge them; and the other, to commence in the kitchen and cut a deep trench or countermine of considerable length parallel with the river. The battery was accordingly erected on the kitchen roof some six feet high, when something of the enemy's movements was observed and dirt was seen as they cast it from the mine into the stream.

That night was the severest firing on both sides that occurred during the siege; commingled reports of the firearms and the vivid flashes of powder in

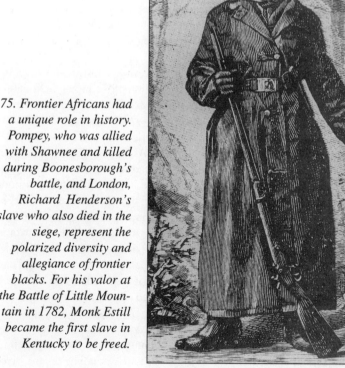

75. Frontier Africans had a unique role in history. Pompey, who was allied with Shawnee and killed during Boonesborough's battle, and London, Richard Henderson's slave who also died in the siege, represent the polarized diversity and allegiance of frontier blacks. For his valor at the Battle of Little Mountain in 1782, Monk Estill became the first slave in Kentucky to be freed.

quick succession, the one echoing back from the surrounding hills and the other partially exhibiting the dark forest in the distance, rendered the scene one of solemn grandeur. The constant flashes of the guns made it so light in the fort that the smallest article could be seen in every part. During the night an Indian crept up to within fifteen steps of the north-west bastion and posted himself behind a tree near where the fence had been fired the preceding night and there kept up a warm fire on the garrison. There was in the fort a Negro servant of Colonel Henderson's named London, who was a real soldier. He imprudently crept into the passage dug the previous night under the sill of Henderson's kitchen, when the little sortie was made to remove the fence, and there in a prostrate condition waited to get a good shot at the bold Indian and fired at the flash of his gun; and London, in turn, became a target for his foe. They snapped their guns several times at each other, and finally the Indian fired clear, and London was shot in the neck, killing him instantly. It was a chance shot aimed only at the snapping of London's gun, but it proved fatal; and the loss of so good a soldier was a source of unfeigned regret to the whole garrison.

Another tragic event occurred during that busy and exciting night. While David Bundrin, a Dutchman who was posted in the south-west bastion, was looking through a port-hole partly closed with a stone, a ball struck close and split, one half penetrating his forehead, producing a mortal wound and rendering him speechless.[8] A little before day, Boone called out to his men to cease firing, as they were necessarily shooting at random and were uncertain of producing any good effects. Though there was plenty of ammunition in the fort, Boone thought it not prudent to expend it in this doubtful way. When the garrison ceased firing, the Indians followed their example.

Perseveringly did the enemy labor at their mine, not venturing, however, to expose themselves as they had done before the erection of the battery. On Saturday morning, Pompey was seen in the opening of the mine near the river, occasionally thrusting up his head to make discoveries or gratify his curiosity. Two or three ineffectual shots were fired at him from the fort, and in each case the balls were observed to strike the water in the river below. At length, William Collins, a fine marksman, took careful aim when Pompey's head was again seen to pop up and fired; the bullet did not, as the others had done, strike the water, and poor Pompey was neither seen nor heard any more. During the three days of the attack, his voice had been constantly heard, sometimes calling upon the garrison to surrender and sometimes engaged in a species of blackguarding or bandying words with the men in the bastions. Hearing no more from that loquacious and important personage, and presuming he had been killed, the men in the fort would call out jeeringly, "Where's Pompey?" In broken English, the Indians would reply that he had gone after more Indians; or that he had "gone hog-hunting"; and sometimes, "Pompey ne-pan"—*he's asleep;* and finally, before their departure, frankly acknowledged, "Pompey nee-poo"—*he is dead.*°

Boone and his companions prosecuted their countermine with energy, commencing in Henderson's kitchen or block-house, and extending up the river through several adjoining cabins, some two or three feet wide and about ten feet deep; and while they kept steadily at work, they at the same time acted in the additional capacity of a guard against the sudden approach of the enemy emerging like so many locusts from the bowels of the earth. While in the trench, the digging of the Indians could be distinctly heard. Boone had a box so adjusted with ropes and fastenings as to be able to raise a portion of the dirt to the top of the palisades and throw it over, that the Indians might be convinced that their scheme was fully understood and the proper means taken to frustrated their designs.

The men would sometimes bawl out to the Indians below, "What are you doing down there?" "Digging a hole," they would reply—"blow you all to hell before morning, may be so! And what are you doing?" "O, as for that," retorted the whites, "we are digging to meet you and will make a hole large enough to bury five hundred of you sons of bitches!" Holder and some others possessing strong muscular powers cast large stones over the cabins and palisades and down the river bank, when the Indians would curse and swear at a round rate and taunt the whites to "come out and fight like men and not try to kill them with stones, like children." Old Mrs. South, in the simplicity of her heart, earnestly besought the men "for God's sake not to throw stones at the Indians, for they might hurt them, make them mad, and then they would seek revenge." The good old lady's humane remark evincing her tender regard for the feelings of the Indians became a by-word among the men and a theme for many a gibe and jeer.

For several days the enemy seemed to toil unceasingly at their mine and penetrated about forty yards or fully two thirds the distance from the river to the fort. It seemed as if by a special interposition of Providence in favor of the beleaguered garrison there were showers almost every night of the siege, and one night towards the close, a very heavy rain fell, which caused large quantities of earth to cave into the subterranean passage and thus put an end to the scheme, whatever it may have been. They probably designed, by springing a mine, to endeavor to blow up a portion of the fort and secure an easy entrance; and failing in this, to penetrate upwards from the subterranean passage to the surface near the fort and thrust through the aperture several long poles and rails all covered with flax and the dry, scaly bark of the hickory securely fastened on, to be set on fire and leaned against the outside of the cabins and palisades and produce a general conflagration. Such huge torches, ready for use, were found near the entrance to the mine after the departure of the Indians, and this was the object for which they were conjectured to have been designed. But all these ingenious plans of the enemy, fraught with so much evil, came to naught.

Failing in their underground operations, the Indians again resorted to their guns, with which they were more familiar. In the center of the fort stood the flagstaff some fifty feet high, from which floated the American colours, and on the top of the staff was a small wooden gun made by Squire Boone, which served the purpose of a weather cock. For several days the Indians fired at the flag and at length cut off the small stem just below the flag with their bullets and raised a great rejoicing when the colours fell. The men in the fort soon took down their

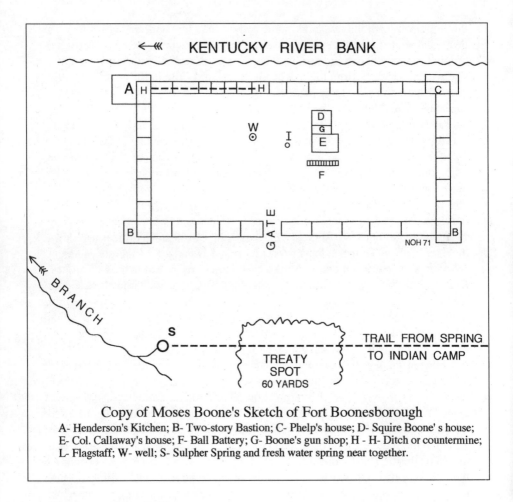

Copy of Moses Boone's Sketch of Fort Boonesborough

A- Henderson's Kitchen; B- Two-story Bastion; C- Phelp's house; D- Squire Boone' s house;
E- Col. Callaway's house; F- Ball Battery; G- Boone's gun shop; H - H- Ditch or countermine;
L- Flagstaff; W- well; S- Sulpher Spring and fresh water spring near together.

76. MAP BY NEAL O. HAMMON.

pole, replaced their ensign, and again it floated gracefully over their heads when they in turn raised a loud huzza. At this demonstration, the Indians remained quiet and made no further attempts to shoot it down again.

Prior to the siege, Squire Boone had constructed a wooden cannon from a tough black-gum tree and strongly banded it with iron, but upon trial it cracked. Then making another, which was twice tried, it was found to answer a very good purpose. During the siege, seeing quite a group of Indians together at the lower part of the nursery nearest the fort, something like two hundred yards distant, the black-gum cannon was brought out, loaded with a swivel ball and some twenty leaden bullets, and fired. The Indians made a prodigious scampering in every direction, and several of them were thought to have been killed and wounded, and certainly considerable havoc was made among the peach trees. Either at that shot or a second one, the cannon cracked and was laid aside, but the Indians were afterwards very cautious about collecting together. Sometimes they would enquire, "Why don't you fire your big wooden gun again?" They were told in reply that they would whenever they could catch the Indians grouped together, but that it was not worth while to be shooting the cannon at a straggling Indian dodging and running about.

Besides preparing refreshments for the men, two women were much engaged in running bullets and making ball-patches. While Captain Boone's daughter Jemima Callaway was standing in her cabin door, which opened within the fort, with her face inside, busily engaged in supplying her father with ammunition, she was struck in the back by a spent ball, which scarcely buried itself in the flesh, carrying with it her linen undress, and in adjusting the linen, the ball fell out. During the whole siege, she partook largely of her father's fearlessness and seemed to expose herself more than other females in carrying ammunition and refreshments to the brave defenders of the garrison.

Between the adjoining cabins, doors were cut during the siege so a passage could be effected nearly around the fort without exposure to the Indian sharpshooters. But this arrangement afforded no protection to the horses and cattle, a few of which were killed and others wounded by shots from the bluff over the river and the hill south-west of the Lick.[9] Having had but little food and water, the cattle had become thin and gaunt; and poor as they were, the garrison would dress the beef of nights when thus killed by the enemy and make meat of them. They were the more ready to do this, as the buffalo meat they had on hand was not only scant in quantity but of a poor quality. During the siege, the Indians wounded a cow outside the fort; the frightened arrival, running to the fort gate, was let in and slaughtered, making the best meat the garrison had pending the attack.

Anticipating the probable attempts of the Indians to set the fort on fire, Squire Boone had, previous to their arrival, unbreeched several old musket barrels and provided them with pistons which would force out from a pint to a quart of water at a time. These squirt guns were distributed among the women in the different cabins so that they might be prepared to extinguish any fire the enemy might communicate to the roofs; and the roofs for additional safety were generally put on in shed style, sloping but one way, and that within the fort. Covered with long shingles which were fortunately fastened but slightly with a single wooden peg at the upper end, they could readily be knocked loose by a pole from within.

For several successive nights the Indians made the greatest efforts to fire the fort. They would collect the long, dry, loose bark of the shell-bark hickory with small splints and sometimes flax, well rubbed with dampened gunpowder, and tie the whole around a stick, which served for a handle, with the end of the torch or faggot left loose and set on fire; and with these the enemy would approach the fort as near as they would dare venture and, from behind some tree or the river bank, would aim to hurl them upon the roofs of the cabins. They were almost invariably hurled with such force that they would pass entirely over the cabins into the fort; and if they happened to lodge, the squirt guns were brought into requisition or the shingles punched off with a pole. These torches were well-calculated to produce mischief, prepared, as they were, with much care and from such combustible materials, and were a foot and a half or two feet in length and five or six inches in thickness.

On one occasion such a torch lodged against the outside door of a cabin, when John Holder, seizing a bucket of water, opened the door and dashed out the blazing faggot; and in doing which he made use of some rough language, for which the good Mrs. Colonel Callaway, who was as much shocked at hearing profanity as she was pained to witness Prock's cowardice, faithfully chided him for want of proper reverence to his Creator.[p] Another plan of the Indians was to fasten smaller sized torches to arrows and shoot them from the bluff over the river. One day an arrow struck a cabin roof and lodged, which had attached to it a small quantity of powder tied up in a rag with a piece of lighted punk; shortly the powder ignited and set the neighboring shingles on fire, when the Indians raised a triumphant shout and at once commenced firing rapidly at the spot to deter the men from venturing there to extinguish it. But the burning shingles were in a few moments loosened from their wooden fastenings and slid off harmlessly to the ground. The showers which so providentially fell almost every night served to keep the cabin roofs more or less dampened and thus rendered them more difficult to set on fire.[10] The enemy were evidently dispirited with their repeated failures to fire the fort.

In these night attacks, the Indians would sometimes attempt to conceal their torches under their blankets and, rushing up as near as they thought prudent, hurl their faggots into the fort. Several in this way lost their lives, as the blazing torches served to render their bodies visible to the marksmen in the bastions. William Hays, Boone's son-in-law, one night saw three Indians approaching with their torches and fired at them; they disappeared, and the signs at the spot next morning indicated that one of them must have been killed. An Indian more daring than his fellows ventured one night to run up directly under one of the projecting bastions and kept so near the wall that the whites could not get a fair chance to shoot him; he at length passed under Stephen Hancock, who fired, when the Indian fell beside a stump as though dead but was seen to draw himself up behind it. Hancock directed a young man near him to shoot the fellow through the head, which he did, and that was the only ball that touched him.

Another adventurous Indian frequently placed himself in the fork of a standing tree on the edge of the bluff over the river and would fire from his eyrie into the fort and sometimes change the scene by pulling up his breech-clout and exhibiting his person in a bantering, derisive manner.[q] Several shots had been ineffectively fired at him, when Captain Boone's famous *Tick-Licker,* as he termed it,[r] a gun of more than common calibre carrying an ounce ball, was obtained, an extra charge of powder was put in, and the bold, saucy fellow was soon seen to tumble lifeless from the tree and roll well nigh two hundred yards to the river.[s]

Such a fatal shot deterred the other Indians from venturing up to remove the body of their fallen comrade till after nightfall, and the hogs meanwhile rooted about the corpse.[11]

Above the fort a hundred yards or more, and near the river bank, was a large, prostrate sycamore which afforded shelter from which for the Indians to fire upon the garrison. They aimed to watch as well as they could and, when a gun was discharged from a port-hole and before the gunner had time to close it, to fire back through the aperture, in which manner Bundrin had been mortally wounded. Two Indians had been posted behind the sycamore, one of whom had a wooden false-face, which he would adroitly expose as though making a preliminary peep in order to secure a good shot and in this way draw the fire of one of the whites in the nearest bastion, when the sham Indian would disappear to make way for the real one to fire into the port-hole. After a few such demonstrations, the man in the fort happened to discover the real state of affairs by discovering the live Indian partly exposed to view while intent on exhibiting to good advantage his wooden humbug; the white marksman now shot at the right one and killed him. The other Indian behind the sycamore now evidently became alarmed for his safety and scampered off. After the siege, signs of blood were found at the spot, as well as the veritable false-face punctuated with two or three bullet holes.

William Hays, discovering an Indian posted behind a stump, sitting upon the ground, loading and shooting frequently with one of his knees exposed, said he would try that fellow's knee; he fired, when it became apparent from no more shots proceeding from that quarter that he was disabled. It was subsequently ascertained that his knee was badly shattered and eventuated in his death. At another time, an Indian was observed sitting carelessly on the fence near the place where the Indian flag-staff was planted, about three hundred yards from the fort. Three men in the garrison, putting heavy charges in their guns, all fired simultaneously at him, when he tumbled off the fence, apparently dead. Such repeated instances of marksmanship had the effect to make the Indians, towards the close, extremely cautious of exposing themselves and probably hastened their departure. In the earlier part of the siege, they had been very garrulous in blackguarding and tantalizing, frequently calling upon the garrison to surrender, promising good treatment, but at length they seemed to get out of heart and said but little.

On Thursday night, the 17th of September, the enemy made their expiring effort. They appeared fully determined to fire the fort and would boldly rush up with their torches and hurl them with all their might towards the denoted cabin roofs. The hideous yelling of the Indians was answered by the screams and yells of the whites within, who after the first day's attack were in high spirits, confident that they could successfully repel any assault or frustrate any stratagem that their enemies could make. It was so light in the fort from the blazing faggots and the constant discharge of musketry that it was said a fire could have been seen any where within the palisades.

Their efforts were of no avail, and they were thought to have lost several warriors that night. William Patten, who lived at Boonesborough and was out hunting when the Indians first appeared, afterwards approaching the fort, discovered the enemy. He lingered near by till this night's attack, when he ascended a hill and witnessed as well as he could, in the night and at a distance, the repeated rush of the Indians with their torches, and hearing the frightful yells and screams, he sorrowfully concluded that the fort was taken and all the garrison, men, women, and children put to death. With this belief, he hastened to Logan's Fort with the sad intelligence.

Early the next morning, the 18th of September, but few Indians were to be seen; they killed some cattle that had not been taken into the fort to provide themselves with a supply of meat for their return march. They did not all depart at once, but gradually, the few remaining occasionally firing a gun to keep up the appearance of a continuance of the siege. When the sun was an hour high that morning, not an Indian remained, and a few guns only were heard far away in the distance. The last party that left were about thirty in number, who crossed the river and bent their course up the stream, and as their trail was found to continue many miles in that direction, they were believed to have been Cherokees.

Again Boonesborough was free, having passed through the longest ordeal of any attack ever made in Kentucky. It proved the last effort of the savages against the home and fortress of Captain Boone. Black Fish and his warriors retired to their homes over the Ohio with no trophies to grace their return and no tidings of victory to convey to their "father," Governor Hamilton of Detroit; yet some remained to disperse themselves around the other stations and waylay their solitary hunters.

Scarcely had the Indians departed, and before the garrison was really aware of it, when some of the men ventured into the garden adjoining the fort, procured a quantity of cabbages, and fed the more than half-starved cattle. During the siege, but little corn had been doled out to them, as it was scarce and was carefully husbanded, not knowing how long they might be compelled to remain cooped up in the garrison. The enemy had taken some cattle away with them, and the third day after their departure, a young cow that had thus been carried into the captivity returned with a buffalo tug three feet in length dangling from her horns, with which she had evidently been tied of nights and managed to get away; and when the poor creature got back to the fort, she capered about, manifesting the greatest possible ecstasy and delight.

"During this dreadful siege," as Daniel Boone justly termed it, "which threatened death in every form," the garrison lost but two men killed, Bundrin and London, and "four wounded," as Boone had recorded it, probably counting himself, brother, daughter, and Rollins, and omitting Major Smith, whose wound must have been very slight.[12] Boone thought there were thirty-seven of the enemy killed and a great number wounded, and this opinion is fully corroborated by the survivors of that memorable siege. When the Indians departed, many of the men who remembered to have had fair shots during the beleaguerment now examined the places the Indians occupied at the time and found many signs of blood. Not one of the enemy's dead was found; as usual, they were carried off, some probably sunk in the river and others thrown into crevices of the rocks some distance from the fort over the Kentucky, whose burial place was pointed out by the numerous buzzards in that quarter.

The enemy had been prodigal in the use of their powder and lead, of which they appeared to have a bountiful supply and which they wasted in the most careless manner, burning and squibbing the powder to no possible purpose. "After they were gone," says Boone, "we picked up one hundred and twenty-five pounds weight of bullets, besides what stuck in the logs of our fort; which certainly is a great proof of their industry." The upper bastion nearest the river, which was commonly spoken of as Phelps' house, was thought to have had a hundred pounds of lead shot into it—evidence of the industrious operation on the part of the Indians of burning powder and whirling leaden bullets from behind the large fallen sycamore in that direction. Around the port-holes particularly, the bullets were thickly studded and had so often struck against other balls and fallen to the ground that whole handfuls of these battered bullets could be scraped up beneath the port-holes of the bastions.

Two or three days after the raising of the siege, Kenton and Montgomery arrived one morning at Boonesborough. They had safely returned from the Paint Creek Town, where Boone and his party had left them. On their way back, with a couple of horses which they had levied from the Indians, they discovered the large Indian trail leading to Boonesborough and, turning their course, went to Logan's Fort. There they learned Patton's doleful report and, wishing to know the truth of the matter, rode over on their Indian ponies, found the fort safe, the Indians gone, and all happy in their deliverance from the hands of the merciless savages. And a few days after, Capt. Thomas Dillard arrived with a small company from Virginia.[13]

A detachment of the Indians hovered around Logan's Fort some time, and every preparation was made there for a protracted siege; a covered way was constructed to the spring, and meat, vegetables, and water [were] provided. Captain Logan went out alone on horseback to drive in the cattle, when he was waylaid and shot at by nine or ten Indians and received two or three dangerous wounds. He escaped to the fort with one of his arms broken and his white horse quite bloody from the rider's wounds. John Martin was dispatched as an express to Virginia for relief at a time when it was thought Boonesborough had fallen. When Manifee and his party, who had gone to aid in the defense of Boonesborough, returned, they came in Indian file and were taken to be Indians. The twenty-four defenders of Logan's Fort took their places at the bastion and, uttering half suppressed curses upon the supposed Indians, said they were ready for them—let them come on, when the women in the garrison were the first to discover their true character [and] exclaimed, *"Why, they are our boys!"* The gate was instantly thrown open and a joyous meeting ensued, which was doubly gratifying, as they were all believed to have been massacred at Boonesborough. After doing some further mischief around Logan's, the Indians departed.[14]

Shortly after, Captain Boone was arraigned before a court-martial convened at Logan's Fort, on charges preferred by Colonel Callaway. These charges were:

i. That Boone had taken out twenty-six men to make salt at the Blue Licks, and the Indians had caught him trapping for beaver ten miles below the Licking, and [he] voluntarily surrendered his men at the Licks to the enemy.

ii. That when a prisoner, he engaged with Governor Hamilton to surrender the people of Boonesborough, to be removed to Detroit, and live under British protection and jurisdiction.

iii. That returning from captivity, he encouraged a party of men to accompany him to the Paint Lick Town, weakening the garrison at a time when the arrival of an Indian army was daily expected to attack the fort.

iv. That preceding the attack on Boonesborough, he was willing to take the officers of the fort, on pretense of making peace, to the Indian camp beyond the protection of the guns of the garrison.

Colonel Callaway said that he [Boone] was in favor of the British government and had sought opportunities to play into its hands and therefore ought to be broken of his commission. Boone defended his conduct at length upon all these charges and maintained that he only aimed at the true interests of his country; that he had used policy, nay duplicity, in trying to win the confidence of the enemy when in their power, he frankly confessed, but contended that it resulted favorably, as he was thereby enabled to escape at a most critical time to give notice of the intended expedition against Boonesborough and have the fort put in proper order for their reception. That the unusual delay of the enemy warranted him in making the little Scioto expedition to learn their movements; and that at the parleying preceding the attack on Boonesborough he had ventured more than he deemed for his personal safety, but he wished to impress on the minds of the Indians his confidence in them and "fool them," as he termed it, as long as possible, all to gain time for the arrival of the anxiously expected reinforcement from Holston. His escape from Indian captivity, his toilsome expedition to Scioto and bold attack on the Indians there, the wound he received, and sleepless watchfulness and sagacity he had exhibited during the unexampled siege of Boonesborough he thought were sufficient evidences of his devotion to the American cause.

After a full investigation, he was honorably acquitted by the court-martial on every charge and at the same time advanced to the rank of major. Though Colonel Callaway, from some unfounded prejudice,[1] and Captain Logan were not exactly pleased with the result, all classes generally confided unhesitatingly in Boone's sagacity and patriotism.[15] It is the pleasing province of the historian, after a lapse of over three fourths of a century, and after a thorough sifting of the whole matter, to declare that not the least criminality attaches to Boone in all these various transactions.

With his conduct fully vindicated, and warm in the affections of the people, Boone now turned his thoughts towards the Yadkin. The Indians had mostly left the country, and Captain Dillard had arrived with a small party of men for the protection of Boonesborough, reporting additional companies on their way to the other stations. On the Rock Castle, Boone met Maj. Daniel Smith with three small companies under his command, consisting of Capt. George Adams, Capt. John Snoddy, and Captain Hays, with eighty men, who marched to Logan's Fort and Harrodsburg, remained awhile, and returned to the Holston.[16] Boone went by way of Watauga and was there enabled to make such representations to his old friend Capt. James Robertson as induced him the following year to visit the Cumberland country and become the pioneer father of Middle Tennessee.[u] In due time, Boone arrived at the Bryan settlement in the Forks of the Yadkin, where he found his wife and family, as well as his daughter, Mrs. [Susannah Boone] Hays, all living comfortably in a small cabin at their kinsman William Bryan's, whose wife was a sister of Daniel Boone. They could not have been much more surprised had he risen from the dead. William Hays had accompanied Mrs. Boone and family from Kentucky shortly after Captain Boone's captivity, and leaving his wife with her mother, Hays immediately returned to Boonesborough. Remaining awhile at William Bryan's, Major Boone removed his family to his father-in-law, Joseph Bryan's, eight miles distant, and where we shall leave them for the present.[17]

Of the remaining events of the year connected with Kentucky, it may be mentioned that by great efforts Colonel Bowman, who made his headquarters at Harrodsburg, procured a quantity of salt from Colonel Clark in Illinois, it is believed, to cure meat for the several garrisons; otherwise they would have been compelled to abandon the country. Kenton, George Clark,[v] and Alexander Montgomery went in October to the Indian country, secured a number of horses, and were overtaken on their return, Montgomery killed, Kenton captured, and Clark escaped. After a great variety of fortune, Kenton at length ran away and safely reached Kentucky.[w] In the latter part of the year, General McIntosh advanced from Pittsburgh with a large army as far as the Tuscarawas River in Ohio, erected and garrisoned Forts McIntosh and Laurens, which served to attract for a time the attention of the Indians from Kentucky.[x]

DRAPER'S NOTES: CHAPTER 16

1. Copies of these two documents have been preserved in the MS. Fleming Papers. They were sent to Colonel Fleming by Col. Arthur Campbell on the 31st of July, when the latter observed: "Would it not be an opportunity for an enterprising officer from Greenbrier or Point Pleasant, in the absence of the Shawanoes [against Boonesborough], to make an incursion over the Ohio? A Captain

and eleven men from Kentucky went within five miles of Chilliacotha lately undiscovered, and returned safe."

2. MS. notes of conversations with Col. Nathan Boone; Capt. John Gass; Joseph Jackson; William M. Kenton and his sister, Mrs. Sarah McCord; Daniel Trabue's MS. memoir; Daniel Bryan's MS. Statement; Boone's Narrative; vol. iii of Hunt's *Western Review;* McClung's *Sketches;* McDonald's *Kenton;* Bradford's Notes; and Perkins' *Pioneers of Kentucky.*

Of this Paint Creek expedition, the following notice appeared in a Williamsburg, Virginia, paper October 9th, 1778, copied into the 7th vol. of Almon's *Remembrance:* "Captain Boone, the famous partisan, has lately crossed the Ohio with a small detachment of men, and nearing the Shawanese towns, repulsed a party of the enemy, and brought in one scalp, without any loss on his side."

3. Col. Daniel Trabue, who was then at Logan's Fort, says the Indian army numbered about one thousand; Bradford's *Notes on Kentucky* says from five to seven hundred; Joseph Jackson, then living with the Shawanoes, says some five or six hundred; Maj. W. B. Smith, who figured in the siege but who was given to exaggeration, says there were not less than six hundred; Colonel Bowman, who wrote from Harrodsburg the month following the siege, says three hundred and thirty Indians and eight Frenchmen; John Gass, then in the fort, a youth of nearly fourteen, says three hundred Indians and forty Canadians; Mrs. Lucy Brashear, also in the fort, and then sixteen years of age, says three hundred and forty altogether; Daniel Boone says the Indian army consisted of 444, commanded by Captain Duquesne, eleven other Frenchmen, and some of their chiefs; Daniel Bryan, who was much at the fort before and after the siege, says upwards of 400 Indians, with some Frenchmen, making nearly 450 altogether; Moses Boone, then in the fort, says 400 Indians and forty Canadians; Isaiah Boone, also then in the fort, says [*wm*]; Col. Nathan Boone always understood his father to say about 400 Indians and about forty Canadians; Robert Hancock, then a child in the fort, says 440 altogether, of whom eleven were Frenchmen and one Negro. Amid such a diversity of opinion, it is natural to presume that Daniel Boone had quite as good an opportunity as any to form a correct estimate. When he spoke of the 12 Frenchmen, he did not say they were all of that class, but that so many were in command.

4. "Kentucky," says the venerable Col. John Johnston, who was for many years [an] Indian agent among the Shawanoes, "is a Shawanoese word, and signifies *at the head of a river.* Kentucky River was formerly much used by the Shawanoese in their migrations north and south; hence the whole country took its name." With this definition before him, Rev. Dr. J. M. Peck remarks, "The repeated statements that it meant 'Dark and Bloody Ground,' is a fiction." Let us see. Filson, who was intimate with Boone, Clark, Harrod, Todd, and other pioneers of Kentucky, and wrote his work from their information and his own observations, says: "The region now called Kentucke, was known to the Indians by the

name of the Dark and Bloody Ground, and sometimes the Middle Ground." At the treaty of Watauga, the Cherokee chief Dragging Canoe said, "The country below the Kentucky was the *Bloody* Ground, that a black cloud hung over it, and it would be found dark and difficult to settle." An aged chief addressed Boone at the same treaty: "Brother, we have given you a fine land, but I believe you will have much trouble in settling it." Commenting on this, Boone adds, "My footsteps have often been marked with blood, and therefore I can truly subscribe to *its original name.*" The late Rev. Dr. John P. Campbell learned from Gen. George Rogers Clark, who was often brought into contact with the Indians, and whose inquisitive mind led him to derive much curious information from them, that "Kentucke, in the language of the Indians, signified *the River of Blood.*" "The Kentucky country," wrote Isaac Morrison, an early pioneer of that country, and published in Casey's American Museum, "in the Indian language implies bloody." "The land of blood.—the name by which Kentucky was at first designated," says the learned Dr. H. McMurtire in his early history of Louisville. "Kentucky," says the venerable Rev. James B. Finlay in his history of the Wyandot Mission, "was the battle ground in the long and bloody wars between the Northern and Southern Indians." Some of the Sacs informed the lamented Col. Joseph Hamilton Daveiss in 1800 that "Kentucky had been the scene of much blood, and was filled with the manes of its slaughtered inhabitants." Heckewelder observes that the Six Nations "insinuated that all the land of the Ohio country was stained with blood, and that even the rivers were of the colour of blood—figurative expressions when speaking of a country in which bloody wars had been carried on." And now, as we see, Black Fish declares to Boone, on this bank of the Kentucky, "This is the *Bloody Land,* you know."

TFB: *For a revisionist analysis and more modern attempt to refute the use of the expression "Dark and Bloody Ground," see A. Gwynn Henderson, "Dispelling the Myth: Seventeenth- and Eighteenth-Century Indian Life in Kentucky," Register of the Kentucky Historical Society 90 (1992): 1–25.*

5. From the records before us and the recollections of Captain Gass, Moses and Isaiah Boone, Col. Nathan Boone and lady, Daniel Bryan, Col. Daniel Trabue, Mrs. Lucy Brashear, and others, we are enabled to present a list of the most of the noble defenders of Boonesborough, whose names and memories deserve to be immortalized:

Daniel Boone, his son Israel Boone, his two sons-in-law, William Hays and Flanders Callaway, his brother Squire Boone, their nephew Daniel Wilcoxen, Col. Richard Callaway and his son Caleb Callaway, Maj. William B. Smith, Capt. David Gass and his nephew John Gass, Capt. William Buchanan, John Holder, John South Sen., Samuel South, Edward Bradley, [*wm*] Crabtree, William Stafford, Ambrose Coffee, Pemberton Rollins, William Collins, Thomas Phelps, Joseph Phelps, William Cradlebaugh, William Bush, Jesse Hodges, Joseph Proctor, William Beasley, Reuben Searcey, Richard Searcey, William Hancock, Stephen Hancock, Morris Hancock, Samuel Henderson, John Callaway, Ephraim

Drake, John Hill, Oswald Townsend, John Bryan, Edward Nelson, John Bullock, Reuben Doblin, William Manifee, John King, David Bundrin, and the Negro London, the two latter of whom were killed. King and Manifee were of the Logan's Fort party. Here we have the names of forty-four; to these should be added the venerable Capt. John Gass, who still survives, a son of Capt. David Gass, and who performed all the duty that could be expected from a youth in his fourteenth year. Moses and Isaiah Boone, sons of Squire Boone, though old enough to fully comprehend all that transpired, were yet too young to render any martial service.

6. McClung, in his *Sketches of Western Adventure,* characterizes this treaty as a contest of folly between Boone and the French commander "as to which should display the quantum of shallowness"; and adds, "we look here in vain for the prudence and sagacity which usually distinguished Boone." Butler and others have taken the same view. The censure is plausible from the statements then given, but they were incorrect and incomplete. As Simon Kenton remarked to the Hon. John H. James, "They may say what they please of Daniel Boone, he acted with wisdom in that matter." Succor was momentarily expected, and the project of the treaty served to gain time for the arrival of the reinforcement. William D. Gallagher, Esq., in an article in the *Hesperian Magazine* for December 1838, was the first writer on western history after McClung who hesitated to censure Boone's conduct in this transaction, as he thought that the published facts were then too meagre to form a correct opinion. The fact of an express having been sent to Col. Arthur Campbell on Holston for assistance, and hence the motive for staving off the attack as long as possible, was communicated by the one of the authors of this work to the Reverend Dr. Peck for his memoir of Boone. We hope that our hero, Boone, is fully exonerated from Mr. McClung's hasty animadversions.

7. Shortly after the siege, a fine horse of Colonel Callaway's was missing, and after a long and vigilant search, he was finally discovered by someone taking a peep of curiosity into the new well, into which the horse had fallen, probably in the night, without injury. So circumscribed was his strange domicil that the poor animal's neck was uncomfortably twisted around to adjust himself to his new quarters. A passage was dug down and the prisoner released. Tice was mightily pleased that Colonel Callaway had, as he said, "got come up with" for making him dig the well. Prock in after years went to Tennessee, probably the Elk River region, and has long since passed away at a good old age but was fond, it is believed, of recounting his exploits at the siege of Boonesborough.

8. He lived a number of hours, all the while resting his forehead in his hands and his elbows upon his knees, constantly rocking his body in a sitting posture until all his brains by the action had apparently worked out of the wound, sometimes wiping away the oozing brains with his hand. His simple-hearted wife, while her husband was in this dying condition, would consolingly remark, "It vas Got's plessing dat de pall didn't hit 'im in de eye." Bundrin was a good soldier and had been wounded in the thigh when at work in the field the preceding spring.

9. Among the wounded cows was Squire Boone's "Old Spot," in the udder. She was retained in the family during all their changes and removals for many years; and finally, when Squire Boone resided in what is now Shelby County, she got crippled and had to be shot, much to the grief of the whole family.

10. These rains, too, and more especially towards the close of the siege, enabled the garrison to catch rain water for the half-furnished cattle, while the old well furnished a bare sufficiency for drinking and cooking purposes.

11. Peck evidently alludes to this incident but makes a Negro instead of an Indian the victim, and adds that the body was left by the Indians, who would not touch a Negro's remains, and that he had deserted from the fort during the parleying preceding the siege. This is a singularly confused statement. If the Negro Pompey is referred to, the only Negro known to have been with the Indians, and who was killed during the siege, it is certain that he never deserted from Kentucky; he had been many years with the Indians, having been probably taken when young on the frontiers of Virginia during the old French and Indian War. He was not killed over the river but at the mouth of the subterranean passage, as survivors of the siege can testify, and his body was never seen after he was killed.

12. Maj. William Bailey Smith was born in Prince William County, Virginia, in 1738, and prior to the Revolution migrated to North Carolina. He accompanied Colonel Henderson to Watauga and was present at the purchase of the Kentucky country from the Cherokees in March 1775, and his name appears as one of the witnesses to the treaty. He appears to have gone on to Boonesborough in Colonel Henderson's rear party and that year explored the country as far as Green River. The next year, he assisted in recovering the captive girls and was at the time quite smitten with one of them; and in 1777, when Boonesborough was infested by Indians, he went to the Yadkin and raised a company for its relief. Early in 1778 he was appointed major of Clark's Illinois regiment and raised some men for that corps; and early in June, after returning to Boonesborough, he headed a party to the Ohio in pursuit of Indians and in a skirmish defeated them. The details show that he was prominent in the big siege of Boonesborough, which was his last military service.

Returning to North Carolina, he was appointed a commissioner in conjunction with Colonel Henderson to extend the western boundary between North Carolina and Virginia and was engaged in this service during the hard winter of 1779–'80. Receiving from Col. John Luttrell as a compensation for services rendered him a tract of land on Green River in Kentucky, about sixteen miles from Henderson, he settled on it in 1794. He never married but raised some nephews whom he adopted, and died at his residence on the Green River in October 1818, at the age of eighty years. He was a man of intelligence and good sense, of fair character, rather fond of the bowl, and somewhat inclined to exaggerate his pioneer services. Though living as a recluse for many years, he was cheerful and social. In appearance, he was about six feet in height, of slender form, fine forehead, sandy hair, and blue eyes. His old papers were unfortunately destroyed by the burning of his old mansion several years after his death.

13. This detailed account of the *big siege of Boonesborough,* as it has long been designated by the pioneers of Kentucky, has been drawn up from the following sources: MS. Fleming Papers; MS. letter of Col. John Bowman in the Clark Papers; MS. statements of Daniel Bryan, Capt. John Carr, Mrs. Lucy Brashear, Robert Hancock, Man. John L. Martin, Wyatt H. Ingram; MS. notes of conversations with Gen. Simon Kenton by Hon. John H. James, furnished by the latter to Mann Butler, the historian of Kentucky, and by Mr. Butler for this work; Trabue's MS. Narrative; Virginia MS. Archives; MS. notes of conversations with Col. Nathan Boone and lady, Moses and Isaiah Boone, Capt. John Gass, Joseph Jackson, Maj. George M. Bedinger, Capt. Henry Wilson, Capt. Benjamin Briggs, and W. M. Kenton. Of these, Captain Gass, Moses and Isaiah Boone, Mrs. Brashear, and Robert Hancock were in the fort during the siege, and the others enjoyed fine opportunities of learning the facts they furnished. The principal printed authorities consulted are Boone's Narrative; an account of the siege detailed by Maj. William B. Smith and published in Hunt's *Western Review* for January 1821; Bradford's *Notes on Kentucky,* Marshall's *Kentucky*, McClung's *Sketches,* McDonald's *Kenton,* Dr. Peck's memoir of Boone, and Perkins' *Pioneers of Kentucky.*

Mrs. Brashears, the daughter of Thomas Phelps, was born in what is now Campbell County, Virginia, in July 1762, was early taken to Boonesborough, and shared in the troubles of that garrison during the successive Indian attacks. She is said to have been the first woman married at Louisville, Kentucky. Her death occurred in Madison County, Kentucky, June 18th, 1854, at the advanced age of almost ninety-two years; and to the last, she was a sprightly, active, cheerful Christian lady of the old pioneer school.

14. MS. Narrative of Col. Daniel Trabue, who was then stationed at Logan's Fort.

15. Trabue's MS. Narrative is our only authority for this court-martial. Colonel Trabue was present at the trial, and he was an intelligent, truthful witness. He was much engaged in public life and was many years a member of the Baptist denomination. He was a relative of Chesterfield County, Virginia, where he was born March 31, 1760; he came to Kentucky in the spring of 1778 and on the way killed an Indian in a skirmish. He was also at the capture of Cornwallis. This meritorious pioneer died in Adair County, Kentucky, in 1840, at the age of eighty years.

16. These troops had been sent out by Col. Arthur Campbell of Washington County, Virginia. When he received Captain Boone's letter, with Boone's and Hancock's deposition, the last of July, he immediately forwarded them by express to the governor and Council of Virginia, who on the 12th of August "directed Col. Campbell to send not under one hundred, nor more than one hundred and fifty militia, officered in the usual manner, for the relief of Kentucky."

17. MS. statements of Daniel Bryan, Cornelius Carmack, Mrs. John B. Craighead, and conversations with Col. Nathan Boone and lady.

EDITOR'S NOTES: CHAPTER 16

    a. Alexander McKee (?–1799) was of mixed-blood parentage. His father was Irish trader Thomas McKee; his mother was Shawnee. During Lord Dunmore's War (1774), he was living in Pennsylvania with a Shawnee wife and working as a trader and deputy Indian agent. Confined to Fort Pitt by American soldiers, McKee, Elliott, and Girty made their escape on the night of March 28, 1777, and fled to Detroit to defect to the Crown. McKee served as captain and commissary in the British Indian Department and became an important mediator among the Algonquians, inciting and leading raids on Ohio's frontier. By 1794, as deputy superintendent of Indian Affairs, McKee was working to build native resistance against American intrusion in the Old Northwest, but his efforts dramatically crumbled near his home and trading post on the Maumee at the Battle of Fallen Timbers (1794). Two years later he moved to Malden, Ontario, where he died in 1799.

    b. Matthew Elliott (1739–1814) was an Indian agent with strong native ties and an Indian wife. Prior to Lord Dunmore's War, he had fought French-allied Indians while serving under Gen. Henry Bouquet. After fleeing to Detriot with McKee and Girty, Elliott defected and served the British Indian Department. Captain Elliott fought in key Kentucky campaigns, including Bird's siege of Forts Martin's and Ruddell's (1780) and the Battle of Blue Licks (1782). He served with Tecumseh at Detroit in 1812 and died in 1814 in Ontario.

    c. See chapter 15, note i.

    d. George Rogers Clark's military career reached its zenith with his bold invasion of the Old Northwest. The exploit began auspiciously on June 24, 1778, under the dark skies of a full solar eclipse that to his men portended great things to come. On July 4, 1778, Lieutenant Colonel Clark's motley, poorly provisioned army of 178 soldiers captured Kaskaskia; shortly thereafter, a contingent of Clark's men led by Capt. Joseph Bowman seized Cahokia and other small Illinois French communities; on February 25, 1779, Lt. Gov. Henry Hamilton, commandant of Detroit (whom Clark dubbed the "Hair Buyer"), en route to attack Clark on the Wabash, badly miscalculated and, in a stunning reversal, was forced to surrender Fort Sackville (Vincennes) to Clark and give himself up as a hostage.

    Though Draper declares that Clark's actions put "an end to British rule and influence in the Illinois country," the impact of his feat was short-lived for several reasons: Clark's newly garrisoned forts were far from aid; inflated Continental currency kept Americans stationed in the Old Northwest from procuring food and supplies from Virginia and the local French *habitants;* having no money, Clark's forces could not sustain good relations with the Indians through gift giving. British-allied warriors so harassed Clark's Illinois outposts that the Americans had to withdraw by 1781.

    e. Draper, as in most other places, corrected Boone's spelling and grammar in this letter.

f. Swivel guns, also called rampart guns, amusettes, or wall guns, were modified large-bore muskets (though some were rifled), balanced on an easily maneuverable mechanism. Transported by canoe or horseback, swivels were used throughout the fur trade. Volleys from swivel guns loaded with buck or ball or any combination thereof devasted vessels, cabins, and forts, as well as human flesh. That the Indians boasted to have such weaponry was sheer braggadocio. Had the Kentuckians' British-allied native foes been so armed, the outcome of the siege of Boonesborough and the fate of its occupants and perhaps even of Kentucky and the Ohio country might have been radically different.

g. In this letter Draper modified Callaway's grammar to his own nineteenth-century tastes.

h. Selling Indian wares seized by Kentuckians during raids on native towns in the Ohio lands gave frontier Anglo settlements a novel source of lucre as well as bestowing a sense of vicarious bravado to the buyer. Wampum, sterling ear-bobs and brooches, blankets, clothing, shot bags, powderhorns, peltry, bows and arrows, guns, war clubs, brain-tanned deerskin bags dyed black in boiled black walnut hulls and garnished with deerhair tufts and embellished with porcupine quillwork, dried scalps stretched on hoop frames, ponies, spirit effigies—all such booty and more fetched high prices when "sold at vendue" at forts and stations. Revenue from the loot auctions not only helped to pay militia fighters but also to incite future forays of such thievery.

In one such act of looting for profit, during Clark's 1782 Shawnee campaign, William Clinkenbeard watched as Michael Cassidy, a short, chunky Irishman, ran back from the first wave of assault "with his fingers all bloody . . . he had cut off their fingers and noses and earbobs to get their trinkets. . . . Had a whole handfull of trinkets that he got." See William Clinkenbeard to Rev. John D. Shane, c. 1843, DM 11CC:54–66.

i. Traveling "Indian file" meant traveling single file, with one or two warriors on point, flank scouts to the sides, the rest of the band spaced eight to ten paces apart, not only to conceal numbers but also to give the appearance of greater numbers. One or two trusted scouts lagged behind in the party's rear to spy out the back trail.

j. Boone, upon his return to Boonesborough from his Shawnee captivity, tacitly assumed command; people trusted him, aside from a vocal few, and he was their natural leader. But Maj. William Bailey Smith made a handy foil to help Boone sidestep his word to Black Fish to capitulate. The Kentuckians presented Smith as the fort's new commandant who had taken Boone's place. Smith played his role well to impress the Indians with his high rank and status, resplendently attired in full regalia, "dressed up in a red scarlet coat, and macaroni hat, with an ostrich feather in it." (Rev. John D. Shane, c. 1843, DM 11CC:13.)

k. See chapter 4, note g, for more on wampum.

l. In May 1763 Ottawa war leader Pontiac proposed to meet in the fort with Detroit British commandant Maj. Henry Gladwin under the guise of treaty making. On the appointed day, Pontiac came with his men, bearing underneath their blankets weapons—cut-down muskets, tomahawks, knives, war-clubs. Alerted to the scheme hours before Pontiac entered, Gladwin made a bold show of his men parading with muskets with fixed bayonets, the whole time keeping his cannon aimed at Pontiac's milling throng. The display was not lost on Pontiac, who never again came so close to taking Detroit.

Kentuckians at Boonesborough in 1778 feared such subterfuge from Black Fish. For this reason, the whites parleyed about sixty yards from the fort, well within range of the fort's marksmen perched along its log walls and concealed in corner blockhouses.

m. Pemberton Rollins (also spelled Rollings or Rawlings) survived this episode as one of Boonesborough's few casualties in that fateful September 1778 siege. But in March 1780 Shawnee warriors shot him on the banks of the Kentucky a mile and a half from the fort at the site of Col. Richard Callaway's newly established ferry. Rollins sprinted a quarter of a mile, then fell to the earth in a swoon, living just long enough to tell his tale of horror to rescuers who ran to his aid when they heard the shots.

Colonel Callaway was with Rollins and died that day too, killed in the skirmish's opening volley. Warriors cut him up badly with knives and tomahawks, scalped the long black and silver mane from his head, stripped the big pale corpse naked, and rolled it down the Kentucky's muddy bank. Years later, John Gass told Rev. John D. Shane that Callaway was "the worst barbequed man" he ever saw (DM 11CC:16).

The Indians kidnaped the two African slaves working at the site.; they were never seen again. A fifth man, who escaped injury, was the only survivor.

n. Even at these ranges, Indian sharpshooters could do much more than lob "an occasional ball into the fort." According to Neal Hammon, who has measured the distance, "the hills on the far side of the river were actually 260 yards from the fort, and the hills on the same side were over 300 yards away."

Musket and rifle fire would have been difficult at such long ranges. Nevertheless, propelled by extra-heavy black powder charges, 60-caliber lead balls are certainly able to kill a man. Hundreds of well-armed Indians blazing away at a three-quarter-acre clearing would have kept the fort's defenders and livestock scampering for cover.

o. This officious black man turned Indian, who was perhaps a runaway slave and now was threatening, with his Indian brothers, to lay siege to a fort full of white defenders, was an inviting target. The Shawnee left him lying on the battlefield when they retreated.

But who actually killed Pompey? Five men have been credited by historians, writers, and in folklore: Simon Kenton, who was not in the fort during the siege; Daniel Boone, who did not take credit for the shot (and Nathan denied that his father had shot Pompey); William Hancock, who believed he did it; John Martin, who thought he had nailed Pompey with his Germanic, long-range Jaeger rifle; and William Collins, a noted Boonesborough sharpshooter whom Draper, after interviewing thirty-eight sources, including five eyewitnesses who were in the siege, believed was Pompey's true slayer. See also Ted Franklin Belue, "Did Daniel Boone Kill Pompey, the Black Shawnee, at the 1778 Siege of Boonesborough?" *Filson Club History Quarterly* 67 (1993): 5–22.

p.   John Holder reportedly raised cursing to a high art. Here, when his mother-in-law, the pious Mrs. Callaway, beseeched him to pray for help, he allegedly retorted, "I've no time to pray, goddammit!" See John Gass to Rev. John D. Shane, c. 1843, DM 11CC:14.

q. In other words, "Kiss my ass!"—a common native insult in time of war to whites and to each other. In another such Anglo-Native exchange during the siege, Draper recorded (DM 4C:26{11–12}), Joseph Jackson—one of Boone's salt boilers turned Shawnee who fought against the Kentuckians—told him he saw a treed Indian "come down from the tree, turn the insulting part of his body to the besieged and defiantly pat it."

r. I have yet to find any other mention of Boone naming his gun; this may be apocryphal, much like Cooper's Natty Bumppo and his trusty rifle "Kill Deer." If "Tick-Licker" shot a one-ounce ball (approximately .66-caliber), that is not necessarily "a gun of more than common caliber," but it is a big-bore rifle. British "Brown Bess" and Dutch muskets ranged from .73- to nearly .80-caliber, as did their American-made Committee of Safety counterparts. French muskets and fusils—like the Charleville and the Tulle—were slightly less hefty, averaging .62- to .66-caliber. If Boone's rifle shot a one-ounce ball, then he must have backed it with a black-powder charge of 70 to 90 grains. Draper says he doubled the charge for his crack shot at this insulting "bold, saucy fellow."

s. Draper's rendition of Boone blasting the treed Indian sounds too much like an earlier tale (partially cited in note q, this chapter) that he collected near the time he began writing *Life, viz:*

> They discovered an Indian in a tree watching the movements of the besieged. One of the men named [Stuffly] Cooper had a long range yagur [Jaeger rifle]. . . . There was a stump in the fort yard and they brought out a chair and placed [it] at the stump in which Cooper seated himself and placed his gun upon the stump. The Indian . . . came down from the tree, turned the insulting part of his body to the besieged and defiantly patted it. Cooper took deliberate aim and at the crack of his gun, the Indian jumped into the air.

This tale and the one of Boone and "Tick-Licker" sounds a lot like another one that in April 1844 Joseph Jackson told Draper and in whose collection it appears in DM 11C:62(16): "A couple of Indians was seen on the hillside. . . . [John] Martin, with his old yagur and one-ounce balls, leveled away and shot one. . . . Martin raised his back sight to take aim for so long a shot." A common thread seems to run through these three tales but one is hard-pressed to know which may have begotten which.

t. Col. Richard Callaway, who was some twenty years older and outranked Captain Boone, resented his rise as a leader. And that the Shawnee still held Callaway's teenage nephews, Micajah and James, two of the captured salt boilers, fired his rancor toward Boone. Callaway's attempt to humiliate him before his peers via court-martial was one of Boone's darkest hours.

There is no record of Boone ever talking about the ordeal. Daniel Trabue, a young Huguenot hunter living at Logan's Station, observed the proceedings. Trabue's autobiographical narrative (1827; DM 57J) is the only eyewitness account. After listing the four charges, Trabue notes Boone's defense of his actions:

> The reason he give up these men at the blue licks was that the Indeans told him they were going to Boonsbourough to take the fort. Boon said he thought he would use some stratigem. He thought the fort was in bad order and the Indeans would take it easy. He (Boon) said he told the Indians the fort was very strong and too many men for them (and the officers at Detroyt) and he would go and shew them some men—to wit, 26—and he would go with them to Detroyt and these men also, and when they come to take Boonsbourough they must have more warriors than they now had. Boon said he told them all these tails to fool them. He also said he Did tell the Britesh officers he would be friendly to them and try to give up Boonsbourough but that he was a trying to fool them.

u. Capt. James Robertson (1742–1814) was a frontier leader, farmer, hunter, and Indian fighter–diplomat of Scotch-Irish lineage who hailed from Brunswick County, Virginia. He moved to North Carolina's Upper Neuse River as a youth and by 1771 had built a cabin on the Watauga. He fought in the east Tennessee theater of Lord Dunmore's War (1774) and reputedly fired the opening shot in the war's last fight at Point Pleasant. His singular efforts in bringing settlers to the Cumberland earned him the title "Father of Middle Tennessee."

v. George Clark, who accompanied Simon Kenton and Alexander Montgomery on this horse-stealing mission, was a new arrival and scout at Logan's Station, not the Virginia military leader George Rogers Clark.

w. Simon Kenton and two of the captive salt boilers, Nathaniel Bullock and Jesse Copher, escaped from Detroit in June 1779. Though they were aided by American sympathizers at the fort, who got them guns and provisions and sent them southwest to the Wabash to avoid the Indian towns along the Scioto and Great Miami, their thirty-day trek back to Boonesborough was not easy. The famished, half-sick trio dodged Indians, slept during the day and traveled at night, and lived off slippery elm bark, one porcupine, and an occasional coon.

x. In 1778 Congress ordered the Continental Army's commander in chief, George Washington, to launch a western offensive to put an end to the Ohio Indians attacking Pennsylvania's western borders. Washington ordered Scottish expatriate Brig. Gen. Lachlan McIntosh (1725–1806) to leave Fort Pitt to campaign in the Upper Ohio Valley—to build a series of forts, cut a supply road, and if possible, to attack Detroit. That October McIntosh's troops descended the Ohio and, at the mouth of the Beaver River, erected Fort McIntosh, manned by Col. Daniel Brodhead. A month later McIntosh was at the site of present-day Bolivar, Ohio, building Fort Laurens—named for his friend Henry Laurens (1724–92), South Carolina's esteemed Revolutionary War statesman—on the banks of the Tuscarawas, to be garrisoned by Col. John Gibson and 150 Virginians. Due to repeated attacks, lack of provisions, poor morale, and inept planning, by the following October both outposts were abandoned.

Thus concludeth Dr. Draper's chronicle. Had he finished it, it would have been an extraordinary effort—the Boone book of the nineteenth century, a landmark work on the pioneer.

Though the narrative of "The Life of Daniel Boone" ends in 1778, Boone's days numbered two score and two years more. His life, he once said, was like a leaf skimming down a pulsing creek, snagging here and there on rocks and clutter, spinning, turning, upending, but always moving on—forward.

And so thus it was.

Boone emigrated to Spanish Missouri in 1799 and died there in 1820. By the time of his death, the old woodsman had become a legend.

He still is. New Boone books appear with regularity and remain strong sellers, Boone societies abound, and mysteries about his life spark debate. After his move west of the Mississippi, did he visit Kentucky to pay off his debts? Did he meet Lewis and Clark in 1804 on the Missouri's banks and pass the torch? Did his pale blue eyes behold the majestic Rocky Mountains? And the greatest and most controversial mystery of them all: Where is he buried? Both Kentucky and Missouri claim that distinction.

No matter where his bones lie, Boone's spirit lives on and embodies the best of what makes America proud—honesty, determination, undaunted courage in the face of adversity, triumph of the human will, and always, the restless push to the mountaintop to see what lies beyond. And then to go there. Such is the true legacy of America's first frontier hero, Daniel Boone.

*John Peter Salling.—Dr. Thomas Walker.—Boone Genealogy.—Col.
William Preston.—Col. Arthur Campbell.—Gen. William Russell.—Gen.
Daniel Smith.—Sketches of the Members of the Transylvania
Convention.—Col. Thomas Slaughter.—Col. James Harrod.—Col.
Richard Callaway.—Col. John Floyd.—Col. John Todd.—Col. William
Cocke.—Alexander Spotswood Dandridge.—Dr. Samuel Henderson.—
Isaac Hite.—James Douglas.—Azariah Davis.—Capt. William Moore.—
Nathan Hammond.—Rev. John Lythe.—Samuel Wood.—Daniel and
Squire Boone, and Valentine Harmon.—Sketches of the Members
of the Transylvania Company.—Col. Richard Henderson.—
Col. John Williams.—Thomas Hart.—Col. David Hart.—Capt. Nathaniel
Hart.—Col. John Luttrell.—James Hogg.—William Johnson.—
Leonard Henley Bullock.*

JOHN PETER SALLING

Salling was a native of Germany and upon his arrival in this country first settled in or near Williamsburg, Virginia, where he seems to have followed the occupation of a weaver. There he became acquainted with Thomas Marlin, a peddler who traded in a small way from Williamsburg to the newly settled region where Winchester has since grown up; and probably Marlin told him of the beautiful country of the valley beyond the Blue Ridge. Anxious to learn more about it, Salling joined Marlin, and the adventurers soon crossed the Blue Ridge and passed up the charming valley as far as the fine bottom lands in the Forks of James River, a little below the Natural Bridge. This must have been about the year 1732. Salling returned to Williamsburg, and he and his brother, whose name was probably Adam, entered a large tract of land in the Forks of James River and soon settled there. Adam Salling died unmarried. While yet at Williamsburg, John Peter Salling met John Lewis and John Mackey, who had just arrived from the mother country, and imparted to them such information of the Virginia Valley as led them to settle there. Lewis was the father of Gen. Andrew Lewis, who commanded at the battle of Point Pleasant.

The name of John Peter Salling appears among the militiamen in or prior to 1742, commanded by Capt. John McDowell, in the beat which has since furnished territory for Rockbridge County. If we may credit the tradition of Salling's descendants and the aged people of his neighborhood, when Salling and his party of explorers in 1742 arrived near the present town of Salem on the Roanoke

River, they were made prisoners by the Cherokees and taken down the New and Kenhawa rivers to the Ohio in a buffalo-skin boat and thence to the Mississippi and were taken by the French. A son of Salling's, who was one of the captives, soon died, and the father was put on board of a vessel to be sent to France as a spy and also to be interrogated with regard to the designs of the British government. Luckily, the vessel fell into the hands of some British cruiser, as Great Britain had recently declared war against France, and Salling was soon landed at Charleston, South Carolina. He reached home, after an absence of over three years, on the very evening that had been appointed for the marriage of his good spouse to another, for she had long given up her John Peter as lost or dead. She instantly recognized his well-known voice on the south-western bank of the James River, when a boat was quickly despatched to convey him over; and although the wedding was singularly frustrated, the occasion nevertheless proved one of real heart-felt joy to his family and all the assembled neighbors.

In a manuscript diary among the Preston Papers, written by Col. John Buchanan, it is recorded that while the writer was spending a couple of days with the old pioneer in October 1745, he copied "Peter Salling's Journal." In September 1747 Salling was a captain of militia; he probably died before the breaking out of the French and Indian War of 1754, as his name does not appear in any of the printed or manuscript records of that period. Dr. William Fleming, who subsequently distinguished himself in the battle of Point Pleasant, in a manuscript letter to William Preston, December 17th, 1756, after mentioning the return of "the manuscript Journal of Salling's trip to New Orleans," which he had loaned, remarked: "It is not well done, and contains some contradictions; yet some part of it is of use to me." This journal is probably lost.

John Peter Salling, or Peter Salling ,as he was usually called, left one son, George, and three daughters, all of whom had families; one of the girls married a Kilgore. The late Rev. Archibald Alexander says in a manuscript letter written in 1849: "The Salling family, were I believe, famous for their daring enterprise. I recollect when a child to have heard my father giving an account of the way which old George Salling, a noted hunter, took to teach his boys to swim. He would take them to deep water and throw them in, and leave them to get out as they could, unless they appeared in real danger, when he would go in after them."

The name is vulgarly pronounced Sallee or Salley, though uniformly written Salling by the family. Several of George Salling's grandchildren are yet living, some on the ancient homestead in the Forks of the James River and in that neighborhood, while others have emigrated to the West—MS. Preston Papers; MS. correspondence of the Rev. Samuel D. Campbell of Rockbridge County, Virginia, and of the late venerable Professor Alexander of Princeton.

DR. THOMAS WALKER

Dr. Walker's ancestors emigrated early from England to Virginia—how early, tradition does not inform us. Among the Virginia adventurers of 1620 there was a George Walker;[1] and in 1667 there was a Maj. Thomas Walker representing

Gloucester County in the Virginia Assembly, who produced satisfactory evidence that he had, three years before, upwards of seventy thousand mulberry trees in successful cultivation and claimed the bounty offered for the encouragement of the culture of silk.[2] This latter person was most likely the ancestor, perhaps the grandfather, of Dr. Thomas Walker, whose father's name was also Thomas.

His son, the subject of this sketch, was born about the year 1710 in King and Queen County, Virginia, in or near the little hamlet of Walkerton on the Mattaponi. His father, it is believed, died while the son was yet young, who, having received a respectable education for that day, was sent to Williamsburg, the capital and metropolis of the colony, and placed in the drug-store of Dr. George Gilmer. With Dr. Gilmer, who married his sister Sarah and was his guardian, young Walker studied physic and became one of the most skillful physicians of his day. The celebrated Dr. William Baynam of Virginia was one of his early pupils.[3]

There is reason to suppose that Dr. Walker first located himself in Hanover County, Virginia, and there for awhile practiced his profession; and while there, married Miss Mary Winston, daughter of Langaloo William Winston, the maternal uncle of the renowned orator Patrick Henry;[4] and having borne him four sons, died, and he was subsequently united in marriage with Colonel Syme's widow, who was the daughter of Nicholas Meriwether. Langaloo Winston was a great hunter and had a quarter in Bedford or Albemarle, where he sometimes spent half a year in deer-hunting, mixing with the Indians and dressing in their costume, and it is quite probable it was from this Langaloo Winston that Dr. Walker first learned of the fine country skirting the mountains in Albemarle and Louisa.[5] He selected a lovely spot at the eastern base of the south-west Mountains for his future home, which he named Castle Hill and where he soon settled. It was many years within the limits of Louisa County but was at length set off to Albemarle and is now the residence of the Hon. William C. Rivers, whose lady is Dr. Walker's grand-daughter.

Engaging early and extensively in the business of a land-monger led him to make his exploring trip in 1748 to the Holston Valley and to Kentucky in 1750—the latter of which, so fully for the first time noticed in this work, has given to his name a notoriety for enterprising adventure it would never otherwise have obtained. Upon the breaking out of the French and Indian War, he was appointed commissary general for Virginia and served in that capacity seven years, having deputies where needed along the frontiers. In fulfilling the duties of his office, he accompanied Braddock's ill-fated expedition and shared in the disasters of the memorable defeat at the Monongahela on the 9th of July, 1755. In the flight which ensued, he found himself in company with a soldier to whom he offered a large sum in gold if he would stop long enough to aid him in getting off his boots, which greatly retarded his progress; but the soldier's fear of the tomahawk and scalping knife was stronger than his avarice. He left the doctor, who hid in a ravine till a swarm of Indians had passed, when, ridding himself of his troublesome boots and, soon after, cutting a horse from one of the baggage-wagons, he escaped.[6]

Reaching a band of fugitives, the doctor began to make inquiry for his missing servant, a favorite Negro slave. He was grieved to learn that the poor fellow
was among the slain and when last seen was lying between two dead horses; but
to the no small surprise and delight of his master, the Negro came up with the retreating army in a few days. When interrogated about it, he frankly confessed he
had lain down between the dead horses to shelter himself from the flying bullets.
Twenty-one years after, Dr. Walker was at Pittsburgh and, visiting the fatal battlefield, gave to his companions a warm and glowing narration of that day's mourn-
ful events, pointing out the ford where the army crossed the Monongahela,
describing the noble sight the troops presented, the burnished muskets, the clean-
liness and excellent order of the soldiery, with joy depicted on every countenance
at being so near Fort Duquesne, the object of all their toils and wishes; with the
pealing music was re-echoing through the mountains, woods, and vallies. How
brilliant the morning—how melancholy the evening![7]

During the whole of that long war, Dr. Walker labored incessantly to procure
supplies and means of transportation for Washington, Braddock, Forbes, Byrd,
and Stephen. Oftentimes straitened for funds with which to purchase provisions,
he nevertheless, by his extensive acquaintance and great energy of character, succeeded far better probably than any other person could have done in the colony.
He merited as he received the gratitude of the people who knew full well his
faithful labors in the public service. In addition to his services as commissary
general, he represented his county of Louisa at least one year during the war, that
of 1758, in the Virginia Assembly. It is said that in 1760 he made a second visit to
Kentucky, penetrating as far as the Dick's River.

In 1768 he was appointed one of the Virginia commissioners to attend the
treaty with the Six Nations at Fort Stanwix; and immediately on his return, he was
despatched at the very close of the year in connection with Col. Andrew Lewis on
a mission to Capt. John Stuart, southern Indian Agent, with reference to an extension of the boundary line between Virginia and the Cherokees.[8] The commissioners returned and reported in February 1769; and though the object sought was not
gained at once, the way was paved for its ultimate accomplishment.

Dr. Walker was a member of the Assembly in 1769, when Patrick Henry's
celebrated resolutions declaratory of the rights of the people were passed, and
gave them his decided support; and when in consequence the governor dissolved
the Assembly, he was among that determined band who re-assembled at a private
house and, forming themselves into the first revolutionary Convention in Virginia,
renewed their declaration of wrongs and entered into a non-importation compact,
pledging themselves to frugality, to import no taxed article, and none of the man-
ufactures or products of Britain, until the northern country should return to the
practice of justice. Among the signatures to this solemn agreement was that of
Thomas Walker.

He also proved himself a devoted patriot during the intervening years until
the final resort to arms. In the Assembly of 1774, he took a leading part, and so
bold were the members in expressing their sentiments and feelings against the

tyranny of the king and ministry that Governor Dunmore abruptly dissolved them. They at once formed themselves into a convention and renewedly pledged their devotion to freedom and their sympathy with their oppressed brethren of Massachusetts. We find him again in the Virginia Convention in July 1775, and the next month, having been appointed a commissioner to hold an Indian treaty at Pittsburgh, together with his son John Walker, [he] obtained leave of absence for that purpose and in the autumn concluded a treaty with the western Indians. In the ensuing December he was again filling his place in the Convention.

During the summer of 1776 he once more repaired to Pittsburgh, where the Indians were again convened, and among them the celebrated Logan, when Dr. Walker used his best endeavors to preserve peace along the frontiers. In both 1776 and 1777 he was chosen by the Legislature a member of the Council of State, an important and arduous office; and in the fall of 1779 he entered upon his duties as one of the Virginia commissioners for running the western extension of the boundary line between Virginia and North Carolina. The "hard winter"[a] caught them in the wilderness; snow fell to an unusual depth, the streams were frozen solidly, and they had to excavate the snow to pitch their tents. So severe was the cold that though they had immense log fires all the time, yet the snow did not melt at all from around their tents. The raccoons and opossums came into their tents at night in search of food, so pinched were they by hunger. During this severe cold weather of about forty days, they were without bread and subsisted entirely on venison and other wild meat. Dr. Walker's son Francis accompanied his father on this perilous service and, being the youngest of the mess, was honored with the post of cook. Upon the opening of spring, the work was re-commenced and soon completed. While engaged in this labor, Dr. Walker in the spring of 1780 visited the infant settlement at the French Lick, now Nashville, from which he wrote to his old friend Colonel Preston assuring him that notwithstanding his advanced years and hardships of the winter, he was yet "hearty."

Having been sometime deprived by death of his old bosom companion, he was united in marriage in January 1781 to a cousin of General Washington's, Mrs. Elizabeth Thornton, whose maiden name was Gregory and who was one of three sisters who married three brothers of the name of Thornton of Spotsylvania. The unceremonious visit Dr. Walker received from Colonel Tarleton and his Legion in June 1781 has been elsewhere in this volume particularly noticed. The Revolutionary War soon after closed, bringing peace and freedom to his native land. For several years after this happy event, he spent his time chiefly at home and amidst his descendants and in acts of kindness to his less fortunate fellows. At an early day, he erected an Episcopal church in his neighborhood known as Walker's church, to which he was warmly attached. His reverence for the Sabbath is sufficiently indicated in the journal of his primitive exploration of Kentucky.

His son Francis Walker wrote in December 1791 to Gen. Daniel Smith, the doctor's fellow commissioner in running the boundary in 1779–80: "My good father, your old friend, is in better health than he has been in several years. He still possesses all that life and good humor by which we were kept alive in the woods.

How happy is the man who, at his age, can, with pleasure, look on a well-spent life; and, without distress, meet the awful moment which is to deprive his dependents of so inestimable a friend." Thus peacefully passed away his closing years. He lived to see his country independent, Washington a second time chosen president, Kentucky a member of the Republic, his oldest son filling a seat in the Senate of the United States, and his youngest in the House of Representatives, and all his children, three sons and eight daughters, grown up and happily settled around him; and, like good old Simeon,[b] he was ready to depart. He paid the debt of nature at Castle-Hill in September 1794, at about the age of eighty-four years. No stone marks the old patriot's grave. But every work commemorative of the interesting story of Kentucky will prove a fitting memorial of his early enterprise and uncommon hardihood.

Dr. Walker was a spare built man, about five feet, seven inches in height, with small blue eyes and, in his latter years, his hair gray and head bald. His nose was uncommonly large, and the general contour of his countenance presented anything but a handsome appearance; but the good qualities of his heart and his uniform kindness to all, which were of far more importance, he possessed in an eminent degree. His great physical strength was remarkable for one of his size. It is related of him that being once with his laborers and overseer at work on the county road, passing a gorge in the mountains near Castle Hill and a large rock lying in the way, he ordered one of the black men to roll it away. The fellow tugged at it in vain. The overseer joined him, and still it proved too much for their united strength. The doctor leaped from his horse and alone removed the stone from the road. It was called *Tom Walker's Rock* for half a century, and to lift it constituted a test of strength among all who passed the road. Few were even found who could raise it; and it still lies by the roadside, we are told, the reproach of the men of "these degenerate days."

In his manners and habits, Dr. Walker was plain and simple and disliked all parade and show. He wished his daughters to become buxom lasses and notable house-keepers rather than fine ladies. But they had their father's respectable library to furnish food for their minds, and the elegance and refinement of their manners was proverbial. Their father would never buy a carriage for them to ride in, though possessing great wealth in lands of baronial extent, telling them they were so many he should never be able to marry them to husbands who could afford them a carriage and they should learn in time to walk. It was afterwards the boast of all his daughters that they lived to ride in their own carriages.

Though his penmanship was usually plain and neat, it was sometimes exceedingly careless and almost illegible. He once wrote a note to his son-in-law Mr. Maury, who, being unable to decypher it, tore off the signature and afterwards showed it to the doctor, who could not make it out. When told that it was his own hand-writing, he pleasantly replied, "It was my business to write the note— yours to read it." At another time, when Mrs. Walker was sick and some lemonade was desired for her, the doctor despatched a servant to a neighboring merchant with a note running in this wise: "Haste, haste, post-haste—if you have none, send a dozen," and signed his name; and then, glancing his eye hastily over it, discovered he had omitted to tell what it was he wanted in such haste: So he took his pen and added by way of postscript, "Lemons or limes, I mean." The merchant was a shrewd, clever young man and was smart enough to comprehend the doctor's meaning and afterwards to marry one of his daughters.

Benevolence was a striking trait of Dr. Walker's character. He loved to aid and encourage the worthy poor. After he had quit the practice of medicine, a young man came to his house after night on his way to Dr. Gilmer's, a son-in-law of Dr. Walker. The invalid had been benighted and missed his way; and of course, he was invited to stay all night. Upon inquiry, the doctor learned from him that his name was Robin Hernsberger, that he was a blacksmith and resided in Augusta County; that he was but recently married and had nothing with which to support himself and wife but his own labor, and his poor health now forbade him working at his trade; that he had expended all his means in doctors' fees without receiving the least benefit, and as a last hope, he was going to consult Dr. Gilmer, whose reputation was widely extended. Dr. Walker examined into his case and told him he could effect a cure as well as Dr. Gilmer, and could afford to do it for nothing, while Dr. Gilmer would necessarily need some remuneration. With these hopeful assurances, the stranger placed himself under Dr. Walker's treatment; [he] remained at Castle Hill a couple of weeks, when he was so far recovered that he left for home supplied with medicines and instructed how to use them. Nothing was charged either for himself or horse, medicines, or advice. He became strong and hearty, and by industry and sagacity amassed a fortune, and died but recently in Augusta County at a good old age.

The doctor's fondness for joking and good humor always made him the life and delight of every social and fire-side circle. On one occasion he sent for the acceptance of some of his neighbors what they took to be a nice piece of fat mutton. Meeting one of them a few days after, he was kindly thanked for the present, and the quality of the mutton was highly extolled. The doctor dryly told his friend he need not be so grateful, for it was not mutton at all—it was only a piece of *"Old Fowler,"* a fat cur dog well known to visitors at Castle Hill. At another time, when the doctor's relish for eating rattle-snakes had provoked the raillery of his family and friends, to play them a prank, he had a rattle-snake beheaded and placed in the large tea-kettle, and the needful quantity of water poured into the vessel, and when boiled, [it] was made into coffee and served up to his family and guests. After they had all partaken freely of it, the doctor pulled out the snake, much to their horror and qualms of stomach.

In the latter part of his life, when he had given up the management of his plantation to his son Frank, riding out with him one day, in company with some other gentlemen, as they passed a certain tree in the woods, the old doctor galloped up to Frank and gave him several snug blows with his horse-whip before he could escape beyond the old man's reach. When Frank demanded the reason for all this, the old gentleman pointed to the tree and said, "My son, that is one of the corner-trees of your estate, and I wanted you to remember it." Frank never forgot the tree, nor the flogging. And to the last, the old doctor was fond of all kinds of sports. On every occasion when it snowed, he would have a grand time in getting up a general snow-ball battle in which all the children, boys and girls, as well as all the guests made up the combatants.

These anecdotes give us some views of the man but show nothing of the great points of Dr. Walker's character and the comprehensiveness of his mind. His sagacity and mighty will are best seen in his fearlessly heading a party and pushing his way over the mountains into Kentucky, evincing a spirit of far-seeing penetration and hardy enterprise far in advance of the age. His various public missions led him at different times as far north as Albany, as far south as Charleston, and nearly to the Mississippi on the west. His election to a seat in the Assembly by both Louisa and Albemarle counties the same year shows the estimation in which he was held by those who knew him best. Nor was his popularity won by the usual trickery and liberal promises of demagogues but was the result of honest worth, stern integrity, and [wi] practical intelligence, and the generous practice of kindly charities, for all of which traits there were constant demands in the border counties. In the best sense of the term, Thomas Walker was a man of more than common distinction in his day, and worthily did he employ his powers and means of usefulness.[9]

BOONE GENEALOGY

It is proper that some notice of the authenticity of this curious document and some account of the writer should precede the Narrative itself. Jonathan, eldest son of Squire Boone, the brother of Col. Daniel Boone, was sent in or about the year 1787 to Berks County, Pennsylvania, to attend school; and there residing among his relatives, received the instructions of his father's cousin, James Boone; and returning home to Kentucky the next year, brought with him this Genealogical Narrative, written by the said James Boone, as endorsed on the instrument, March 21st, 1788.[10] It is a beautiful specimen of chirography, as hundreds can attest who have seen it. "I can truly say," declares Mr. Charles Cist, the well-known statistician of Cincinnati, "I never examined a more remarkable manuscript document." This genealogical account has been preserved in Jonathan Boone's family, and from his grandson, Col. William P. Boone, a prominent attorney at law of Louisville, Kentucky, the original has been obtained. This document is fully corroborated by another, though briefer, sketch, in precisely the same handwriting, preserved by the late aged Miss Susannah Boone, raised in Berks County, Pennsylvania, and obtained from her half brother, James W. Biddle, Esq., editor of the *Pittsburgh Daily American*. The dates are precisely the same, so far as they go, in both papers. The same general dates also appear in a similar record preserved by a nephew of said James Boone, Mr. John Boone, of Berks County, Pennsylvania.[11]

James Boone, the writer of this Boone Genealogy, who was born in Exeter, Berks County, Pennsylvania, January 26th, 1743–'4, O.S.,[c] spent the most of his life in school-teaching in his native region and became distinguished for his extensive knowledge of mathematics. He was never married but made his home with his kindred on the place where his father and grandfather had lived and died, and there he died on the 16th of October, 1795, in his 52nd year, and was interred in Friends' burial-ground at Exeter. Nearly all his life was devoted to the study of books, of which the Bible claimed a large share of his attention; and with reference to the latter, there are many interesting remarks interspersed through his mathematical writings, some of which are still preserved in manuscript.[12]

> *Our Genealogy, or Pedigree; traced as far back as had come to the knowledge of John Boone (the son of George and Mary Boone): Wrote by James Boone, (grandson of the said George and Mary Boone).*

> *George Boone,* I, (that is, the first that we have heard of) was born in England.

> *George Boone,* II (son of *George Boone* the First) was born in or near the city of Exeter, in Devonshire, being a blacksmith; his wife's maiden name was *Sarah Uppey.* He died aged 60; and she died aged 80 years, and never had an aching bone or decay'd tooth.

> *George Boone,* III (son of *George* and *Sarah Boone*) was born at Stoak, a village near the city of Exeter, in A.D. 1666, being a weaver; his wife's maiden name was *Mary Maugridge,* who was born in Bradninch (eight miles from the city of Exeter), in the year 1669, being a daughter of *John Maugridge* and Mary his wife, whose maiden name was *Milton.* They (the said George and Mary Boone) had nine children that lived to be men and women, namely, *George, Sarah, Squire, Mary, John, Joseph, Benjamin, James,* and *Samuel,* having each of them several children, excepting John, who was never married. The said *George* and *Mary Boone* with their family, came from the town of Bradninch, in Devonshire, Old England (which is a town at 8 miles distance from the city of Exeter, and 177 measured miles westward from Loudon); they left Bradninch the 17th of August, 1717, and went to Bristol, where they took shipping, and arrived at Philadelphia in 1717, September 29th, Old Style, or October 10th, New Style; three of their children, to wit, *George, Sarah,* and *Squire,* they sent in a few years before. From Philadelphia they went to Abington, and staid a few months there; thence to North Wales, and lived about two years there; thence to Oley, in the same county of Philadelphia, where *Sarah* (being married) had moved to, some time before.

This last place of their residence (since the divisions made in the township of Oley, and county of Philadelphia), is called the township of Exeter, in the county of Berks. It was called Exeter, because they came from a place near the city of Exeter. And he, the said *George Boone* the Third, died on the sixth day of the week, near 8 o'clock in the morning, on the 27th of July, 1744, aged 78 years; and Mary, his wife, died on the second day, on the 2d day of February, 1740–1, aged 72 years; and were decently interred in Friends' Burying-Ground, in the said township of Exeter. When he died, he left eight children, fifty-two grand-children, and ten great-grand-children, living—in all, seventy, being as many persons as the house of Jacob which came into Egypt.

George Boone, IV (the eldest son of *George* and *Mary Boone*), was born in the town of Bradninch aforesaid, on the 13th of July, 1690, about half an hour past five o'clock in the afternoon; and died in Exeter township aforesaid, on the 20th of November, 1753, in the 64th year of his age. He taught school for several years near Philadelphia; was a good mathematician, and taught the several branches of English learning, and was a magistrate for several years. His wife's maiden name was *Deborah Howell.* She died in 1759, January 26th.

George Boone, V (the eldest son of *George* and *Deborah Boone*), was never married, and died in Exeter township aforesaid, aged about 24 years.

Sarah Boone (daughter of *George* and *Mary Boone*), was born on the fifth day of the week, about half an hour past eleven in the forenoon, on the 18th of February, 1691–2.

Squire Boone (son of *George* and *Mary Boone*), was born on the fourth day of the week, between eleven and twelve in the forenoon, on the 25th November, 1696.

Mary Boone (daughter of *George* and *Mary Boone*), was born September 23d, A.D. 1699. She was the wife of John Webb, and departed this life on the 16th of January, 1774, in the 75th year of her age; her husband died in the same year, October 18th, in the 80th year of his age.

Joseph Boone (son of *George* and *Mary Boone*), was born between four and five in the afternoon, on the 5th of April, 1704; and he departed this life on the 30th January, 1776, in the 72d year of his age. His wife, *Catherine Boone,* died on the 31st of January, 1778, and was interred at Exeter the next day, exactly two years after the burial of her husband.

Benjamin Boone (son of *George* and *Mary Boone*), was born the 16th of July, 1706; and he died on the 14th of October, 1762, in the 57th year of his age. *Susannah Boone,* (his widow), died on the 5th November, 1784, in the 76th year of her age.

Samuel Boone (the youngest son of *George* and *Mary Boone*), departed this life on the 6th of August, 1745, and was buried at Exeter the next day, aged about 34 years.

James Boone, Senr. (the sixth son of *George* and *Mary Boone*), was born in the town of Bradninch, in Devonshire, in Old England, about half an hour past 2 in the morning, on the 7th of July (O.S.) or the 18th of July (N.S.) Anno Domini, 1709. And in 1735, May 15th (O.S.) he married *Mary Foulke,* by whom he had fourteen children, and nine of them lived to be men and women, namely, *Anne, Mary, Martha, James, John, Judah, Joshua, Rachel,* and *Moses.* The said *James Boone, Senior,* and *Mary* his wife lived together 20 years, and eight months, and twenty-five days; and she departed this life on the 6th day of the week, at twenty minutes past one o'clock in the afternoon, on the 20th day of February, 1756, aged 41 years and eleven weeks, and was decently interred in Friends' Burying-Ground, at Exeter, on the first day of the next week. And in 1757, October 20th, he married *Anne Griffith,* being just twenty months after the decease of his former wife.

And here, for the satisfaction of the curious, I shall insert a few chronological remarks, viz:

1. The said *Mary Boone* deceased in 1756, February 20th, at twenty minutes past one in the afternoon, which wanted but two minutes and sixteen seconds of 20 o'clock according [to] the Italian manner of reckoning (for the Italians, Jews, and some others, always begin their day at sun-set); which was the 20th day of the Jewish month Adar, when the moon was twenty days old, and four weeks after the Vernal Equinox.

2. The said *James Boone, Senior,* married *Anne Griffith* in 1757, October 20th, at 20 minutes past one in the afternoon; that is, he was married to his second (or last) wife, exactly

twenty months after the decease of his first, and four weeks after the Autumnal Equinox.

James Boone, Senior, departed this life on the 1st day of September, A.D. 1785, on the fifth day of the week, at ten minutes after nine o'clock at night, in the 77th year of his age; and was decently interred in Friends' Burying-Ground, at Exeter, on the seventh day of the same week. He (with his parents, and etc.), left Great Britain in the ninth year of his age, and lived almost sixty-eight years in Pennsylvania.

N.B. When he was born, it was between 9 and 10 at night here in Pennsylvania (allowing for the difference of longitude), and he died between 9 and 10 at night.

John Boone, Senior (the third son of *George* and *Mary Boone*), was born in the town of Bradninch, in Devonshire, in Old England, on the seventh day of the week, about 10 or 11 o'clock in the forenoon, on the 3d of January, 1701–2, O.S.; or, A.D. 1702, January 14th, N.S. And he departed this life on the 10th day of October, 1785, on the second day of the week, sixteen minutes after midnight, in the 84th year of his age (being the oldest of our name and family, that we have heard of), and was decently interred in Friends' Burial-Ground, at Exeter, the next day. He (with his parents, and etc.) left Great Britain in the 16th year of his age, and lived *exactly* 68 years in North America from the day he landed at Philadelphia. He lived only 5 weeks and 4 days after the decease of his brother James.

N.B. All our relations of the name of Boone, who were living after 1785, October 10th, are American born, as far as we know.

Now, I shall conclude this paper, after I have set down the time and place of my own nativity, viz: I, *James Boone* (the eldest son of *James Boone, Senior,* and *Mary* his wife), was born in the township of Exeter aforesaid, on the fifth day of the week, about five o'clock in the morning, on the 25th day of January, 1743–4, O.S.; or, A.D. 1744, February 6th, N.S. The geographical situation of the place of my birth, is nearly as follows, viz:

	Deg.	Min.
Latitude	40:	22 North.
Longitude from London	75:	43$^1/_2$ West.

So that, the meridian passing through said place, is 5 hours, 2 minutes, and 54 seconds west from the meridian of London; or nearly so, if otherwise.

Endorsed: *"Our Genealogy,* and etc. Wrote 1788, March 21."

The other paper on *Boone Genealogy,* preserved by the late Susanna Boone, who was born in Berks County, Pennsylvania, May 1st, 1771, and died in Pittsburgh, March 8rd, 1847, is subjoined—all of which, except the closing paragraph relative to Judah Boone, is in the hand-writing of James Boone, the school-teacher and mathematician:

> *James Boone, Senior* (son of *George* and *Mary Boone*), was born in the town of Bradninch, eight miles from the city of Exeter, in Devonshire, in Old England, about half an hour past 2 in the morning there, A.D. 1709, July 18th (N.S.). And he departed this life, A.D. 1785, September 1st, at the 9th hour, and ten minutes, at night, in the 77th year of his age.

> *Mary Foulke* (daughter of *Hugh* and *Anne Foulke*), was born at North Wales, in Philadelphia County, A.D. 1714, December 5th (N.S.) James Boone, Senior, and Mary Foulke were married A.D. 1735, May 26th (N.S.); and lived together twenty years, eight months, and twenty-five days. She departed this life, A.D. 1756, February 20th, at one o'clock and twenty minutes in the afternoon, in the 42d year of her age.

> The times of the births of the children of the said James Boone, Senior, and Mary (his first wife), set down according to the New Style. The place of their births is Exeter Township, Berks County, in Pennsylvania.

> *Anne Boone* was born, about 5 in the afternoon, 1737, April 14.

> *Mary Boone* was born, about 1 in the morning, 1739, January 28.

> *Martha Boone* was born, about 5 in the afternoon, 1742, July 11.

> *James Boone, Junior,* was born, about 5 in the morning, 1744, February 6.

> *John Boone, Junior,* was born, about 2 in the morning, 1745, November 28.

Deceased at 10 o'clock at night, in the 28th year of his age, 1773, March 29.

Judah Boone was born, about 3 in the morning, 1746, December 19.

Dinah Boone was born, 1748, March 19. Deceased 1748, July 17.

Joshua Boone was born, about 4 in the morning, 1749, April 4.

Rachel Boone was born, about 3 in the afternoon, 1750, April 21.

Moses Boone was born, about 3 in the morning, 1751, August 3.

Hannah Boone was born, 1752, June 16. Deceased 1752, August 15.

Nathaniel Boone was born, and died, in the year 1753, being 5 weeks old at his decease.

The said *James Boone, Senior,* and *Anne Griffith* were married, A.D. 1757, October 20th, being just 20 months after the decease of his former wife. She the said Anne Griffith was born, A.D. 1713, January 29th, New Style.

John Boone, Junior (son of *James Boone, Senior,* and Mary his wife), when he died, left three children, the times of whose births were so hereunder mentioned, viz:

1. *Hannah Boone* was born on the 6th day of the week, about 4 o'clock in the afternoon 1765, November 1st

2. *James Boone,* III, was born on the 7th day of the week, 15 minutes after noon, 1769, January 21

3. *Susanna Boone* was born on the 4th day of the week, 45 minutes past 10 o'clock at night, 1771, May 1st

John Boone, Senior (son of *George* and *Mary Boone,* and brother of the said *James Boone, Senior*), was born in the town of Bradninch, in Devonshire, in Old England, on the seventh day of the week, about 11 in the morning, A.D. 1702, January

14th, New Style. And he, the said *John Boone, Senior,* departed this life, in the township of Exeter, on the 2d day of the week, 16 minutes after midnight, on the 10th of October, 1785, in the 84th year of his age. He left Old England in the 16th year of his age, and he (with his parents, and etc.) arrived at Philadelphia, in 1717, October 10th, New Style, and lived here, in North America, exactly 68 years; he died within 5 weeks and 4 days after the decease of his brother James.

Judah Boone (son of *James Boone, Senior,* and *Mary* his wife), departed this life on the 15th day of May, A.D. 1787, on the 3d day of the week, at fifteen minutes after midnight, aged forty years, four months, three weeks, and five days, that is, he was in the 41st year of his age; and was interred in the Friends' Burying-Ground, at Exeter, on the fourth day of the same week.[d]

COL. WILLIAM PRESTON, COL. ARTHUR CAMPBELL, GEN. WILLIAM RUSSELL, and GEN. DANIEL SMITH

COL. WILLIAM PRESTON

William Preston was born in Donegal County, Ireland, December 25th, 1729, and was brought by his parents to Virginia in 1740, who settled in the frontier county of Augusta in that province. When he had attained the age of sixteen years, his father, John Preston, died, after which he received an excellent English education under the instruction of Rev. John Craig, pastor of the Tinkling Spring congregation. His first public service was acting as secretary to the commissioners, of whom his uncle, Col. James Patton, was one, at the Indian treaty at Logstown on the Ohio in June 1752; and the same year, he was appointed a deputy surveyor of Augusta County under Thomas Lewis. In 1755 he was made a justice of the peace and also commissioned captain of a company of rangers; and the following year led his company on the disastrous Sandy Creek expedition against the Shawanoes, when officers and men had to eat horses, buffalo tugs, and even shot-pouches—and such was the extent of their hunger, as Preston records in his manuscript journal of the expedition, "that any man in the camp would have ventured his life for a supper."[e]

Captain Preston was unceasing in his efforts for protecting the frontiers and repelling the enemy until 1759, when he was appointed sheriff of Augusta County. He continued to serve as a member of the justices' court until 1767, about which time he removed to the region which was in 1770 organized into the county of Botetourt; and in that county, as in the counties of Fincastle and Montgomery, which were successively carved out of it, he held the highest and most lucrative offices and often represented them in the Virginia Assembly. While the troops were absent on the Point Pleasant campaign in 1774, he had an extensive frontier to protect and was untiring in the discharge of his duties. He was an active friend of freedom during the Revolutionary War and distinguished himself at the head of a regiment of riflemen at the battle of Whitsell's Mills,[f] March 6th, 1781, shortly anterior to the battle of Guilford.[g]

His death occurred by apoplexy shortly after superintending a military review near his residence, which was at Smithfield, Montgomery County, Virginia, June 28th, 1783, in his fifty-fourth year. His widow survived him forty years. Colonel Preston was above the ordinary height of men—about five feet, eleven inches, and inclined to corpulency; ruddy, pleasing countenance, fair hair, and hazel eyes. His manners were easy and graceful, and his intellect, naturally strong, was well cultivated. His descendants are very numerous in the southern and western states and have filled many of the highest offices of the country— among them, James P. Preston, James McDowell, and John B. Floyd, governors of Virginia; William Preston, United States senator from South Carolina, and William Ballard, secretary of the Navy under President Taylor.

COL. ARTHUR CAMPBELL

The Campbells from whom Arthur Campbell descended were originally from Inveraray in the Highland of Scotland, whence they migrated to Ireland in the latter part of the reign of Queen Elizabeth. In 1726 John Campbell left Ireland and settled awhile near Lancaster, in Pennsylvania, and subsequently, when the valley of Virginia began to attract adventurers, he removed into what became Augusta County. His youngest son, David, was the father of Arthur Campbell, who was born in the county November 14th, 1742. Serving as a volunteer on a tour of militia duty in the early part of the summer of 1756, when only in his fourteenth year, he was slightly wounded in the knee, while plucking fruit in a wild plum tree, by a party of Indians in ambush near a fort on Cow Pasture River and unhappily made their prisoner. Loaded with Indian packs, he was conveyed to the Wyandotte towns, where James Smith speaks in his Indian Narrative of meeting him and alludes in high terms to his manly deportment. When something over four years a prisoner, hearing that an Indian army was approaching the Indian country, he escaped from his captors and met the troops under the command of Maj. Robert Rogers at Presque Isle[h] on Lake Erie and piloted them to Detroit, where he witnessed, on the 29th of November, 1760, the French flag give place to that of England. For this service, he subsequently received a thousand acres of choice land near Louisville, Kentucky.

Having settled on the ancient survey of the Royal Oak on the Holston in 1769, he was the next year appointed a captain of Botetourt County militia, a justice of the peace of Fincastle County in 1773, and a major in 1774. He was a member of the Convention in 1776 which formed the first constitution for Virginia and served a few terms in the General Assembly. When Washington County was organized in 1777, he was appointed county lieutenant and served in that position throughout the trying period of the Revolution and the succeeding years of Indian warfare. In 1780 he was particularly active in suppressing the rising of the

Tories on New River and led the Virginia troops on a successful campaign against the Cherokees during the winter of 1780–'81. He continued for many years to take an active part in public affairs.

A little less than six feet in height, with dark, piercing hazel eyes, long chin and nose, gait erect and lofty, and manners very graceful, he was well calculated to impress the beholder with the idea that he was looking upon no ordinary man. His reading was extensive and his conversational powers very superior. Yet with the mass of society, he was not popular, because he would not relax in his manners to do court to their ignorance and prejudices. A few years [later], he removed to Knox County, Kentucky, and settled on Yellow Creek between Cumberland Gap and Cumberland Ford, where he died of cancer in the face, calmly and in Christian faith, August 8th, 1811, in his sixty-ninth year. His widow, who was a sister of Gen. William Campbell, survived him a few years. Of their six sons and six daughters, Col. John B. Campbell became the most conspicuous—a lawyer of distinction at Russellville, Kentucky, he commanded the expedition in November 1812 against the Mississinewa Indians[i] and was mortally wounded at the battle of Chippewa, July 5th, 1814, and died shortly after at the Williamsville cantonment near Buffalo.

GEN. WILLIAM RUSSELL[13]

At an early day, William Russell, a native of England, migrating to Virginia, obtained a grant of land in Culpeper County and there married and settled. His oldest son, William, the subject of this notice, was born in that county in or about the year 1738; and his father, possessing considerable wealth, sent his son to William and Mary College, where he received a liberal education. His father dying about this period, young Russell, when only seventeen years of age, was united in marriage to Tabitha Adams, daughter of Samuel Adams, a respectable farmer of that county. The ensuing thirteen years were mostly spent, we presume, on the farm, providing for his own and mother's families. Having now a growing family, Mr. Russell concluded to remove to the western waters and first settled on New River in 1768; and the next year [he] push[ed] on to the extreme frontier and located Castle's Woods on the eastern side of the Clinch River, west of the present town of Lebanon, Russell County, in south-western Virginia, and subsequently obtained a pre-emption of one thousand acres of land for having made this early settlement.

A man of such cultivation and enterprise proved a real acquisition to the country. About this period, he was sent on a public mission to the Creek Indians, accompanied by two men; and in consequence of swollen streams, some of which they crossed with great difficulty and danger, their progress was greatly retarded, but at length [they] reached the Indian towns well nigh starved. After an absence of several months, Russell safely returned. He kept a journal of this adventurous trip, which is now believed to be lost. Anterior to the Revolutionary War, he served in the Virginia Assembly—perhaps in 1770, as his name was in June of that year appended to the Non-importation agreement entered into at

Williamsburg by the members of the House of Burgesses and merchants of the colony. When Fincastle County was organized in 1773, he was appointed in the first commission of justices of the peace and was that year defeated in his conjoint plan with Daniel Boone for settling Kentucky.

We find him in the following year both deputy surveyor of the county and a captain of the militia; and, withal, a sturdy signer of the Continental Association of the leading men of Fincastle, giving their hearty acquiescence in favor of the non-importation of merchandize from Great Britain and its dependencies, until the mother country should cease her oppressive acts against the colonies. Captain Russell fought with distinguished bravery at the battle of Point Pleasant, October 10th, 1774, and was selected by Governor Dunmore to command the troops left to garrison Fort Blair at Point Pleasant, in which service he was still engaged as late as June 1775. Early in this latter year, he was chosen a member of the Fincastle Committee of Safety and was faithful in his attendance on its meetings, though he had nearly a hundred miles to travel and the same to re-travel on each occasion. In June 1776 the Virginia Convention appointed him lieutenant colonel to command the militia ordered out for the defense of Fincastle County, and in July [he] relieved Watauga fort and settlement when beleaguered by the Cherokees and in the autumn accompanied Christian on his successful expedition into the Cherokee country.

Having been appointed to the command of the 12th Virginia regiment on continental establishment, he was ordered in February 1777 to join the main army under Washington and shared in the battles of Brandywine[j] and Germantown[k] during the campaign of that year; and in the latter conflict, General Stephen, in his official report, stated that "Colonel Lewis and Colonel Russell, of Green's division, Colonel Wood with his regiment, and Major Campbell of the Eighth, behaved gallantly during the action." Colonel Russell took part in [the] Monmouth battle in June 1778; and his regiment formed part of Muhlenberg's brigade, which supported Wayne in his attack on Stoney Point in July 1779. Early in 1780 he was detached under General Woodford to the relief of Charleston, which, after sustaining a long siege and much hard fighting, had finally to surrender to the British. We find him next at Yorktown, the closing active scene of the Revolution. Continuing in the army until its disbandment, he was brevetted a brigadier general by Congress November 3d, 1778.

During the whole seven years he served in the Continental Line, except when detached to Charleston, he was immediately under the eye of Washington, sometimes commanding the brigade to which he belonged, and always zealous and efficient in his country's service. His having been among the faithful few connected with the main army, fighting its battles, suffering uncomplainingly at Valley Forge, and seldom engaged on independent service, coupled with his modest, unobtrusive manners, and dying early on the frontiers, have contributed to render his name, merits, and services far less known than many who never served their country half so long nor half so well. Yet Mr. Headley[l] flippantly tells his readers that General Russell's services were too insignificant to deserve notice!

His wife dying in April 1776, leaving him thirteen children, he married after the war the widow of Gen. William Campbell, a sister of Patrick Henry, by whom he had five others. After this marriage, he generally resided at the Salt Works in Washington County, Virginia; and died of a fever January 17th, 1793, in about his fifty-fifth year, while on a visit to Col. Thomas Allen, whose daughter General Russell's son Robert had married in then Shenandoah, now Warren County, Virginia. He died in Christian hope, and his remains still rest with only fading tradition to mark the spot in the family burying-ground of the Allens, one mile west of the village of Front Royal. In height he was about six feet, noble and commanding in appearance, and his manners, rare in his day, were considered of the courtly order. A county in Virginia commemorates his name.

Among his descendants who have risen to distinction was his son William Russell, who commanded a company at King's Mountain and at Whitsell's Mill, headed a battalion on Wayne's Indian campaign, and served as a colonel on the frontiers of Indiana and Illinois during the war of 1812–'15, and often served in the Legislature of Kentucky; the late John A. Bowen, who served in Congress from Tennessee during the last war with England; Col. John H. Moore, who distinguished himself in the Texican war of independence;[m] and lastly, Gen. William B. Campbell, of Tennessee, who served with high distinction in the last Seminole War[n] and on General Scott's remarkable campaign in the valley of Mexico,[o] rendering credible service also in the halls of the legislature of his native state and of Congress and more recently as governor of Tennessee—everywhere proving himself a lover of his country rather than a blind devotee of party.

GEN. DANIEL SMITH

Henry Smith migrated from Stafford County, England, and settled at an early period in Stafford County, Virginia. His son Henry was the father of Daniel Smith, the subject of this sketch, who was born in Stafford County, in the Old Dominion, October 29th, 1748. He was early sent to Baltimore to acquire an education but, it seems, did not long enjoy his advantage and was mainly indebted to his private application for his very respectable literary acquirements. He studied law with Steven Thompson Mason, afterwards a member of the United States Senate from Virginia; and about the time he reached his majority, he went to Albemarle County and there formed an intimate acquaintance with Dr. Thomas Walker, with whom he studied physic and also engaged in surveying and mercantile transactions for him for several years. During this residence in Albemarle, he made the acquaintance and secured the friendship of Thomas Jefferson, who many years after assured Mr. Smith that he was "remembered with esteem" in the neighborhood of Monticello.

Having married Miss Sally Mickie in 1773, he soon after settled on the frontiers of the Clinch River, and we find him the following year acting vigilantly in defense of the Upper Clinch settlements and uniting with Boone in repelling their savage enemies. In 1776 he commanded a company on Christian's Cherokee campaign and was a major of militia in 1777 when Washington County was organized and, as such, led a party to the relief of Kentucky the ensuing year. During the latter part of the year 1779 and into the summer of 1780, he was engaged in conjunction with Dr. Walker in extending the dividing line between Virginia and North Carolina to the Mississippi—a toilsome, self-denying labor, subsisting in camps on the Cumberland River during the hard winter of 1779–'80. Upon his return from this service, he found that he had in April 1780 been promoted to the rank of lieutenant colonel, and in March 1781 he joined General Greene and fought in the battles of Whitsell's Mills and Guilford and received the thanks of the general for his good conduct. During the same month, he was advanced to the full rank of colonel of the 2nd regiment of Washington County.

Allured by the fine appearance of the Cumberland country while acting as a commissioner in extending the boundary line, he removed there in 1783 and was a member of the justice court when Davidson County was organized in October of that year, and shortly after was appointed surveyor of the county; and in the autumn of 1784, while engaged with several others on a surveying tour on Bledsoe's Creek, he received two wounds, and one William McMurry was at the same time killed by the Indians. When Sumner County was organized early in 1787, he was made justice of the peace and represented that county in the Legislature of North Carolina and aided in procuring a repeal of the cession act of 1789. He was also a member of the North Carolina Convention, which ratified the Federal Constitution. When the Cumberland counties were formed into Miro District in November 1788, he was appointed the first brigadier-general and continued to act in that capacity till the organization of the Territory South of the Ohio in 1790, when he was appointed territorial secretary by President Washington, often acting as governor in the absence of Governor Blout, and served till Tennessee became a state in 1796. He was in this latter year a member of the Convention which formed the constitution of Tennessee and was one of the electors of president and vice president, voting for the Jefferson in opposition to the Adams ticket. He was chosen to fill an unexpired term in the Senate of the United States in 1798–'99; and from 1805 till 1809 he again filled that distinguished position.

General Smith's death occurred at his seat on Drake's Creek, Sumner County, Tennessee, June 18th, 1818, in his seventieth year. He was a fine mathematician, a devoted student, an example of virtue, and a lover of his country. In size he was nearly six feet in height, well made, with hazel eyes, and presented altogether a fine and prepossessing appearance. His son, the late Col. George Smith of Sumner, served as a lieutenant-colonel under General Jackson[p] in the Creek war and was a most amiable and worthy man.

SKETCHES OF THE MEMBERS
OF THE TRANSYLVANIA CONVENTION
COL. THOMAS SLAUGHTER

Robert Slaughter was among the early settlers in that part of Spotsylvania which now forms Culpeper County, Virginia, and there his son, Thomas Slaughter, the chairman of the Transylvania Convention, was born about the year 1734. It is not certainly known that he served in the old French and Indian War, but probably he did; he was, at all events, many years a colonel of militia of Culpeper and was always very popular in the county. His early trip to and exploration of Kentucky exhibit the energy of the man; and though he contracted for ten thousand acres of land of Henderson and company on condition of bringing out from Virginia a certain number of families and settling them in Kentucky, there is no evidence that he ever returned. Perhaps his health failed him or the troubles of the country prevented. He died in Culpeper County at about the age of sixty-five, leaving two sons and five daughters.

COL. JAMES HARROD

The father of James Harrod came from England about the year 1734 and settled among the very first adventurers on the Shenandoah in the valley of Virginia; and being a young widower, with two young sons, he there married Sarah Moore, and there his oldest son, Samuel, was born—the same who, in 1767, accompanied Stoner to the West on a hunting and exploring trip, as we have already mentioned. Mr. Harrod then removed to the Big Cove, within the limits of the present county of Bedford, Pennsylvania, where his son William, who served with so much reputation under George Rogers Clark, was born December 9th, 1737. Here too, a young son, James Harrod, whose name is so intimately connected with the early settlement of Kentucky, was born in the year 1742. About the commencement of the French and Indian War, when James was about twelve years of age, his father died, leaving a large family. The celebrated Indian chief Shingas[q] headed a party of warriors and made a bloody descent upon the Great Cove Settlement in November 1755, killing some and capturing others, while another portion were so fortunate as to escape with their lives, when their cabins, with their little [*wm*] all, fell a prey to the flames. The Harrod family were among those who escaped, and then, or soon after, took refuge in Fort Littleton in that region.

When James Harrod was sixteen years of age, he as well as his brother William served on Forbes' campaign and probably performed other services during that protracted Indian war. Reared on the frontiers and early inured to border military service, he contracted a fondness for hunting and wild-woods life and became, like Boone, unsurpassed in all that related to woodcraft. In 1772 he accompanied his brother William, who settled on the South Fork of Ten Mile Creek of Monongahela; and in the following year, James Harrod, with several others, explored Kentucky and returned home by the Greenbriar River in West Virginia. About this period he visited his elder half-brother Thomas Harrod, who resided on the frontiers of North Carolina.

In 1774, as we have seen, he again went to Kentucky as the leader of a party of hardy adventurers; and when the Indian war[r] broke out, he retired with his men to the Holston and, forming them into a company, joined Colonel Christian's regiment and went on the Point Pleasant campaign but arrived a few hours too late to participate in the memorable battle of the 10th of October. Re-commencing his

Kentucky settlement early in 1775, he was at once regarded as a conspicuous person in the colony and chosen to a seat in the Transylvania Convention.

From its very infancy, he faithfully watched over the interest and safety of the Harrodsburg settlement.[s] In 1776 he and Benjamin Logan transported a quantity of lead from the Long Island of Holston for the defense of the country; and [he] was, early the following year, appointed one of the justices for Kentucky County. When Harrodsburg was attacked in 1777, he was active in repelling the Indians. He commanded a company on Bowman's campaign in 1779 and a regiment on Clark's Indian campaign of 1780. When Kentucky County was subdivided in 1781, he refused a commission of major of Lincoln as not the rank to which he was fairly entitled. Had his health permitted, he would doubtless have played well his part with his friends and neighbors at the sanguinary battle of the Blue Licks in August 1782; and he patriotically served as a private in Clark's Indian campaign in the fall of that year. He was a member of the Kentucky Convention that met at Danville in December 1784; and once served as a Kentucky representative in the Virginia Legislature. About 1790 he volunteered his services on one or two occasions to pursue Indians who had committed depredations in the Green River settlements. In November 1791 Colonel Harrod appeared at Washington, Kentucky, made his will, and proceeded in February 1792 to the Three Forks of the Kentucky in search of a silver mine,[t] accompanied by two men. He was either killed by the Indians, or sickened and died, or was treacherously murdered by his companions; the latter, from several circumstances, was strongly suspected at the time, and his widow, only daughter, and son-in-law always thought he fell by the assassin's hand. Thus perished at about fifty years of age one of the noblest of the pioneer fathers of Kentucky.

James Harrod was a fine-looking, well-proportioned man, six feet in height, with dark complexion, hair, and eyes, an aquiline nose, with a firm, manly gait, animated countenance, and grave deportment. Yet he was kind and social in his intercourse without being obtrusive and would, in a mild and conciliating manner, express his opinions freely. With scarcely any early advantages, he could yet read and write—he had, however, more faithfully studied men and nature than he had books. He was more ambitious to do a good act than to fill high positions among his fellows. Gen. George Rogers Clark, the Father of the West, often consulted him in times of difficulty and danger. When young Ray was killed four miles from Harrodsburg[u] and it was thought best to venture to send out a party—"Boys," said Harrod to those around him, "let us go and beat the red rascals," and suiting the action to the word, snatched his gun, always ready, and took the lead of his confiding followers. A man on a campaign in the Indian country got lost, when Harrod, kind-hearted as he was, went alone in search of him and was gone two days and finally found him half-bewildered up a tree, snugly ensconced among its entangled branches. Once, going to New Orleans with a flat-boat load of produce, one Frank Wilson, who had pushed ahead some distance in a canoe, was unfortunately drawn by the current upon a sawyer, which, rising several feet, tossed the frail boat and solitary voyageur high in the air. Wilson was, of course, plunged into the turbid stream and, in rising to the surface, grasped hold of the sawyer, which would alternately take him to his chin under water and then toss him a considerable distance above. Harrod hastened to his relief and toiled several hours before he succeeded in getting Wilson released from his perilous situation, as the waves made by the sawyer would drive off Harrod's canoe. Again, he hears that a family in the station is in want of meat, almost the staff of life; and another accosts him, "My horse not having come up, I cannot plow today." "What kind of a horse is yours?" enquires Harrod; he is informed—he disappears and in a little time the horse is driven to the owner's door and a load of buffalo meat or venison is presented to the needy family. But even these acts of kindness were not attended with great personal danger, alike from the lurking Indians and from the perils incident to the chase; but from the fearlessness of his character, he esteemed these dangers but lightly. Once on horseback he fired at game, his horse jumped at the flash and report of the gun, threw him, and broke one of his thighs; and at a subsequent period, the other was broken in the same way. "These traits," says Marshall, "not only portray the character of Harrod, but they also delineate the circumstances of the country, therefore they belong to history: A man may be useful without book learning—usefulness is merit."

In 1778 Colonel Harrod was married to Mrs. Ann McDaniel at Logan's Station, Robert Todd, one of the magistrates of Kentucky County, officiating on the occasion. She had come into the country with her former husband, James McDaniel, and reached Harrodsburg in February 1776, and he was killed by the Indians the same year at Drennon's Lick. With her, Colonel Harrod left an only daughter, Margaret, and a fine patrimony in the rich lands of the country. She became the wife of Maj. John T. G. Fauntleroy and died August 25th, 1841, at Harrod's Old Station, Boyle County, Kentucky, at the age of nearly fifty-six years, leaving a large number of worthy descendants. Her venerable mother, Mrs. Harrod, lived almost to patriarchal years and died at the same place, April 14th, 1843, in the eighty-eighth year of her age. She was among the very last of the venerable pioneer women of Kentucky.

COL. RICHARD CALLAWAY

The memory of Richard Callaway deserves a better historical memorial than has hitherto been reared. His grandfather, Joseph Callaway, early emigrated from England to Virginia. He had an only son, Joseph, who settled in Caroline County in that colony while it was yet a frontier wilderness, and there were born to him seven sons and two daughters. Richard Callaway, the sixth son of the family, was born about the year 1724. His father, mother, and a brother all sickened and died of fever within a period of six weeks, while Richard was yet a mere youth. The children continued to live several years on the old homestead, when, finding themselves straitened for land, [they] concluded to sell out and remove farther west. They accordingly sold and started about the year 1740 and settled on Big Otter River, then in Brunswick, afterwards Lunenburg, and finally Bedford County, Virginia, at the eastern base of the noted Peaks of Otter. They were the first men who cleared land and raised corn on Otter River. Here, about the commencement of the French and Indian War, Richard Callaway married Elizabeth, a daughter of George Walton. His brother, Thurwood Walton, being then the county surveyor, enabled all the Callaways to secure a competent share of the rich lands of that region.

When the war broke out in 1754, the country where the Callaways resided had become considerably populated, and the people for several years collected in forts, which Washington occasionally visited. Richard Callaway and his two elder brothers, Thomas and William, each held the commission of captain, Richard having the command at the Black Water Fort, Thomas at Hickey's Fort, and William at Pig River Fort. From the outbreak of the war till the capture of Fort Duquesne in 1758, the frontiers were constantly alarmed and marauding parties of Indians were frequently pursued and sometimes overtaken and chastised. For their services, Capt. Richard Callaway was subsequently raised to the rank of colonel of the militia of Bedford County.

In 1775 Colonel Callaway went out with Boone and the road-markers to Kentucky and became one of the founders of Boonesborough, was a member of the Transylvania Convention and soon after returned to Virginia, and in September of the same year arrived at Boonesborough with his own and other families. In July 1776, when his two daughters and Jemima Boone were captured, he headed a party in pursuit of the marauders and the next spring aided in the defense of Boonesborough when attacked by the Indians. He and John Todd were elected the first burgesses from Kentucky County to the Virginia Legislature in April 1777; and in June following, he was appointed a justice of the peace and colonel of the county. He was prominent and active in the defense of Boonesborough during the long siege of September 1778. During the session of the Virginia Legislature of October 1779, he was appointed one of the trustees of Boonesborough and authorized to establish a ferry across the Kentucky at that place.

On the 8th of March, 1780, while Colonel Callaway and others were at work about a mile above Boonesborough, engaged in constructing his ferry-boat, they were fired on by a party of Shawanoe Indians, the colonel killed on the spot, Lt. Pemberton Rawlings badly wounded, who, after running a quarter of a mile, was overtaken, tomahawked in the back of his neck, and scalped. Two Negroes were taken prisoners and never heard of afterwards, while the fifth person of the party safely escaped to the fort. A party consisting of Captain Holder, Bland W. Ballard, and others immediately repaired to the scene of the tragedy, found Colonel Callaway scalped, his head shockingly cut and mangled, and his body stripped and rolled in the mud. Rawlings was conveyed to the fort but lived only a few hours. Two days after, the remains of Callaway and Rawlings were buried in one grave just back of the fort. When Colonel Callaway's scalp was taken to the Indian towns, the peculiarly long and mixed grey appearance of the hair was recognized by Joseph Jackson, then a prisoner who had been captured with Boone's salt-boilers at the Blue Licks.

Colonel Callaway left a widow, who was his second wife, and several children by both marriages; and their descendants are scattered in Kentucky, Tennessee, Alabama, and Mississippi. The late Hon. Richard French, who was several years a judge in Kentucky and a member of Congress from that state, was a grandson. Colonel Callaway has been represented as a man of fine appearance, rather tall, and weighing about 180 pounds, with a character happily blending the moral, patriotic, and benevolent virtues. He was a fine representative of the early law-givers and defenders of Kentucky. A county in the western part of that state deservedly perpetuates his name.[v]

COL. JOHN FLOYD

Early in the eighteenth century, the ancestors of John Floyd emigrated from Wales and settled on the eastern shore of Virginia. His father, William Floyd, had two brothers, one named John, who went north and was lost sight of; and the other, Charles, went to Georgia, and was the ancestor of Gen. Charles Floyd of that state. William Floyd wended his way to that part of Albemarle at the eastern base of the Blue Ridge which has since been formed into Amherst County and which was then a very wild frontier region. Here he met with a family of the name of Davis, who descended from Welsh ancestry and who had carried on a profitable trade with the Catawba Indians and had accumulated quite a [bit of] property in that way. The immediate ancestor of Robert Davis married a half-breed Indian girl whose father was a Catawba chief; and this Robert Davis had a daughter Abadiah, whom William Floyd married. Davis owned many of the rich lands of Amherst, and his other daughters also married respectably and from them descend the Venables, Breckenridges, Shelbys, and others.

In what is now Amherst County, Virginia, *John Floyd*, the oldest son of William Floyd and Abadiah Davis, was born in 1751; and like many others of his day, his education was limited to a plain English one, including surveying, and his earliest employment was school-teaching. At the age of eighteen, he married a Miss Buford, who lived but a year, leaving a young daughter named Mourning, who was taken in charge by her grand-mother Davis, intermarried with General Stewart of Georgia, and raised a large and respectable family. Shortly after the death of his wife, Floyd went over the Blue Ridge into Botetourt County and engaged in the business of teaching school in the family and writing in the office of Col. William Preston, who was then the county surveyor. In 1772 we find him the deputy surveyor of that county. He devoted a portion of his time also in performing the duties of deputy sheriff under Col. William Christian; and in the autumn of 1773 he was engaged on the Clinch River in Colonel Preston's employment. Early in 1774 he was one of Colonel Preston's deputy surveyors locating lands in the Kentucky country and was recalled by Boone and Stoner in time to raise a company and serve in Colonel Christian's regiment on the Point Pleasant campaign, and reached the battle-ground at the mouth of the Great Kenhawa at midnight after the battle.

Early in 1775 Captain Floyd went to Kentucky at the head of thirty adventurers, who settled St. Asaph's, near where Logan's Fort was subsequently located; he held a seat in the Transylvania Convention and spent most of the year locating and surveying lands on the north side of the Kentucky. Near the close of the year, he was appointed surveyor of the new colony upon the recommendation of the people in convention, and appointing six deputies, he returned to Virginia. But the next spring he hastened back to Kentucky and in July accompanied Boone's party and distinguished himself in rescuing the captive girls from the Indians. He returned to Virginia in the fall and engaged with the late Col. John Radford and others in a privateering adventure, twenty partners having purchased the privateer *Phoenix* at £200 per share, and sailed near the close of December 1776 on a three or four months' cruise. Floyd's letters to Colonel Preston,[w] written just before his departure on this voyage, exhibit not a few misgivings as to its wisdom and propriety, and a firm resolve, whatever might be its results, never again to try his fortune at sea.

Sailing for the West Indies, a rich prize was captured, and among the articles on board the merchantman was a very fine wedding suit for a lady. Floyd was at this time engaged to Miss Jane Buchanan, daughter of the late Col. John Buchanan and the kinswoman and ward of Colonel Preston. He thought his fortune was made in the valuable cargo taken, but when nearing the capes of Virginia, the *Phoenix* was overhauled by a British man-of-war and captured. Floyd was at the time confined to his bed by illness, but this did not mitigate the severity of his treatment—for he was not only ironed, but one of the officers, pointing to him, observed, "he shall hang at all events." In six weeks they arrived in England, and poor Floyd and his companions were thrown into prison to await their trial. Meanwhile, some books and papers were granted the prisoners, and Floyd divided his time between "reading and serious meditation," not knowing but he might yet have to swing for it; and one day, to his great joy, he read in a newspaper that the *Phoenix* had been re-taken by the Americans, for, while there was no prospect of his getting possession of his property again, he was gratified that it had passed from the hands of his proud enemies into those of his needy countrymen.

Captain Floyd was the first of his party to be summoned to trial and plead his own cause. He stated that he was from the frontier parts of America and had been unengaged in the war then raging in the colonies; that feeling the pressing want for the necessaries with which his vessel was laden, a few of his friends and neighbors had joined to seek them in the West Indies; that on their return, they were seized, their property taken, and they sent in irons to England; and conscious of his innocence, he strongly asserted that no evil intention could be proved against him. The judge, fixing a stern look on Floyd, exclaimed, "What you have said may be true, but I doubt it much." He was, however, acquitted. When Floyd bid his fellow prisoners adieu, they all shed tears, so greatly was he endeared to them.[14]

The judge refusing Floyd a passport, he wended his [way] towards Dover and hoped thence, in some way, to reach the shores of France. On the road, he happily met a generous tar who had formed one of the crew of the British vessel that had captured Floyd—they recognized each other, and the old sailor seemed fully to understand and sympathize in Floyd's objects and wishes. He not only gave him his last guinea but imparted to him advice how best to avoid the press-gang[x] by stopping only at respectable houses and even went with him several miles, more fully to explain these matters. He succeeded quite well at first but was finally twice successively caught by the dreaded press-gang, sent to London, and each time released, and persevering, he at length reached Dover. There he learned of a person who had a vessel with which he occasionally made trips to Calais—probably of a semi-clandestine character, for this was not very long before the treaty between France and the United States which so soon eventuated in an open rupture between France and England. Though the man himself was absent, probably on a trip to Calais, his good angel of a wife was at home, of whom Floyd made cautious enquiries about the chances of a passage across the channel and asked if there was no danger of capture by the French. Looking him archly in the face, she said with a smile, "I fancy, sir, that nothing would afford you more pleasure than such a misfortune." Floyd attempted no further concealment and artlessly told her the whole story of his unhappy adventures. The good woman, touched with his simple narrative, secreted him from the press-gang and promised him her best offices of kindness. After repeated failures, she at length procured a passport for her friend—her husband returned, entered as warmly as his wife into the feelings and wishes of the unfortunate adventurer, conveyed him to Calais, gave him a guinea, when Floyd was left to wend his way as best he could to Paris. This was the vintage season in the autumn of 1777. With no knowledge of the French language, simply pronouncing the word Paris, he finally reached there, found Dr. Franklin, our ambassador there, and obtained from him the loan of ten guineas.[15]

While in Paris, he was attacked with the small pox, which nearly cost him his life; and during his sojourn there, he secured a beautiful scarlet coat and other wedding clothes for himself and an elegant pair of shoe-buckles for his intended bride. He soon sailed for home, landed at Charleston early in 1778, and hastened to Colonel Preston's in West Virginia. As no intelligence of the *Phoenix* or its crew had been received, it was reluctantly concluded that all had perished at sea. Miss Buchanan had, with a sad heart, given up her first love as lost. Robert Sawyers, a distant kinsman of hers who was both wealthy and worthy and then serving as an officer in the American army, paid his addresses to her. He had one day requested her to walk with him in the garden at Smithfield, Colonel Preston's residence, which resulted in a matrimonial engagement. In an hour after, John Floyd arrived at Colonel Preston's, much to the surprise and joy of all the family. Miss Buchanan's newly made engagement was canceled; she, admiring Floyd all the more for the dangers through which he had passed, readily acknowledged his superior claim to her heart and hand, and they were united in marriage the ensuing November.

Settling temporarily on John's Creek, in Botetourt County, where his father was then residing, Captain Floyd acted as commissary to supply the militia in service for the defense of the frontiers until the autumn of 1779, when he migrated with his family to Kentucky; and on the 8th of November of that year, commenced the settlement of *Floyd's Station,*[y] six miles from Louisville up Beargrass. His cabin was lined with deer-skins, and his family at one period were nine months without bread; and when a traveller presented Mrs. Floyd with two ears of corn, she carefully kept them in case of sickness. This was in 1780, after the preceding "hard winter."

Floyd was placed in command of a regiment of militia and served on Clark's campaign against the Shawanoes in the summer of 1780; and early in 1781 he was, upon General Clark's recommendation, appointed county lieutenant of Jefferson County, of which county he was also a justice of the peace. When in September of that year the inhabitants of Squire Boone's Station were attempting to remove to a place of greater security and were intercepted and defeated on the way, Colonel Floyd immediately collected a party of seventy-seven men and went to the relief of the survivors;[z] and this party was drawn into an ambuscade and fourteen killed and some taken; and Floyd himself was only saved from the tomahawk when nearly exhausted by Samuel Wells dismounting and placing Floyd upon his horse, while Wells himself escaped by running by his side and holding to the stirrup. This noble act was rendered doubly magnanimous from the fact that but a short time before the two had a violent personal rencontre in which Wells was roughly handled by Floyd. All enmity was now subdued; Floyd presented Wells a fine tract of one hundred acres of land; they lived and died friends.

When the Indian bands who, in August 1782, were returning from their attack on Bryan's Station and the defeat of the Kentuckians at the Blue Licks, about one hundred and fifty of the western warriors passed through Jefferson County, Floyd called out the militia, scoured the country along the Salt River; the Indians, however, managed to evade him, fell upon and captured Kincheloe's Station,[aa] and hastened over the Ohio. On Clark's retaliatory campaign that fall, Colonel Floyd again headed his Jefferson County militia and rendered efficient service.

He was appointed a judge of Kentucky District and assisted in holding the first district court in Harrodsburg, early in March 1783. This was his last public service. On his way from his station to Bullitt's Lick, in company with his brother, Charles Floyd, Alexander Breckenridge, and two others, they were fired upon by a party of Indians on the 8th of April, about three miles north of the present village of Shepherdsville, one of the men shot dead, and Colonel Floyd mortally wounded. Every horse of the party was shot except Colonel Floyd's; and the colonel wore that day his scarlet coat which he had purchased in Paris, which probably rendered him a more conspicuous mark. He was shot through the arm, the ball then entering the body. His brother, observing him reeling on his horse, dismounted from his own wounded animal and mounting behind the colonel, sustained him, and rapidly retraced their trail to a house about five miles distant. Here, nearly exhausted, he was taken from the horse in an apparently dying condition, but recovering somewhat, he survived till the 10th, when he expired. His remains were interred on an eminence which he had selected for the purpose at his station on Beargrass. His widow subsequently married Alexander Breckinridge and died May 14th, 1812; and at her own request, the scarlet coat which Colonel Floyd wore at their wedding and in which he received his death-wound was placed in her coffin, and she was buried near Colonel Floyd's grave.[bb]

Of Colonel Floyd's three children, the eldest died in infancy; the second, George Rogers Clark Floyd, who was distinguished in the battle of Tippecanoe,[cc] died in Jefferson County, Kentucky, in June 1823 and was buried near his parents; the younger son, John Floyd, a native of Kentucky, was educated to the profession of medicine, settled in Virginia, held a seat in Congress from 1817 to 1829, and from 1829 to 1834 was governor of that state, and died at the Sweet Springs, Virginia, August 16th, 1837, in the fifty-fifth year of his age. His widow, a daughter of Col. William Preston, still survives, and their son, John B. Floyd, has recently served a full term as governor of Virginia, and another son, B. R. Floyd, has often served in the Virginia Legislature.

Colonel Floyd was upwards of six feet high, somewhat slender, straight as an Indian and almost as dark as one, indicative of his aboriginal descent; [with his] brilliant black eyes and very black straight hair, presenting altogether a handsome appearance. He possessed a fine natural understanding, great integrity of character, and displayed on all occasions cool, undaunted courage and a heart full of the milk of human kindness. He and his connections suffered greatly from the Indians. Five of his relatives of the Davis family were killed by them; his brother Joshua Floyd, and his brothers-in-law, Le Master, Asturgus, Pryor, Drake, William and John Buchanan, were all victims to Indian warfare; and finally Colonel Floyd himself, at the early age of thirty-two, fell by their hands, but he had lived long enough to make a name that shall long remain illustrious in the early annals of the West.

COL. JOHN TODD

This conspicuous Kentucky pioneer descended from Irish-Welsh parentage,[dd] and was born on the Schuylkill, in Berks County, Pennsylvania, March 27th, 1750. His father, David Todd, born in Ireland, April 8th, 1723, emigrated to Pennsylvania about 1745 and there married Hannah Owens, a Welsh lady two years his junior. David Todd was a farmer and also kept a turner's[ee] shop and brought up [his] sons to industry. John Todd grew up nearly to man's estate with such an education as he could acquire in the ordinary schools of the country, with some scientific and mathematical instruction obtained from his relative, Robert Porter, a practical surveyor. He was then sent to learn the languages and complete his studies with his uncle, Rev. John Todd, in Louisa County, Virginia. He afterwards studied law with a Mr. Lewis and was admitted an attorney to practice in Botetourt court in 1771 and located in the town of Fincastle; and when Fincastle County was organized two years later, he also practiced in the courts of that county. His *debut* at the bar was not very flattering, having been discomfited in a case by a competitor much his inferior; but gaining confidence and self reliance by experience, he soon rose to distinction. He volunteered as a cadet in Capt. Philip Love's company in Col.

William Fleming's regiment and had his first *bout* in Indian fighting in the memorable battle of Point Pleasant on the 10th of October, 1774.

Lured by the captivating accounts he heard of Kentucky, he hastened there with Captain Floyd's party early in 1775 and held a prominent place in the Transylvania Convention. During that and the succeeding years, he was chiefly engaged in exploring the country and aiding in the defense of the settlements. Heading a party of ten men, he started to convey from the Ohio near Limestone some ammunition brought down the river and hid there by George Rogers Clark; but his (Todd's) party was ambuscaded near May's Lick, December 25th, 1776, two of his men killed and two taken prisoners, while Todd and the rest made good their escape. On the 19th of April, 1777, Capt. John Todd and Colonel Callaway were chosen to represent Kentucky County in the Virginia Legislature; and on the 24th of that month, Captain Todd, Daniel Boone, and two others were badly wounded and one man killed in a skirmish with the Indians at Boonesborough. He had so far recovered as to be able to set off for Virginia by the 23d of May ensuing and while in the Legislature was constantly attentive to the wants of the Kentucky settlements.

In 1778 he served on Clark's Illinois campaign and shared in the capture of Kaskaskia and Cahokia; and when the newly conquered county was organized by Virginia into the county of Illinois, Todd was, December 12th, 1778, appointed county lieutenant or commandant, with civil and military powers. The most of the year 1779 was spent in fulfilling the duties of his station in the Illinois country. In the spring of 1780 he was chosen to represent either Illinois or Kentucky County in the Virginia Legislature and while in Virginia was married to Miss Jane Hawkins, to whom he had been many years engaged, and arrived with his bride in Kentucky at the close of that year or beginning of 1781 and settled at Lexington. During that winter, provision became so scarce at the Lexington fort that Mrs. Todd was able to present her husband on his return home one night with his servant, George, with a small bit of bread about two inches square and about a gill[ff] of milk. On accepting it, Colonel Todd asked if there was nothing for George. "Not a mouthful," she answered. The colonel called George and handed him the bread and milk without taking any of it for himself. Such was the habitual benevolence of his heart.

When Kentucky County was divided early in 1781 and Fayette County formed, Colonel Todd was placed at the head of the commission of justices and also appointed county lieutenant. He was that year very active in securing men and preparing meat and canoes for Clark's intended campaign against Detroit, which, however, from various causes proved abortive. Colonel Todd's relief of Bryan's Station and his pursuit of the enemy to the Blue Licks, his defeat and death there August 19th, 1782, have long been matters of historic notoriety. His widow and only daughter survived him many years, the latter of whom was first married to James Russell, a lawyer, and he dying, she became the wife of the Hon. Robert Wickliffe[gg] of Kentucky.

Colonel Todd was a man of fine personal appearance, about five feet six or seven inches high, well formed, and was considered among the swiftest on foot of his day and excelled in all athletic exercises. Once, when surveying on Licking with a party of men under him, and dispersed by a superior body of Indians and each man pursued by separate Indian parties, Todd kept beyond their reach with considerable ease on foot and in cold winter weather with snow on the ground, swam the Licking in the presence of his pursuers, holding his rifle and equipment in one hand out of water, and when out of danger, quietly built his fire and encamped for the night. Such a man, rich in expedients, brave, generous, and talented, devoting his time and services to his country, cut down in the flower of his age, was a serious loss to the infant settlements of Kentucky.

COL. WILLIAM COCKE

The youngest of eleven brothers and descended from an ancient Virginia family, William Cocke was born in Amelia County in that colony in 1744. Though his education was very defective, he yet acquired a practical knowledge of men and books that enabled him to fill, respectably and usefully, a more than ordinary position among his followers. He was among the adventurers in 1773 to the Holston country. Early distinguishing himself in opposition to the arbitrary acts of the mother country, he boldly met the charge of high treason preferred by Governor Dunmore and council December 6th, 1773, and defended the patriotic efforts and aspirations of the people in a speech, unaided by the presence and power of Dunmore himself, and even by the eloquence of Patrick Henry.[16]

Returning to Amelia in March 1774, Governor Dunmore sent him a captain's commission in the militia, with a request to visit him at Williamsburg; and attending him, the governor endeavored by every art and promises of promotion and British gold, intermingled with strong intimations of the power of England and even threats of intimidation, to attach him to the royal interests. But the young backwoodsman was not thus to be swerved from his principles, and frankly told his excellency so. Upon his return to Fincastle County on the Holston, Captain Cocke assembled his company and forcibly endeavored to impress upon their minds the value of their liberties and the necessity of firmness and union. During the Indian war of that year, he was vigilant and once pursued the bloody Logan after one of his murderous inroads into the Holston settlements.[17]

Captain Cocke's daring adventure as a messenger from Colonel Henderson to Boone in April 1775 has been well related in Henderson's diary, and his services in the Transylvania Convention have already been adverted to in the sketch of the proceedings of that body. Returning in June 1775 to the Holston, he was suddenly again made a participant in Indian warfare on the route in Powell's Valley. During the Cherokee outbreak of 1776, he was engaged in four contests with the Indians; and in July 1780 Captain Cocke then, with the force of Colonel Shelby and Sevier, was sent to demand the surrender of Boston post Thicketly Creek in South Carolina, and seeing the place surrounded by the mountain riflemen, Capt. Patrick Moore at once surrendered the fort. In 1782 he was admitted to the practice of law in the courts of the western counties of North Carolina.

In 1786 Colonel Cocke, in connection with Colonel Outland, led a force against the Cherokee town of Coya-tee, which was burned and the Cherokees compelled to sue for peace. During the short-lived republic of Franklin,[hh] he was one of its chief supporters, figuring in its conventions, serving as one of its generals, and acting as its ambassador both to Congress and the government of North Carolina. In 1796 he was a member of the Convention that formed the first constitution for Tennessee and was chosen one of the senators in Congress for the new state, serving a short term and subsequently a full term of six years. In 1809 he was elected a circuit judge; in 1813 he was a member of the Legislature and, at its close, when nearly seventy years of age, joined the army under General Jackson and signalized himself in the battle of Enotachopco[ii] January 24th, 1814— when, says General Jackson, he "entered into the engagement, continued in the pursuit of the enemy with youthful ardor, and saved the life of a fellow soldier by killing his savage antagonist." He served as a commissary for General Jackson during the year 1814. He was subsequently Indian agent to the Chickasaws and, settling in Mississippi, was chosen a representative to the Legislature, and died in Columbus in that state of bilious fever August 21st, 1828, in his eighty-fourth year. In height he was fully six feet, with light hair, blue eyes, full face, heavy frame, kind, benevolent, and full of sociality and good humor.

General Jackson calling on his old friend at Columbus a few years before his death, who was then keeping a small house of entertainment for a livelihood, the old judge enquired of the general if he had, according to promise, made application in his behalf to government for the services he had rendered during the Cherokee war. The general apologized for his neglect, pleading his numerous public duties. "I am glad, General," sarcastically and feelingly replied the old patriot, "that you have been so much engaged in your country's service as to be compelled to neglect the poor old soldier." Cocke was not a man to complain. He had served his country in her hour of need, not for mere lucre, but because he was impelled to do so by the promptings of a patriotic heart. His eloquent appeals in times of danger had sent many a man to the field and served them in the performance of duty.

John Cocke, a major general in the Creek war and since a member of Congress from Tennessee, and ex-chancellor Stephen Cocke, of Mississippi, are sons of the old pioneer.

ALEXANDER SPOTSWOOD DANDRIDGE

Nathaniel West Dandridge [came] from a prominent early Virginia family and married, in 1747, Dorothea, the youngest daughter of Gov. Alexander Spotswood, who was distinguished while governor of Virginia for having led forth a party of explorers beyond the Blue Ridge into the valley of Virginia in 1714 and instituted in consequence an order known as *Knights of the Horse-Shoe*. Alexander Spotswood Dandridge, the third child of this marriage, was born in Hanover

County, Virginia, August 1st, 1753, where he grew to manhood and studied the profession of law. His sister Dorothea became the second wife of the celebrated Patrick Henry.

In the spring of 1774 Mr. Dandridge, inheriting something of the spirit of western enterprise and adventure that had actuated the bosom of his grandsire after whom he was named, joined Capt. John Floyd and party with a view to explore Kentucky, but having descended the Ohio to the Little Guyandott,[jj] and hearing of Indian disturbances, he thought it most prudent to return to the settlements, which he did by penetrating the trackless forests. But early in 1775 we again find [him] associated with the adventurers under the leadership of Floyd in the settlement of St. Asaph, which he in part represented in the Transylvania Convention. Returning to Virginia not long after, he joined the main army under Washington and served till near the close of the war as a captain and distinguished himself as a chivalric soldier; and tradition adds that he served a portion of the time as an aid to General Washington, whose lady was his near kinswoman.

About the year 1780 he was stationed in Winchester, Virginia, and there met and soon after married Ann, the only daughter of Gen. Adam Stephen, and died in the adjoining county of Jefferson in 1785, leaving an only son, Adam Stephen Dandridge, who has left many descendants, among them the lady of Hon. R. M. T. Hunter. Of handsome features, graceful manners, amiable disposition, and possessed of an enterprising spirit, Alexander Spotswood Dandridge may well be classed among the young chivalry of Virginia of the period of the Revolution.[18]

COL. SAMUEL HENDERSON
Samuel Henderson, whose father bore the same name, was born in Granville County, North Carolina, February 6th, 1746. He accompanied his brother Col. Richard Henderson to Watauga early in 1775 and was present at the treaty. He formed one of Colonel Henderson's rear party that followed Boone's trail to the Kentucky and arrived there on the 20th of April. The following month he occupied a seat in the Transylvania Convention. Remaining in the country, he aided in the pursuit and re-capture of the three captive girls in July 1776 and was shortly after united in marriage to Elizabeth Callaway, one of the heroines. He aided in the defense of Boonesborough during the attacks on that place in 1777 and 1778, and the next year went with his family on a visit to North Carolina. Hearing of the death of her father, Colonel Callaway, by the Indians in March 1780, Mrs. Henderson chose to remain in Carolina; when her husband engaged in the service of his country, raising a party of one hundred men and securing the Guilford region for the suppression of the Tories. He served in the battle of Guilford in March 1781, and being well acquainted with the localities, he acted as General Green's pilot in guiding the army the night after the battle to Troublesome Creek Iron Works.

Near the close of 1784, then known as Major Henderson, he was sent by Governor Martin of North Carolina to ascertain the injuries inflicted by the people of the Franklin republic, now east Tennessee, upon the Cherokees and learn the extent of the disaffection of the Franklinites to the government of North Carolina. This mission was faithfully performed. He afterwards held the office of colonel of militia of his county. In 1807 he removed to Tennessee, first locating in Hawkins, and then in 1811 migrating to Franklin County. Aside from the offices indicated and that of a magistrate, he was not engaged in public life, preferring to spend his days as an independent cultivator of the soil. His death occurred in Warren County, Tennessee, December 16th, 1816, at about the age of sixty-five years. He had blue eyes, was six feet in height, well proportioned, possessing great muscular powers, weighing about two hundred pounds, [and was] fearless, kind, affectionate, and humane. His wife preceded him to the grave, having died in Franklin County, Tennessee, about [wm] years of age. They raised three sons and six daughters, of whom one son and three daughters yet survive.[19]

ISAAC HITE

Isaac Hite was a native of Hampshire County in the valley of Virginia and was a son of Col. Abraham Hite and a grandson of Joist Hite, an enterprising German who migrated from Pennsylvania and became the pioneer in settling the Virginia Valley. In 1773 Isaac Hite embarked at Fort Pitt and overtook Capt. Thomas Bullitt's party near the mouth of the Big Miami and was that season engaged in surveying lands in Kentucky. The succeeding year, he again repaired to Kentucky as a surveyor, and upon learning of the rupture between the borderers and the Indians, he returned with others by the way of the Ohio and Mississippi to New Orleans and thence by sea to Virginia.

Early in 1775, nothing daunted, he again visited Kentucky and was chosen from the Boiling Spring settlement to a seat in the Transylvania Convention and appears to have remained permanently in the country. On the 24th of April, 1777, he was wounded with Boone, Todd, and Stoner in the defense of Boonesborough and served on Clark's Indian campaigns of 1780 and 1782. He was a member, from Lincoln County, in the Kentucky Convention that met at Danville in December 1784 and died in 1794. He was for many years largely engaged in locating lands for himself and others and was a prominent and useful pioneer of Kentucky. His brother, Col. Abraham Hite, Jr., was an early and leading citizen of Jefferson County, Kentucky.

JAMES DOUGLAS

James Douglas, another member of the Transylvania Convention, was a native of Scotland, and successively visited Kentucky as an enterprising surveyor in 1773, 1774, and again in 1775. He resided in Williamsburg, Virginia, where he was living near the close of 1778. "It was his intention," says Marshall, "to have settled in Kentucky, but life failed, and with it all his purposes."

AZARIAH DAVIS

Azariah Davis, a native of Pennsylvania, first visited Kentucky in 1774 and [was] among the followers of James Harrod and, returning in 1775, was chosen to a seat in the Transylvania Convention, was among the heroic defenders of Logan's Station when attacked in 1777, and often served against the Indians. He never married and was much of a misanthrope on account of an early love disappointment and died in Mercer County, Kentucky, July 11th, 1808, at the age of seventy-five years. He was a man of small size, worthy, honest, and unambitious.

CAPT. WILLIAM MOORE 0

Capt. William Moore had a fort located near the southern bank of the Clinch River in which Daniel Boone, David Gass, and others took refuge with their families during the Indian War of 1774; and in 1775 we find him following Boone to Kentucky and holding a seat in the Transylvania Convention. Of him we can only further add that he served faithfully in the defense of the country, was on Clark's campaign of 1780 and probably others, and settled and died near Crab Orchard in Lincoln County, Kentucky.

NATHAN HAMMOND

Nathan Hammond came from Virginia and first visited Kentucky as one of Captain Bullitt's party in 1773 and again in 1775, when, locating at the Boiling Springs settlement, afterwards known as Harrod's Station, four miles north-west of the present village of Danville, he was sent as one of the delegates to the Transylvania Convention. He was several years a drummer in Harrodsburg Fort and was ultimately, it is believed, killed by Indians. Hammond's Creek, a tributary of Salt River, in Anderson County, Kentucky, commemorates his name and perhaps the region where he lost his life.

REV. JOHN LYTHE

Rev. John Lythe, of the Episcopal church, was the first minister of the gospel who penetrated the wilds of Kentucky. The fact that he was chosen to a seat in the Transylvania Convention from the Harrodsburg settlement—served on important committees, and officiated as chaplain—are evidences that he was a man of talent and influence. He returned to Virginia whence he came sometime during the year 1775; and it is to be regretted that so little is known of the man who first performed "divine service" in Kentucky.

SAMUEL WOOD

Samuel Wood, one of the delegates of the St. Asaph settlement, we have failed to gain any very particular information. He remained in the country but was little known to the public; he lived to a good old age and died in Mercer County about the year 1815. He is represented as a man of good mind, and though he as an early settler obtained a settlement and pre-emption in the rich lands of the country, he died poor.

DANIEL and SQUIRE BOONE, and VALENTINE HARMON

Daniel and Squire Boone, and Valentine Harmon were the remaining members of the Convention. The two sturdy brothers, we hardly need say, seemed to have well discharged the new duties which the occasion imposed; and while this work is intended especially to perpetuate Daniel Boone's memory and services, it will at the same time commemorate the name and worth of his worthy brother. A succinct sketch of Squire Boone will be found in the appendix notice of the Boone family. Valentine Harmon has already been noticed among the Long Hunters.

SKETCHES OF THE MEMBERS OF THE TRANSYLVANIA COMPANY.
COL. RICHARD HENDERSON

Of Col. Richard Henderson, whose career has already in part been sketched, it only remains to be added that in 1799 he was one of the North Carolina commissioners for extending the western boundary between that state and Virginia. Some difficulty arising in determining the true latitude of a particular point, Colonel Henderson and his coadjutor abandoned the service. He went on to Boonesborough, where he spent the winter, and the next spring proceeded to the French Lick on the Cumberland, where settlements were just commencing; and establishing a land office there under Transylvania authority, [he] returned home in the summer of 1780. In 1781 he served in the House of Commons of North Carolina, after which he lived in retiracy until his death, which occurred at his seat in Granville County, January 30th, 1785, in the fiftieth year of his age, leaving four sons and two daughters. He was a man of giant mind—one of nature's noblemen. Two of his sons rose to distinction—Archibald and Leonard; the former thrice held a seat in the Legislature of his native state and twice represented his district in Congress and was pronounced "the most perfect model of a lawyer" North Carolina ever produced—he died at Salisbury in October 1822, at the age of fifty-four years. Leonard Henderson studied the profession of law and was chosen as judge of the Superior Court of North Carolina in 1808 and resigned in 1816; and in 1818, on the formation of the present Supreme Court of that state, he was elected one of the judges, and upon Chief Justice Taylor's death in 1829, he was appointed his successor, and died at his residence in Granville County in August 1833, in his sixty-first year, leaving behind him a character second to none for intellectual greatness and generosity.

COL. JOHN WILLIAMS

Col. John Williams was a native of Hanover County, Virginia. His early education was defective, and he learned the trade of a house-carpenter; but afterwards studying the profession of law, he settled in North Carolina. In 1770 he became in some way obnoxious to the Regulators, who fell upon and beat him in a furious manner. Taking an active part with the patriots of the Revolution, he was chosen a member of the Convention at Hillsboro in August 1775 and in the latter part of that year repaired to Boonesborough as the agent of the Transylvania Company. In 1777 he was appointed one of the first judges under the new state constitution and served as a member of the Continental Congress in 1778–'9. He was a man of high standing in society, greatly distinguished for his sound judgement and plain common sense. He died at his residence in Granville County in October 1799.

THOMAS HART

Thomas Hart was a prominent citizen of Hanover County, Virginia, who had six children, all natives of Hanover, John, Benjamin, Thomas, David, Nathaniel, and Susanna—the latter the grandmother of the present Hon. Thomas Hart Benton. Their father dying, the whole family removed prior to 1756 to North Carolina. Thomas, David, and Nathaniel Hart were members of the Transylvania Company. *Thomas Hart, Jr.,* was born December 11th, 1730, and when he migrated to North Carolina, he settled near Hillsboro and married a lady of fortune. In the conventions which met at Newbern and Hillsboro in April and August 1775 he represented the people of Orange and in the fall of that year visited Kentucky. When Cornwallis invaded North Carolina, Colonel Hart made a hurried sale of his estate and removed to Hagerstown, Maryland, intending shortly to settle in Kentucky, but the death of his brother Nathaniel by the Indians and the continued attacks of the Indians in Kentucky deterred him from migrating there till the spring of 1794, when he settled in Lexington and there died June 22nd, 1808. Mrs. Henry Clay is one of his daughters, and his son, Capt. Nathaniel Gray T. Hart, deputy inspector-general of the North Western Army, was killed at the massacre of the River Raisin in January 1813.[KK]

COL. DAVID HART

Col. David Hart was born about the year 1732. He settled on Country Line Creek in what is now Caswell County, North Carolina. The Transylvania Company was divided into eight shares—and each of the nine shareholders owned a full share, except David Hart and L. H. Bullock, who had but a half-share each. Mr. Hart visited Kentucky in the spring of 1776; and in 1781 he was chosen lieutenant-colonel of a regiment of light-horse and shared in the defeat of the Tories at Holt's and took part in the battle of Guilford, behaving with much gallantry. He continued to reside on his estate in Caswell until his death about the year

1791. His grandson, Hon. Archibald Dixon, is now a member of the U.S. Senate from Kentucky.

CAPT. NATHANIEL HART

Capt. Nathaniel Hart, who was born May 8th, 1734, was married in 1760 and settled on Country Line Creek, North Carolina, and there built and resided in the noted *Red House*. He commanded a company under Governor Tryon at the defeat of the Regulators at Alamance, May 16th, 1771. He went to Kentucky with Colonel Henderson early in 1775 and spent most of his time in the country until he finally removed his family there in the fall of 1779. While out to drive up his horses, he was killed by the Indians on Otter Creek, two or three miles from Boonesborough, July 22nd, 1782, in his forty-ninth year. Excepting perhaps Colonel Henderson, Captain Hart had been the most active member of the Transylvania Company; and in the final settlement of the affairs of the company, the sum of two hundred pounds was allowed for Captain Hart's extraordinary services rendered and risk incurred in effecting the settlement of Kentucky. He had fourteen times passed [through] the wilderness between Kentucky and the old settlements. His wife survived him but two short years, leaving nine children, most of whom were young; but the connection formed by the second daughter, Susan, with the late Gov. Isaac Shelby, gave the younger members of the family a home, a protector, and a friend. His son, the late Nathaniel Hart, of Woodford County, Kentucky, served on Wayne's campaign and died February 7th, 1844, leaving several children—among them Col. Nathaniel Hart, and William P. Hart, of Woodford, and the lady of the Rev. R. J. Breckinridge, of Kentucky.

COL. JOHN LUTTRELL

Col. John Luttrell married the only daughter of John Hart and settled in Chatham County, North Carolina. He accompanied Colonel Henderson to Kentucky in the spring of 1775. During the Revolution, he was much engaged against the Tories; and when David Fanning, the noted Tory partizan, captured Governor Burke and others at Hillsboro September 13th, 1781, Gen. John Butler and Colonel Luttrell hastily raised a party and the next day attacked the retreating foe on Cane Creek, in which engagement Colonel Luttrell was shot through the body with two balls and died the following day, greatly lamented. He left no children, and his widow subsequently married Dr. John [wi].

JAMES HOGG

James Hogg was a native of Scotland. He received a superior education and, migrating to North Carolina, settled as a farmer near Hillsboro. He was chosen to represent the Transylvania Company in the Continental Congress but thought it not prudent to ask for a seat in that body. He died at his residence about the year 1804, aged about seventy-five years. His wife's maiden name was Alves, and to perpetuate that name, Mr. Hogg had the name of his son, Walter Alves Hogg, changed by legislative enactment to Walter Alves; and James Alves, a son of the latter, now resides at Henderson, Kentucky.

WILLIAM JOHNSON

William Johnson was also a Scotsman and early settled in Orange County, North Carolina, where as a merchant, mill-owner, and farmer with a large landed estate, he became extensively known as a businessman of great energy of character. He was a member of the Provincial Congress at Halifax in April 1776 and died at his residence in Orange County in May 1785.

LEONARD HENLEY BULLOCK

Leonard Henley Bullock appears not to have figured in public life. He resided in Warren County, North Carolina, where he died in the year 1797 at the age of about sixty years. His son Richard Bullock, now (June 1855) in his 82nd year, resides where he was born, upon the old homestead.

DRAPER'S NOTES: APPENDIX

1. Burk's *Virginia,* i:347.
2. Burk, ii:140, 142.
3. Allen's *American Biographical Dictionary,* 86.
4. Charles Campbells' *Virginia,* note 132, gives her name as Fanny, but the Winston Family Record calls her Mary. MS. letter of C. D. Fontaine, Esq., of Mississippi, a lineal descendant of both the Winston and Henry families.
5. Campbell's *Virginia,* note 122.
6. This horse was a remarkable animal. He lived to a great age and was carried to Kentucky when nearly forty years old.
7. Letter of Judge Yeats, Pittsburgh, August 21, 1776, in Hazard's *Register,* vi:104.
8. In Peck's revised edition of Perkins' *Annals of the West,* it is stated that Dr. Walker was employed from about 1750 as an agent among the Cherokees on the Holston; and about 1758 was appointed commissioner to take certain Cherokee chiefs to England; and while there, organized a land company, of which the duke of Cumberland was patron, for settling the wild lands of western Virginia and Carolina; [wi] returning to Virginia as general agent, Dr. Walker subsequently explored the West, and gave the name of his patron to the Cumberland River and Mountain, and the name of Louisa to the Kentucky River in honor of the duchess of Cumberland. There is nothing to show that Dr. Walker was even an Indian agent or ever visited England; nor did his descendants credit either assertion. The formation of a Land Company in Virginia has been already adverted to; the time of the naming of the Cumberland River and Mountain in 1750 Dr. Walker's Journal, with other contemporaneous correspondence, sufficiently prove; and that the duke of Cumberland was never married and consequently had no duchess [wi].

9. Besides scattering facts from various printed authorities, this sketch has been mainly made up from the MS. notes furnished for this work by Franklin Minor, Esq., of Albemarle County, Virginia, a descendant of Dr. Walker; some facts were also derived from the Hon. W. C. Rives and lady; others from MS. letters of Dr. Walker to Col. William Preston; and yet others from the MS. records of Botetourt County, Virginia.

10. Notes of conversations with the venerable Isaiah Boone, a brother of Jonathan Boone, and also with Col. W. P. Boone, of Louisville, Kentucky.

11. MS. letter of Thomas E. Lee of Berks County, Pennsylvania

12. Ibid.

13. This sketch revised for *Border Forays and Adventures.*

14. Colonel Radford, one of the number, so related to the venerable Mrs. Floyd, a daughter of Colonel Preston.

15. Dr. Thomas Walker, the early explorer of Kentucky, writing from Williamsburg, Virginia, July 9th, 1778, to Colonel Preston, says: "Please give my compliments to Captain Floyd, and tell him I have paid the ten guineas, he had of Dr. Franklin, to the Treasurer, who is thought the proper person to receive it." — MS. Preston Papers.

16. Cocke's Mss.

17. Ibid. (Memorandum for Mr. Lossing's eye: I don't like exactly to give this allusion to Patrick Henry, but so Cocke states it; and I suppose Henry was employed somewhat as John Adams was to defend the British authorities connected with the Boston riots and murders of March 1776.)

18. MS. Preston Papers and MS. correspondence with the late Col. Patrick Henry Fontaine of Mississippi, Adam S. and Philip P. Dandridge, and William Spotswood Fontaine of Virginia.

19. MS. letters of Alfred Henderson, Mrs. Elizabeth Dixon, and Mrs. Eudocia Estill, surviving children of Col. Samuel Henderson. Ramsey's *Tennessee,* 304, 306, 307.

EDITOR'S NOTES: APPENDIX

a. Ohio Valley settlers marked the Hard Winter of 1779–80 as the hardest they ever endured. The Ohio and Cumberland froze, stopping the flow of supplies to Kentuckians. Heavy snows that fell in October did not melt in some areas until March. Weeks of below-freezing temperatures wiped out livestock and wildlife, creating starving times for folks west of the Blue Ridge; many people froze to death or died from exposure or sickness.

b. The Bible lists five different men named Simeon. The context suggests the devout Simeon of Jerusalem in Luke 2:25–32.

c. Old Style, or Julian style of dating, as opposed to N.S., meaning New Style, or Gregorian style of dating. (See chapter 1, note e.)

d. James Boone's precise family chronology is the basis for all modern Boone genealogies, the two most useful and best known being Lilian Hays

Oliver's *Some Boone Descendants and Kindred of the St. Charles District* (Rancho Cordova, CA: Dean Publications, 1984) and Hazel Atterbury Spraker's *The Boone Family,* 2nd ed. (Baltimore: Genealogical Publishing Company, 1974).

e. The Sandy Creek expedition (in present-day Logan County, West Virginia) against the Shawnee was a grim affair of no lasting consequence. Starving times beset the 340 troops, forcing them to subsist on whatever they could find. A small band of the men discovered two buffalo hides high in a beech tree where they had hung them weeks before. The soldiers cut the hides down and singed off the wool to slice the hides into tugs (thongs) to boil and eat. They named the site Tug Fork.

f. The skirmish at Weitzel's Mill, North Carolina, on March 6, 1781, cost the British, led by Lord Cornwallis, and the Americans, commanded by Col. William Preston, Col. Otho Holland Williams, and Col. William Campbell, thirty to forty men each. The little-known fight had several important consequences: it revealed the strategic value of the rifle over the bayoneted smoothbore musket, in the form of Preston's riflemen, who briefly held back Col. Banastre Tarleton's flank assault. The engagement allowed Brig. Gen. Nathaniel Greene to mobilize the main army and evade Cornwallis's grasp. Cornwallis lost his chance to defeat Greene's undermanned force, and nine days later Cornwallis and Greene collided at Guilford Court House.

g. Cornwallis defeated Greene's reinforced army on March 15, 1781, at the Battle of Guilford Court House, but his Pyrrhic victory cost him one-fourth of his army—93 dead, 439 wounded. "Another such victory," observed British statesman Charles Fox, "would destroy the British army." Said Cornwallis: "I never saw such fighting since God made me. The Americans fought like Demons."

h. As a New Hampshire teenager, Robert Rogers (1731–95) had his first taste of military life while serving in the ranks of the local militia during King George's War (1744–48). During the French and Indian War (1755–63), Rogers' crack squads of guerilla-style woodland commandoes—dubbed "Rogers' Rangers"—lived by a strict code that helped set the precedent for modern-day military special forces like the U.S. Army's Rangers and Green Berets and the Navy's Seals. Controversy, legal intrigues, and personal problems mar much of his later career from the Revolution to his death. But whatever his flaws, and despite his poor administrative skills, it cannot be denied that in his prime, Rogers was blessed with a streak of military genius.

Abandoned by the French in March 1760 and rebuilt that autumn by the British, Fort Presque Isle, near present-day Erie, New York, was the southern gate to the eastern portion of Lake Erie and commanded portage routes leading to the Ohio's tributaries during the French and Indian War. Major Rogers had a garrison of men stationed there in the latter part of 1760. In June 1763, during the short-lived Pontiac's Rebellion, Indians burned the fort to the ground.

i. Miami Indians living in the Indiana country at the confluence of the Wabash and Mississinewa.

j. The September 11, 1777 Battle of Brandywine, Pennsylvania, was one of the most hotly contested engagements of the Revolution. General Howe suffered

576 casualties, the Americans about 1,400. As General Washington ordered the American army to retreat, the day, bitterly gained, belonged to the British.

k. The October 4, 1777 Battle of Germantown, Pennsylvania, marked a show-down between Gen. Sir William Howe's forces of 9,000 and Washington's 8,000 Continentals and 3,000 militia. A dense fog settled on the battlefield, hampering fighting, and in the end, the Americans retreated. Casualties are uncertain. Estimates of British losses range as high as 800; Howe reported 537 of his men dead. American reports of losses are more vague—about 150 killed, more than 500 wounded, almost 400 missing. Americans lost Germantown but proved their mettle and thus influenced the French to come to the aid of the Patriot cause.

l. Joel Tyler Headley (1813–97), a former Presbyterian minister who forsook his New York pulpit to write. In 1846 he became associate editor of the *New York Tribune*. During his lifetime he authored twenty-four works, which sold by the hundreds of thousands, including *Napoleon and His Marshals* (2 vols., 1846) and *Washington and His Generals* (2 vols., 1847). Headley's morally high-toned, sentimentalist approach to history writing gained him critics besides Draper, who deemed him no scholar. Edgar Allan Poe called him "The Autocrat of all the Quacks."

m. Texicans—Americans living in Texas prior to statehood—declared their independence from Mexico on March 2, 1836. After the devastating siege of the Alamo, ending March 6, 1836, and following Sam Houston's capture of Mexican war leader and dictator Santa Anna at the Battle of San Jacinto on April 21, 1836, Texas remained an independent republic until December 29, 1845, when it was admitted into the Union. (See chapter 15, note w.)

n. The Seminole Wars lasted well into the nineteenth century and represent one of America's most ignoble chapters in its frontier history. Precipitating the first Seminole War (1817–18) was the incendiary issue of slaves fleeing from the southern states (largely Georgia) into Spanish Florida. As a result of this conflict, Spain ceded Florida to the United States in 1819. The Second Seminole War (1835–42) resulted from the energetic, often ruthless efforts of the United States government to remove the Seminoles to the Oklahoma Indian Territory. Though most Seminoles were captured and sent west, a remnant band fled to Florida's southernmost swampland from Okeechobee to the Everglades, where some of their reservations are today.

o. Winfield Scott (1786–1866) was commanding general of the U. S. Army (1841–61) and Whig presidential nominee in 1852. Nicknamed "Old Fuss and Feathers" because of his emphasis on discipline and appearance, Scott was twice wounded in the War of 1812 and served in the Seminole and Creek Wars (1835–36). Under the orders of President James K. Polk, on March 26, 1847, Scott made an amphibious assault on Vera Cruz and captured Mexico City September 14.

p. Gen. Andrew Jackson led numerous forays in the American Southeast against British-allied Indians during the Creek War (1812–15), which culminated in the final British offensive against the United States, ending with the famous Battle of New Orleans on January 8, 1815.

q. Shingas (also spelled Chingas or Shingiss) was a much heralded Delaware chieftain of the Turkey Clan, who in Pennsylvania in 1755 had a bounty of £200 levied on his head. "Were the war exploits of Shingas all on record," reported Moravian minister John Heckewelder in the early 1800s, "they would form an interesting document, though a shocking one. [Pennsylvania settlements such as] Conococheague, Big Cove, Sherman's Valley, and other settlements along the frontier, felt his strong arm sufficiently [to know] that he was a bloody warrior, cruel his treatment, relentless his fury. His person was small, but in point of courage and activity, savage prowess, he was said to have never been exceeded by anyone." For Heckewelder's recollections and a biographical sketch of Shingas, see C. Hale Sipe, *The Indian Chiefs of Pennsylvania,* 2nd ed. (Baltimore: Gateway Press–Wennawoods Publishing, 1995), 287–305.

r. Lord Dunmore's War (1774).

s. For more on James Harrod and the Kentucky settlement of Harrodsburg, see chapter 11, note x, also see chapter 13, note n.

t. Jonathan Swift's fabled silver mines. See Introduction, note x.

u. Early in 1777 Black Fish's warriors killed William Ray and mutilated his body at a sugar-making camp near Harrod's Town. His brother, James, and one William Coomes barely escaped the ambush, which sparked a series of raids against Kentucky settlements.

v. It is interesting that Draper, who is complete to a fault in his encyclopedic research and biographical sketches, omits the well-established fact that Col. Richard Callaway was one of the main instigators of Boone's court-martial.

w. Col. John Preston engaged in transporting passengers to America for indenture. He was Anglo-Irish, with strong British ties.

x. "Press-gang" refers to the involuntary impressment of men into the British Navy. Impressment of Americans on the high seas by British sailors became so commonplace that it was one of the primary factors that ignited the War of 1812.

y. In 1774 John Floyd went to Kentucky as a deputy surveyor under William Preston. After traveling to the Falls of the Ohio (Louisville), he staked a 2,000-acre claim on the Middle Fork of Beargrass Creek. There in 1779, near present-day St. Matthews, Floyd began building an outpost to secure his claim from squatters and guard against raids. Beginning as a lone cabin in 1779, by the time of Floyd's death by an Indian bullet in April 1783, Floyd's Station (sometimes called Beargrass Station) was a garrisoned military headquarters for Jefferson County, with a series of cabins and a stockade. Colonel Floyd, his wife, Jane Buchanan Floyd, and some of his kin are buried at the fort site in Breckinridge Cemetery, now on the west side of Breckinridge Lane in the Louisville suburbs.

z. In the spring of 1780 Squire Boone, Jr., erected his outpost at the Painted Stone site on the north bank of Clear Creek in Shelby County, twenty-five miles east of the Beargrass settlements. Squire Boone's Station covered about an acre and consisted of cabins arranged in a square protected with pickets.

Draper is referring to a skirmish called the Long Run Massacre, a bloody, now little-known affair. Indian raids in the Painted Stone region were especially brutal in 1781; by midsummer settlers there began fleeing for safety. But the loss of manpower weakened Squire Boone's Station, and on September 14, fearing attack, the rest of the families fled to Linn's Station on the Beargrass. Alexander McKee's Shawnee scouts spotted them, and his large band of warriors reinforced by British soldiers attacked. Col. John Floyd's militiamen rushed to the settlers' aid, and the forces clashed eight miles east of Linn's Station. Sixty Kentuckians —men, women, and children alike—were killed that day.

aa. On December 1, 1826, John Bradford, founder of Kentucky's first newspaper, the *Kentucky Gazette,* described the attack on Kincheloe's. See Thomas D. Clark, ed. *The Voice of the Frontier: John Bradford's Notes on Kentucky* (Lexington: University Press of Kentucky, 1993, p. 59).

> On the night of the 1st of September, 1782, a party of Indians broke into Kincheloe's Station on Salt River, whilst the people were asleep, and killed seven, and no doubt would have killed or taken the whole, had not the darkness of the night favoured their escape. A man by the name of Thompson Randolph defended his family with great bravery, and it was believed killed several Indians. His wife with an infant in her arms were killed by his side—with their remaining child he got into the loft of his cabbin, and made his escape through the roof; but as he jumped from the roof to the ground, he was attacked by two Indians, one of which he stabed, and the other he struck with his empty gun, upon which they both left him.

bb. For more on the interment of Col. John Floyd and his wife, see note y.

cc. On November 7, 1811, Tecumseh's British-allied pan-Indian alliance clashed with William Henry Harrison's American troops in the Old Northwest Territory of Indiana at the confluence of Tippecanoe Creek and the Wabash. Harrison's victory at Tippecanoe catapulted him to a short-lived term in the presidency and also was a harbinger both of the brewing hostilities that led to the War of 1812 and of the U. S. policies of Indian removal.

dd. Historian Neal Hammon (unpublished notes) observes that "Todd is a Teutonic name, meaning Fox, introduced into England by the Anglo Saxons and the Danes. It is not an Irish name."

ee. An early American or European artisan whose work involves turning, such as one who shapes pottery, stone, or wooden items (such as bedposts) on a lathe.

ff. A British unit equal to $1/4$ imperial pint (8.669 cubic inches) or a liquid unit equal to $1/4$ pint (7.218 cubic inches).

gg. Robert Wickliffe (1775–1859), of Lexington, Kentucky, U.S. attorney, legislator, and staunch pro-slavery Democrat who upon his death freed his favorite slave and gave the rest of them a three-day holiday.

hh. The "Lost State of Franklin" was an attempt in the early 1780s by backcountry Middle Tennesseans to form a new state called Franklin. These

"Franklinites" were especially aggressive in forcing Old Tassel's Cherokee neutralists to cede to them land protected by treaty, and their actions led to further Indian-Anglo wars in the area. In November 1784 the Franklinites elected for their governor famed Revolutionary War hero and Indian fighter Col. John "Nolichucky Jack" Sevier (1745–1815), a position he held until the demise of Franklin in 1788.

ii. On January 23, 1814, in the Battle of Enitachopco Creek (a northern tributary of the Coosa in Alabama), Gen. Andrew Jackson's outnumbered troops routed the Red Stick Creeks, killing nearly 200 and giving the United States a much-needed morale boost during the Creek War of 1812–15.

jj. The Little Guyandotte (or Guyandot) is a branch of West Virginia's Guyandotte River, which empties into the Ohio about forty miles east of the Big Sandy, the river defining Kentucky's eastern border.

kk. On January 22, 1813, on Michigan's River Raisin, eighteen miles from British Fort Malden, Gen. Henry Proctor's force of 1,400 British and Indians defeated Gen. James Winchester's 1,300 Kentuckians, killing more than one-third of his men. "Remember the Raisin" became the Kentucky troops' rallying cry in all subsequent War of 1812 engagements.

INDEX

Numerals in bold typeface indicate an illustration.